J2EE™ Open Source Toolkit:

Building an Enterprise Platform with Open Source Tools

J2EE™ Open Source Toolkit: Building an Enterprise Platform with Open Source Tools

John T. Bell
Stanford Ng
James T. Lambros

Wiley Publishing, Inc.

Vice President and Publisher: Joseph B. Wikert
Executive Editor: Robert M. Elliott
Developmental Editor: James H. Russell
Editorial Manager: Kathryn A. Malm
Production Editor: Felicia Robinson
Media Development Specialist: Greg Stafford
Text Design & Composition: Wiley Composition Services

Published simultaneously in Canada

Library of Congress Cataloging-in-Publication Data:

ISBN: 0-471-44435-9

Printed in the United States of America

10 9 8 7 6 5 4 3 2 1

To Tammy and my girls, Kristine, Rebecca, and Joanna,
and to the little one soon to come.

– John T. Bell

This book is dedicated to all my family and friends who have supported me through the years. Special thanks goes to out to Judy, whose care packages and wit have brightened up my day more times than I can recall. Thank you all!

– Stanford Ng

I dedicate my portion of the book to my mother, Dolly Ratliff. Without her sacrifice and perseverance early in my life, none of this would have been possible.

– James T. Lambros

Contents

Acknowledgments

John T. Bell would like to gratefully acknowledge the capable assistance of his editors, Bob Elliott and James Russell. Without their guidance this book would not be what it is.

Stanford Ng would like to acknowledge the help of his colleague and friend, Mr. Stephen Holder, whose technical expertise proved invaluable.

James T. Lambros acknowledges the patience of his wonderful son Ryan, who tolerated the many evening hours he spent writing this manuscript.

About the Authors

John T. Bell has over two decades of software development experience. Currently he is an instructor in server-side Java technologies for the Center for Applied Information Technology at Towson State University in Maryland and serves as a technical architect for a major hospitality company. He has a master's degree in Computer Systems Management and a bachelor's degree in Electrical Engineering, both from the University of Maryland.

Stanford Ng is currently the cofounder of Nuglu, LLC and is directing software development at ciMediaGroup, a division of Creative Images. A veteran of the software industry, he's been involved with companies ranging from small startups such as NetGUI to giants such as TriCon. Stanford is a graduate of the University of California at Irvine and a co-conspirator, with Dr. Robert Nideffer, behind the international award-winning Proxy/MAM research project.

James T. Lambros is a software architect and analyst for Caterpillar Financial Corporation. In addition to his work for Caterpillar, Jim has been involved with several exciting software development projects during his career with IBM. His current interests are Java Design Patterns and the whole open source software movement.

Introduction

Your beginnings will seem humble, so prosperous will your future be.
Job 8:7

Installing and configuring even commercial enterprise platforms is often a challenge. Configuring the J2EE environment to work with the needed databases and messaging systems and making certain that everything is working is often difficult, even when most of the components come from the same vendor. This task is made more difficult when each of the components is separate and derived from an independent source, and that difficulty is exacerbated when you're dealing with open source software to boot.

The focus of the book is on platform architecture and assembling and validating the components required to build a platform that can be used to develop and deploy Java-based, enterprise-class applications using open source and freely available tools and components.

The following sections discuss the contents of this book and show you how to get the most out of it.

Why You Need This Book

This book is about architecture. More specifically, the book is about creating platform architecture by selecting the right components for the platform, combining them, and making certain that all of the integrated components work together. It is also about open source Java and the components that can be selected to build the platform.

The purpose of this book is to enable you to select and assemble various open source components needed to demonstrate and build applications using Java 2 Enterprise Edition (J2EE) technologies by creating a Java platform that's suitable for enterprise-class applications.

NOTE ***Enterprise-class applications*** **are distinguished from other applications by their need to be integrated into multiple systems within an enterprise or organization.**

Your Java platform can be used to build and deploy applications using enterprise Java technologies. This follows industry trends of using Java for enterprise applications as well as increased support for the widespread use of open source software.

Hopefully, reading this book will help you to avoid some of the pitfalls that we have encountered and at the same time give you a better understanding of platform architecture or integration of open source Java components.

About the Book

This book is about making the right choices for creating an enterprise platform from open source components. In short: Where there's a need for an affordable alternative to commercial J2EE platforms to evaluate technologies, to provide training, and to jump start development teams, that need can be met by using open source tools.

To state it more concisely, this book is about:

- Creating a Java enterprise platform
- Selecting the right open source components for the platform
- Combining those components with other components
- Making certain that all of the components work together

NOTE **The principles that we apply in this book are not limited to open source components. The processes and practices we develop for selecting, combining, and testing components apply to any architecture, be it commercial or open source. The programs that we develop to demonstrate and test platform features are also useful for demonstrating and testing platform features with commercial J2EE platforms.**

Who Should Read This Book?

This book is targeted toward readers who may have a familiarity with information systems but are not necessarily familiar with enterprise Java technologies and architectures. The book does assume that the reader has a basic familiarity with Java and does not provide an introduction to Java programming or to programming for J2EE platforms. Source-code examples are designed either to provide a basic understanding of the capabilities of a component or to provide testing, diagnostic, and troubleshooting support.

You should read this book if you want to:

- Learn about systems architecture
- Access to an affordable Java Enterprise platform
- Learn about open source Java components
- Create your own Enterprise platform
- Learn about Java Enterprise components

It is our hope that everyone who reads this book will gain some benefit from it. Certainly you should gain a deeper knowledge of open source components and enterprise architectures. More importantly, though, we want to help you solve real problems that you may encounter with real systems that you are developing or supporting. To that end we offer this practical guide for those people who want or need to use enterprise Java components.

Industry Trends

There are many books that cover application development. There are a few books that discuss application architecture. There are very few books available that discuss platform architecture and building complex systems from existing components. I believe that this is the first book to cover platform architecture and building a complex system entirely from existing open source Java components. For everything, there is a season, and there are a number of major industry trends that make a book like this one particularly relevant:

- The first industry trend is the maturing nature of the Java 2 Enterprise Edition platform and its demonstrated effectiveness at addressing enterprise-class problems. Enterprise Java is becoming increasingly recognized as a superior platform for developing and delivering enterprise applications. Java has several distinct advantages over other platforms, including:

  Platform independence. Java solutions can be created to run on the entire variety and spectrum of hardware and operating systems that can be found in many large organizations. This is the famous "write once, run anywhere" mantra and methodology of Java.

  Distributed computing support. Java has always had strong support for distributed computing. J2EE enhances this with Enterprise Java Beans, one of the easiest to use distributed component capabilities ever invented.

Web-based delivery tools. Java servlets and JavaServer Pages (JSPs) provide the ability to deliver enterprise applications through Web browsers. Web-based delivery has a large impact on reducing the total deployment costs of an enterprise application.

- The second trend is the high cost of commercial enterprise Java platforms. In many companies, purchases of expensive items and software prices above set limits must be approved at higher levels of management than the department charged with creating an application. This requires more effort to justify the cost and often slows the purchasing cycle. Information systems managers and technology leads in many companies are frustrated by delays in development projects caused by long procurement cycles and a lack of the ability to get tools into developers' hands. These high costs tend to be a concern for smaller companies and delay development projects in larger companies. Justification for the use of Java in these environments is further complicated by the fact that many organizations already have Windows-based departmental servers that come with a Web server solution preinstalled. Often it is difficult to justify to management the expense of a Java application server (JAS) just to write the program in Java, which leads us nicely to the third trend.
- The third trend is the growing recognition by many companies of the value of open source software. Ten years ago, most companies wouldn't even have considered using open source software. Five years ago, the information technology (IT) departments were using Linux, Apache, and other open source applications, but management didn't want to know about it. Today, many companies recognize open source software as a viable alternative to commercial products for cost-effectively solving real corporate computing concerns.
- The fourth trend is the increasing amount of high-quality Java software that is being created by the open source community. Open source projects such as the Jakarta/Apache projects have helped to establish high standards for open source Java software. I believe that there are several reasons for how this has come about:
  - First, Sun decided to make the Java development environment free to use, making Java an easily accessible language for programmers. That is, programmers do not have to purchase an expensive development environment to get started writing Java programs.
  - Using open source projects to create reference implementations of Java standards also has helped open source Java. For example, the Apache Tomcat server is the reference implementation for the servlet specification. In addition to helping with funding for open

source development, this practice helps establish open source Java projects as reliable tools. Corporate sponsorship by large Java vendors of major open source initiatives has also played a role.

CROSS-REFERENCE **Chapter 4 discusses two excellent open source Integrated Development Environments that were developed with funding from IBM and Sun.**

- Java came along at the right time. The proliferation of the World Wide Web and the strength of the Apache Web server running under Linux raised the visibility of Linux from that of technologists' toy to IT department tool.

Conventions

In this book, we use various methods of calling text out for various reasons. For example, when we want you to type something, we bold the text that we want you to type, as in, "Type in **ls –l**, and press Enter." When we mention commands, filenames, or directories, we use what's called monofont (or a fixed-width font). For example: "As you can see, the `ls` command lists two files: `fileone.txt` and `filetwo.lgz`, both of which are located in the `directoryone` directory." Finally, when we discuss a variable that you need to replace with something, such as *JAVA_HOME*, we put an underscore between the words to show that the words are linked and then italicize it.

How This Book Is Organized

The book is divided into four parts that form a logical progression that leads you from learning the basics to building an integrated development environment of your own. The following sections discuss each part briefly.

Part I: At the Starting Gate

This part covers material that is used throughout the book. It introduces several open source Java projects, covers the basics of enterprise architectures and provides an overview of open source developer tools.

NOTE **We recommend that all readers read Chapters 2 and 3 to get an overall view of the platform components and to understand the process we used to guide our specific component selections.**

Part II: Integrating the Web Tier

This part covers components of the architecture that are involved in delivering Web-based applications, Web servers and servlet containers, template tools, Web application frameworks, and portal software.

The chapters in this part and in Part III cover individual components that provide a specific functionality for the enterprise platform that we are creating. Each of these chapters provides a brief overview of the technology and the way it is used within the platform, and then compares various open source components that implement that functionality. Each chapter covers one specific component, which is given a detailed examination and then integrated with the other components discussed in earlier chapters. Source-code examples are also provided to demonstrate the use of the component and test the integration of the component within the platform.

Part III: Building the Infrastructure

This part covers components that form or are used to communicate with the enterprise infrastructure. It covers relational databases, messaging, Enterprise Java Beans (EJBs), Extensible Markup Language (XML), and Web services.

As in Part II, the chapters in this part cover components that provide a specific functionality for the enterprise platform that we are creating. These chapters provide a brief overview of the technology and the way it is used within the platform, and compares various open source components that implement that functionality. Each chapter covers one specific component that is given a detailed examination. That component is then integrated with the other components discussed in earlier chapters. Source code examples are also provided to demonstrate the use of the component and test the integration of the component within the platform.

Part IV: Test Driving the Platform

This part provides complete integrated examples of the primary platform components working together. It also covers issues that may be encountered when moving an application from a development environment to a production environment hosted on the platform that we created.

The chapters in this part provide more comprehensive code examples than earlier chapters, demonstrating the integration of the platform components working together within the enterprise platform environment.

Technical Considerations

This book focuses on open source software. That is not to say that open source software represents the only affordable J2EE solution for the many types of people or organizations that may need a J2EE platform. For example, Sun provides the J2EE reference environment for free. Although it cannot be used to deploy an application, the J2EE reference environment is suitable for learning purposes.

The products evaluated and discussed in this book are all open source. All discussion is based on the latest stable version of each product at the time of writing. For some products this may mean that the product is a beta release; however, our focus is on stable releases. Alpha and unstable products that may have merit are discussed more briefly so that the reader knows to monitor the project for potential future application.

What You Will Need

First and most obviously, if you want to build and run the platform we create in this book, you will need a computer. Because we want to be able to accommodate a wide variety of users, we have tried to make the computer requirements very minimal by today's standards. As a minimum to install the platform and run the examples, we recommend a Windows- or Linux-based computer with 128 MB of RAM running on a 350-MHz or faster CPU. A more typical developer configuration might be to have a 1.5-GHz CPU with 512 MB of RAM. Most developers using Windows will benefit from using Windows 2000 or Windows XP rather than Windows 98.

CROSS-REFERENCE **Deployment configurations are covered in detail in Chapter 15.**

The computer will also need a network connection. That is not to say that the computer must actually be connected to a network, but the network software to support TCP/IP connections must be installed and configured to work on the computer. Fortunately, this is common on modern computers. This is needed because many of the components in an enterprise system assume that they will use the network to communicate with other components deployed in a distributed environment. These components often make use of the network software infrastructure even if the components they need to communicate with are on the same machine. If the network software is not there, the component will fail.

NOTE If your computer does not have a network card (or modem), then look for documentation on installing the network loopback connector for your operating system.

You will also need to install the Java 2 Software Development Kit (JDK). This is the set of tools provided by Sun that enables you to compile and execute Java code. The JDK can be downloaded by following the links at `http://java.sun.com`.

NOTE Make sure to download and install the JDK and not just the Java Runtime Environment (JRE). The JRE does not include the Java development tools that are needed compile a Java program, but the JDK does include the JRE, which is needed to run Java programs. If you can compile a Java program, then you have the JDK installed.

Supported Platforms

This book is designed to be a practical tool for use by developers with varying needs. Even though the book emphasizes open source tools, the practical reality is that many developers must use various versions of Windows for their development systems, while many others increasingly prefer to use Linux, given its open source status as well as its reputation for stability and performance. For this reason, we cover both Windows and Linux platforms in this book.

One of the great features of Java is that it is mostly platform independent. In most cases, any differences in the behavior of Java programs have to do with differences in installation and in the security models on the two systems. Where there are differences, we try to identify those differences.

NOTE All of the software in this book has been tested under Windows 2000, Windows XP, and Linux. Most of the software has also been tested under Windows 98. When a component does not work under Windows 98 or when Windows 98 operation is not supported that fact is mentioned in the component summary.

NOTE Mandrake Linux version 9.0 was the specific version of Linux used for development and testing of the software in this book; however, no Mandrake-specific extensions were used, and all examples should work on any current release of Linux that supports JDK 1.3 or later.

We have not tested any of the software on other operating systems. However, most of the software should work on any Java Standard Edition–supported platform. We try to identify cases where a component is documented to specifically support platforms that we have not tested.

NOTE All code for this book has been written for and tested with the Java 2 Software Development Kit (JDK) version 1.4.1. However, 1.4 features were not specifically used, so the code should also run on older version 1.3 JDKs.

Beyond the Book

Although the focus of this book is not on application development, this book will give you a good start on developing enterprise applications, but the help doesn't end here. From here, you can look at the book's Web site or at a companion book in the Java Open Source Library.

For starters, this book has a companion Web site that's located at the following URL:

```
http://www.wiley.com/compbooks/bell
```

Featured at the site are:

Java source code examples for most chapters. For the most part, the examples are designed to demonstrate the integration of the various components or to aid in troubleshooting. For example, Chapters 13 and 14 provide significant examples designed to demonstrate the platform's capabilities. The source code for this application is available at the site.

Where to get the software. A URL is provided to the home page for each software component referenced in the book. The individual tools and components can be downloaded directly from these sites or in some cases mirrors of these sites. Code samples provided in the book can be downloaded from the book's companion Web site.

CROSS-REFERENCE Although this book gives you a good overview of how to build an application with open source tools, *Java Open Source Programming* by Joe Walnes et al., a companion book to this one that's also part of the Java Open Source Library, discusses the topic in far more detail.

PART One

At the Starting Gate

Everything has to have a beginning. This first part forms much of the basis for the rest of the book. It introduces the concepts that will form the basis for the chapters in the later parts. We start by examining open source software and software projects and communities, and discussing some of the issues related to using open source software in a commercial environment. We continue by covering enterprise platform architecture from the Java perspective. We look at the decision-making process used to decide which components will be selected for use in our platform, and, finally, we examine some developer tools that will be useful for developing software for the enterprise Java platform.

CHAPTER

1

Leveraging Open Source Software

Everything that is really great and inspiring is created by the individual who can labor in freedom.

Albert Einstein

Historically, enterprise software has been expensive and proprietary. Furthermore, if you needed to modify the software to suit your specific business needs, you had to contract with the vendor to make changes. Even worse, if there were errors, you were dependent on the vendor to address them in a timely fashion. Open source software has changed all of that.

This chapter examines the question "What is *open source software*?" To answer the question, we briefly describe some of the history of and concepts behind open source software. We also discuss the nature of open source software and the licenses that govern its use. Finally, we provide an overview of the major open source projects supporting Java development.

What Is Open Source Software?

Questions and misunderstandings about open source software and what it is abound. Many people associate open source software with its being free and think that any software that is given away is open source. Although open source software is free, just being free does not make the software open source. To be open source software, the software must meet certain criteria. In general, these can be stated as:

- Open source software allows free redistribution of source code and binaries.
- Open source software provides source code.
- Open source software allows modification and redistribution of the modified source code.

The formal definition of open source software is that open source software is software that is copyrighted and licensed under a license that meets the criteria outlined in the Open Source Definition, which can be found at the following site:

```
http://www.opensource.org/docs/definition.php
```

An alternative definition, known as the Debian Free Software Guidelines, can be found at the following site:

```
http://www.debian.org/social_contract.html#guidelines
```

Origins of the Open Source Movement

Conceptually, the open source software movement began with the GNU project started by Richard Stallman in 1983. GNU was a project established to create a Unix-compatible system of software that would be completely free, to be copied and given away, and that would provide access to all of the source code. Linux exists today mainly because of the tools created for the GNU project. The statements from the GNU Manifesto below describe Richard Stallman's view of Free Software.

> *GNU is not in the public domain. Everyone will be permitted to modify and redistribute GNU, but no distributor will be allowed to restrict its further redistribution. That is to say, proprietary modifications will not be allowed. I want to make sure that all versions of GNU remain free.*

The Free Software Foundation was formed to aid in the coordination, development, and maintenance of the GNU project. The Free Software Foundation (FSF) identifies their products as "free software." However, when the FSF refers to "free software" they state that "free" does not refer to "price" but rather to freedom. The FSF compares free software to "free speech" (as opposed to "free beer").

Prior to GNU and FSF, free software was generally "public domain." The FSF addressed the issues of public domain software by copyrighting all of their software. Along with the copyright is a license allowing the use of the software but including certain restrictions. The GNU General Public License, or GPL, enforces the goals of the FSF by ensuring that the software can be copied, distributed, modified, and extended, but requires that the software always be free and include source code (which the FSF sees as a condition of software freedom). Applying the GPL is often referred to as "copylefting."

The Open Source Software Movement Today

Free software was firmly established in 1998 when the term "open source" was coined. A group of people actively involved in working with Linux and other "free" software projects determined that a new name was needed that could be used to identify all software projects that provided access to source code without restrictions on changes or redistribution. They wanted to include the broader spectrum of free software, not just those programs covered under the GPL. They also wanted to make these software projects more palatable for businesses in the software industry. The FSF with its philosophy and rhetoric about free software had gone a long way toward endearing some programmers, but had alienated many, including businesses. The open source movement grew out of a desire to promote the concepts of free software but to avoid its confrontational past. They wanted to help businesses understand how this free software could be used to their benefit. This new name, open source software, quickly spread and was adopted by many. The Open Source Initiative (OSI) was formed to promote open source software and the concepts behind it. The OSI Web site can be found at the following URL:

```
http://www.opensource.org
```

FSF elected, however, to continue using the term "free software" to describe the programs that are covered by GPL-compatible licenses.

Open Source Licenses

In the previous discussion, we mentioned the GNU Public License, or GPL. The GPL works because of the power of the copyright laws. The copyright establishes ownership. The holder of the copyright is the owner of the software. The owner of the software is able to establish the rules for allowable use of their property by others. These rules are stated in a license. A license is a legal document that gives permission to do specified things or defines restrictions on what can be done.

In the following sections, we look at several of the most popular open source software licenses. Many open source programs share or reuse the licenses from other projects. The GPL for example is used by many projects that are not a part of the GNU project or other FSF efforts. For each license, we try to cover the most important features of the license and discuss any issues that may arise when combining products with different licenses.

Many of the licenses have similarities. Almost all of the licenses have a provision that states that the software is not covered under any warranties and that use of the software constitutes acceptance of the license. Some licenses also require that changes to the code be clearly marked and distributed separately to avoid confusion with base distributions.

All of the licenses that we discuss in the following sections are recognized by the OSI as open source licenses.

NOTE We are not lawyers. The discussion in this chapter is based on frequently asked questions (FAQ) documents available online and is not intended for use as legal advice. Licenses are, after all, legal documents.

NOTE There are many more open source licenses than those covered here. We have tried to focus on those licenses that we encounter most frequently with the software used throughout this book. Any specific piece of software may have a unique license of its own or a different variant from those covered in this chapter. You should always read and understand the software license before you commit to using a piece of software for any project or endeavor, even if it is an open source license.

Apache

The Apache software license was created originally for the Apache Web server but now applies to all projects hosted under the Apache umbrella. Basically, the license does not have any restrictions on the redistribution of source code or binaries other than the inclusion of a required disclaimer statement. It does require that if Apache software is used in a product the use must be acknowledged in the documentation for the product. The FSF recognizes the Apache license as a "free" license but also states that the Apache license is not compatible with GPL. FSF does not provide a specific reason why the Apache license is not compatible. On the other hand, the Apache License FAQ states that the Apache license is compatible with GPL as far as they can tell and states that FSF has not provided them with an explanation for why it is not GPL compatible.

Artistic

The Artistic License is commonly associated with the Perl programming language. The license is designed to provide the copyright holder with a form of "artistic control" over the development of the software. It allows redistribution of the software in original or modified form for free or for a fee. It does provide restrictions on how modified versions can be redistributed. These restrictions cover several common scenarios and are mostly oriented toward making certain that modified versions are not confused with the original version. The FSF recognizes the Artistic License as a free software license that is compatible with the GPL.

BSD

The BSD License was created for the University of California at Berkeley. It is a license template. The template is used to generate a license by substituting values for *OWNER, ORGANIZATION,* and *YEAR* with ones that are appropriate for the copyright holder. The license provides only three restrictions summarized here:

- Binary distributions must reproduce the copyright notice, the license conditions, and the disclaimer.
- Source distributions must reproduce the copyright notice, the license conditions, and the disclaimer.
- The names of the organization or contributors cannot be used for endorsements without permission.

The FSF recognizes the BSD license as a free software license that is compatible with the GPL.

GNU General Public License (GPL)

The GPL is the primary license of the Free Software Foundation and the GNU project. Many other projects have also adopted the GPL as their standard license. The primary features of the GPL are:

- The program can be copied and redistributed as long as copyright notices, disclaimers, and references to the license remain intact.
- Changes to the program are allowed as long as the changes are identified.
- The modified program must also be licensed under GPL and be freely distributed.
- Copyright notice, disclaimers, and references to the license need to be displayed by the program when practical.
- When distributing binaries, either the source code or an offer to provide source for copying costs only must be provided.

The GNU license clearly states that GPL programs can be included with other programs as parts of larger aggregate collections of programs as long as the GPL programs and the other programs are independent of each other. This allows the GNU programs to be included in Linux distributions that also include non-GPL-compatible programs, for example.

The Free Software Foundation also provides a FAQ document about the GPL to clarify questions about the license. This FAQ can be found at the following URL:

```
http://www.gnu.org/licenses/gpl-faq.html
```

In these FAQs, the FSF makes it clear that linking a program to a GPL library constitutes a derivative work that must also be covered under GPL. In general, if two programs are tightly coupled and share the same process space, and one of the programs is covered under the GPL, then they both must be covered under the GPL. However, if the two programs are loosely coupled and communicate using pipes, sockets, or other means of interprocess communications, they do not both have to be under the GPL. Interpreted programs and scripts that require an interpreter that is covered by the GPL do not themselves have to be covered under GPL.

Another point made clear in the FAQ documents is that the copyright holder is free to release a software product under several licenses. This allows a company, organization, or individual to release a free and open source version of a product under GPL but also release the same product under a different license to those willing to pay not to be under the GPL restrictions. The MySQL database is an example of software that uses this multiple license model.

GNU Lesser General Public License (LGPL)

As stated in the previous section, programs that are linked to GPL libraries are required to also be covered by the GPL. This became problematic for people who wanted to use the GNU compilers to move software to Linux. They could not use the GNU compiler unless the software itself was open source. This could have had a profound effect limiting the use of GNU tools. Instead the FSF created the Lesser GPL (also called the Library GPL) known as the LGPL. This variant has provisions to allow programs to be linked with libraries and redistributed under a separate license. The library itself still needs to be made available as source code under the LGPL, but the combined executable and the library do not.

Mozilla Public License (MPL)

The Mozilla license was created to support the open source release of the Netscape browser. Other companies have used variations on the Mozilla Public License as a model license when they have wanted to release their products as free software. The primary features of the Mozilla license are:

- The MPL allows the use, modification, and redistribution of code.
- The MPL requires that modifications to source code also fall under the same license.
- The MPL requires that source code be documented and made available.
- The MPL allows sections of a program to be covered under multiple licenses.

The FSF recognizes the Mozilla license as a free license but also states that the Mozilla license is not compatible with GPL—with one exception. The latest version of the Mozilla license provides a clause that allows different portions of a software product to be covered under multiple different licenses. This can allow products to be partially Mozilla and partially licensed with a GPL-compatible license.

Open Source Communities

Another common question about open source software is "Where does it come from?" There is often a subtle hint of "Can I trust it?" in that question. The answer to this last question is yes, you can trust open source software, because it is open and free for examination. The answer to the first question is that open source software comes from people, organizations, and companies that invest their time and money in developing these projects. Some projects are sponsored by large reliable companies such as IBM (Eclipse), Sun (NetBeans), SAP (SAP DB), and Netscape Communications (Mozilla). Others are developed by individuals (McKoi comes to mind). Still others are parts of larger open source communities (Apache's Jakarta for example).

Open source software projects have infrastructure needs just as any other project would. Many of these efforts are very large and complex and require coordination among many developers. The open source community provides this infrastructure for the developers. Once established, many projects can often share the same infrastructure, forming a community. These open source communities often serve as incubators for new ideas.

In the following sections, we look at some of the open source communities that have formed over the years to develop and support open source Java development. These communities represent good places to start when searching for open source software. Mostly, our focus will be on projects and communities with a focus on open source Java software.

Apache

The Apache project was originally created to support the development of the Apache Web server. Apache got its name from the fact that it started as a series of patches to the original Cern Web server. The name was a play on words on "a patchy" Web server. Apache is a proven product and has been the most widely used Web server on the Internet for several years, with more sites running Apache than all other Web servers combined. Apache has also become an umbrella for a large number of open source projects that share the Apache license. Often these projects are technology leaders, proving technologies before they are standardized. The Apache project has had a large impact on the open source Java community, initially with the jServ servlet container and now through the Jakarta project. There is more than just one major project under the Apache umbrella that has an impact on Java; we discuss these in the following sections. The main Apache Web page is found at the following site:

```
http://www.apache.org
```

Jakarta

Jakarta is a primary project within the Apache group. Jakarta is focused on developing open source Java code. The primary page for the Jakarta project can be found at:

```
http://jakarta.apache.org
```

Table 1.1 below provides a brief overview of just some of the many subprojects hosted under Jakarta. Some of these subprojects have further subprojects below them. Currently Jakarta represents the largest coordinated community of open source Java projects.

XML

Not all of the open source Java software from the Apache project can be found under Jakarta. A number of Java projects are found under the XML Apache banner at `http://xml.apache.org`. These projects are all of course related to processing XML files. These projects include those shown following in Table 1.2.

Table 1.1 Jakarta Subproject Summary

SUBPROJECT	WHAT IT IS
Commons	Commons is best described as a large collection of small Java utilities. Commons provides a place for those small little classes that are reused time and time again within other Jakarta projects.
James	An email, news, and messaging server written entirely in Java.
Jetspeed	A Java-based Web portal.
Jmeter	A Java-based load-testing tool. Jmeter is covered in Chapter 4.
Log4J	A standard logging library for Java programs.
Struts	A Web application framework used to ease the creation of Web applications. Struts is covered in more detail in Chapter 7.
Taglibs	The taglibs set of projects provides standardized groups of tag libraries for use in developing JavaServer Pages.
Tomcat	An open source Java servlet container and Web application server. Tomcat is covered in more detail in Chapter 5.
Turbine	An alternative Web application framework to Struts. The Jetspeed portal is based on Turbine. Turbine is covered briefly in Chapter 7.
Velocity	A macro-expansion program. Velocity replaces special tags within a document with values that are generated by a Java program. Velocity is covered in Chapter 6.

Table 1.2 XML Apache Projects

SUBPROJECT	WHAT IT IS
Xerces	A Java-based XML parser
Xalan	A Java-based XML style sheet processor
Cocoon	An XML-based Web publishing system written in Java

Web Services

Apache provides a number of projects designed to support Web services. All of the current projects are Java based. These projects can be found at `http://ws.apache.org` and are listed in Table 1.3.

Table 1.3 Web Services Apache Projects

SUBPROJECT	WHAT IT IS
Axis	SOAP-based Web Services for Java.
XML-RPC	XML-RPC-based Web Services for Java.
WSIF	The Web Services Invocation Framework (WSIF) provides a mechanism for creating clients for distributed-processing services by using Web Service Definition Language (WSDL) files.

Ant

Ant is the tool that is most commonly used to build large Java projects. Ant used to be a part of the Jakarta project, but has been promoted to a primary project below Apache. Ant is discussed in more detail in chapter 4 and can be found at: `http://ant.apache.org`.

ExoLab

ExoLab is an informal group focused on developing open source enterprise software projects. ExoLab is probably best known for Castor, a tool that enables XML document binding to Java classes. ExoLab is also responsible for projects such as OpenEJB, OpenJMS, OpenORB, and Tyrex, and contributes to external open source projects such as Tomcat, James, Xalan, and Xerces, which are all a part of the Jakarta project.

The ExoLab Group licenses the code it develops under the ExoLab Public License, which is similar to the Apache License. ExoLab can be found at `http://www.exolab.org`.

GNU

Although the GNU project is not well known for its Java contributions, the GNU project does boast quite a number of ongoing Java efforts. These are mainly focused around providing a pure open source implementation of Java. Many of the Java projects under GNU are hindered by the fact that the Java compiler and JVM are not open source. However, there are still several interesting GNU projects going on, using Java as the core language. The GNU Compiler for Java (GCJ), for example, has the ability to compile Java source code into either Java byte code or machine-native code. The following URL provides a list of Java programs that are linked through the GNU site and are distributed under the GPL.

```
http://www.gnu.org/software/java/java-software.html
```

ObjectWeb

ObjectWeb is an open source community created by a consortium of companies. They have the stated goal of creating and developing Open Source middleware. Two of the more interesting projects are described in Table 1.4. ObjectWeb can be found at `http://www.objectweb.org`. ObjectWeb is now also the hosting organization for the Enhydra project.

Enhydra

Enhydra was one of the first Java-based Web application servers. Enhydra was sponsored by a company known as Lutris that used open source as a means of creating demand for their products. Lutris failed sometime during the dot-com crash, and now the ObjectWeb consortium hosts the Enhydra projects. However the ObjectWeb consortium still host Enhydra at `http://www.enhydra.org`.

Over the years, the Enhydra project has added a number of interesting subprojects. The community now supports a set of projects designed to provide application server capabilities and Web services to Java 2 Micro Edition (J2ME) platforms. Barracuda is a well-regarded Web application framework hosted on Enhydra. XMLC, which provides a clean separation between Web page design and the generation of dynamic content, is also a project worth looking into. Using XMLC a Web page can be mocked up by a Web designer, and the dynamic content can be generated by a servlet. XMLC marries the servlet to the page mockup, replacing the fake values with the real values as the page is served through the application server. This technology can be used to reduce the cycle time on projects using a "visual design, code, and then integrate" cycle.

SourceForge.net

SourceForge.net serves as an open source project incubator, offering free hosting for projects with licenses accepted as open source by the OSI. SourceForge.net is the largest open source community in existence. SourceForge.net currently claims over 56,000 separate projects, over 7,900 of which are Java based. SourceForge.net is owned by OSDN, which in turn is a wholly owned subsidiary of VA Software Corporation. VA Software is known for VA Linux. SourceForge.net can be accessed at (surprise) `http://www.sourceforge.net`.

Table 1.4 ObjectWeb Projects

PROJECT	WHAT IT IS
JonAS	An open source Enterprise Java Bean container
JORAM	An open source implementation of the Java Messaging Service

What makes SourceForge.net so popular? The site's popularity is due to a combination of things. SourceForge.net offers many things that an open source project needs to get started and succeed, and it offers them to open source developers for free. Smaller projects that do not have any funding can get started on SourceForge.net with no startup costs. For example, SourceForge.net provides free Web site hosting for SourceForge.net projects. As a part of this free hosting service, the site offers 100 MB of storage per project. This storage can be used for project-oriented Web content, project files, and documentation. This hosting service also supports CGI and PHP scripting.

SourceForge.net also eases user access to hosted projects by offering a standardized summary page for each project that provides links to the major areas within a project. An example of a summary page is shown in Figure 1.1.

The summary also provides a brief summary of project status and current project issues.

Projects on SourceForge.net are provided with database access to a MySQL database. The database can be used by the project Web site or for developing and testing the project itself. Developers on active SourceForge.net projects also have access to shell accounts through SSH. Tools are available to allow compiling projects directly on the SourceForge.net machines. This means that binaries can be provided for machines and operating systems that normally would not be available to smaller projects.

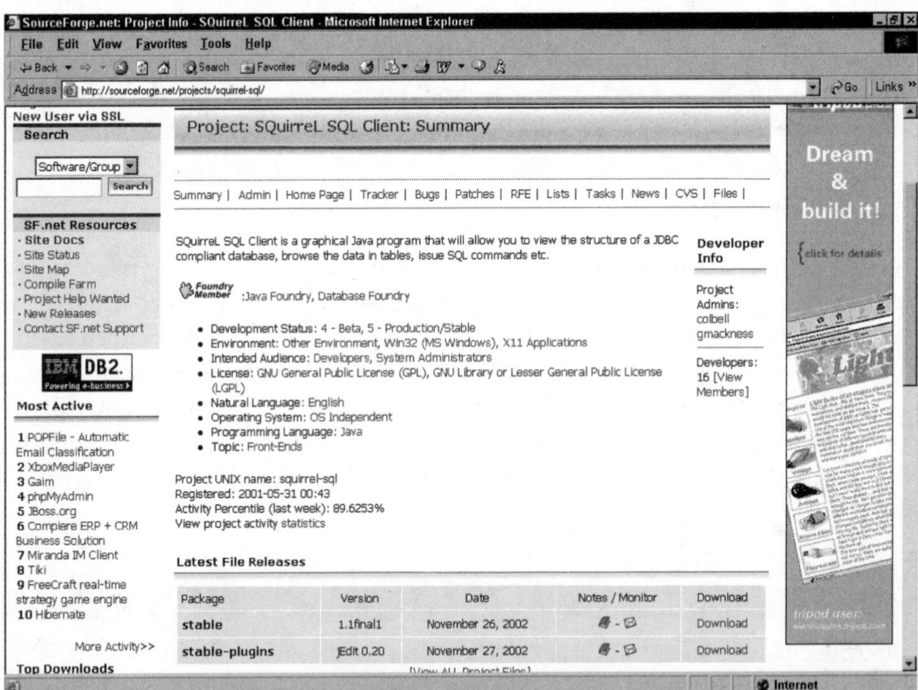

Figure 1.1 Source Forge Project summary page for Squirrel.

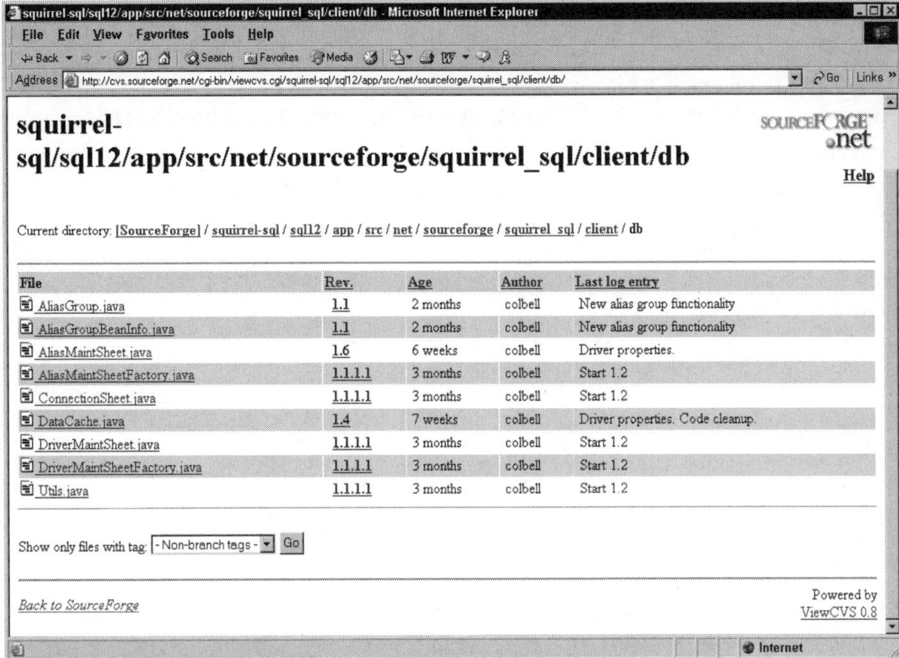

Figure 1.2 Source Forge CVS repository browser.

Each project is provided with a bug-tracking system. The bug tracker allows bugs to be reported by users and tracked by the project team. As progress is made on addressing bugs, the status can be reported back, providing feedback to users, who are able check on the status of the reported bug.

Collaboration is a necessary part of the product mix for any open source community. SourceForge.net provides mailing list support and forum discussion software for each project. The mail list has spam-protection features and is automatically archived providing convenient access to previous list traffic.

SourceForge.net has not forgotten the need for configuration management. It provides each project with a CVS repository. The CVS repositories can be accessed using standard CVS clients. SourceForge.net also provides a Web-based repository browser (shown in Figure 1.2) that allows you to navigate the repository source code tree and view or download individual files as needed.

Summary

In this chapter, we examined the definition of open source software and explored the differences between various open source licenses. These open source licenses will be important to us as we select components to build an enterprise platform. Most of the components we will use come from the open source communities that we briefly explored in this chapter.

In Chapter 2, we will establish the architecture of the platform that we will be creating, and we will identify the components that we will need to create it. In Chapter 3, we will look at the decision-making process for selecting the right components and take a look at some of the factors involved in using open source components in an enterprise setting.

CHAPTER

2

Java Enterprise Architecture

This book focuses on the creation of an enterprise platform from open source Java components. To create an enterprise platform, we become architects. According to the American Heritage Dictionary, *architecture* is "the orderly arrangement of parts," or, more specifically for computer applications: "The overall design or structure of a computer system, including the hardware and the software required to run it." Thus, architecture is the technology framework or infrastructure that systems solutions are built upon. The architecture we create is determined by the needs of the solution and the constraints imposed by technology, resources, and organization.

In this book, we use Java as a basis for our platform and impose two primary constraints:

- We use Java 2 Enterprise Edition (J2EE) as a base for our architecture.
- We use open source software.

These constraints limit the selection of "parts" for us to arrange. However, we will use these constants as guidelines and not as hard and fast rules.

This chapter describes the architecture of the enterprise platform in the context of the J2EE specifications and the other tools that are available that enable you to build and deploy complex enterprise applications.

Examining the Different Types of Platforms

A *platform* as it relates to software development is the combination of hardware and software that is used to develop and/or deliver a software application. This is normally thought of as a combination of hardware and an operating system. For example, Linux running on an Intel Pentium 4 constitutes a platform. Add the GNU development utilities to Linux, and you then have a development platform. Other examples of platforms are Solaris running on Sun hardware or Windows running on Intel hardware. The following sections discuss the various types of platforms.

Development Platforms

A development platform is software used to develop software. Typically, the software is developed for deployment in a specific environment. The development platform normally includes a compiler or interpreter and may also include other programming tools such as debuggers, and editors. The Java Developers Kit (JDK) is the basic development platform for Java programs. The JDK provide basic tools such as a Java compiler and the jar tool. These are designed to execute from a command line.

CROSS-REFERENCE **A development environment normally includes more advanced tools that assist in the development process. These will be examined in more detail in Chapter 4.**

Delivery Platforms

Sometimes a software environment—notably Java—is designed to be independent of the hardware and operating system it is executed on. This hardware-independent "platform" executes on, or is hosted by, another platform, thus achieving platform independence at one level.

Java is a good example of a platform that achieves platform independence. *Platform independence* means that it is possible to write applications in Java that are not dependent on the underlying hardware and operating system that the Java Virtual Machine (JVM) executes on because the JVM itself is a platform. In this case, the JVM is called a *delivery platform,* a term for the software that provides services needed to run or execute an application.

Most operating systems are delivery platforms in themselves. Some languages need an interpreter, runtime environment, or virtual machine to run programs written in that language. In these cases, these other components either form a delivery platform or become part of the delivery platform.

The JVM is a part of the virtual delivery platform for Java. The entire Java delivery platform is known as the Java Runtime Environment, or *JRE*. The JRE provides all of the components needed to run a program written for the Java 2 Standard Edition (or J2SE).

NOTE The JRE does not provide the tools needed to develop Java programs, only to run them.

As just mentioned, the JDK provides the tools to develop Java software. However, the JDK by itself does not provide the tools needed to develop enterprise-class applications. For that we need an enterprise platform.

Enterprise Platforms and Applications

The first thing that may spring to mind when you hear the word enterprise is a starship with the mission to "Boldly go where no one has gone before." However, that particular "Enterprise" is not what we're talking about here; going back to the American Heritage Dictionary an enterprise is "an undertaking, especially one of some scope, complication, and risk."

This more apropos definition accurately reflects the nature of enterprise systems, but the dictionary also provides a less-interesting definition of an enterprise as a "business organization." In this context, then, an enterprise is where we work, go to school, or volunteer.

An enterprise normally has many computing systems. Each system may have specific jobs for which it is used. For example, there are likely to be systems for accounting and human resources. There are probably systems to provide services for corporate email and to use for archival document storage. An enterprise platform provides the ability to deploy or deliver software that integrates these various separate systems. This is the trait that most distinguishes an enterprise platform from other software-delivery platforms.

An *enterprise application*, then, is an application that supports a business or enterprise undertaking. Most large organizations already have systems in place to assist with the daily needs of the business. However, because these organizations are constantly evolving to better meet the needs of their customers, these systems are also constantly evolving. For this reason, an enterprise platform must not only support the delivery of enterprise applications but also enable the building of enterprise applications that can leverage the existing infrastructure and applications within the organization. This brings us back to the first definition of enterprise, involving scope, complication, and risk.

Enterprise applications are created using an enterprise platform. An *enterprise platform* is the software infrastructure that provides the services necessary to deliver applications, integrating the various systems within an enterprise. In other words, an enterprise platform is a delivery platform that interacts with and integrates various other systems within, and external to, an enterprise or organization. To do this, an enterprise platform provides intersystem connectivity, allowing new applications to be built that combine information stored on many disparate systems. This connectivity needs to be flexible enough that it can be used by many different applications.

But the enterprise platform goes beyond simple connectivity; it must also provide a means of delivering applications to end users. End users are the ultimate consumers of the information provided by the system. Although some enterprise systems may be small, most enterprise applications must be able to scale to support a large numbers of users.

Java 2 Enterprise Edition as an Enterprise Platform

We mentioned earlier in the chapter that the JRE is a delivery platform for platform-independent Java applications. The Java 2 Enterprise Edition, or J2EE, is the Java enterprise platform. J2EE is designed as a platform that can be used to integrate the various systems within an enterprise. In many ways, Java is uniquely suited to this task. The Java language was designed to be independent of the hardware and operating that it executes on. This makes it possible to use one language to write components for each of the various other platforms that may exist within the enterprise. Java has some features for distributed processing built into the language. Java also has a very strong set of libraries that can be used for database access and network communication.

Still, an enterprise platform needs more than these basic libraries, and J2EE provides much of its required functionality. The primary components that make up a J2EE platform are:

Java servlets	Dynamic Web content generation
JavaServer Pages	Dynamic Web pages
Enterprise Java Beans	Distributed component technology

Additionally, J2EE defines a number of standard services that must be available for use by the primary components. These are:

Java Mail	Sending email messages
Java Messaging Services	Asynchronous processing
JNDI (Java Naming and Directory Interface)	Java naming and directory interface services
Java Transaction API	Transaction management
JDBC API (Java Database Connectivity)	Java database connectivity

XML Processing	Information exchange between systems
Web services	Language-independent distributed processing

Many of these services are now standard features of the J2SE platform, with the primary exception being Java Mail and Java Messaging Services. The rest of this chapter explores how these technologies can be combined with other technologies and how they can be used to build a platform for delivering enterprise applications.

Requirements and Goals for an Enterprise Platform

Before moving on from the topic of platforms, let's review our initial goals, requirements, and constraints for an enterprise platform.

- We want to create a platform that is suitable for the development and deployment of enterprise applications.
- We want to minimize dependencies on hardware and operating systems.
- We want to minimize dependencies on any specific choice of platform component.
- The platform should be scalable to support large complex applications and to support a large base of users.
- We want to constrain ourselves (for the most part) to using Java and open source components.

There are several reasons for these goals and constraints:

Promoting the use of Java. We want to enable companies and individuals that need to deliver enterprise applications to do so with a Java platform. To this end we want to provide a platform that can be used for development and delivery of J2EE applications.

Providing cost-effective development solutions. In some cases, J2EE is not used for smaller enterprise applications because of the expense associated with commercial J2EE platforms. By providing an alternate, cost-effective solution we get all of the advantages of the J2EE platform without the associated cost.

Reducing time to market. When an organization decides to embark upon a new J2EE project, sometimes there is a delay between the time the developers are available to staff a project and when the platform is available for them to use. This delay is often due to the lengthy procurement cycles for the purchase of expensive J2EE software. In these cases, it is possible to start development on an alternate compatible platform that is immediately available, and complete the development and deployment on the commercial platform when it is available. This is a good way to jump-start a development team that will be using the J2EE environment but does not currently have a commercial solution in place.

Providing a suitable learning platform. Enterprise applications are, by their nature, complex, and enterprise application development is not a task that is easily mastered. We want to provide a platform that offers the opportunity for developers to sharpen their enterprise-development skills on systems already available to them.

Platform Users and Stakeholders

Our discussion so far in this chapter has centered on the platform we will build for creating and delivering enterprise software. The platform itself is an enterprise system. In addition to having an idea of what you are going to build, it is always a good idea to have an understanding of whom you are going to build for—the stakeholders for the platform. *Stakeholders* are those people or organizations that have a vested interest in a system. Examples of stakeholders include users, developers, management, vendors, and customers.

Most enterprise systems have many stakeholders. Some stakeholders are not or will not be users of the system but they have an interest in the system for one reason or another. For example, developers sometimes never use an application that they have developed once it has been deployed, yet they clearly have an interest in the system as it is being developed. When creating any system, it is important to understand who are the stakeholders in a system, and what their interests in the system are.

The following sections discuss the general categories of typical stakeholders in an enterprise system. Because we are building a general-purpose platform that is also an enterprise system, we will take a generic view of the stakeholders that applies to most enterprise systems and applications.

End Users

The term *end user* refers to the consumer who ultimately uses the applications that are delivered through an enterprise system. If the system is a public Web site then end users are those people who access the site. Frequently, the end user is not paying for the application being developed, but just benefits from using the application in some way.

Keep in mind that often the end user is not the customer. Many enterprise systems are not created for use by the general public but are instead targeted at specific classes of users, such as employees, vendors, or dealers. These users are considered end users.

The Customer

The customer can be many things to many projects. The approach we will take to customer is that the *customer* is the organization or person responsible for paying for the development, deployment, and operation of the enterprise system or application. Typically the customer desires to see a direct benefit from the system or application that justifies the expense of development and deployment.

Developers

The word *developer* brings to mind programmers, the people who create the code for a system. However, a developer does not necessarily have to be a programmer. Most enterprise systems have a number of different types of developers who have varying responsibilities for adding features to an application. We will divide developers into the following four categories:

- Enterprise developer
- Application developer
- Web developer
- Content developer

These categories are roles that developers fulfill. Not every team will have separate individuals in each of these roles, and not all roles will be needed for every project. Also, this is not a list of all of the roles that might be included in a project team, but is rather a model of the types of roles that will typically be needed for an enterprise-development project.

The next sections will examine each of these developer roles in more detail.

Enterprise Developer

The enterprise developer develops the components that connect to the databases and systems that are used by the business, enterprise, or organization. From the enterprise developer's viewpoint, the platform must provide a means to expose interfaces to the underlying business systems. For this reason, these components are often referred to as the *business layer* of a software project, and typically have the following characteristics:

- They expose the business systems so the information can be used and exchanged by applications.
- They must enforce the business rules for access to and use of the information.
- They do not normally have a user interface but are intended for use by other programmers.
- They should be implemented as flexible and reusable components that can support many applications.
- They must have the ability to enforce the business rules that govern the access to the underlying systems, information, and data.
- They are specific to the organization but are general purpose in the sense that they are intended for use by many applications.

Application Developer

The application developer creates the specific components and logic for the implementation of specific applications. An application uses the components developed for the business layer, but the application's components are specific to a given application.

NOTE In non-Web-based applications, the application developer often also implements the user interface (UI). In other cases, there can be a separate developer or team of developers who focuses on just the UI.

The enterprise platform needs to provide tools to the application developer that supports the integration of the application logic with the enterprise of the business logic, while at the same time maintaining a loose coupling between them. By *loose coupling*, we mean minimizing dependencies between the layers. This is important because, from an organizational view, it is desirable to minimize the effect of changes in the underlying business systems on the applications, and vice versa.

Web Developer

In a Web-based system, the Web developer is responsible for the user experience. The Web developer creates the code, templates, style sheets, and forms that will be used to collect and render information provided by the end-users. The Web developer creates the user interface that will be rendered by the user's Web browser.

The enterprise platform needs to provide access to and expose the components provided by the application developer, while minimizing the need for the Web developer to understand the underlying application or business logic. That is, it should be possible to completely change the look and feel of an application without changing the underlying application or business components.

Content Developer

The content developer creates the content for the system. *Content* is the data and information that is available to the users of the system, such as images, text, or records in a database, for example. A content developer does not have to be a programmer. In many organizations, the content developer knows little or nothing about the actual mechanics of delivering the content the to end user. This is much the same as an author who knows little about the actual process of typesetting or printing a book or magazine article. It is even possible for a content developer to not recognize that they are performing that role.

The content developer's concern is typically (but not always) the content and not the presentation or the way that the content is going to look. Once again, this is much like a writer who creates an article for a magazine. The writer has little input into the page layout, font selection, or other presentation concerns for the article. These chores are left for others like Web developers.

Operations

Operations run an enterprise system once it is deployed. These are the system administrators, database administrators, network engineers, and other people that must install the system and its components and keep it all working with everything else in the enterprise. Sometimes, it is easy for a developer to forget about the costs associated with the installation, configuration, and maintenance of a program, but there are cases where a little foresight on the developer's part can significantly reduce costs and problems associated with installing and operating the software.

Enterprise

In some ways the enterprise may be thought of as the customer because ultimately the enterprise is writing the check, but normally the customer is an organization within an enterprise that directs the money to be spent. The enterprise, however, is still a stakeholder, for a number of reasons. Any enterprise system may have an effect on other systems deployed within the enterprise. This effect has to be considered as new systems are deployed. For example, an application that ties up a database for reporting purposes could prevent other applications from accepting orders. If accepting orders is more important than generating reports from that database, a solution must be found that does not affect the order-taking process.

There are other factors to consider. As a new application is being developed, the developers need to consider what components can be published and made available to other applications in the enterprise. The customer may not be concerned about paying for features that benefit others, although the enterprise may well be. Often it is better and less expensive to make components broader in scope so that they can be more easily reused. This is typically an enterprise concern.

Application Architecture and Layers

Most applications can be organized to support a common set of layers. In using layers to describe an architecture, each layer below the top layer provides a set of services for the layer immediately above it. Figure 2.1 shows a common set of layers for enterprise applications.

The *presentation layer* provides the logic needed for the user interface. Much of this is oriented towards formatting and displaying information. The presentation layer also exposes actions implemented by the application layer.

The *application layer* implements the logic needed for the specific application. It serves as an interface between the presentation layer and the business layer.

The *business layer* enforces business rules and protects the data layer. The business layer provides a common set of shared components for revealing and changing the data layer. The business layer may also provide conglomeration and aggregation services when the information will be needed by more than one application.

The *data layer* represents the underlying data that is accessed by the business layer.

The following sections describe each layer in more detail.

The Presentation Layer

The presentation layer provides for the generation and presentation of the user interface. Today, most enterprise applications are designed for Web-based delivery over the Internet.

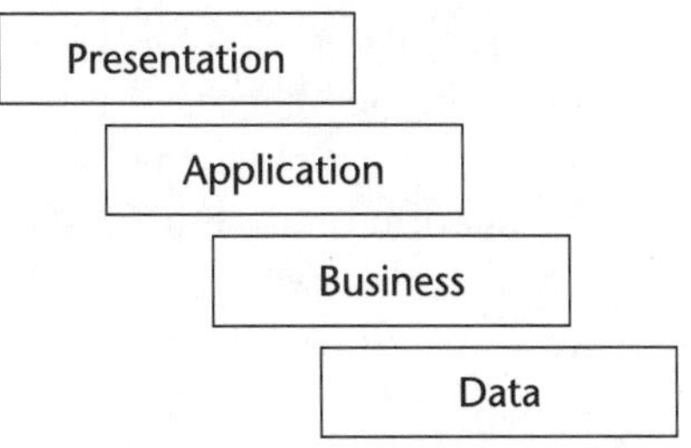

Figure 2.1 Enterprise application layers.

NOTE Web-based development does not mean that the application itself is available over the Internet, just that the underlying technology is the same that would be used to deliver it over the Internet. It is common for companies to have Web-based applications that are only available within the companies' own internal network or intranet.

The user interface of a Web-based application is delivered through a Web browser instead of through a custom client application. The application and business logic for a Web application is provided by software components running on Web application servers and other centrally controlled and managed machines.

Web-based delivery of applications makes sense for a number of reasons:

- Web-based delivery reduces deployment and maintenance costs.
- The application does not have to be installed and configured on the computers of each user who will use the application. Instead, the application is installed and maintained on a small number of Web application servers. The user just needs a Web browser to access the application. Today, Web browsers are a standard software component available on all personal computers.
- When the application is updated there is no need to distribute the update for installation on each users computer. Instead, each user gets immediate access to the update through the browser.
- Information updates can be made in a more timely fashion. When the information or data within an application is changed, the new data can be made available to all users at the same time. This means that everyone can access the most current and timely information, and everyone has access to the same data.

- Web applications can easily be made to be very accessible. If a company wants to make an application available to users who need access from outside the company network, the company can create a presence on the World Wide Web. Users can access this application using whatever means they have of connecting to the Web. The company no longer needs to be concerned about specialized network access, or banks of modems and telephone lines.

The Application Layer

The specific logic that governs an application is implemented in the application layer. The application layer forms an interface between the presentation layer above it and the business layer below it. The application layer may create new ways of looking at information by aggregating and conglomerating information retrieved from business layer components. See the "Aggregation and Conglomeration" sidebar for more information on aggregation and conglomeration.

Because the application layer sits between the presentation and business layers, the application layer normally controls the flow of the application, or the navigation through the application. The application layer also manages changes in the state of the application.

The Business Layer

The business layer serves as an interface and adapter layer between the application layer and the underlying data. The business layer enforces *business rules* for accessing and modifying the data in the layer below. An example of a business rule might be that delivery dates are only scheduled on Monday through Friday. A business object used in a shipping program would know this rule and be responsible for enforcing it. Objects in the business layer also serve to isolate the application layer from changes to the data layer. In this way, an underlying database can change the way that data is stored without affecting applications that access the database through business components.

The Data Layer

The data layer represents the underlying data used within a system. Typically, this data is stored in relational databases. However, it is possible that this data is stored in nonrelational data files or comes from applications running on other systems.

AGGREGATION AND CONGLOMERATION

Data aggregation **is the combining of similar types of data collected from different sources. For example, hotel room rate information might be collected from a number of different sources and then combined to provide a rate comparison between hotels in a region.**

Data conglomeration **is the collection and combining of dissimilar kinds of data. The data may or may not be related. For example, hotel listings, restaurants, tourist attractions, history, and current news about Frederick, Maryland might be collected in a travel application. These are different types of data, but are related by the common city.**

Often, portal applications aggregate and conglomerate data. An application designed to support salespeople in an automobile showroom might include local weather information alongside inventory levels and lease and loan rates. Even though these items are not directly related, they provide the information that is most important to the salesperson.

Distributed Computing Architectures

An enterprise platform is, by its nature, a distributed-computing platform. *Distributed computing* divides computing tasks among a number of computers. Each computer has specific roles and implements specific layers of the architecture. This allows a computer to be specialized and optimized for its specific roles. Although there have been many variations on distributed computing architectures in the past, we will only look at three: client/server (or two-tiered), three-tiered, and *n*-tiered.

Client/Server

The client/server architecture was the first generation of a common distributed-computing architecture. Figure 2.2 represents the client/server, or two-tiered, architecture. In a typical two-tiered application, the client software has the responsibility for implementing the presentation and application layers of an application. Often, the client also implements the business layer as well, which can have severe consequences. Making changes to the data layer means that all clients have to be updated. Furthermore, because most of the application logic resides on the client, code is implemented with dependencies among the presentation, application, and business layers, making the code for many applications very fragile. Each change therefore tends to have large effects on the system.

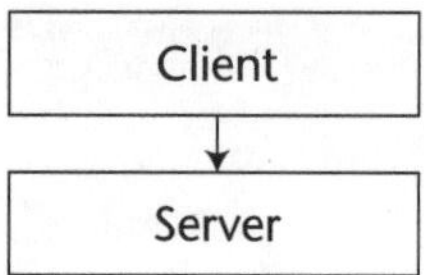

Figure 2.2 Client/server architecture.

Three-Tiered

The three-tiered architecture evolved to address the shortcomings of the client/server architecture. Figure 2.3 illustrates the three-tiered architecture. The primary difference between the client/server and three-tiered architectures is the separation of the business logic from the application layer on the client and the data layer. The business logic has become *middleware* and is no longer implemented on the client. Normally, the business logic is also separate from the databases and other repositories making up the data layer. Moving the business logic has two major advantages:

- It's now possible to make changes to the data layer and only affect the business layer.
- It's easier to share business components across the enterprise.

LAYERS VERSUS TIERS

Many people use the terms "layers" and "tiers" interchangeably. You can distinguish them this way: layers are associated with applications, and tiers are associated with platforms. Both applications and platforms have an architecture. Layers are used as a means to describe the logical segmentation and organization of the application. An application is deployed on a platform. Tiers are used to describe the logical segmentation and organization of the platform.

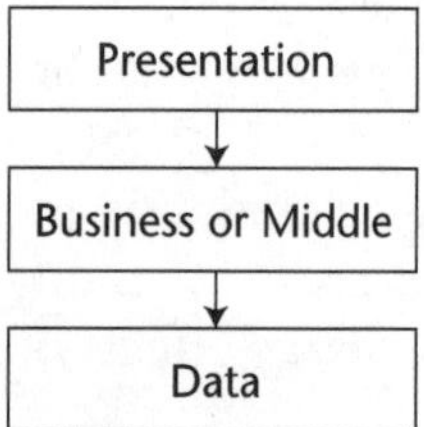

Figure 2.3 Three-tiered architecture.

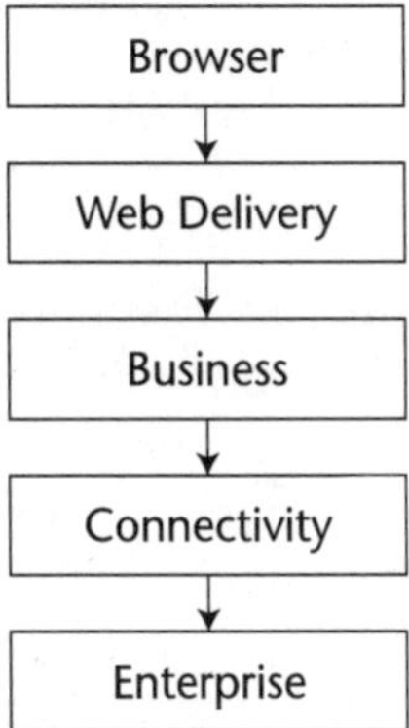

Figure 2.4 An *n*-tiered architecture.

n-Tiered

The *n*-tiered architecture follows naturally from three-tiered architectures. The *n*-tiered architecture may add any number of tiers needed to decouple software layers. Decoupling layers provides for better software design. Adding tiers provides more opportunities to decouple software layers and move them from the client to the server. As is shown in Figure 2.4, an *n*-tiered architecture can be made to more closely match the layers of an application's architecture. In many cases, changes on the server are easier to manage than changes on the client because servers tend to be centralized. A few servers handle many times more clients.

Decoupling also offers more opportunities to share components. Three-tiered systems make it much easier to share just the business logic between applications. Now, with *n*-tiered systems, there are many more opportunities to share; it is often even possible to share application logic between applications.

Tiers of an Enterprise Platform

Figure 2.5 shows the logical organization of an *n*-tiered enterprise platform and the various tiers. In an enterprise platform, each tier has a specific purpose and role within the architecture. We show five tiers; however, others may represent the same architecture differently. Our diagram is designed not just to help illustrate the logical tiers but to position the various components that make up the tiers. The five tiers we show are:

- Browser tier
- Web tier

- Component tier
- Connection tier
- Enterprise tier

Each tier supports different components of the architecture. The five tiers are grouped into three groups, front, middle, and back. This is a convenience that allows us to work with the *n*-tiered architecture as if it were a simpler three-tiered one. The front group consists of the browser and Web tiers. This group is where the presentation layers of an application are deployed.

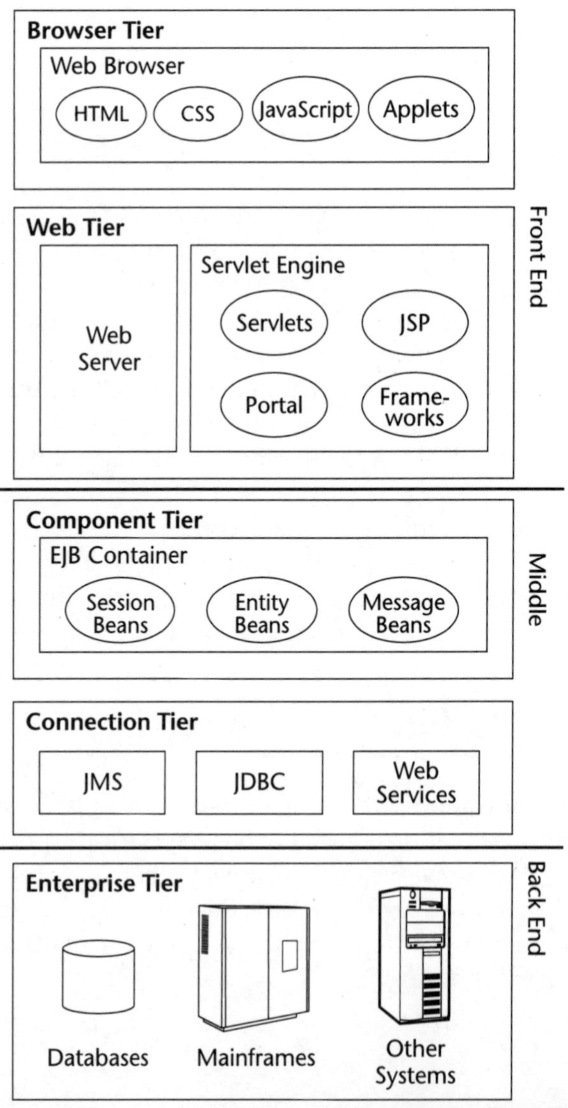

Figure 2.5 Logical organization of an enterprise platform.

The application layer of an application is often divided between the front and the middle tiers. Our preference is to put as much of the application layer as possible into the middle tier. The business layer is deployed to the middle group, or component tier. Enterprise applications typically have more than just a relational database in the back end. For this reason, we divide the back end into two tiers: the connection tier and the enterprise tier. The connection tier connects the components in the component tier to the data sources in the enterprise tier. The enterprise tier is where the data layers of an application are deployed.

The following sections discuss each of these tiers in more detail.

The Browser Tier

The browser tier is used to represent the components that execute within a Web browser. This tier includes Hypertext Markup Language (HTML), Cascading Style Sheets (CSS), JavaScript, Java applets, and other elements that execute within the Web browser environment. For the most part these elements are developed by Web developers and are delivered through the Web tier. With few exceptions, the browser tier supports elements of the presentation layer.

The Web Tier

The Web tier is the dynamic page-generation portion of an application server. This serves as the "front end" for most Web-based applications. For J2EE, this is implemented using servlets and JavaServer Pages.

The Web-Tier Components

Web-tier components are all either part of the Web application server or implemented as components of the Web application server. In our discussion, we will not be including applets and other browser-based components. Our emphasis instead will be on the server side of the platform.

The primary focus of Web-tier components is in support of the presentation and application layers of an application. Most of the components are used either to generate HTTP responses or to determine which pieces of application logic need to be invoked or collected to generate the HTTP response.

Servlets and Servlet Containers

Java servlets are designed to generate dynamic responses to HTTP requests. When an HTTP request is made, the servlet container executes the servlet, which builds the HTTP response. Often, this response is an HTML document, however it could be an XML document, image, or any other allowable HTTP response.

Servlet technology serves as an improvement over the original Common Gateway Interface (CGI) capability that is available on most Web servers. Instead of just serving static HTML files, Web servers can run a CGI program to generate the response to an HTTP request. The CGI program generates a dynamic response based on the values passed to it in the HTTP request. Although CGI was innovative at the time it was created, CGI programs also suffer from some severe limitations. For example, each time a request is made that accesses the CGI program, a new process is started that repeats execution of startup and initialization code, which can be a time-consuming process.

Like a CGI program, a servlet can generate a dynamic response to an HTTP request. However, a servlet container manages a servlet. The servlet container efficiently manages servlet initialization and threading. Typically, initialization is performed only once, when the container first loads the servlet. The container will run the servlet code responsible for generating a response in a thread. Threads are more efficient than processes and can be created in advance and pooled.

The servlet container provides some additional benefits as well. HTTP is a stateless protocol. Most applications require several interactions in order to complete an action by the user. This makes it necessary to maintain state across several HTTP exchanges. The servlet container provides a session manager that deals with the specifics of how to handle state for Web applications.

Template Engines

When writing servlets, many programmers found that much of what they were doing was copying lines of HTML into their Java code. This was awkward for a number of reasons but the biggest concern was that the HTML could not be managed and maintained separately from the Java source code. Changes to the HTML required a Java programmer to become involved, making it difficult to separate the roles of the application programmer and Web developer. Minor changes to the Web page become a major effort. It occurred to some people that the HTML could be read into the Java program from a separate file and then be modified separately as needed. Thus the template engine was born.

A *template engine* reads a template file, which is typically an HTML file with special markers. The application program builds a set of values that the template engine uses to replace the markers in the file. The resulting output file has the markers replaced with the values generated by the application.

This is sort of like the Madlibs game, where you are prompted to enter specific types of words such as nouns or adjectives. The words you provide are used to fill in the blanks within a story. The text combined with the words that you provide creates a new, sometimes humorous story.

A simple example may make this clearer. Following is a template where the values between the $ characters will be replaced.

```
Hello $username$! Welcome to our site. You have been here $numVisits$
times.
```

If we use "John" for the username value and "2" as the number of visits, the result will be:

```
Hello John! Welcome to our site. You have been here 2 times.
```

Most template engines provide additional tools that allow conditional processing of replacement values and iteration through collections of values. These simple constructs are designed to deal with problems such as table generation, and reflect only the needs of the presentation layer. The primary purpose of template engines remains the separation of the presentation logic from the application logic.

JavaServer Pages

JavaServer Pages (JSP) is the technology that is the Java response to various server-side scripting solutions. Originally with JSP, instead of putting the HTML into the Java code, as is done in servlets, the Java code was inserted into the HTML. This reflected the practices of developers using Microsoft's ASP and Netscape's server-side JavaScript technologies. Using JSP technology the developer would create a JSP page that mixed HTML and Java code, which would then be compiled to generate a servlet. (The compiling step is automatic on most application servers).

Many felt that this was a simpler way to do things. The Java code inside these pages tended to be simple, and the compiling process hid many of the concerns that Java programmers deal with. However there was still the problem of separation of the Web developer role from the Java programmer role. True, the Web developer did not have to know much about Java, but there was still a Java programming aspect to developing the Java code in the Web page.

Fortunately, JSP technology has matured. The first change was a different view of applying the same technology. A JSP compiles to a servlet, and one servlet in turn can forward a request to another servlet. With the goal of minimizing HTML inside of the servlet code and minimizing Java in the JSP, we can perform most of the application logic in a servlet and then forward the request to a JSP just to format the response. This allows the servlet and the JSP to work together in a Model-View-Control (MVC) design pattern. The JSP provides the view, the servlet provides the control, and the business classes invoked by the servlet represent the model. This way of using a JSP to render the view with a servlet as a controller has become known as *Model 2*. A design using stand-alone JSP is known as *Model 1*. The Model 2 approach to using JSP technology gives JSP many of the same benefits as template technologies, but with a slightly more complex syntax.

Still, a Model 2 design may need to support Java code inside of a JSP, particularly for conditional logic and looping for tables and other repetitive structures. The answer to this dilemma was taglibs. Taglibs provide the ability to add new JSP tags that can be used within a JSP page. In addition to the taglib capability, which allows the developer to extend the JSP set of tags, a standardized set of tags has been developed that addresses many common issues faced by Web designers. These tags handle situations that require conditional logic and looping, but do so without the need for Java code.

Application Frameworks

An *application framework* recognizes that most applications have a number of common needs. The framework tries to provide a single solution for these common needs that can be shared by all applications. A framework combines and integrates technologies in a reusable way. The framework reduces development time and eases maintenance of Web applications by establishing a common set of tools that can be applied to common concerns.

Most Web application frameworks are an implementation of the Model-View-Controller design pattern. They provide good separation of the code needed to create the view from that needed to represent the model. Often, the framework itself becomes the controller portion of the pattern. Web frameworks are most often implemented as servlets and are either combined with template engines to render the view or with JSPs and custom taglibs.

CROSS-REFERENCE **Web frameworks are covered in more detail in Chapter 7.**

The Middle, or Component, Tier

The component tier is the home for reusable components that implement application and business logic. In our architecture, we use Enterprise Java Beans (EJBs) to implement the component tier. We can also use ordinary Java classes or beans in those cases where EJB technology is too much, for example, when the physical architecture is not a good match for the logical architecture.

NOTE Components can also be built using Remote Method Invocation (RMI) and Common Object Request Broker Architecture (CORBA); however, our discussion will not focus on CORBA or RMI, primarily because they do not add any perceived value beyond that offered by current EJB technology.

The component tier is where business objects are used to expose the underlying enterprise tier through the connectivity tier. Business objects isolate applications from changes that may be made to underlying systems, and have the responsibility of enforcing the business rules that apply for accessing and using the underlying information. Business objects may also synthesize new information by combining information gathered from different systems.

Business objects can deal with data conversion concerns and provide services such as data caching and data isolation. Data caching is important in situations where the cost in time and performance to get the data is high, yet the data changes relatively slowly as compared to how often the data needs to be read. Data isolation is needed when the effect of reads on a system negatively affects other systems that need to access and update the same data. These services become invisible to the application layers above these business components but can be essential to the smooth operation of an enterprise system within the framework of the enterprise as a whole.

The component tier can also serve application components. There are a number of situations in which applications may have common needs. For example, most Web sites of businesses with a network of retail outlets will include the ability to find an outlet location nearest to the user. There might also be a need to locate the nearest authorized repair and service center. These applications serve different purposes and may have different user interfaces, but the logic behind the application is essentially the same. Supporting the application logic in the component tier makes the service application easier to implement because it can reuse some of the application logic of the previous application.

This brings us to the question, what is the difference between the application and business layers (not tiers)? The answer is that the application layer sits between the presentation layer and the business layer. The business layer sits between the application layer and the data layer. In the locator example discussed earlier, both applications also need to access the data layer, but the business component that they access may be different. One application will access a business component that uses a database of all of the retail locations, the other accesses a component that uses a database of all of the service centers. These databases in the enterprise tier may be maintained by different organizations within the enterprise and may be on different servers and different types of databases.

The Connectivity Tier

The connectivity tier provides connections between the business tier and the underlying systems of the enterprise. These enterprise systems reside in the enterprise tier and represent the databases, mainframes, ERP software, and other systems within the enterprise. The connectivity tier connects the business components in the component tier to these systems. There are three primary technologies that are used in this tier:

- JDBC is used for database connectivity.
- Messaging is used for asynchronous message exchanges.
- Web services (typically XML-based) are used for remote procedure calls.

NOTE There are other ways of connecting systems; for example, Common Object Request Broker Architecture (CORBA) or Remote Method Invocation (RMI) technologies can also be used to remotely execute components; however, these technologies tend to be tightly coupled to the business logic and rightfully belong in the component tier.

XML is discussed along with Web services because XML is a primary component within Web services. However, XML, by its nature, also provides services that can ease the exchange of information between systems. Although XML may be useful at several layers of an application's architecture, it is placed here in the connectivity tier for the platform architecture. See the *Web Services, SOAP, and XML* section later in this chapter for more information.

The Java Database Connectivity (JDBC) Layer and Databases

The Java Database Connectivity (JDBC) layer, as its name implies provides a uniform means of accessing databases from Java programs. JDBC is oriented towards accessing relational databases and supports the use of SQL as the query language. For the most part, JDBC handles issues such as conversion from database column types to Java types, but JDBC does not define a mapping between objects and relational databases.

A JDBC driver is necessary to use JDBC with a particular database. In most cases, this driver is specific to the database product being accessed. A driver known as the JDBC-ODBC bridge provides connectivity to databases that support an ODBC (Open DataBase Connectivity, a Microsoft database connectivity technology) interface but not a JDBC one. Use of this driver is often discouraged because it suffers from performance issues. JDBC drivers exist for most commercial and open source databases. There are several pure Java databases that use JDBC as the primary means of accessing the database.

Although the enterprise tier represents the connection layer to the enterprise, most enterprise applications require a relational database as part of the supporting infrastructure.

CROSS-REFERENCE **Because relational databases themselves can be a very expensive proposition for many companies, Chapter 8 examines open source databases as well as the JDBC drivers that are used to access them.**

Messaging

Messaging provides the ability for asynchronous interactions between systems. Unlike Web Services or RMI, where a process or program must be available to generate a response, with messaging, a message can be left in a queue and processed at a later time. Therefore, one component can send a message to another component even if the target component is not available. The source, or sending, component for the message does not need any knowledge of the target, or receiver. The only knowledge required by the sender is the format for the message and the destination for the message. Messages can be sent in a reliable fashion that guarantees message delivery and ensures that messages are received once and only once.

Messaging is built upon Java Messaging Service (JMS). JMS provides a common means of accessing a lower-level messaging service, allowing Java programs to use technologies, such as IBM's MQSeries or other messaging infrastructures through a uniform interface. The JMS API isolates dependencies upon the underlying messaging system similarly to the way that JDBC isolates database dependencies.

Web Services, SOAP, and XML

Web services provide the ability to use the common infrastructure of the Internet or World Wide Web to remotely execute programs that are distributed on machines located across the network. More concisely, a *Web service* is a computer program, function, or procedure that can be executed remotely by another computer program, using the same protocols and infrastructure that is used to deliver Web pages over the Internet.

Today, when we speak of Web services, we are typically talking about the Simple Object Access Protocol (SOAP). SOAP is a messaging standard based on XML. SOAP messages can be exchanged through the Hypertext Transport Protocol (HTTP). SOAP messages normally represent remote procedure calls or the return values of remote procedure calls. A remote procedure call occurs when a program on one machine executes a function that runs on another machine.

SOAP has a number of advantages as a distributed-computing solution:

- SOAP is independent of the underlying implementation layer.
- It is possible to access Enterprise Java Beans, CORBA components, and Distributed Component Object Model (DCOM) components, or programs written in any language, through a SOAP interface.
- SOAP is supported on all major Web-hosting environments.
- The technologies that SOAP depends on are ubiquitous.
- SOAP is built on XML and can use HTTP as a transport protocol. This means that SOAP solutions can be developed to leverage an existing Web infrastructure.
- SOAP has wide industry support from companies such as IBM, Sun, and Microsoft.

For these reasons, SOAP and Web services have become an important factor in both enterprise and Internet computing. SOAP provides a common layer for executing remote procedure calls that are hardware, software, and programming language independent. Instead of requiring expensive middleware tools, SOAP builds upon the common infrastructure of the Web.

Although SOAP is the direction that most current Web services implementations are taking, SOAP is not the only Web services solution. Many companies saw the need for Web services before standards were formalized. These companies created XML documents that could be exchanged as messages between machines. The difference between this approach and the SOAP approach is primarily standardization. SOAP-based messages can use a common parsing infrastructure, whereas custom XML messages require the XML to be parsed and manipulated. Thus, developers need more information when exchanging custom XML documents than they do when using methods invoked via the SOAP protocol.

There are other places where XML is useful in an enterprise system. For example, XML documents are easy to transform into other documents using technologies such as XML stylesheets. These transformation abilities make XML a good candidate for content representation. For example, content that is stored in an XML document format can be easily transformed for rendering on a browser, a printer, or a wireless device. Each of these devices has its own peculiarities that can be addressed during the transformation.

The Enterprise Tier

The enterprise tier is the backbone of everything; it is where the information used by the applications resides. The data layer of an application is deployed in the enterprise tier. The enterprise tier may consist of more than just databases. In most enterprise environments at large corporations, for example, there are mainframe computers and other systems that reside in this enterprise layer. In most cases, the enterprise layer already exists and represents something that you are building upon or adding to. The primary piece of enterprise-layer software that we look at in this book is the relational database.

CROSS-REFERENCE **Relational databases are examined in detail in Chapter 8.**

Platform-Architecture Views

When discussing architecture from different perspectives, we call these *perspective views*. So far in this chapter, we have discussed the stakeholder views and the logical views of the architecture, although we did not identify them as such. In this section, we will examine the physical and process views. The physical view is related to how the various components are intended to be deployed on actual hardware. We provide a general discussion here and a more detailed coverage of this topic in Chapter 15. Our discussion of the process view discusses the internal processes of an application running within the platform.

The Physical View

The physical view of a platform architecture shows and explains how the platform will be deployed on actual hardware. If this were an architecture document for a specific instance of a platform, the *physical view* of the architecture would show exactly the hardware components that would be used for each of the tiers. Brand, model, and other specific characteristics would normally identify these machines or physical components. In our situation, though, the physical view can vary widely. A student or developer for example might want to deploy all of the layers on a single machine that he or she already owns. A small business or a department within a larger business might wish to divide the functionality between two or three machines. Two or three machines might even be adequate for applications that are made available to the Web if only a moderate number of users are expected to use the system. Larger deployments might add additional machines to better share the load.

In general, the single machine deployment is designed to support the individual developer. The two- and three-machine systems are suitable for supporting team development and integration-testing environments. Depending on the application, these configurations may also be useful for stage testing (*stage testing* is the final phase of testing immediately before code is placed into actual production; stage testing is normally done in an environment that is structurally the same as the deployment environment, but on a smaller scale). There are also a number of situations in which any of these configurations could be used for actual application deployment; however, these situations are very dependent on the nature of the specific applications and the way they will be used. This issue is considered in more detail in Chapter 15.

CROSS-REFERENCE **In this section, we examine physical architectures that match the normal requirements of a single developer or small development team. Larger-scale deployments and issues that need to be considered and addressed are discussed in more detail in Chapter 15.**

In this discussion, we will not consider specific hardware (or operating systems). For our purposes, it is enough just to identify the number of machines that will be used and what components each machine will support. As a point of reference, however, all of the components examined in this book have been tested running on standard Intel- and AMD-based personal computers running Windows and Linux operating systems.

Also, for the most part, this discussion does not cover topics such as load balancing (except very briefly), firewalls, message routing, or the other topics you might normally expect to see in a discussion of the physical architecture view. These topics require an understanding of specific application needs and are beyond the scope of this chapter.

Single-Machine Deployment

Deploying a platform on a single machine sounds contrary to the basis of an enterprise platform; however, this is actually a common need for several reasons:

- Developers find it convenient to be able to develop, deploy, and test their components without the need to coordinate with other developers on a project. This is possible if the entire enterprise platform exists on their development machine.

TIP **This is actually one of the advantages that can be realized by the platform developed in this book. It allows developers to work independently, deploying and testing their code as they move forward without affecting the other developers.**

- Students and those who want to experiment with the technology can install and learn from the system without a massive infrastructure deployment.

> Single-machine deployment also provides a platform that can be easily used for demonstration purposes. This is very important for those creating commercial software because the single-machine platform makes it easy to be prepared for conferences and sales presentations. For example, when supporting the development of commercial eLearning products, John found it much easier to run demonstrations from his laptop than to depend on the Web infrastructure, which may or may not exist at any client site or venue.

Other than to provide the rationale for why a single-machine deployment is useful, there is not much else to say. All of the components are deployed on one machine. That's it! The machine must still have the network software installed so that the machine acts as though it were on a network, even if it's just a network of one machine. This is required because most of the components are designed for distributed computing and are dependent on the network infrastructure. This is not usually an issue if the machine you are using is normally connected to a network; if this is so, it typically has the required network software already installed.

Two-Machine Deployment

When more machines are added to the mix, the physical architecture for an enterprise platform becomes more complex. Figure 2.6 demonstrates a very common deployment scheme for two machines.

As you can see, Machine 2 only supports a relational database and represents the enterprise tier. Machine 1 supports everything else and supports all other tiers. This configuration does not include support for Web services or JMS messaging to Machine 2; however, many enterprise applications do not need to use these features. Also, note that all of the servlet engines that we will examine fully support HTTP. This makes the Web server an optional component; therefore, it is shaded. This architecture works well for applications that require a large database or are database intensive. It does not, however, support all of the features that might need to be used or tested.

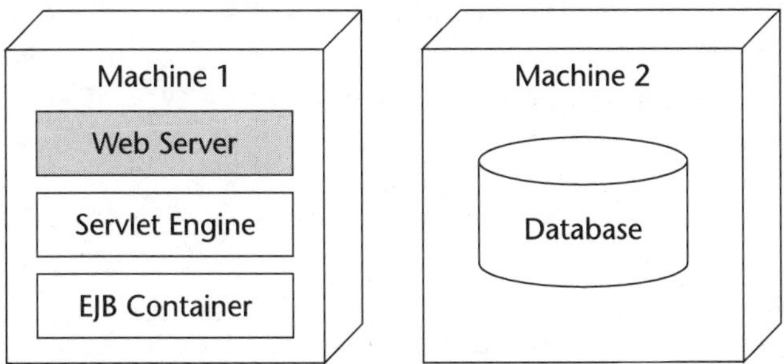

Figure 2.6 Simple two-machine deployment.

A more complex deployment on two machines is shown in Figure 2.7. This architecture places the entire front-end processing onto Machine 1 and all of the middle and back-end features onto Machine 2. Support for Web services and messaging is also included. Machine 2 also has a servlet container, but this servlet container is a convenience for use by the Web services components. This configuration is useful for applications that are heavy on the user interface and presentation layers, but do not require a lot of back-end processing power.

Deployment on Three or More Machines

When you are deploying an enterprise platform on three or more machines, as shown in Figure 2.8, the physical architecture can map very closely to the logical three-tiered architecture discussed earlier in the chapter. In this case, Machine 1 is used for the front end, machine two is used for the middle tier with connectivity, and Machine 3 serves as the back end or enterprise tier. Although not shown, it would be just as reasonable to move the Web services and JMS support infrastructure to Machine 3, but because databases typically consume more resources than other components it's usually preferable to leave the database by itself.

Adding additional machines requires a more intimate understanding of the specific applications and the way they will be used. Typically, more machines are used to either replicate a tier or to split a tier. When a tier is *replicated*, the load is balanced (using another hardware or software component) across the duplicate machines. When a tier is *split*, application components are divided among machines according to specific application or domain needs. It is most common to replicate the front end and to split the middle and back-end machines. For example, if an application is database intensive and uses two databases, it might make sense to locate each database on a separate database server to split the back end.

The Process View

The architectural process view shows the processes involved in the applications that run within that architecture. This section covers this topic in a general sense for Web applications built on an enterprise platform. Figure 2.9 is a diagram showing how various components might interact in a typical Web-based enterprise application.

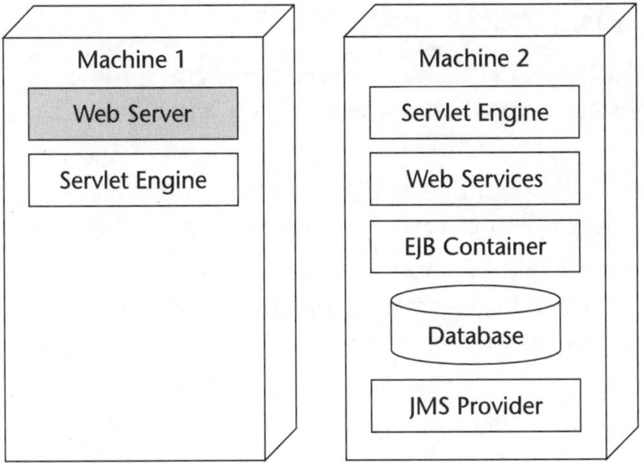

Figure 2.7 Complex two-machine deployment.

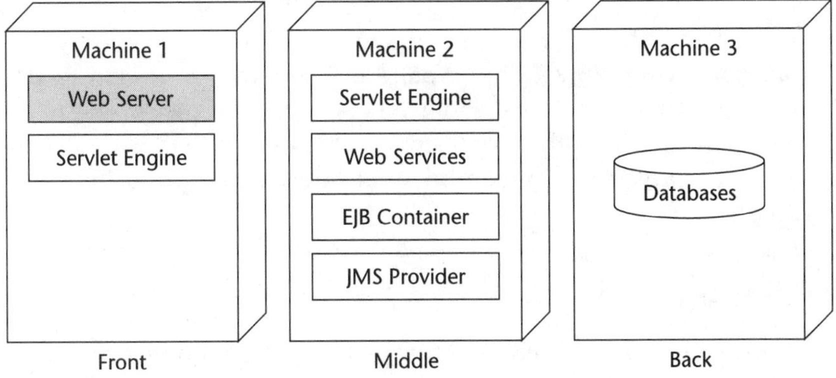

Figure 2.8 Three-machine deployment.

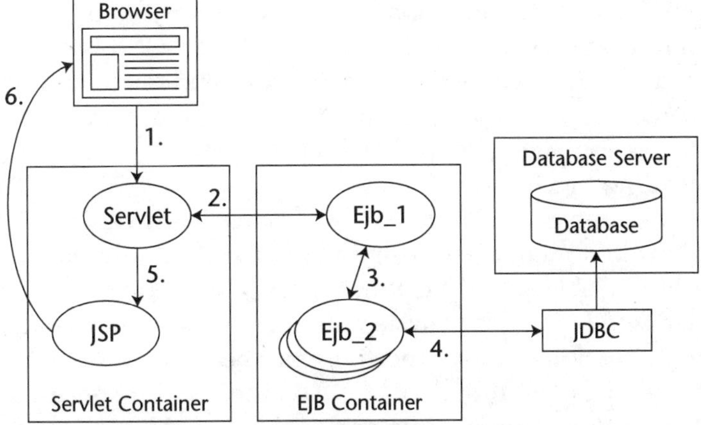

Figure 2.9 Typical application process.

The steps in the diagram are as follows:

1. Each action begins with an HTTP request from a Web browser to a servlet. It is not important here whether the request is a POST or a GET request.
2. The servlet invokes an EJB (identified as EJB_1). This is most likely a session bean that is implementing some portion of the application logic.
3. This first EJB, in turn, executes one or more other beans identified as EJB_2. These beans represent beans that implement business logic and will most likely be a mix of session and entity beans, depending on the application.
4. The beans implementing the business logic reference the database through JDBC.
5. The servlet now forwards the information to a JSP.
6. The JSP creates an HTML document that is returned as the HTTP response.

Most applications will follow a similar pattern. There will, of course, be differences within specific applications. Some may be more complex and involve larger numbers of beans and other connectivity channels; others may be simpler. This, however, provides a general view of how many applications will operate under the architecture.

What's Missing?

In any software architecture, there are things that fall through the cracks. These things tend to be application or component specific or do not fall neatly into one of the tiers or layers. XML parsers and XML utilities are good examples. There are situations where an XML parser may be used at almost any layer of the architecture. XML transformation through stylesheets into HTML might be used for the front end. XML messages sent by old-style Web services might need to be decoded in the middle tier. Even the back end might need to encode XML documents or may depend on an XML database. Potentially, there are other utility classes that may need to be considered, such as encryption utilities. So where do we include these tools?

In general, these tools cross tiers. They are often modeled as a vertical bar going from the top to the bottom of a tier diagram. Specifically, it is important to note utilities that are available at each tier when those utilities are necessary for a common function within the tier or system. In the case of XML parsing, we included it in the discussion of the connectivity tier because connectivity requires that capability in order to support SOAP-based Web services. If objects in a specific tier need encryption components, they should be included in that tier. If encryption is needed at several tiers, then it should be included at each tier for which it is required.

In this book we look at open source tools for dealing with XML documents. We will not be discussing open source tools for encryption. (Basic encryption tools are now included in the JDK anyway.) The rationale for this is that although encryption is an important technology, it is already provided in the platform and is not essential to most enterprise applications. The basic XML tools, on the other hand, are also now provided by the JDK, but we still cover XML because its use is so widespread and is required by a large number of enterprise applications.

There are two other specific capabilities that are commonly needed in enterprise environments but that are not covered here:

File transfer. Specifically, we mean file transfer via the File Transfer Protocol, or FTP. FTP is often used as a file exchange mechanism between corporations or machines. However, FTP is not supported as part of the enterprise Java platform. Because of that we have not included it as part of our platform.

JavaMail. Java Mail is a required service for an enterprise Java platform; however, the Java Mail API is designed to work with many existing mail platforms. Most companies and individuals already have access to an email infrastructure that is supported by the Java mail API. Although some of our examples may use the Java Mail API, we did not feel that it was important to look at Java products that implemented the service layers below the API. Therefore we do not include a chapter on Java Mail, and we do not examine the open source Java Mail products. If you need a mail platform, then you are encouraged to look at the James project, which is part of the Apache-Jakarta suite of products. James can be found at:

```
http://jakarta.apache.org/james/index.html
```

Benefits and Risks

It is our opinion that every architecture document should discuss the benefits and risks of the architecture. This chapter serves as the architecture document for this book. However, it is different from a typical architecture document in many respects because it does not cover specific products, hardware, or software. Normally, you would expect to see a list of all the infrastructure components. In this case, however, these topics are what make up the other 500 or so pages in the rest of this book. Still, it is appropriate to discuss the potential benefits and risks associated with what you are attempting to accomplish, that is, the creation of an enterprise platform from open source Java products.

So, what is the downside; what are the potential risks associated with this project to build an enterprise platform? There are several risks. Some risks are general risks related to all software acquisition. Others are unique and specific to open source. These are covered in more detail in Chapter 3, where we discuss the decision-making process for selecting software components.

Specific risks of this architecture are not significantly different from those of any other J2EE-based architecture:

- There is a risk of complexity that is inherent in all enterprise development. This platform does not suffer any more or any less from that risk than any other enterprise platform.
- In certain cases, there may be concerns about the performance and scalability of the platform; these are discussed in Chapter 15. Certainly, most of the benefit scenarios do not require the platform to be very scalable, and if scalability is a requirement, then there are always commercial alternatives that can be used for deployment.
- Support for and compatibility with Java and J2EE standards are two other considerations.

These risks can be managed by careful component selection, which is also addressed in the next chapter. At this point, it is sufficient to say that the potential benefits of the platform outweigh the risks.

Summary

As we've stated before, the goal of this book is to work the reader through the process of building an enterprise Java platform from freely available open source components. The potential benefits of a platform of this nature are:

- A low-cost platform for training and learning purposes
- An affordable platform that can be used to jump-start enterprise Java development efforts
- A platform that can be used as a tool to support individual developers
- An inexpensive platform that can be used as a tool to develop applications that will be deployed on other J2EE-based platforms
- A platform that can be used for proof of concept development of enterprise Java applications
- A reasonable platform for hosting enterprise Java applications

The primary benefits are realized by the fact that the platform does not cost thousands, or even hundreds, of dollars and can be downloaded from the

Internet in a few minutes (depending of course on your bandwidth). This enables any project that might have been hampered by the cost or purchase of a commercial J2EE product to move forward with a viable alternative. Yet, due to the nature of J2EE, that application can be moved to a commercial product if requirements demand such a move or if one becomes available for the project at a later date.

In this chapter, we have described the architecture of the platform we are going assemble as well as the various potential stakeholders and their interests in the system. We have also discussed the layers of a typical application architecture for applications that will be hosted by this system.

We have discussed distributed architectures in general and specifically covered the *n*-tiered architecture of the platform we are creating. The specific components that make up the J2EE environment and the components we will be using in our platform were explained. We provided a discussion of several potential physical deployment architectures and concluded with a section on the potential benefits and risks of the platform.

In the next chapter, we look at the decision-making process we will use to select our platform components.

CHAPTER

3

Selecting the Right Platform Components

Every software developer needs to be able to make decisions. Software development involves decision making, from deciding on the right programming language to use to selecting the developer tools, or deciding on how best to deploy and distribute an application. This chapter introduces the process that we will use throughout the rest of the book for selecting components for our enterprise platform.

Decisions, Decisions, Decisions

As we discuss in Chapter 1, the focus of this book is on building an enterprise software platform. As demonstrated in that chapter, an enterprise platform comprises a large number of independent components, each of which contributes capabilities to the overall platform. Selecting the components to be used to establish a platform is typically the role of a software architect. The architect uses his or her knowledge of the system to be delivered and the needs of the stakeholders to help make choices about which components to use. The architect must be able to explain the choices to others, such as programmers, customers, and management, in order to achieve the acceptance needed to make the project a successful one.

As software architects, we need to select which components will compose our enterprise platform. For example, if you know that the applications that will be created for this platform will use a Web-based interface, you will want to make sure that you have a servlet container as one of the platform components. After you determine the need for a servlet container, you need to decide among the many choices of servlet containers.

There may be a wide variety of choices for any single component in your platform. Because you have a large number of components that can be applied to your architecture, you want to make sure that you have a consistent means of deciding which component implementation you will select and use, and then be able to communicate the reasons for your choices to other stakeholders in the project. A consistent and documented product-selection process eases this communication task by making it possible to explain to all involved parties how the decision to use a specific component was reached.

This decision-making process is not unique to the use of open source software, but applies to the selection of any software component or application. However, this book is primarily about using open source software, so the first decision we will examine is the decision to use open source software.

Choosing Open Source Software

Why choose to use open source software? Although this question may offend some open source zealots, open source software is not the right choice in every situation. It is good to know when open source software is the right choice and be able to defend the decision to other stakeholders in a project. So, in this light, let's examine why people choose to use—or not use—open source solutions.

So what are the factors that push companies to choose the open source alternative to commercial software? How does open source software compare to commercial software in the areas of cost, fitness, quality, risk, and time? When you are making a decision to purchase or use any product, there several things of interest to consider:

- Cost
- Suitability
- Quality
- Risk
- Time

Weigh the needs and features of your product against each of these points when making a product decision. In some cases, cost may be the driving factor in making a product decision; in others cases, it may be suitability, quality, level of risk, or time. The following sections examine each of these factors briefly to help you understand how they affect a project decision.

Cost

Cost reflects the entire cost of owning and using the software. This is much more than just the initial cost of purchase. Cost includes cost of acquisition, cost of use, cost of training, and cost of maintenance. Taking all these costs into account, you come up with what's called the total *cost of ownership* for the time that the product will be used. Cost applies directly to a project's budget, and so in general we want to minimize costs when possible.

During the height of the "dot-com" era, Linux was heralded by many as *the* choice operating system for many of the newly formed and cash-tight startup companies. The rationale was simple, Linux met the software needs of these companies and could be acquired for free. In these cases, the initial cost of product acquisition was a driving factor in the decision-making process.

Most open source software is available for free. There may be restrictions placed on how the software or resulting products are used commercially, but the software is typically free of acquisition costs. That is not to say that there are no costs involved in using open source software, but the initial cost of purchase is zero.

Let's examine these costs as they relate to open source software. The cost of purchase is, of course, zero. There are, however, costs associated with:

Training. Initially, the cost of training for an open source application is likely to be higher than for commercial applications. This is because often there are limited training resources specializing in providing training for open source applications. However, for a large organization with many users, an initial investment in the development of training materials may be less costly than the purchase cost of the alternative commercial software.

Operations. It is difficult to determine operational cost differences. Initially, any new software will have higher costs associated with operations as the staff becomes more familiar with the software and the way it can be configured and used. Commercial products often offer or work with add-on tools (such as monitoring programs) that can be used to reduce operational costs. These tools often support open source products as well. For example, Apache is well supported by third-party Web monitoring tools. In general, the operational costs of open source software should not be substantially different from those of commercial equivalents.

Maintenance. Commercial software products normally charge annual fees to cover maintenance of the software and provide regular updates. Active open source projects maintain the software and provide updates for free. If a company wants to pay a fee for software maintenance, most open source products have developers who are willing to accept the money and address company-specific problems.

To summarize, open source software wins on initial acquisition costs, but loses on training costs. It ties with commercial software on operational costs but wins on maintenance costs. Overall, in most cases open source software will be less expensive for companies to use.

Suitability

Suitability is the measure of how well suited a given product is to the requirements that it is being applied against. A software product that is not a good fit for a given project can adversely affect both budget and time. In general, you want the product that best satisfies your project's needs.

As long as we are focused on enterprise Java and we select components that conform to the standards, we know that we have achieved a certain amount of suitability for our purpose of building an enterprise platform. Suitability has to be measured against each project's individual needs. As a very basic example, if you want to pound a nail into a board, you don't use a pot, you use a hammer. If you're making soup, though, a hammer will do you no good at all, but a pot will be quite useful.

For a platform developer, suitability is normally based on product features that relate to conformance to standards and performance metrics. If the primary purpose is to use the open source platform as a development environment and deployment will be done on a different platform, then most performance considerations typically do not apply. If open source components *are* to be used for deployment, then the suitability of the platform needs to be evaluated against the requirements for deployment and compared to competing products to determine the best value for the deployment solution.

CROSS-REFERENCE **Deployment concerns are covered in detail in Chapter 15.**

Quality

Obviously, the higher the quality of your chosen software, the better. There are three major quality concerns you need to consider when evaluating software: robustness, reliability, and reparability. These concerns are discussed in detail in the following sections.

Robustness

Robustness is a measure of how well a product withstands abnormal situations. Sure, we've established that open source software is typically zero initial cost and subsequently fast to acquire. But does it follow, as the saying goes,

"You get what you pay for"? In other words, can we expect low quality from free software just because we pay nothing for it? The answer is that quality is just as much an issue with open source software as it is with commercial software, and that the money you pay for a given piece of software does not in any way determine its quality.

Reliability

Reliability is a measure of how often the product breaks. First, the source code of an open source product is open to scrutiny. Many people can review and comment on the source code. You can even review the source code for a product before you decide to use it. Because of this, developers are often able to offer fixes as software problems are found. This means that many times problems are found and fixed faster in open source programs. It also means that, if needed, you can fix the software yourself.

Now, compare this to the commercial software. The software is reviewed internally by the vendor and depends on the quality assurance (QA) process within the vendor. In this model, with many fewer people testing the software, bugs may or may not be caught, just as with open source software. The difference is that the eyes that are looking over the code are those of the QA employees of the company that makes the software; with open source software, the reviewers are typically those who are using the software. If a bug does make it into a release, the size of the vendor's available workforce limits its ability to fix the bug and make the fix available to the user community. This means that a typical vendor has to decide which bugs to fix and which ones to ignore or postpone fixing until a later release. Even worse, the vendor may decide to no longer support a particular version of the software, and a fix may never be released or you may be forced to upgrade the software to a newer release. Microsoft, for example, collects all fixes (in particular those that don't have to do with security) into yearly releases called *service packs*, meaning that if you find a bug in Windows you may well have to wait up to a year to get the fix, if not longer. Or, sometimes the company will fix the bug in a new release of Windows, forcing you to pay for the upgrade if you want to get a fix for a problem you had with a previous release.

Reparability

Reparability is a measure of how long it takes to repair a product once it is broken. In general, open source software is more repairable because the source code is available, and this property typically means that bugs have often been discovered and repaired before you encounter them.

As you can see, open source products can have some advantages over typical commercial software products. The bottom line is that any particular open source product may or may not have a quality advantage over any specific commercial product. In many cases, the quality of open source products is at least comparable to that of their commercial counterparts. Often, it is superior. The issue is not black and white; you have to judge each piece of software on its own merits against its competition to determine the quality of that software, regardless of how much it costs to acquire.

Risk

Risk is the measure of how probable it is that things will go wrong with a given piece of software. There are many risks that may need to be taken into account when making a product decision, including the ability of the vendor to support the product, the stability of the vendor, and the ability to move to another product in the future. Naturally, you want to minimize risk to your projects.

So what are the potential risks associated with using open source software and do those risks outweigh those of using commercial software? There are several common risks associated with open source software:

- Insufficient technical support
- The lack of proper documentation
- Dubious longevity of the software

The following sections discuss each of these risks in more detail.

The Risk of Insufficient Software Support

The types and availability of support for a specific open source product is something that should be evaluated when making an open source product decision. When a commercial software package is purchased, it is normally expected that a certain level of technical support will come with the package or is available for purchase from the manufacturer or vendor. In some cases, this may include installation and configuration of the software in the customer's environment and investigation and resolution of problems. The level of technical support is something that is often negotiated along with the price of the software.

Support is normally available for open source software products as well, but there are differences in how that support can be had. Unless a separate support contract is negotiated with an open source consultant or vendor, support for an open source product is most likely to come from newsgroups, mailing lists, and online documentation. While this avenue can provide rapid response for more common issues, there are occasions when problems or concerns are never addressed because they affect too few people and no one has the time or inclination to research the issue.

One advantage open source software does have regarding support is that because the source code is available, users or developers can always research the issue themselves. A disadvantage is that you must bear the costs of finding that solution.

The Risk of Documentation Issues

The support issue is sometimes made worse by a lack of high-quality documentation or training for many open source projects. Although this is not true in many cases, especially for the larger projects such as Linux, Apache, or Mozilla, it often *is* true for smaller open source projects. The manufacturers of most serious commercial products spend a great deal of time developing documentation, and many commercial vendors use product training as a major source of revenue. The quality and availability of product documentation is another area that should be considered when choosing among open source products.

The Risk of Undetermined Longevity

In the commercial world, it is possible for a company to go out of business, creating a product orphan. This is a risk that should be weighed with any large commercial software purchase. For example, if you had switched your entire user base to the Be operating system (OS), you'd now be suffering from the effects of that OS becoming, essentially, an orphan. This same risk applies to open source projects. The development team may lose interest or because of other circumstances may no longer be able to provide continued development and support for the project. Again, this is less likely to be true of the larger projects such as Linux, which most likely isn't going to be orphaned anytime soon (if ever). Many of these larger projects have corporate or university support to help sustain development and support efforts.

Also, if an open source product is orphaned, anyone with an interest in maintaining the project can do so because the source code is available. For example, with the Hypersonic Java database, the original developer could no longer spend the time to maintain the product, but the community has since picked up and maintained the project and has even been releasing new versions.

Time

Time is often a factor in product decisions. Think of time as availability of the product. For example, if it will take six weeks to purchase and install a product but a solution is required in two days, then an alternative product that can be available immediately is a better choice. In general, we want the most expedient product.

Zero initial cost of purchase has another effect: a short purchasing cycle. This can be illustrated by John's experiences on several large J2EE-based projects. Each of these projects encountered long delays in purchasing popular commercial J2EE platforms. The reasons for the delays were varied, but in many cases the delay was caused by the fact any enterprise software procurement must consider the needs of the entire enterprise. The many organizations that make up the enterprise need to be involved in the decision-making process. In turn, the procurement cycle is slowed down drastically. When a decision on software purchasing is pending, naturally any individual projects that need the software to build their application are left waiting. This creates a situation in which a project is staffed but tools to start work are not available. With free software, approval of the purchase doesn't take nearly as long because the software is free. All that has to be considered is the quality of the software as weighed against the goals of the project.

In our case, we are focused on enterprise Java. Because J2EE creates a standardized platform for delivering solutions, it is possible to start development on one platform and deploy the application on another. Instead of having to wait for the purchasing process to be completed, a development team can get started working right away with available open source tools, and then the end product can be deployed on another platform altogether. To ensure this, strict compliance to standards should be enforced, but that's a good idea anyway.

Putting All the Factors Together

This section summarizes what the previous sections covered to give you sort of an aerial view of what those sections covered:

- Open source software has low initial acquisition costs, but may have a longer learning curve if staff is unfamiliar with the tools.
- Open source software is usually faster to acquire than commercial products because there is no procurement cycle.
- The quality of open source software is at least as good as, if not better than, comparable commercial products.
- Risks associated with using open source software are comparable to similar risks using commercial software.
- Suitability and features such as standards conformance and performance metrics are likely to vary widely among products, whether open source or commercial.

So, the best product for a given project is normally the one with the lowest cost, lowest risk, highest quality, and immediate availability, and one that does exactly what you need. In practice, of course, you often end up having to come up with the best compromise in all of these areas. If the features of an open source component meet the development or deployment requirements of a project, then open source software represents a high-value solution to addressing the project's needs.

The Product-Selection Process

You'll want to establish a process for selecting software components that ensures you are consistent in your decision making. The process must also provide you with a means of demonstrating that the decision you make is not flawed. Or, if the decision was flawed, the process should then help you to fix the mistakes so that they are not repeated. The process should minimize dependency on special skills or knowledge by the people involved in the decision-making process. However, special skills and knowledge can certainly benefit you by reducing the time to complete the selection process.

This product-selection process is designed to work in any situation where a product is an integral part of a software project. It has the following four stages:

- Market survey
- Features and needs analysis
- Evaluation
- Selection

Each of these stages is discussed in detail in the following sections.

The Market Survey

The first step in selecting a product or software component is discovering the choices that exist for that component. This part of the software-selection process is called the *market survey*. Essentially, a market survey is a search for all products that fit within a particular product category. Use the search to collect and organize information about the products. At this point, you're not usually weeding out any products, but rather trying to collect as much information as you can about as many relevant products as possible.

Years ago, this might have been accomplished by reviewing magazine advertisements and reading reviews. Today, though, the Web makes this process much faster and easier. Typically, it is possible to find a large list of matching products by conducting a few simple searches on your favorite search engine (a really good one is found at `http://www.google.com`).

The Features and Needs Analysis

After the market survey is completed, you need to determine the breadth of features available within the product category. Each product will have features or attributes that help distinguish it from the other products. These features should be noted. A good way to do this is to create a table. Table 3.1 illustrates features of various Java-based text editors. In this case, the features are listed down the rows, and the products are listed across the columns. An X in a cell indicates that the product in that row contains that feature; a blank space in a column indicates that the feature is missing from that product.

Typically, the list of features for a product category will be much longer. We have shortened the list for illustrative purposes. If you are already aware of the features that are important to your project, then you may decide to limit the list to only those features. If you are not aware of the types of features that a product is likely to offer, you may find it helpful to list all the features available in all products and then select those that are most important to your project. Many features will also have some attribute or unit of measurement associated with them. For example, the levels of undo capability shown in the chart above have varying values; these should be captured whenever possible.

Table 3.1 Feature Summary of Java-Based Editors

FEATURE	JPEDIT	JEXT	JEDIT
Java Syntax Highlight	X	X	X
HTML Support	X	X	
XML Support		X	
Regular Expressions		X	X
Extensibility		X	X
Templates	X		X
Undo	1 level	10 levels	Unlimited
License	GPL	GPL	GPL
JVM Required	1.3	1.2	1.3

Licensing (versus Cost) Considerations

When comparing commercial software, one of the features that would normally be represented is purchase price. Most open source software is free. Instead of price, what becomes important is the open source license used to distribute the software. As discussed in Chapter 1, different licenses have different limitations on how the product can be used. Let's say, for example, that you are evaluating database products for inclusion as an embedded part of your application, and you want to be able to distribute your application commercially without revealing the source code to your customers. In this case, you might want to avoid using products with the GNU Public License (GPL) because the GPL requires derivative works to also be published under GPL. This was among the reasons that Apple chose FreeBSD over Linux for the base of Mac OS X; FreeBSD is under a less-restrictive license (the FreeBSD license) that does not require derivative works to be published, as the GPL does. As you can see, it is important to understand the various open source licenses and treat the license as a feature or attribute of the software component.

Portability Considerations

Java is of course known as the "write once, run anywhere language." In reality, we do need to have an awareness of how the various components we want to use will interact with the operating system, the Java Virtual Machine (JVM), the hardware we plan to use, and with any other components that we will select. For example, it would not be good to select a component that requires a version 1.2 or later JVM if the only JVM supported on the hardware platform you are developing for is version 1.1. Although this seems obvious, you might be amazed at how many projects that have failed because the developers developed an application on one platform for deployment on another platform that only supported an earlier version of the JVM.

The issue of compatibility is exacerbated by the widespread use of heterogeneous computing environments. In many environments (universities, for example), the machines may be running operating systems such as Windows 98, which have different capabilities than more advanced operating systems such as Linux or Windows XP. Any or all of these systems may be present within the institution. If supporting all of these machines and operating systems is important for your purposes (for J2EE training, for example), then it is important to note any operating system or hardware issues with the component. In heterogeneous environments such as these, you'll have to make a choice between programming for the lowest common denominator (say JVM 1.1) and having multiple versions of your software available for different clients.

Other Features

There are other things that are not exactly project features, but may be important in the decision-making process. Some of these were discussed in the *Choosing Open Source Software* section earlier in this chapter. Addressing these "other features" in the software selection process includes obtaining answers to questions such as the following:

- What are my options for technical support?
- Is the product supported by a well-established organization?
- Are support issues answered quickly?
- Is the product still being maintained and supported?
- Does the necessary technical documentation exist?

These questions apply equally to open source and commercial products. Because this information is an important part of the decision-making process, it should be collected prior to the evaluation process.

Needs Analysis

It might seem obvious that you should know what you need before you start looking for a solution that properly addresses those needs. In reality, though, you often have only a general understanding of your needs before the project begins; other needs don't rear their ugly heads until the project is already underway.

The initial goal of the feature analysis is to gain a better understanding of the types of features that are available in a group of related products. These features often exist because others trying to solve similar problems have encountered the same needs. Often, understanding the features offered by a set of products provides new insights into how those features can be applied to your application. Also, you don't want to limit yourself by a lack of foresight. If a feature is very common across products, it is likely that it will be desirable to have it available for your project at some point in the future. In other words, we can use the features analysis to aid us in our needs analysis by highlighting what others have needed.

A good way to track the project's needs is to add a needs column to your earlier table and check any feature that you must have to support your project. It is also useful to provide a weight or score for each need to serve as a measure of how important the need is for our project. Many ways to rank these exist; we prefer a simple scheme of "required," "nice to have," and "not needed." An example based on our earlier feature summary example is shown in Table 3.2.

Table 3.2 Java Editors with Needs Column

FEATURE	JPEDIT	JEXT	JEDIT	NEEDS
Java Syntax Highlight	X	X	X	Required
HTML Support	X	X		Nice
XML Support		X		Nice
Regular Expressions		X	X	Required
Extensibility		X	X	Not needed
Templates	X		X	Not needed
Undo	1 level	10 levels	Unlimited	Three or more
License	GPL	GPL	GPL	N/A
JVM Required	1.3	1.2	1.3	1.3+

The Evaluation Process

After you have collected the features and needs information for your project, you need to evaluate the various products to determine the best choice. This evaluation is focused on the following three steps:

1. The first step to ranking products is to narrow the list of features to those features that are most critical for decision making. You can narrow the features by weighing or ranking them from most important to least important and then picking a cutoff point where the features are no longer relevant to your project goals or no longer have an effect on your decision-making process. You want to make certain that you consider things such as organizational stability, project size, and other factors here. Do not forget to identify your project's needs in these areas and the product's assessment in these areas.

NOTE If the project's needs are weighed as discussed in the previous section, then at this point, you'll already have an initial ranking of importance for each feature.

2. The next step, eliminating products, reduces the effort required for a more complete evaluation. Ultimately, you want to compare your project's needs with the capabilities of the products discovered in the market survey, eliminating products that are not a good match. Ideally, this will narrow the field down to one or two products, or three or four products at most.

If it has not been done before this point, make sure that the product documentation for the products is reviewed and that it is sufficient to meet the needs of the project teams. Also, review the support lists and online forums that cover the product to get an impression of the experiences others have had with the product.

What if none of the products meets all of your needs? In that case, you need to determine which products come closest to meeting those needs and then select those products for further evaluation. If all of the products are missing a required feature, you might have to start investigating to see if there's another type of product somewhere that you can acquire to cover that feature.

3. The third step is the testing process, where you make certain that products you're interested in actually do meet your needs. Testing involves acquiring and installing the products and then creating a typical application scenario that exercises the features that the project is most dependent upon. This may be a proof of concept application or a technical prototype that is intended to exercise or demonstrate specific features. Some tests may involve performance measurements, while others may only demonstrate that a certain feature works as expected. At a minimum, pass or fail information for specific tests should be captured and recorded. The amount of time spent testing must be in proportion to the overall project size.

The Selection Process

At this point, the products are now ranked and all but the most promising candidates have been eliminated, and those candidates have been tested and their documentation reviewed. If the choice is still not clear, other factors need to be considered. These include:

- Team experience with the product
- Team comfort level with the product
- Organizational experience with the product

Ultimately, if the team is experienced with a product or more comfortable with one product over another, defer to the team. They will have to use the product. If there is no team experience, then look for organizational experience. If there are others within the organization who have used the product, they may be able to lend a hand during the learning curve.

Applying the Process

Much of the rest of this book demonstrates this product-selection process at work. As we show you how to build your platform, we will apply this process to select the components that make up the platform.

The Sample Application

It should be clear from the previous discussions that product selection is very dependent on the projects that the platform will have to support. For this reason, we have decided to use a concrete sample project that will be referenced throughout this book. Although the sample project itself is fictional, it is designed to reflect many of the real situations that we have observed in actual projects. At the same time, this sample project is small enough so that project issues and concepts can be quickly understood.

The following sections introduce you to the sample project.

The Scenario

Our sample application is a reunion-management system. Our fictional company, Old Friends Incorporated, has decided to create a Web-based application to enable groups such as high schools or colleges to plan and coordinate reunions on the Web. The company plans to offer the product in two different ways: as a hosted service and as a Web-based application that a small college or high school can easily deploy using its own Internet-hosting capabilities.

Because the company wants the ability to deploy the system on a wide variety of Web platforms, Java is a natural choice for the development platform. However, there are two concerns:

- This is a marketing experiment, and the company is interested in limiting early investment in infrastructure until it has a better idea of the total market value. The company intends that the hosted version of the product will be eventually deployed on a commercial J2EE platform but wants to wait as long as possible before it commits to the final product decision.
- The company is also concerned that the high price of many commercial J2EE offerings may limit acceptance of the product by the smaller organizations that it sees as its initial marketing thrust.

The company is willing to use open source products at least through the delivery of the initial application in order to control costs. Although the company may consider making source code available to partners in the future, the company is, in general, not planning to make the source code for the application available.

The next section is intended to provide some background for understanding the sample application and the requirements it must meet.

System Roles and Functions

The following roles are supported within the system supporting the use cases as described.

Visitor Role

A visitor is someone who has not yet registered to use the site. A visitor's actions are limited to viewing selected informational content and participating in self-registration.

Alumnus Role

The alumnus is the primary user of the system and is a registered user of the site. The functions that can be performed by an alumnus are:

- Modifying user information
- Registering for reunion event
- Purchasing merchandise
- Viewing news
- Viewing the alumni address book

Administrator Role

The administrator is the privileged user of the system. An administrator can perform all the actions of all other roles. Additionally, the administrator has the ability to add classes and subgroups (for example, "marching band" or "cheerleaders") that might receive specially targeted information.

Content Administrator Role

The content administrator has the ability to add, update, and delete content and news items.

Event Coordinator Role

The event coordinator's primary functions are to add, modify, and remove events. Events may be ticketed, and tickets may be sold as merchandise.

Merchandise Administrator Role

The merchandise administrator can add, modify, and remove merchandise items from the merchandise catalogue.

System Interfaces

The Reunion Management System (RMS) has four interface points with external systems. The first interface point is a batch-initialization capability. This is to be provided through a standard set of XML files that can be used to initialize the databases in the system. The system must also be able to export these files so the information can be exported to other systems.

The next two interfaces are related to the fulfillment of merchandise sales. Many products that will be available for sale through the site are provided through external merchants. These merchants fall into two categories: those that can accept orders for single or bulk items using Web services and those that only accept bulk orders or do not have support for ordering through Web services.

The final interface is an interface to an email system. This allows confirmation of actions such as registration or purchase completion to be sent to an email address.

Platform Considerations

The Reunion Management System should support deployment in a J2EE 1.3 or later environment and should have minimal dependencies on the hardware or operating system for correct operation. The company does not want to purchase new equipment for development, so the developers will work on the existing desktop computers running the Window 2000 Professional operating system.

A Couple Final Notes

The following sections discuss a couple final notes that don't fit anywhere else in the chapter, but that we wanted to impart to you anyhow.

A Word about Operating Systems

While it may seem that a book focused on development using open source tools should focus on Linux, the reality is that most companies use Windows on the desktop. Although support for Windows 9*x* platforms is not a requirement in our scenario, there is still a great demand for people who want to do J2EE development work on the Windows 9*x* platforms. We also recognize the large number of Linux devotees who will want to make certain that they can duplicate what we do in this book for their Linux platform. As we progress through this book and evaluate products, we will annotate any variations or dependencies on operating systems and strive to choose products that are not only the best open source products available for our needs but are also compatible with the widest variety of operating systems possible.

Changing Open Source Code

A final comment on using open source code: There may be many good reasons to change the code for a product. The product might not exactly meet your needs and you know that with a small change you can address this. You may have discovered a bug and decide to fix it. Or you may feel that the product should be modified to suit your particular purposes. This is all well and good, but remember that if you make a change and it is not accepted by the general user community, you will become dependant on a custom version of the product that no one else is willing or able to support. This, in turn, can affect your ability to integrate your application with other products or to upgrade it in the future. Most open source projects have a mechanism in place to implement changes to the products that consider the effects of those changes on the entire user community. If you feel that you must make a change to a product, try to work within the framework of the open source project and make your contributions to the community. This way, you will learn from their experience as they learn from yours.

Summary

In this chapter, we provided a rationale for the use of open source products in an enterprise setting, showing that open source products often offer cost-effective solutions for information technology concerns. In many cases, open source solutions are comparable to commercial products in terms of quality, risk, and suitability of purpose. Open source products offer an advantage in cost and time to acquire.

We also established a four-step process that will be used throughout the book to aid in the selection of the tools that will be used to assemble our open source enterprise platform. The steps can be described as:

- Survey products
- Assessment of needs
- Evaluation of products
- Selecting a product

To focus our selection criteria, we established an application scenario for an application to be hosted on our platform. This hypothetical application (which we will call Old Friends Incorporated) is designed to manage high-school and college reunions.

In the next chapter, we look at some of the open source tools available to aid application developers in their task of developing applications that will run on the J2EE platform.

CHAPTER

4

Choosing Your Developer Tools

Starting a programming team on a new project can be an expensive undertaking. Normally, it is necessary to make sure that everyone on the team has access to the tools needed to complete the project. Commercial development tools can cost hundreds to thousands of dollars per copy. To make matters worse, team members often need to have multiple types of tools to address various development concerns. This chapter gives you a brief look at the types of tools that are typically used in large software development projects and explores some of the open source tools that have been created to address these needs.

Tools of the Trade

Once, while waiting in the lobby of Chrysler Headquarters in Auburn Hills Michigan, John noticed a display case that contained a toolbox and several apparently high-quality precision tools. As he read the tag, he learned that the toolbox and the tools themselves had been handcrafted by the founder of Chrysler. In those early days of the automotive industry, the machinists who created the engines, transmissions, and other parts of those early automobiles had to start by creating their own tools.

Today, things have changed; even if you were to build an automobile by hand, you would most likely use tools created by others. Although today's craftsman is not likely to have to build his own tools, he knows the tools and understands how and when to use them.

Similarly, years ago in the software field, many of us started out by creating our own programming tools. Now, more often than not, we use tools created by others, and we benefit from what has been learned by those who have gone before us.

The Religion of Development Tools

Although there is much science in creating programs, programming itself still remains a creative process. Many programmers are craftsmen, putting a piece of themselves into their work. The best programmers, like the best craftsmen, learn their tools. They develop a deep understanding of each tool's strengths and weaknesses, and they develop a certain level of comfort in using the tool. Because of this personal comfort level, some programmers tend to feel that their selected tool is the best, and for them, that may be true. People are often more productive when they are using tools with which they are most familiar and comfortable. The point of all of this is that the tools we use every day are often a matter of personal choice and preference.

There is another point of view. Many organizations see the advantage in having a standardized set of development tools. The advantages of this include: a shared common team experience, group learning, and mentoring. This can be especially important to large project teams where tool differences can pose barriers to sharing code and shifting responsibilities. In these cases, it is often acceptable to sacrifice certain amounts of short-term individual productivity to improve the overall productivity of the team.

So which point of view is better? The answer is: it depends. Just like any other decision in the software development process this one depends on the people involved. In many cases, developers are more productive when using the tools with which they are most familiar. New tools can be added to the mix, and as developers decide that new tools are better than the old ones, they will usually switch.

New tools can change the way we work. For example, for years when John wrote programs, he kept language and library references right next to him. When he could not remember the syntax for a rarely used statement, or the parameters for a particular function call, he would look them up in the book. Now, if John is using an Integrated Development Environment (IDE), all he has to do is start typing the command and hit a single key to instantly see the reference or have the editor complete the statement for him. This is an important timesaver: He no longer has to remember the syntax for the language he's programming in because the tool will remember it for him. For complex Web applications, you may have to program in several languages at the same time, including HTML, XML, Java, Javascript, Perl, PHP C++, and Visual Basic for Applications.

New tools can also add new capabilities. For example, many seasoned developers have learned the importance of testing their own code. When you develop new classes, you may regularly create main methods just to exercise the class and make sure that it works as expected. (Frankly, this was easier in C and C++, where you could use a compiler switch to determine if the main function would be compiled into the module). There are now tools, such as jUnit, which allow you to create a suite of tests. You can write individual tests for each class and method and then exercise all of your classes at once.

In light of this, it makes sense to allow developers to use the tools that they are most comfortable with, and also to encourage experimentation with new tools. However, for teams, certain tools need to be standardized. The tools that need to be standardized are the ones that will be shared across the team. Source code repositories are an example. The entire team must be able to retrieve code from the repository and update code within the repository. However, there is little need to standardize the client used as long as the team can share the same repository.

In summary, tools that are team oriented need to be selected for the team and should be common to all members. Developers should be able to select the tools that are individually focused.

Which Tools Will You Need?

In light of this, what tools does a developer need? The obvious tools for the Java developer are the compiler and the editor. The Java Developers Kit (JDK) provides a base set of tools, including the compiler, the runtime environment, and a number of other useful utilities. A JDK is a requirement for doing Java development. Most operating systems provide a very basic text editor that can be used for the creation of Java source code files. But these are very basic tools and are tedious to use for anything but small programs. Large or complex projects require a good development environment, which provides more than just editing and compiling.

Development Environments

A good development environment needs to support the programmer during the edit, build, and run and test cycle. Much of the focus of a development environment is on the actual creation of code. This, of course, can be done with a simple text editor. But there is a lot that a simple text editor does not do that can assist developers in their tasks.

Development environments tend to fall into two categories: text editors used with other supporting tools and IDEs. Most IDEs provide text- and code-editing capabilities but also handle other chores such as code organization, automatic compiling and building, and debugging. Text editors often provide the ability to compile code within the editor but are less likely to have integrated debugging capabilities. Text editors are normally smaller and faster to start up than an IDE and typically do not impose rules on file locations or project organization.

NOTE Although debugging and building tools are not normally integrated into a text editor, often editors provide a capability that allows external tools to be launched from within the editor.

Source Code Editors

The text or source code editor is the most commonly used tool for programmers. As a result there are many free editors available. Because of their wide popularity and availability, two editors should be specially noted, Vi and Emacs. We will also take a look at a couple of pure Java editors.

Text editors and programming tools have an advantage over other software applications in that programmers write editors and development tools for the audience they know best: other programmers. The programmers add features that they know they would like to have, as well as features that will minimize the effort they have to expend on developing software. They try to create their tools to make their lives, and those of their comrades, easier.

So what makes for a good program editor? What do we need beyond Windows Notepad? A good program editor helps the programmer write code. For Java, a good editor helps the programmer write Java code. But Java code is not enough. Most enterprise-class applications also require HTML, XML, JSP, property files, batch files, and script files to be written in addition to Java. A good editor needs to be able to assist the programmer with all of these technologies.

All editors support basic features such as navigation through a document and the ability to insert, edit, and delete text. Even the early line-oriented editors did that. The tools we use today need to offer much more. They need to understand the language we are programming in and suggest ways to help. They need to assist us in avoiding common mistakes and pitfalls. A good editor needs to help us get our work done and yet not get in the way while we are doing it. Some of the features we desire in a program editor are:

Auto-indent. Automatic indentation of code lines appropriately for the language.

Beautification. Automatic reformatting of source code to certain standards.

Brace match. Mismatched braces and parentheses are automatically identified.

Code assistance. Pop-up, just-in-time help to inform the programmer about the arguments needed for various method calls.

Code completion. Completes method signatures automatically as they are being typed in.

Color syntax highlighting. The editor has at least a rudimentary understanding of the syntax of the language being edited and changes the color of the code to reflect the language's grammar.

Macro capability. Allows repetitive tasks to be automated through some simple scripting capability.

Regular expression search and replace. Supports regular expressions for the search and replace functions.

Spell checking. Checks spelling for comments and string constants.

Templates. Automate generation of standard code fragments or method bodies.

Undo. Allows the previous operations on the document during the current editing session to be reversed.

Can we expect every editor to have these features? The answer is no. But these features are the ones we will look for as we compare tools. The choice of editor can be both the most personal tool decision and the most important. It is personal because it is used so much during the development cycle. Because of this a good developer will know his or her editor well and that is what makes it a personal choice. Does that mean that a developer should use only one editor? No, of course not! That's like asking if a carpenter should use only one saw. Different tools offer different advantages and features over other tools. A good developer will know which capabilities each tool has and then select the right tool for the job at hand.

The Attack of the Vi Clones: Vim

Vi is the "visual editor" that has been around on Unix and Unix-like operating systems (such as Linux) for decades. As a result, many people are familiar with it. As people moved to other operating systems, there was a desire to bring the familiar Vi editor with them. This need spawned a large number of Vi clones. If you are running Linux or almost any other Unix variant, you already have at least one Vi clone. There are several clones available for Windows as well. Of these, my personal favorite is Vim (which stands for Vi improved) and its graphical user interface sibling, Gvim. From here on, when we reference Vim we are referring to both Vim and Gvim.

Vim is supported well in all Windows and Linux environments with both command-line and graphical user interface (GUI) versions. In a GUI environment, Vim can be configured so that the user can use the mouse to highlight text and perform familiar cut-and-paste operations. Indeed, in a GUI environment, Vim can work almost just like any other standard GUI editor without the need to learn most of the Vi commands. Color syntax highlighting is supported for Java as well as XML, HTML, and many other languages. Vim can be configured to format source code and compile code automatically. Vim also has a simple programmable macro capability that is surprisingly powerful. The following table gives you a summary of Vim.

Product	Vim
Category	Text editor
URL	http://www.vim.org
Supported Platforms	MS-DOS, Windows 9*x*/Me/NT/2000/XP, Cygwin, Linux, and most Unix Systems
License	GPL
Features	Auto-indent, brace matching, color syntax highlighting, macros, regular expressions, templates, and undo capability

Vim has some nice features for Windows users, including a standard Windows installation utility and the ability to edit a file by right-clicking the file in Windows Explorer and choosing Edit with Vim from the context menu.

To install Vim under Windows, first download the file `gvim61.exe` from `http://www.vim.org` or one of its mirror sites. Run the program and select the typical options when prompted. When the installation is complete, there should be three icons on the desktop and a Vim 6.1 item under the programs folder on the Start menu. Figure 4.1 shows Gvim running on Windows.

Windows allows associations to be created between files and programs. To associate Java files with Vim on Windows 9*x*/Me platforms, navigate to a Java file in Windows Explorer, right-click on the Java file, and choose Open with... from the context menu. On Windows 9*x*/Me, you will be presented with a dialog box that allows you to select of a program to use to open the file. If Gvim does not appear, then click the Other... button to navigate to the Gvim executable. On Windows NT/2000/XP, you will be given a short list of programs and an option to choose a program. Selecting Gvim will associate Vim with your Java source code files, allowing the editor to be opened automatically when you click on a Java file.

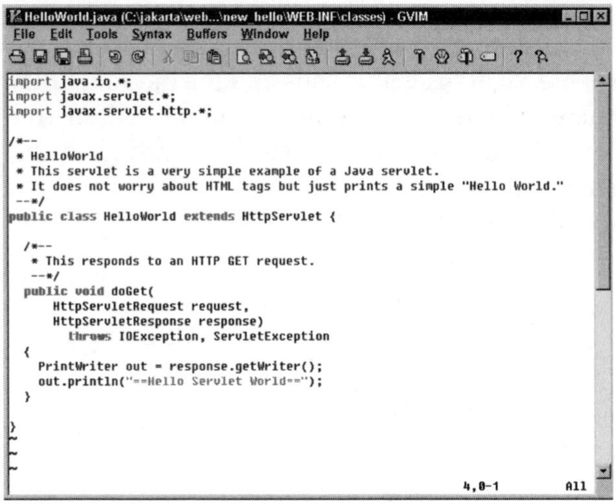
HelloWorld.java (C:\jakarta\web...\new_hello\WEB-INF\classes) - GVIM
File Edit Tools Syntax Buffers Window Help
import java.io.*;
import javax.servlet.*;
import javax.servlet.http.*;
/*--
* HelloWorld
* This servlet is a very simple example of a Java servlet.
* It does not worry about HTML tags but just prints a simple "Hello World."
--*/
public class HelloWorld extends HttpServlet {
/*--
* This responds to an HTTP GET request.
--*/
public void doGet(
HttpServletRequest request,
HttpServletResponse response)
throws IOException, ServletException
{
PrintWriter out = response.getWriter();
out.println("==Hello Servlet World==");
}
}
4,0-1
All

Figure 4.1 Gvim running under Windows.

Even if you do not enable the file association, Vim provides a quick edit feature associated with the right mouse button. When you right-click the mouse over a file in Windows Explorer, there will be an option to edit it with Vim. Selecting this option immediately opens the file inside of Vim for editing.

To create a new file choose File ➪ New from the menu or enter the characters:

```
:enew
```

Vim is a mode-oriented editor. It has four modes: insert, replace, command, and ex (or colon command) mode. Vim normally displays the mode it is in at the bottom of the screen (although this feature can be disabled). When it is in command mode, most letters on the keyboard correspond to commands that operate on the text at the current cursor location. For example, pressing the X key will delete the character under the cursor. Most commands can be preceded by a number to repeat the command that number of times, or by a cursor movement command to apply the command until the cursor stops moving. For example, typing **5x** deletes the character under the cursor and four additional characters to the right. To undo the last command, type a lowercase **u**. You can undo all changes to the current line by typing an uppercase **U**.

The command `i` (among others) puts the editor into Insert mode where text can be entered. Vim differs from Vi in insert mode because Vim allows full cursor movement in insert mode without returning to command mode. The `r` command puts Vi into replace mode. This is similar to overtype in most editors. Instead of inserting new characters for each keystroke, Vi overtypes, or replaces, the characters under the cursor. You can toggle between insert and replace modes by pressing the Escape (ESC) key.

Vim also has a command mode that is started with a colon. This is a holdover from the original Vi, which had a line editor mode called ex. For this reason, these colon commands are called ex commands and the mode is called ex command mode. ex commands provide access to a number of editor configuration attributes and other advanced features such as keyboard mapping. For example, to change the number of spaces represented by a tab from the default of eight to four, you would enter the following:

```
:set tabstop=4
```

Vim comes preconfigured to support compiling Java using Ant or the Jikes compiler. To compile code using the Ant build tool (Ant is discussed in more detail later in this chapter), prepare Vim by entering the command:

```
:compile ant
```

Then, when you are ready to compile the code, just enter the command:

```
:make
```

Vim also supports a simple yet powerful macro language. The Vim macro language reflects the fact that Vi commands are mostly single-letter commands. A macro in Vim can be as simple as repeating the same set of keystrokes that would have been typed if the command were being entered manually. There are also some simple extensions that provide for repeating steps a specific number of times and performing tests and conditional branching. As it turns out, these are often not needed due to the richness of the Vim command set.

Emacs

Emacs has been around as long as Vi (both were first created in 1976). Emacs was originally created by Richard Stallman, who is best known for founding the Free Software Foundation and the GNU project and is considered by many to be the father of the open source or free software movement. Stallman describes free software as "being a matter of liberty and not price." GNU Emacs is currently the best-known and most widely distributed version of Emacs. The following table provides a summary for the Emacs editor.

Product	GNU Emacs
Category	Text editor
URL	http://www.gnu.org/software/emacs/emacs.html

Supported Platforms	MS-DOS, Windows 9x/ NT/2000/XP, Cygwin, Linux, and most Unix Systems
License	GPL
Features	Auto-indent, brace matching, color syntax highlighting, macros, regular expressions, spell checking, templates, and undo capability

Emacs is distributed as a gzipped tar archive. This is a common format on Linux machines but it is less common on Windows platforms. The files can be recognized by a .tar.gz or .tgz file extension. The shareware package WinZip recognizes and extracts gzipped tar archives. WinZip prompts you and asks if you want to create a temporary file as it opens the archive. Respond with "yes," and WinZip will decompress the archive and allow you to browse through the resulting .tar file as if it were a .zip file.

The files can also be extracted under Windows if you are using Cygwin. Cygwin is an open source Windows port of many of the tools that are available to Linux users. (Cygwin can be found at `http://www.cygwin.com` . First, copy the `emacs*.tar.gz` file to the directory that you want to extract the files into, and then use the following commands to extract the software using Cygwin utilities:

```
gunzip emacs-21.2-fullbin-i386.tar.gz
tar xvf emacs-21.2-fullbin-i386.tar
```

The first command decompresses the file, leaving a tar archive. The second command extracts the tar archive. Note that the filenames may change and that you should use the filenames for the distribution that you downloaded.

After the files have been extracted, navigate to the `bin` directory below the directory where the files were installed. In the `bin` directory is a program called `addpm.exe`. Running this program adds a GNU Emacs shortcut to the Windows Start menu. You can start Emacs either by selecting Emacs from the Start menu or by double-clicking on `runemacs.exe` (also found in the `bin` directory). Figure 4.2 shows Emacs running in Windows.

Emacs comes with a complete tutorial and reference manual built in and uses its own hypertext language called *info* for documentation. Linux users will be familiar with info because many of the help pages for Linux commands are implemented as info pages. Most Emacs commands are key combinations, using the Control and Alt keys found on most keyboards.

Associations between Java source code files and the Emacs editor for the Windows operating systems can be made in a fashion similar to that described for Gvim in the previous section.

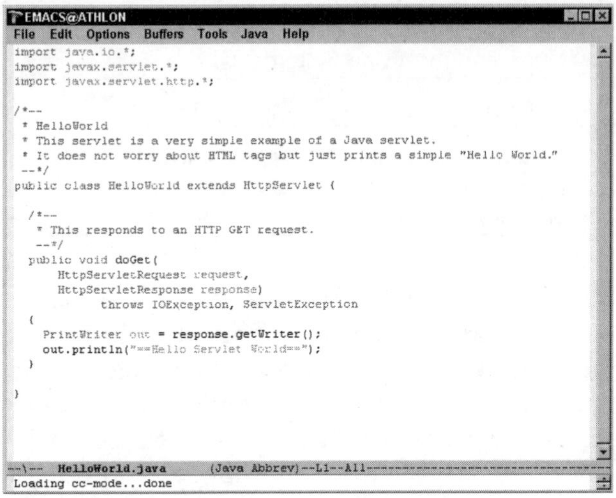

```
EMACS@ATHLON
File Edit Options Buffers Tools Java Help
import java.io.*;
import javax.servlet.*;
import javax.servlet.http.*;

/*--
 * HelloWorld
 * This servlet is a very simple example of a Java servlet.
 * It does not worry about HTML tags but just prints a simple "Hello World."
 --*/
public class HelloWorld extends HttpServlet {

  /*--
   * This responds to an HTTP GET request.
   --*/
  public void doGet(
      HttpServletRequest request,
      HttpServletResponse response)
          throws IOException, ServletException
  {
    PrintWriter out = response.getWriter();
    out.println("==Hello Servlet World==");
  }

}

--\-- HelloWorld.java      (Java Abbrev)--L1--All-----------------------------
Loading cc-mode...done
```

Figure 4.2 Emacs running under Windows.

To associate Java files with Emacs on Windows 9*x*/Me platforms, navigate to a Java file in Windows Explorer, right-click on the Java file, and choose Open with... from the context menu. On Windows 9*x*/Me, you will be presented with a dialog box that allows you to select a program to use to open the file. If Emacs does not appear, then click the Other... button to navigate to the Emacs executable. On Windows NT/2000/XP, you will be given a short list of programs and an option to choose a program. Selecting Emacs will associate Emacs with your Java source code files, allowing the editor to be opened automatically when you click on a Java file.

Emacs supports many of the same features as Vim. It supports color syntax highlighting for Java code and provides a specialized Java menu that eases navigation through large Java source code files. Like Vim, Emacs can be configured to compile the source code from within the editor. However, Emacs is the only editor that we are aware of that also includes an integrated spell checker. Options exist for spell checking just the comments, or for checking the word currently under the cursor. Dictionaries are provided for a large number of languages.

Emacs also supports a powerful macro language based on a variant of Lisp. Lisp is an old but powerful programming language for list processing. Most of the actual Emacs editor code is itself written in the macro language. The language is so powerful that Emacs comes with a number of games and utilities written in that language that run inside the editor.

Java Editors

Emacs and Vim are general-purpose text editors with some specific features that support Java code development. Both editors are written in C and are designed for easy porting to other platforms. As a result, both editors are available on a very wide range and variety of platforms.

But are there open source editors written specifically to support Java development? The answer to these questions is yes! Several editors can be found written in Java to specifically support the needs of the Java developer. In the following sections, we will look at two of these editors: jEdit and Jext.

jEdit

jEdit is a Java-based text editor for programmers. As a Java editor, jEdit is targeted at Java developers and allows developers to extend the jEdit environment with plug-ins. The following table summarizes information for jEdit.

Product	jEdit
Category	Text editor
URL	http://www.jedit.org
Supported Platforms	Java 1.3 and 1.4
License	GPL
Features	Auto-indent, brace matching, color syntax highlighting, macros, regular expressions, templates, and undo capability

jEdit Features

By itself, jEdit supports many of the same features as those found in Vim or Emacs. The jEdit keys can even be configured to emulate many of the commands of these other editors. The brace matching is especially noteworthy. Instead of just highlighting the matching brace if the braces are on different source code lines, jEdit draws a line in the left margin between the top opening brace and the bottom brace. This makes it very easy to visualize the structure of the code. jEdit is shown in Figure 4.3.

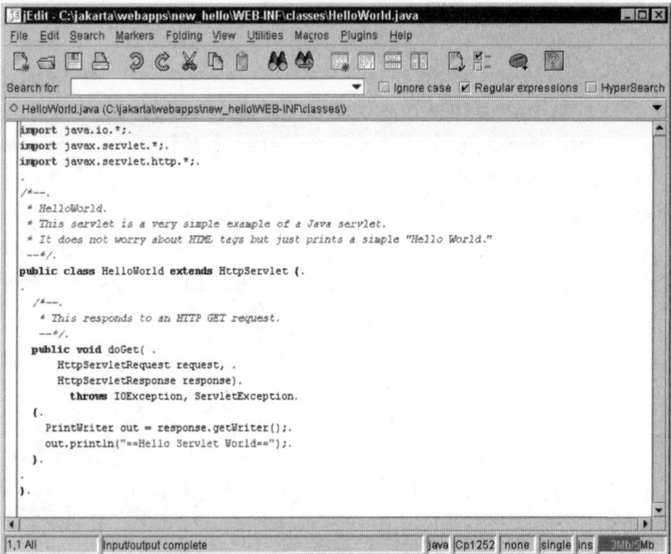

Figure 4.3 jEdit.

Also, like Vim and Emacs, jEdit has a macro feature. The jEdit macro facility is implemented using another open source product called BeanShell (`http://www.beanshell.org`). BeanShell is a Java-based scripting language. Basically, if you know Java you know BeanShell. However, unlike Java, which requires Java code to be compiled into byte codes, BeanShell interprets the Java source code as it executes the code. BeanShell also adds some common scripting features such as dynamically typed or untyped variables, arguments, parameters, and return values. BeanShell is designed to have much of the same power as Java but provides language features that make it easier to use for scripting applications. Macros can be created automatically by recording keystrokes. Once created, the macro is available to be reviewed and edited.

jEdit offers plug-ins as another means of extending the editor's capabilities beyond those provided by its powerful macro capability. Plug-ins are Java classes written to a specification that allows interaction with the editor. By using plug-ins, jEdit adds features such as source-code formatting, code completion, and spell checking to the editor. There are an impressive number of plug-ins for jEdit, and the program makes it easy to download and install the plug-ins using the built-in plug-in manager. Each plug-in supports its own set of help pages and configuration dialog boxes.

NOTE **Some plug-ins also have dependencies on other products; for example, the AntHill plug-in is dependent on the Apache Ant Build tool. Ant needs to be downloaded and installed separately for the AntHill plug-in to work.**

Installing jEdit

To install jEdit, first download the file `jEdit403install.jar`, and then execute the file. The .jar file is executed on any platform by running the following command:

```
java -jar jEdit403install.jar
```

This command starts a Java-based installation program that extracts the required files. For Windows operation, jEdit provides a launcher package that eases launching on Windows and installs shortcuts on the Start menu. Like Gvim, jEdit also installs shortcuts on right-click context menus so that files can be easily selected and opened using Windows Explorer.

Jext

Jext is also a Java-based programmer-centric text editor. (Interestingly, Slava Pestov, the creator of jEdit, is also given credit as being a major contributor to the Jext source code.) Jext demonstrates a principle that is commonly found in less-mature open source products. The product may show its immaturity in the lack of high-quality documentation or features that may not be fully implemented. But certain features are innovative and unique, and serve to set the product apart from the rest. Open source code provides a method for this type of experimentation without every project having to reinvent everything from scratch.

The following table summarizes Jext, and the following sections discuss Jext in more detail.

Product	Jext
Category	Text editor
URL	http://www.jext.org
Supported Platforms	Java 1.2 through 1.4
License	GPL
Features	Auto-indent, brace matching, color syntax highlighting, macros, templates, and undo capability

Jext Features

Jext takes a slightly different approach from the other editors we have examined. Jext has an user interface that is designed for rapid coding. By choosing File ➪ New From Template you can create a basic Java class instantly. Templates exist for servlets, applets, main Java programs, and other common Java programs. Templates also exist to support JSP creation and many other types of files.

Jext also provides the ability to organize a group of related files into a project. It is easy to switch between files in a project; just click on the filename in the project pane. Like jEdit, Jext also supports plug-ins. However, Jext and jEdit use two different interfaces for implementing plug-ins, so Jext plug-ins are not compatible with jEdit plug-ins. Jext is packaged with two plug-ins preinstalled. Hypertyper provides a facility for completing partially typed strings. A keystroke-recording facility is provided by the other plug-in.

Jext provides not one but two separate scripting languages for entering macros. Jext comes with jPython, which is a Java implementation of the Python programming language. It also comes with a language called Dawn. Dawn is a custom scripting language that uses a Reverse Polish Notation (RPN) based syntax. RPN is the stack-oriented way of programming that was popular on Hewlett-Packard calculators and in the Forth programming language.

One very nice feature of Jext can be found on the XInsert tab of the panel to the left of the application window. This can be seen in Figure 4.4. XInsert provides a series of templates and wizards that can be used to create common code skeletons. For example, choosing Templates ➪ Servlet instantly places the source code for a simple class based on HttpServlet into the edit buffer. The real power of this tool can be seen when creating XML files for Ant or when creating JavaServer Pages. Now, individual tags can be created to serve specific purposes, and the cursor is left positioned at the first attribute for the tag.

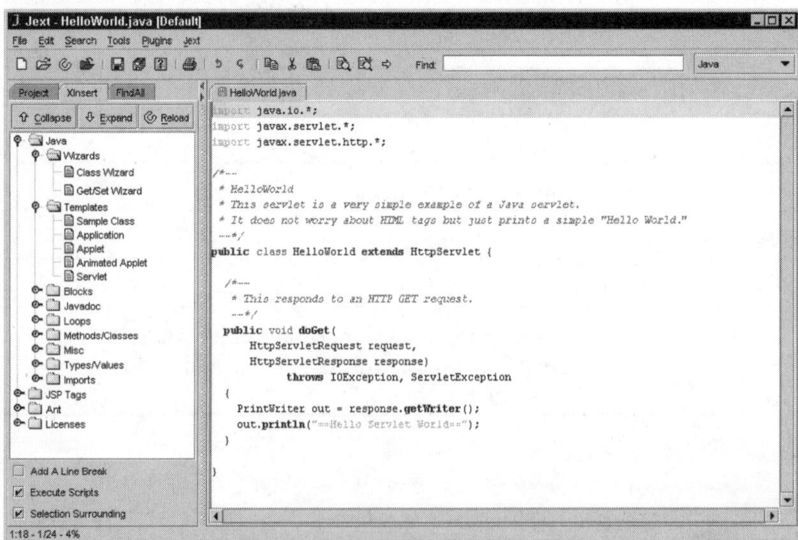

Figure 4.4 Jext, with XInsert tab selected.

Jext Shortcomings

Although Jext does provide some tools that speed up the programming process, Jext suffers from a number of problems, including the following:

- Jext does not have an integrated help system. Instead, Jext provides a brief series of Web pages that are installed along with the editor.
- The help Web pages are poorly organized and have no search capability.
- At this time, the documentation also must be downloaded separately from the program.

Installing Jext

Installing Jext is reasonably easy. Download the `jext-install.jar` file from `http://www.jext.org`, and run the following command line:

```
java -jar jext-install.jar
```

This will run the Java-based installer program. Jext comes with several files to make Windows operation easier, most notably a `Jext.exe` program launcher that eliminates the needs for unreliable batch files. Once installed, download the documentation file, and extract the documentation.

Integrated Development Environments

Integrated Development Environments (IDEs) are sort of the shopping malls of software development tools. An IDE normally includes:

- Source-code editing
- Class browsers
- Debuggers
- Build tools
- Packaging tools
- Integrated reference documents

Although a source code editor allows the programmer to create source code and sometimes supports compiling the program and correcting the errors, an IDE goes much further. The IDE also provides tools that reduce the complexity of the compiling, the building, and the test cycle. Some tools aid in organizing source code modules by maintaining and managing projects. The IDE understands how to build a project consisting of many files and only builds the files that have changed or been modified since the previous build. The

IDE is also integrated with a debugger, allowing code to be executed and debugged immediately after building. In addition, a typical IDE is much more closely integrated with the compiler (or has a better understanding of the language syntax) than a text editor. This allows for advanced editing features such as automatic code completion and language-specific context-sensitive assistance for functions and language features.

The time for each compile, build, and test cycle is decreased using an IDE because the programmer never leaves the development environment. The editor component provides language-specific assistance for developing programs, which speeds up the coding process. The IDE project component understands how to organize and build complex projects, building only those components that have been modified. The debugging component understands how to execute and debug the code. With the push of a single button, the programmer can move from editing to building and then to debugging code. The IDE handles the building process, immediately flagging errors and matching them to the source code. If no errors are found and the application is built successfully, then the debugging environment is started within the IDE so the code can be observed as it is running.

So one may ask, if the IDE includes text-editing features and is so powerful, why is a text editor needed? The answer is simple. Most IDEs are very large. If all that is needed is a quick change or to quickly browse a file, a text editor will load the file and have it ready to view almost instantly. An IDE may take 15 to 20 seconds or longer to load even on a moderately fast machine. Also, an IDE may impose a project structure on your source files, making it difficult to browse a file that is not already contained within a project.

There are many well-known and excellent commercial IDEs. Some of the companies that make these commercial products even provide for free licenses for noncommercial use of their most basic editions. In the past couple of years, through corporate sponsorships by Sun and IBM, two excellent free and open source IDEs have appeared specifically for Java development. These are Eclipse and NetBeans, which are discussed in the following sections.

Eclipse

Eclipse is not a typical open source project in that IBM has reportedly invested more than 40 million dollars in its development. Conceptually Eclipse is intended to be an open source platform for developing IDEs. Eclipse is also the basis for IBM's WebSphere Advanced Developer (WSAD). Although Eclipse is designed to be a platform for developing IDEs, it is also a Java IDE and is developed in Java. However instead of using the Java Swing or AWT (Abstract Window Toolkit) classes to implement the user interface, Eclipse uses a package called the Standard Widget Toolkit, or SWT. SWT replaces AWT or Swing, providing a thin wrapper over the native operating system calls for accessing GUI resources. This has a dramatic impact on performance and the look and feel of the user interface. Unlike other Java-based applications, which seem a little sluggish, Eclipse is fast and responsive even on slower workstations. Another effect is that, when running on Windows, Eclipse has the feel and behavior of a native Windows application, yet when running under Linux, Eclipse has the feel and behavior of a native Linux application. The following table provides summary information for Eclipse.

Product	Eclipse
Category	Integrated Development Environment (IDE)
URL	http://www.eclipse.org
Supported Platforms	Java JDK 1.2 through 1.4, Windows 9x/NT/2000/XP, Linux, Solaris, QNX, AIX, HP-UX
License	Common Public License
Features	Auto-indent, beautification, brace matching, class browsing, code assistance, code completion, color syntax highlighting, remote and local debugging, macros, regular expressions, templates, and undo capability

The licensing model for Eclipse allows extensions to the IDE to be repackaged with the IDE and the resulting products sold commercially. This has encouraged support for integration of a number of commercial and open source extensions to the product, which is a good thing. Out of the box, Eclipse does not come with support for easily building Web-based applications using servlets or JavaServer Pages; however, there are several plug-ins available to add this support.

As a native Java IDE, Eclipse provides the extended tools for editing Java language-specific source code files that developers have come to expect from professional development environments. These include features such as code assist and code completion. Eclipse does have one feature that is different from most other development environments: Eclipse tries to compile the code each time the code is saved, which has the effect of ensuring that you always have code that compiles.

Installing Eclipse

Eclipse can be downloaded from `http://www.eclipse.org`. For Windows platforms, it is downloaded as a compressed ZIP archive (.zip file). Note that this file is large, over 50 MB. To install Eclipse, simply extract the .zip file into the `c:\eclipse` folder. Navigate to the `c:\eclipse` folder and click on

`Eclipse.exe` to launch Eclipse the first time. A message should appear that says "Please wait completing install..." and shortly the IDE will be started with the Welcome page in the editor window.

NOTE Eclipse does not install any items into the Windows Start menu or onto the desktop. This must be done manually. Adding an icon to the Windows Desktop is easily done by right-clicking on the Desktop and choosing New ⇨ Shortcut and then browsing to `eclipse.exe`**.**

Eclipse is shown in Figure 4.5. The Eclipse Welcome screen provides a means of navigating and exploring the documentation that is provided with Eclipse. The documentation includes a tutorial on getting started and information on perspectives. *Perspectives* is the term used by Eclipse to refer to a specific customizable arrangement of windows and tools within the IDE. After the initial installation, there are perspectives for Java programming, and building Eclipse add-ons or plug-ins.

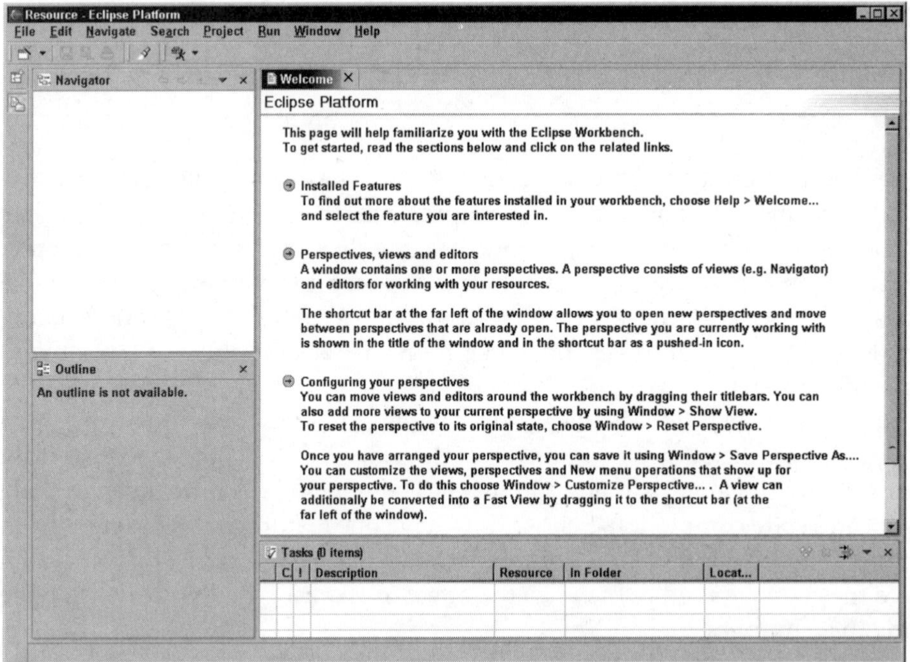

Figure 4.5 Eclipse.

Configuring Eclipse

Before moving on with Eclipse, you need to make some configuration changes. When Eclipse is installed, it defaults to using the Java Runtime Environment instead of the JDK. Eclipse has its own Java compiler built into the IDE and so does not need the JDK to compile. However, you want to ensure that Eclipse is using the JDK to avoid any other potential problems, so you need to change the Eclipse configuration slightly by following these steps:

1. Choose Window ➪ Preferences from the Workbench menu bar.
2. Open the Java node of navigation tree on the left side of the new window.
3. Select the installed JRE's node of the tree.
4. Select the Add... button on the right.
5. For JRE Type select Standard VM.
6. For JRE Name enter **JDK 1.4.1** (or whichever JDK you are using).
7. The JRE Home directory should be set the same as the `JAVA_HOME` directory for the JDK. This is the base directory where the JDK is installed. On my system this is `c:\jdk1.4.1`.

You may also want to examine the Workbench node of the tree and check to make sure that the box next to Perform build automatically on resource modification is checked.

Creating Hello World in Eclipse

As a brief introduction to the IDE, we will build the classic Hello World application. Eclipse starts with the Welcome screen, as seen in Figure 4.5. The Eclipse application refers to the application window as the *workbench*. A workbench may have one or more perspectives. A perspective defines the layout and views of the various windows within the workbench. Perspectives are organized to help with specific tasks.

Our task is to create a HelloWorld Java program, so we start our task by selecting a perspective by choosing Window ➪ Open Perspective ➪ Java. After you do so, the arrangement of the Windows changes and some icons are added to the shortcut bar on the left side of the workbench. The icons on the border represent the currently available perspectives.

Now, we want to create a project for our code. To do so, choose File ➪ New ➪ Project to bring up the dialog box, as shown in the Figure 4.7. Choose Java ➪ Java Project, and then click Next. The next screen prompts you for a project name; we will call our project HelloWorld, and click Next. Then, accept all of the defaults on the screen, and click Finish.

When the wizard finishes, you are returned to the workbench. The Package Explorer window now shows your project. Clicking on the node reveals the full path to the runtime package `rt.jar`. This is a good way to make sure that you are using the correct JDK. Highlight the project node and right-click it, then choose New package from the menu. When prompted for the name enter the following:

```
com.wiley.freej2ee.ch4.eclipse
```

Then, click Finish. A new package is added to the project. Right-click the new package, and choose New ➪ Class. Use HelloWorld as the class name and check the box next to public static void main... Leave everything else as it is, and click Finish. A new class is generated and displayed in the editor window.

Position the cursor within the editor to start adding code to the main method. Start by typing **System**. As you pause, notice that the IDE displays a list of the methods available for the System class. Select "out" from the list of methods, and the editor will fill in the next part of the line. Add the next dot, and the system will again show a list of the methods. Select `println(String)`, and enter "Hello World" as the argument. Do not add the semicolon at the end of the line, and save the source code by either choosing File ➪ Save or by clicking on the disk icon on the tool bar. Notice that now a red circle with a white x appears at the border of the editor window on the line below the one you just edited. This is showing you a compiler error and indicating that you need to complete the expression; so, add the semicolon and resave the file.

After the program has been saved, the compiler errors are cleared. Now, you are ready to run the program. This is done through the Run menu. Choose Run ➪ Run As... ➪ Java application or click the running man icon on the toolbar. A console window will overlay the task and error window at the bottom of the screen and should now read "Hello World".

Congratulations! You have just written your first application using the Eclipse IDE.

Installing the Sysdeo Plug-in

Eclipse is a very powerful IDE in many ways; however, in other ways Eclipse only comes with very basic tools. For example, when Eclipse is first installed, there is no GUI design tool and there is no inherent capability for developing J2EE or Web applications. A number of plug-ins are available that extend these basic capabilities. In this section, we will install and use a plug-in that allows Eclipse to be used with the Tomcat servlet container and develop and use servlets and JavaServer Pages.

The plug-in we will install can be found at the following URL:

```
http://www.sysdeo.com/eclipse/tomcatPlugin.html
```

The plug-in is distributed as a .zip file and requires that Tomcat already be installed on the computer. The `plugin` file should be downloaded and extracted to the Eclipse `plugins` folder. When you extract the file, be sure to retain the directory structure of the .zip file. If Eclipse is running, it needs to be shut down and restarted; otherwise start Eclipse.

Inside Eclipse, choose Window ➪ Customize Perspective ➪ Other, then check the Tomcat check box, and click OK. Next, choose Window ➪ Preferences. Select the Tomcat node, which appears at the bottom of the tree structure. The dialog box (shown in Figure 4.6) allows setting the Tomcat version and base directory. Set these values to the values that are appropriate for your system, and be sure to click the Apply button before exiting the screen.

CROSS-REFERENCE **Tomcat is discussed in detail in Chapter 5.**

Building a Servlet

Now, you are ready to build a servlet in Eclipse. To start, create a new project (an old project can be closed by selecting Project ➪ Close Project). Selecting File ➪ New ➪ Project summons the Project wizard. Notice that a new type of project appears, the Tomcat project as shown in Figure 4.7. A Tomcat project automatically creates the correct directory structure for a Web application. Select the Tomcat Project. On the next screen, enter **HelloServlet** as the project name, then click next. Accept /HelloServlet as the context name, and click Finish. The package Explorer should now show your new project. If you expand the HelloServlet project, you will see that `servlet.jar` is included in the project that also includes a `WEB-INF` subdirectory. With the HelloServlet project root highlighted, right-click it, and select New ➪ Class.

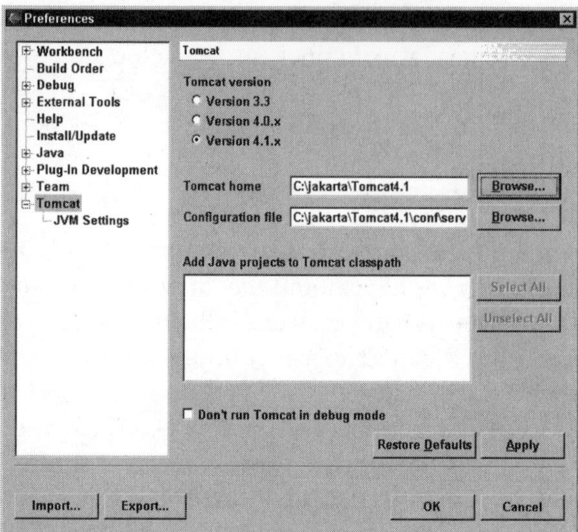

Figure 4.6 Eclipse configuration for Tomcat plug-in.

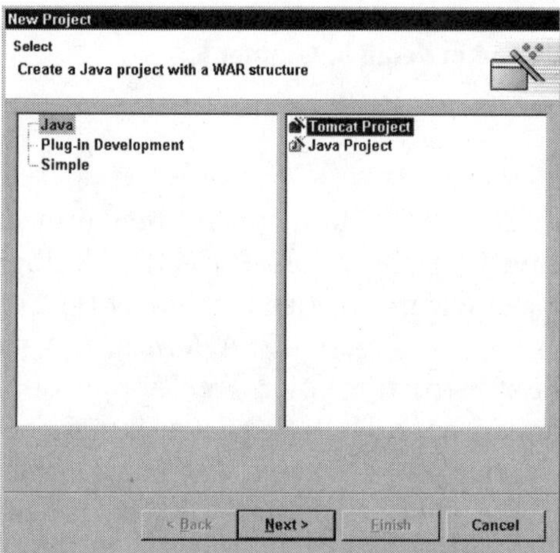

Figure 4.7 Eclipse Project wizard.

When the New Class wizard starts, use the default package, and then enter HelloServlet as the class name. Set the superclass to `javax.servlet.http.HttpServlet`. The Browse button can be used to do this as well. Clicking Browse presents the dialog box shown in Figure 4.8.

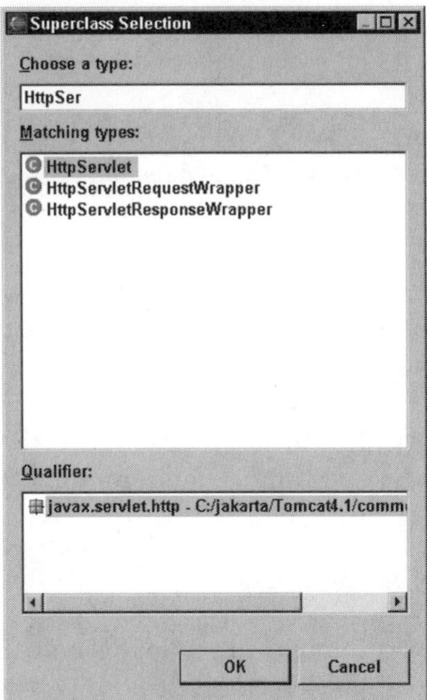

Figure 4.8 Looking up a superclass in the Class wizard.

Entering **httpserv** and pressing Enter will bring up a list of class names that match the screen. Select the HttpServlet class from the list, uncheck the boxes at the bottom of the dialog box, and click Finish.

The editor window should now contain a class called HelloServlet with no code inside. Place the cursor of the editor inside the curly braces, and type **doGet**. Hold the Control key down, and press the space bar. The editor will fill in the method definition based on the method in the superclass. Change protected to public and change arg0 and arg1 to request and response, respectively. Also, remove the call to the superclasses `doGet`, and then edit the `doGet()` code to look like the following:

```
public void doGet(HttpServletRequest request, HttpServletResponse
response)
throws ServletException, IOException
{
  PrintWriter out = response.getWriter();
  out.println("Hello World");
  out.close();
}
```

TIP After you type the line:

```
PrintWriter out = response.getWriter();
```

a lightbulb appears on the left margin of the editor. Clicking on the light bulb provides an opportunity for the editor to automatically add the needed import statement at the top of the file as follows:

```
import java.io.PrintWriter;
```

Save the file (remember that saving also compiles the file), and if there are any errors, correct them. Tomcat can be started by clicking the Start Tomcat button on the toolbar. Starting Tomcat rearranges the windows, showing the Tomcat console at the bottom of the workbench. Test the application by starting a browser and entering the following URL (assuming a standard Tomcat development configuration):

```
http://localhost:8080/HelloServlet/servlet/HelloServlet
```

When you're finished testing, clicking the Stop Tomcat button on the toolbar stops the Tomcat server. Clicking the button on the left border of the workbench restores the Java perspective.

To export the project to a Web Archive (or .war) file, right click on the project, and select properties. Select the Tomcat node in the navigation pane, and then enter the name of the .war file that will be created. After clicking OK, right-click on the project again and select the Tomcat project, then export to a war file.

There are several things that we should note about the Eclipse environment. First is that the plain vanilla environment is very basic and does not support such common tasks as designing a Java GUI or building HTML, XML, or JSP files. The Sysdeo plug-in is just one plug-in that can extend the Eclipse IDE to support J2EE or Web-application programming tasks. Many other plug-ins, both commercial and open source, exist or are being developed for Eclipse. A list of currently available plug-ins can be found at the community plug-ins page at the following URL:

```
http://www.eclipse.org/community/plugins.html
```

NetBeans

NetBeans is Sun's entry into the open source IDE fray. NetBeans has been around since 2000 and so has a year head start on Eclipse. In practice, this means that NetBeans currently offers much more functionality out of the box for the programmer.

NetBeans also has a different purpose. Rather than being a platform for developing IDEs, NetBeans is designed to be an application platform or framework that can be used to develop any application. The IDE is just another application using the NetBeans development framework. Unlike Eclipse, NetBeans is also strictly standard Java. The user interface is implemented using the swing class. The following table summarizes NetBeans.

Product	NetBeans
Category	Integrated Development Environment (IDE)
URL	http://www.netbeans.org
Supported Platforms	Java JDK 1.2 through 1.4, Windows 9*x*/NT/2000/XP, Linux, Solaris, Mac OS X, and most other platforms supporting a 1.2 or later JDK
License	Sun Public License (based on Mozilla Public License)
Features	Auto-indent, beautification, brace matching, class browsing, code assist, code completion, color syntax highlighting, remote and local debugging, macros, regular expressions, templates, and undo capability

Like Eclipse, NetBeans comes configured as a Java development environment when it is downloaded. NetBeans can also be extended by using plugins. However, NetBeans comes with a lot more functionality preinstalled into the environment than Eclipse provides. Once installed, NetBeans supports the development of Java programs, servlets, JavaServer Pages, XML, and HTML files. NetBeans includes support for the graphical development of Java applications. Many other tools come as part of the standard installation.

NetBeans offers a standard installation program for Windows. Linux and Unix users can either simply extract the `tar.gz` distribution or run an installer package. After it is installed on Windows, NetBeans provides an icon on the desktop and entries on the Windows Start menu to launch the IDE.

Creating Hello World in NetBeans

As an introduction to the Netbeans IDE, you will create the same Hello World application that you did with the Eclipse IDE. To start, you need to create a project. This is done by selecting Project ➪ Project Manager from the menu and then selecting the New... button. Name the project HelloProject, and click OK.

The Explorer pane on the left of the workbench displays a disk icon representing the root of all file systems. You need to mount a file system for your project. To do this, right-click the drive and choose Mount ➪ Local Directory. The resulting dialog box can be used to select a directory to host your project (for example, `c:\mysrc\helloProject`). If there are no directories mounted, you are forced to mount a directory before you can create files for your project. After the directory is mounted, select the directory.

The File ➪ New menu item presents a tree with templates that can be selected to create source code files. Select the Java classes node, expand it, and then select the main node. The description for this node states "Using this template, you can create a new Java class with a main method permitting it to be run as a console application." Click next. For the name enter **HelloWorld**, for the package enter **com.wiley.freej2ee.ch4.netbeans**, then click Next to go to the Basic Class Definition screen. You don't need to do anything here, so you may either click Next to see the other screens in the wizard or just click Finish to start the code generation.

After you click Finish, you will be returned to the workbench. The Explorer pane shown in Figure 4.9 shows the subdirectory structure created to support the package, and the editor pane shows the generated source code. Add the following line to the main method:

```
System.out.println("Hello World");
```

Then, choose Build ➪ Compile to compile the program and then choose Build ➪ Execute to run the program.

Building a Hello World Servlet

Unlike Eclipse, you do not need to install any additional software to build a servlet in the NetBeans environment. To start, you need to create a new project called HelloServlet. When you create a new project, you need to mount a directory, as in the previous section. This time, create and mount the directory HelloServlet (for example, `c:\mysrc\HelloServlet`). After the directory is mounted, right-click on the directory in the Explorer pane and choose Tools ➪ Convert Filesystem into Web Module. This generates a message informing you of multiple ways to view the file system. Dismiss the message by clicking OK.

The Explorer pane now shows two views of the file system. Also note that expanding the mounted directory node reveals a `WEB-INF` subdirectory and the other associated subdirectories below `WEB-INF`. If the WEB-INF node is selected, the properties at the bottom of the Explorer pane reflect the `web.xml` file. Editing these properties changes the `web.xml` file that will be generated.

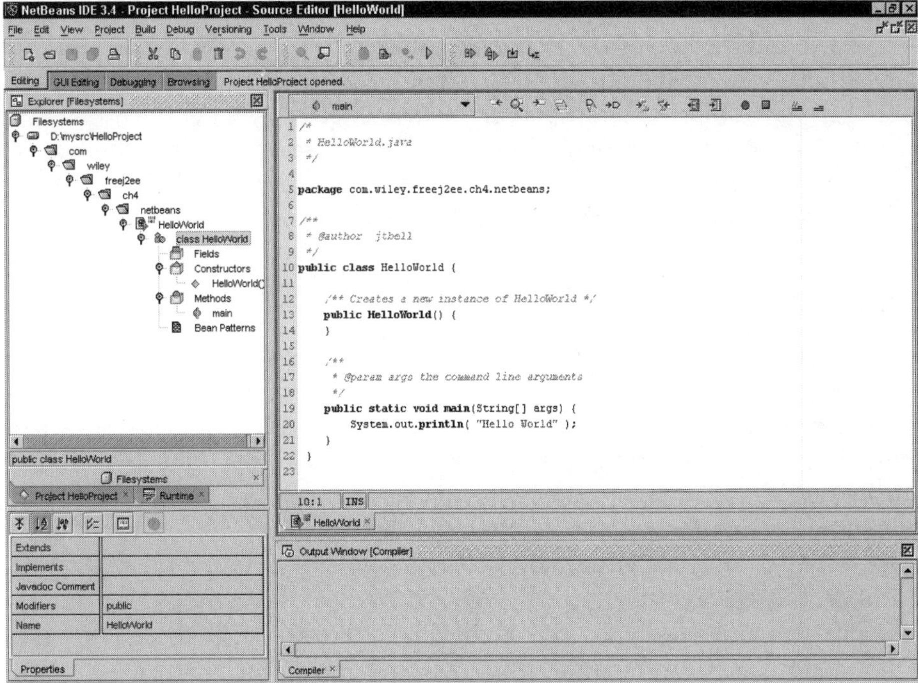

Figure 4.9 NetBeans IDE.

Choose File ➪ New to bring up the new file dialog box again. This time, scroll down if needed to find the node that is titled "JSPs and Servlets." Open this node and select servlet. Enter **helloServlet** as the servlet name, and select the classes directory as the target location. Clicking Next brings you to a deployment configuration panel. No changes are needed here, so click Finish.

The source editor pane now shows the source code for a fully functional servlet that doesn't do anything. Modify the code in the `processRequest()` method by adding the following line after the line defining the PrintWriter:

```
out.println( "Hello World");
```

The project can be built by choosing Build ➪ Build.

NetBeans comes with its own integrated version of Tomcat. To run the servlet, just choose Build ➪ Execute, and NetBeans will start the internal Tomcat and deploy the Web application to that instance. An instance of the browser pointed to the URL where your Web application is deployed is also started for you. Messages sent to the Tomcat console are displayed in a pane below the Editor pane. When you are finished with testing, Tomcat can be stopped and started manually through the Runtime tab located below the Explorer pane. To do this, expand the Server Registry node, the Installed Servers Node, and the Tomcat node and then right-click on the Internal node. The menu provides options to start, stop, or restart the server as needed.

NetBeans can also export the .war file. To do so, right-click the project directory in the Explorer panel, and select Tools ➪ Export WAR file. NetBeans prompts for a filename and then generates the war file.

Which IDE Should You Use?

So which IDE is better? Well, both NetBeans and Eclipse have their strengths and weaknesses. Eclipse is a solid product and works well even on slow hardware. Eclipse looks and feels like any other native application in Windows or Linux. But Eclipse is lacking a number of useful features "out of the box," which must be added in by installing and configuring plug-ins.

On a fast enough machine, NetBeans' slower user interface is not bothersome. But the feature set built into NetBeans is clearly more complete than the default features currently offered by Eclipse. NetBeans also provides a plug-in capability allowing it to be extended like Eclipse. However, NetBeans provides tools to automate the installation of the plug-ins within the NetBeans environment, making even this process easier than Eclipse. NetBeans is clearly a more mature product than Eclipse at this time. NetBeans also supports a broader variety of hardware and operating system platforms than Eclipse does at this time.

The bottom line here is that both IDEs are excellent products, so the decision depends on platform compatibility for the platform you must use and your own personal preferences.

Build Tools: Ant

Build tools are used to compile and build large complex projects. A build tool will typically do more then just compile code. A build tool creates directory structures, deletes unneeded files, copies files between directories, and performs many of common routine tasks that are needed for managing the building of projects.

Programmers have used the Unix make tool and various work-a-likes for years to build their complex C and C++ programs. But make has it limitations. Make is not standardized across platforms, and make syntax is quirky and can be difficult to read. On many implementations, errors in makefiles can occur because of arcane errors such as using spaces instead of tabs. Make has another limitation that does not make sense for Java programmers: Make is designed to execute operating system shell commands, meaning that makefiles are not portable across operating systems. Java of course is designed to be a platform-independent programming language, and as such Java requires platform-independent build tools. This was a real problem with people working on various Jakarta projects, and so the Jakarta project gave us Ant.

NOTES FOR WINDOWS USERS

Ant is a command-line-oriented tool that is normally used from the command prompt (`command.com` for Windows 9*x* and `cmd.exe` for Windows NT, 2000, and XP). Often, it is desirable not to change the global Windows environment through `autoexec.bat` or by making changes in the Windows Control Panel, especially when there is a requirement to support multiple versions of the JDK and other tools. Environment variables set in an instance of the command prompt are local to that instance. This allows you to create shortcuts that will start the command prompt with the environment variables set the way we want them. To do this, first create a batch file that sets the variables as needed. The following is a sample batch file:

```
rem === save as JavaDev.bat ===
rem configures environment for Java
set JAVA_HOME=c:\jdk1.3.1_06
set ANT_HOME=c:\ant
PATH %PATH%;%JAVA_HOME%\bin;%ANT_HOME%\bin
```

For example, we store the batch files in the `c:\batch` folder, which is also on the system path. After this file has been created, a shortcut can be added to the desktop. To add the shortcut, right-click on the desktop and choose New ➪ Shortcut. When prompted, browse to the batch file just created. After the shortcut has been saved, the command line will have to be edited. The command line can be edited by right-clicking on the shortcut and selecting properties and then selecting the program or shortcut tab. The command line for Windows 9x/Me platforms should look like the following:

```
C:\WIN98\COMMAND.COM /E:2048 /K c:\batch\JavaDev.bat
```

And for Window NT/2000/XP it should look like:

```
C:\windows\system32\cmd.exe /K c:\batch\JavaDev.bat
```

The `/E:2048` increases the environment space for environment variables. Many Java programs require a number of large environment variables, so this is recommended for Windows 9x platforms, which by default only provides 256 characters of environment space. The `/K` keeps the command prompt active after completion of the batch file.

After this is done, it will be easy to access Java-specific functions from the command prompt launched from the shortcut.

Ant is new kind of build tool. Ant uses XML configuration files to describe the project to be built. Instead of executing shell commands, Ant executes Java classes. The following table summarizes Ant.

Product	Ant
Category	Build tool
URL	http://jakarta.apache.org/ant
Supported Platforms	Java 1.2, 1.3, 1.4
License	Apache
Features	XML-based build files, Java-based support

After the files are downloaded, unzip them into the directory where you want Ant installed. If you are using Windows 98/Me, you we suggest that you install Ant into a directory with a short pathname such as `C:\ant` to avoid issues with filename mangling in the Windows 98/Me command line. You will want to create an environment variable ANT_HOME and add the `%ANT_HOME%\bin` directory to your path. Under Windows 98/Me, adding the following line to the `autoexec.bat` file can do this:

```
set ANT_HOME=c:\ant
PATH %PATH%;c:\ant\bin
```

In other versions of Windows, you can do this via the System icon in the Control Panel. Under Linux (and Bash) you can do this by adding the following line to the profile in the user's home directory:

```
ANT_HOME=/usr/local/java/ant;export ANT_HOME
PATH= $PATH:/usr/local/java/ant/bin
```

This assumes that Ant was installed into `/usr/local/java/ant` directory on your Linux machine.

After Ant is properly installed, it can be executed by using the `build` command. `build` is a batch file on Windows or a shell script under Linux that sets the environment variables and launches the Java runtime.

Ant uses XML files to control the build process. Normally, an Ant build file is named `build.xml`. The root element of the build file is the project element. The primary elements are:

Project. The *project* is the root element of an Ant build file. The project identifies the default target and the base directory used for the build.

Target. A *target* is something that can be built or done within a project. Targets may include things like generating directory structures, compiling Java code, or deleting old class files. A project may have many targets. Targets can have dependencies on other targets, forcing a target to wait to be built until the targets it depends on have been built.

Task. A *task* is not the actual element name but rather describes a class of elements. Tasks are pieces of code that can be executed. These are the commands or operations that are used to build targets. Ant has many built-in tasks including Copy, Zip, and Javac. New tasks can be added and are written in Java.

Property. *Properties* are similar to variables. Properties are named and have values. Properties can be expanded within attributes of other tags. Properties can exist outside of a target.

A more detailed look at Ant syntax is beyond the scope of this chapter; however, Ant is revisited in later chapters, where it is used to compile the code examples in the book.

If you are planning to use open source tools and you want to be able to rebuild them, Ant is not an option, it is a requirement. Ant is also required for running some tools. Ant is so pervasive for open source Java that support for Ant is built into almost every Java development tool, commercial and open source. Ant support is provided for all of the editors and IDEs discussed in this chapter.

Revision Control and Code Repositories

Any serious programming project of any size needs to be concerned about configuration management and control. A configuration management (CM) system or revision control system (RCS) tracks changes to software as it is being developed. Most CM systems allow only one programmer to check out a module for editing at a time. Checking out a module locks the module and prevents others from changing it. Other programmers can get copies of the module, but they are not allowed to make changes to their copy. This allows many programmers to work on a single project without stepping on each other's toes. It also provides a central repository where anyone on the project team can go to retrieve the latest version or any previous version of the source code.

After the changes to a module have been completed the programmer checks in the module. Checkin unlocks the module and makes the changes available to the rest of the team. It allows someone else to check the module out to make further changes as needed. As changes are checked into the system, the programmer provides information or documentation about the changes that were made. These comments form a history of the changes that were made to the system as the system was developed. Most systems automatically add this historical documentation as comments to the source code files involved in the change.

The CM system also allows changes to be rolled back. Most systems allow a rollback to any previous code revision. The easiest way to do this is to keep a copy of each version of each file as it is checked in. Although that is a simple approach, it also consumes a lot of storage space for large projects. CM systems realize that most source code is stored as simple text files. Instead of storing the complete file in the repository, the CM system just stores the changes to the file. When a file is checked out, the CM system builds the requested version of the file by applying all of the changes made to that file since it was originally checked in. This approach allows for space-efficient storage of all previous versions of a source code file. In other words, a CM system maintains a complete history of your source code.

At certain points along the development cycle, you will normally want to make a release. A CM system will allow you to mark a version of the source code as a release. From that point, you can then continue making changes as before. You can also elect to split off into two or more directions, starting from the same source code base. This feature is called *branching*. Sometimes, you will want to recombine two different branches back into a single version. This is called *merging*.

A CM system does not build or compile your code. It does not provide bug tracking, change management, or collaboration features. But what it does do is critically important for any large software project.

CVS

CVS is the most common open source CM system. It has been around in one form or another since 1986. It is very stable and robust. CVS can be found at `http://www.cvshome.org`. The following table gives the product summary for CVS.

Product	CVS
Category	Source code configuration control and management
URL	http://www.cvshome.org and http://www.cvsnt.org
Supported Platforms	Java 1.2, 1.3, 1.4
License	GPL
Features	Tracks changes to source code files

CVS takes a different approach to revision control than many other CM systems. Instead of locking a source code file to prevent others from modifying the file, CVS allows everyone to access, or *check out*, a file. However, when code is checked back in, CVS warns the developer if someone else has already updated the code. CVS attempts to merge any code changes with the changes already made. If the merge fails, then CVS prompts the user to merge the code manually. This is done by checking out the code again and then using a difference utility (diff or WinDiff, for example) to merge the changes to the source code.

CVS can operate as a standalone, single-user application or it can be configured to support a distributed client-server model. The same CVS program can act as a client or a server. In general, CVS is a command-line-based application; however, a number of graphical shells have been created to support CVS. Although CVS primarily supports Linux and other Unix-like operating systems, it is available for all Windows platforms.

NOTE CVS works well as a client or standalone application on most Windows platforms, but it is not supported for use as a server under Windows 9x–based computers. A closely related product CVS NT (`http://www.cvsnt.org`) does work well as a server on Windows NT/2000/XP.

Installing the CVS Server on Windows

CVSNT is a specialized version of CVS designed especially for Windows NT–based platforms, including Windows 2000 and Windows XP. Although CVSNT does come with a standard Windows-style installer, the installation is not as simple as just running the setup program. The following instructions assume that you have downloaded `CVSNT1_1.11.1.3.exe` or the most current distribution of CVSNT (available at `http://www.cvsnt.org`).

1. Determine the drive that will be used for source code repositories. The rest of this discussion assumes that the C: drive has been selected.
2. Create two directories: `c:\cvsrepo` and `c:\cvstemp`. Set the permissions on these directories so that all users can have full access.

NOTE These directories cannot be located below `C:\Documents and Settings` or `C:\Windows\temp` due to security restrictions in these directories.

3. Install CVSNT by running the setup program. (It is recommended that instead of using the default installation directory that you use the directory `c:\tools\cvsnt`. There may be problems using directories with spaces embedded in the name.)
4. Open the Control Panel, and double-click the CVS for NT icon.
5. On the Service Status tab, make certain that everything is stopped.
6. On the Repositories tab, select the Repository Prefix check box and navigate to the `c:\cvsrepo` directory you created in Step 2.
7. Click the Add button to add a new repository root and append the name **test** to the prefix shown. Click Yes to create the directory.
8. Click Apply, and then select the Advanced tab.
9. Select all the check boxes, and set the temporary directory by navigating to the `c:\cvstemp` directory you created in Step 2.
10. The CVS Server port should be set to 2401, and the Lock Server port should be set to 2402.
11. Click Apply, then select the Service Status tab.
12. Start the CVS Locking service, and then start the CVS Service.
13. After the services have been started, close the window and close the Control Panel.
14. Add a user to the CVS users list by opening a command prompt window and entering the following commands:

    ```
    set cvsroot=:ntserver:<machinename>:/test
    cvs passwd -a <your windows login name>
    ```

15. Enter a password when prompted, and then close the command window.

At this point, the CVSNT installation is complete and ready to be tested. The easiest way to test the installation is from the command line version of CVS that's already installed. To do so, open a new command prompt window, and enter the following commands:

```
set cvsroot=:pserver:<user_name>@<machinename>:/test
cvs login
cvs ls -R
```

This should generate a response similar to the following:

```
Directory CVSROOT

checkoutlist
commitinfo
```

```
config
cvswrappers
editinfo
loginfo
modules
notify
rcsinfo
taginfo
verifymsg
```

The preceding output indicates a successful CVS installation. You can now execute the CVS logout command and close the command windows.

Basic CVS Commands

There are a few commands that need to be understood to use CVS. Although we do not intend to use CVS from the command line, it is still helpful to understand these commands to provide context for using CVS from any interface. These commands are described fully in the CVS documentation provided with CVSNT or downloaded from `http://www.cvs.org`.

Import. Copies a directory structure and files into a CVS repository, creating a new module. This is the best way to insert a new source code project into a CVS repository.

Add. Adds a single new file or directory to a repository.

Commit. Refreshes the repository with the changes made to code previously checked out.

Checkout. Retrieves a module from the repository and places it in a local directory.

Update. Synchronizes the local copy of the code with the code in the repository. This only makes changes to the local copy and does not affect the repository.

Users of other configuration management systems should be reminded that CVS does not lock a file that has been checked out. This means that it is possible for multiple developers to check out the same files and make changes to them. However, CVS does not let you check a file back in if it has been altered since you last checked it out.

A repository in CVS is treated as a collection of modules. A module, in turn, has a mapping between a subdirectory structure on the server and one on the client. When a module is imported into CVS, the subdirectory structure from the client is placed into the repository on the server. When the module is then checked out, that subdirectory structure is recreated on the client and all of the files copied. A module must be checked out before it can be committed or updated. This is true even if the module was imported from the current client machine.

CVS maintains information on the client by adding CVS subdirectories to each directory it is managing. This information is used to help with the synchronization process, and these directories should not be deleted.

CVS Clients

There are a number of graphical shells for CVS available. These shells are designed to act as clients to a CVS server. Most can also be configured to work with a standalone CVS. We will briefly look at three of these:

- WinCVS
- Tortoise
- jCVS

WinCVS

WinCVS is actually one of a suite of related GUI shells for CVS. The other members of this group include MacCVS for the Macintosh and gCVS for gtk+ running under Linux and other Unix-like operating systems.

WinCVS can be found at `http://www.wincvs.org` and installs onto a Windows system using a standard Windows installer. It supports Windows 9*x*/Me/NT/2000/XP. WinCVS is a graphical shell for CVS. It works as a client to a CVS server but also comes with a standalone version of CVS. This is ideal for users of Windows 9*x* platforms who do not have a server installed on another machine. WinCVS provides a scripting capability that supports both Python and Tcl as scripting languages.

Tortoise CVS

Frankly, Tortoise CVS is a good graphical CVS shell for day-to-day use available under Windows. Tortoise CVS can be found at:

```
http://www.tortoisecvs.org
```

Tortoise does not do everything that you might need to do in CVS but it easily performs all of the most common chores. Tortoise integrates directly into the Windows Explorer and provides right-click menu items for automating the most common CVS tasks of checkout, update, and checkin. Tortoise also colors file icons, making it easy to see which directories and files are controlled by CVS. Tortoise installs using a simple Windows setup program.

jCVS

Except for the IDE products, jCVS is the only Java CVS client entry. Unlike WinCVS, jCVS does not operate as a standalone CVS tool. It requires an available CVS server to be accessible from the current machine. The jCVS client provides a number for dialog boxes for executing the primary CVS commands. After a module has been checked out, jCVS provides a browser for the local file system. The browser can be configured to automatically launch programs based on the filename or mime type. Using JCVS is a definite improvement over entering commands on the command line, but it is not as powerful WinCVS or as convenient as Tortoise. jCVS can be found at:

```
http://www.jcvs.org
```

NOTE One feature of jCVS is noteworthy. There is a servlet version of jCVS. This version allows repository browsing through a Web browser. Unfortunately, the documentation for this feature is very limited.

CVS Integration with IDE

Both NetBeans and Eclipse have integrated support for CVS built directly into the IDE. The following sections describe how CVS is integrated into Eclipse and NetBeans, respectively.

CVS and Eclipse

Eclipse provides one advantage over other CVS clients that we have seen to date: Eclipse supports a convenient repository browser. Most CVS clients focus on the client side and the files that have been checked out. Eclipse allows the user to browse the repository on the server. This is very useful when you are first starting to work on an existing project that already has a repository.

To use CVS from Eclipse choose Window ➪ Open Perspective ➪ CVS Repository Exploring, and then right-click in the CVS repositories panel and choose New Repository Location. Enter the information needed to access the CVS server and repository. After you have clicked the Finish button, the repository will be represented as a tree in the left panel, as shown in Figure 4.10.

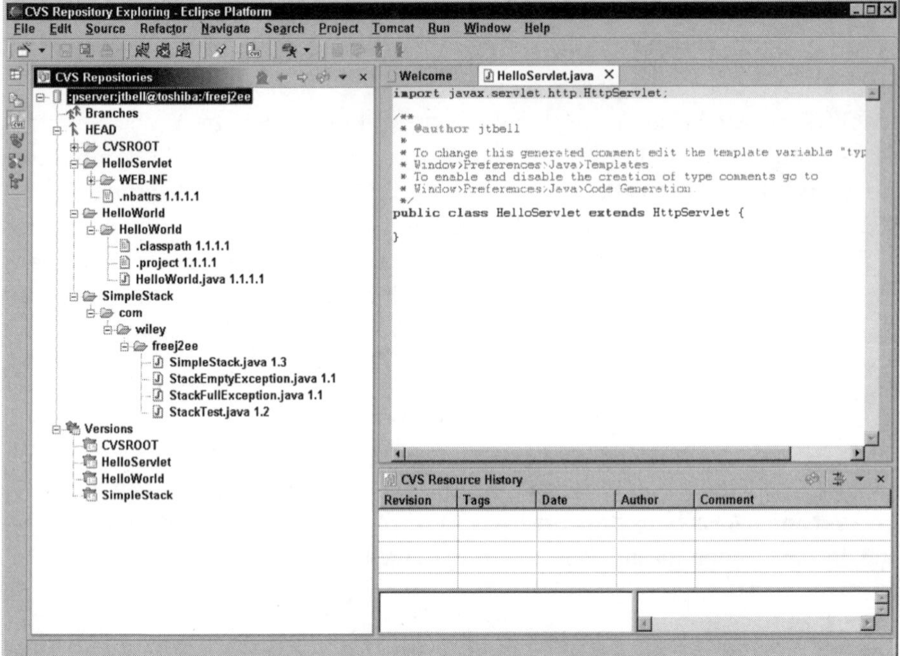

Figure 4.10 Browsing a CVS repository in Eclipse.

From here, you can expand the tree and explore the modules stored within the repository. Right-clicking on a module provides a menu item to check out the module as a new project.

New modules can be added to the repository by selecting a project node, right-clicking, and choosing Team ➪ Share project. The dialog box will prompt you to select a repository. After a project has been associated with a repository, the team menu offers the ability to commit and update the project with the repository.

CVS and NetBeans

NetBeans takes a different approach to CVS integration. In NetBeans, you mount a CVS repository just as you would a local directory or a .jar file. A CVS repository can be mounted from the Explorer pane by right-clicking on the root node and choosing Mount, or by using the menus and selecting Versioning ➪ Mount Version Control ➪ CVS. This starts New Wizard - CVS. The wizard first prompts you for the working directory. This is the directory that will be used as the CVS sandbox on your local system. The next dialog box prompts you for the CVS connection information. The home directory screen only appears for Windows 98 and ME users. The CVS client dialog box allows you to choose between the built-in CVS client or an external CVS client, defaulting to the built-in client. The login dialog box allows you to enter a password and log into CVS. It also shows if you are already logged in. Finally, the initial checkout screen gives you an opportunity to check out the entire repository to your local system. In many situations, this is undesirable, so leave the box blank and select finish.

Modules can be checked out of CVS by choosing Versioning ➪ CVS ➪ Checkout. In the default configuration, this will give you a warning that the default values will be used unless you held the Control key down when you selected the menu item. Unfortunately, the default seems to be to check out the entire repository. The way to fix this behavior is to choose Tools ➪ Options ➪ CVS Client Settings, and change the item labeled User Interface Mode to GUI Style. Now you will always be prompted for checkout arguments before the checkout begins. Once again, be aware that the default values in the dialog box will check out the entire repository. At this point, the you should replace the value in the module field with the name of the module that will be checked out.

Getting started in CVS with NetBeans can be a little awkward, primarily because the user interface provides little easy control of what is copied from the repository. If the modules have already been checked out of the repository using another CVS client, NetBeans becomes a little easier to work with. If the directory is mounted as a CVS directory, then NetBeans will provide access to the CVS commands, maintaining the coordination of the directory with the repository. Unfortunately, NetBeans does not automatically recognize when a file system is already under configuration management control. This means that it is up to the user to manage the file system and its relationship with CVS by mounting the system as a CVS-controlled system.

Subversion

Subversion is a project at `http://subversion.tigris.org`. The idea behind Subversion is to create a new version control or configuration management tool that is platform independent and addresses some of the inconveniences of CVS. A major issue being addressed by Subversion is the ability to version control directory structures. Subversion makes reconfiguring a directory structure the same level of task as changing a source module within the system. Directory changes can be managed and controlled like other files in a project. This is very difficult to do in CVS.

Another important feature is that commits in Subversion are atomic. That is, if a commit fails for any reason the entire commit fails. If a commit succeeds, the entire commit succeeds. This is different from CVS, which allows each file to succeed or fail individually.

Subversion is still a new project, but seems to be stable. Unfortunately, the broad set of tools that exist for CVS will not be available for Subversion for some time. Subversion can be hosted through a Web-based interface, making it a good candidate for use by development teams that are geographically separated.

Testing

Testing is a critical component in any large-scale software-development project. Unfortunately, testing is often the first component to be tossed when a project starts to fall behind schedule. This always seems to haunt the project team later in the life cycle. Reasons for abandoning testing seem to be that testing tools tend to be expensive, and quality assurance tends to be a separate concern from developing and delivering a final product. Open source products provide solutions here because they offer a means of placing affordable testing tools into the hands of the developers. This allows testing to work concurrently with development, ensuring a higher-quality product at the end of the development effort.

Unit Testing: JUnit

Testing is one way to ensure software quality. Languages like Java make it easy to test code while it is being developed because the language supports encapsulation and code independence. Testing a single functional piece of code is known as *unit testing*. JUnit is a set of utilities designed to aid in unit testing Java classes. The philosophy behind JUnit is that as developers create methods for a class they can also create tests to ensure that each method works as designed. These tests can be executed as a collection in a test plan. The test plan is executed on classes each time a class is changed to ensure that the changes have not broken other elements of the code. If a bug or anomaly is found that was not caught by the test plan, then a new test can be added to the test plan to specifically test for that bug. Future changes will continue to execute all tests in the plan to ensure that a future fix does not break earlier ones. This execution of all previous tests is sometimes known as regression testing. The following table provides a product summary for JUnit.

Product	JUnit
Category	Java unit testing tool
URL	http://www.junit.org/
Supported Platforms	Java 1.2, 1.3, 1.4
License	Common public license
Features	Supported in Eclipse, NetBeans, and Ant

To gain a better understanding of unit testing with JUnit, let's work through a simple example. Our sample code will be a class called Palindrome. Palindrome stores a single string object and returns that string either the way it was stored or reversed. The class definition follows:

```
/*== save as Palindrome.java */
/**
 * Palindrome is a demonstration class for use
 * in demonstrating the use of the jUnit testing framework.
 * @author jtbell
 */
public class Palindrome extends java.lang.Object {

    private StringBuffer s = null;

    /** Creates a new instance of Palindrome */
    public Palindrome() {
    }

    public Palindrome( String aString ) {
        s = new StringBuffer( aString );
    }

    void setString(String aString) {
        s = new StringBuffer( aString );
    }

    String getString() {
        if( s != null)
            return s.toString();
        else
            return null;
    }

    String getReverse() {
        if( s != null)
            return s.reverse().toString();
        else
            return null;
    }
}
```

There are two methods that we want to test in Palindrome: `getString` and `getReverse`. In the past, good programmers would test their code by creating main methods that exercised the class. JUnit goes beyond this type of testing by providing a testing framework that allows multiple complex tests to be defined and easily combined. To start creating a JUnit test, we need to derive a new class from the junit.framework.TestCase class as follows:

```
import junit.framework.*;

public class PalindromeTest extends TestCase {
    public PalindromeTest(java.lang.String testName) {
        super(testName);
    }
}
```

Next we define some class variables and a `setUp` method that initializes the data we will use for testing. We could also add a `tearDown` method to perform any tasks that might be needed to gracefully shut down the test sequence.

```
    String aString = null;
    Palindrome palindrome = null;
    public void setUp()
    {
        aString = new String("Madam Im Adam");
        palindrome = new Palindrome( aString );
    }
```

Test code is added to test each method.

```
    public void testGetString()
    {
        Assert.assertEquals( aString, palindrome.getString());
    }

    public void testReverseString()
    {
        StringBuffer sb = new StringBuffer( aString );
        sb.reverse();
        Assert.assertEquals(sb.toString(), palindrome.getReverse());
    }
```

We added one function for each method we wanted to test. For some complex methods, we might want to add multiple methods to cover special circumstances; in our simple case this is not needed. JUnit makes use of a specialized naming convention in order to streamline the testing process. Methods that are used to test individual features or methods should all have the lowercase test prefix so they appear in the form `testXXX`, where `XXX` is the name of the method being tested.

Running tests one at a time can be tedious. JUnit provides a capability to define a suite of tests to execute. A *TestSuite* is a composite or collection of TestSuites and TestCases. Both TestSuite and TestCase implement the Test interface. The Test interface is used to run the tests. Test suites can be defined in two ways: statically or dynamically. In the sample code that follows we have defined the suite dynamically. The framework uses introspection to find all of the methods that need to be executed and then executes them. The suite method is defined as a public static method and is used by the framework to launch the tests.

```
public static Test suite() {
 TestSuite suite = new TestSuite(PalindromeTest.class);
 return suite;
}
```

A main method is added to run the test within the framework.

```
public static void main(java.lang.String[] args) {
    junit.textui.TestRunner.run(suite());
}
```

This example can be executed directly from the command line.

TIP Eclipse and NetBeans both have integrated jUnit directly into the IDE environments. This allows unit testing to be done as a part of the develop, compile, and test cycle without ever leaving the development environment.

Web Testing

Testing for Web applications falls into two primary categories, functional testing and load, or performance, testing. Functional testing is testing to determine whether the Web application operates as designed and intended. This type of testing ensures that the application presents the correct data and that the expected actions occur within the application. Load testing, on the other hand, measures the performance characteristics of a Web application. Load testing evaluates how many users can access a Web application before there is a noticeable performance degradation or failure.

jUnit with HttpUnit

JUnit can be configured to perform a number of Web-based functional-testing tasks by using the HttpUnit add-in module. HttpUnit, available at `http://httpunit.sourceforge.net/`, is a free open source API for accessing Web sites without a browser. HttpUnit provides methods for sending HTTP requests, and processing and analyzing the responses. HttpUnit handles cookies, browser redirects, HTTPS, and many of the features needed to writes tests for Web applications. Utilities are also provided that can be used to compare a Web response against the expected result. HttpUnit is designed to work within the JUnit framework and can be used to build a comprehensive functional-testing tool for Web applications.

HttpUnit combined with JUnit is a very powerful testing tool, but creating tests for Web applications this way requires a great deal of effort. Essentially, you must create a test program for each element of a Web application that will be tested. This adds time and expense to a project. HttpUnit and JUnit represent one approach for functional testing of Web sites. Another approach is offered by jMeter.

jMeter

The jMeter tool is another product from the Jakarta-Apache group. Currently, jMeter is designed to be a load-testing tool. As a load-testing tool jMeter can simulate many users accessing a system at the same time. For testing Web applications, it is necessary to simulate the HTTP `GET` and `POST` requests that are made by the browser to the Web servers. JMeter provides the capability to do this in two different ways. You can manually add each HTTP request by completing a form-based interface. Alternately, you can configure the built-in proxy and allow jMeter to capture the information it needs from the requests and responses created as you browse through the application, using your favorite Web browser. The following table provides a summary of jMeter.

Product	jMeter
Category	Load testing tool
URL	http://jakarta.apache.org/jmeter
Supported Platforms	Java 1.2, 1.3, 1.4
License	Apache
Features	Provides a proxy to record progress through a Web application and generate user simulation; supports distributed testing clients

Installing jMeter

jMeter can be installed by unzipping the file into the appropriate directory. A shell script is provided for launching jMeter under Linux, and a batch file is used to launch jMeter under Windows NT/2000/XP. In spite of the fact that the Web site claims that jMeter works on Windows 98, the batch file provided does not work under Windows 98 and thus will likely not work under Windows 95 or Me. jMeter is shown in Figure 4.11.

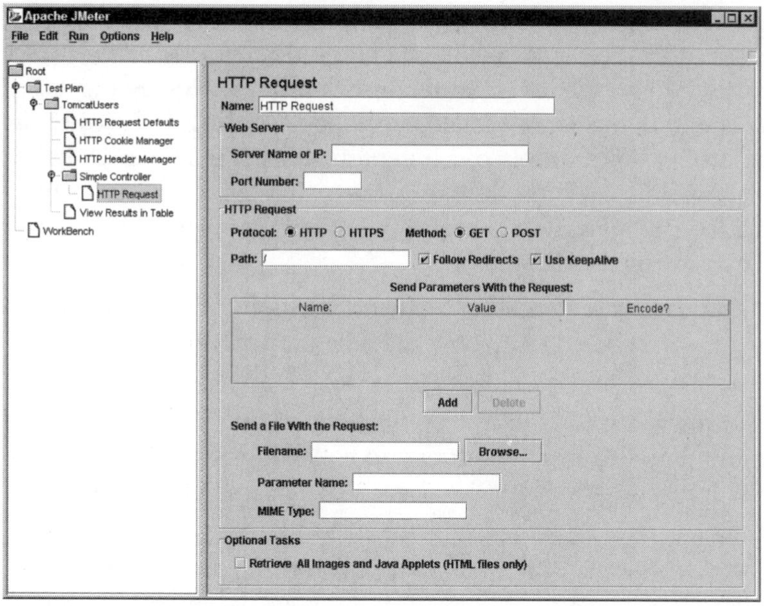

Figure 4.11 jMeter.

When jMeter is launched, there are two panes. The left pane has a tree with a root node and two nodes below it labeled Test Plan and Workbench. This is called the test tree. The right pane shows details for the currently selected node. With the root node highlighted, the name for the project or root node can be edited. To build a test plan, we will add nodes to this tree. A node can be added by selecting a node and using the right mouse button or the Edit menu item and choosing Add.

Test Plans

The first thing a test plan needs is a thread group. Thread groups represent groups of virtual users; each thread corresponds to another user of the system. Each thread group will prompt you for a number of threads, a ramp-up period, and a loop count. The ramp-up period is divided evenly among all the users. Remember that each thread counts as one virtual user, so if there are five threads and a ramp-up time of five seconds, the users will ramp up at an approximate rate of one new user per second. To a thread group, we can add:

Configuration elements. Configuration elements are helpers that provide support for samplers within the same subtree. Some of the uses of configuration elements include setting default values for samplers and collecting and storing cookies for Web requests.

Logic controllers. Logic controllers provide a means to customize the logic that is used by jMeter to decide when to send requests. Logic controllers can also be thought of as containers for other testing elements. The elements within the container are executed according to the rules of the logic controller. An example of a logic controller is the Once Only controller. Once Only executes the samplers within the controller only once during the test plan. This is useful for situations such as site logins, where the user should only login once.

Listeners. Listeners provide access to the information collected as jMeter runs. Listeners can be used to display the data graphically or to save the results in a file.

Samplers. Samplers are used to collect information for jMeter. Samplers exist for sending requests to the server and collecting responses. There are samplers for testing Web applications, Web services, JDBC, and FTP requests.

Assertions. Assertions are not added to a thread group but are added to samplers. Assertions are added to test if the response from the server was the expected response.

Timers. Timers are used to provide delays between requests. jMeter sends requests one immediately after another by default. A timer adds a delay between requests on a thread or by a virtual user.

For a quick demonstration, the following instructions show you how to perform a quick test of the `Tomcat index.html` page.

1. Start by adding a thread group and naming it TomcatUsers. Set the number of threads to 5, the ramp-up period to 0, and the loops to 2.
2. To this thread group, add these three config elements:
   - HTTP Request Defaults
   - HTTP Cookie Manager
   - HTTP Header Manager
3. Edit the HTTP Request Defaults so that the server is the server where Tomcat is installed and the port is the port configured for Tomcat requests (normally Tomcat uses port 8080 by default). The values set here will become the default values for all HTTP request samplers that we will add later. No changes need to be made for the cookie or header managers.
4. Add a logic controller to the thread group. To do this, select the TomcatUsers Node and add the "Simple Controller" from the Logic

Controllers menu. This controller isn't strictly required but it serves as a container for the samplers that we will add shortly.

5. Add an HTTP request sampler to the Simple Controller. To do so, in the path field just enter a "/" and select the GET request button.
6. Next, you need a listener. (Remember, a listener provides access to the data collected by samplers. If a listener is not present, then there will be no way to observe anything as the test progresses.) Because you will be running just a small number of samples, you can use the View Results In Table listener. You can add the listener directly to the TomcatUsers node. If you want to save the data and share it across listeners, you should provide a filename in the Write All Data to a File portion of the panel. Providing a filename here also allows you to view the results in other listeners after you have executed the test.
7. You are now ready to run the test. To do so, choose Run ➪ Start. A small green square at the top-right corner of the window indicates that a test is currently in progress. If the View Results in Table node is selected, the results of each test will be added as the tests are completed. If the individual tests are successful, then a check mark will appear in the right-most column of the result table.

Adding Assertions

If the test ran successfully, then you are ready to start adding to it. First, add an assertion. The assertion should be added to the HTTP Request node. The assertion will be applied to the response generated for the request. Assertions accept Perl-style regular expressions. If you want to check that the response contains a particular string you can add the string or a pattern that will match the string. For your test you will look for the title of the page. The title of the Tomcat root page is as follows:

```
<title>Jakarta Project - Tomcat</title>
```

You need to escape the greater than and less than signs, so when you add it into the patterns list you need to enter it as:

```
\<title\>Jakarta Project - Tomcat\<\/title\>
```

After this has been entered, select the TomcatUsers node again, and add an Assertion Results listener. Next, clear all of the data from the previous run by choosing Run ➪ Clear All, and then rerun the test. The results of the assertions will be displayed in the Assertion Results listener panel.

Using the Proxy to Build a Web Test

jMeter also provides a tool that allows it to quickly build a test plan for a Web site. The tool is a proxy server that captures the entire conversation between the browser and the server. To configure the proxy server, select the Workbench node and click Add ➪ Non-Test Element ➪ HTTP Proxy Server to the node. By default, the proxy is configured to listen to port 8080; however, port 8080 is also the default port for standalone Tomcat installations. (John normally changes the port setting to 8088.)

There are lists in the panel for patterns to include and patterns to exclude. These lists determine which requests will be added to the test plan. Most of the time, we want to ignore requests for images and style sheets. For example, to ignore GIF and JPEG images, you would add:

```
.*\.gif
.*\.jpg
.*\.jpeg
```

as patterns to the exclude list. These are also Perl-style regular expressions. If you were only interested in requests for HTM documents, you could add an include pattern such as:

```
.*\.html
```

The Start button at the bottom starts the proxy server.

After the proxy has been configured, you must also configure the browser to use the proxy. In Internet Explorer, this can be done by choosing Tools ➪ Internet Options and then selecting the Connections tab. Select LAN Settings, and then check the Use a proxy server... box. Use localhost and 8088 for the address and port. On other browsers, you will have to look for the settings that allow you to manually configure your proxy settings. Netscape and Mozilla users will typically find this under Edit ➪ Preferences ➪ Advanced ➪ Proxies.

After the browser is configured and the proxy server has been started, browse to the Tomcat application (make sure Tomcat is running too). Click the Servlet Examples link, then select Execute beside the cookies sample line. Fill in the form, and press Submit.

Now, look at your test plan. The pages that you visited have been added as HTTP Request nodes to the test plan. The values entered into the forms have also been entered into each node. Now when the test is executed, all of these pages will be visited and the post requests will send the data captured during the browsing session.

NOTE **When your are finished, do not forget to reset the browser and turn off the proxy server.**

We have demonstrated how jMeter can be used for load testing. Asserts can also be used to verify the information returned on a Web page, providing an effective means of functional testing as well. jMeter is not currently as powerful as commercial tools such as Load Runner, but jMeter can be a useful tool when Load Runner or another commercial tool is not available and load testing must be done. jMeter also has some limitations. Currently, the proxy does not support browsing to pages served with the secure HTTPS protocol. This may limit some of its functionality to preproduction testing purposes. jMeter is easy to extend. Developers are encouraged to add listeners, samplers, and other elements to jMeter by writing new Java classes. The stated goal of the jMeter project is to become one of the best functional-testing tools for Web applications. It appears as if the product has a good start.

Summary

In this chapter, we have examined a number of developer tools that are designed for use as part of the development process and are not intended, for the most part, to be part of the enterprise platform. However, these tools are necessary to build a successful development team and will help us as we move forward building our enterprise platform. In general, the developer tools we covered fall into these categories:

- Editors
- IDEs
- Build tools
- Source code control and management
- Testing tools

There are other tools to consider. Most notably, we did not cover profiling and debugging tools. Debugging tools are included within an IDE and so standalone debugging tools are less common. Both of the IDEs we discussed have full debugging support for Java built in. We did not cover source-code formatters, (also built into the IDE) or documentation generators and add-ins. We did not discuss the variety of open source Java compilers and other specialty language add-ins. These tools tend to be more specialized, and although they may be a good fit for certain teams and projects, we decided not to cover them here.

The personal nature of developer tools was discussed along with the effects that tool selection can have on personal and team productivity. The bottom line here is to select the tools that are best for the project and for the developers. When there is room for developer individuality, provide leeway for the developer, but not at the expense of the team.

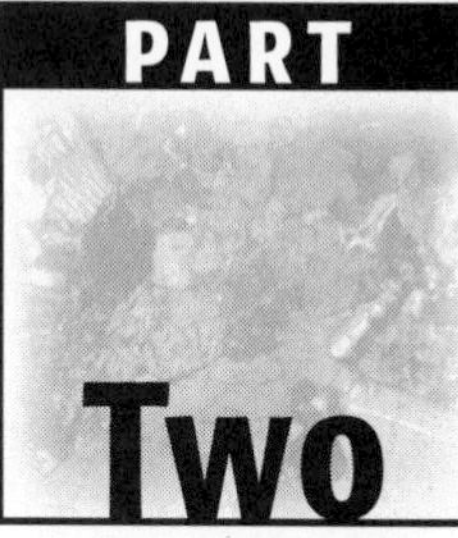

Integrating the Web Tier

Many of today's enterprise applications are delivered through a Web-based interface. In an enterprise application, the Web tier serves to implement the portions of an application that are used to deliver the user interface through a Web browser. In this part, we look at open source implementations of the primary J2EE component used to implement the Web tier, the servlet container. However, we do not stop here. Most Web-tier technologies are best utilized by separating the business logic from the application logic through the implementation of the Model View Controller design pattern. We examine open source tools that provide two approaches for doing this: template engines and Web application frameworks.

CHAPTER

5

Powering the Web Tier with a Server Container

Web servers and servlet containers work hand in hand to deliver Web-based applications. Today, Web-based applications are a common way to deliver enterprise applications. There are a number of reasons why this is true:

- Web-based applications can be centrally maintained and updated, reducing the support and maintenance costs of delivering an application to many desktops.
- Information presented in Web-based applications can be published faster through the Web, making the information more timely.
- Information is updated simultaneously for all users, so all users act on the same information.
- Users do not have to be tied directly to a corporate local area network (LAN) or wide area network (WAN) because the applications can be accessed through the ubiquitous World Wide Web.

This chapter looks at open source servlet containers and their relationship to Web servers.

Web-Tier Architecture

The Web tier contains the elements of an enterprise platform that are responsible for delivering the presentation layers of an application. The foundation of the Web tier is the Web server. In the J2EE world, the servlet container may supplement, or even implement, the Web Server. In this section, we explore the relationship between the Web server and the servlet container by defining these components and gaining an understanding of how they interact with each other. We also position these components within our J2EE platform.

Defining Architectural Pieces

In a Web-based application, the Web server receives HTTP requests. The browser creates the HTTP request and directs it to a server based on a Uniform Resource Locator (URL). When the Web server receives the request from the browser, it then determines how to respond to the request (see Figure 5.1). If the request is for a file then the Web server returns that file. This is the way that most static HTML files are handled.

However, there is an alternate method of handling requests: the request may be to execute a program that will, in turn, generate the response. The Web server executes that program, and the program then generates the response for the request. The response generated is often an HTML text, but it could also be an XML document, an image, or anything else that can be transferred through HTTP.

One popular technology for these Web-server-executed programs is known as CGI (Common Gateway Interface). When a CGI program is requested through a URL, the Web server launches and executes the program to generate the response. CGI programs can be written in almost any language, including Perl, Java, and C/C++. Each time a request is made for a CGI program, a new process is created and the program must be initialized. Initialization can be a time-consuming process that may include establishing database connections and/or reading in files and other tasks that need to be repeated each time the program is started.

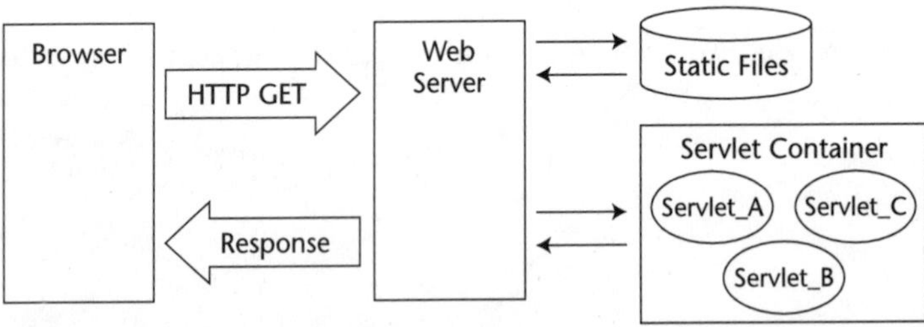

Figure 5.1 Processing requests with servlets.

Java has replaced CGI programs with Java servlets. *Servlets*, a key element in enterprise Java, provide a means of creating dynamically generated Web pages, Web pages that respond to user input and control. A servlet is typically used to dynamically generate a response for an HTTP request. For example, if a user enters a city and state into a Web form to look for a hotel, a servlet might be used to generate the list of hotels within the specified city. This list is then dynamically created and returned to the browser based on the user's input of city and state.

Servlets run within a servlet container; that is, a *servlet container* acts as a host for Java servlets and manages the life cycle of those servlets. Servlet containers (sometimes called *engines*) are a standard component in the J2EE architecture. Most servlet containers are designed so that they can be integrated with an existing Web server. However, many servlet containers can also be configured to behave as Web servers themselves. This configuration is often preferable for development environments because it is easier to configure and maintain.

It is possible to create very complex applications using just servlets. This is common for what we call "Web applications." These applications are just that, Web applications with little or no integration with the rest of the enterprise. By contrast, in a full-scale enterprise architecture, the Web server and servlet container work together in the front end of an enterprise architecture and form the Web tier (see Figure 5.2). The Web-tier is responsible for most of the user interface generation and delivery (the browser renders the user interface). The Web tier handles HTTP communication between the applications and the browsers or agents.

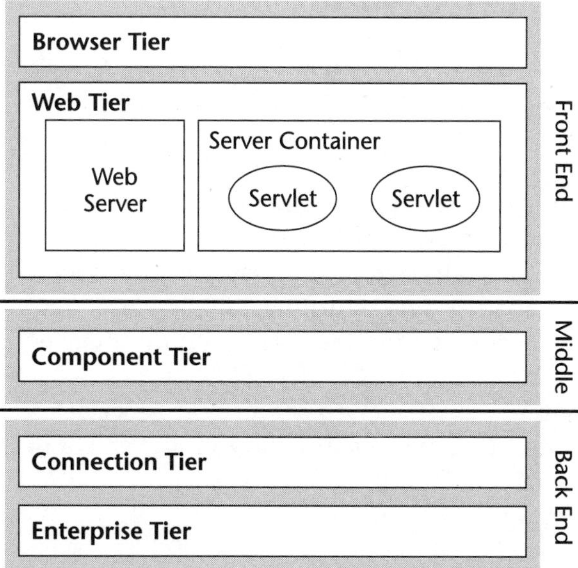

Figure 5.2 Servlet container with enterprise platform.

Putting the Pieces Together

Now that you've got a handle on the different pieces of the architecture, here's how those pieces work together:

1. A request comes in to a Web server.
2. If the requested URL is for a servlet, the Web server sends the request on to the servlet container.
3. The servlet container locates the servlet referenced by the URL.
4. If the servlet has not been initialized, the container executes the servlet's `init()` method. It does this only once during a servlet's lifetime in the container. This allows the servlet to generate dynamic content without repeating the initialization process.
5. The container executes the `service()` method of servlet. In most servlets (based on the HttpServlet class), the service method will then call the `doGet()` or `doPost()` method on the HttpServlet.
6. The servlet does whatever application processing it needs to do to generate the response. This may include connecting to databases or invoking Enterprise Java Beans for example.

A servlet must implement the javax.servlet.Servlet interface. The container calls the methods defined in this interface to manage the servlet's life cycle. The `init()` and `service()` methods mentioned previously are two of the methods defined by the servlet interface.

Web Servers versus Servlet Containers

In Figure 5.1, we show the Web server as a front end for the servlet container. This seems to be the most common configuration for production-based deployment, but note that this configuration is optional for many servlet containers. Most servlet containers have the ability to handle HTTP directly instead of relying on the Web server to do so. Remember: the Web server returns a file or executes a program based on the request. Because the servlet container also understands HTTP, it's fairly simple to create servlets to look up files and return them or execute programs returning the standard output. These functions are now typically built in and provided with most currently available servlet containers.

So the question is: Why continue to use a Web server with a servlet container? The answer is that you often don't need to use the Web server. For most development uses, there is no need for a separate Web server at all. The servlet containers we will look at handle static content just as well as servlet-generated content.

But for production purposes, having a Web server, such as Apache, deal with static content can be beneficial. For example, the Web server is often optimized for serving static files and can do this faster than the servlet container. There are also techniques that can be used with Apache for supporting load balancing and other features that may help a site to be more scalable. These come at a cost of complexity, but that is the trade-off.

TCP/IP, NETWORKING, AND THE INTERNET

Networking protocols are often built one on top of another. The protocol used by the World Wide Web is the Hypertext Transfer Protocol, known as HTTP. HTTP, in turn, uses the TCP/IP (Transmission Control Protocol/Internet Protocol) protocol. Many other protocols are also built on top of TCP/IP, which is the basis for Internet communication between machines. TCP/IP identifies machines by a unique address called the IP address. The IP address is represent by four numbers, each representing a string of 8 bits (octets). The IP address is normally represented in print as something like:

```
192.168.0.1
```

Most people find it difficult to work with or remember numbers. They prefer names. The Internet allows us to identify computers by using names. This is commonly seen when we type a URL into a browser. A URL can be broken up into parts as follows:

```
  1          2          3       4
|===|===================|==|=================|
http://jakarta.apache.org:80/tomcat/index.html
```

The first part (Part 1 above) is the protocol. In this case, it says that the browser will communicate with the server using HTTP. Part 2 identifies the machine that will receive the request. The browser, working with other networking protocols, converts this name into an IP address. In this way, we can simply remember names, and the computer converts those names into the numbers it needs.

Part 3 shown in the example is the port. Normally, this is not entered because the port defaults to port 80 for HTTP. The port is a logical connection point on that machine. Most services or protocols running on a server listen to "well-known" ports for connection requests. The service that handles HTTP, for example, normally listens on port 80.

Part 4 is the resource. In this case, it is a filename for the file `index.html` located in the `tomcat` directory.

BENEFITS OF USING A WEB SERVER ON UNIX/LINUX

On Linux and other Unix-like systems there is another reason to front end a servlet container with a Web server. (For this discussion, when we refer to Linux, we mean all Unix-based or similar operating systems).

As you may already know, a port is a logical connection point on a machine. TCP/IP supports over 65,000 (2 to the 16th power) ports. All "well- known" ports exist between the numbers 0 and 1024. Most services or protocols running on a server listen to well-known ports for connection requests. The service that handles HTTP, for example, normally listens on port 80. On Linux systems, only programs that are running as root can access these well-known ports.

As most Unix administrators already know, the root user of a Linux system can do anything without restriction. A program running with root privileges could possibly be taken over, or hijacked, giving root access to the hijacker. Most applications designed to work with these lower ports are aware of this as a security concern. These programs start as root but then immediately lower their access levels once the port has been opened. Unfortunately, the servlet containers don't do this or can't do this because of current limitations in Java. This means that to run a servlet container on port 80, the container must be running as root, and this is an unacceptable security risk for most Web-facing sites.

There is no need for a servlet container to run as root if the port being used for communication is above 1024. The default for most servlet containers used in development, is to use port 8080. This allows the servlet container to be used directly. In cases where the servlet container is not Web-facing (for example, on a company intranet), some companies allow the servlet container to run as root. This practice is questionable and should never be done for a Web-facing site.

There are a couple of workarounds for this issue. One is to configure a non-Java-based Web server, such as Apache, to forward requests (based on URLs) to the servlet container. The Web server handles the traffic coming in on port 80 and uses another means to communicate with the servlet container. This solution has advantages for large systems because Apache has load-balancing capabilities that allow a site to scale for more capacity by adding machines. Apache can also be configured so that it handles all static files, only redirecting servlet and JSP requests to the servlet container. This may improve performance in cases where a site has many static files in relation to dynamic content.

Another solution is based on the fact that most modern Linux kernels have built in firewall capabilities. This solution requires the firewall to be configured to forward or reroute all traffic addressed to port 80 so that it goes to another port above 1024, typically 8080. Specific instructions for doing this will vary from system to system and are beyond the scope of this chapter.

JavaServer Pages

JavaServer Pages (or JSP) is Java's Web-page-scripting technology. JSP provides the ability to create dynamic Web content by embedding Java code directly into the HTML of a Web page. In this respect, JSP is similar to Active Server Pages (ASP), PHP, and server-side JavaScript technologies. Unlike those technologies, though, JSP also provides a custom tag capability that allows complex dynamic Web pages to be developed without using Java code within the page itself. This feature allows a clean separation between page design tasks and application development tasks.

CROSS-REFERENCE **For more information on dynamic content, see Chapters 6 and 7.**

JavaServer Pages have a close relationship to servlets and servlet containers: specifically, a JSP is compiled into a Java servlet. A JSP can be precompiled into a servlet before deployment, or the container can handle this task automatically when the page is requested for the first time. Because of the close relationship between JSP technology and servlet technology, all of the current servlet containers include JSP capability as an integral part of the container.

Selecting Your Tools

Now that we know what the different pieces of our architecture are and what they do, it's time to choose the specific tools we'll use. The tools we have to decide upon are as follows:

Web server. This chapter assumes that you either do not need a Web server or that you have chosen the Apache Web server. By virtue of the fact that this book supports the use of open source tools and that the Apache Web server is the most popular Web server in the world today, we assume that if you do need a Web server it will be Apache. Apache is free, open source, and available for most popular operating systems.

Servlet container. We will follow the process outlined in Chapter 3 in order to decide which servlet engine will be used for the platform. As a reminder, this process goes through four steps:

- Survey the products.
- Determine the project's needs.
- Evaluate the products.
- Select a product.

A Survey of Servlet Containers

A survey of the currently available open source servlet containers yields only a few products. This was not always the case. In the early days when the servlet specification was fairly new, many people created servlet containers. As the specification matured, it took more effort to keep up with the technologies demanded by the specification and by competing open source projects. Some efforts went by the wayside and disappeared. Others merged with other open source projects to share the development load. In at least one case, the free open source container project was closed and the company attempted to make it a fee-based open source project. The products left to choose from today are:

- Enhydra
- Jetty
- Paperclips
- Tomcat

NOTE There may be other free servers or servers that may have been open source in the past (Resin comes to mind), but at this time these are the only servers that are both free and currently available under open source licenses. Of these four, only Jetty and Tomcat seem to be enjoying steady uninterrupted development and continue to conform to the latest servlet specifications.

At this writing the GNU Paperclips product apparently has not been updated for almost 2 years. Enhydra has recently completed a transition to a new open source community and has fallen far behind the other containers. Hopefully, in this new development community, Enhydra will quickly start moving forward again, but in the meantime we're left with Jetty and Tomcat as the products to evaluate.

Jetty

Jetty is the primary servlet engine distributed with the jBoss project and is one of the most popular servlet engines around. Jetty is small enough to be used for embedded systems or to be included as a part of another software package. Don't let its size fool you, however, Jetty's performance compares with the best of them. The following table gives a summary of Jetty.

Product	Jetty (version 2.4.2)
Category	Servlet container and HTTP server
URL	http://jetty.mortbay.org

Supported Platforms	Windows 9x/NT/2000/XP, Linux, and most Unix systems
License	Artistic
Features	Servlet spec 2.3 with enhancements, suitable for embedding into other applications, Jasper JSP compiler, HTTP server support

Today Jetty is the default servlet container for JBoss and boasts a number of supporting developers that help enhance Jetty. This means that project continuity is likely to continue if the project's owner stops maintaining the system.

The current version of Jetty can be used on almost any platform that supports a 1.2-compliant JDK. This includes Windows 98/Me/NT/2000/XP and most current Linux platforms. Jetty supports JSP, but uses a slightly modified version of the Apache-Jakarta product called Jasper, which is the same JSP compiler used for Tomcat.

Jetty can be downloaded as a standalone product or as part of the JBoss open source J2EE environment. There is also a version of Jetty that is integrated with the Jonas EJB container.

Tomcat

Tomcat is a product of the Apache-Jakarta Project. The Tomcat servlet container also serves as the industry standard reference implementation of the servlet specification. This means that Tomcat is normally the most up-to-date container as far as the specifications go. In the past, this sometimes meant that performance took a back seat to specification compliance. Since the release of Tomcat 4, though, this has not been an issue. In our experience, Tomcat performs as well as any other servlet container in the market. The summary information for Tomcat is provided in the following table.

Product	Tomcat (version 4.1.24)
Category	Servlet container
URL	http://jakarta.apache.org/tomcat
Supported Platforms	Windows 9x/NT/2000/XP, Linux, and most Unix systems
License	Apache
Features	Servlet spec 2.3 (version 5 supports servlet spec 2.4), Jasper JSP compiler, HTTP server support, specification reference implementation

Tomcat uses Jasper for processing JSPs. Jasper is another product from the Apache-Jakarta group. The Jetty servlet container also uses Jasper.

Tomcat is available for all platforms that support a JDK 1.2 or later environment and is specifically supported for all 32-bit Windows platforms and Linux. Tomcat can be downloaded from the Jakarta site at the following URL:

```
http://jakarta.apache.org/tomcat
```

Here you'll find several choices of binary distributions specific to the version of Java and the platform, be it Windows or non-Windows. Tomcat provides an XML parser and a JNDI provider for older JDK 1.2– and 1.3–based deployment. These features are built into the JDK for Java 1.4 and later, so Tomcat provides distributions that leave these features out for these implementations. These "light" distributions have the letters "LE" in their filenames.

The Windows distribution is available as a .zip archive file or as a self-installing executable (.exe) file. Linux versions are available as compressed .tar archive files or as Red Hat Package Manager (.rpm) files.

Needs and Features Analysis

In the previous section, we discussed the many benefits of offering a Web-based interface for enterprise applications. So, what are the things that we are looking for in a servlet container? What features are required, and which would we just like to have? Simply stated, the basic requirements for a servlet container are as follows:

Support for Java servlets and JavaServer pages. First and foremost, we need the basic functionality of a servlet container with JSP support. This is the most basic requirement.

Conformance with J2EE standards. We may not require conformance to the most current version of the standard but we do want a conforming implementation. The rationale here is that we want to be able to develop software on this platform that can be easily rehosted if necessary. If the container conforms to the standards, and we restrict our development teams to staying within the scope of the standard, we can achieve this. The standards in question here are version 2.3 of the Java Servlet specification and version 1.2 of the JavaServer Pages specification. We need the product that we select not only to conform to these standards but also to be developed to support the future changes in the standard.

Support for standalone operation. Standalone operation of the servlet container is important for developers and for small applications. It is easier to configure and maintain a servlet container if it does not need to be integrated with a Web server. We should potentially be able to allow each developer to have a personal copy of the servlet container.

Support for integration with Web servers. In addition to wanting to be able to have standalone operation, we also want to have the ability to integrate the product with a Web server. This is important for large-scale deployment. The Web server can be used to provide load balancing and to reduce the load on the servlet container by handling static content.

Project stability and continuing support. The servlet container is a core piece of functionality in our platform. We want to make sure that development on the product is not likely to end and that there will be continuing support for it. Remember that we pointed out earlier that there have been a number of servlet containers that were created and are now orphaned or are not being maintained—we don't want this to happen to the product we chose.

Evaluating Servlet Containers

Both Jetty and Tomcat meet all of the criteria outlined in the previous section, as follows:

- They provide servlet and JSP support conforming to the current specifications.
- They are evolving to meet the next generation of specifications.
- Both products can operate on a standalone basis or be integrated with popular Web servers.
- Both products are a part of sizable open source development communities with commitments to continue development and support into the future.

Other important features that these products have in common:

- They both work on JDK 1.2 and later Java platforms.
- They both support all Windows platforms from 9*x* through XP, and they both support Linux.

The bottom line: Both products meet our requirements. This means that we will need to gather more information to choose between the two products, namely by installing each product and comparing certain features. The features we are most interested in now are:

- Ease of installation
- Ease of operation

- Ease of application deployment
- Anything else relevant that we may learn about the system

In this case, our objectives are simple, we want to install the software and observe its basic operations. We are not going to go through a complex deployment but rather a simple one for personal use. We will save the more difficult stuff for later.

Installing Jetty

In order to install Jetty you will first need to download the files for your system. The files can be accessed from `http://jetty.mortbay.org`. If you are using Windows, Jetty is available as a .zip archive file. It is also available as a gzip-compressed .tar archive file for Linux systems. Other than the compression mechanism, these files are the same. You will also need to have previously installed and tested the Java Developers Kit (JDK). We suggest using JDK 1.4 or later.

For Windows, use your favorite unzipping tool to unzip the package, preserving the subdirectory names. We suggest that Jetty be placed in a subdirectory named `jetty` below the root directory of a drive. On Linux, Jetty can be unpacked using the command:

```
tar zxvf Jetty-2.4.2.tgz
```

This will decompress and de-archive the file in one step. We suggest that this be done either in a directory named `jetty` below your home directory (for personal use) or in `/usr/local/jetty`.

Once Jetty has been unpacked, it can be started on any platform by using the command:

```
java -jar start.jar
```

from the `jetty` subdirectory. The file `start.jar` should be in this directory.

The default configuration for Jetty listens on port 8080. The installation can be tested on the server by entering the following URL into a browser running on the same machine:

```
http://localhost:8080
```

If Jetty is running, you should see the screen similar to the one shown in Figure 5.3.

> **WARNING FOR WINDOWS**
>
> **Most servlet containers need access to a full JDK in order to compile JSP files. When the JDK is installed on Windows the Java plug-in is also installed. The Java plug-in installs a Java Runtime Environment (JRE) into the** `Program Files` **directory and places** `Java.exe` **into the** `C:\windows\system32` `directory`**. The** `system32` **directory normally appears before the** `%JAVA_HOME%\bin` **directory in the program path. The** `Java.exe` **found in** `system32` **uses the JRE for the Java plug-in and not the JDK. If this happens, then JSP files will not be served correctly and a "500 server error" will be returned instead of the expected JSP-generated response. There are two easy ways to avoid this: either make sure that** `%JAVA_HOME%\bin` **is first in your program path or use the fully qualified name to run Java. Assuming that you have the JDK installed in** `C:\j2sdk1.4`**, you would use the following command to start Jetty:**
>
> ```
> c:\j2sdk1.4\bin\java -jar start.jar
> ```
>
> **This will ensure that you are using the correct Java runtime.**

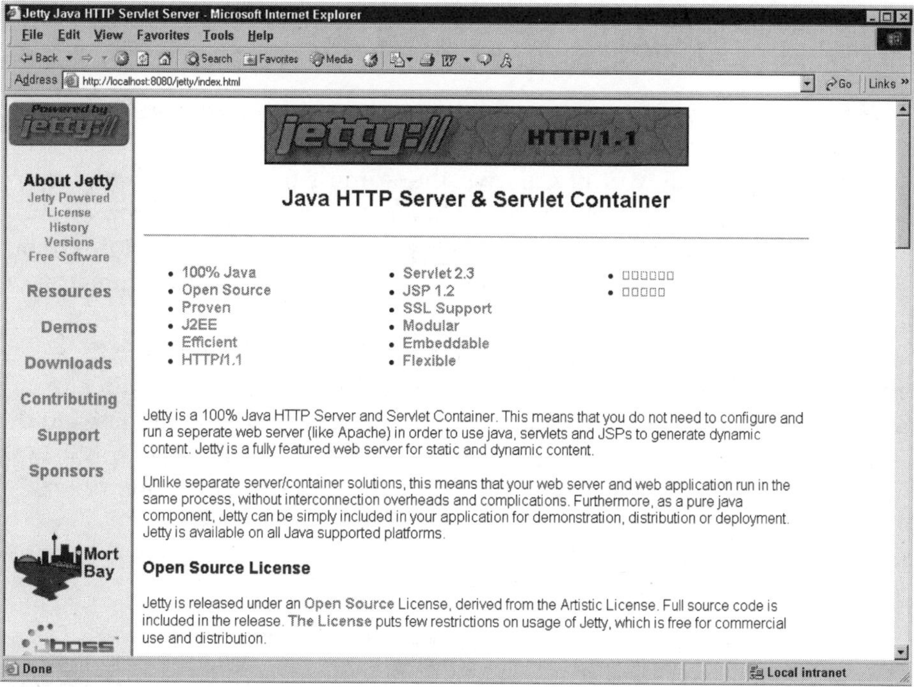

Figure 5.3 A successful test of Jetty.

You should also test to make sure that JavaServer Pages are working. To do this, enter the following URL or follow the Demo link on the left of the startup page and then follow the JSP link.

```
http://localhost:8080/jetty/demoJSP.html
```

This provides a short list of JSP examples that are installed into jetty. We suggest that you try the snoop example and make sure it works. Snoop returns information about the HTTP request that invoked the page.

If you want to change the port that Jetty uses, edit the file `jetty.xml`, which can be found in the `jetty/etc` directory. This is important if you want to test another servlet container that may also use port 8080 (like Tomcat for example). We normally change Jetty to use port 8186. Just search on the string 8080 and replace it with the new port number.

You should also add a line to the file `jetty/etc/demoRealms.properties` in order to add yourself as an administrator. The following line appended to `demoRealms` adds a user named `super` with a password of `boss` and both administrator roles recognized by Jetty.

```
admin:adminpasswd,server-administrator,content-administrator
```

After this is done and the container is restarted, you will be able to use Jetty's simple administration screen shown in Figure 5.4.

Jetty's administration utility allows the administrator to stop and stops almost any activity within the server. This feature allows us to stop an individual application, update it in place on the server, and then restart it without affecting the rest of the applications running on the server. The administration page can also be used to shut down the server.

Deploying a new Web application on Jetty requires additions to Jetty's configuration files. The configuration files can be found in the `/etc` directory in the Jetty installation directory. For example, adding the following lines to the "add contexts" section of the file `demo.xml` will install the Web application `myapps` located in the `/webapps/myapps` directory below `JETTY_HOME`.

```
<Call name="addWebApplication">
    <Arg>/myapps/*</Arg>
    <Arg>
        <SystemProperty name="jetty.home" default="."/>
        /webapps/myapp
    </Arg>
</Call>
```

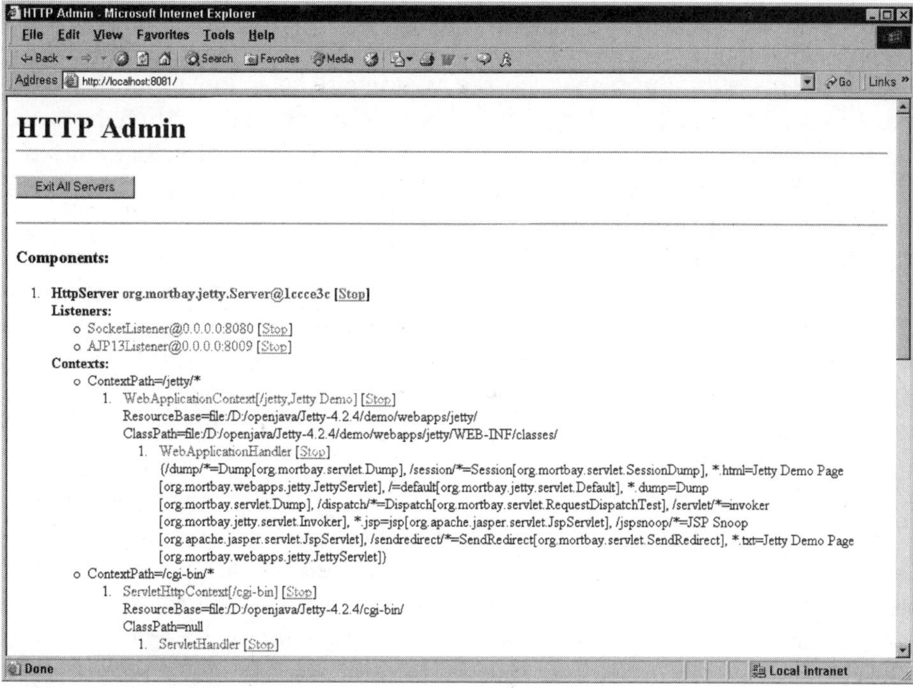

Figure 5.4 Jetty administration utility.

Although this may seem complicated at first, the configuration language is well documented and easy to learn.

Installing Tomcat on Windows

The best way to install Tomcat on Windows is to download the self-installing executable file. This program works like many Windows installer programs and should be easy to use. The first thing the installer does is detect the JDK. If you have more than one version of the JDK, make sure to note whether the one it finds is the one you want Tomcat to use and click OK. The next screen is the license screen. Accept the license by clicking OK. The next screen provides the installation options. The Normal option is fine for most users. If you want Tomcat to install itself as a Windows service then you should check the NT Service box. We do not recommend this for development purposes, but if you were to configure a Windows-based production server you would want to do this to ensure that Tomcat ran whenever Windows was restarted. Click Next to move to the next dialog box.

This dialog box allows you to select the directory that will be used to install Tomcat. The default for this is `C:\Program Files\Apache Group\Tomcat 4.x`. This is an unfortunate choice as a default selection. Often Java programs have difficulty dealing with spaces embedded in directory and filenames. We recommend that you change the default directory and use one that does not have mixed case or spaces. Our choice is normally `c:\jakarta\tomcat4.x`.

Selecting install will begin the installation process. After the files are copied, you will be prompted for a connection port. The default of 8080 is fine unless you are running another servlet container (Jetty for example) on the port. You are also prompted for an administrator password. Be sure to enter one that you will remember. For later examples, we will use `adminpasswd` as the password. After this is done the installation will complete. Click Close to end the program.

The install program adds the menu Start ➪ Programs ➪ Apache Tomcat to the Start menu. This menu provides convenient shortcuts to the Tomcat documentation and to start and stop the servlet container. To start Tomcat, click the Start button and choose Programs ➪ Apache Tomcat ➪ Start. A command prompt window will open with output similar that shown in Figure 5.5.

Test the configuration by opening your browser and pointing it to:

```
http://localhost:8080
```

You should see the response shown in Figure 5.6.

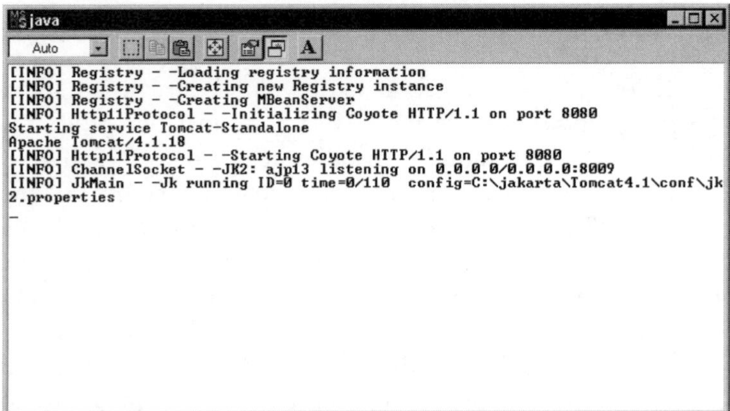

Figure 5.5 Starting Tomcat under Windows.

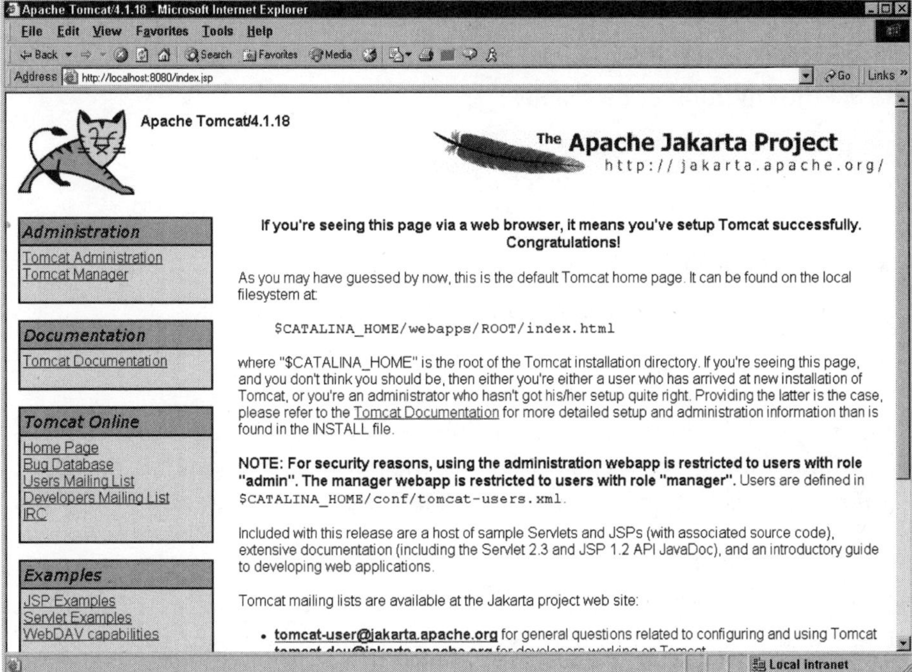

Figure 5.6 Tomcat Web page.

We should also test to make sure that JavaServer Pages are working. To do this, click the JSP Examples link on the startup page or enter the following URL:

```
http://localhost:8080/examples/jsp/index.html
```

This will provide a list of JSP examples that are installed in Tomcat. We suggest that you try the snoop example and make sure that it works. Snoop returns information about the HTTP request that invoked the page.

Installing Tomcat under Linux

For evaluation purposes, it is sufficient to only install a personal copy of Tomcat within your Linux home directory. The steps for doing this are described briefly in the following list and in more depth in the sections following it.

1. Download the compressed .tar archive.
2. Check to make sure that the JDK is installed.

3. Create a deployment directory.
4. Extract the files from the archive.
5. Set the environment variables.
6. Add an administrator.
7. Start Tomcat.

Step 1: Download the Archive

The archive file can be downloaded from the following URL:

```
http://jakarta.apache.org/tomcat
```

The name of the archive varies according to the version number. For the purposes of illustration, we will assume that the name of the .tar archive file will be `jakarta-tomcat.tar.gz` and that it is located in your home directory.

Step 2: Check the JDK

You need to have a JDK installed to use Tomcat. To ensure that the JDK is installed and you are configured to use it, enter the following command:

```
java -version
```

This command should return a message like the following:

```
java version "1.4.1_01"
Java(TM) 2 Runtime Environment, Standard Edition (build 1.4.1_01-b01)
Java HotSpot(TM) Client VM (build 1.4.1_01-b01, mixed mode)
```

Now, you need to ensure that the `JAVA_HOME` environment variable is set. The echo command can be used to do this.

```
echo $JAVA_HOME
```

This should print the path to the root directory where Java is installed. If it does not, then this environment variable will have to be set. The following shows how JAVA_HOME would be set on your system. This is dependent on how the JDK is installed your system and may need to be modified for your system.

```
export JAVA_HOME=/usr/java/j2sdk1.4.1_01
```

Placing this line in the `.profile` file will make certain it is set each time you log into the system.

Step 3: Create the Deployment Directory

You want to install Tomcat into a directory located below your home directory. You will use the directory named `jakarta/tomcat`. You only need to create the `jakarta` directory for now.

```
md jakarta
cd jakarta
```

Step 4: Extract the Files

The following command extracts the .tar archive into a directory in your new `jakarta` directory. You will then rename the directory as `tomcat`.

```
tar -zxvf ../jakarta-tomcat.tar.gz
mv jakarta-tomcat tomcat
```

Step 5: Set Environment Variables

You need to set the environment variable `CATALINA_HOME`. This should be set to the directory where Tomcat has been installed. The following command does this.

```
export CATALINA_HOME=$HOME/jakarta/tomcat
```

If you add this command to the `.profile` file, then you won't have to set it manually in the future. The following `echo` command can be used to check that `CATALINA_HOME` has been set properly.

```
echo $CATALINA_HOME
```

Step 6: Set up an Administrator

You want to add an administrator password so you can use the administration tool built into Tomcat. To do this you need to edit the file `tomcat-users.xml`. This file is found in the `jakarta/tomcat/conf` folder. Add the lines shown in bold in the following code.

```
<?xml version='1.0' encoding='utf-8'?>
<tomcat-users>
  <role rolename="admin"/>
  <role rolename="manager"/>
  <role rolename="role1"/>
  <role rolename="tomcat"/>
  <user username="admin" password="adminpasswd" roles="admin,manager"/>
  <user username="both" password="tomcat" roles="tomcat,role1"/>
  <user username="role1" password="tomcat" roles="role1"/>
```

```
  <user username="tomcat" password="tomcat" roles="tomcat"/>
</tomcat-users
```

Step 7: Run Tomcat

Now, you are finally ready to start Tomcat and see if it works. The following command will start Tomcat:

```
cd $HOME/jakarta/tomcat/bin
./startup.sh
```

You can test to make certain it is working by opening your browser and pointing it to:

```
http://localhost:8080
```

Using the Mozilla browser on Linux, you should see the response shown in Figure 5.7.

You should also test to make sure that JavaServer Pages are working. To do this, click the JSP Examples link on the startup page or enter the URL:

```
http://localhost:8080/examples/jsp/index.html
```

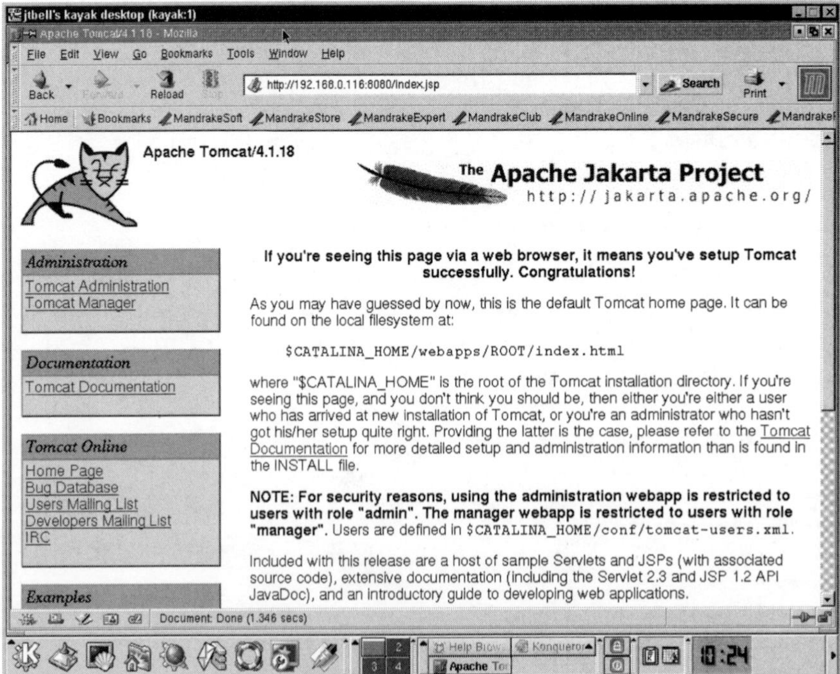

Figure 5.7 Tomcat Web page on Mozilla.

This will provide a list of JSP examples that are installed in Tomcat. As mentioned earlier, we suggest that you try the snoop example and make sure it works. Snoop returns information about the HTTP request that invoked the page.

Tomcat Manager and Administration Tools

Tomcat 4.1 provides two tools to assist you with controlling the application server. These tools are Web-based and accessible from the Tomcat startup page. The tools are the Tomcat Administration Tool and the Tomcat Manager Tool. We will discuss the Manager Tool first.

Start the Manager Tool by selecting this option from the startup page. You will be prompted to enter a username and password. The username is `admin` and the password is the value you entered as you were installing the program (`adminpasswd`). After this is done, you should see a page similar to the one shown in Figure 5.8.

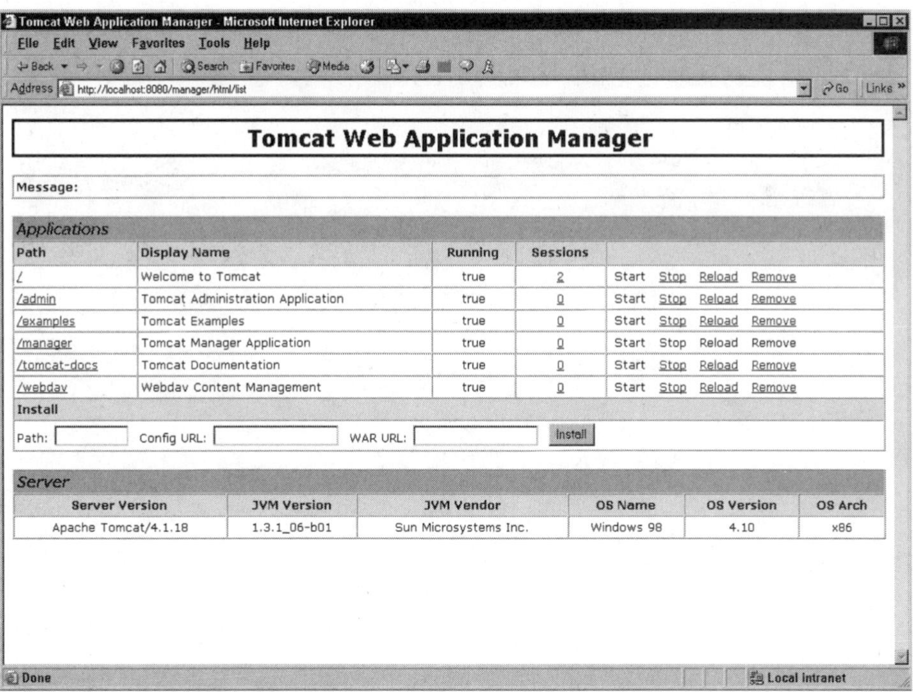

Figure 5.8 Tomcat Manager page.

This page shows a table of each of the application contexts that are currently controlled by Tomcat. It also provides functions to start, stop, reload, and remove an application. There is a line allowing for the installation of a new application and a summary line that describes information about the server.

The Administration tool requires a separate login, but because you have configured your `admin` user to support both administrator and manager roles you can use the same username and password as before. Access the Administrator tool by clicking on a context in the Manager Tool or by selecting the tool from the startup page. After you have logged in, you should see something like Figure 5.9.

The page is divided into three panes. The top pane simply has buttons to submit changes or to log out. The left pane is a tree-based representation of the server configuration. The tree has three primary nodes:

- Tomcat Server node
- Resources node
- User Definitions node

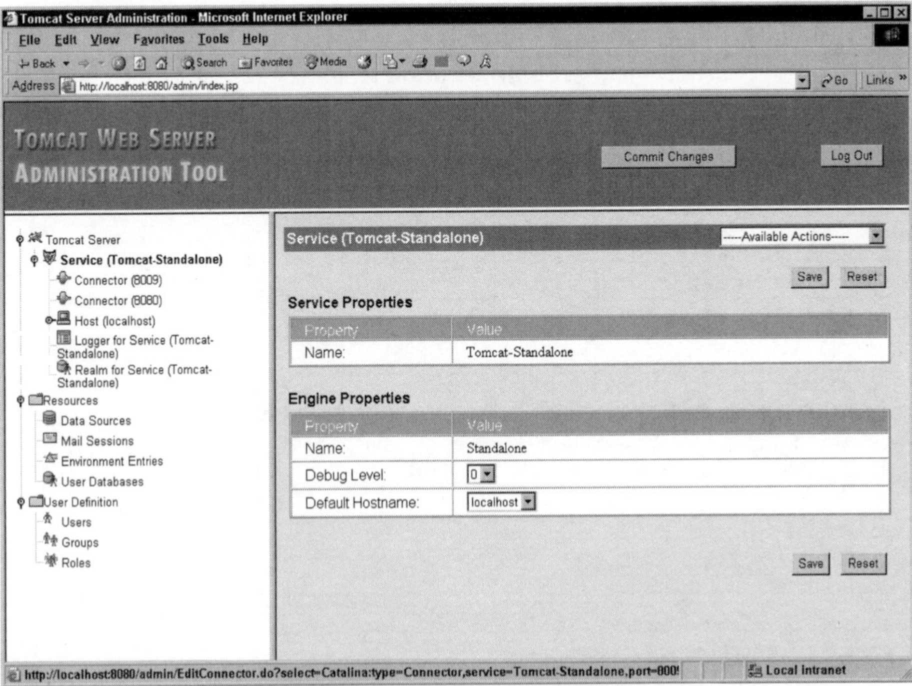

Figure 5.9 Tomcat Administration tool.

The User Definitions node provides a view into the user file. The default for this file can be found in the `conf` subdirectory of the Tomcat installation. It is named `tomcat-users.xml`. The Administration tool allows these values to be viewed and edited through the browser.

The Resources node allows us to view, edit, and add resources in the JNDI provider. This would be used, for example, to set up a database connection pool for use by hosted Web applications.

The Tomcat Server node allows you to edit the configuration of the Tomcat server and of the Web applications it is hosting. The server configuration items correspond to the elements of the `server.xml` file found in the `conf` directory of the Tomcat installation. Each context that is being managed by Tomcat is also shown. The Administration application allows you to manage the resources used by each context and change the context configuration.

Deploying a Web application in Tomcat turns out to be easy even without the management tools. If your Web application is configured as a .war file, it is simply a matter of copying the .war file into the `webapps` directory in the Tomcat installation and restarting Tomcat. Tomcat automatically detects and deploys the .war file under the application context matching the name of the file.

Selection

Both Jetty and Tomcat are excellent products. Both meet our primary criteria and requirements. Either product would be a suitable choice. This gives us the advantage that either decision can be viewed as the right one. However, we must select one product to use as we move forward. In this case, we select Tomcat.

There are several reasons for selecting Tomcat over Jetty:

- Tomcat is a more popular application server than Jetty and so it should be easier to find people who are familiar with it and who can support it.
- Tomcat and Jasper are also the official reference implementations of the Servlet and JSP specifications, respectively. This implies that there should be a commitment by both the Tomcat team and those that contribute to the specification to make sure that Tomcat evolves with the specifications.
- As part of the Apache project, it is expected that Tomcat will also continue to support integration with the Apache Web server as it and the connectors to it mature.
- Finally, Tomcat's built-in management tools seem to be more mature and functional than those provided by Jetty.

So, for our purposes in this book, we select Tomcat. However there are a number of times when Jetty may be the better choice. Jetty would be the preferred choice if server size were a constraint. It would also be the choice if we needed to embed an application server into a larger software product. Jetty's size and its support J2ME also make it the choice for embedded and palm-size applications.

Building a Tomcat Server

Previously, you performed just a simple installation of Tomcat designed for personal use. Now that we have made our decision to use Tomcat, you need to go through the process of reinstalling Tomcat as a server. Before you get started, you will need:

- An installed J2SDK version 1.3 or later
- The Tomcat binaries for your platform
- Administrator or Root privileges for the server
- (Optional) Apache Web Server 1.3 or later installed
- (Optional) The Ant build tool

The Tomcat binaries can be downloaded from `http://jakarta.apache.org/tomcat`. Please download the executable (.exe) file for Windows or the tar.gz files for Linux. The Apache Web server is optional and can be downloaded from `http://www.apache.org`. Ant can be downloaded from `http://jakarta.apache.org/ant`.

CROSS-REFERENCE **Ant is discussed in more detail in Chapter 4.**

Installing Tomcat under Windows

The installation of Tomcat under Windows is almost identical to what we covered earlier in this chapter. There are only a few differences.

NOTE **While Tomcat will work on a Windows 98 system, it needs to be installed onto Windows NT, 2000, or XP to act as a service. Furthermore, Microsoft limits the ability of some of its operating systems to act as servers. If you want a fully scalable production capable server, you will need to use Windows NT Server or Windows 2000 server. Although Tomcat installs and runs as a service on Windows 2000 Professional and all editions of XP, these platforms have limited networking capabilities when compared to server products such as Windows 2000 Server.**

Prior to installation, make sure you are logged in as an administrator. If you have previously installed Tomcat, you may want to uninstall it first. This is done by running the uninstall program that was installed into the Start menu during the previous install.

Start the installation by running the Tomcat executable; this time, however, you want to make sure that the NT service option is selected. Installing Tomcat as a service allows Tomcat to be started automatically by the operating system as the operating system is started. Complete the installation as before, remembering to change the installation directory to `c:\jakarta\tomcat4` and enter an administrator password for Tomcat. If you want to run Tomcat on port 80 and you are not running IIS or Apache on port 80, then feel free to change the default port. We normally leave Tomcat running on port 8080 and then reconfigure it to the new port after we are certain everything else is working.

The installation program installs Tomcat as a Windows service and then starts the server before it completes the installation. Tomcat will now automatically restart each time the system is rebooted. This behavior can be changed by going into the Windows Control Panel and selecting Services and then modifying the service for manual start instead of automatic start (see Figure 5.10). The Services Panel also allows you to provide Tomcat with startup options and set the user that Tomcat will run as.

If Tomcat will be used for an Internet-facing site, for security reasons it is best to establish a local user login account with limited system abilities and run Tomcat as this user. You will want to make sure that Tomcat has all privileges for its installation directory and the directories below it, but limited access to the rest of the system. This way, if Tomcat is compromised, the potential damage will be minimized.

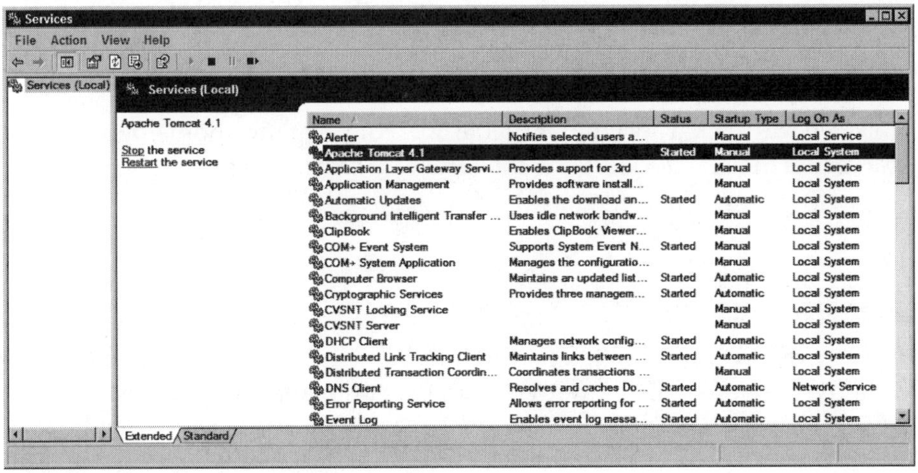

Figure 5.10 Windows Services panel.

Installing Tomcat under Linux

The steps for installing Tomcat as a server under Linux start off being similar to those we performed under Linux previously; however, we need to add some significant steps to this process. We will skip the first couple of steps from the previous example, assuming that you have already installed the JDK and downloaded the Tomcat binary tar.gz file. Instead, you will start by creating the new deployment directory. You need to be logged in as root for this installation. The new steps are:

1. Create a deployment directory.
2. Extract the files from the archive.
3. Add an administrator.
4. Add a Tomcat user and group.
5. Change the owner and group on all files and directories.
6. Create and install an initialization script.
7. Set the user environment.

Step 1: Create the Deployment Directory

We normally install Tomcat into the `/usr/jakarta/tomcat` directory. Your organization may have different rules for the installation location. Other common locations that we have seen are:

- `/usr/tomcat`
- `/usr/local/tomcat`
- `/usr/local/jakarta/tomcat`
- `/var/tomcat`
- `/var/jakarta/tomcat`

You need to pick a location suitable for your organization's deployment rules. Create the directories using the Linux `md` command as follows:

```
md /usr/jakarta
```

Step 2: Extract the Files

First copy the distribution (tar.gz) file into the `/usr/jakarta` directory created in the previous step. Now, the following command can be used to extract the files:

```
tar -zxvf jakarta-tomcat.tar.gz
```

This also creates a directory with the name of the .tar file. We want to rename this directory with the following command:

```
mv jakarta-tomcat tomcat
```

We should now have all of the distribution files extracted into the directory /usr/jakarta/tomcat.

Step 3: Add a Tomcat Administrator

This is identical to the step shown earlier. You need to add an administrator password so the Tomcat Manager and Administration tools can be used. To do this, edit the file tomcat-users.xml. This file is found in the /usr/jakarta/tomcat/conf folder. Add the lines shown in bold in the following code.

```
<?xml version='1.0' encoding='utf-8'?>
<tomcat-users>
  <role rolename="admin"/>
  <role rolename="manager"/>
  <role rolename="role1"/>
  <role rolename="tomcat"/>
  <user username="admin" password="adminpasswd" roles="admin,manager"/>
  <user username="both" password="tomcat" roles="tomcat,role1"/>
  <user username="role1" password="tomcat" roles="role1"/>
  <user username="tomcat" password="tomcat" roles="tomcat"/>
</tomcat-users>
```

Be certain to select a password that is appropriate for your site. Please do not use the same password shown here.

Step 4: Add a User and Group for Tomcat

If you already have Apache installed, you should use the apache user and apache group that should already exist on the system. Otherwise, you should add a user and a group to your system specifically for Tomcat. This is a security precaution. It effectively limits the ability of a hijacker to access other parts of the system. Tomcat should always and only be run by this special user. The special user and group should be created with numbers that identifies them as a system accounts. The commands to do this will vary from system to system. On Mandrake 9.0 the following command creates both the tomcat user and tomcat group.

```
useradd -c "Special Tomcat user" -r tomcat
```

You may have slightly different commands on your system (or you may have a graphical interface for adding new users to your system). If you are unfamiliar with these commands try searching the manual pages for `adduser` and `addgroup` or `useradd` and `groupadd` commands.

Step 5: Change File and Directory Owner and Group

Now that you have a user and group for Tomcat you want to set all of the files and directories so they are owned by the `tomcat` user and group. The following command does this.

```
chown -R tomcat:tomcat /usr/jakarta/tomcat
```

While you are at it, you should examine the file permissions. The directories should have the attributes set as shown here:

```
drwxr-xr-x    2 tomcat   tomcat       4096 Jan  4 23:52 bin/
drwxr-xr-x    5 tomcat   tomcat       4096 Dec 19 09:08 common/
drwxrw-r-x    4 tomcat   tomcat       4096 Jan  6 23:03 conf/
drwxrwxr-x    2 tomcat   tomcat       4096 Jan  7 22:19 logs/
drwxr-xr-x    5 tomcat   tomcat       4096 Dec 19 09:08 server/
drwxr-xr-x    4 tomcat   tomcat       4096 Dec 19 09:08 shared/
drwxr-xr-x    2 tomcat   tomcat       4096 Jan  6 23:03 temp/
drwxrwxr-x    6 tomcat   tomcat       4096 Jan  2 11:56 webapps/
drwxrwxr-x    3 tomcat   tomcat       4096 Jan  6 01:31 work/
```

Use the `chmod` command to set permissions as needed.

Step 6: Initialize Scripts

You want Tomcat to start when the system is started and shut down when the system is shut down. To do this under Linux, add a script to the `/etc/init.d` directory and run the `chkconfig` command to install the scripts into the `rc.d` directories. The following script (named `tomcatd`) was created for this purpose.

```
#!/bin/sh
#
# Startup script for the Tomcat servlet container
#
# chkconfig: 345 80 20
# description: Tomcat is a Java Application Server and servlet container
#       HTML files and CGI.
# processname: tomcat
# pidfile: /var/run/tomcat.pid
# config: /usr/jakarta/tomcat/conf/server.xml
```

```
#========================================================================
#=== IMPORTANT NOTE:
#=== The comments above are required for the chkconfig script to work
#=== correctly. Please do not remove them. Read the man pages for
#=== chkconfig if you need to know more.
#========================================================================

# Source function library.
# Set environment variables needed by JVM and Tomcat
JAVA_HOME=/usr/java/j2sdk1.4.1_01
CATALINA_HOME=/usr/jakarta/tomcat

#========================================================================
# This function will be executed when the system is starting up.
#========================================================================
start() {
  # Start daemon
  echo "Starting Tomcat: "
  su -l tomcat -s /bin/bash -c "/usr/jakarta/tomcat/bin/startup.sh"
  RETVAL=$?
  if [ $RETVAL -eq 0 ]; then
    echo "Tomcat started!"
  else
    echo "Tomcat failed to start!"
  fi
  echo
  touch /var/lock/subsys/tomcat
}

#========================================================================
# This function will be executed when the system is stopping
#========================================================================
stop() {
# Stop daemon.
  echo "Stopping Tomcat: "
  su -l tomcat -s /bin/bash -c "/usr/jakarta/tomcat/bin/shutdown.sh"
  RETVAL=$?
  if [ $RETVAL -eq 0 ]; then
    echo "Tomcat stopped!"
  else
    echo "Problem stopping Tomcat!"
  fi
  echo
  rm -f /var/lock/subsys/tomcat
}


restart() {
  echo "Stopping Tomcat for restart..."
  stop
```

```
    sleep 15
    echo "Restarting Tomcat:"
    start
}

# See how we were called.
case "$1" in
  start)
  start
  ;;
  stop)
  stop
  ;;
  restart)
    restart
  ;;
  *)
  echo "Usage:" "$0" "{start|stop|restart}\n"
  exit 1
esac

exit 0
```

Please note the warning in the comments. The comments at the top of the file are required for the `chkconfig` program to work properly. The line that reads

```
# chkconfig: 345 80 20
```

has special meaning. The 345 tells `chkconfig` that the service should be started at runlevels 3, 4 and/or 5. The 80 and 20 provides a means to control the order that the script should be executed in relation to the other startup scripts. These numbers were picked for our system because Tomcat should start before Apache is started and be shut down after Apache has been shut down.

There are a couple of other items to note. You must set the `JAVA_HOME` and `CATALINA_HOME` environment variables here since the script is running before any shell variables have been set. Also, the script starts Tomcat with the command shown below:

```
su -l tomcat -s /bin/bash -c "/usr/jakarta/tomcat/bin/startup.sh"
```

By using `su` to start Tomcat, you can start Tomcat as the `tomcat` user that you created earlier. This allows Tomcat to be executed safely as the `tomcat` user even though the script is executed by root during system initialization. This is also a handy command to use instead of the usual Tomcat `startup.sh` and shutdown.sh. I normally create two scripts, tomstart and tomstop to ease the starting and stopping the Tomcat server using the correct user.

Once the initialization script has been created and tested, it should be copied to the /etc/init.d directory and named tomcatd. The script then needs to be installed using the following command:

```
chkconfig -add tomcatd
```

After this is done, a reboot will automatically start Tomcat. Before you start Tomcat by rebooting however you should start Tomcat manually to make sure that there are no other problems. To do this, enter the following command:

```
su -l tomcat -s /bin/bash -c "/usr/jakarta/tomcat/bin/catalina.sh run"
```

This starts Tomcat running as the tomcat user in the current shell. Its startup messages will be sent the terminal on stderr instead of the file $CATALINA_HOME/logs/catalina.out. This can help you find any problems that Tomcat might have reading or writing to the directories it needs.

Step 7: Set up the User Environment

If you want a user to be able to run the Tomcat startup and shutdown scripts, then you should set the CATALINA_HOME environment variable to reflect the new installation. The user also needs to have the JAVA_HOME environment variable set. Adding the following commands to a users profile script does this:

```
export JAVA_HOME=/usr/java/j2sdk1.4.1_01
export CATALINA_HOME=/usr/jakarta/tomcat
```

Remember to adjust the values to reflect the appropriate ones for your system.

A user that needs to add applications to the Tomcat webapps directory can be added to the tomcat group. If the permissions are set correctly this, will give write access to webapps to the user because webapps is configured for group write. The command to do this under Linux is:

```
usermod -G tomcat username
```

Configuring Multiple Instances of Tomcat

On Linux, Tomcat provides a means to run a user-customized instance of Tomcat from a single Tomcat installation. This is useful if there are many developers who need to share a single installation, but need their own unique instances. For this to work, a new environment variable, CATALINA_BASE, is created.

```
export CATALINA_BASE=$HOME/tomcat
```

CATALINA_BASE is automatically set to CATALINA_HOME if it does not exist in the environment.

Next, you will need to create a Tomcat directory below your home directory and create or copy certain directories, as follows:

```
cd $HOME
md tomcat
cd tomcat
cp $CATALINA_HOME/conf .
md logs
md webapps
md work
md temp
```

If you want a copy of the contents of the Tomcat webapps directory, then you should copy them into your new webapps directory.

You may also need to change the ports that Tomcat uses so that your instance does not conflict with the core Tomcat installation. You can do this by editing the file conf/server.xml. Search for strings like port= and replace them with unique ports. If Tomcat is configured to listen on port 8009 for Apache, you can disable the connector by commenting out the element in server.xml. The other ports that you are likely to have to change are:

8080. The default connection port

8443. The port for SSL connections

8009. The port for connections to Apache

8005. The port used for stopping Tomcat

After these changes have been completed, you can start and stop Tomcat by using the normal startup.sh and shutdown.sh scripts found in the CATALINA_HOME/bin directory. You do not want to use the tomcat user in this case because the file permissions should be set for your use.

Troubleshooting Your Tomcat Installation

There are only a few things that are likely to go wrong with a Tomcat installation. First, you should know that Tomcat logs error messages to the file catalina.out in the CATALINA_BASE/logs directory. This is the first place to look for clues if Tomcat does not seem to be working. The most common installation problems for Tomcat are:

- The server port is occupied.
- Tomcat is using the JRE and not the JDK.
- Directories are configured with the wrong access privileges.
- The network configuration on the machine is incorrect.

We will look at this last problem first. If you are sure Tomcat is running but Tomcat does not generate a response to the localhost URL in the previous paragraph, then you can check the network by entering the following command at either a Linux or Windows command prompt:

```
ping localhost
```

If you get a "request timed out" response, then there is a problem with your network configuration that needs to be addressed. Further troubleshooting of this issue is beyond the scope of this book.

If the server port is occupied or in use by another process, Tomcat places a message in its output log (`catalina.out`). Look for a message that says something like:

```
java.net.BindException: Address already in use: JVM_Bind:8080
```

Often, this means that Tomcat was already started and is running as a service under Windows or Linux. You can run the Tomcat shutdown script (`shutdown.bat` for Windows and `shutdown.sh` for Linux) to end any other Tomcat instance that may be using the port. The `netstat` command can also be used to see if another process is listening on the port. Use the command:

```
netstat -a
```

on either Windows or Linux to see if another process is listening on the port in question.

The final common problem is Tomcat's using the JRE instead of the JDK. The primary symptom of this is that servlets work fine but JSPs do not. The error message in the log file will complain that the classloader cannot find `com.sun.javac.Main`. Jasper may even diagnose the problem and suggest that the JRE is in use instead of the JDK. The fix is to check that the JDK is actually installed (and not just the JRE) and make sure that `JAVA_HOME` is set correctly to use the JDK.

Integrating Tomcat with Apache

So far, we have looked at configuring Tomcat as a standalone server. There are several reasons why we might want to configure Tomcat to work with a Web sever such as Apache. We have already discussed the restrictions under Linux on access to ports below 1024 and security concerns with running any server application as a root or administrative user. This issue is unique, however, to Linux and other Unix-based operating systems. There are other reasons to run Tomcat with a Web server. Often, a Web server will deliver static content faster than Tomcat can. If a site has a large amount of static content in proportion to its dynamic content, using a Web server to deliver the static content may result in better performance. This, of course, is specific to the application. However, it is not an uncommon occurrence when you think about the fact that HTML files, graphics, Cascading Style Sheets, JavaScripts, and applets are all usually served as static content. Most Web pages are built from many of these static files that are combined.

In this section, we will cover the basics of integrating Tomcat with the Apache Web server. The steps are similar for both Windows and Linux. We assume that Apache is already installed and configured as a service running on port 80. There are basically six steps to this process:

1. Download the connector binaries.
2. Copy the connector module to the Apache modules directory.
3. Edit the Apache configuration file.
4. Edit the Tomcat configuration file.
5. Create a workers.properties file.
6. Restart Tomcat and Apache.

Step 1: Finding and Downloading the Binaries

You will be installing the `mod_jk` connector for Apache. The required file is normally called `mod_jk.so` for Linux and `mod_jk.dll` for Windows. These files can be found at:

```
http://jakarta.apache.org/builds/jakarta-tomcat/release/v3.3/bin/
```

You should read the `README` file found in the directory to make sure that you download the correct file for your Apache configuration. Most Linux users with Apache installed with Secure Sockets Layer (SSL) support or the Extended Application Programming Interface (EAPI) should download the file:

```
mod_jk-3.3-ap13-eapi.so
```

or if EAPI is not installed download:

```
mod_jk-3.3-ap13-noeapi.so
```

Once the file is downloaded, Linux users should rename the file as `mod_jk.so`.

Windows users should download the file:

```
mod_jk.dll
```

Step 2: Copy the File to the Apache Modules Directory

Do just as the title says. Copy the mod_jk file to your Apache modules directory. Under Linux this is normally /usr/lib/apache.

Step 3: Edit the Apache Configuration File

Apache will need to know about Tomcat-based applications. Tomcat will dynamically create a configuration file for Apache to use, but you must tell Apache how to find it. Edit the Apache configuration file httpd.conf and append the following line to the end of the file:

```
Include CATALINA_HOME/conf/auto/mod_jk.conf
```

Replace CATALINA_HOME with the name of your Tomcat installation directory. You will configure Tomcat to dynamically generate the file mod_jk.conf in the next step.

Step 4: Edit the Tomcat Configuration File

Now, you need to tell Tomcat to dynamically generate a configuration file for Apache that reflects the applications installed in Tomcat. Tomcat needs to start before Apache does to ensure that this file is created and up to date for Apache when Apache starts.

Edit the file $CATALINA_HOME/conf/server.xml and look for a line that reads:

```
<Server port="8005" shutdown="SHUTDOWN" debug="0">
```

Immediately after this line define a server listener by adding:

```
<Listener className="org.apache.ajp.tomcat4.config.ApacheConfig" />
```

Next, look for:

```
<Host name="localhost" debug="0" appbase="webapps" >
```

and add:

```
<Listener
  className="org.apache.ajp.tomcat4.config.ApacheConfig"
  append="true"/>
```

Step 5: Create a workers.properties File

The file `worker.properties` is used to control which threads handle which requests. We will create a workers file supporting a single thread, or worker. For the default configuration, this file must be named `workers.properties` and must be placed in the `CATALINA_HOME/conf/jk` directory. Create the file with the following lines, changing `tomcat_home` and `java_home` to reflect the values for your system:

```
workers.tomcat_home=/usr/jakarta/tomcat
workers.java_home=/usr/java/
ps=/
worker.list=ajp12, ajp13
# Definition for Ajp13 worker
#
worker.ajp13.port=8009
worker.ajp13.host=localhost
worker.ajp13.type=ajp13
```

Step 6: Restart the Servers

Now, you are ready to restart the servers. Remember to start Tomcat first and then start Apache. This will give Tomcat the opportunity to generate the configuration information that Apache needs. After the servers are running, you should be able to hit the Tomcat examples applications. Note that you will not get the Tomcat start page as before unless you changed Apache's document root to be the same as Tomcat's. This is so because there can only be one root context. Open your browser and enter the URL:

```
http://192.168.0.143:8080/examples/jsp/index.html
```

Run the snoop JSP to make sure it is working too.

Testing Tomcat

At this point, we should have Tomcat installed as a server. Once again we can test to make sure Tomcat is installed correctly by entering the following URL in a browser running on the system that Tomcat is installed on.

```
http://localhost:8080
```

If you changed the port that Tomcat listens on then the 8080 will have to be replaced with the number for the new port. You should also test that JSPs are working. Assuming that everything works, we can move on to integrating Tomcat with Apache.

Assuming that your machine is connected to a network, you should also be able to access Tomcat from any other machine by using the machine name or local IP address for the machine.

Next, we'll create the code for a pair of useful utility servlets. When developing Web applications, it can be useful to have a handful of useful utilities to help diagnose problems with the application server environment. We normally start each application with a HelloWorld servlet. The source code for this simple servlet was demonstrated in Chapter 4 and won't be repeated here. We find HelloWorld useful because it tells us that the basics of the servlet environment are set up and configured correctly. The `snoop.jsp` example provided with both Jetty and Tomcat can also be a useful debugging tool. Often, however, it is useful to have a snoop servlet instead of or in addition to `snoop.jsp` to identify differences in the handling of context names and relative paths. It can also be handy to have a servlet that exposes information about the Java environment that the container is running in. For this reason, we created the SuperSnoop servlet, as shown in the following code:

```
import java.io.*;
import java.net.*;
import java.text.DateFormat;
import java.util.Date;
import java.util.Enumeration;
import java.util.Properties;

import javax.servlet.*;
import javax.servlet.http.*;

public class SuperSnoop extends HttpServlet
{

  private String makeTitle( String title )
  {
    return new String("<H2>"+title+"</H2>\n");
  }

  private String makeRow( String left, String right )
  {
    StringBuffer sb = new StringBuffer(128);
    sb.append( "<tr>\n" );
    sb.append( "\t<td>"+left+"</td>\n");
    sb.append( "\t<td>"+right+"</td>\n");
    sb.append( "</tr>\n" );
    return sb.toString();
  }
```

```
private String today()
{
  Date now = new Date();
  DateFormat dateFormatter = DateFormat.getDateTimeInstance();
  return dateFormatter.format( now );
}

private String showHeaders( HttpServletRequest request )
{
  StringBuffer sb = new StringBuffer(512);
  Enumeration e = request.getHeaderNames();
  String key = null;
  String value = null;
  sb.append( makeTitle("Request Headers"));
  sb.append("<table>");
  while( e.hasMoreElements() )
  {
    key = (String)e.nextElement();
    value = request.getHeader(key);
    sb.append( makeRow( key, value ));
  }
  sb.append("</table>");
  return sb.toString();
}

private String showRequestInfo(HttpServletRequest request)
{
  StringBuffer sb = new StringBuffer(512);
  sb.append(makeTitle( "Request Info"));
  sb.append("<table>\n");
  sb.append(
  makeRow( "ContextPath", request.getContextPath() ));
  sb.append(
  makeRow( "Method", request.getMethod() ));
  sb.append(
  makeRow( "RequestURL", request.getRequestURL().toString()));
  sb.append(
  makeRow( "ServletPath", request.getServletPath() ));
  sb.append(
  makeRow( "CharacterEncoding", request.getCharacterEncoding()));
  sb.append(
  makeRow( "ContentType", request.getContentType() ));
  sb.append(
  makeRow( "RemoteAddress", request.getRemoteAddr() ));
  sb.append(
  makeRow( "RemoteHost", request.getRemoteHost() ));
  sb.append(
  makeRow( "Scheme", request.getScheme() ));
  sb.append(
  makeRow( "ServerName", request.getServerName() ));
```

```
    sb.append(
    makeRow( "ServerPort",
    Integer.toString(request.getServerPort()) ));
    sb.append("</table>\n");
    return sb.toString();
  }

  private String showRequestParams( HttpServletRequest request )
  {
    StringBuffer sb = new StringBuffer(512);
    Enumeration e = request.getParameterNames();
    String key = null;
    String value = null;
    sb.append(makeTitle("Request Parameters"));
    sb.append("<table>");
    while( e.hasMoreElements() )
    {
      key = (String)e.nextElement();
      value = request.getParameter(key);
      sb.append( makeRow( key, value ));
    }
    sb.append("</table>");
    return sb.toString();
  }

  private String showSysProps()
  {
    StringBuffer sb = new StringBuffer(512);
    Properties p = System.getProperties();
    Enumeration e = p.propertyNames();
    String key = null;
    String value = null;
    sb.append(makeTitle("System Properties"));
    sb.append("<table>");
    sb.append(makeRow("System Time", today() ));
    while( e.hasMoreElements() )
    {
      key = (String)e.nextElement();
      value = p.getProperty( key );
      sb.append( makeRow( key, value ));
    }
    sb.append("</table>");
    return sb.toString();
  }

  private String showInitParams()
  {
    StringBuffer sb = new StringBuffer(512);
    ServletContext context = getServletContext();
    Enumeration e = context.getInitParameterNames();
```

```
    String key = null;
    String value = null;
    sb.append(makeTitle("Initialization Parameters"));
    sb.append("<table>");
    while( e.hasMoreElements() )
    {
      key = (String)e.nextElement();
      value = context.getInitParameter(key);
      sb.append( makeRow( key, value ));
    }
    sb.append("</table>");
    return sb.toString();
  }

  private String showServletContextInfo()
  {
    StringBuffer sb = new StringBuffer(512);
    ServletContext context = getServletContext();
    sb.append(makeTitle("Servlet Context"));
    sb.append("<table>");
    sb.append( makeRow( "Server Info", context.getServerInfo()));
    sb.append( makeRow(
    "Servlet Context Name",
    context.getServletContextName()));
    sb.append( makeRow( "Real Path", context.getRealPath("/")));
    sb.append("</table>");
    return sb.toString();
  }

  private String showContextAttributes()
  {
    StringBuffer sb = new StringBuffer(512);
    ServletContext context = getServletContext();
    Enumeration e = context.getAttributeNames();
    String key = null;
    String value = null;
    sb.append(makeTitle("Servlet Context Attributes"));
    sb.append("<table>");
    while( e.hasMoreElements() )
    {
      key = (String)e.nextElement();
      value = context.getAttribute(key).toString();
      sb.append( makeRow( key, value ));
    }
    sb.append("</table>");
    return sb.toString();
  }

  private String showSessionAttributes(HttpServletRequest request)
  {
    StringBuffer sb = new StringBuffer(512);
    HttpSession session = request.getSession();
```

```
    Enumeration e = session.getAttributeNames();
    String key = null;
    String value = null;
    sb.append(makeTitle("Session Attributes"));
    if( session==null )
      return "No session attributes";
    sb.append("<table>");
    while( e.hasMoreElements() )
    {
      key = (String)e.nextElement();
      value = session.getAttribute(key).toString();
      sb.append( makeRow( key, value ));
    }
    sb.append("</table>");
    return sb.toString();
  }

  public void doGet(
  HttpServletRequest request,
  HttpServletResponse response)
  throws ServletException, IOException
  {
    response.setContentType("text/html");
    PrintWriter out = response.getWriter();

    out.println("<html>");
    out.println("<head>");
    out.println("<title>SysProps Servlet</title>");
    out.println("</head>");
    out.println("<body>");

    out.println( today() );
    out.println( showHeaders(request) );
    out.println( showRequestInfo(request) );
    out.println( showRequestParams(request) );
    out.println( showSessionAttributes(request) );
    out.println( showServletContextInfo() );
    out.println( showContextAttributes() );
    out.println( showInitParams() );
    out.println( showSysProps() );

    out.println("</table>");
    out.println("</body>");
    out.println("</html>");

    out.close();
  }

  public void doPost(
  HttpServletRequest request,
  HttpServletResponse response)
  throws ServletException, IOException
```

```
  {
    doGet(request, response);
  }

  public String getServletInfo()
  {
    return "Prints Java System Properties";
  }
}
```

SuperSnoop shows information about the

- HttpRequest that invoked it
- Current session
- ServletContext
- Java environment

This code is not complex, but being able to see the information it presents can be very useful when you are trying to solve difficult problems with servlet and container configurations. You can include a copy of SuperSnoop in my `classes` directory for any new Web application that you're developing. Use the following `web.xml` file for deployment:

```
<?xml version="1.0" encoding="UTF-8"?>

<!DOCTYPE web-app
    PUBLIC "-//Sun Microsystems, Inc.//DTD Web Application 2.3//EN"
    "http://java.sun.com/dtd/web-app_2_3.dtd">

<web-app>
  <servlet>
    <servlet-name>Snoop</servlet-name>
    <servlet-class>SuperSnoop</servlet-class>
  </servlet>
  <servlet-mapping>
    <servlet-name>Snoop</servlet-name>
    <url-pattern>/servlet/Snoop</url-pattern>
  </servlet-mapping>
</web-app>
```

The following command line can be used to compile the program on Windows:

```
javac -classpath %CATALINA_HOME%\common\lib\servlet.jar SuperSnoop.java
```

The command for compiling under Linux is:

```
javac -classpath $CATALINA_HOME/common/lib/servlet.jar SuperSnoop.java
```

CATALINA_HOME represents the base installation directory for Tomcat. This can normally be found set in the CATALINA_HOME environment variable.

After the code has been compiled, follow these steps to install the code:

- Create a directory below the Tomcat webapps directory, and name it snoopy.
- Below the snoopy directory create another directory, and name it WEB-INF. Note that the name WEB-INF must be entered as uppercase even on Windows.
- Copy the web.xml file into this WEB-INF directory.
- Create a new directory named classes below the WEB-INF directory.
- Copy the SuperSnoop.class file into the classes directory.

Restart Tomcat, and it should now recognize the new Web application. The application can be executed by entering the following URL into your browser:

```
http://localhost:8080/snoopy/servlet/Snoop
```

A sample of the output screen is shown in Figure 5.11.

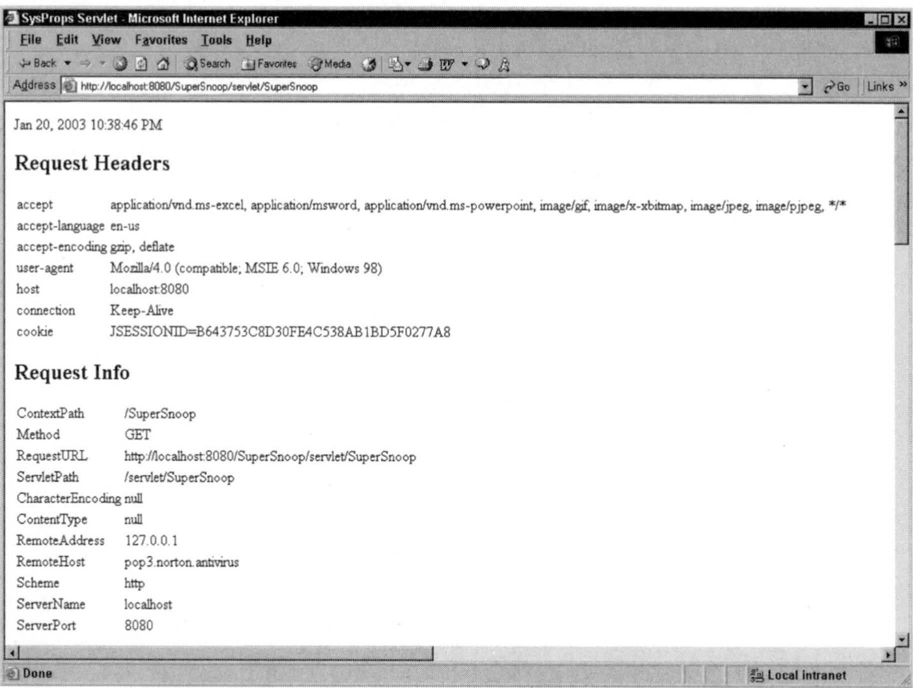

Figure 5.11 SuperSnoop.

Summary

In this chapter, we have examined Web servers and servlet containers. The servlet container is the primary component of the presentation tier of our platform architecture. All of the other components in this tier depend on the servlet container. We examined two open source servlet containers and selected Tomcat for our platform by virtue of its popularity and standards conformance. We installed Tomcat as a standalone server and integrated it with the Apache Web server. Finally, we provided a useful utility that can be used for diagnosing servlet issues as we move forward.

CHAPTER

6

Creating Dynamic Content Using Template Engines

A well-known tennis personality once told us "Image is everything!" This quip could just as easily be applied to the art of Web-application development. The presentation layers of an application are ultimately what determine the perceived success or failure of the development effort. The effort to create the presentation layers of an application is hardly trivial, and as we shall see, is often encumbered by the marriage of two sometimes completely different cultures: that of the Web-page designer and the Java developer. This chapter looks at template engines and how they can be used to significantly reduce the agony and programming effort needed to create the presentation layers of an application by separating the responsibilities of the Web-page designer from those of the Java developer.

What Is a Template Engine?

If you have ever played the game Madlibs, then you should have a conceptual grasp of what a template engine does. A template is a document, in our case typically a Web page, with placeholders (spaces) for certain information. Template engines are typically deployed within the servlet container and used as part of the presentation layer of an enterprise application. The template engine combines the template with the information needed to fill in the spaces. For example, the line below represents a simple template:

```
Hello my name is ${name}. I live in ${state}.
```

If we give the line above to a template engine as a template with values of `name=Jim` and `state=Tennessee`, the template engine would create the document shown below as output:

```
Hello my name is Jim. I live in Tennessee.
```

In this case `${name}` is used as the placeholder that is replaced with data. This capability is very useful for creating dynamic content for Web-based applications.

NOTE Template engines are not a part of the J2EE specification or architecture. However, template engines are a very useful component for creating Web applications, representing an alternative to JavaServer Pages.

Architectural Considerations

Template engines support a design pattern known as the Model-View-Controller (MVC) architecture. MVC is the most-used architecture for constructing Web applications today. MVC separates the logic for delivering a user interface (the view) from the underlying business logic (the model), connecting the two with a controller. The typical way of implementing MVC in a servlet environment is:

1. A request comes to the controller (a servlet), which then collects the information from the underlying business systems and packages it into one or more Java Beans.
2. The controller forwards the request to a JSP that invokes methods of the Java Bean to render the data into HTML.

Figure 6.1 shows a schematic illustrating this architecture.

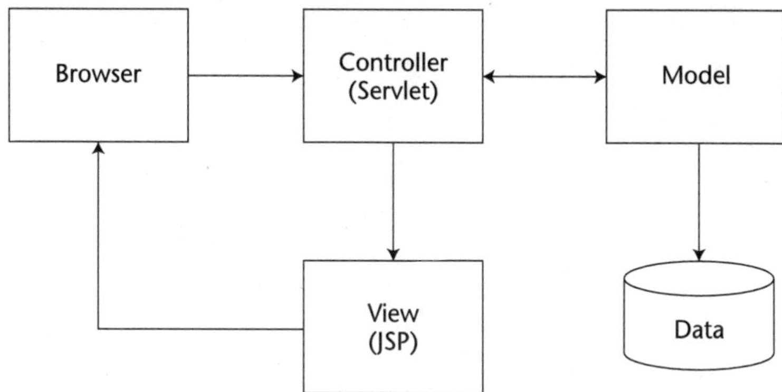

Figure 6.1 Standard Model-View-Controller (MVC) architecture.

The idea here is that by segmenting the design using the MVC architecture, the various components can be developed independently, while promoting reusability. The introduction of JavaServer Pages (JSPs) enables development duties to be better separated between the technical talent of the Java developer and the creative talents of the Web-page designer. Clearly, this provides a significant improvement over early development practices in which the servlet was used as the controller *and* model and provided the view through a series of `System.out.println()` statements.

Typically, a template engine is used as a replacement for JSP in the MVC architecture. Even though the JSP has significantly enhanced the development process, JSPs still leave many complexities for the developer to deal with. Following is a typical example of JSP code:

```
<HTML>
<BODY>
  <jsp:useBean id="dataBean" scope="page" class="EventsSearchBean" />
  <jsp:setProperty name="dataBean" property="*" />
  <HR>
  <P>Events in process:</P>
  <%
    Events[] Ev = dataBean.executeSearch();
    if Ev.length > 0) {
  %>
  <TABLE WIDTH='100%' BORDER='1'>
  <TR>
    <TH ALIGN='left'>Contact</TH>
    <TH ALIGN='left'>Description</TH>
    <TH ALIGN='left'>E-Mail Address</TH>
  </TR>
```

```
<% for (int i = 0;i < ev.length; i++){ %>
<TR>
  <TD><%= Ev.getContact() %></TD>
  <TD><%= Ev.getDesc() %></TD>
  <TD><%= Ev.getEmailAddress() %></TD>
</TABLE>
<%   }
}
%>
</BODY>
</HTML>
```

The preceding code illustrates a couple of well-known controversies with JSPs. The first issue has to do with embedding Java code within the JSP. MVC purists maintain that this violates the convention established by the MVC paradigm, and that the commingling of HTML and Java violates the separation of the model and controller components from the view layer.

The introduction of Java code to a JSP now requires that the Web-page designer know both Java and HTML. Although the model and view are separate, the skill sets required for implementation of each piece have not changed. Furthermore, the temptation to abuse Java code in JSPs and implement business and control logic within the JSP makes this a greater concern. The other problem evident from our example, and most developers would agree, is the terse and somewhat confusing nature of the looping construct with JSPs. It is simply messy and hard to read! Finally, add to this the somewhat ambiguous messages generated when error-laden JSPs are compiled, and it is clear why developers have sought an alternative to JSPs.

Template engines avoid the potential problems of using JSPs and are designed to support the Web developer. They are also designed to be simpler and easier to use, and they do not support the embedding of Java code into the page. This means that they strictly enforce the separation of business logic from presentation logic.

Defenders of JSPs will point out that the just released JSP 1.2 standard provides for the Java Standard Tag Libraries (JSTL 1.0). JSTL 1.0 provides a standard set of tag libraries that enable HTML developers to access objects stored in attribute values. JSTL also supports an expression language that allows access to objects stored in the standard session, page, request, and application contexts. We present examples of JSTL later in the chapter as an alternative to template engines.

Selecting Your Tools

Now it is time to apply the process presented in Chapter 3 for evaluating and selecting a template tool. The steps we will follow are:

- Determine project needs.
- Evaluate the products.
- Select a product.

A Survey of Template Engines

A quick survey of Template Engines yields three primary candidates:

- Tea
- WebMacro
- Velocity

In this case, we will defer providing more detail about the products until we are ready to evaluate the products.

Needs and Features Analysis

The desire to provide a more manageable and efficient development environment has provided template engines with a motivated user community. At this point, we must ask ourselves what we would like to have in a template engine? What are the needs that must be satisfied? The following list answers these questions.

- We need a product that allows separation of duties, minimizing the interface between the software developer creating the business and application layers and the Web-page designer creating the presentation layer.
- We need to be able to easily create the dynamic Web pages from static prototypes.
- We want to avoid requiring Web-page designers to know Java.
- Our template language needs to be powerful enough that it provides access to objects that have been exposed to the Web, but simple enough so that Web-page developers are capable of using the scripting language without developing programming skills.

- We need a template engine that works well in varied application-development environments, not just with those applications that are geared toward presentation on the Web.
- We would like to have the flexibility of writing one data model and invoking various templates based on the evaluation of key data elements.

Evaluating the Template Engines

Now that we have stated our needs, it is time to evaluate the products. We assume that the Tomcat servlet container has already been installed as described in Chapter 5.

Tea

Tea is a simple template language that, when used in conjunction with the TeaServlet, can be used to create powerful, dynamic Web applications. Tea was originally created by the Walt Disney Internet Group and is distributed under The Tea Software License, Version 1.0, which is based on The Apache Software License. Summary information about Tea can be found in the following table.

Product	Tea
Category	Template languages
URL	http://teatrove.sourceforge.net/
Supported Platforms	Java 1.2 and above, Servlet 2.1 and above
License	Tea Software License, an Apache variant
Features	Simple yet powerful template language. Supporting applications include Tea Kettle IDE and Tea servlet.

The Tea architecture is divided into two general areas, the Tea compiler and Tea runtime (see Figure 6.2). Tea templates consist of *code regions* and *text regions*. Code regions contain programming instructions based on the Tea template language, and text regions contain text, which is output without modification by the template engine. Once coded, the Tea template is compiled with the aforementioned Tea compiler and generates standard Java byte-code for use by the host JVM.

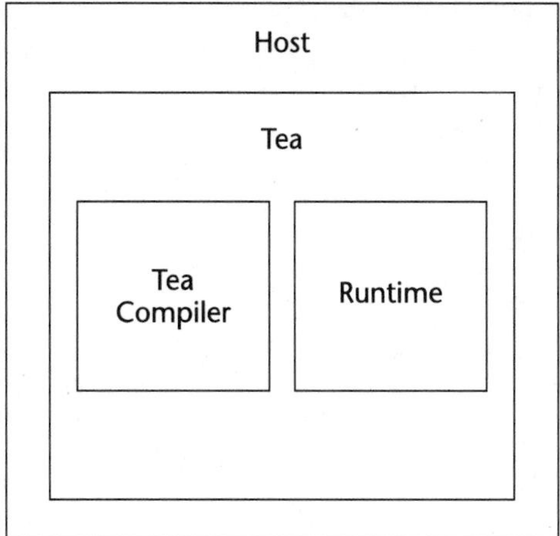

Figure 6.2 Tea architecture.

The runtime environment configures and executes the context class, which provides the `print(Object)` and the `toString(Object)` functions. The Tea model enforces the separation between data acquisition and data presentation. The purpose of the template under the Tea architecture is truly that of a template; it can't retrieve or modify data, it depends on the host environment to provide data to it. Let's take a look at how this is accomplished within the Tea architecture. We will start by setting up our Tea environment.

Installing the Tea Servlet

To install Tea for the examples that follow, you will need to download both the TeaKettle and TeaServlet files. Unzip these files into separate directories. TeaServlet needs to be installed into the Tomcat environment. Follow these steps to install the TeaServlet into Tomcat:

1. Set up the following directory structure within your Tomcat container:

   ```
   <tomcat_root>\webapps\tea
   <tomcat_root>\webapps\tea\WEB-INF
   <tomcat_root>\webapps\tea\WEB-INF\classes
   <tomcat_root>\webapps\tea\WEB-INF\templates
   <tomcat_root>\webapps\tea\WEB-INF\templateClasses
   <tomcat_root>\webapps\tea\WEB-INF\lib
   ```

2. Create the `TeaServlet.properties` file as shown in the following code, and place it into the `\WEB-INF` directory.

   ```
   # TeaServlet properties.
   # Path to locate Tea templates, in .tea files.
   template.path = /jakarta/tomcat4.1/webapps/tea/WEB-INF/templates
   ```

```
# Optional path to write compiled templates, as .class files.
template.classes = \
/jakarta/tomcat4.1/webapps/tea/WEB-INF/templateClasses

# Applications to load into the TeaServlet.
applications {
  "System" {
    # The SystemApplication provides TeaServlet
    # administration support.
    class = com.go.teaservlet.AdminApplication

    init {
      # The security key for the Admin page.
      admin.key = admin
      admin.value = true
    }

    log {
      debug = true
      info = true
      warn = true
      error = true
    }
  }
  "HelloMyCity" {
    class = HelloMyCityApplication
  }
}
log.debug = true
log.info = true
log.warn = true
log.error = true
```

NOTE You may want to edit the sample `properties` file, which can be found in the `samples` directory below where `TeaServlet.zip` was unzipped.

The values for `template.path` and `template.classes` should be adjusted to match your system.

3. Copy the `TeaServlet.jar` file from the directory where you unzipped the `TeaServlet.zip` file, and place it into the `\WEB-INF\lib` directory.

4. Create a `web.xml` file in the `TOMCAT_ROOT/webapps/teaservlet/WEB-INF` directory, as follows:

```
<?xml version="1.0" encoding="UTF-8"?>
<!DOCTYPE web-app PUBLIC
  "-//Sun Microsystems, Inc.//DTD Web Application 2.3//EN"
  "http://java.sun.com/dtd/web-app_2_3.dtd">
<web-app>
  <servlet>
    <servlet-name>
      teaservlet
    </servlet-name>
    <servlet-class>
      com.go.teaservlet.TeaServlet
    </servlet-class>
    <init-param>
      <param-name>properties.file</param-name>
      <param-value>c:/jakarta/tomcat/webapps/tea/WEB-
INF/TeaServlet.properties</param-value>
    </init-param>
  </servlet>

  <servlet-mapping>
    <servlet-name>teaservlet</servlet-name>
    <url-pattern>/dynamic/*</url-pattern>
  </servlet-mapping>

  <servlet-mapping>
    <servlet-name>teaservlet</servlet-name>
    <url-pattern>*.tea</url-pattern>
  </servlet-mapping>
</web-app>
```

   Note that the parameter `properties.file` needs to be set to the location of the `TeaServlet.properties` file on your system.

5. Restart Tomcat.

6. To ensure that the installation process was successful, invoke the TeaServlet Administration Console with the following URL:

```
http://localhost:8080/tea/dynamic/system/teaservlet/Admin?admin=true
```

   If the installation was successful, you should see the screen shown in Figure 6.3.

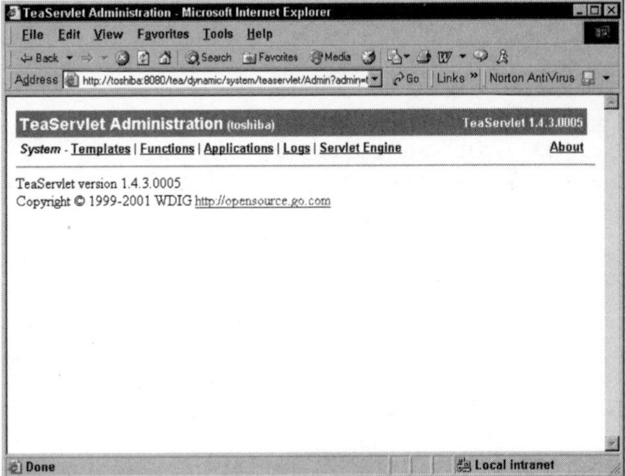

Figure 6.3 The TeaServlet Administration Console.

Creating a Tea Application

After you have satisfied yourself that you have a working Tea servlet environment, you can embark on your first development effort. We start by implementing Tea's Application interface. Following is the source code for `HelloMyCityApplication.java`:

```
package freej2ee;

import com.go.teaservlet.*;
import javax.servlet.ServletException;
public class HelloMyCityApplication implements Application
{
  public HelloMyCityApplication()
  {
    super();
  }

  // Return an instance of the class that contains the functions
  public Object createContext(
    ApplicationRequest request,
    ApplicationResponse response)
  {
    return new HelloMyCityContext(request);
  }

  public void destroy()
  {
  }
```

```
    // Returns the class that contains the functions
    public Class getContextType()
    {
      return HelloMyCityContext.class;
    }

    public void init(ApplicationConfig config) throws ServletException
    {
    }
  }
```

This is a very basic Tea application and as such does not require any special processing in the `init()` and `destroy()` methods. In fact, the only function of `HelloMyCityApplication` is to serve as a factory for creating the `Context` class that follows. The TeaServlet is configured to look for this class by the `TeaServlet.properties` file. After successful compilation, be careful to place the compiled class file in the `WEB-INF/classes` directory.

The `Application` class serves as a class factory to create `Context` classes. The `Context` class does the real work of generating the data that will be used to fill in the template at run time. Following is the `Context` class for our sample application:

```
package freej2ee;

import javax.servlet.http.*;

public class HelloMyCityContext
{
  HttpServletRequest mRequest;

  public HelloMyCityContext()
  {
    super();
  }
  public HelloMyCityContext(HttpServletRequest request)
  {
    // Save the user's request object.
    mRequest = request;
  }

  public String getMyCity()
  {
    // Get  "myCity" parameter from the URL.
    String myCity = mRequest.getParameter("myCity");
    // If it is null, then make Fort Myers the default city.
    if (myCity == null)
    {
      myCity = "Fort Myers";
```

```
        }
        return myCity;
    }
}
```

The Context class HelloMyCityContext contains the methods that will be exposed to the HelloMyCity template for the purpose of delivering data to the template.

After compiling this class be careful to place the compiled class file in the classes directory alongside your application class.

Creating the Tea Template

Tea provides an excellent Integrated Development Environment (IDE) with which to manage the development of Tea templates, called the Kettle IDE. Kettle requires Java 1.3 or greater (even though Kettle runs on Linux, Windows is the preferred operating environment). Figure 6.4 shows the Kettle IDE. We start Kettle by executing the following command:

```
java -cp Kettle.jar com.go.kettle.Kettle
```

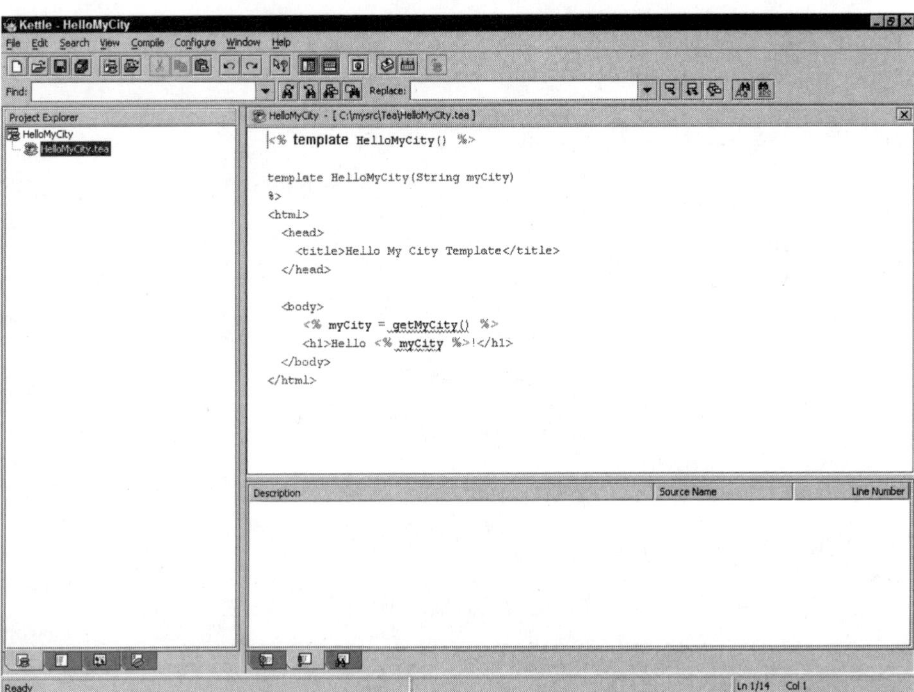

Figure 6.4 The Kettle IDE.

NOTE You will need to have Tomcat running with the TeaServlet installed in order to make effective use of the Kettle IDE.

Create a new project by selecting File ➪ New Project. Enter the name **HelloMyCity** for the project, and make sure it is in the following directory:

```
TOMCAT_ROOT/webapps/tea/WEB-INF/templates
```

After the project has been created, use Configure ➪ Project Properties, and make sure to select Link Project to Tea Servlet and enter the URL for the TeaServlet Administration Console. This URL should be the same one you used to test the servlet earlier and is repeated below for convenience:

```
http://localhost:8080/tea/dynamic/system/teaservlet/Admin?admin=true
```

Next, create a new template by selecting File ➪ New, and enter **HelloMy City** for the template name. Enter the code shown below:

```
<% template HelloMyCity(String myCity) %>
<html>
  <head>
    <title>Hello My City Template</title>
  </head>
  <body>
    <% myCity = getMyCity() %>
    <h1>Hello <% myCity %>!</h1>
  </body>
</html>
```

You will notice code regions within the template that start with "<%" and terminate with "%>". Within these code regions are where functions are invoked and logical operations are performed. All Tea templates must have a template declaration (within the code region), and the declaration must be the same name as the template file. The template declaration in our example is:

```
<% template HelloMyCity(String myCity) %>
```

The template file is saved as HelloMyCity.tea. This particular template accepts a single parameter, myCity, which can be defined in the URL when invoking the template. Two other code regions appear in our example, <% myCity=getMyCity() %> and <% myCity %>. The <%myCity =getMy City() %> code region invokes the user-defined function that's defined in the Context class created earlier. The value returned is assigned to the variable myCity. In our case, the code for the Context class examines the request to see if a city was provided as a parameter, and if not, supplies the string "Fort Myers". The `<% myCity %>` code region tells the template to insert the value assigned to this variable into the template's output. Anything outside of these code regions is considered the text region, and is output by the template in the servlet response without modification.

The template can be compiled using Compile ➪ Template. If everything was entered correctly, Kettle should compile the template and output the compiled template class file into the `templateClasses` directory. This directory was created when we installed the servlet and configured in the `TeaServlet .parameters` file.

NOTE It is much easier to link your project to a TeaServlet in order for Kettle to get configuration information such as the Template Path and ClassPath, otherwise you will have to manually configure these yourself. Manual configuration is discussed in the Kettle user manual.

If all is well, you should be able to invoke the following URL from your browser and see your first Tea application in action.

```
http://localhost:8080/tea/dynamic/HelloMyCity
```

We can see from Figure 6.5 that the output is what we expected. Because the request parameter was undefined, the value of `myCity` was evaluated as null and was changed programmatically by our application to be "Fort Myers."

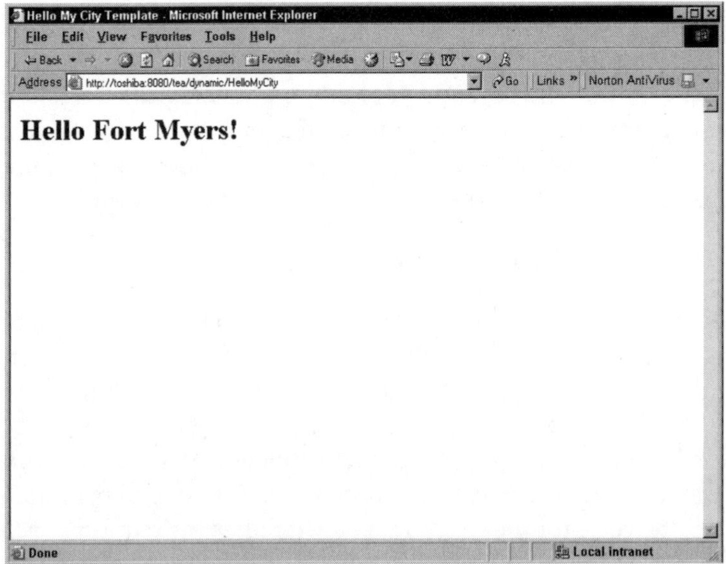

Figure 6.5 A Tea application.

Now, pass the name of your city to the application from the command line; if your city is Nashville, the command would look like the following:

```
http://localhost:8080/tea/dynamic/HelloMyCity?myCity=Nashville
```

As you can see in Figure 6.6, when you define the city parameter (`Nashville` in this case), the application passes it to the template and subsequently returns it to the browser. These simple examples show how the Tea environment provides a simple framework for creating Web applications that enforce the separation of data acquisition from the presentation layer. There are many powerful features we have not shown in this chapter, such as sophisticated flow-control capabilities and a rich set of standard functions that can be used to access request parameters and aid in sending a response to the client.

One other interesting piece of the Tea environment is the Trove library. The Trove library consists of:

- A logging API useful for configuring and capturing events to be logged
- Utility classes that are useful for thread, HTTP, socket management, and other tasks
- A Class File API useful for creating Java Class files from high-level methods

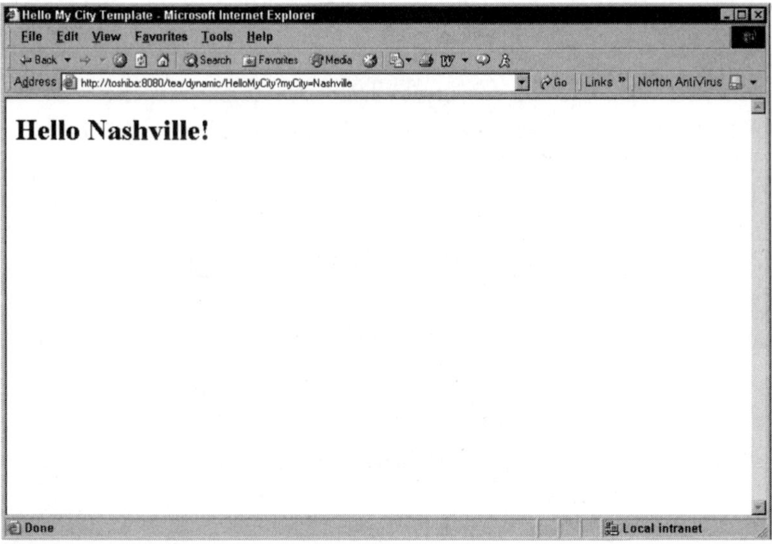

Figure 6.6 Another Tea example.

Clearly, the powerful tools provided by the Walt Disney Internet Group in the Tea suite of products, its simplicity, and its enforcement of separation of data and presentation makes it a good potential choice for Web-application development.

WebMacro

WebMacro is an extremely popular Web-development framework that has been developed by Semiotek Inc. and is available for use under the GNU GPL and/or the Semiotek Public License. The design concept for WebMacro, like that of Tea, is to enforce the separation of presentation code from data acquisition code. This separation is accomplished through the use of the WebMacro template language, which allows designers to embed macros into their page design. The macro expansion process is performed by a servlet that extends the `org.webmacro.servlet.WMServlet` class. This WebMacro servlet processes user requests, acquires data from JavaBeans and other sources, and loads the data into the WebMacro `WebContext`, where the data is visible to the WebMacro template. The WebMacro servlet then loads the template containing the embedded macros, and expands the macros before presenting the rendered HTML back to the browser. A summary for WebMacro is shown in the following table.

Product	WebMacro
Category	Template languages
URL	http://www.webmacro.org
Supported Platforms	Java 1.2 and above, Servlet specification 2.1 and above
License	Either GPL or Semiotek Public License
Features	Simple, yet powerful template language

The WebMacro environment used for the examples presented in this chapter is the latest as of this writing, version 1.1.

Following are the basic steps needed to install WebMacro:

1. Unzip the WebMacro distribution file into a working directory (not in `TOMCAT_ROOT\webapps`).

2. Create the following directories:

```
<tomcat_root>\webapps\wm
<tomcat_root>\webapps\wm\WEB-INF
<tomcat_root>\webapps\wm\WEB-INF\classes
<tomcat_root>\webapps\wm\WEB-INF\lib
```

3. Copy WebMacro.jar from the distribution archive, and put it into the TOMCAT_ROOT \webapps\wm\WEB-INF\lib directory.
4. Compile and install the HelloWorld.java sample application located in the wm_examples directory by putting the class file into the TOMCAT_ROOT \webapps\wm\WEB-INF\classes directory.
5. Copy the helloWorld.wm templates file in the TOMCAT_ROOT \webapps\wm directory.

We are now ready to test our WebMacro environment by running the HelloWorld example:

```
http://localhost:8080/wm/servlet/HelloWorld
```

Your browser should look like Figure 6.7 now, proving that the WebMacro environment is functional.

Moving on, let's take a look at the HelloMyCity program we used in the previous section and see how to use WebMacro to accomplish the same task. First, we will create our template file, HelloMyCity.wm, and put it into our application root TOMCAT_ROOT \webapps\wm.

```
<html>
<head><title>Hello My City!</title></head>
<body>

#set $Response.ContentType = "text/html"

<h1>Hello $myCity!</h1>

</body>
</html>
```

Notice that the first and last line of our template is simple HTML, and as such it will simply be rendered as is without modification to the browser. The second line is a directive to set the content type, informing the browser what type of document it is receiving. The third line is a small demonstration of WebMacro's macro-substitution capability. The myCity variable is put into the WebContext by the WebMacro servlet and is expanded when the template is processed. Following is the source for the WebMacro servlet to help you get a better understanding of what is going on:

```
// Import the WebMacro core interfaces.
import org.webmacro.*;

// Import the WebMacro servlet classes.
import org.webmacro.servlet.*;

public class HelloMyCity extends WMServlet {
```

```
    public Template handle(WebContext context) throws HandlerException {
      String myCity = context.getRequest().getParameter("myCity");
      if(myCity == null)
        myCity = "Fort Myers";

      context.put("myCity", myCity);

      Template view;

      try {

        // Get the "HelloMyCity.wm" template.
        view = getTemplate("HelloMyCity.wm");

      } catch (ResourceException e) {

        throw new HandlerException(
        "HelloMyCity loaded and executed OK, but was unable to load \n"
        + "the HelloMyCity.wm template", e);
      }

      return view;
    }
  }
```

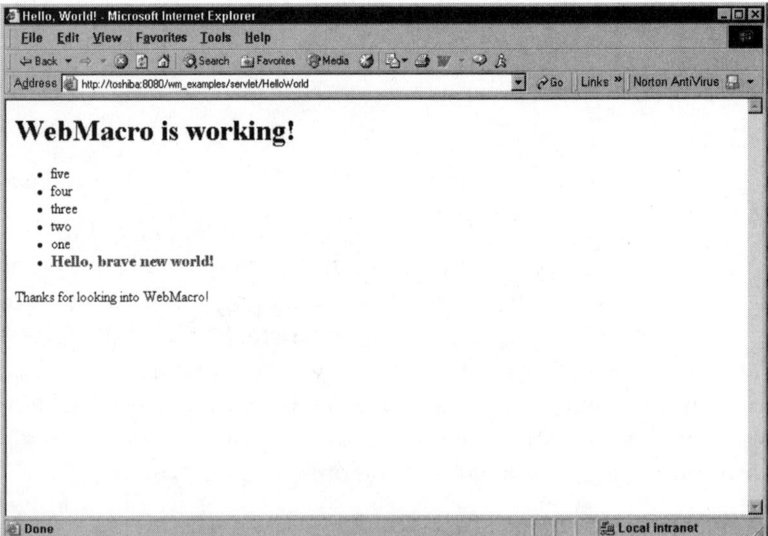

Figure 6.7 A sample WebMacro application.

From the WebMacro servlet code we see that we our servlet is subclassed by extending `WMServlet`, which derived from `HttpServlet`, thus we inherit the `getParameter()` method used to extract the `myCity` parameter that was passed by the browser. After testing for a null condition and putting our value into the `WebContext`, we return the expanded view to the browser. Execute the following command to take a look at the finished product:

```
http://localhost:8080/wm/servlet/HelloMyCity
```

The result is shown in Figure 6.8.

The versatility and power of the WebMacro environment is truly impressive, but a more thorough discussion is outside the scope of this book. Considering the simplicity and power of WebMacro, coupled with the widespread following it enjoys, the application framework can be considered a desirable development environment on those merits alone. WebMacro also seems to be considerably easier to learn, set up, and use than Tea.

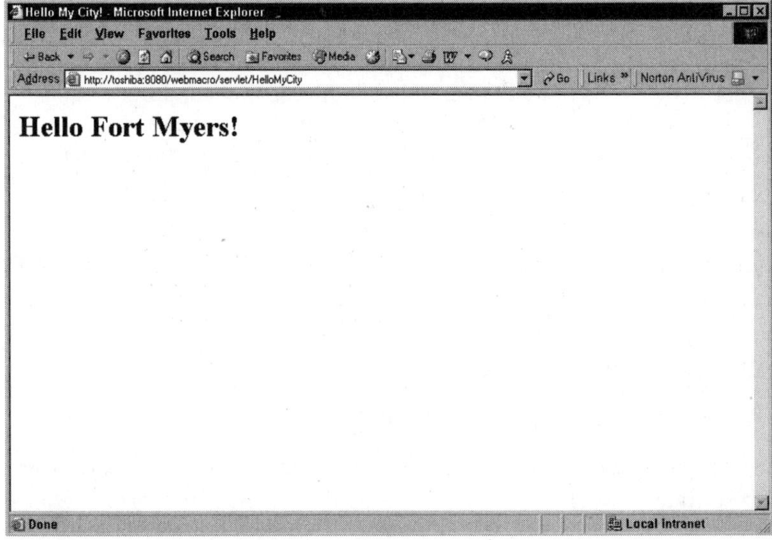

Figure 6.8 Another WebMacro example.

Velocity

When discussing template engines, there's no way we could forget to discuss the Jakarta-Apache group's contribution: Velocity. Velocity is a Java-based template engine similar to the previous templates engines we have examined; in fact its concept came from WebMacro. Also, like Tea and WebMacro, Velocity enforces the separation of the presentation and data-acquisition layers. Velocity provides some truly stellar capabilities, including the ability to generate SQL, PostScript and XML, and also serves as the template engine for the Turbine development framework. Velocity can also be very useful outside the Web application development arena. The summary information for Velocity is shown in the following table.

Product	Velocity
Category	Template languages
URL	http://jakarta.apache.org/velocity
Supported Platforms	Java 1.2 and above
License	Apache
Features	Powerful template language that supports generation of many file types; used as a component in XDoclet, Turbine, and many other open source projects

We will install Velocity version 1.3 within the same Tomcat servlet container we used for the Tea and WebMacro demonstrations. The prerequisites for building the Velocity environment are Ant version 1.3 or later and the Java 2 SDK. The installation process involves the following steps:

1. Uncompress the Velocity archive to a work directory.
2. Change to the `build` directory and execute `./ant`. This will build the Velocity executable .jar file and place it into the `/bin` directory.

CROSS-REFERENCE **Ant is discussed in Chapter 4.**

Velocity comes with two .jar files in the distribution: one that contains the core Velocity classes without any external dependency classes (they are included but in separate jars) and one that contains the core classes along with the external dependency classes. This gives developers flexibility in using various versions of the collections classes and other dependent classes without having to deal with collisions.

After Velocity has been compiled, perform the following steps:

1. Create the following directory structure in your servlet container:

```
TOMCAT_ROOT/webapps/velocity
TOMCAT_ROOT /webapps/velocity/WEB-INF/classes
TOMCAT_ROOT /webapps/velocity/WEB-INF/lib
```

2. Place the Velocity jar into the `TOMCAT_ROOT/webapps/velocity/WEB-INF/lib` directory.

NOTE Because the default dependency classes were fine for our purpose, we used the `velocity-dep-1.2.jar` that came with the distribution.

3. Switch back to your working directory and compile the examples that came with this distribution by going into the `\build` directory and executing the `ant examples` command.
4. Test your Velocity installation by installing the `SampleServlet` application that came with the distribution by copying `SampleServlet.class` to `TOMCAT_ROOT \webapps\freeJ2EE\WEB-INF\classes`, and `sample.vm` to the `TOMCAT_ROOT \webapps\freeJ2EE` directory.
5. Create the following `web.xml` file, and place it into the `WEB-INF` directory.

```
<?xml version="1.0" encoding="UTF-8"?>

<!DOCTYPE web-app PUBLIC
  "-//Sun Microsystems, Inc.//DTD Web Application 2.3//EN"
  "http://java.sun.com/dtd/web-app_2_3.dtd">

<web-app>
  <servlet>
    <servlet-name>Servlet_SampleServlet</servlet-name>
    <servlet-class>SampleServlet</servlet-class>
  </servlet>
  <servlet-mapping>
```

```
        <servlet-name>Servlet_SampleServlet</servlet-name>
        <url-pattern>/servlet/SampleServlet</url-pattern>
    </servlet-mapping>
</web-app>
```

6. Restart Tomcat to allow it to register the new application.
7. After you've restarted Tomcat, test the Velocity installation by executing the following URL from your browser:

   ```
   http://localhost:8080/velocity/servlet/SampleServlet
   ```

   If everything goes as expected, you should see the screen shown in Figure 6.9.

In keeping with the format for presenting the previous template engines, we will show you how to develop and deploy the HelloMyCity application as we did previously. First, we will develop our template file, HelloMyCity.vm.

```
<html>
<head><title>Hello My City</title></head>
<body>

<h1>Hello $myCity!</h1>
</body>
</html>
```

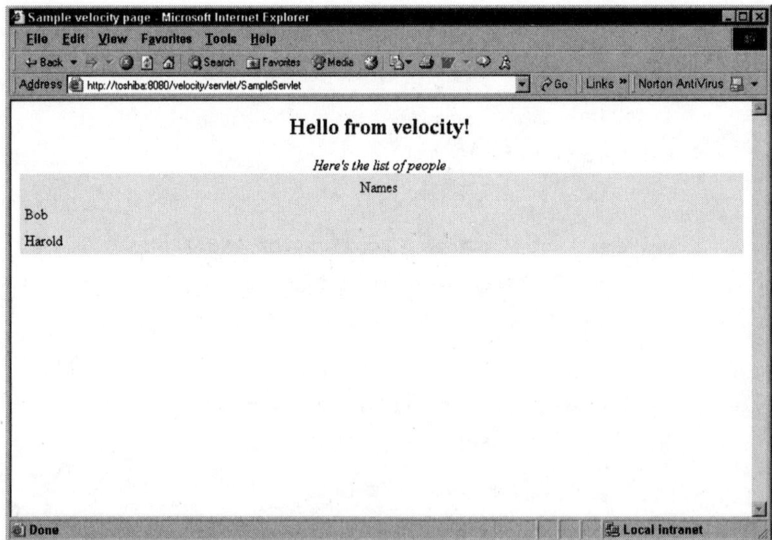

Figure 6.9 A sample Velocity application.

You will notice that the format is similar to that of the WebMacro template; basically, the only difference in this trivial example is that there is no need for a directive to set the content type. Also, similarly to the WebMacro template, the `$myCity` variable is expanded by the application prior to being presented to the user. The Velocity `HelloMyCity` servlet looks like this:

```
import java.io.*;
import java.util.Properties;
import javax.servlet.ServletConfig;
import javax.servlet.http.*;
import org.apache.velocity.Template;
import org.apache.velocity.context.Context;
import org.apache.velocity.servlet.VelocityServlet;
import org.apache.velocity.app.Velocity;
import org.apache.velocity.exception.ResourceNotFoundException;
import org.apache.velocity.exception.ParseErrorException;

public class HelloMyCity extends VelocityServlet
{

  // Configure so that templates will be found in the application root

  protected Properties loadConfiguration(ServletConfig config )
  throws IOException, FileNotFoundException
  {
    Properties p = new Properties();

    String path = config.getServletContext().getRealPath("/");

    if (path == null)
    {
      path = "/";
    }

    p.setProperty( Velocity.FILE_RESOURCE_LOADER_PATH,  path );
    return p;
  }


  public Template handleRequest( HttpServletRequest request,
  HttpServletResponse response, Context ctx )
  {

    String myCity = request.getParameter("myCity");

    if(myCity == null)
      myCity = "Fort Myers";
```

```
        ctx.put("myCity", myCity );

        // Get the template.

        Template out = null;
        try
        {
          out =  getTemplate("HelloMyCity.vm");
        }catch( ParseErrorException pee )
        {

          System.out.println("HelloMyCity : template error");

        }catch( ResourceNotFoundException rnfe )
        {

          System.out.println("HelloMyCity : template not found");

        }catch( Exception e )
        {

          System.out.println("Error " + e);
        }
        return out;
      }
    }
```

The loadConfiguration(ServletConfig) method is called by init() of the superclass, enabling you to configure the location for templates; in this case, the application root. The main workhorse is the handleRequest (HttpServletRequest, HttpServletResponse,Context) method. You can see that this is very similar to the doGet and doPost methods of a conventional servlet, except for the addition of the Context parameter. After we retrieve the value for the parameter and check its value, we put it into the Context. We then define our template and return it so that it can be merged with the data context before it is presented to the user. We invoke our Velocity application as follows:

```
http://localhost:8080/velocity/servlet/HelloMyCity
```

The result should look like Figure 6.10.

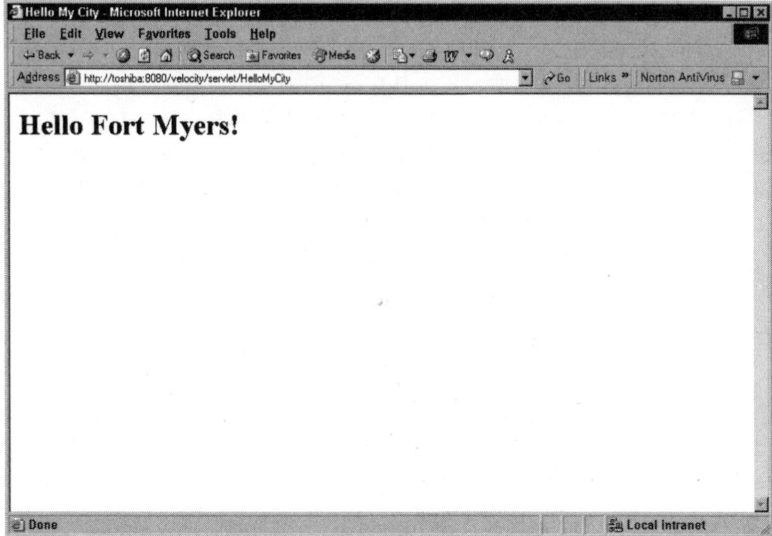

Figure 6.10 A sample Velocity application.

As you can see from this short presentation, Velocity is a very capable player in the template engine space. In fact, Velocity has become so popular so quickly that it has generated some lively discussions on Web forums, particularly regarding its comparison to WebMacro. In the next section, will make our selection, comparing Velocity with WebMacro and Tea.

Product Selection

All of the template engines we have presented in this chapter are stellar performers; there's no doubt about that. There are also some good template engines (such as Tapestry) that have not been presented here. Ultimately, all of the template engines we have mentioned could have a role in your development shop. The applicability of a particular template engine will probably be dependent on the needs of and features that are required by the user for a particular application. We will base our decision primarily on two factors:

Ease of use. The three template languages seem to offer the same complexity in the template languages themselves. However, Tea seems to be the most cumbersome of the three products to set up and support. Both WebMacro and Velocity are easy to set up and start using, with the edge here going to WebMacro.

Project viability. There do not seem to have been any new Tea releases in the past couple of years. Tea has also recently been moved away from its original home to SourceForge.net, which may indicate that Disney and its original creators are abandoning the product. WebMacro currently boasts five active developers and continues to release new versions. WebMacro seems to be used primarily for Web development and does not seem to have been widely used as a component in other significant open source projects. Velocity is a part of the larger Jakarta project and is used in several other visible open source projects both internal and external to the Apache group. Because of this, we think Velocity has a lead over WebMacro in project viability.

For our purposes, we have to give Velocity the win. In addition to its wide popularity as demonstrated by the number of projects that have used it as a component, we feel that the support of the Jakarta group will help to ensure that Velocity will remain compatible with other Jakarta-based products. Because Jakarta is a major provider of open source Java tools, we feel this gives the edge to Velocity.

Coding, Integration, and Testing

Now that we have decided on Velocity as a template engine for our project, let's take a detailed look at the development of one of our views for the Old Friends Incorporated application described in Chapter 3. Old Friends Incorporated has a dual business model, one offering is a hosting service for institutions that choose to outsource the development and management of their site to a third party and one that involves selling the software and license outright to the customer, where the customer manages the site themselves. Either way, it is desirable to be able to configure the site for an institution without having to resort to custom programming. Through the use of a properties configuration file and the Velocity template engine, this is easy to manage.

Consider the default page for an institutional Web site; our example will use Jim's alma mater, Mullins High School. We have decided to use the `java.util.Properties` classes to retrieve the institution name from a configuration file named `OldFriends.properties`. The `OldFriends.properties` file will reside in the root directory for our application `TOMCAT_ROOT \webapps\ROOT`.

`OldFriends.properties` contains a single entry:

```
oldfriends.institution=Mullins High School Tigers
```

This entry defines our institution as the Mullins High School Tigers. Let's take a look at our Velocity template `OldFriends.vm`, which will use this information from the properties file:

```
<!DOCTYPE html PUBLIC "-//W3C//DTD HTML 4.01 Transitional//EN">
<html>
  <head>
    <meta name="generator" content="HTML Tidy, see www.w3.org">

    <title>$customer</title>
  </head>

  <body bgcolor="#FFFFFF">
    <table width="100%" height="100%">
      <tbody>
        <tr>
          <td height="20%" bgcolor="#999999">
            <center>
              <h2>$customer</h2>
            </center>
          </td>
        </tr>

        <tr>
          <td height="80%">
            <table width="100%" height="100%">
              <tbody>
                <tr>
                  <td height="100%" width="15%" bgcolor="#999999">
                    <table border="0" width="138">
                      <col span="1" align="center" valign="middle">

                      <tbody>
                        <tr>
                          <td height="27">UserID</td>
                        </tr>

                        <tr>
                          <td height="24">
                            <form>
                              <input size="15" type="text" name=
                              "USERID">
                            </form>
                          </td>
                        </tr>
```

```
            <tr>
              <td height="30">Password</td>
            </tr>

            <tr>
              <td height="34">
                <form>
                  <input size="15" type="text" name=
                  "PASSWORD">
                </form>
              </td>
            </tr>

            <tr>
              <td height="69">
                <form>
                  <input type="button" name="Login"
                  value=" Login ">
                </form>
              </td>
            </tr>

            <tr>
              <td height="69">
                <form>
                  <input type="BUTTON" value="Register"
                  onclick=
                 "window.location.href='/servlet/Register'">
                </form>
              </td>
            </tr>

            <tr>
              <td height="89">
                <form>
                  <input type="button" name=
                  "AboutButton" value=" About ">
                </form>
              </td>
            </tr>
          </tbody>
        </table>
      </td>

      <td height="100" width="80%" bgcolor="#cfe7e7"
      valign="top">
        <center>
          <h3>Welcome $customer Alumnus!</h3>
        </center>
        <br>
         <br>
```

```
                    <h3 align="left">We hope you enjoy YOUR
                    Web site. Registration is free (after all, you
                    provide our content)!<br>
                    <br>
                    If you have already registered, please log in
                    using the menu on the left. If you are new to
                    our site, please take the time to register.
                    Registered members have access to the alumni
                    directory, access to our souvenir shop, and
                    many other member privileges!<br>
                    <br>
                     Don't delay! Your long-lost schoolmate is
                    waiting to hear from you!</h3>
                    <br>
                     <br>
                     <br>
                     <br>


                    <h3 align="bottom">Copyright Old Friends
                    Incorporated</h3>
                  </td>
                </tr>
              </tbody>
            </table>
          </td>
        </tr>
      </tbody>
    </table>
  </body>
</html>
```

You will notice the bold references to `$customer` in the above template; these will be expanded into the name of our institution after it is retrieved from the properties file and put into our context. Let's take a look at the `OldFriends.java` source and see how this is done.

```
import java.io.*;
import java.util.Properties;

import javax.servlet.ServletConfig;
import javax.servlet.http.HttpServletRequest;
import javax.servlet.http.HttpServletResponse;

import org.apache.velocity.Template;
import org.apache.velocity.context.Context;
import org.apache.velocity.servlet.VelocityServlet;
import org.apache.velocity.app.Velocity;
import org.apache.velocity.exception.ResourceNotFoundException;
import org.apache.velocity.exception.ParseErrorException;
```

```
public class OldFriends extends VelocityServlet
{
  protected Properties loadConfiguration(ServletConfig config)
  throws IOException, FileNotFoundException
  {
    Properties p = new Properties();

    String path = config.getServletContext().getRealPath("/");

    if (path == null)
    {
      System.out.println(
      "loadConfiguration() : unable to "+
      "get the current webapp root. Using '/'.");

      path = "/";
    }

    p.setProperty(Velocity.FILE_RESOURCE_LOADER_PATH, path);
    p.setProperty( "runtime.log", path + "WEB-INF/oldfriends.log" );

    return p;
  }

  public Template handleRequest(
  HttpServletRequest request,
  HttpServletResponse response,
  Context ctx
  )
  {
    try
    {
      Properties p = new Properties();
      String path = getServletContext().getRealPath("/");
      FileInputStream is =
      new FileInputStream(path + "OldFriends.properties");
      p.load(is);

      String customer = p.getProperty("oldfriends.institution");
      if (customer == null)
      {
        customer = "Unable to" + " find OldFriends.properties";
      }
      is.close();
```

```
            ctx.put("customer", customer);
        } catch (IOException ioe)
        {
            ctx.put("customer","Exception:Contact " + "Administrator");
        }

        // get the template

        Template out = null;

        try
        {
            out = getTemplate("OldFriends.vm");
        } catch (ParseErrorException pe)
        {
            System.out.println("OldFriends : Error parsing" +
            "template " + pe);
        }
        catch (ResourceNotFoundException rnf)
        {
            System.out.println("OldFriends : template not " + "found " + rnf);
        }
        catch (Exception e)
        {
            System.out.println("Error " + e);
        }
        return out;
    }
}
```

Let's take a look at what is happening here. The first thing that occurs is that the `loadConfiguration` method is invoked by `init()` of the superclass VelocityServlet. It creates a Properties object that contains the contents of the file `velocity.properties`. The Properties object is used by the VelocityServlet's `init()` method during setup. It also ensures that the path information for the `velocity.properties` file and the directories named in Velocity loader path are relative to the Tomcat application home directory.

The `handleRequest` method provides the HttpRequest and HttpResponse objects along with the Context object from the Velocity superclass. This method retrieves the institution name from our `OldFriends.properties` file and puts it into our context. The method then retrieves the template file and merges the context and template through macro expansion and emits the resultant output to the user's browser.

Let's take at look at the finished product, but before we do, make sure your web.xml file is properly configured and in the WEB-INF directory. Here it is:

```
<?xml version="1.0" encoding="ISO-8859-1"?>

<!DOCTYPE web-app
    PUBLIC "-//Sun Microsystems, Inc.//DTD Web Application 2.3//EN"
    "http://java.sun.com/dtd/web-app_2_3.dtd">

<web-app>
  <servlet>
    <servlet-name>OldFriends</servlet-name>
    <servlet-class>OldFriends</servlet-class>
    <init-param>
      <param-name>properties</param-name>
      <param-value>/velocity.properties</param-value>
    </init-param>
  </servlet>
  <servlet>
    <servlet-name>Register</servlet-name>
    <servlet-class>Register</servlet-class>
  </servlet>
  <servlet-mapping>
    <servlet-name>OldFriends</servlet-name>
    <url-pattern>/OldFriends/*</url-pattern>
  </servlet-mapping>
  <servlet-mapping>
    <servlet-name>Register</servlet-name>
    <url-pattern>/Register/*</url-pattern>
  </servlet-mapping>
</web-app>
```

Now we are ready to execute our URL; to do so use the http://localhost command.

In Figure 6.11, you can see that our template engine worked flawlessly. We were able to completely separate the delicate presentation work (working with those nasty tables) from the data acquisition code (setting up retrieval of the data from the properties file). Both teams were able to work independently from a set of specifications without having to step on each other's toes during development. Because this is so much fun, let's take a look at what the registration module would look like!

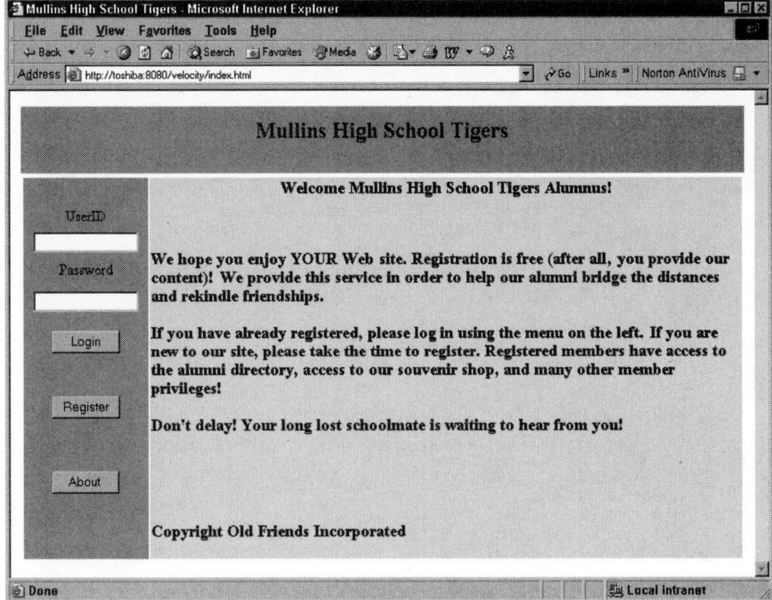

Figure 6.11 The Mullins High School default page.

In order to gain membership, we require applicants to fill out a registration form with their personal information. Access to the registration screen is from a button on the main menu on the left side of the page (the button is visible in Figure 6.11). The registration template, `Register.vm`, looks like this:

```
 <!DOCTYPE HTML PUBLIC "-//W3C//DTD HTML 4.0 Transitional//EN">

<html>
  <head>
    <meta name="generator" content="HTML Tidy, see www.w3.org">

    <title>$customer</title>
  </head>

  <body bgcolor="#999999">
    <table width="100%">
      <tbody>
        <tr valign="top">
          <!-- row 2 -->
```

```
<td colspan="4">
  <table border="0" width="100%">
    <col span="1">
    <col span="1" align="center">

    <tbody>
      <tr valign="middle" align="center">
        <td valign="bottom" align="center">
          <form>
            <input type="BUTTON" value="Home" onclick=
            "window.location.href='OldFriends'">
          </form>
        </td>

        <td valign="top" align="center"><font size=
        "-1"><font size="5">Registration for $customer
        Alumnus and Faculty</font></font></td>

        <td valign="top" align="right">$date</td>
      </tr>
    </tbody>
  </table>
  <hr>

  <form method="POST" name="REGISTER" onsubmit=
  "return REGISTER_onsubmit()" action="/JavaServlet">
    <table width="100%">
      <tbody>
        <tr>
          <td align="left" width="35%"><font size=
          "3"><b>First Name</b></font></td>

          <td width="65%"><input size="30" type="text"
          name="FNAME"></td>
        </tr>

        <tr>
          <td align="left" width="35%"><font size=
          "3"><b>Middle Name</b></font></td>

          <td width="65%"><input size="30" type="text"
          name="MNAME"></td>
        </tr>

        <tr>
          <td width="35%"><font size="3"><b>Last Name
          (Graduation Name)</b></font></td>
```

```
  <td width="65%"><input size="30" type="text"
  name="LNAME"></td>
</tr>

<tr>
  <td width="35%"><font size="3"><b>Married Name
  (if applicable)</b></font></td>

  <td width="65%"><input size="30" type="text"
  name="MDNAME"></td>
</tr>

<tr>
  <td width="35%"><font size="3"><b>Grad
  Year</b></font></td>

  <td width="65%"><select name="GRADYR">
    <option selected>1960s</option>
    <option>1970s</option>
    <option>1980s</option>
    <option>1990s</option>
    <option>2000s</option>
    <option>Faculty</option>
    <option>N/A</option>
  </select></td>
</tr>

<tr>
  <td width="35%"><font size=
  "3"><b>Faculty</b></font></td>

  <td width="65%"><select name="FACULTY">
    <option>
      Yes
    </option>

    <option selected>
      No
    </option>
  </select></td>
</tr>

<tr>
  <td width="35%"><font size=
  "3"><b>City</b></font> (Current)</td>

  <td width="65%"><input size="23" type="text"
  name="CITY"></td>
</tr>
```

```
<tr>
  <td width="35%"><font size=
  "3"><b>State</b></font> (Current)</td>

  <td width="65%"><select name="STATE">
    <option selected>Alabama</option>
    <option>Alaska</option>
    <option>Arizona</option>
    <option>Arkansas</option>
    <option>California</option>
    <option>Colorado</option>
    <option>Connecticut</option>
    <option>Delaware</option>
    <option>District of Columbia</option>
    <option>Florida</option>
    <option>Georgia</option>
    <option>Hawaii</option>
    <option>Idaho</option>
    <option>Illinois</option>
    <option>Indiana</option>
    <option>Iowa</option>
    <option>Kansas</option>
    <option>Kentucky</option>
    <option>Louisiana</option>
    <option>Maine</option>
    <option>Maryland</option>
    <option>Massachusetts</option>
    <option>Michigan</option>
    <option>Minnesota</option>
    <option>Mississippi</option>
    <option>Missouri</option>
    <option>Montana</option>
    <option>Nebraska</option>
    <option>Nevada</option>
    <option>New Hampshire</option>
    <option>New Jersey</option>
    <option>New Mexico</option>
    <option>New York</option>
    <option>North Carolina</option>
    <option>North Dakota</option>
    <option>Ohio</option>
    <option>Oklahoma</option>
    <option>Oregon</option>
    <option>Pennsylvania</option>
    <option>Rhode Island</option>
    <option>South Carolina</option>
    <option>South Dakota</option>
    <option>Tennessee</option>
    <option>Texas</option>
    <option>Utah</option>
```

```
    <option>Vermont</option>
    <option>Virginia</option>
    <option>Washington</option>
    <option>West Virginia</option>
    <option>Wisconsin</option>
    <option>Wyoming</option></select></td>
</tr>

<tr>
  <td colspan="2">
    <hr>
  </td>
</tr>

<tr>
  <td width="35%">
  </td>

  <td width="65%">
  </td>
</tr>

<tr>
  <td width="35%"><font size="3"><b>E-Mail
  Address</b></font></td>

  <td width="65%"><input size="58" type="text"
  name="EMAIL"></td>
</tr>

<tr>
  <td width="35%">
  </td>

  <td width="65%">Choose a user ID and password
  that you will use to access the members section
  and to update your user information.</td>
</tr>

<tr>
  <td width="35%"><font size="3"><b>User
  ID</b></font></td>

  <td width="65%"><input size="15" type="text"
  name="USERID"></td>
</tr>

<tr>
  <td width="35%"><font size=
  "3"><b>Password</b></font></td>
```

```
                <td width="65%"><input size="15" type=
                "password" name="PASSWD1"></td>
              </tr>

              <tr>
                <td width="35%"><font size="3"><b>Verify
                Password</b></font></td>

                <td width="65%"><input size="15" type=
                "password" name="PASSWD2"></td>
              </tr>

              <tr>
                <td colspan="2">
                  <hr>
                </td>
              </tr>

              <tr>
                <td width="35%"><input type="submit" name=
                "SUBMIT" value="Submit"></td>

                <td width="65%"><input type="reset" name=
                "CANCEL" value="Cancel"></td>
              </tr>
            </tbody>
          </table>
        </form>
      </td>
    </tr>
  </tbody>
</table>
</body>
</html>
```

On this page, we are using the customer object and a date object, which is being placed in the Velocity context by our Register servlet. Following is the source for `Register.java`:

```
import java.util.Date;

import javax.servlet.ServletConfig;
import javax.servlet.http.HttpServletRequest;
import javax.servlet.http.HttpServletResponse;

import org.apache.velocity.Template;
import org.apache.velocity.context.Context;
import org.apache.velocity.servlet.VelocityServlet;
import org.apache.velocity.app.Velocity;
import org.apache.velocity.exception.ResourceNotFoundException;
```

```
import org.apache.velocity.exception.ParseErrorException;

public class Register extends VelocityServlet
{
  protected Properties loadConfiguration(ServletConfig config)
  throws IOException, FileNotFoundException
  {
    Properties p = new Properties();

    String path = config.getServletContext().getRealPath("/");

    if (path == null)
    {
      System.out.println(
      "loadConfiguration() : unable to "
      + "get the current webapp root. Using'/'.");

      path = "/";
    }

    p.setProperty(Velocity.FILE_RESOURCE_LOADER_PATH, path);
    p.setProperty( "runtime.log", path + "oldfriends.log" );

    return p;
  }

  public Template handleRequest(
    HttpServletRequest request,
    HttpServletResponse response,
    Context ctx )
  {
    try
    {
      Properties p = new Properties();
      String path = getServletContext().getRealPath("/");
      FileInputStream is = new FileInputStream(path +
        "WEB-INF/OldFriends.properties");
      p.load(is);

      String customer= p.getProperty("oldfriends.institution");
      if (customer == null)
        customer = "Unable to find " + "OldFriends.properties";

      is.close();

      ctx.put("customer", customer);

      Date dte = new Date();
      ctx.put("date",dte.toString());
    }
```

```
        catch (IOException ioe)
        {
          ctx.put("customer", "Exception - Contact Administrator");
        }

        // get the template
        Template out = null;
        try
        {
          out = getTemplate("register.vm");
        }
        catch (ParseErrorException pe)
        {
          System.out.println("Register : Error parsing template " + pe);
        }
        catch (ResourceNotFoundException rnf)
        {
          System.out.println("Register : template not found " + rnf);
        }
        catch (Exception e)
        {
          System.out.println("Error " + e);
        }
        return out;
      }
    }
```

You can see that we have added a `"date"` element to our context for this screen. The `java.util.Date()` library is used to format a Date object and store it in our context. We can now execute the registrations screen from our main page. The result is shown in Figure 6.12.

The examples covered here only scratch the surface of the capabilities of Velocity. What hasn't been demonstrated is the fact that the Velocity engine can be used for far more than generation of Web pages. For example, Velocity is used in Torque (another Jakarta project) to generate database-specific SQL. It can also be used to create XML or PostScript files. In XDoclet, Velocity is even used to generate Java programs. Velocity however has a new competitor in the Web-page-generation arena, and it is not a template engine.

JSTL

We put on hold earlier an example of the JSP 1.2 standard and the services provided by the JSTL 1.0 specification, in order to evaluate template engines, the services they provide, and the problems they solve. As it turns out, the Java Community Process (JCP) standards group has been addressing the very same issues.

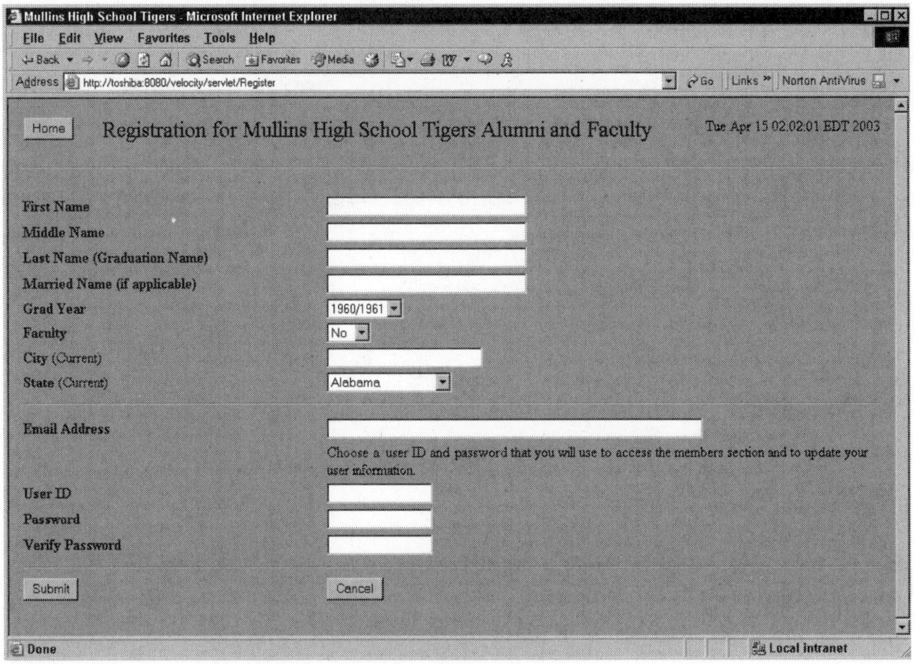

Figure 6.12 The Mullins High School registration page.

The JSTL specification provides standard libraries to provide support for iteration, conditional logic (if/else), manipulation of XML, internationalization, text formatting, and access databases through SQL (structured query language) tags. Prior to this standardization, custom tag libraries were developed by various vendors to solve similar problems, but moving between applications was confusing due to the inconsistent tags being employed.

JSTL is available today from the Jakarta project for the JSP 1.2 and Servlet 2.3 containers. The summary information for this JSP implementation is shown in the following table.

Product	JSTL (from the Jakarta Taglibs project)
Category	JSP tag library
URL	http://jakarta.apache.org/taglibs/doc/standard-doc/intro.html
Supported Platforms	Java 1.2 and above, Servlet 2.3 and above
License	Apache
Features	Soon to be a standard part of JSP

Like Template engines, JSTL can be used to enforce the separation of Java code from Web-page development. JSTL even has a feature that will enforce the rule of allowing no Java scriptlet code within a JSP. In the interest of making a comparison of the subset of services we looked at in template engines; we make a similar comparison of the services found in the JSTL.

The if tag, as demonstrated in the following code, supports conditional logic with a JSP:

```
<c.if test="${myproject.proglang == 'Java'}">
        Excellent choice
</c:if>
<c.if var="${myproject.proglang == 'C'}">
    <c:set var="warnings"
           scope="session"
           value="You are responsible for your garbage collection." />
</c:if>
```

The choose tag handles cases where there is a choice between multiple elements. The example below adds to the HTTP response a value that represents the way each language would print "Hello World."

```
<c:choose>
  <c:when test="${lang.Java}">
      System.out.println("Hello World")
  <c:when test = "${lang.C}">
      printf("Hello World")
  <c:otherwise>
      cout << "Hello World"
</c:choose>
```

Iteration is also supported by JSTL. JSTL can be used to iterate over elements of a Java collection or array, as follows:

```
<c:forEach items="${languages}" var="lang">
<c:out value="${lang}"/>
</c:forEach>
```

JSTL also supports an iteration construct that is similar to a for loop.

```
<c:forEach begin="0" end="10">
Java rocks!
</c:forEach>
```

The forTokens tag allows simple parsing and iteration through short embedded lists.

```
<c:forTokens items="red:green:blue" delims=":" var="token">
  <c:out value="${token}"/>
</c:forTokens>
```

The idea is that with the JSTL installed it is now possible to address our page, session, application, and request context with a macro language similar to what we have seen in our previous template engine examples. Let's take a look at what the first few lines of our default page for Old Friends Incorporated would look like using the JSTL:

```
<%@ taglib uri="http://java.sun.com/jstl/core" prefix="c" %>

<HTML>
<TITLE><c:out value = '${sessionScope.customer}' /></TITLE>
</HEAD>
<BODY bgcolor="#FFFFFF">
<TABLE width="100%" height="100%">
  <TBODY>
    <TR>
      <TD height="20%" bgcolor="#999999"><CENTER>
         <H2><c:out value='${sessionScope.customer}'/></H2>
      </CENTER></TD>
   </TR>
. . . code skipped . . .
  </TBODY>
</TABLE>
```

We can see this is an improvement over the older method of retrieving information from the session context. The real potential of JSTL will be realized with the implementation of the JSP 2.0 specification and the services provided by the Expression Language. The above snippet of code could then be written as follows:

```
<%@ taglib uri="http://java.sun.com/jstl/core" prefix="c" %>

<html>
<TITLE><${sessionScope.customer}></TITLE>
</HEAD>
<BODY bgcolor="#FFFFFF">
<TABLE width="100%" height="100%">
  <TBODY>
    <TR>
      <TD height="20%" bgcolor="#999999"><CENTER>
         <H2><${sessionScope.customer}></H2>
      </CENTER></TD>
    </TR>
. . . code skipped . . .
  </TBODY>
</TABLE>
```

We can see that syntactically, this is an even better improvement and much easier for content developers to manage. Going forward with the development of Old Friends Incorporated, we can still make a strong argument for the services of our Velocity template engine from the standpoint of the services it provides beyond HTML generation (PostScript support, for example). Velocity remains a valuable tool because of its compatibility and ease of integration with our production Apache environment. However, the introduction of JSTL as a standard extension to JSP eliminates the need to use a template engine to enforce separation of our code and content in Web development projects.

Summary

What should be clear from our examples in this chapter is that, through the use of templates, one can clearly separate the duties of Web development from software development. The presentation aspects of the templates involved no introduction of Java whatsoever, and, likewise, the Java servlets used to acquire data for our templates were not encumbered with HTML.

Clearly, template engines are a useful addition to the view component of the MVC design architecture. When templates are coupled with a good specification, the development of high-quality, timely, and cost-effective Web applications has never been easier.

The JSTL now offers a viable standard alternative to template engines for Web-page generation: however, template engines are still a useful tool for generating other types of output.

CHAPTER

7

Adding a Web Application Framework

In Chapter 6, we looked at separating the duties of the Web designer from those of the software developer by applying the Model-View-Controller (MVC) design pattern. The template engines covered in Chapter 6 were oriented toward providing the view or presentation elements of MVC. In this chapter, we look at Web frameworks that provide a more complete implementation of the MVC pattern. Frameworks can speed up all aspects of MVC development. We will briefly cover the most notable frameworks, but will concentrate on a particular framework offered by the Jakarta Apache group, Struts.

Architectural Considerations

In the Java community, the MVC design pattern is widely recognized as the way to go for developing medium to large-scale enterprise Web applications. The MVC design pattern is associated with the JSP Model 2 development approach. In JSP Model 2 development, the JavaServer Page is used strictly to render the output of a Web page. A servlet is used to act as a controller, determining which page to generate and gathering the information to be rendered into HTML by the JSP.

Someone just being introduced to application frameworks will naturally want to know answers to questions such as, "What does a framework do for me?" and "Why should I want to use it?" The answer to these questions, as we shall see, is that this approach speeds up the development process and helps in the creation of higher-quality and easier-to-maintain software.

After the MVC design architecture became a de facto standard, it became clear after its repeated use on application after application that there were similar activities being performed within each of these applications. A Web browser normally issues a request to a servlet; the servlet instantiates a JavaBean that encapsulates the business logic and data, which in turn will be handed over to the JSP for presentation back to the browser. Any time a pattern or repeatable series of events can be identified, there is usually a way to construct a device or mechanism with which to automate a process. The realization of this automation for Web application development manifests itself as a *Web application framework.*

Advantages of a Framework

Web application frameworks are quickly becoming the standard architecture for Web application development. Most frameworks provide a uniform and consistent implementation of the MVC design pattern that leverages servlets and JavaServer Pages. Many frameworks also support other features like:

- Internationalization
- Localization
- Connection pooling
- Security and SSL support
- File uploading support
- Logging

These features typically add complexity to a Web application, but having the features provided by the framework allows us to benefit from them without adding complexity to our development effort.

Using these frameworks minimizes the development effort required to create large, complex applications because the developer does not have to focus on addressing or creating general-purpose services that resolve common issues. This leaves the developers free to focus on implementing business requirements.

These frameworks are tried-and-true products that enjoy a large and ever-expanding community of developers who are familiar with these platforms and continue to add functionality and third-party tools. Certainly, one of the greatest benefits of all is that these extremely stable products are open source and available free of charge through projects like those sponsored by the Apache Group.

Selecting Your Tools

In this section, we apply the process presented in Chapter 3 to examine several available Web application frameworks and select one for more detailed coverage. We start this process with a quick survey of some of the available products.

Web Application Framework Product Survey

A brief search of the available open source products uncovers four products for us to examine:

- Barracuda
- Expresso
- Struts
- Turbine

There are some interesting relationships among these projects. Struts and Turbine are competing frameworks that are both offered by the Apache-Jakarta project. Expresso predates Struts but now incorporates Struts as part of its framework. The next sections will examine these products a little more closely.

Barracuda

Barracuda is a first-class framework that comes from the Enhydra project that was originally created by Lutris Technologies. Although Lutris Technologies did not survive the dot.com crash, the open source Barracuda framework that Lutris created did survive. ObjectWeb now sponsors Barracuda and the other Enhydra-related projects. Barracuda, much like the other frameworks we discuss, provides classes that allow the developer to develop Web applications faster, more easily, and with fewer bugs. The product summary is provided in the following table.

Product	Barracuda
Category	Web application framework
URL	http://www.barracudamvc.org
Supported Platforms	Java 1.3 (issues with 1.4) and Servlet 2.2 and above
License	Enhydra Public License
Features	"Push" model, DOM modification, XMLC support, form mapping and validation, globalization and localization support

The primary mechanism for implementing the framework in Barracuda is the utilization of the server-side component model that itself implements widgets such as tables, lists, and templates to manipulate XML/HTML (*ML) templates that have been compiled into Document Object Model (DOM) objects. A tool supplied with Barracuda called XMLC handles the compilation of these *ML templates.

The idea behind Barracuda is to provide a cleaner separation of code and content because there is no need to introduce scriptlets, or for that matter any server-side programming logic, into the markup. The "View" does not "pull" data from the model object similarly to most template engines or conventional JSP and Java Beans. Under Barracuda's "push" model, the controller (servlet) is used to manipulate the view directly through the DOM interface.

Another nice feature is the Barracuda Event Model, which allows the developer to design events into the Web client application. These events are analogous to the event mechanism provided by the Java AWT user interface. The firing of an event on the client component notifies a server-side event handler so that it can invoke its event logic.

Most applications that are international in scope are faced with language issues that need to be dealt with. The solution to this problem is commonly referred to as *localization*. Historically, two approaches have been taken to deal with this issue:

- The designer develops duplicate versions of the content, and the appropriate version is served up depending on the target client locale. Clearly, from a maintenance standpoint this is not desirable.
- The content is served dynamically, depending on the target client locale; of course, this solution suffers from the cost of high overhead.

Barracuda's approach to localization is novel to say the least: The user develops his or her base content HTML/XML file and a suite of property files with appropriate keys and text for the various locales supported. It is important to note that the original base HTML/XML file *does not* contain any ID tags that correlate to the keys in the property files. It is also important for the base locale properties file to contain text that is exactly the same as that in the base *ML file. The XMLC compiler can then use this comparison to derive the appropriate key for the subsequent locales. After this has been done, the XMLC will then recognize all of the locales and, with the help of the XMLC Localization Taskdef, produce compiled output for each of the locales. Working in a fashion similar to the way GUI-based Java programs use the Java Resource Bundles, the DOMLoader returns the previously compiled output based on the requested class name and locale automatically, alleviating the aggravation to the developer of determining the locale and calculating the appropriate template name.

The final feature we must mention is the Barracuda Form mapping and validation framework. *Mapping* involves taking an HTTP request form and mapping the form elements into Java objects. These objects can then be validated by subclassing the DefaultFormValidator class and writing specific validation logic for the mapped fields.

Expresso

Expresso started out as an independent framework. The original framework predates Struts and Turbine. At one time, the Expresso site used to comment that Struts features were a subset of those offered by Expresso. However today, the current version of the Expresso framework is essentially a large collection of classes that is built on top of the Struts application framework and other open source libraries. The summary for the Expresso Framework appears in the following table.

Product	Expresso
Category	Web application framework
URL	http://www.jcorporate.com
Supported Platforms	Java 1.3+, Servlet specification 2.3
License	Apache Style (Expresso License)
Features	Built on Struts and leverages other open source projects to provide a comprehensive Web-development platform

Expresso extends the basic Struts framework by adding components for developing database-driven applications. It includes 16 core business application components that support the Expresso framework. These components are:

Controller objects. Encapsulates the application logic.

Database objects. Maps relational database tables to Java objects and associates actions of business logic to their storage (analogous to an entity EJB).

DB connection pooling. Handles multiple database connections and manages their respective connections to and from the pool.

Email connectivity. A base-level email class provides support for event notifications, login verification, and attachments.

Security. Security classes that provide login, database object, and application security.

Logging. Integrates Apache Log4j.

Job control. Enables a job queue where jobs can be scheduled for future execution.

Registration and login. Classes that leverage the Struts /Login and /Register actions to perform Express and Extended registration.

Caching. Classes to implement a caching facility for providing fast lookups for frequently used data; features automatic and custom caches.

Health check. Utilities to monitor Web services and components.

Taglibs. A custom tag library that includes action, input, and error tags.

XML. Provides capabilities for importing and exporting DB objects to XML format streams and/or files.

Event notification and error handling. Provides capabilities for sending email notifications based on system events.

Unit testing. Extends JUnit to provide an Expresso unit-testing environment.

Configuration values. Facility to manage configuration data for an application, such as information needed to connect to databases, email servers, and so on.

Workflow. Feature to facilitate and encourage proper screen-flow logic.

If your needs are a database-driven application, Expresso's feature-rich framework is a good fit. Although the Expresso framework is available under the Jcorporate Apache Style Software License, a premium commercial support license is also available. Developer documentation is excellent and is available from the Jcorporate Web site.

Turbine

Turbine is an application framework similar to Struts and the other frameworks presented here. Like Struts, Turbine is also developed by the folks at the Jakarta-Apache project. Turbine also provides MVC-style support and allows Java developers to quickly build Web applications based on a known and proven model. The Turbine approach to the view layer is a "pull" (servlet places data into a context where it can be "pulled" by the view) as opposed to a "push" (the servlet "pushes" data directly into the view). Thus, Turbine works extremely well with many popular presentation alternatives such as

WebMacro, Velocity, FreeMarker, Cocoon, and JSP. The following table gives a summary of Turbine's characteristics.

Product	Turbine
Category	Web application framework
URL	http://jakarta.apache.org/turbine
Supported Platforms	Java 1.3+, Servlet specification 2.2
License	Apache
Features	Support for template engines, built-in object/relational mapping tool, content caching

As far as functionality is concerned, Turbine is one of the front-runners in its application space, providing over 200 classes in its toolkit. These classes provide support for security, database connection pooling, template-based email using many of the common template engines, and logging support based on Log4J. Additionally, the Torque classes are easily integrated to provide object relational mapping. These object relational mapping tools provide for auto-generation of SQL and Java code for databases, which makes it easy to build object relational systems.

Turbines downfall is its complexity. Turbine has a much steeper learning curve than its sibling project Struts. Many of the features offered in Turbine (Torque, for example) can be extracted and used independently of the rest of the framework.

Struts

The Struts framework is another offering from the Jakarta-Apache project and so is a sibling of Turbine. Struts is similar to Turbine in that it provides MVC Model 2 support in solving many of the same problems in Web-application development, and does so by providing Java developers with a robust, proven framework for their development effort. Struts differs from the Turbine framework in that it does not contain some of the same functionality; such as the robust security provided through Access Control Lists (ACLs), the superior integration with various template engines for processing the view layer, and the robust services found in Turbine. See the following table for a summary of Struts characteristics.

Product	Struts
Category	Web Application Framework
URL	http://jakarta.apache.org/struts
Supported Platforms	Java 1.3+, Servlet specification 2.2
License	Apache
Features	Stable, most popular framework, easy to learn

One the other hand, Struts is much easier to learn and use. Like Turbine, the Struts view layer can leverage technologies provided by JSP, XSLT and the Velocity template engine. The difference is that Struts seems to offer just about the right mix of power, flexibility, and ease of use. As a result, Struts is the most popular open source Java Web application framework being used today, and has the largest current following in the construction of corporate intranet/Internet Web-based applications with an application framework.

Struts includes a set of custom JSP taglibs that make Web-page creation easier. Struts also includes a tag library called "tiles" that provides for portal-like application windows. Although Struts does not come integrated with things like logging libraries and database-mapping tools, Struts does not prevent the use of these tools and is normally easy to integrate with them. This allows Struts to be a base platform that can be extended using the tools and libraries that best suit a project, corporate environment, or development team.

Needs and Features Analysis

Before we examine the current field of application frameworks, you should ask yourself this question: What features would I like to have in an application development framework?

If you prefer, as we do, to use a framework that has already been developed, you probably want the following things:

- The framework should be mature and stable.
- The framework should have a large installed base of existing users to draw upon in order to staff our development needs.
- From a managerial and developers standpoint, we would like for the framework to be easy to grasp for new developers making the transition from other development groups. Easy to grasp translates into a reduced learning curve and keeping management happy by reducing startup costs.

- Good documentation and readily available example applications are a must.
- Preferably, the framework we use should be supported or maintained by the technical mainstream.
- A record of changes in technical standards or direction for the framework should be maintained or updated by third parties and contributors in a timely fashion.
- The framework should be feature-rich, leaving our developers free to work on developing solutions for business requirements rather than spending time working on tool development.
- Although the framework should be feature rich, we do not want it to lock us in to core libraries. For example, we may have a corporate standard for logging tools. We do not want a logging tool forced upon us by a Web-application framework.

So, now that we know what we have to choose from and we know what we are interested in, let's select the framework that is right for us.

Evaluation and Selection

All of the frameworks that we have discussed are mature and stable. Struts has the largest estimated installed base and offers the most available resources for support. Struts is also the easiest of the frameworks to learn and start using. All of the frameworks have good documentation available. The Expresso documentation is especially noteworthy. In addition to the provided documentation, Struts also boasts a number of books that have been published about the framework and Struts is covered in many books on servlets and J2EE. Both Struts and Turbine are maintained by the well-regarded Jakarta project. Barracuda seems to be free of its earlier relationship with Lutris and appears to be doing well under ObjectWeb. Expresso boasts the support of jCorporate; however, jCorporate seems to be more of a consulting company than an independent source of open source projects. All of the frameworks are feature rich, with both Expresso and Turbine offering the most features.

Considering all of this, we select Struts as the Web application framework for our platform. The rational is this: Struts has the broadest user base, is easiest to learn, and is maintained by a stable open source community. Although Expresso is built upon Struts, Expresso also adds a lot of features that we may not need at this time. This wealth of features represents more for us to learn and maintain. Also, we are not sure that the additional components selected by the Expresso project will fit our future needs. By selecting Struts, we can still move to Expresso if we need to in the future. Turbine is too complex, and the Barracuda model of DOM manipulation does not seem to fit as well with the standard J2EE components and architectures that we would like to use (JavaServer Pages, for example).

Working with Struts

Now, it's time to take a more in-depth look at Struts and show how it can be used to build a Web application. Before we start, we assume that you already have a working Tomcat environment as described in Chapter 5. You should also download the Struts distribution from the Jakarta Web site and decompress it into a working directory.

A Struts Overview

To provide a very simple overview of how Struts works we will break down the MVC design pattern into the Struts components used for its implementation. This is done, as follows:

The controller. Handles the requests between the user (Web browser) and the application, executing the appropriate business logic and then invoking the appropriate view component to communicate the result of the user request. The primary component of the controller is a servlet that is subclassed from ActionServlet. The actions that will be performed by the ActionServlet are defined in a subclass of the Action class. These objects encapsulate the business logic, determine the outcome, and invoke the appropriate View component to create the response. The validation of form data is performed by subclassing the ActionForm class, once the ActionForm has successfully executed it's validate method, the ActionForm, is passed on to the Action class. The contract or mapping between the ActionServlet and the Action class are defined by the ActionMappings, which are defined in `/WEB-INF/struts-config.xml`.

The model. Encapsulates the state of the system and the methods that change the state of the system. The classic example is that of the shopping cart, which contains properties that represent the current list of items the user has purchased. The beans expose methods that enable items to be added, deleted and processed for checkout. The Action object we discussed for the controller would be responsible for instantiating and invoking the methods of the bean.

The view. The view is most often constructed using JavaServer Pages in conjunction with the standard tag libraries or the custom tags that are included with Struts. The tags are used to dynamically pull data from the model object into the view before it is presented to the user.

Building a Sample Application with Struts

For this exercise, we will take our example application Old Friends Incorporated and develop the entry screens for the application. This will consist of the entry point and login for the application `[index.jsp]` as well as the registration screen for those who have yet to register `[registration.jsp]`. Before we start developing, we need to install the base Struts framework in our Tomcat servlet container. We will be using the latest version as of this writing, Struts 1.1. Installation is very easy: it entails simply copying the `/webapps/*.war` files from the distribution to the Tomcat `TOMCAT_ROOT/webapps` directory. The Tomcat servlet container will automatically expand the .war files into their respective directory structures.

The quickest way to start developing with Struts is to shut down your servlet container and copy the `struts-blank.war` file from your Struts distribution into the `TOMCAT_ROOT/webapps` directory. Decide on the name for your application and rename the copy of `struts-blank.war` with that name. For the application we are developing here, we will rename it `oldfriends.war`. Then, restart the Tomcat servlet container, and it will automatically expand the `oldfriends.war` into the directory structure `TOMCAT_ROOT/webapps/oldfriends/`. We can test to see if the template for our Old Friends Incorporated application is correctly installed by invoking it from our browser as follows:

```
http://localhost:8080/oldfriends
```

If everything is installed correctly, the page shown in Figure 7.1 should be displayed in the browser.

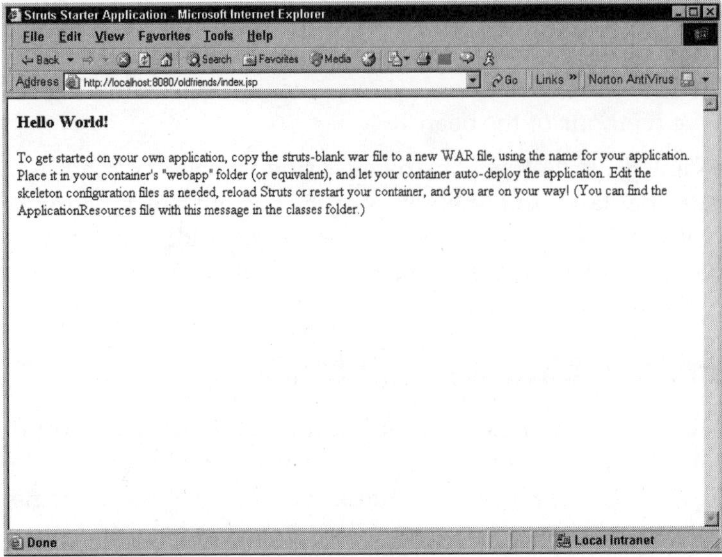

Figure 7.1 Default page for the Struts-Blank application.

That was easy! Now that we are confident that we have a good starting point, we will proceed to modify this base application to give us the functionality that is required for our Old Friends Incorporated application.

The entry point of our application will be `index.jsp`, which will present the user with the screen shown in Figure 7.2.

Users who have already registered previously will log into our application by entering their user ID and password and clicking the Login button. First-time users will be able to register with Old Friends Incorporated by clicking the Register button, and they will be presented with a registration screen. Users have a third option in that they can find out more information about Old Friends Incorporated before registering by clicking the About button.

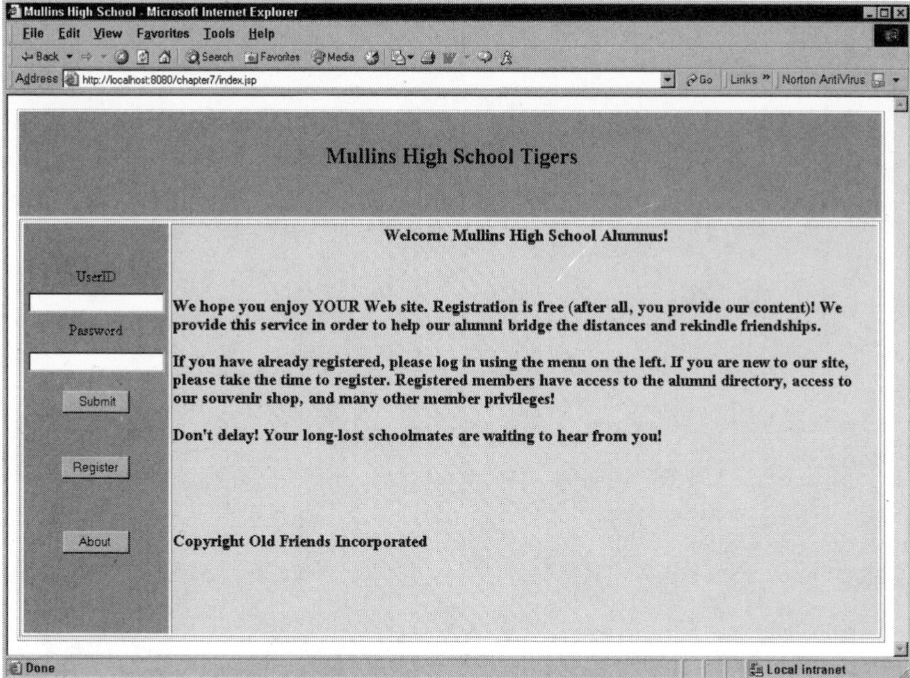

Figure 7.2 Old Friends Incorporated login screen.

Our next step will be to create a Form class for this application screen so that we can validate our data prior to passing it to our Action class. Before doing this, we take an accounting of the fields for this screen, and determine that we need to define two fields, UserID and Password. As we mentioned during our earlier discussion of Struts, the Form class is created by subclassing the Struts ActionForm class. Here is the source for our ActionForm class:

```
import javax.servlet.http.*;
import org.apache.struts.action.*;

public class OldFriendsForm extends ActionForm
{
  private String mUserID = null;
  private String mPassword = null;

  public String getUserID()
```

```
    {
      return mUserID;
    }
    public void setUserID(String aUserID)
    {
      mUserID = aUserID;
    }

    public String getPassword()
    {
      return mPassword;
    }
    public void setPassword(String aPassword)
    {
      mPassword = aPassword;
    }

    public ActionErrors validate(
    ActionMapping aMapping,
    HttpServletRequest aR)
    {
      ActionErrors err = new ActionErrors();
      if ((mUserID == null) || (mUserID.length() < 1))
        err.add("userid", new ActionError("error.userid"));
      if ((mPassword == null) || (mPassword.length() < 1))
        err.add("password", new ActionError("error.password"));
      return err;
    }

    public void reset(ActionMapping aMapping, HttpServletRequest aR)
    {
      mUserID = null;
      mPassword = null;
    }
  }
```

The primary purpose of our ActionForm class is to transfer data from the input screen to our business logic. The class contains getter and setter methods for our data field, but the most important services are the `validate()` and `reset()` methods. The `reset()` method is called by the controller, just before transferring our data from the request object into our ActionForm object. After the data is transferred, validation is performed via the `validate()` method.

Next, we need to construct our OldFriendsAction class by extending the Struts Action class. Normally the OldFriendsAction class invokes classes that encapsulate the business logic for our application. In our case, we have not implemented any business logic so the OldFriendsAction class is left with just having to manage error-handling and control-forwarding duties. Chapter 14 provides a more detailed example that includes the business logic associated the Action class. Following is the source for our `TOMCAT_ROOT/oldfriends/WEB-INF/classes/OldFriendsAction` class:

```
import javax.servlet.*;
import javax.servlet.http.*;
import org.apache.struts.action.*;

public class OldFriendsAction extends Action
{
  public ActionForward execute(
    ActionMapping aMapping,
    ActionForm aForm,
    HttpServletRequest aRequest,
    HttpServletResponse aResponse)
  throws ServletException
  {
    OldFriendsForm f = (OldFriendsForm) aForm;
    String userid = f.getUserID();
    String password = f.getPassword();
    return aMapping.findForward("main");
  }
}
```

The execute method of the Action class is where we would perform an operation such as authenticating our userID and password against a database before returning a Success or a Failure. A Success would cause the controller to forward to a view that would allow the user to continue his or her use of the application, a Failure would cause control to go back to the Login screen.

The purpose of the Action class is to allow us to decouple the request from the model. This allows more than one request to use a given action. In our subclass OldFriendsAction, we retrieve our UserID and Password from the Form object and then use that data to authenticate the user.

The opening screen for the application is created by a JSP file `index.jsp`. The source code for `index.jsp` is as follows:

```
<%@ taglib uri="/WEB-INF/struts-html.tld" prefix="html" %>
<%@ taglib uri="/WEB-INF/struts-bean.tld" prefix="bean" %>
<HTML>
```

```
<HEAD>
  <TITLE><bean:message key="oldfriends.highschool"/></TITLE>
</HEAD>

<BODY bgcolor="#FFFFFF">
<TABLE width="100%" height="100%" border="1">
  <TBODY>
    <TR>
      <TD height="20%" bgcolor="#999999">
        <CENTER><H2>
            <bean:message key="oldfriends.highschool"/> Tigers
        </H2></CENTER>
      </TD>
    </TR>

    <TR>
      <TD height="80%">
        <TABLE width="100%" height="100%" border="1">
          <TBODY>
            <TR>
              <TD height="100%" width="15%" bgcolor="#999999">
                <TABLE border="0" width="138">
                  <COL span="1" align="center" valign="middle">
                    <TBODY>
                      <TR>
                        <TD height="27">UserID</TD>
                      </TR>

                      <TR>
                        <TD height="24">
                          <html:form action="oldfriends">
                            <html:text property="userID" />
                        </TD>
                      </TR>

                      <TR>
                        <TD height="30">Password</TD>
                      </TR>

                      <TR>
                        <TD height="34">
                          <html:password property="password" />
                        </TD>
                      </TR>

                      <TR>
                        <TD height="69">
                          <html:submit value="  Submit "/>
```

```
                    </html:form>
                  </TD>
                </TR>

                <TR>
                  <TD height="69">
                    <html:form action="startregister">
                      <html:submit>Register</html:submit>
                    </html:form>
                  </TD>
                </TR>

                <TR>
                  <TD height="89">
                    <html:form action="about">
                      <html:submit value="  About   ">
                      </html:submit>
                    </html:form>
                  </TD>
                </TR>
              </TBODY>
            </TABLE>
          </TD>

          <TD height="100"
              width="80%"
              bgcolor="#cfe7e7"
              valign="top">
            <CENTER>
<H3>Welcome <bean:message key="oldfriends.highschool"/> Alumnus!</H3>
            </CENTER>
<BR><BR><H3 align="left">
We hope you enjoy YOUR Web site. Registration is free
(after all, you provide our content)! We provide this service
in order to help our alumni bridge the distances and rekindle
friendships. <BR><BR>

If you have already registered, please log in using the menu
on the left. If you are new to our site, please take the
time to register. Registered members have access to the
alumni directory, access to our souvenir shop, and many other
member privileges! <BR><BR>

Don't delay! Your long-lost schoolmates are
waiting to hear from you!<BR><BR>
</H3><BR><BR>
<H3 align="bottom">Copyright Old Friends Incorporated</H3>
            <html:errors/>
```

```
                </TD>
              </TR>
            </TBODY>
          </TABLE>
        </TD>
      </TR>
    </TBODY>
  </TABLE>
</BODY>
</HTML>
```

We have completed the construction of the major pieces of our initial screen for the Old Friends Incorporated application; we now need to take a look at how we glue them together. In other words, how does the Struts controller know which Action to invoke for a given request? This *gluing* (or *mapping*) of the actions is defined in the file `struts-config.xml` that can be found in the `WEB-INF` directory of the Web application. Here is a look at the complete `struts-config.xml` file:

```
<?xml version="1.0" encoding="ISO-8859-1" ?>

<!DOCTYPE struts-config PUBLIC
  "-//Apache Software Foundation//DTD Struts Configuration 1.1//EN"
  "http://jakarta.apache.org/struts/dtds/struts-config_1_1.dtd">

<struts-config>
  <!-- Form Bean Definitions ================================= -->
  <form-beans>
    <form-bean name ="oldfriendsForm" type="OldFriendsForm" />
    <form-bean name ="emptyForm" type="EmptyForm" />
    <form-bean name ="registerForm" type="RegisterForm" />
  </form-beans>

  <!-- Global Forward Definitions ========================== -->
  <global-forwards>
  </global-forwards>

  <!-- Action Mapping Definitions ============================-->
  <action-mappings>

  <action path="/about"
          type="EmptyAction"
          name="emptyForm">
    <forward name="Success" path="/about.jsp"/>
  </action>
```

```
<action path="/mainscreen"
        type="EmptyAction"
        name="emptyForm"
        validate="false"
        input="/register.jsp">
  <forward name ="Success" path="/index.jsp" />
</action>

<action path="/oldfriends"
        type="OldFriendsAction"
        name="oldfriendsForm"
        input="/index.jsp">
  <forward name ="main" path="/main.jsp" />
</action>

<action path="/startregister"
        type="EmptyAction"
        name="emptyForm"
        validate="false"
        input="/index.jsp">
  <forward name ="Success" path="/register.jsp" />
</action>

<action path="/registerform"
        type="RegisterAction"
        name="registerForm"
        validate="true"
        input="/register.jsp">
  <forward name ="main" path="/main.jsp" />
</action>

</action-mappings>
<message-resources parameter="ApplicationResources"/>

</struts-config>
```

Near the beginning of our configuration file, you will notice the section for our Form bean classes, which we list by itself here:

```
<!-- Form Bean Definitions ================================ -->
  <form-beans>
    <form-bean name ="oldfriendsForm" type="OldFriendsForm" />
    <form-bean name ="emptyForm" type="EmptyForm" />
    <form-bean name ="registerForm" type="RegisterForm" />
  </form-beans>
```

This snippet of XML describes the bean names for our action mappings and the accompanying class that contains the Form bean.

The other significant part of the configuration is the action mappings, an example of which follows:

```
<action path="/oldfriends"
  type="OldFriendsAction"
  name="oldfriendsForm"
  input="/index.jsp">
  <forward name ="main" path="/main.jsp" />
</action>
```

The Struts servlet uses the action mappings to determine how to handle a request. In the example above, the Struts servlet will handle a request for the URL ending with `oldfriends.do` by:

- Creating an instance of the OldFriendsForm class
- Populating it with the fields from the `input.jsp` page
- Sending it to the OldFriendsAction form

The OldFriendsAction form can then send the application on to `main.jsp` or back to `index.jsp`, depending on how it handles the content on the form.

There are a couple of other configuration files that we need to look at before launching our application. The `web.xml` file that was provided by the Struts-Blank project that we started with should be okay with no changes.

Next, we create the `ApplicationResources.properties` file in the classes directory. This file was specified in the following line that appears in the `struts-cfg.xml` file:

```
<message-resources parameter="ApplicationResources"/>
```

The file is a standard Java resource bundle and provides the message text that will be used in our application. The contents are shown below:

```
error.userid=<li>UserID is required.</li>
error.password=<li>Password is required.</li>
errors.header=<h3>Errors:</h3><ul>
errors.footer=</ul>
oldfriends.highschool=Mullins High School

error.register.useridpasswd=<li>UserId and Password are required.</li>
error.register.userfname=<li>First Name is required.</li>
error.register.userlname=<li>Last Name is required.</li>

errors.register.header=<h3>Errors:</h3><ul>
errors.register.footer=</ul>
```

Running the Application

Now, we are ready to launch our application! We invoke our application from our browser with the following URL:

```
http://localhost:8080/oldfriends
```

Figure 7.3 shows the resulting output of `index.jsp`. Let's examine what went on here. The Tomcat servlet container invoked `index.jsp` because it is configured in the welcome-file in `web.xml`. The first couple of lines in `index.jsp` are references to the Struts tag libraries, `struts-html.tld` and `struts-bean.tld`. The HTML tag libraries provide tags that can be used to provide basic functionality in the creation of HTML screens, such as forms, input fields, links, and so on. The bean tag libraries provide functionality for accessing the properties of Java Beans, and as we saw earlier, Java Beans are prevalent in the Struts architecture. You will notice that the declaration begins with `taglib uri=`, telling where the tag library descriptor is located; the `prefix=` simply tells us how we can reference the tags in our JSP.

```
<%@ taglib uri="/WEB-INF/struts-html.tld" prefix="html" %>
<%@ taglib uri="/WEB-INF/struts-bean.tld" prefix="bean" %>
```

The name of our organization, "Mullins High School" is not embedded in `index.jsp`. Instead, we make use of the `ApplicationResources.properties` file to define our organization.

```
oldfriends.highschool=Mullins High School
```

This allows us to repurpose the application for another school without making changes to the code. With the information stored the properties file, we can use the convenience of our bean tag libraries to extract it and insert it into our output, as shown below.

```
<TITLE><bean:message key="oldfriends.highschool"/></TITLE>
```

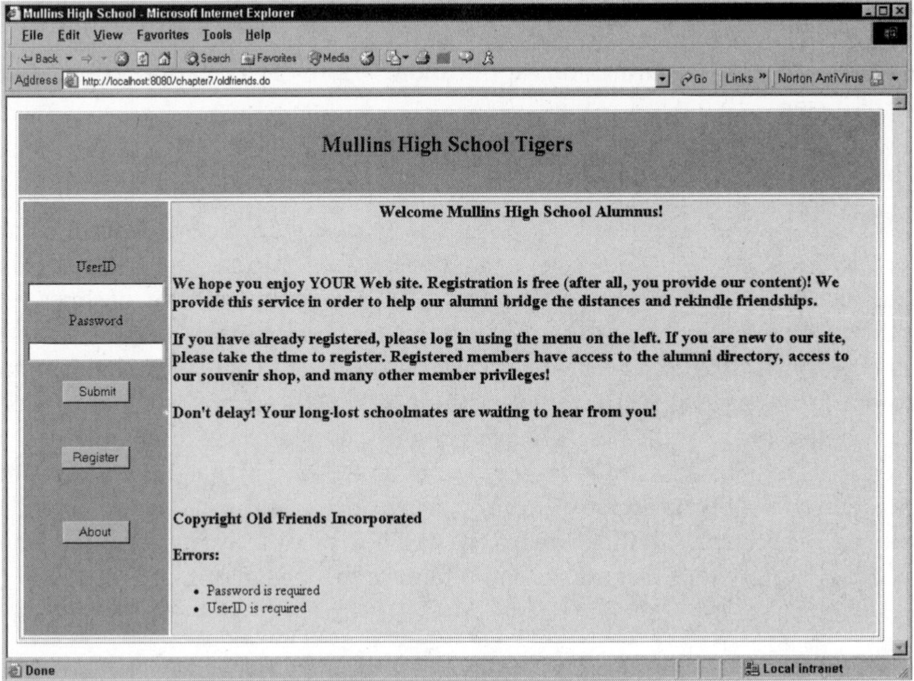

Figure 7.3 Old Friends Incorporated login screen with errors shown.

We have leveraged the Struts HTML tag libraries to construct the form:

```
<html:form action="oldfriends.do">
```

the input fields:

```
<html:text property="userID" />
<html:password property="password" />
```

and links for getting to other parts of our application (which we will look at later):

```
<html:form action="startregister.do">
  <html:submit> Register </html:submit>
</html:form>
```

Understanding Error Handling with Struts

New users need to register with Old Friends Incorporated before receiving services. Before we look at the registration form, let's examine the error-handling facility provided by the Struts framework. First, attempt to log into the site without a UserID or password defined by pressing the Submit button (this logic will eventually consult a security database of some sort and apply to invalid logins as well; however, we are just demonstrating basic Struts functionality for now).

Once again, let's drill down through the details of what the Struts framework is doing to trap this error condition. Following is the pertinent section of `index.jsp` that submits the form for processing:

```
<html:form action="oldfriends">
    .
    ... code skipped here ...
    .
<html:submit value=" Submit "/>
</html:form>
```

Our HTML taglib specifies "oldfriends" as an action for this form. This action generates a request for the relative URL `oldfriends.do`. Because of the servlet mapping in the `web.xml` file, the Struts ActionServlet handles all requests for URLs ending with ".do". The Struts ActionServlet uses the action mappings in the `struts-config.xml` to determine how to process the request. It finds the mapping for oldfriends (matching the URL pattern `oldfriends.do`) and processes that action. We show only the relevant parts of the `struts-config.xml` in the following code to help with the explanation.

```
<form-beans>
  <form-bean name ="oldfriendsForm" type="OldFriendsForm" />
</form-beans>

<action-mappings>
  <action path="/oldfriends"
    type="OldFriendsAction"
    name="oldfriendsForm"
    input="/index.jsp">
    <forward name ="main" path="/main.jsp" />
  </action>
</action-mappings>
```

The path attribute in the action mapping, informs the ActionServlet that requests for `oldfriends.do` will be handled by this action. The name attribute maps oldfriendsForm to the OldFriendsForm class listed as a form bean. This mapping provides flexibility when a single ActionForm class is used for handling multiple forms. The servlet creates an instance of the OldFriendsForm class and populates it with the data from the browser provided in the request. This population is accomplished by matching the property names of the form fields with corresponding get and set method names on the ActionForm class. The relevant tags from `index.jsp` are as follows:

```
<html:text property="userID" />
<html:password property="password" />
```

These names match the `setUserID()` and the `setPassword()` methods of the OldFriendsForm class. If the validate attribute is set for the action (it is by default), the servlet then attempts to validate the form by calling the `validate()` method of the form class. If the validation succeeds, then the servlet calls the execute method of the class defined in the type attribute of the action mapping. If the validation fails, the servlet forwards the request to the page defined by the input attribute and the action class never sees it. The `validate()` method of the OldFriendsForm class is shown below for convenience.

```
public ActionErrors validate(
  ActionMapping aMapping,
  HttpServletRequest aR)
{
  ActionErrors err = new ActionErrors();
  if(( mUserID == null ) || ( mUserID.length() < 1 ))
    err.add("userid", new ActionError("error.userid"));
  if(( mPassword == null ) || (mPassword.length() < 1))
    err.add("password", new ActionError("error.password"));
  return err;
}
```

You can see that the validation criteria we established earlier are tested against the data that came over from our request. Because we did not enter values for UserID and password, they both evaluate to null. The error messages `error.userid` and `error.password` are retrieved from the properties file we discussed earlier and then added to a list of errors before being returned to the controller.

A common error for new users is to omit the `errors.header` and `errors.footer` definitions in the properties. This results in <null> being displayed for the header when the <html:errors/> tag processes the error map. The relevant portion of `ApplicationResources.properties` is shown below:

```
error.userid=<li>UserID is required.</li>
error.password=<li>Password is required.</li>
errors.header=<h3>Errors:</h3><ul>
errors.footer=</ul>
```

Handling the Registration Form

Now that we have seen how the error processing works, let's examine how we handle the registration screen in Struts. As you may recall from our initial login screen, we provided a Register button to allow a user to register for the services of the site. Following is the relevant section of code from `index.jsp`:

```
<html:form action="startregister ">
  <html:submit> Register </html:submit>
</html:form>
```

Our tag specifies `startregister` as the action for this form. Even though we are not dealing with a form in the conventional sense, we use the <html:form> taglib to define the action for the Register button. The pertinent configuration associated with the `startregister` action is shown below for convenience.

```
<form-beans>
  <form-bean name ="registerForm" type="RegisterForm" />
</form-beans>

<action-mappings>
  <action path="/startregister"
          type="EmptyAction"
          name="emptyForm"
          validate="false"
          input="/index.jsp">
  <forward name ="Success" path="/register.jsp" />
  </action>
</action-mappings>
```

The above configuration tells the controller that when a request comes in from the browser for the URL `startregister.do`, the EmptyForm should be used to receive the form data. The EmptyForm class does nothing, and only exists to short-circuit ActionServlet in situations like this when we do not require form processing. The code for the EmptyForm class is as follows:

```
import org.apache.struts.action.*;

public final class EmptyForm extends ActionForm
{
}
```

We do not perform validation, so the servlet will send the request on to our action class, EmptyAction. In this case, the only action we need is to forward the request to our target JSP. The code for the action class is as follows:

```
import javax.servlet.*;
import javax.servlet.http.*;
import org.apache.struts.action.*;

public class EmptyAction extends Action
{

  public ActionForward execute(
  ActionMapping aMapping,
  ActionForm aForm,
  HttpServletRequest aRequest,
  HttpServletResponse aResponse)
  throws ServletException
  {
    return aMapping.findForward("Success");
  }
}
```

Again, our implementation of the Action class does nothing but forward to the Success view, which we see is configured for `register.jsp`.

Now that we have everything set up, go ahead and click the Register button and you should see the registration form, as shown in Figure 7.4.

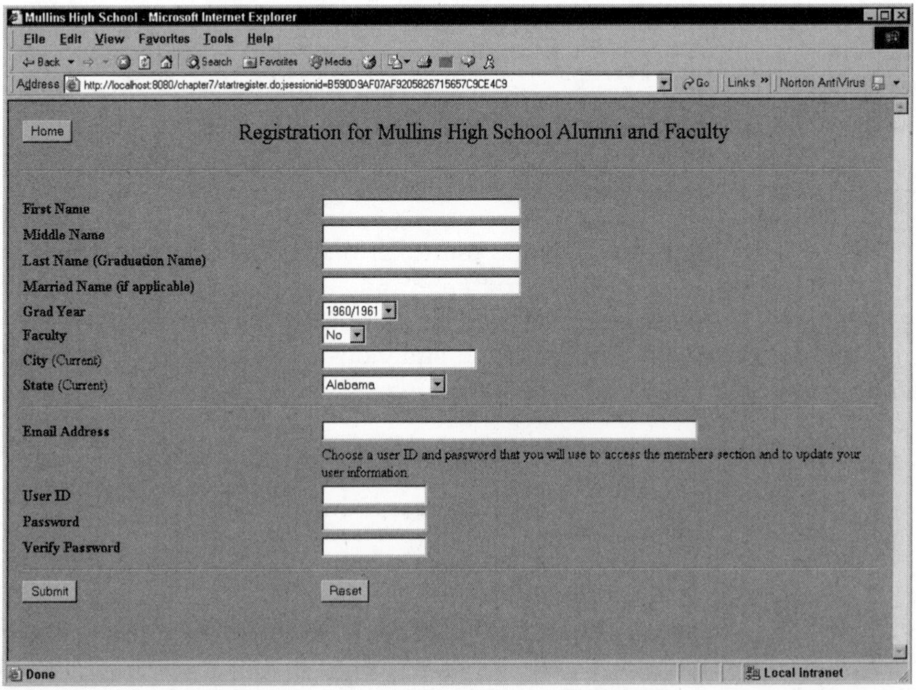

Figure 7.4 Registration form.

We now have an interface that we can use to collect registration information from our prospective members. Let's look at the code for `register.jsp` in order to look at the functionality.

```
<!DOCTYPE HTML PUBLIC "-//W3C//DTD HTML 4.0 Transitional//EN">
<HTML>
<HEAD>
<%@ taglib uri="/WEB-INF/struts-html.tld" prefix="html" %>
<%@ taglib uri="/WEB-INF/struts-bean.tld" prefix="bean" %>
<TITLE><bean:message key="oldfriends.highschool"/></TITLE>
</HEAD>
<BODY bgcolor="#999999">
<TABLE width="100%">
  <TBODY>
    <TR valign="top"><!-- row 2 -->
      <TD colspan="4">
      <TABLE border="0" width="100%">
        <COL span="1">
        <COL span="1" align="center">
        <TBODY>
          <TR valign="middle" align="center">
            <TD valign="bottom" align="left">
              <html:form action="/mainscreen">
                <html:submit>Home</html:submit>
              </html:form>
            </TD>

            <TD valign="top" align="center">
              <FONT size="5">Registration for
              <bean:message key="oldfriends.highschool"/>
              Alumnus and Faculty</FONT>
            </TD>
          </TR>
        </TBODY>
      </TABLE>

      <HR>
      <html:form action="registerform.do">
      <TABLE width="100%">
        <TBODY>
          <TR>
            <TD align="left" width="35%">
              <FONT size="3"><B>First Name</B></FONT>
            </TD>
            <TD width="65%">
              <INPUT size="30" type="text" name="FNAME">
             </TD>
          </TR>
```

```
<TR>
  <TD align="left" width="35%">
    <FONT size="3"><B>Middle Name</B></FONT>
  </TD>
  <TD width="65%">
    <INPUT size="30" type="text" name="MNAME">
  </TD>
</TR>

<TR>
  <TD width="35%">
    <FONT size="3"><B>Last Name (Graduation Name)</B></FONT>
  </TD>
  <TD width="65%">
    <INPUT size="30" type="text" name="LNAME">
  </TD>
</TR>

<TR>
  <TD width="35%">
    <FONT size="3"><B>Married Name (if applicable)</B></FONT>
  </TD>
  <TD width="65%">
    <INPUT size="30" type="text" name="MDNAME">
  </TD>
</TR>

<TR>
  <TD width="35%"><FONT size="3"><B>Grad Year</B></FONT></TD>
  <TD width="65%"><SELECT name="GRADYR">
    <OPTION selected>1960</OPTION>
    <OPTION>1960</OPTION>
    <OPTION>1970</OPTION>
    <OPTION>1980</OPTION>
    <OPTION>1990</OPTION>
    <OPTION>2000</OPTION>
    <OPTION>FACULTY</OPTION>
    <OPTION>N/A</OPTION>
  </SELECT></TD>
</TR>
<TR>
  <TD width="35%">
    <FONT size="3"><B>Faculty</B></FONT>
  </TD>
  <TD width="65%">
```

```
    <SELECT name="FACULTY">
      <OPTION>Yes</OPTION>
      <OPTION selected>No</OPTION>
    </SELECT>
  </TD>
</TR>

<TR>
  <TD width="35%">
    <FONT size="3">
      <B>City</B>
    </FONT> (Current)
  </TD>
  <TD width="65%">
    <INPUT size="23" type="text" name="CITY">
  </TD>
</TR>

<TR>
  <TD width="35%">
    <FONT size="3"><B>State</B></FONT> (Current)
  </TD>
  <TD width="65%"><SELECT name="STATE">
    <!-- Note: some states omitted for brevity -->
    <OPTION selected>Alabama</OPTION>
    <OPTION>Delaware</OPTION>
    <OPTION>District of Columbia</OPTION>
    <OPTION>Florida</OPTION>
    <OPTION>Georgia</OPTION>
    <OPTION>Kentucky</OPTION>
    <OPTION>Maryland</OPTION>
    <OPTION>Ohio</OPTION>
    <OPTION>Tennessee</OPTION>
    <OPTION>Virginia</OPTION>
    <OPTION>West Virginia</OPTION>
    <OPTION>Other</OPTION>
  </SELECT></TD>
</TR>

<TR>
  <TD colspan="2">
    <HR>
  </TD>
</TR>
```

```
<TR>
  <TD width="35%"></TD>
  <TD width="65%"></TD>
</TR>

<TR>
  <TD width="35%">
    <FONT size="3"><B>Email Address</B></FONT>
  </TD>
  <TD width="65%">
    <INPUT size="58" type="text" name="EMAIL">
  </TD>
</TR>

<TR>
  <TD width="35%"></TD>
  <TD width="65%">
    Choose a user ID and password that you will
    use to access the members section
    and to update your user information.
  </TD>
</TR>

<TR>
  <TD width="35%">
    <FONT size="3">
      <B>User ID</B>
    </FONT>
  </TD>
  <TD width="65%">
    <INPUT size="15" type="text" name="USERID">
  </TD>
</TR>

<TR>
  <TD width="35%">
    <FONT size="3"><B>Password</B></FONT>
  </TD>
  <TD width="65%">
    <INPUT size="15" type="password" name="PASSWD1">
  </TD>
</TR>

<TR>
  <TD width="35%">
    <FONT size="3">
      <B>Verify Password</B>
```

```
            </FONT>
          </TD>
          <TD width="65%">
            <INPUT size="15" type="password" name="PASSWD2">
          </TD>
        </TR>

        <TR>
          <TD colspan="2">
          <HR>
          </TD>
        </TR>

        <TR>
          <TD width="35%"><html:submit /></TD>
          <TD width="65%"><html:reset /></TD>
        </TR>
      </TBODY>
    </TABLE>
    </html:form>
    <html:errors/>
    </TD>
  </TR>
 </TBODY>
</TABLE>
</BODY>
</HTML>
```

From a brief inspection of the preceding source code, we see that when our form is submitted, the HTML taglib specifies the action `registerform`. The action mapping follows for convenience.

```
<action path="/registerform"
    type="RegisterAction"
    name="registerForm"
    validate="true"
    input="/register.jsp">
    <forward name ="main" path="/main.jsp" />
</action>
```

Our registration form will be validated with the registerForm form bean, which is mapped to the RegisterForm class instance. The `validate()` method will be invoked because the validate attribute is set to `true`, and if an error occurs, control will be transferred back to the `register.jsp` view. The code for the RegisterForm class is shown below:

```
import javax.servlet.http.*;
import org.apache.struts.action.*;

public class RegisterForm extends ActionForm
{
  private String mFName = null;
  private String mMName = null;
  private String mLName = null;
  private String mMDName = null;
  private String mGradYear = null;
  private String mFaculty = null;
  private String mCity = null;
  private String mState = null;
  private String mEmail = null;
  private String mUserID = null;
  private String mPasswd1 = null;
  private String mPasswd2 = null;

  public String getFNAME()
  {
    return mFName;
  }
  public void setFNAME(String aFName)
  {
    mFName = aFName;
  }

  public String getMNAME()
  {
    return mMName;
  }
  public void setMNAME(String aMName)
  {
    mMName = aMName;
  }

  public String getLNAME()
  {
    return mLName;
  }
  public void setLNAME(String aLName)
  {
    mLName = aLName;
  }

  public String getMDName()
  {
    return mMDName;
  }
  public void setMDName(String aMDName)
```

```
{
  mMDName = aMDName;
}

public String getmGradYR()
{
  return mGradYear;
}
public void setGradYR(String aGradYR)
{
  mGradYear = aGradYR;
}

public String getFaculty()
{
  return mFaculty;
}
public void setFaculty(String aFaculty)
{
  mMName = aFaculty;
}

public String getCity()
{
  return mCity;
}

public void setCity(String aCity)
{
  mCity = aCity;
}

public String getState()
{
  return mState;
}
public void setState(String aState)
{
  mState = aState;
}

public String getEmail()
{
  return mEmail;
}
public void setEmail(String aEmail)
{
  mEmail = aEmail;
}
```

```
    public String getUSERID()
    {
      return mUserID;
    }
    public void setUSERID(String aUserID)
    {
      mUserID = aUserID;
    }

    public String getPASSWD1()
    {
      return mPasswd1;
    }
    public void setPASSWD1(String aPasswd)
    {
      mPasswd1 = aPasswd;
    }

    public String getPASSWD2()
    {
      return mPasswd2;
    }

    public void setPASSWD2(String aPasswd2)
    {
      mPasswd2 = aPasswd2;
    }

    public ActionErrors validate(
    ActionMapping aMapping,
    HttpServletRequest aR)
    {
      ActionErrors err = new ActionErrors();
      if ((mUserID == null) || (mUserID.length() < 1))
        err.add("useridpasswd",
          new ActionError("error.register.useridpasswd"));
      if ((mFName == null) || (mFName.length() < 1))
        err.add("userfname",
          new ActionError("error.register.userfname"));
      if ((mLName == null) || (mLName.length() < 1))
        err.add("userlname",
          new ActionError("error.register.userlname"));
      return err;
    }

    public void reset(ActionMapping aMapping, HttpServletRequest aR)
    {
      mUserID = null;
      mPasswd1 = null;
    }
  }
```

The RegisterAction class would normally invoke the application and business logic in the underlying application layers. In this simple case, all we do is populate the login information. Normally, we would update a database or perform some other operation on the data. A more complete example of this is provided in Chapter 14. The code for the RegisterAction class follows:

```
import javax.servlet.*;
import javax.servlet.http.*;
import org.apache.struts.action.*;

public class RegisterAction extends Action
{

  public ActionForward execute(
  ActionMapping aMapping,
  ActionForm aForm,
  HttpServletRequest aRequest,
  HttpServletResponse aResponse)
  throws ServletException
  {
    RegisterForm f = (RegisterForm) aForm;
    String userid = f.getUSERID();
    String password = f.getPASSWD1();
    return aMapping.findForward("main");
  }
}
```

Upon successful processing of the form and the business model, the Action class forwards to the main view (shown in Figure 7.5), which we saw from the action mapping above is `main.jsp`.

```
<%@ taglib uri="/WEB-INF/struts-html.tld" prefix="html" %>
<%@ taglib uri="/WEB-INF/struts-bean.tld" prefix="bean" %>
<!DOCTYPE HTML PUBLIC "-//W3C//DTD HTML 4.0 Transitional//EN">
<HTML>
<HEAD>
<TITLE></TITLE>
</HEAD>

<BODY BGCOLOR="#FFFFFF">
  <TABLE border="1" width="100%" height="100%">
    <TBODY>
      <TR>
        <TD></TD>
        <TD></TD>
        <TD></TD>
      </TR>

      <TR>
        <TD></TD>
```

```
          <TD align="center">
            <H2>Welcome
            <bean:write name="registerForm" property="FNAME"/>
            <bean:write name="registerForm" property="LNAME"/>
            to<BR> OLD FRIENDS INCORPORATED</H2><BR>
          </TD>
          <TD></TD>
        </TR>

        <TR>
          <TD></TD>
          <TD></TD>
          <TD></TD>
        </TR>
      </TBODY>
    </TABLE>
  </BODY>
  </HTML>
```

An interesting feature to note, and the hallmark of the MVC architecture, is the way we are able to pull data from our ActionForm. The `bean:write` taglib is used to place the users first and last name on the main screen by leveraging the getter methods that are exposed in our ActionForm bean.

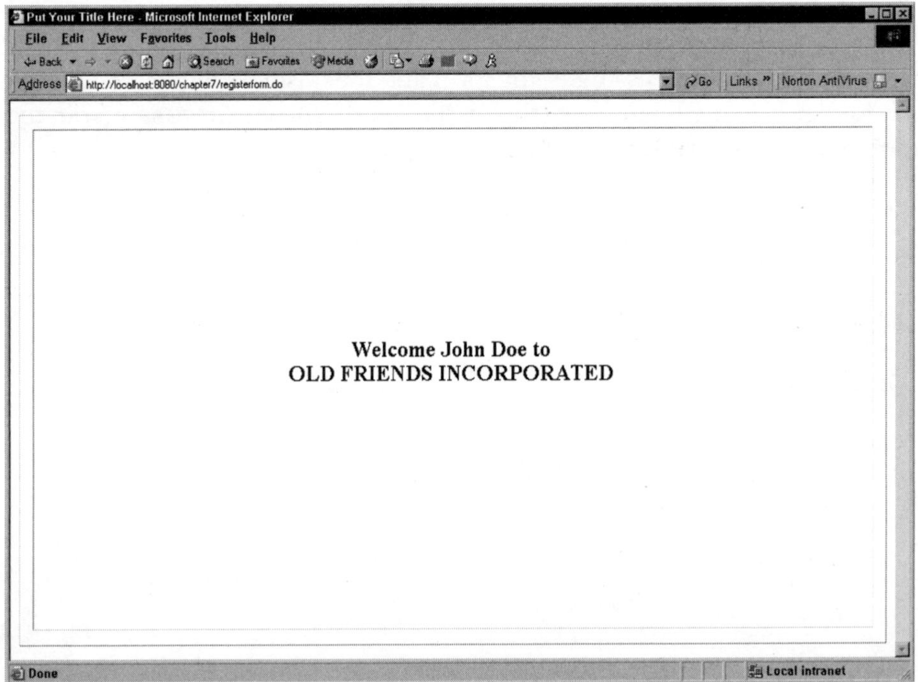

Figure 7.5 Main screen.

Summary

The Model-View-Controller design pattern is one of the primary application design patterns in use today for Java-based Web-application development. Web-application frameworks provide standardized implementations of the MVC design pattern. Using a framework reduces errors and improves the application's quality, while allowing developers to focus on the project-specific needs of the application.

In this chapter, we briefly examined four different application frameworks and selected Struts as the framework to use within our platform. The decision to use Struts was based on the popularity of Struts and its relatively short learning curve. Finally, we created a sample Web application to gain a better understanding at how the Struts framework operates.

Building the Infrastructure

While it is possible to build application using only servlets, JSPs, and the technologies presented in the previous section, most enterprise-class applications benefit from being built upon a robust infrastructure. In this part, we look at open source tools to build that infrastructure. We start by looking at databases and messaging systems, then we examine open source implementations of Enterprise Java Bean containers and show how to publish Web services using open source tools. Finally, we demonstrate some of the open source tools available for working with XML documents.

CHAPTER

8

Managing Data Using JDBC and Databases

Any application of reasonable complexity needs to have a means of organizing and storing information. A database provides a repository for information, allowing the information to be organized and accessed efficiently. Although there are several types and forms of databases, over the years the relational database has emerged as the workhorse of the software industry. Today, the relational database is the foundation for most enterprise applications. Thus, when we refer to a database in this chapter, we will always be discussing relational databases.

For Java to be useful as an enterprise language, Java must be able to access data from relational databases. The JDBC API (Java Database Connectivity application programming interface) was created to provide the ability for Java programs to access relational databases in a uniform and consistent manner. Most modern databases provide Java support via a JDBC driver. A number of relational database products have also been created in the Java language. This chapter looks at open source Java databases and other open source databases that support JDBC connections.

Databases and the Platform Architecture

The database can be thought of as the base layer for all enterprise applications. It is where data is stored and organized to create information. Relational databases, the most commonly used type of database, are normally "back-end" components along with other enterprise systems. Figure 8.1 shows databases existing in the bottom, or enterprise, tier of a platform.

JDBC also resides in the back end; however, JDBC provides the connection between the components in the higher tiers to the databases.

Relational Databases

Relational database theory is based on the mathematics of relational algebra. A relational database can be thought of as a collection of tables. Each table has a set of columns and rows. Each row within a table shares the same set of columns as all of the other rows within that table. The columns define the type of data that can be found within the corresponding column of a row. The rows themselves represent the individual records of information within the database.

Table 8.1 below illustrates these points. This might represent a table in a database supporting the Old Friends Incorporated Reunion application that we described in Chapter 3. Each column is associated with a name and a data type. Columns like FIRSTNAME and LASTNAME are character based, VISIT_COUNT is numeric, and LAST_VISIT represents a date.

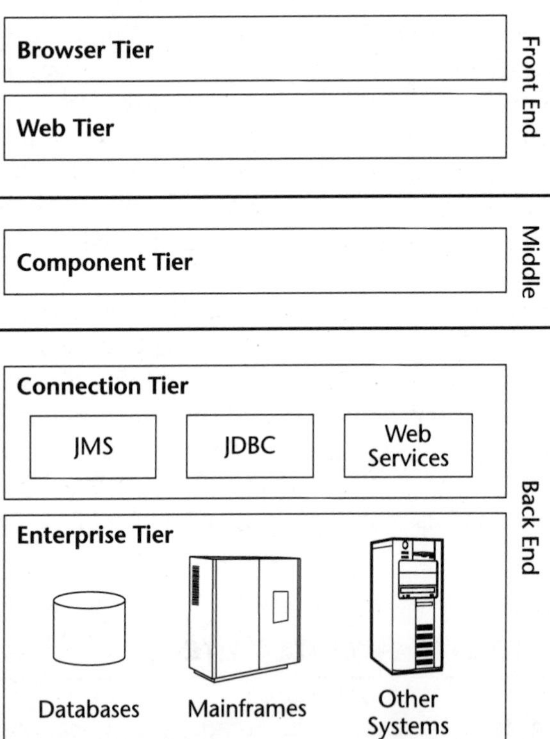

Figure 8.1 Databases in the enterprise tier.

Table 8.1 Sample Database Table

USER_KEY (INTEGER)	LOGIN_ID (CHAR)	FIRSTNAME (CHAR)	LASTNAME (CHAR)	VISIT_COUNT (INTEGER)	LAST_VISIT (DATE/TIME)
1	jdoe@someisp.com	John	Doe	1	1/2/03
2	jdough@someisp.com	Jane	Dough	2	3/31/03
3	jsmith@someisp.com	John	Smith	1	2/2/03

Each record in a table should be unique. In the example, we use the USER_KEY column as the unique identifier. (In this case, we could have also used the LOGIN_ID column because it too should be unique). This unique identifier is known as the *primary key*. The primary key uniquely identifies a specific individual row in the table. Any specific individual record or row of a table can be selected using its primary key.

Table 8.2 illustrates a table that might be used to track login history. It uses VISIT_KEY as a primary key. It also has a column for the USER_KEY. In this case, USER_KEY is a foreign key. By using the primary key from the user table and the foreign key of the history table a *relationship* can be established between the two tables. In this case, we have a one-to-many relationship. Each user may have many visits, but each visit is associated with exactly one user.

In this example, the user identified with the USER_KEY value of 2 (Jane Dough) has logged into the application twice, most recently on March 31.

This example demonstrates a simple one-to-many relationship between two tables. Relational databases also support one-to-one and many-to-many relationships between tables. By using a third table that has a separate one-to-many relationship with each of two other tables a many-to-many relationship can be created between the two tables. Although the proof is beyond the scope of this text, it can be demonstrated that relations between tables can be used to describe any arbitrarily complex structuring of data.

SQL

Most relational database products available today use a standardized language for manipulating the data within a database. This language is known as the Structured Query Language, or SQL (often pronounced as "sequel"). Although the SQL language is standardized, most implementations conform only to a subset of the complete standard language known as SQL-2 Entry Level. The subset serves as a least common denominator between most database products. The databases then create their own extension beyond this standardized subset. In practice, this means that each dialect of SQL is slightly different, although the basic syntax remains the same.

Table 8.2 Visit Table

VISIT_KEY (INTEGER)	USER_KEY (INTEGER)	VISIT_DATE (DATE/TIME)
1	1	01/02/03
2	2	01/15/03
3	3	02/02/03
4	2	03/31/03

There are three primary parts to SQL:

DDL. Data Definition Language

DML. Data Manipulation Language

DCL. Data Control Language

The DDL provides commands that are used to create, modify, and remove tables in the database. Some typical DDL commands include:

CREATE TABLE. Creates a new table in the database

ALTER TABLE. Makes changes to an existing database table

DROP TABLE. Removes a table from the database

The DML provides commands to retrieve records, insert new records, and change and delete existing records within the tables of a database. Typical DML commands include:

SELECT. Selects rows of data for viewing or processing

INSERT. Inserts new rows of data into a table

UPDATE. Modifies existing rows of data

DELETE. Deletes rows of data from a table

The DCL provides commands that control access to the database or data within the database. Typical DCL commands are:

CONNECT. Makes a connection to a database

GRANT. Gives access privileges to database users

REVOKE. Removes user access privileges

The commands listed above are just a representative set of commands from each group. The actual commands available will vary from database product to database product. The syntax for these commands also varies somewhat from database to database. We recommend that you become familiar with the specific dialect of SQL required for the target database.

JDBC helps to isolate some differences between dialects. JDBC drivers convert SQL statements made in the JDBC-supported subset into the dialect supported by the target database.

Transactions

Most databases need to support transactions. *Transactions* ensure data integrity during complex database changes. An easy example to consider is moving money from one bank account to another, as illustrated in Figure 8.2.

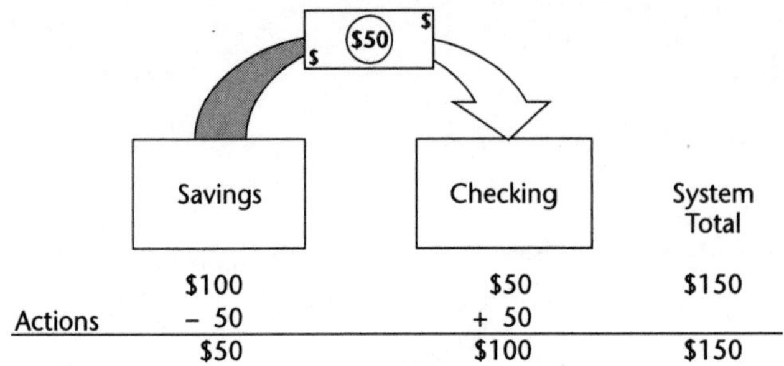

Figure 8.2 Moving money between accounts.

Say for example, that there is $100 in your savings account and you want to move $50 into your checking account. This requires two separate operations, removing $50 from savings and then depositing it into checking. When the operations are complete, you should have $50 less in savings and $50 more in checking. If either operation fails, the system is wrong and out of balance. For example, if the removal of the $50 from savings succeeds but adding it to checking fails, you're short $50. If the removal fails instead, but you still add $50 to checking, the bank is out $50. (Although you might not mind that, the bank would certainly be unhappy). In short, in order to keep everyone happy and to keep the system in a balanced, or consistent, state, both actions must succeed or both must fail. This is the basic requirement for a transaction.

Transactions enforce four rules, known as the ACID properties, for each letter of the acronym:

A. Atomic property ensures that actions all succeed or fail as a group within a transaction.

C. Consistent property states that the system will be in a consistent state both before the transaction begins and after it is completed.

I. Isolated property ensures that one transaction does not affect other transactions as they are occurring.

D. Durable property ensures that once a transaction has been completed it is permanent.

In some dialects of SQL, transactions can be marked with a BEGIN TRANSACTION statement prior to the statements that will be incorporated within the transaction. At the end of the transaction a COMMIT keyword is used to complete the transaction. If the transaction cannot be completed, the ROLLBACK keyword is used to reverse the actions that make up the transaction.

The java.sql.Connection interface provides several methods for handling transactions. We will briefly examine four of these:

```
java.sql.connection.setAutoCommit( boolean )
java.sql.connection.getAutoCommit( boolean )
```

```
java.sql.connection.commit()
java.sql.connection.rollback()
```

The `get` and `set AutoCommit` methods determine the transactional behavior of each statement submitted to the database. With `AutoCommit` set to `true`, (the default) each statement is included in its own transaction. With `AutoCommit` set to `false`, each statement is included in a single transaction until either the `commit()` method is invoked completing the transaction (and starting the next one) or the `rollback()` method is invoked, aborting the transaction.

JDBC

JDBC is the Java Database Connectivity API. JDBC allows Java programs to connect to and access any database supporting a JDBC driver. Although JDBC is traditionally used to access relational databases, a JDBC driver can be created to access almost any information that is organized in a tabular format.

A JDBC Driver that is compliant with the JDBC standard must support the ANSI 92 SQL-2 Entry Level standard commands. This ensures that it will be possible to write database code that is not dependent on the underlying database platform. However, this also means that the code will not be able to leverage any of the advanced features of a specific database and maintain that portability. On the bright side, JDBC allows any command to be passed into the database engine. The command is not even required to be a SQL command. This allows JDBC to be used with proprietary extensions even at the cost of portability.

There are basically four types of JDBC drivers: Type 1 through Type 4.

- The Type 1 driver is the JDBC to ODBC (Open DataBase Connectivity) bridge. This was an early driver designed to leverage the availability of the existing set of ODBC drivers. Type 1 drivers are normally very slow and are drivers of last resort.
- Type 2 drivers are essentially Java wrappers around native database interfaces. The Type 2 driver converts JDBC calls into native database API function calls using JNI (Java Native Interface). Type 2 drivers are no longer very common.
- Type 3 drivers are pure Java drivers that use a middleware component to translate JDBC calls to a database-generic communication protocol. The middleware then converts this to the specific protocol required by the target database.
- A Type 4 driver is a native Java driver designed specifically to interact with the target database. Now that JDBC has matured, Type 4 drivers are the most common.

Connections

A JDBC driver provides a connection to a database for a Java program. The connection is the means that Java uses to interact with the database. The following code fragment illustrates one way of making a connection to a supported database using JDBC:

```
Class.forName("org.hsqldb.jdbcDriver");
conn = DriverManager.getConnection(
  "jdbc:hsqldb:c:/openjava/hsqldb/data/hsqltest",
  "sa",
  "");
```

This example loads the driver for the HsqlDb database. The following line loads the JDBC driver into the JVM:

```
Class.forName("org.hsqldb.jdbcDriver");
```

The DriverManager then uses the driver to get a connection. The `getConnection` method of the DriverManager class requires three arguments, a connection URL for the database, a username, and a password. The URL follows the same basic rules as a URL that would be used for the Internet.

```
jdbc:hsqldb:c:/openjava/hsqldb/data/hsqltest
```

The `jdbc:` portion of this string is the protocol (exactly as `http:` is the protocol in a URL requesting a Web page). The `hsqldb:` portion of the string is the sub-protocol. The DriverManger looks for a loaded JDBC driver that understands the requested subprotocol. After the subprotocol is the subname. The subname provides information to the driver that is needed to connect a specific driver to a specific database. In this case the subname represents the absolute path to a database file on a file system. The subname information and how it is formatted within the string is driver specific and varies from driver to driver. The subname may, for instance, include information needed to make a network connection to the database, such as machine name and port. For this reason, most programs to not code the string directly but instead read the connection strings from parameter files or some other configuration technique. Reading the string as a parameter allows connection to other database instances without recompiling the program.

Connections, DataSources, JNDI, and Pooling

As JDBC evolved, the awkwardness of using the previously demonstrated means for obtaining connections in server-side programs became more apparent. The previous connection process requires registering a specific driver class by name at run time. It also requires driver-specific URL strings. Furthermore, the URL strings are often specific to a particular installation because database resources may be located on differing machines using different connection parameters throughout an organization. Every program written this way needs a means to manage and modify the connection information. JDBC 2.0 addressed many of these concerns by introducing the concept of the DataSource.

A DataSource is a factory for creating database connections. By a factory we mean that a DataSource is an implementation of the factory design pattern. A DataSource is an implementation of the javax.sql.DataSource interface. The vendor (creator) of the JDBC driver normally implements DataSources specifically for the driver and provides it as part of the driver. The properties of a DataSource object can be modified as needed. If a database is moved to another server (or if you want to use a different database for testing for example), the properties specific to that DataSource can be changed. Any code accessing the DataSource does not need to be changed.

There are three types of DataSource implementations

- A Basic implementation provides a standard connection.
- A Connection Pooling implementation that provides a connection from a cache or pool of connections. This will be discussed in more detail later in this section.
- A Distributed Transaction implementation, which creates a connection suitable for distributed transactions.

DataSources are designed for use with the Java Naming and Directory Interface (JNDI). The DataSource is configured within the JNDI provider and bound to a JNDI name. The code for getting a database connection from a DataSource normally looks similar to the following:

```
Context ctx = new InitialContext();
DataSource ds = (DataSource)ctx.lookup("jdbc/TestDataSource");
Connection con = ds.getConnection("sa", "");
```

This gets a connection just as in the previous example that did not use a DataSource; however, in this case, the Java program is not required to know any of the specifics of the database other than the user ID and password. Everything else has been configured in JNDI. Each DataSource configured in JNDI represents a database that can be accessed by the program. (We will cover configuring DataSources later in the chapter).

The lookup method of the context retrieves a resource by looking up the name bound to the resource. JNDI supports a hierarchical structure to names similar to a file system. In this case the name is TestDataSource. By convention, the name is contained in the "jdbc" subcontext of JNDI. A subcontext is like a folder in a file system. The jdbc subcontext is normally found immediately below the JNDI root context.

The resource returned by the lookup method is a generic object that must be converted or cast as the DataSource interface so that it can be used. After the DataSource has been retrieved, the program can get a database connection from the DataSource interface.

The pooled DataSource is another type of DataSource implementation. A pooled DataSource stores connections in a pool. A *pool* is similar to a cache. Unlike a cache, however, a pool is normally prepopulated with a number of items. The items are handed out from the pool when requested. If there are no longer any items available in the pool, then either the pool adds more items or it fails.

In the case of DataSources, connections are handed out from a pool of premade connections. This represents a significant performance increase when databases connections are needed frequently by several threads or processes. For example, in a servlet environment, a servlet can request a connection from a pool (often managed by the servlet container) instead of directly opening the database connection. The pool is initialized and connections made when the servlet container starts. This makes connections instantly available to servlets that need them. Closing the connection automatically restores the connection to the pool.

NOTE The connection itself is not normally closed, but remains open for the next time a connection is needed from the pool.

Beyond SQL Entry-Level Commands

JDBC also requires support for certain nonstandard extensions beyond those supported by the minimal ANSI standard. In order to use these extensions, JDBC defines a standard "escape" clause that is used to provide information directly to the JDBC driver. The driver uses this information to build the database-specific command. The syntax for the escape is:

```
{keyword ... parameters ... }
```

where `keyword` is the name of the command or function, and the parameters are specific to the specific command.

SERVLETS AND CONNECTION POOLS

Normally a servlet that needs database connections should get the connections from within the appropriate `doPost` or `doGet` method and not during the `init` of the servlet. These connections come from the DataSource pool implemented by the container and should always be closed (returned to the pool) before exiting the servlet method.

However, the DataSource itself is normally retrieved during the servlets `init` method because the InitialContext and DataSource lookups are only needed once. After the DataSource has been retrieved, it can be reused many times to provide connections from the connection pool.

Java Databases

We treat Java databases separately from other databases because open source pure Java databases are not as mature or as powerful as the non-Java databases. However, the Java databases do offer some advantages for the Java programmer. The Java databases are platform independent and easily run the system being used for development. The databases also tend to be small, making it easy to directly incorporate or embed the database as part of the application. Their small size, however, does not mean they are limited in the size of the database that they can handle. Most of these databases can handle files that are large enough for many applications. Some Java databases offer a feature allowing the data within the database to be completely stored in random access memory (RAM). This is great for performance but may cause problems if the system goes down before the disk files are written. This feature would normally be used for small very high-speed read-only database applications.

Survey of Open Source Java Databases

Our survey of open source Java databases comes up with quite a number of products. Many of these, however, are no longer being maintained. By using the most recent release date as a discriminator and checking the activity on the mailing lists, we can narrow the choices down to three products.

Axion

Axion is a product of Tigris.org. Tigris is the same open source community that brings us the Subversion products discussed in Chapter 4. Axion is a relational database system written in Java and described as being a "lightweight, scalable, modular, and complete relational database." The following table provides a brief overview of Axion.

Product	Axion
Category	Java database
URL	http://axion.tigris.org/
Supported Platforms	JDK 1.2
License	Other OSI-certified license
Features	Embedded Java database with support for file- or memory-based tables

At this time, Axion seems to be the least mature of all of the Java database products that we cover in this section. Although it can be a useful product in situations where memory is a concern, the other products have more features. We hope that this situation will change as the Axion project moves forward.

The Axion project has submitted a proposal to become part of the newly formed `http://db.apache.org`. If the proposal is accepted, then it is likely that Axion will mature quickly as its visibility to the open source community is increased. Axion has a number of dependencies on Apache projects already. In order to install and run Axion, you must also install two .jar files from the Jakarta Commons project.

To install Axion, download the current distribution from Tigris.org and decompress the file into a subdirectory. You will also need to download the following files:

- `commons-collections.jar`
- `commons-logging.jar`

These files can be downloaded from the Jakarta Commons project at `http://jakarta.apache.org/commons`.

Entering the following command for Windows starts Axion:

```
java -cp axiondb.jar;commons-collections.jar;commons-logging.jar \
org.axiondb.Axion dbname [dbpath]
```

The command is the same for Linux, except for replacing the classpath separator with colons as follows:

```
java -cp axiondb.jar:commons-collections.jar:commons-logging.jar \
org.axiondb.Axion dbname [dbpath]
```

The parameter `dbname` is the name of the database that will be opened or created. This name is used to reference the database using the JDBC driver. The optional parameter `dbpath` is for persistent or disk-based databases. It provides the filename and path for the database.

Axion provides a simple command-line interface that accepts SQL commands. Axion also supports access by those using products such as Squirrel (discussed later in this chapter). However, Axion currently only works as an embedded database and does not have a server mode. This essentially limits Axion databases to access by a single JVM at a time. This may not be an issue for applications that need to embed a database into a servlet environment or a standalone Java application, but for many purposes this is too restricting.

HSqlDb

HSqlDb is the continuation of Thomas Mueller's Hypersonic database. Thomas Mueller originally created the popular Java database and brought it up to version 1.43. The original product was used in a number of other open source projects such as the Jakarta Turbine and Jetspeed portal projects. When Mr. Mueller decided to abandon the project, a number of people jumped in and created the HSqlDb project on SourceForge.net. This project now represents a true example of the value of open source community. The project has moved from a single developer to a group of developers and has matured considerably under this new group. HSqlDb now represents one of the best Java-based open source database products around. A summary appears in the following table.

Product	HSqlDb
Category	Java database
URL	http://hsqldb.sourceforge.net/
Supported Platforms	JDK 1.2 and later; many Java environments are supported (see text)
License	BSD-based
Features	In memory- and disk-based databases, transaction support, JDBC 2.0 (and partial 3.0) support, embedded, standalone, server, and HTTP server modes

Like Axion, HSqlDb offers support for both in memory- (transient) and disk-based (persistent) databases. HSqlDb is small and suitable for embedded environments. However, HSqlDb has a number of advanced features that don't exist in Axion.

HSqlDb Features

HSqlDb supports two modes of operation, in process and client/server. In process mode allows HSqlDb to be run as a standalone database, embedded inside a Java product. Calls to the database are handled as function calls and do not require a network connection. This mode limits access to an HSqlDb database to one application at a time. HSqlDb also offers a client/server (or just server for short) mode. In server mode HSqlDb runs in its own JVM. A JDBC client connects to the database using a network connection. As a server, HSqlDb supports database access by multiple applications simultaneously.

Server mode is available using two protocols. One protocol is unique to HSqlDb, but is very efficient. The JDBC driver understands this protocol, so the details of the protocol implementation are not important for most developers. The other supported protocol is HTTP. HTTP is, of course, the protocol used for the World Wide Web. The HSqlDb HTTP server is not designed to serve HTML files or for use as a Web server. It is actually designed so that an HSqlDb client can access a database server even if the server is located behind a firewall or proxy. This Web-server mode does has some limitations, most important of which is that transactions are not currently supported.

HSqlDb supports a wide variety of Java environments. In order to do this efficiently, it provides a build tool called Code Switcher. Code Switcher acts in a similar fashion to the C or C++ preprocessor, except that it only serves to comment and uncomment out blocks of Java code. This allows HSqlDb to be built to support the more recent versions of Java and also support earlier versions from the same code base. The binary distribution presently supports the 1.3 JDK by default but source code can be easily rebuilt to support the 1.1 JDK by using Code Switcher.

If you attempt to open a database that does not exist, HSqlDb automatically creates a database for you. The following code fragment provides an example of how to create and connect to a HSqlDb database.

```
Connection conn = null;
try
{
  Class.forName("org.hsqldb.jdbcDriver").newInstance();
  conn = DriverManager.getConnection(
    "jdbc:hsqldb:c:/openjava/hsqldb/data/hsqltest", "sa", "");
}
catch (Exception e)
{
  e.printStackTrace();
}
```

The URL in the above example will create a database in the `c:/openjava/hsqldb/data` directory that will be named `hsqltest`. By default HSqlDb tables are created in memory. By providing a filename for the database, the memory-based database is persisted, or saved to disk. As the database is modified a transaction log of SQL commands is written to disk as a script file. When the database is reloaded, this script is executed to automatically reload the memory-based database.

The database would not be saved to disk if the URL parameter had been specified as:

```
jdbc:hsqldb:.
```

This default behavior of memory-based tables being rebuilt through transaction logs can be modified on a table-by-table basis. Each table can be stored as a data file or as a comma-delimited text file. Unfortunately, this behavior can't be configured but is accessed through specialized commands. The syntax for the `CREATE TABLE` command in HSqlDb is:

```
CREATE [ MEMORY | CACHED | TEMP | TEXT ] TABLE name
( columnDefinition [, ...] [, constraintDefinition...]);
```

An example for a normal command for creating a table in a SQL database is:

```
CREATE TABLE USERS(
  ID INTEGER PRIMARY KEY,
  USERID VARCHAR(32),
  PASSWD VARCHAR*(32)
);
```

In HSqlDb, this will create, by default, an in-memory table that is automatically regenerated from a SQL script each time the database is started. In order to create a disk-based table, the command needs to be modified by adding the keyword `CACHE` between `CREATE` and `TABLE` as follows:

```
CREATE CACHE TABLE USERS(
  ID INTEGER PRIMARY KEY,
  USERID VARCHAR(32),
  PASSWD VARCHAR(32)
);
```

Now, the table will be disk-based but caching will be used to improve performance. Replacing the keyword CACHE with the keyword TEXT creates the table on disk as a comma-delimited file. A comma-delimited file is a file of comma-separated values (CSV), where each column is separated from the others by a comma. The CSV file format is a common means of exchanging data between applications, and the files can be read directly by many products—for example, Microsoft's Excel spreadsheet program.

MEMORY and TEMP keywords are also supported. MEMORY is used for explicitly creating a memory-based table (the default behavior) that is reloaded automatically from a script file. The TEMP keyword is for creating a memory-based table, but this table is not recreated and a script file is not maintained.

Although these commands reflect a powerful ability to create a mixture of storage types within the database, not being able to determine a default behavior in the absence of a keyword limits script portability.

Installing and Running HSqlDb

HSqlDb is installed simply by downloading and decompressing the binary distribution file. HSqlDb provides a manager utility that can be used test the database installation. From the data subdirectory, launch the HSqlDb Manager application using the following command:

```
java -classpath ..\lib\hsqldb.jar org.hsqldb.util.DatabaseManager
```

The dialog box shown in Figure 8.3 prompts you for the database connection information. The default arguments create a temporary memory-based database. Replacing the URL string with `jdbc:hsqldb:hsqltest`, as shown in the figure creates (or opens if the database has already been created) a database named "hsqltest" in the current directory.

The manager application is a useful tool and can be used with other JDBC-supported databases as well. The tool provides a means to quickly generate a test database by choosing Options ➪ Insert Test Data. After this has been done, the manager application shows the structure of the database in the left pane, as shown in Figure 8.4.

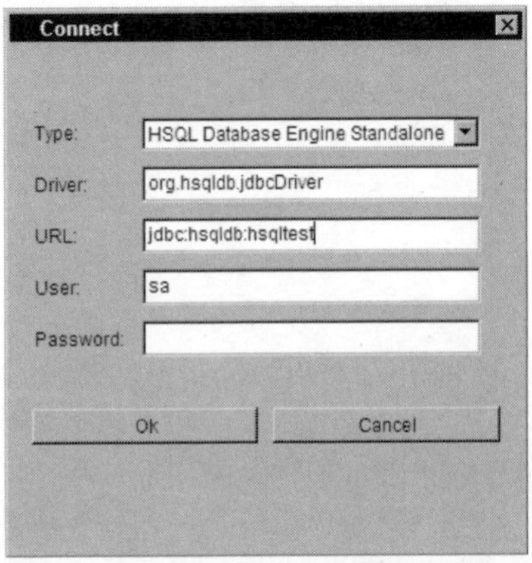

Figure 8.3 HSqlDb manager application Connect dialog box.

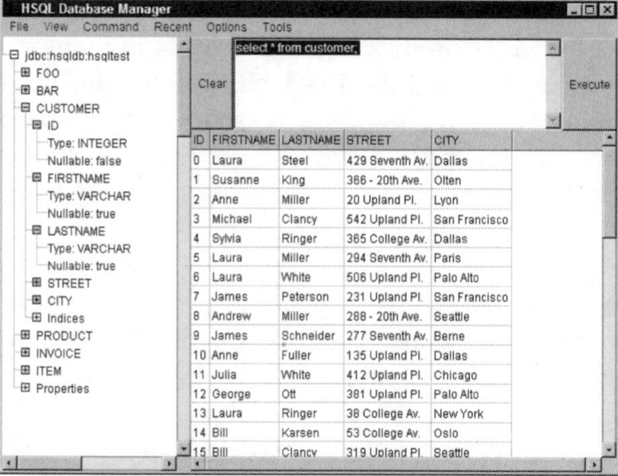

Figure 8.4 HSqlDb manager application.

The manager application provides a tool for building and executing database commands. The results are displayed in the pane on the right side below the text box that allows entering and editing commands. Entering the following SQL command and clicking the Execute button displays a list of the test data loaded into the customer database.

```
SELECT * FROM CUSTOMER
```

McKoi

McKoi is an open source Java database released by Diehl and Associates, Inc. under the Gnu Public License. McKoi is not a part of a larger open source project or community but seems to be primarily supported by an individual developer. The product summary for McKoi can be found in the following table.

Product	McKoi
Category	Java database
URL	http://www.mckoi.com/database/
Supported Platforms	JDK 1.3
License	GPL
Features	Transaction support, embedded or client/server modes, JDBC 3.0 support

McKoi is more of a traditional database than HSqlDb and is more full featured that Axion. McKoi stores data files on disk and caches data in memory. Like HSqlDb, however, McKoi can be used as a database embedded into another program or as a standalone server that is accessed via a database client. McKoi provides a separate file for the JDBC driver, providing a smaller footprint for JDBC client-only applications.

License Issues

Unfortunately, both the McKoi server and the JDBC driver are covered under the GPL license. This forces products that want to use and distribute McKoi to use a license that is GPL compatible. Unfortunately, the Apache license is not considered GPL compatible. This causes problems for those projects that would benefit by combining GPL-protected software with software covered under the Apache license. This would not have been a problem if McKoi had been released under the LGPL license or if the JDBC driver had been released as LGPL. Because it is impossible to access the McKoi database without linking to either the McKoi server or the JDBC client, McKoi shouldn't be used with Tomcat or any other Java application covered under the Apache license. This is unfortunate because McKoi is a very attractive product from a standpoint of features and performance.

NOTE **This license-compatibility problem only affects programs that will be distributed to others. It does not affect personal software or programs that are private to a business and will not be distributed to other users.**

McKoi Installation

McKoi can be installed by downloading the distribution and decompressing it into the directory of your choice. After the files have been copied, a new empty database can be created using the following command:

```
java -jar mckoidb.jar -create "admin" "admin_pass"
```

`admin` is the name to use for the administrative user and `"admin_pass"` should be replaced by an appropriate password. To start McKoi running in server mode use the following command.

```
java -jar mckoidb.jar
```

The running server can be accessed from a McKoi command tool. This tool is started by the following command:

```
java -cp mckoidb.jar com.mckoi.tools.JDBCQueryTool \
-u "admin" -p "admin_pass"
```

The McKoi command tool shown in Figure 8.5 is considerably more primitive than the tool provided by HSqlDb. Fortunately, the HSqlDb tool also works with McKoi in both server and nonserver modes of operation.

To stop the McKoi server, use the following command:

```
java -jar mckoidb.jar -shutdown admin admin_pass
```

Use the following class and URL to access a McKoi database with McKoi running as a server from a Java program using JDBC:

```
com.mckoi.JDBCDriver
jdbc:mckoi://localhost/
```

where *localhost* is the machine name of the server.

Note that McKoi, by default, stores its configuration information in the file called `db.conf`. There are several values that may be of interest here. First, note that the references to the `database_path` and `log_path` are relative. If you will be running McKoi from a different working directory than the one used when the database was created, these should be made absolute. For example, instead of:

```
database_path=./data
log_path=./log
```

you might want to use:

```
database_path=c:/openjava/mckoi0.94h/data
log_path=c:/openjava/mckoi0.94h/log
```

The other value that you may want to change is:

```
ignore_case_for_identifiers=disabled
```

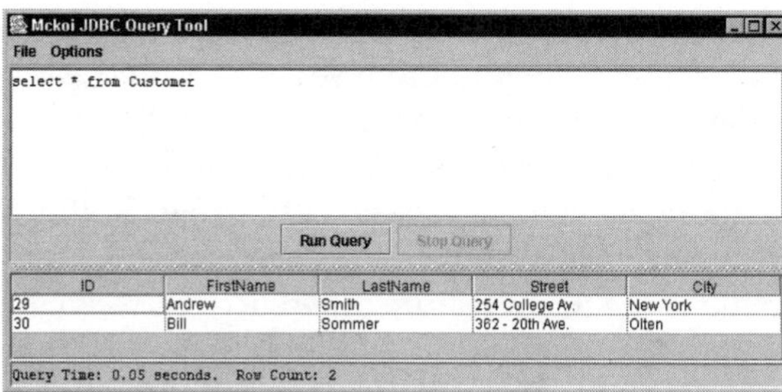

Figure 8.5 McKoi command tool.

By default, McKoi is case sensitive for table names. However most SQL environments are case insensitive. Changing `disabled` to `enabled` addresses this issue.

Needs and Features Analysis

What are the reasons we might need a Java database? There are other non-Java databases that are better suited to handle large enterprise applications. These other databases support Java using JDBC drivers. Why do we need a lightweight Java alternative?

There are several reasons why we might elect to use a Java database:

- If the database needs of an application are light, then a Java database is normally easier to set up, configure, and maintain than the heavyweight alternatives.
- Two of the Java databases also support memory-based tables. This feature might come in handy for fast lookups of commonly needed data.
- It might also be advantageous to use a lightweight database for specialized installations of our application. John has often installed sales versions of applications onto a laptop computer for demonstration purposes. The laptop can be easily used for conferences or sales presentations and the database quickly restored for the next demonstration.
- It is even possible to deploy the database as a part of a Web application, including it in the .war file.

In light of these uses, the closer the database is to conformance with the SQL Entry Level specification and with the required JDBC 2.0 subset, the better. The database should also provide support for transactions. Support for both memory- and disk-based databases is nice but is not mandatory. Product stability and reliability is a concern that also needs to be considered.

Evaluation

All three databases support at least the bare minimum set of DDL and DML commands. In evaluating the databases, we are more interested in the extensions beyond the basic support. The more features beyond the basics that are supported by the database, the more likely the database will be able to fulfill a role as an alternative to a more powerful enterprise database. Table 8.3 provides a quick comparison of some of the major feature differences between the database products.

Table 8.3 Major Feature Differences between Java Databases

FEATURE	AXION	HSQLDB	MCKOI	COMMENTS
Embeddable	X	X	X	
Server Mode		X	X	
HTTP Server Mode		X		
Transaction Support	*	X	X	* limited
Memory Tables	X	X		
Disk-Based Tables	X	X	X	
JDBC Version	JDBC 1.0	JDBC 2.0+	JDBC 3.0	
Minimum JDK Required	JDK 1.2	JDK 1.1*	JDK 1.3	* HSqlDb must built from source for 1.1 support
Triggers		X	X	
SPECIAL TYPES				
Blob Support	X	X*	X*	* Uses LONG VARBINARY Type
Java Object	X*	X	X	* Must register as new type
DDL COMMANDS				
ALTER TABLE		X	X	
CREATE INDEX	X	X		
CREATE VIEW		X	X	
DML COMMANDS				
Inner Joins	X	X	X	
Outer Joins		X	X	
GROUP BY		X	X	
ORDER BY	X	X	X	
DCL Commands				
GRANT		X	X	
REVOKE		X	X	

(continued)

Table 8.3 *(continued)*

FEATURE	AXION	HSQLDB	MCKOI	COMMENTS
Schema Support			X	
Triggers		X	X	
Stored Procedures		X		
License	OSI	BSD*	GPL	* BSD based
Documentation	Sparse	Full	Full	

This comparison does not highlight the differences in structure between the databases. It does show that each of these products has it own set of strengths and weaknesses. However, it is apparent that McKoi and HSqlDb have a far richer set of features than the set currently offered by Axion. This table provides us with all of the information that we need to make a selection. There is no need for further evaluation.

Selection

For our platform, we select HSqlDb as our choice for an embedded Java database. The reasons for this selection are discussed in this section.

First, the selection of GPL as the license for McKoi limits our ability to use it with Tomcat or commercial application server environments.

NOTE This is not a limitation of the technology, but is rather an artificial limitation imposed by the use of the GPL license. In our opinion, the LGPL license would have been a more appropriate choice for McKoi.

Another reason for not selecting McKoi is that fact that it is not maintained by an open source project, but is maintained by an individual developer or company. This tends to increase risk that the product will someday be abandoned and become unsupported.

Eliminating McKoi leaves Axion and HSqlDb. Axion is clearly a less mature product with fewer features to offer than HSqlDb. Although Axion is a product that is worth keeping an eye on for future applications, the differences in capabilities clearly point towards the selection of HSqlDb.

Relational Databases with JDBC Drivers

The current crop of available Java databases is suited for many purposes but they are limited in their ability to scale and handle very large applications.

Fortunately, JDBC allows Java programs to connect to any database with a supported driver. JDBC support exists for most commercial databases, including Oracle, DB2, and Microsoft's SQL Server. In the following sections, we examine non-Java databases and JDBC support for these databases. Our need for the non-Java database is to provide a scalable database alternative to commercial database products that we can use in our platform.

Survey and Analysis

A quick view of the Google category Computers ⇨ Software ⇨ Databases ⇨ Open Source reveals five potential candidates:

- Firebird
- GNU SQL
- MySQL
- PostGres
- SAP DB

Development of the GNU SQL database seems to have stalled several years ago, so it will not be considered further. All of the remaining products have large followings and active developer communities. We might expect that we could eliminate some choices based on availability of JDBC drivers: however, all of the databases provide some form of JDBC level 4 JDBC driver support. So with this in mind, we will take a brief look at each of these products.

FireBird

Firebird is based on a Borland product called Interbase. Interbase had been available as a commercial product for many years. During July of 2000, Borland decided to release Interbase version 6.0 as an open source project. This new project attracted a large following of open source developers who were already familiar with Interbase. However, this community did not see eye to eye with the way Borland wanted to manage the project. Instead, they created their own open source community around the product, and named the new product Firebird. This new project is hosted on Source Forge. Because Borland's open source effort never quite took off, Borland abandoned its open source support and moved back into providing commercial support for the Interbase product. The open source community, on the other hand, has continued development and support of their own open source development branch separately and divergently from Borland's. Attempts to merge the efforts so far have failed. The Firebird product summary is shown in the following table.

Product	Firebird
Category	Relational database with JDBC driver
URL	http://firebird.sourceforge.net
Supported Platforms	Windows 9*x*, 2000, XP, Linux, most forms of Unix, and Mac OS X
License	Interbase Public License (Similar to Mozilla Public License)
Features	SQL 92

Because of its heritage as a commercial product, there is a rich set of professional-quality document files for Firebird. Most of these are available as .pdf files that can be downloaded from the project site. The current Firebird project boasts the participation by an active community of over 60 developers. These are not corporately sponsored developers, but are developers who also actively use the product. Third-party service and support for Firebird and Interbase can be purchased from IBPhoenix (`http://www.ibphoenix.com`).

MySQL

MySQL is, by most measures, the most popular open source database available today. MySQL is available from `http://www.mysql.com`. It is developed and maintained by MySQL AB, a Swedish company founded by the original creators of the product and is released under the GPL and LGPL licenses. The following table provides a summary of the MySQL information.

Product	MySQL
Category	Relational database with JDBC driver
URL	http://www.mysql.com
Supported Platforms	Windows 98, 2K , XP, Linux and many forms of Unix, and Mac OSX
License	GPL (server components), LGPL for client components
Features	Fast, reliable database; recently added transaction support; most common open source database

MySQL has a reputation for being fast, reliable, and easy to use. Binary installations are provided for many platforms, including most Linux and Windows systems.

MySQL AB is an example of a company that thrives on free software. It generates most of its income from sales of support contracts and training for supporting the MySQL product in commercial environments. It also sells alternative licenses for MySQL to cover those situations where a company wants to distribute the MySQL product but does not want their products to fall under the GPL restrictions. At less than $400 per server, even these licenses are reasonably priced when compared to the competition. Especially when you consider that there are no extra charges for additional CPUs.

Although MySQL has earned a reputation for being a reliable database with good performance, it has also received criticism for lack of transaction support and support for advanced features such as foreign keys, user-defined functions (UDFs), triggers, and stored procedures. Recent versions of MySQL, however, do provide support for transactions and foreign keys by using data engines provided by InnoDB. A MySQL database can be configured to use a mix of these tables, allowing considerable flexibility in situations where transaction support is not important for every table. The current version of MySQL also provides UDF support. Stored procedures and triggers are expected to be included in MySQL version 5.0.

For quite a while, Java JDBC support for MySQL was handled separately by outside developers. One of these drivers mm.MySQL developed by Mark Mathews became more popular than the rest. In June 2002, MySQL AB hired Mark Mathews and acquired the driver. The driver is now available directly from the MySQL site and is currently available under the LGPL. Development on the driver has continued, and a MySQL has recently released a version supporting JDBC 3.0.This new driver has been released under the more restrictive GPL license.

PostgreSQL

PostgreSQL seems to be the granddaddy of all open source database projects. PostgreSQL evolved from database research at the University of California at Berkeley that began in the late 1970s and spawned a number of commercial products. In 1996, it became clear that there was great demand for an open source relational database. The PostgreSQL project was born. The work was based on efforts that had been performed earlier at Berkeley but the new effort was to occur outside of Berkley. The following table provides a summary of PostgreSQL.

Product	PostGreSQL
Category	Relational database with JDBC driver
URL	http://postgresql.org
Supported Platforms	Linux, other Unix platforms
License	BSD

The PostgreSQL community inherited a huge project. It took a while for the PostgreSQL community to develop and master the large code base that they had inherited. Initially, the community focused on problem resolution and bug fixes. As the project matured, the developers had a better grasp of the structure of the code and now PosgreSQL development continues at a rapid pace. Unfortunately, although several companies produce commercial Windows ports of PostgreSQL, there is no open source implementation of the PosgreSQL server available for Windows (there are an ODBC driver and a Windows client available).

Because of its history as an object-relational database, PostgreSQL boasts some of the richest support for new data types of any database software. The project has also paid close attention to detail in implementing the SQL standards and represents one of the most complete SQL implementations available.

PostgreSQL is an open source project in the truest sense of open source community. No one individual company sponsors development; and developers and contributors from all over the world participate in its development.

SAP DB

While PosgreSQL is the granddaddy of open source databases, SAP DB is the new kid on the block. Most people familiar with information technology within large companies are familiar with SAP. SAP practically defines enterprise resource planning (ERP) software. ERP software is used by most of the world's largest companies to do everything from project planning to purchasing to payroll. Most enterprise systems in large companies must integrate applications with that company's ERP software. Of course, ERP software is itself heavily dependent on underlying databases. That is where SAP DB comes in. The following table provides a summary of SAP DB.

Product	Sap DB
Category	Relational database with JDBC driver
URL	http://www.sapdb.org
Supported Platforms	Windows, Linux, others
License	Server GPL, clients LGPL

Why would SAP release this software as open source, and what makes this a good choice for an open source database? SAP says that they believe that databases are becoming a core part of the technical infrastructure and as such, they should not be proprietary or complex. The feeling is that, by releasing a commercial-grade database to the open source community, they can help this process along. We remain skeptical of their motivation, but impressed by the product.

SAP DB does represent an "industrial strength" database. It also provides some features that are unique and may make it the preferred choice for some projects. In particular SAP DB can be made to understand the dialects of SQL that are supported by Oracle (version 7) database products and by IBM's DB2 (version 4) database. This is a very valuable feature if you need to migrate an application developed using those older commercial products to an open source platform. With over 1,300 registered installations SAP DB also has a proven track record supporting commercial installations.

In some ways, it may sound as if SAP is dumping their product into the open source community, similarly to what Borland attempted with Interbase. SAP claims that this is not true and further states that they have over 100 programmers who are dedicated to continuing development and maintenance of the product. It does not seem, however, that SAP DB has attracted a large number of volunteer programmers to help with the open source effort. Granted, any database product of this size will take a while for a community to learn how to manage and make changes to the source code. This was the same problem encountered by the PostgreSQL community. Although SAP DB is, by any measure, a powerful and robust database product, it remains to be seen how it will fare in the long term as an open source product.

Needs and Features Analysis

Our requirement is for a robust, scalable, and portable relational database platform that can support development and hosting large complex applications. The system must provide support for the SQL 92 Entry Level specification at a minimum. Our rationale for this is that SQL 92 Entry Level is the common subset of SQL that should be implemented by all databases that claim to support SQL. Many businesses and government agencies require conformance to this specification for their enterprise systems. If we want to create a platform that is suitable for use within an enterprise environment, it should meet this standard.

We also require transaction support. Transaction support is necessary for many business scenarios, and a database that does not have transaction support will be difficult to use in these circumstances.

The system must also provide a JDBC 2.0 or later driver. JDBC 2.0 is the minimum version of JDBC that provides support for DataSources. This is necessary to use the database effectively in a connection-pooled environment. The ability to pool connections is critical for the scaling and performance of J2EE applications. Although JDBC 2.0 support is the minimum required, we certainly prefer having a JDBC 3.0–compliant driver with transaction support within the driver.

Evaluation

All four of these databases offer similar feature sets that differ only in the details. In some cases, though, those specific details may be important. For example, if you are porting an application from an Oracle or DB2 database, you might want to use SAP DB because of its capability to recognize the various SQL dialects. However, in our case, we have not identified any specific requirements that force us to select one product over the other strictly due to a support technology feature.

The most glaring limitation between products for our purposes is the fact that there is no server support for running PostgreSQL on Windows. This is unfortunate because PostgreSQL is widely recognized as a full-featured robust product.

NOTE **Obviously, if you are planning on doing development and hosting under Linux, then this should not be a concern, but because this violates our goal of creating a platform that is operating system and hardware independent, we will rule out PostgreSQL.**

Eliminating PosgreSQL still leaves us with three database products to select from. From a technology standpoint, all three seem to be able to support most of our needs.

This brings us to nontechnology issues. All three remaining products offer excellent resources for support and documentation. Each project offers a much richer documentation package than is seen in most open source Java products. Furthermore, unlike the embedded Java database issue discussed in regards to McKoi's use of GPL, we do not have to be concerned with the GPL license restrictions here because we are connecting to the database and not embedding it into our platform. The licenses on the JDBC drivers (LGPL, BSD, and Mozilla based) are all compatible with the rest of the products in our platform.

NOTE **MySQL has recently changed the licensing on their latest JDBC driver to be GPL instead of LGPL. However, the documentation on their site makes it clear that using the JDBC driver does not imply a requirement to make the client software GPL unless the client software will be distributed with the**

driver. It is not clear that this view of the GPL license is compatible with the view offered by the GNU organization. It would be nice if MySQL would restore the LGPL license and remove any questions about the use of the driver with commercial products. This is different from the issue discussed for McKoi and embedded Java databases because as an embedded product the Java database would be required to be distributed with the product.

Firebird and PosgreSQL both have true open source communities supporting them. MySQL, although maintained by MySQL AB, has done an excellent job of involving outsiders. SAP DB seems to provide good support for users (application developers) but it is unclear if a development community is being created around the project.

In short, all three choices are good choices for us. In others words, we can't make the wrong choice here. That is a nice position to be in.

Selection

Although there is no wrong choice, we still must make a selection and be able to justify our reasons. In this case, we select MySQL. Our justification for this is as follows.

At the time of this writing MySQL clearly seems to be the most widely supported open source database project available. This minimizes our risk. PostgreSQL is easily eliminated because of its limited Windows support. Although SAP DB is a powerful option, it has a smaller following than the other products, which can pose difficulties when trying to purchase learning materials or hire programmers who are experienced with the product and technology. Although Firebird has an excellent development community, MySQL resources are more plentiful and easier to find.

Finally, MySQL has been documented by several independent sources to perform as well as any commercial database product in the market. This means that we do not have to compromise performance to use an open source solution. MySQL benchmarks their product against others and publishes these benchmarks regularly. The other products have not documented their performance quite so well.

This does not mean of course that MySQL is the best choice for every project. In our case, we are focused on developing new code in a Java enterprise environment. This allows us to address database platform limitations through software design. MySQL gives us quite a bit of flexibility in terms of designing a system for performance or accepting a reduction in performance when data integrity is paramount. However, its lack of support for stored procedures means that many database access rules will need to be enforced in places other than the database. Fortunately for us, our focus on delivering a Java platform provides us natural places to enforce these rules (for example in Enterprise Java Beans). In a broader language-heterogeneous environment, the cost of this approach is that core business rules need to be developed and enforced in each language that accesses the database.

There is another consideration to take into account. When developing a software project, there is a lag between the time development starts and the time the product is delivered. During this time, the platform itself is going through changes. With a little foresight and planning, development projects can anticipate these changes and plan to leverage them just in time for deployment. This is one reason that platform developers provide early beta access to their products: application developers using the platform can come out with applications that leverage a platform's strengths at the same time as the platform is released to production. This can be risky if the platform is not delivered on schedule, so a risk-mitigation strategy in these cases is warranted. In our case, we recognize the fact that the MySQL team has identified these shortcomings (like lack of stored procedures) within their product and expect to incorporate them in the next major release. In the mean time, we will design our software for the most current stable version of the platform available.

If your project has specific requirements for triggers and stored procedures to be supported in the database, then MySQL may not be the right choice for you and you should look more closely at the other offerings. Remember that no single choice is always the right choice to meet every need. In our case, MySQL meets our current needs.

So the bottom line is that we select MySQL for the quality, depth, and breadth of the support available for the platform due to its current dominance as an open source database and for the flexibility it offers for creating high-performance applications.

Installation

Now that we have completed the selection process for the two database products that will be used in our platform, we need to integrate these products into the platform. Primarily, this means installing the databases and then configuring Tomcat to support the databases. The following sections show you how to perform these tasks.

Installing MySQL on Windows

MySQL supports most versions of Windows, including Windows 98, with some limitations. When running under Windows 98 there is no support for named pipes because named pipes are not available to the operating system, and there is no support for the installation of the database as a service. The database can be started automatically as part of the operating system startup process, but it then runs as the current user. The process described here is for Windows NT, 2000, and XP. Installing MySQL under Windows is a three-step process:

1. Download and Unzip the binary distribution.
2. Run the setup program.
3. Start the database.

Download the Distribution Files

The first step is to download the distribution files. You should, at a minimum, get the MySQL binary distribution and the JDBC driver. These files can be found on the MySQL site at `http://www.mysql.com`. Note that the database and JDBC drivers are separate downloads. If you wish to use Windows programs with the database, then you should also download the ODBC driver as well. The three files you need will be named something like:

- `MySQLversion.zip`
- `MySQL-connector-java-version.jar`
- `MyODBC-version.zip`

After the files have been downloaded, create a temporary directory and use you favorite unzip utility to unzip the `MySQLversion.zip` file.

Run the Setup Program

In the subdirectory where the files were unzipped is a program named `setup.exe`. Double-click this file to run it and install MySQL. The default installation installs MySQL on the C: drive in the `mysql` directory. The installation program provides a note informing you that the initialization file will have to be manually edited if you do not accept the default installation directory.

Starting MySQL

The setup program creates a program subdirectory. By default, this is named `c:\mysql`. Setup does not create any Start menu items or desktop shortcuts. MySQL is automatically installed as a service under Windows NT, 2000, and XP. By default, this service will start automatically each time the system is rebooted. The service can be controlled through the standard service control panel applet or can be started and stopped using the program `winmysqladmin.exe`. The program can be found in the `mysql\bin` directory. This utility also makes it easy to change the configuration information for the database running under Windows.

MySQL can also be started from the command line. To do this change directory to the `MySQL\bin` subdirectory, and enter the command:

```
mysqld-max —standalone
```

The following command can be used to stop MySQL:

```
mysqladmin -u root shutdown
```

Installing MySQL on Linux

MySQL already comes as a standard installation option on many Linux distributions. The easiest way to install MySQL on Linux is to use the standard RPM-based distribution. The RPM files that you will need are:

MySQL-server-VERSION.i386.rpm. This is the MySQL server.

MySQL-max-VERSION.i386.rpm. Extensions to support UDF and other features.

MySQL-client-VERSION.i386.rpm. The standard MySQL client programs.

MySQL-devel-VERSION.i386.rpm. Libraries and include files needed if you want to compile other MySQL clients, such as the Perl modules.

MySQL-shared-VERSION.i386.rpm. This package contains the shared libraries (`libmysqlclient.so*`), which certain languages and applications need to dynamically load and use MySQL.

These files can be downloaded from `http://www.mysql.com` or one of its mirror sites. After these files have been downloaded, MySQL can be installed by first logging in as root and then running the following commands:

```
rpm -i MySQL-server-VERSION.i386.rpm
rpm -i MySQL-max-VERSION.i386.rpm
rpm -i MySQL-client-VERSION.i386.rpm
rpm -i MySQL-devel-VERSION.i386.rpm
rpm -i MySQL-shared-VERSION.i386.rpm
```

The installation process configures MySQL and starts it as a daemon automatically.

Testing MySQL

After MySQL has been installed and is running, we want to check and make certain that we can access it. This is easily done from the command line by running a utility program provided with MySQL. From the Linux or Windows command prompt, enter the following command:

```
mysqlshow
```

If MySQL is running you should see:

```
+-----------+
| Databases |
+-----------+
| mysql     |
| test      |
+-----------+
```

Windows users will want to make sure that the `c:\mysql\bin` directory is in their path.

Install the MySQL JDBC Driver

The MySQL JDBC driver is downloaded separately from the MySQL database distribution. The same file is used for Linux and Windows. The file can be downloaded from `http://www.mysql.com` and is normally named something like:

```
MySQL-connector-java-version.jar
```

This is a .jar file that has the source code and documentation for the driver along with a .jar file that contains the driver itself. To clarify, the driver is a jar file that is contained within the downloaded .jar file. To use the driver, you will first need to extract the driver .jar file from the downloaded jar file. The .jar tool provided with the JDK can be used to extract the entire downloaded .jar file.

```
jar -xvf MySQL-connector-java-version.jar
```

This creates a directory tree that contains the needed .jar file in the topmost directory. The driver is named:

```
mysql-connector-java-version-bin.jar
```

The following program can be used to test the driver and make certain it can connect to the database:

```
import java.sql.*;

public class TestJdbc
{

  public TestJdbc()
  {
  }

  public static void main(String[] args)
  {
    String connectionURL = "jdbc:mysql://localhost:3306/test";
    String driverClass= "com.mysql.jdbc.Driver";
    String dbUser = "root";
    String dbPassword = "";
    Connection conn = null;
    try
    {
      Class.forName(driverClass);
      conn = DriverManager.getConnection(
              connectionURL, dbUser, dbPassword );
      DatabaseMetaData md = conn.getMetaData();
      System.out.println( "Database="+md.getDatabaseProductName());
      System.out.println( "Driver="+md.getDriverName());
    }
    catch( Exception e )
    {
      e.printStackTrace();
    }
    finally
    {
      try
      {
        if( conn != null )
          conn.close();
```

```
        }
        catch( Exception e )
        {
          e.printStackTrace();
        }
      }
    }
  }
```

Useful Tools

There are a number of open source tools that are useful when working with relational databases. We will quickly look at two of them.

MySQL Control Center

The MySQL Control Center is a GUI client for accessing MySQL databases. It provides the ability to easily create databases, add, edit, and delete tables, and execute queries. MySQL Control Center is covered under the GPL and supports both Windows and Linux. MySQL Control Center can be downloaded from `http://www.mysql.com`. The following table summarizes MySQL, and Figure 8.6 shows the Control Center running under Windows.

Product	MySQL Control Center
Category	Relational database access tool
URL	http://www.mysql.com
Supported Platforms	Windows 98/Me/NT/2000/XP, Linux
License	GPL
Features	Provides a GUI for managing MySQL databases

To install the Control Center in Windows, download the binary distribution for Windows, which comes as a .zip file, and unzip it into a temporary directory. Run the setup program to complete the installation.

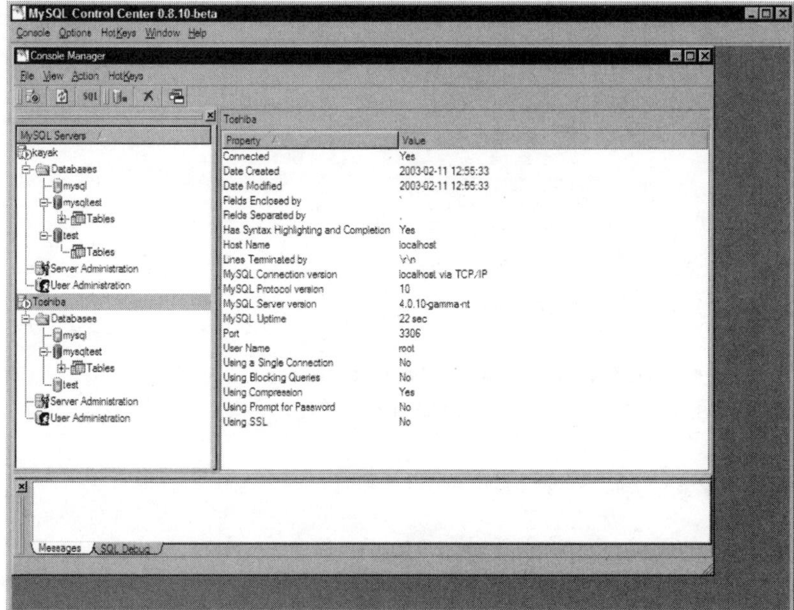

Figure 8.6 The MySQL Control Center.

To install the Control Center in Linux, download the Linux version of the binary distribution. This comes as a compressed .tar archive. From the command prompt, move to the directory that you wish to install the software into, for example `/usr/local`, and then de-archive the distribution file.

```
tar -zxvf $HOME/download/mysqlcc-<version>-<os>-glibc23.tar.gz
```

This creates a directory named `mysqlcc-version-os` with the software installed. We want to provide a simple link to access the program.

```
ln -s mysqlcc-version-os mysqlcc
```

You should now be able to run the program using the command:

```
/usr/local/mysqlcc/mysqlcc
```

Remember that this is a graphical program, and you must be running an X Windows-based GUI to use it.

Squirrel

Squirrel is similar in many respects to MySQL Control Center. It provides a program with graphical interface and the ability to connect to a database. It can be used to browse the structure of the database and execute queries against it. Tables can be created and altered within Squirrel by entering SQL commands in a provided command window. Unlike MySQL Control Center, Squirrel is written solely in Java and uses JDBC for its database connections, which allows it to work with any database supported by JDBC. The following table provides a summary for Squirrel.

Product	Squirrel
Category	Relational database access tool
URL	http://squirrel-sql.sourceforge.net/
Supported Platforms	JDK 1.3
License	LGPL
Features	Provides a GUI for managing databases using JDBC

Installing Squirrel is easy. First, download the binary distribution and decompress it. Inside is Squirrel's self-installing .jar file. To install it, just enter:

```
java -jar squirrel-sql-version-install.jar
```

You will be presented with an installation wizard similar to the one used to install most Windows applications. However, this wizard is written in Java and runs on the current Java platform. You will need to have the appropriate privileges to install the program into your desired target directory.

When running, Squirrel looks like the screen shown in Figure 8.7.

Squirrel also supports a number of plug-ins. One of these is MySQL-specific and seems to provide the MySQL-specific syntax for creating tables. The biggest advantage that Squirrel brings, however, is that it supports both MySQL and HSqlDb, and any other database with a JDBC driver.

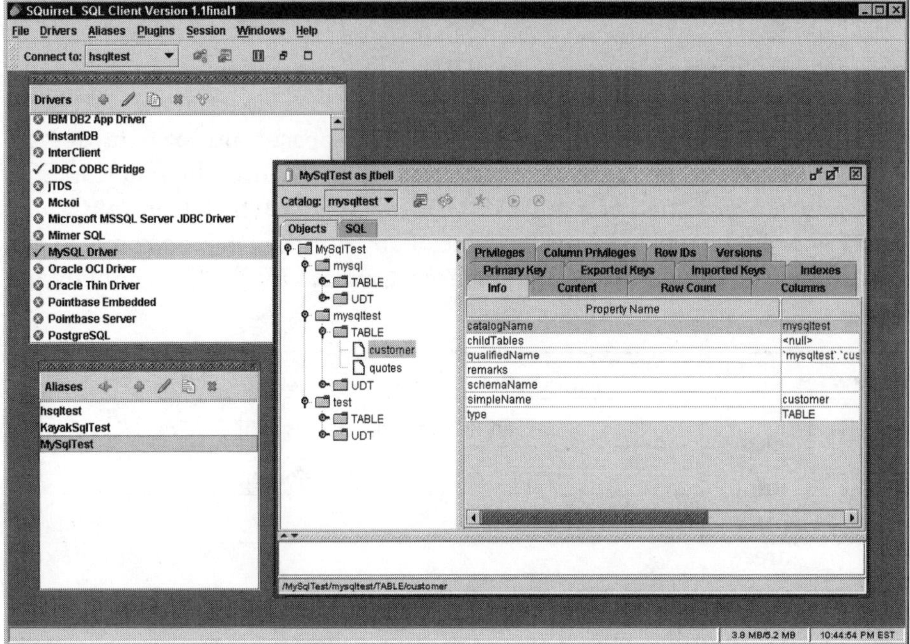

Figure 8.7 Squirrel.

Integration and Testing

Now that the databases are installed, we need to integrate them with the platform as it stands. This involves integrating the databases with Tomcat and configuring DataSources so they can be accessed from servlets and JavaServer Pages.

Integration with Tomcat

In a J2EE environment, we want to have the container manage database connections for us. This means that we need to be able to look up DataSources, and we need to get database connections from a connection pool. The container has to be configured so that it knows how to do this. In this section, we will configure Tomcat so that it can provide our applications with database connections.

Adding Connection Pooling to Tomcat

The current version of Tomcat (4.1.24) has separated the connection-pooling functions from the primary distribution. Tomcat does claim to provide a DataSource implementation without connection pooling; however, this implementation does not seem to be supported by the Tomcat Administration facility. We need connection pooling to properly access databases from servlets and make our applications scalable. Although it would be nice if we were able to use the Admin tool to install and configure DataSources, we can't. Hopefully, Tomcat will fix this in future releases and include the connection-pooling facility as a standard part of the distribution, but in the meantime you'll have to add connection pooling to Tomcat yourself. This section tells you how to do just that.

We will be using the Database Connection Pool implementation from the Jakarta Commons project, referred to as the DBCP. This is the standard connection pool implementation that is supported by Tomcat. The first step is to download three subprojects from Jakarta Commons. Commons can be found at `http://jakarta.apache.org/commons`. Commons is a project within Jakarta designed to be a collection point for those utilities and features that are used and shared across multiple projects. The projects we need are:

- Jakarta Commons DBCP
- Jakarta Commons Collections
- Jakarta Commons Pool

DBCP provides the actual connection-pooling library that we will use but it is dependent on the other two .jar files. Download the binary distributions for each of these projects and decompress the files into a working directory. (It's a good idea to use a common `jakarta` directory for all Jakarta projects that you download.) After the files have been unpacked, we need to install the .jar files for Tomcat to use. The best way to do this is to copy the files into the `CATALINA_HOME/common/lib` subdirectory. On Linux, you need to remember to set the ownership and permissions to match those of the rest of the Tomcat installation. Following is an example of doing this on our system:

```
/usr/jakarta/tomcat4.1/common/lib/#chown apache:apache commons-*.jar
/usr/jakarta/tomcat4.1/common/lib/#chmod 644 commons-*.jar
```

After this is done, Tomcat needs to be stopped and restarted.

Installing the JDBC Drivers

With the DBCP support installed, we are now ready to add the database drivers. We want to add two drivers, one for HSqlDb and the other for MySQL. The HSqlDb driver is built into the `hsqldb.jar` file. There is no need to extract it; we will use the entire .jar file. Copy the entire file into the `CATALINA_HOME/common/lib` subdirectory. Placing the driver here allows access both by Tomcat and by all Web applications. The driver needed for MySQL is the `mysql-connector-java-version-bin.jar` file. This should also be copied into the `common/lib` directory of the Tomcat installation. Once again, if you are using Linux, change the owner and set the permissions to match the rest of the installation.

When this is done, stop and restart Tomcat again.

Configuring JNDI

Now that the pooling software and the database drivers are installed, we are ready to configure Tomcat so that database connections can be retrieved from the connection pool. The following sections show you how to do this.

Creating a Test Database

Before configuring Tomcat, we need a database. For our purposes at this time, a simple database will suffice, so we will create a test database called quotes. Quotes has four columns:

id. An integer to serve as a primary key

author. A name attributed to the quote

quote. A quote

stardate. An optional string representing the time or circumstances when the quote might have been said

First, we need to create a database. The following lines will do this in MySQL.

```
CREATE DATABASE mysqltest;
USE mysqltest;
```

The first line creates the database; the next one makes sure it is the database we are using. We don't need to do this for HSqlDb because it automatically creates a database based on the connection URL. Next, we create the table in the database using the following SQL script:

```
CREATE TABLE quotes(
  ID INTEGER PRIMARY KEY,
  AUTHOR VARCHAR(64),
  QUOTE VARCHAR(128),
  STARDATE VARCHAR(64));
```

The next script loads some test data into the table:

```
insert into quotes (id, author, quote, stardate)
VALUES (1, 'Dorothy', 'This does not look like Kansas', 'Oz arrival');
insert into quotes (id, author, quote, stardate)
VALUES (2, 'Hamlet', '2B or !2B', 'When IMing');
insert into quotes (id, author, quote, stardate)
VALUES (3, 'Macdonald', 'E I E I O', 'When bitten');
insert into quotes (id, author, quote, stardate)
VALUES (4, 'Marcel Marceau', 'Nothing', 'Most of the time');
```

This adds four records into our test database. These scripts can be executed either through the MySQL command-line tool or by using tools such as Squirrel, the MySQL Control Panel, or even the HSqlDb-provided database manager. The scripts are designed to be compatible with both databases.

We may want to add specific users and grant them privileges to access the database. In MySQL, this is done with the following command:

```
GRANT ALL PRIVILEGES ON *.* TO tomcat@localhost
  IDENTIFIED BY 'passwd5' WITH GRANT OPTION;
```

If you are using HSqlDb, then you need to use the following commands to create a user and give the user access to the table:

```
CREATE USER tomcat PASSWORD passwd5
GRANT ALL ON quotes TO tomcat
```

Now that we have a database, we need to be able to access it through a servlet. To do this, we need to configure a DataSource in Tomcat. There are two ways to do this, through the Tomcat Admin tool or by editing Tomcat's configuration file `server.xml`.

Testing the Connection Parameters

Before we get started configuring the Data Sources, we need to know the following things:

- The class name of the JDBC driver
- The connection URL

- The username we will use to connect to the database
- The password for the user

We also need to pick a name that we will use to look up the connection in JNDI. For accessing a MySQL database named mysqltest running on the same computer as Tomcat, we will use the values shown in Table 8.4.

localhost can be replaced by the name of the server running the database if it is not the same machine that Tomcat is running on.

If we were to access the database on an embedded HSqlDb, the values would be as shown in Table 8.5.

Before we configure these into Tomcat, it makes sense to test the parameters to make certain they are correct. The following code is a useful utility that can be run from the command line to test the parameters:

```
import java.sql.*;
public class JdbcTest
{
  public static void main(String[] args)
  {
    String driver = "org.hsqldb.jdbcDriver";
    String url = "jdbc:hsqldb:d:/openjava/hsqldb/data/hsqltest";
    String user = "sa";
    String passwd = "";

    if( args.length > 0 && args[0] != "" )
      driver = args[0];
    if( args.length > 1 && args[1] != "" )
      url = args[1];
    if( args.length > 2 && args[2] != "" )
      user = args[2];
    if( args.length > 3 && args[3] != "" )
      passwd = args[3];

    System.out.println( "Driver: "+driver );
    System.out.println( "URL   : "+url );
    System.out.println( "User  : "+user );
    System.out.println( "Passwd: "+passwd );
    Connection conn = null;
    DatabaseMetaData meta = null;
    try
    {
      System.out.println("Loading Driver: "+driver);
      Class.forName( driver ).newInstance();
      conn = DriverManager.getConnection(url, user, passwd);
      System.out.println( "Got connection" );
      meta = conn.getMetaData();
      System.out.println( "ProductName ==>"+
```

```
        meta.getDatabaseProductName());
      System.out.println( "DriverName    ==>"+meta.getDriverName());
      System.out.println( "DriverVersion==>"+meta.getDriverVersion());
      System.out.println( "URL           ==>"+meta.getURL());
      System.out.println("*** TABLES ***");
      ResultSet rs = meta.getTables(null, null, "%", null);
      while( rs.next() )
      {
        System.out.print( rs.getString("TABLE_TYPE"));
        System.out.print( ":" );
        System.out.println( rs.getString("TABLE_NAME"));
      }
      System.out.println( "Closing connection");
      conn.close();
    }
    catch (Exception e)
    {
      e.printStackTrace();
    }
  }
}
```

Table 8.4 Data Source Configuration for MySQL

NAME	VALUE
JNDI Name	jdbc/mysqltest
JDBC Driver class	com.mysql.jdbc.Driver
Data Source URL	jdbc:mysql://localhost:3306/mysqltest
User Name	tomcat
Password	passwd5

Table 8.5 Data Source Configuration for HSqlDb

NAME	VALUE
JNDI Name	jdbc/hsqltest
JDBC Driver class	org.hsqldb.jdbcDriver
Data Source URL	jdbc:hsqldb:/openjava/hsqldb/data/hsqltest
User Name	tomcat
Password	passwd5

The program accepts four command-line parameters:

- The name of the JDBC Driver class
- The URL for the connection
- The user ID
- The password

If no arguments are passed in, it will try to connect to an HSqlDb database. The following line loads the database driver into the JVM:

```
Class.forName( driver ).newInstance();
```

The driver must be on the classpath. The following line gets the connection, based on the provided URL:

```
conn = DriverManager.getConnection(url, user, passwd);
```

The rest of the program uses the DatabaseMetaData object from the connection to print information about the JDBC driver and the database. To run the program to test the MySQL sample database that we set up earlier, enter the following command at the command-line prompt:

```
java -cp mysql-connector-java-2.0.14-bin.jar JdbcTest \
    com.mysql.jdbc.Driver jdbc:mysql://localhost:3306/mysqltest \
    tomcat passwd5
```

Note that this should be entered all as one line. The result should be something similar to the following:

```
Driver: com.mysql.jdbc.Driver
URL   : jdbc:mysql://localhost:3306/mysqltest
User  : tomcat
Passwd: passwd5
Loading Driver: com.mysql.jdbc.Driver
Got connection
ProductName  ==>MySQL
DriverName   ==>Mark Matthews' MySQL Driver
DriverVersion==>2.0.14
URL          ==>jdbc:mysql://localhost:3306/mysqltest
*** TABLES ***
TABLE:quotes
Closing connection
```

If this works, then we are ready to configure a DataSource in Tomcat.

Using the Tomcat Admin Tool

The Tomcat Administration Tool is a great improvement over the old means of configuring Tomcat by editing configuration files. To start the Admin utility first make certain that Tomcat is running, and then enter the following URL into the browser.

```
http://localhost:8080/admin/login.jsp
```

The machine and port may need to be changed to reflect your configuration. You will be prompted for a username and password. The username and password are the ones you created when installing Tomcat. After you are logged in, you should see a screen that looks like Figure 8.8.

Using the navigation tree on the left-hand pane, select Service ➪ Host (localhost), and open the tree. If a branch does not exist for Default Context, then create one by selecting the Host node and then selecting Create New Default Context from the pull-down menu of available actions on the right. A form appears in the left pane with the values that can be set for the DefaultContext tag. Most of these can be left at their default values, but make certain that the value for Use Naming is set to true. There are Save buttons at the top and bottom of the form that can be used to save the values and create the Default Context.

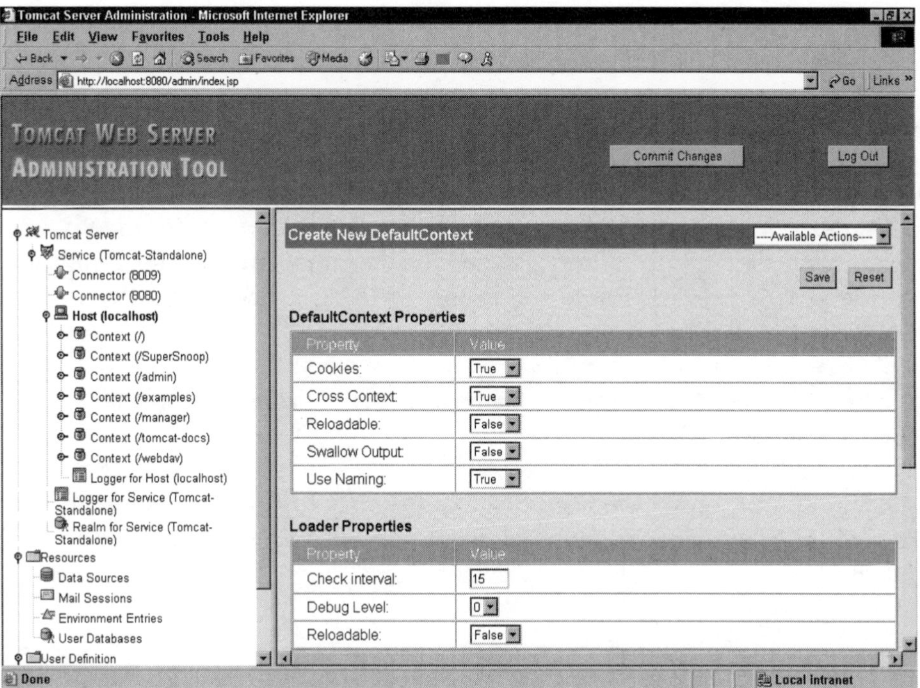

Figure 8.8 Tomcat administration screen.

After the Default Context has been created, we need to add the DataSource to it. Use the Navigation tree on the left to navigate to the Default Context node that we just created, and open it and the Resources node below it. A node for Data Sources should appear below the Resources node. Select the Data Sources node. The Action menu on the right should now have an option to create a new DataSource. Selecting this option presents us the screen shown in Figure 8.9.

Use the values from Tables 8.4 and 8.5 to fill in the form. The other fields can be left at their default values. After the form has been completed, click the Save button and then restart Tomcat.

NOTE A number of people have reported problems using Tomcat's Administration Tool to create pooled connections through Tomcat version 4.1.24. Most who have encountered problems have found a workaround by configuring the resources in the application context or default context instead of configuring them in the Global Resources. This is what we have shown with these instructions. Occasionally, however, even configuring the resource in the default context fails. When that happens, manually configuring the resource by editing `server.xml` will often work. The instructions for doing this are provided in the next section. If you have tried to use the Administration Tool, you may want to reinstall the `server.xml` file in the `conf` directory of the Tomcat installation. The Administartion tool generates a `server.xml` file that is difficult to read.

Editing Tomcat's server.xml

Although some people may find that the Admin utility is the easiest way to configure and manage a Tomcat server, others find it easiest to directly edit the `server.xml` file that Tomcat uses for its initialization. The configuration file `server.xml` is found the in the `conf` directory within the Tomcat installation.

NOTE It is a good idea to always create a backup of the `server.xml` file before you start editing it.

To add a Data Source, we need to add a resource to Tomcat by inserting the Resource element. The Resource element supports the attributes shown in Table 8.6.

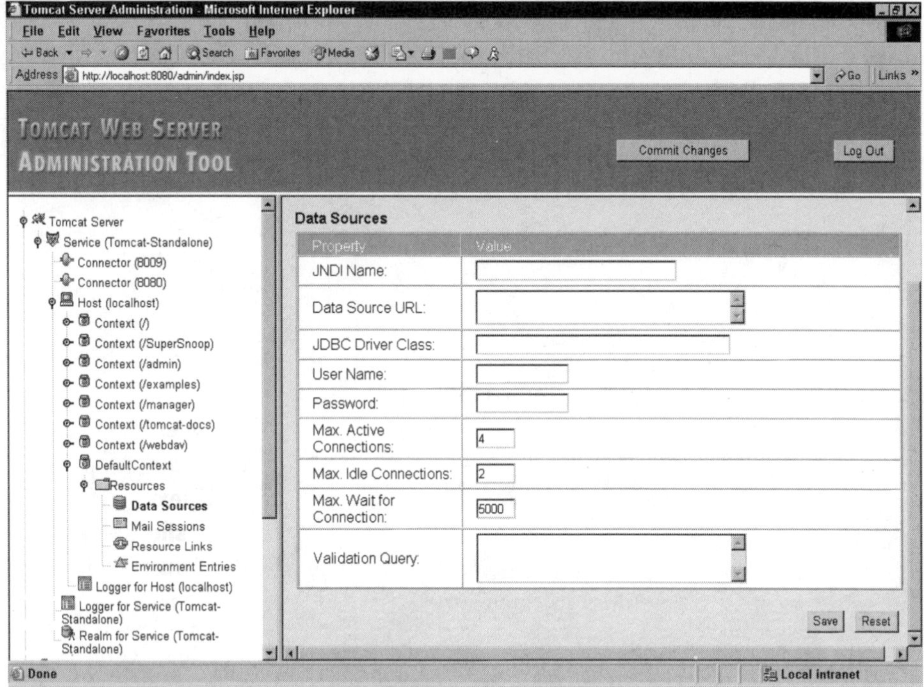

Figure 8.9 Adding a Data Source.

Table 8.6 Tomcat Resource Element Attributes

ATTRIBUTE	DESCRIPTION
`auth`	Legal values are `Application` or `Container`. This attribute determines whether the Web Application code signs onto the matching resource manager programmatically or whether the container signs on on behalf of the application. This attribute is required if the Web application uses a `<resource-ref>` element in the Web application deployment descriptor, but is optional if the application uses a `<resource-env-ref>` instead.
`description`	Optional, human-readable description of this resource.
`name`	This is the JNDI name of the resource to be created. It is relative to the `java:comp/env` context. For Data Sources, this should begin with `jdbc/`.
`scope`	Legal values are `Sharable` or `Unsharable`, and the default is `Sharable`. This attribute states whether connections obtained through this resource manager can be shared.
`type`	The fully qualified Java class name expected by the Web application when it performs a lookup for this resource. For DataSources, this should be `javax.sql.DataSource`.

We also need to add a Parameter element with a set of parameters that describes how to configure the resource. The Parameter element requires a name attribute that must match the name of the associated resource element. The following is an example of the XML for configuring an HSQLDB data source.

```
<Resource
    name="jdbc/hsqltest"
    auth="Container"
    scope="Shareable"
    type="javax.sql.DataSource"
/>
<ResourceParams name="jdbc/hsqltest">
    <parameter>
        <name>url</name>
        <value>jdbc:hsqldb:c:/openjava/hsqldb/data/hsqltest</value>
    </parameter>
    <parameter>
        <name>driverClassName</name>
        <value>org.hsqldb.jdbcDriver</value>
    </parameter>
    <parameter>
        <name>username</name>
        <value>tomcat</value>
    </parameter>
    <parameter>
        <name>password</name>
        <value>passwd5</value>
    </parameter>
</ResourceParams>
```

The above is the bare minimum for configuring the connection. It does not provide any configuration parameters for the connection pool. The parameters for the connection pool can be included with the `ResourceParams`. According to the Tomcat documentation, the supported parameters for configuring the pool are:

maxActive. A number representing the maximum number of active instances that can be allocated from this pool at the same time.

maxIdle. A number representing the maximum number of connections that can sit idle in this pool at the same time.

maxWait. The maximum number of milliseconds that the pool will wait (when there are no available connections) for a connection to be returned before throwing an exception.

validationQuery. A string representing a SQL query that can be used by the pool to validate connections before they are returned to the application. If specified, this query must be a SQL SELECT statement that returns at least one row.

For example:

```
<parameter>
    <name>maxActive</name>
    <value>8</value>
</parameter>
<parameter>
    <name>maxIdle</name>
    <value>6</value>
</parameter>
<parameter>
    <name>maxWait</name>
    <value>5000</value><!-- wait up to 5 seconds ‡
</parameter>
<parameter>
    <name>validationQuery</name>
    <value>SELECT * FROM CUSTOMER</value>
</parameter>
```

After you have created the Resource and Resource Parameters elements, you need to insert them into the `server.xml` file. There are three candidate locations:

- Inside the Global Resources element
- Inside a Default Context element
- Inside the Context element for the Web application

If the new elements are placed inside the Global Resources element, then they can be made visible to all applications. To add a resource to the Global Reference section, search for the `<GlobalResource>` tag and then the matching `</GlobalResource>` end tag. Copy the XML section with the Resource and Resource parameter elements, as shown previously, just before the end tag. Each application that needs to access the resource should also add a `<resource-ref>` tag to the `web.xml` file for that application. An example of a `<resource-ref>` element is:

```
<resource-ref>
  <description>
    Resource for connecting to the mysqltest database
  </description>
  <res-ref-name>
    jdbc/mysqltest
```

```
    </res-ref-name>
    <res-type>
      javax.sql.DataSource
    </res-type>
    <res-auth>
      Container
    </res-auth>
  </resource-ref>
```

NOTE A number of users of Tomcat 4.1.x have experienced problems initializing the database connection pool for DataSources configured in global resources. We recommend configuring DataSources in a default context instead to avoid these problems.

A <resource-ref> element is not necessary if the data source is configured in a default context. The default context establishes default values for all contexts contained in a Tomcat Host or Engine elements. The DefaultContext element is used to configure the default context values for automatically deployed Web applications. Data sources that are established here are visible to all application contexts supported and defined within the current host (or engine) context. This is the preferred means of establishing a data source that is to be shared across applications. To add the Resource and Resource Parameter elements to a default context, search for the <DefaultContext> tag and </DefaultContext> end tag. If a default context is not defined, it can be added inside of a <Host> element or an <Engine> element. The example below shows a sample <DefaultContext> element.

```
<DefaultContext
    cookies="true"
    crossContext="false"
    reloadable="false"
    useNaming="true">
<!-- place Resource elements here -->
<!-- place Resource Parameter elements here -->
</DefaultContext>
```

The `useNaming` attribute of the default context should be set to "true" to enable a JNDI InitialContext. The Resource and Resource Parameter Elements should be placed inside the Default Context element, between the tags, as shown by the comment markers.

A resource can also be added directly within a Context element if an application has a context element within the `server.xml` file. In this case, the resource is specific to that application context and is not shared across application contexts.

Troubleshooting Tools

Two common problems occur when working with Web applications that access databases through JNDI. The first one is that often the JNDI name is mistyped, or the container did not place the data source in the expected position within the JNDI tree. (This later case is a real problem when working with multiple containers.) The second concern is incorrect configuration parameters for the data source or another problem connecting to the database. In this section, we will briefly look at two simple tools that can help to address these problems.

Browsing JNDI

Getting the JNDI name correct in the client code is important. The JNDI name is what the application uses to look up the data source with JNDI. A common mistake is to forget to place `jdbc/` in front of the JNDI name for a Data Source in Tomcat. Some application servers enforce the `jdbc/` subcontext for data sources. Others, like Tomcat, just suggest it. It can be frustrating to know that a data source is supposed to be configured for one name but the lookup fails. This program tries to address this issue by providing a basic JNDI browser. The servlet below is designed to walk through a JNDI context (starting at `java:comp/env`) and print information about any Data Sources that are found. When it encounters a subcontext, it will walk through that as well.

```
import java.io.*;
import java.net.*;
import java.text.DateFormat;
import java.util.Date;
import javax.naming.*;

import javax.servlet.*;
import javax.servlet.http.*;
import javax.sql.DataSource;

public class SnoopJndi extends HttpServlet
{

  private String printJndi( String jndiStart )
  {
    String rStr = null;
    Context initCtx = null;
    StringBuffer sb = new StringBuffer(128);

    try
    {
```

```
            initCtx = new javax.naming.InitialContext();
            NamingEnumeration list = null;

            if( jndiStart.equals("") )
              jndiStart="java:comp/env";
            sb.append("\nContext ==>");
            sb.append( jndiStart );
            sb.append( "\n" );

            list = initCtx.listBindings(jndiStart);
            Binding item = null;
            while (list.hasMore())
            {
              item = (Binding)list.next();
              sb.append( jndiStart );
              sb.append("/");
              sb.append( item.toString() );
              sb.append( "\n" );
              if( item.getObject() instanceof javax.naming.Context)
              {
                sb.append( printJndi( jndiStart+"/"+item.getName()) );
              }
            }
            rStr = sb.toString();
          }
          catch( Exception e )
          {
            rStr = e.toString();
          }
          return( rStr );
        }

        private String today()
        {
          Date now = new Date();
          DateFormat dateFormatter = DateFormat.getDateTimeInstance();
          return dateFormatter.format( now );
        }

        public void doGet(
          HttpServletRequest request,
          HttpServletResponse response)
          throws ServletException, IOException
        {
          response.setContentType("text/plain");
          PrintWriter out = response.getWriter();
          out.println( "Date:"+today());
          out.println( printJndi( "" ) );
          out.close();
        }
      }
```

First, note that the response type is text/plain. This simplifies the servlet by not requiring HTML tags. The simple text output is fine for our purposes at this time. The `printJndi` method builds a string that will be returned and sent as the response generated by `doGet()`.

The `printJndi` method does all of the interesting work. First, it gets an InitialContext (this is necessary because an InitialContext is not synchronized and so should not be shared with all other thread instances). Then, it gets a list of binding within the context as shown in the following line:

```
list = initCtx.listBindings(jndiStart);
```

The argument `jndiStart` provides the initial argument for the function and presents the current base path within the JNDI hierarchy that the list will be generated for. A while loop is used to iterate through the list, using the `toString` method to print a string representation of each binding on the list. The line below shows how each element is tested to see if it is also a context:

```
if( item.getObject() instanceof javax.naming.Context)
```

If the item is a context, the `printJndi` methods recurses and calls itself to add the subcontext information as follows:

```
sb.append( printJndi( jndiStart+"/"+item.getName()) );
```

Any exceptions that may occur are caught and returned as the return string. Once compiled this servlet can be installed into the `classes` directory of any Web application to provide a convenient information tool. The relevant fragment for the `web.xml` deployment descriptor is:

```
<servlet>
    <servlet-name>SnoopJndi</servlet-name>
    <display-name>SnoopJndi</display-name>
    <description>Jndi Snooper</description>
    <servlet-class>SnoopJndi</servlet-class>
  </servlet>
<servlet-mapping>
    <servlet-name>SnoopJndi</servlet-name>
    <url-pattern>/servlet/SnoopJndi</url-pattern>
</servlet-mapping>
```

When deployed with a Web application named snoopy the URL for accessing the servlet is:

```
http://localhost:8080/snoopy/servlet/SnoopJndi
```

The result should look something like the following:

```
Date:Feb 17, 2003 10:10:29 PM

Context ==>java:comp/env
java:comp/env/jdbc:
org.apache.naming.NamingContext:org.apache.naming.NamingContext@969c29

Context ==>java:comp/env/jdbc
java:comp/env/jdbc/hsqltest:
org.apache.naming.ResourceRef:ResourceRef[className=javax.sql.DataSource
,factoryClassLocation=null,factoryClassName=org.apache.naming.factory.Re
sourceFactory,{type=scope,content=Shareable},{type=auth,content=Containe
r},{type=url,content=jdbc:hsqldb:c:/openjava/hsqldb/data/hsqltest},{type
=password,content=},{type=driverClassName,content=org.hsqldb.jdbcDriver}
,{type=username,content=sa}]
```

Note that the line of output that begins with `org.apache.naming` is displayed as a single line in the browser.

Testing the Connection

The other test that is often needed is a test of the data source to make sure that it is working as expected. The following servlet is provided as a simple example of how this can be done. It hard-codes the data source lookup information into the servlet to make the example as simple as possible for explanatory and ease of understanding purposes. In practice, the data source should be extracted form the URL used to invoke the servlet.

```
import java.io.*;
import java.net.*;
import java.sql.*;
import java.text.DateFormat;
import java.util.Date;

import javax.naming.*;
import javax.servlet.*;
import javax.servlet.http.*;
import javax.sql.DataSource;

public class SnoopJdbc extends HttpServlet
{
  private String today()
  {
    Date now = new Date();
    DateFormat dateFormatter = DateFormat.getDateTimeInstance();
```

```
    return dateFormatter.format( now );
  }

  public void doGet(
    HttpServletRequest request,
    HttpServletResponse response)
    throws ServletException, IOException
  {
    Context initCtx = null;
    DataSource ds = null;
    Connection conn = null;
    DatabaseMetaData meta = null;

    response.setContentType("text/plain");
    PrintWriter out = response.getWriter();
    out.println(   "Today     ==>"+today() );
    try
    {
      initCtx = new javax.naming.InitialContext();
      ds = (DataSource)initCtx.lookup("java:comp/env/jdbc/hsqltest");
      conn = ds.getConnection();
      meta = conn.getMetaData();
      out.println( "Database    ==>"+meta.getDatabaseProductName() );
      out.println( "DriverName  ==>"+meta.getDriverName());
      out.println( "DriverVersion ==>"+meta.getDriverVersion());
      out.println( "==== Tables ====" );
      ResultSet rs = meta.getTables(null,  null, "%", null );
      while( rs.next())
      {
        out.print( rs.getString("TABLE_TYPE"));
        out.print(":");
        out.println(rs.getString("TABLE_NAME"));
      }
      out.println( "================" );
      conn.close();
      conn = null;
    }
    catch( Exception e)
    {
      e.printStackTrace(out);
    }
    finally
    {
      out.close();
      try
      {
        if(conn != null)
          conn.close();
```

```
            }catch(SQLException sqle)
            {
              throw new ServletException( sqle );
            }
        }
    }
}
```

This servlet is very similar to the standalone Java program that was shown earlier in the *Install the MySQL JDBC Driver* section. We used this program to test the data source parameters. This new program lists the some of the same database metadata information as that earlier program but adds additional information. The primary differences here are that the program is implemented as a servlet and the connection is retrieved from a data source that was provided via JNDI lookup as shown in the following line of code.

```
ds = (DataSource)initCtx.lookup("java:comp/env/jdbc/hsqltest");
```

Unlike the earlier program, this one also lists the tables contained within the database. This is done by using the `getTables` method of the DatabaseMetaData object as follows:

```
ResultSet rs = meta.getTables(null,  null, "%", null );
```

The `getTables` method returns a ResultSet, just as a query against the database would do. This ResultSet can be looped through to display all of the table information as follows:

```
while( rs.next())
{
    out.print( rs.getString("TABLE_TYPE"));
    out.print(":");
    out.println(rs.getString("TABLE_NAME"));
}
```

In this case, we are primarily interested in the table type and the table names. The table type tells us if this is a system table, a view, or an ordinary table. This servlet can be deployed with the following fragments added to the `web.xml`.

```
<servlet>
    <servlet-name>SnoopJdbc</servlet-name>
    <servlet-class>SnoopJdbc</servlet-class>
</servlet>
```

```
<servlet-mapping>
    <servlet-name>SnoopJdbc</servlet-name>
    <url-pattern>/servlet/SnoopJdbc</url-pattern>
</servlet-mapping>
```

When deployed with a Web application named snoopy, the URL for accessing the servlet is:

```
http://localhost:8080/snoopy/servlet/SnoopJdbc
```

The result should look something like the following:

```
Today         ==>Feb 17, 2003 10:34:07 PM
Database      ==>HSQL Database Engine
DriverName    ==>HSQL Database Engine Driver
DriverVersion ==>1.7.1
URL           ==>jdbc:hsqldb:c:/openjava/hsqldb/data/hsqltest
==== Tables ====
TABLE:FOO
TABLE:BAR
TABLE:CUSTOMER
TABLE:PRODUCT
TABLE:INVOICE
TABLE:ITEM
================
```

Summary

In this chapter, we examined Java Database Connectivity (JDBC) and relational databases for inclusion in our platform. We compared three pure Java relational databases that are suitable for embedded database environments. We also examined four non-Java relational database products that provide Java support through JDBC drivers. We demonstrated configuration of the databases we chose and discussed integration with the Tomcat servlet container. Finally, we provided some tools to assist identifying and resolving problems when connecting through a servlet container.

CHAPTER

9

Messaging with JMS

Enterprise applications often require an asynchronous method of communicating between components. This is addressed within J2EE by the notion of messaging. Messaging comprises two key pieces: JMS (Java Message Service) and message-driven beans. JMS is the standard Java API for messaging, while message-driven beans, which are built on JMS, are the standard J2EE component model for messaging. In this chapter, we will take a look at several open source JMS providers and show you how to use JMS within the J2EE architecture with message-driven beans.

Architectural Considerations

JMS providers, which are servers that implement JMS, are often found as middleware tying together enterprise applications. Messaging allows elements of the enterprise to interoperate. We will learn about the two messaging models supported by JMS and the scenarios where each is appropriate.

JMS Overview

Messaging is a vital tool for linking enterprise applications together in a flexible and reliable manner. The JMS API focuses on exposing two primary messaging concepts: point-to-point messaging (PTP) and the publish/subscribe model (pub/sub).

Say Hi to MOM

JMS is only an API to an underlying piece of software known as message-oriented middleware (MOM), which is responsible for the actual implementation of messaging.

The MOM category of software emerged during the 1980s to meet the growing need of companies to glue together disparate enterprise applications. In normal Java parlance, MOM that implements the JMS API is known as a *JMS provider*.

All of the open source JMS providers are pure-Java solutions, but JMS can also be used to interface with existing non-Java-based message-oriented middleware, such as Tibco Rendezvous or Microsoft's MSMQ.

JMS Providers

Many different JMS providers exist and each has a unique set of trade-offs. There are freely available open source JMS providers such as JBossMQ, JORAM, OpenJMS, and UberMQ. There are also commercial JMS providers such as IBM's WebSphere MQ, Swift MQ, and FioranoMQ. For those applications that need to interoperate with existing MOM, commercial providers may be your only choice. For example, FioranoMQ can interoperate with Microsoft's MSMQ.

By coding against the JMS API, you minimize the costs of switching JMS providers. For example, you could use an open source JMS provider in development and then switch to an MQ-series provider for the final deployment. It's also a boon in benchmarking because you can test your application against a variety of JMS providers and find the best choice for your needs.

Synchronous versus Asynchronous Messaging

When we refer to messaging in the context of JMS, we're referring to asynchronous messaging. That means that things can occur across a span of indeterminate time. In contrast, synchronous messaging is initiated, executed, and returned in a predictable sequence. Asynchronous messaging allows more freedom with regard to timing, allowing messages to be queued and processed as resources permit. This decoupling contributes to increased scalability and load distribution. Another characteristic strength of asynchronous messaging is its ability to bridge gaps in availability. In connecting disparate enterprise applications, you don't want to be waiting until some distant system is finished processing. Overall, JMS messaging is a valuable tool for loosening dependencies between enterprise applications.

Types of Messaging Models

The two types of messaging models, queues and topics, share many similarities. In previous releases of the JMS specification, the two models were treated as entirely separate. Experience has shown that many of the conceptual differences between the queue model and the topic model are unnecessary. Beginning with version 1.1, the JMS specification unifies the queue and topic models.

A *queue* is like a line for messages. When you produce a message, it is added to the queue. When you remove a message from a queue, it is consumed. Between the time a message is produced and consumed, the message waits in the queue.

A *topic* is like a queue, except that it extends the 1:1 model to a 1:*n* model. To receive messages from a topic, a consumer must subscribe to it. Any number of consumers may be subscribed to the same topic. When a new message is produced, each of those subscribers will receive a copy of the same message.

Other Aspects of Messaging

There are messaging aspects that are orthogonal to the messaging model of queues versus topics, also known as PTP versus pub/sub messaging. Notably, these include the following notions:

- *Persistence* guarantees that messages survive the shutdown of the JMS server, whether voluntarily or otherwise.
- *Durability* applies only those who subscribe to a topic and guarantees that the topic will attempt to redeliver messages to a subscriber if the subscriber is temporarily unavailable.
- *Selectors* are used to restrict delivery of messages to just the ones you're interested in. The selector holds a selection expression, based on a subset of SQL. Potential messages are filtered based on that expression and only delivered if they pass.

JMS and Messaging

In the case of JMS, messaging provides for asynchronous, reliable, and transactional-aware point-to-point and publish/subscribe messaging. By providing a standardized interface to messaging services, JMS aids in the adoption of messaging on the Java platform and fulfills a vital need for enterprise applications.

Honestly, messaging and JMS probably sound more complicated than they actually are. As you will see, JMS is a very useful part of the enterprise architect's toolkit.

JMS and Enterprise Architectures

Now that you know what messaging and JMS are, where do they fit into the enterprise architecture? Connecting disparate enterprise components is the primary role of JMS. Naturally, JMS providers are found in the middleware layer. JMS clients, on the other hand, have their place throughout the enterprise architecture.

Overview of JMS within an Enterprise

JMS is a superb mechanism for passing events and data between enterprise components, and because enterprise components are often EJBs, JMS is fairly prevalent among middleware business components. In particular, message-driven beans serve as a great JMS message consumer hook into the typical enterprise application.

Messaging is also useful for standalone Java thick clients. For example, an administration console can benefit greatly from JMS to receive important events or send queries to multiple monitored sources.

JMS messaging can be a useful tool from the Web tier, although this is less common in practice. For example, servlets in the Web tier can use JMS to send messages to components. The servlet can then go about its business without waiting for the operation to be completed. The drawback is that the status of the operation is not available, as it is in the case of a synchronous call, where the return status is known after the call is completed. There are situations where this is acceptable, such as a buy order for a stock, where the status could be marked as pending until the order is processed. The user can check later to find out the status of his or her order.

This is an overview of JMS within the enterprise architecture. There are many places where JMS is a good solution. The best way to see where JMS fits into the enterprise architecture is to look at the problems that JMS solves.

Enterprise Issues Addressed by JMS

There are many situations that benefit from JMS. Proper application of a messaging solution can improve availability, load balancing, and scalability. We'll examine some real-world examples where these factors are improved through the addition of JMS.

JMS is great at pushing out cache invalidations. Enterprise applications often rely on data from other components in an enterprise system. These components are quite often very expensive to communicate with in terms of latency and resource consumption. A cross-JVM invocation might incur serialization and network transfer costs. Performance can be greatly improved by relying on the age-old tradition of local caching to minimize expensive communications. However, the problem with caching is that the data being cached may become outdated. A great pattern for tackling this is to have the owner of the cached data use a JMS topic to push out cache invalidations to any components that may be caching its data locally.

Cache invalidation is an example of using JMS to publish events. Now, let's take a look at how JMS can be used to communicate data efficiently to increase scalability and response time.

The Web is built around HTTP, which is a request/response protocol. In practical terms, this means the logic must finish running before a page can be displayed. You may have seen this problem yourself in some Web sites: you'll click on a link to purchase an item, and the user interface becomes blocked until the order is processed. Messaging can be used to solve this problem. Often, a sale is composed of several logical steps:

1. Checking availability
2. Processing payment information
3. Generating a sales notification
4. Generating a confirmation
5. Adding the order to a sales data warehouse

In this case, Steps 3 through 5 are not necessary to complete the transaction and can require lengthy processing. You can use messaging to defer the processing until after the user interface is handled. This is a server-side analog to the classic multithreaded GUI. The proper use of messaging improves application responsiveness and, more importantly, the user experience.

A task such as transferring funds can depend on multiple remote databases or integration with legacy systems. It might be infeasible to wait until the status of the transaction is known. In such a case, messaging can be used to kick off the processing while the user is informed that the result is pending. That way the user can continue to interact with the system.

If tasks within a single method call can be done in parallel, then messaging can improve scalability and responsiveness. Let's say the requirements state that we need to update information in our database, as well as in the databases of our partners. By using messaging you can simultaneously push out the updates rather than doing them sequentially, as would be required with a session EJB.

Taking the same scenario, you can use reduce coupling by taking advantage of pub/sub, which makes it easy for a new business-to-business (B2B) partner to listen in to updates from our application. It is also easy for a partner to drop out and be removed as a listener. By abstracting the knowledge of consumers out of our logic code, our application gains flexibility and robustness. Moves, adds, and changes of B2B partners won't break things and won't require code changes. All the listener needs to know is the name of the topic.

As you can see, JMS addresses a number of enterprise issues. Often a problem can be solved very elegantly if it is reframed in terms of messaging.

When Is JMS the Right Solution?

As with any tool, there are times when it makes sense to use JMS and there are times when it doesn't.

You would use JMS in situations where loosely coupled communication is beneficial. Queues and topics are fairly independent of the producers and consumers that use them. This buys flexibility in connecting enterprise components at the expense of increased cognitive complexity. You can fall into a tangle of asynchronous communications if messaging is overused without careful planning. It is far more difficult to trace asynchronous communication than it is to trace synchronous communication.

On the flip side, messages can lead to reduced complexity by simplifying the enterprise architecture. You can publish events and forget about them. You can trim away polling and other synchronous hacks in favor of true asynchronous programming.

In situations where components get overloaded by harsh spikes in processing, you can use messaging to distribute and normalize the load. The trade-off is that designing an application around messaging requires a different mindset than a traditional method-driven approach.

Another drawback to JMS is that messaging requires greater resources than a comparable method call. That is to say, in a one-to-one comparison, a message costs more than a method call. Overall, though, the scales may turn in favor of messaging. For example, in a system that sees large spikes in activity, you might be able to allocate fewer resources to handle the same load.

There is no single solution. JMS is a great tool and should be used when it makes sense. Hopefully, knowing what the trade-offs are will aid you in building your enterprise applications.

Selecting Your Tools

In this section, we'll establish our matrix of needs and evaluate the JMS providers to find the one that fits best. As with any endeavor, using the right tool for each situation is critical to your success. From a broad standpoint, we are interested in open source JMS providers that are at least JMS 1.0 compliant. That narrows down the field to several strong candidates. There are four products that stand out in this category: JBossMQ, ObjectWeb's JORAM, Uber Group's UberMQ, and Exolab's OpenJMS. We will consider our messaging needs, look at the factors that differentiate these messaging providers, and finally select one to install and configure.

Needs and Features Analysis

Messaging shares many common criteria for evaluation with other parts of an enterprise solution. In examining a JMS provider, we can ignore the common functionality required by the specification. Usually, any JMS-compliant solution will have strong suitability in enterprise use. In further differentiating the JMS providers, we will look at the following criteria:

- Scalability
- Performance
- Specification compliance
- Interoperability
- Reliability
- Administrative capabilities
- Ease of use/integration
- Development velocity

Scalability is a good differentiator of JMS providers. This is commonly measured in terms of the maximum volume of messages per unit time. As a practical matter, this fact is important to know, but you should also know how scalable the JMS provider is in other terms. How many topics or queues can the JMS provider handle? This is where added features such as JORAM's clusterizable topics can become important.

Performance is always a factor in evaluating products. How much CPU time and memory resources does a JMS provider require? What is the incremental increase in resources for each additional message?

Specification compliance is usually a given, but in this particular case, it is important to note which JMS providers adhere to version 1.1 of the JMS specification and which implement older versions of JMS. This is because JMS 1.1 unified the messaging domains. The main benefit from unification is that you can now use both PTP and pub/sub messaging within the same transaction. The unification also simplifies the development of client code, increases flexibility, and improves reusability because the decision to use either a PTP or pub/sub model is less binding. From a less formal point of view, specification compliance serves as a barometer for the amount of developer activity in a project.

Interoperability is a great differentiator, if only because the open source projects offer so little interoperability. Commercial offerings add value here because they often do work with preexisting MOM such as Microsoft MSMQ and Tibco Rendezvous. It is worth noting that most vendors do offer JMS-compliant interfaces. On the other hand, the open source JMS providers are focused on their implementation of the JMS API and do not feature any interoperability with vendor-specific MOM.

Reliability is always important, but particularly within the scope of JMS providers. It is critical for a JMS provider to remain stable over a large volume of messages. Measuring reliability can be difficult given the velocity of open source development. For example, JBossMQ 3.0.3 was crippled by a memory leak bug that prevented long-term operation. Yet this was rapidly fixed in 3.0.4 release. The thing to keep in mind is test, test, test.

Administrative capability is fast becoming the most important criterion for enterprise systems. As complexity continues to rise, administrators are becoming overwhelmed. JMX (Java Management Extensions) has been great in increasing the visibility of enterprise systems and the entire J2EE industry to moving in that direction for administration. Beyond just a standard for administration, a good set of tools can make a huge difference in choosing one JMS provider over another.

Ease of use and integration are especially important in the context of J2EE development. JMS is one of the foundation elements for J2EE and needs to work with higher-level elements such as EJBs. A reduction in configuration and integration errors translates directly into greater productivity. This is particularly true if you plan on moving the J2EE enterprise application over to a different environment for final deployment.

Evaluating JMS Providers

Now that we've established the criteria for evaluation, we will look at each of the JMS providers in detail. During this examination, we'll weigh the advantages and disadvantages of each.

JBossMQ

JBossMQ is the JMS provider that is bundled with the JBoss J2EE application server. JBossMQ is a clean-room, pure-Java implementation of JMS. Formerly known as SpyderMQ, it was first released to the public in April 2000 and still enjoys high development activity. The following table gives a summary of JBossMQ.

Product	JbossMQ
Category	Messaging/JMS
URL	http://www.jboss.org
Supported Platforms	Java 1.3 and above
License	LGPL Open Source License
Features	JMX management console; integrated with JBoss application server

NOTE One caveat about JBossMQ is that information on the Web site tends to lag behind the development, so the best place to go for the latest scoop is the forums.

The performance of JBossMQ is very good on a single machine, but it has issues scaling under heavy load. Clustering code is being tested at the time of this writing, which may prove to be a useful feature. The optimized invocation layer (OIL), which uses TCP/IP as the basis for the messaging protocol, has excellent performance. JBossMQ holds the performance edge over the other JMS providers when the load is manageable.

There is also another messaging protocol, named UIL, that is supported by JBossMQ for cases where the JMS client is located behind a firewall. This is a nice bonus touch. JBossMQ seems to have a wide variety of protocol support, like OpenJMS, but it fails to trumpet that fact.

JBossMQ is compliant with JMS 1.1, the most recent version of the specification. It was one of the JMS providers to reach compliance, which is impressive.

JBossMQ is used in production environments and has performed admirably in those scenarios. Support for transactions is optional in the specification but possibly critical to an enterprise application. JBossMQ includes transactional support for messaging. As scalability features such as flow control and clustering are added, there is a risk that reliability of JBossMQ will suffer in the short term.

Without a doubt, the JMX feature makes administration a breeze. Both extremely powerful and imminently accessible, JMX is the standard for Java administration. As products continue to add JMX support and generic tools arise for management of any JMX-enabled product, huge improvements in administration can be expected. For now, JBossMQ gets a big thumb's up for its support of JMX.

Because JBossMQ is integrated with the JBoss J2EE application server, integration is not a factor if you are using JBoss; right out of the box; you have a complete J2EE solution ready to run. Unfortunately, newer versions of JBossMQ are only available for download as a part of the entire JBoss bundle. We will examine how to separate out JBossMQ for use with other J2EE application servers.

Ease of use is quite good. The default configuration works well and all the configuration files are in XML. Documentation is available, as are online forums and IRC support. Because JBoss is so widely used, it is easy to find other experienced developers to talk to if a problem is encountered. In fact, it's hard to fault any of the open source JMS providers in this area.

JBossMQ is a great choice if you are running the JBoss Application Server. Unfortunately, it is currently being rewritten to rely on the JBoss CMP for persistence. This means that there is a dependency on the JBoss application server. The JMX interfaces are excellent and performance is good. As a quick ramp-up developer environment, it is a great choice.

JORAM

JORAM is one of the best pure-Java JMS providers available. It was originally developed at Bull, a European consulting firm, and since being open sourced JORAM has incorporated research from INRIA (French National Institute for Research in Computer Science and Control). Since JORAM leverages other open source projects, it is available under a number of different licenses. JORAM is very feature rich and adds many niceties above and beyond what is needed to implement the JMS specification, such as flow control and topic hierarchies distributed over servers. In addition, there is strong developmental activity from the core team. The following table gives a summary of JORAM.

Product	JORAM
Category	Messaging/JMS
URL	http://www.objectweb.org/joram/
Supported Platforms	Java 1.2 and above
License	Joram license, Xerces license, Jakarta-Regexp license, CUP license
Features	Good scalability features; integrated with JOnAS J2EE application server

Scalability is one of JORAM's strong suits. Its ability to cluster topics is a big plus in enterprise applications that require a high level of scalability. The flow control mechanism is great for throttling down an overly active client and maintaining levels of service for other clients. There are also many other features that should contribute to JORAM's dominance in the scalability arena.

JORAM's performance is decent, although the wealth of additional functionality of the product detracts from its overall performance in a simple configuration. As the need for scalability goes up, JORAM's relative performance could be much better than the other JMS providers.

JORAM features its own administration protocol via JMS to make administration easier. A lack of tools undermines this effort to a large extent: you still have to code your own administration interface! Granted, with a little effort, a Java Swing administration client or a Web interface using JMS could be created, and odds are that those administration tools will be added to JORAM in the future. It's worth noting that all JMS providers come with an API that exposes administrative features, so it is possible to wrap the administration API to interface it with JMS. So, although the administration protocol running over JMS is espoused as a feature, it really doesn't add up to much of an advantage.

Setting up JORAM is a snap and having it available integrated with JOnAS, its sister EJB container, is wonderful. Some great sample programs come with it, and the test suite, available through an additional download, is very nice to have.

JORAM has considerable development velocity, with new releases showing up on a regular basis. The code is high quality, and because several of the primary developers are employed by ScalAgent, I would expect to see continued high-quality development. On the other hand, having a corporate backer that could potentially steer the direction of development is a risk. Thus far there has been no reason to worry about that, but it is a potential issue.

Perhaps the most confusing aspect of JORAM is the plethora of licenses. This is so because the JORAM project builds upon several other open source projects, namely from the Xerces and Jakarta-Apache projects. As a result, the JORAM code must also be made available under multiple licenses: the JORAM license, the Open Public License 1.0, and the Apache Software License 1.1. Although this is confusing, it is actually not much of an issue because the licenses share a lot of common ground and don't really put up any noteworthy restrictions. All are open source licenses and should not be an issue.

NOTE **Downloading the free JORAM implementation requires entering your name, email address, and organization, as well as agreeing to the JORAM license; we think this requirement a bit onerous for an open source product.**

JORAM also has a JMS test suite available on the Web site. They used it to test that JORAM's JMS compliance when it was rewritten, and it serves a good measuring stick to check whether other JMS providers are compliant. The results are very nice, and the tests themselves are open source, so you can see what is actually being run. Unlike the download for JORAM, the test suite is available without having to enter any personal information. The test suite is available at the following URL:

```
http://www.objectweb.org/joram/tests/download.html
```

To run the test suite, you will need to have Ant and JUnit installed.

CROSS-REFERENCE **See Chapter 4 for more details on Ant and JUnit.**

TIP **The easiest way to make JUnit available to Ant is to place the** `junit.jar` **file into your** `ANT_HOME/lib` **directory.**

One problem that may crop up after downloading the JORAM files is that they might end up with the wrong extension. The files are typically .tgz, which is in the tar gzipped format. The .tar extension is erroneously appended to the file, and you should remove that part of the filename.

Overall, JORAM is a great product with many advanced features. The lack of good administration tools is JORAM's greatest weakness. If you think that you will hit the scalability limits of the other JMS providers, JORAM is your best bet.

OpenJMS

OpenJMS is an open source JMS provider sponsored by The Exolab Group, who are also responsible for the excellent Castor data-binding framework. Once a leading-edge implementation, OpenJMS seems to have lagged behind its peers in achieving JMS 1.1 compliance. Nevertheless, it is a decent project with some unique features. The following table gives a summary of OpenJMS.

Product	OpenJMS
Category	Messaging/JMS
URL	http://openjms.sourceforge.net/
Supported Platforms	Java 1.2 and above
License	Custom license (similar to the BSD Open Source License)
Features	Impressive array of messaging protocols

One of best things about OpenJMS is the impressive variety of protocol options that are supported, including RMI, HTTP, HTTPS, and TCP/IP. This comes into play when you need to tunnel through firewalls or when the resources used by the protocol become a problem.

Specification compliance is an area where OpenJMS falls short: it supports an older version of the JMS spec, 1.0.2. This means that OpenJMS will not be specification compliant when version 1.4 of the J2EE specification is the norm.

OpenJMS comes with an administration GUI, which makes it easy to browse through the queues and topics. The GUI was nice to have and definitely better than nothing, but it didn't add much value overall.

OpenJMS doesn't come integrated with any J2EE application servers. This is not a problem, because integration with OpenJMS is a straightforward affair. It definitely deserves some points for playing well with others.

Development activity seems to have tapered off, and OpenJMS might be in danger of becoming orphaned software. Again, at the time of writing Open JMS is still stuck on version 1.0.2 of the JMS specification. There has been some good traffic on the mailing lists recently, and hopefully OpenJMS will start making more regular releases.

UberMQ

UberMQ is one of the newest open source JMS providers. The Uber Group recently released version 2.0 of UberMQ, a clean-room, pure-Java implementation of JMS 1.1. They focused on performance, and it really shows. In addition, some nice advanced features such as clustering are provided. The main drawback to UberMQ is that lack of support for transactions. It is difficult to fathom how such a critical feature would have missed the cut. Our hope is that UberMQ will soon add transaction support. The following table gives a summary of UberMQ.

Product	UberMQ
Category	Messaging/JMS
URL	http://www.ubermq.com/
Supported Platforms	Java 1.4.1
License	Custom license (similar to the BSD Open Source License)
Features	GUI admin tools; uses NIO (non-blocking I/O)

UberMQ is based on the new Java NIO (non-blocking I/O) functionality and should be very scalable in a single-server environment. It also offers clustering, and its scalability is very impressive.

Performance was surprisingly average given the amount of attention UberMQ gives to the subject. It was middle of the pack among the other open source JMS providers. The numbers are solid but JBossMQ remains the performance leader.

While not interoperable out of the box, UberMQ does stand out by having pluggable wire and transport protocols. This means that others can develop and add in protocol support for other MOM. There is a high likelihood that in the future, UberMQ will become more interoperable than the other open source JMS providers.

Superb administration tools come with UberMQ, including GUI versions of the administration console and a message viewer that captures all messages moving through the system. This makes it great for providing visibility into the system. Unfortunately, the tools do not offer any active functionality. For example, you cannot use them to add a new queue or topic.

Because of the use of Java NIO, UberMQ requires a fairly new version of Java run time. This can be a major issue for many deployments and is something to keep in mind. The lack of JNDI hooks makes UberMQ the most difficult of the open source JMS providers to integrate into a J2EE application server.

Development velocity on this project is rapid. The entire project only started in August 2002, and the UberMQ developers have already gotten the product in a very competitive state. Hopefully, they can continue the blistering pace and drive innovation in the open source Java JMS space.

Downloading UberMQ from the main Web site requires entering your name, email address, and organization. However, UberMQ is hosted on SourceForge.net and can be reached directly through the following URL:

```
http://sourceforge.net/project/showfiles.php?group_id=59277
```

With its strong feature set that is very performance oriented, UberMQ looks very promising. However, being a relative newcomer to the open source JMS provider arena, UberMQ remains incomplete. A couple of glaring holes are the lack of transaction support and the missing JNDI hooks out of the box.

The jury remains out as to how UberMQ will evolve, but its presence in the open source JMS messaging will hopefully invigorate the category and bring about renewed developer attention.

Product Selection

Of the four open source JMS providers, we feel that JBossMQ and JORAM are the strongest candidates. JORAM adds some very useful functionality beyond just what is required by the specification, such as clusterizable topics. The JMX support provided by JBossMQ makes it much easier to work with and administrate. Both are available integrated with a J2EE application server if you want to get up and running quickly. Scalability favors JORAM with its extensive feature set and clustering abilities. These features are somewhat offset by the lower performance of JORAM; this is where JBossMQ gets the nod. JBossMQ also features the best administration interface through its support of JMX.

UberMQ is a fast rising up-and-comer that you should keep an eye on but the incompatibility with older Java runtime environments are a deal breaker. Meanwhile, OpenJMS development seems to be languishing, and it could well be on its way out.

NOTE **Keep in mind that for mission-critical applications, open source JMS providers still very much lag their commercial counterparts. The commercial JMS providers offer better scalability, provide better performance, and can work with existing pre-JMS MOM products. Open source JMS providers are new to the scene and haven't attracted much developer attention until recently. Furthermore, commercial JMS providers have already established track records in production enterprise environments.**

In the end, all four JMS providers are good products with JBossMQ and JORAM leading the pack. The JMX administration features in JBossMQ make it easy to see what's going on and make it easier to configure. It has high performance, a good feature set, and is an excellent choice if you're planning on using JBoss for the EJB container. JORAM has a vast amount of well-written documentation and a superb test suite. Performance is good, and it has some leading edge features, such as using SOAP as the invocation protocol. The decision between JBossMQ and JORAM is very close. We choose JBossMQ because it is easier to administrate and use, which is important during development.

Installation and Configuration

Given our evaluation of the open source JMS providers (see the previous section), we'll use JBossMQ as an example in the next couple sections. First, we will look at how to install and configure JBossMQ. Then, we'll show some example usage of JMS from a standalone basis and from within the J2EE framework. Like the other parts of J2EE, by design JMS providers are interchangeable. Although we will be using JBossMQ, for these projects, another product can be substituted in if it fits your requirements better.

Installing JBossMQ is a simple matter. First, you need to download the release from the JBoss Web site (`http://www.jboss.org`). Because JBossMQ is not offered as a standalone product, you'll need to download the entire JBoss application server.

Installing JBoss in Windows

After downloading JBoss, unzip the files into the directory in which you want JBoss to be installed. The recommended directory for Windows is `C:\jboss`. The files should be extracted under a folder named `jboss-VERSION`, where *VERSION* is the version number for that release of JBoss. We will refer to this folder as the JBoss home directory, or `%JBOSS_HOME%`[NR2], when it is referred to inside a path.

After extracting all the files, you need to add the JBOSS_HOME variable to your environment. The basic method of doing so in Windows is by changing the settings in the System applet in the Control Panel by choosing Advanced ➪ Environment Variables.

Installing JBoss in Linux

As with the Windows version, first you need to extract all the files into the directory where you want JBoss to be installed. In Linux, the recommended directory, for the time being, is within your home directory, which is typically `/home/MYUSERNAME`. You can do this by running the following command from within your home directory: `unzip jboss-3.0.4.zip -d jboss`, substituting the version you're working with for the 3.0.4. The –d option tells unzip that we want to specify the destination directory.

After extracting all the files, you need to add the $JBOSS_HOME variable to your environment. In Linux, environment variables are usually added into the startup scripts, such as the `.bash_profile` file in your home directory.

Looking at the Default Configuration

At this point, JBoss is already ready to run. Just find the batch file named `run.bat` (`run.sh` in Linux) in the `bin` subdirectory of the JBoss home directory. Executing that will run the JBoss application server, including JBossMQ.

CROSS-REFERENCE **We'll get into configuring and securing JBoss in more detail in Chapter 11.**

For the time being, the default setup will work fine. Before we run JBoss though, we will look at parts of JBoss that are pertinent to our discussion of JMS and MDB.

If you look at the JBoss home directory, you'll find the following directories:

/bin. Holds various batch files and shell scripts, of which we are only interested in `run.bat` (or `run.sh` for Linux).

/client. Contains library jars that are used by client applications. We will need the `jbossall-client.jar` and `log4j.jar` in this directory for our standalone JMS clients. The `jbossall-client.jar` file holds all the classes needed by a standalone JBoss client, including the JBossMQ client classes. The `log4j.jar` file holds classes that handle logging and is also required.

/docs. Includes documentation and is a useful place to check whenever you need more information on JBoss.

/lib. Contains various library jars required by JBoss application server.

/server. This is where all the server stuff resides. There are three subdirectories under server directory, which correspond to various service level configurations for the JBoss server:

/default. Includes the standard J2EE environment for a standalone server.

/minimal. This minimal environment is pretty much useless for our purposes, because it doesn't even start up the EJB services.

/all. Contains everything in default, plus RMI/IIOP and clustering.

We will be sticking with the default service configuration for the purposes of this book.

JBoss Configuration Files

Now, take a look inside the `server\default\conf` directory. This is where the JBoss configuration files are. They are mostly in XML format. For our purposes, `jbossmq-state.xml` is the most interesting of the lot. The JMS users and roles are stored in this file. The other directory worth checking out is `server\default\deploy`. This is the directory where JBoss checks for new .ear, .war, and .ejb jar files. Any files copied here are automatically deployed by the application server. JBoss also stores some configuration files here. In particular, you can find `jbossmq-destinations-service.xml` and `jbossmq-service.xml` files in this directory.

The `jbossmq-destinations-service.xml` file defines all the JBossMQ queues and topics, as well as security permissions for JBossMQ. Open up the `jbossmq-destinations-service.xml` file and take a look. There are several JMS destinations already preconfigured. We'll be utilizing the testTopic topic a lot in our examples because it is available by default.

Here's an excerpt from `jbossmq-destinations-service.xml`:

```
<mbean code="org.jboss.mq.server.jmx.Queue"
    name="jboss.mq.destination:service=Queue,name=testQueue">
  <depends optional-attribute-
name="DestinationManager">jboss.mq:service=DestinationManager</depends>
  <depends optional-attribute-
name="SecurityManager">jboss.mq:service=SecurityManager</depends>
  <attribute name="SecurityConf">
    <security>
      <role name="guest" read="true" write="true"/>
      <role name="publisher" read="true" write="true" create="false"/>
      <role name="noacc" read="false" write="false" create="false"/>
    </security>
  </attribute>
</mbean>
```

The `jbossmq-service.xml` file contains configuration information for the actual JBossMQ service. In particular, you can modify values in here to tweak performance by reducing timeout intervals. However, we won't actually get into that in this book.

Standalone JBossMQ

The default JBoss distribution seems to include everything but the kitchen sink. There are times when all we want or need is a JMS provider. In those cases, the footprint required for a complete JBoss installation is overkill. The flexibility of JBoss is one of its strongest selling points. JBoss was designed to be highly modular, and it is even possible to decompose it down to a tiny microkernel that fits only a single floppy. We won't be doing anything that drastic, but we will be configuring JBoss down to a minimal useful configuration for JBossMQ, the JMS provider.

We will start with the default server configuration, which is contained in the `server/default` directory within the JBoss home directory. Copy the entire directory, and rename it `server/jbossmq`. This will make a replica of the default configuration.

Now, we'll remove the unnecessary services from the `server/jbossmq/deploy` directory. The list below shows the files that we need. Everything else should be deleted from this directory.

- `counter-service.xml`
- `hsqldb-service.xml`
- `jboss-local-jdbc.rar`
- `jbossmq-destinations-service.xml`
- `jbossmq-service.xml`
- `jboss-xa.rar`
- `jca-service.xml`
- `jms-ra.rar`
- `jms-service.xml`
- `properties-service.xml`
- `schedule-manager-service.xml`
- `scheduler-service.xml`
- `user-service.xml`

Next we need to clean up the `server/jbossmq/lib` directory to remove unused library jars. Once again, the list below represents the files that should remain. Unlike the previous step, this one is not strictly necessary. Everything will work properly even if we have extra library jars loaded. It will waste resources and result in a memory footprint that is approximately 3 MB larger than necessary.

- `activation.jar`
- `autonumber-plugin.jar`
- `bcel.jar`
- `counter-plugin.jar`
- `hsqldb.jar`
- `hsqldb-plugin.jar`
- `jboss.rar`
- `jboss-j2ee.jar`
- `jboss-jaas.jar`
- `jboss-jca.jar`
- `jboss-management.jar`
- `jbossmq.jar`
- `jbossmx.jar`
- `jbosssx.jar`
- `jnpserver.jar`
- `jsse.jar`
- `jts.jar`
- `log4j.jar`
- `properties-plugin.jar`

Finally, we need to modify the `server/jbossmq/conf/jboss-service.xml` file. This is an XML configuration file that tells JBoss which services to start up. If you'll recall, JBoss uses a JMX core to make it easy to add, remove, and configure services. This file contains references to the JMX MBeans that JBoss uses. In order to disable some of the services we don't want, we must make some changes here. Most notable among the deleted services are the EJB container, the servlet container, and the Web server.

Find the following elements and delete them from the `jboss-service.xml` file:

- Approximately line 105:

```
<mbean code="org.jboss.web.WebService"
       name="jboss:service=Webserver">
```

- Approximately line 199:

```
<mbean code="org.jboss.ejb.EJBDeployer"
       name="jboss.ejb:service=EJBDeployer">
```

- Approximately line 208:

```
<mbean code="org.jboss.deployment.EARDeployer"
       name="jboss.j2ee:service=EARDeployer">
```

- Approximately line 239:

```
<mbean code="org.jboss.invocation.jrmp.server.JRMPInvoker"
       name="jboss:service=invoker,type=jrmp">
```

- Approximately line 244:

```
<mbean code="org.jboss.invocation.pooled.server.PooledInvoker"
       name="jboss:service=invoker,type=pooled">
```

- Approximately line 248:

```
<mbean code="org.jboss.invocation.local.LocalInvoker"
       name="jboss:service=invoker,type=local">
```

The configuration is complete! To start the standalone JBossMQ server, you must pass the server configuration in the start script.

In Windows, the `run.bat` script is used:

```
%JBOSS_HOME%\bin\run.bat -c jbossmq
```

On Linux, we will use the `run.sh` script:

```
$JBOSS_HOME/bin/run.sh -c jbossmq
```

The examples in the following section will work with the standalone JBossMQ. However, the JMX console will not be available because that service was removed.

Integration and Testing

Okay, now that you've had the basic tour of the JBoss application server and its JBossMQ parts, let's try to get some Java code to work with the JBossMQ JMS service. In this section, we'll be testing JMS usage from all areas of the J2EE framework, from standalone clients to MDBs, and thereby show how they can be used within a J2EE architecture.

We'll perform the following chores in the following sections:

1. We'll first build an EAR containing our MDBs.
2. Next, we'll add a stateless session bean and show how we can improve response time and scalability by using MDBs to queue off expensive operations.
3. Finally, we'll build a standalone Java client that will interact with our MDBs via JMS.

NOTE **For more information on JMS, check out the JMS Tutorial available from Sun's Web site at** `http://java.sun.com/products/jms/tutorial/index.html`.

Standalone JMS Clients

In this section, we'll demonstrate how to write a standalone JMS client just to test that JBossMQ is available and working properly. This is a fairly simple program. For the sake of organization, you will want to create a new directory to hold the JMS test programs. Without further ado, let's see the code for a simple JMS publisher. Here's the code for `SimplePublisher.java`:

```
import java.util.*;
import javax.jms.*;
import javax.naming.*;

/**
 *  Simple JMS Publisher.
 */
public class SimplePublisher
{
  public static void main( String[] args )
  {
    TopicConnection connection = null;
    TopicSession session = null;
    try
    {
      // --- Create default properties to find JBoss's JNDI. ---

      Hashtable default_properties = new Hashtable();
      default_properties.put(
        Context.INITIAL_CONTEXT_FACTORY,
        "org.jnp.interfaces.NamingContextFactory" );
      default_properties.put( Context.PROVIDER_URL, "localhost:1099" );
```

```
    // --- Create and cache various JMS resources. ---
    // -- Note that we are using the transaction aware versions of
    // -- everything.

    Context context = new InitialContext( default_properties );
    TopicConnectionFactory factory = (TopicConnectionFactory)
      context.lookup( "java:/XAConnectionFactory" );
    connection = factory.createTopicConnection();
    session =
      connection.createTopicSession( true, Session.AUTO_ACKNOWLEDGE );
    Topic topic = (Topic) context.lookup( "topic/testTopic" );

    // -- We use topic/testTopic as the topic to publish to because it
    // -- is defined by default by JBossMQ. You can find the queues
    // -- and topics available at JBoss startup time within the
    // -- jbossmq-destinations-service.xml file inside the
    // -- %JBOSS_HOME%\server\default directory.

    TopicPublisher publisher = session.createPublisher( topic );

    // --- Publish a trivial text message. ---
    TextMessage message = session.createTextMessage();
    message.setText( "" + new Date().getTime() );
    publisher.publish( message );
    session.commit();
    System.out.println( "Published " + message );
  }
  catch( Exception e )
  {
    e.printStackTrace();
  }
  finally
  {
    try
    {
      if( session != null )
      {
        session.close();
      }
    }
    catch( JMSException e2 )
    {
      e2.printStackTrace();
    }
    try
    {
      if( connection != null )
      {
        connection.close();
      }
```

```
          }
          catch( JMSException e2 )
          {
            e2.printStackTrace();
          }
        }
      }
    }
```

Now, compile the program. To compile it in Windows, use the following command:

```
javac -classpath .;%JBOSS_HOME%\client\jbossall-client.jar SimplePublisher.java
```

To compile it on Linux, use the following command:

```
javac -classpath .:$JBOSS_HOME/client/jbossall-client.jar SimplePublisher.java
```

After the program is compiled, try running SimplePublisher. Before you do, make sure that the JBoss is running. JBoss is required because it provides the JNDI and JBossMQ JMS services that SimplePubisher relies on.

In Windows, SimplePublisher can be run with following command:

```
java -classpath .;%JBOSS_HOME%\client\jbossall-
client.jar;%JBOSS_HOME%\client\log4j.jar SimplePublisher
```

In Linux, the command is:

```
java -classpath .:$JBOSS_HOME/client/jbossall-
client.jar:$JBOSS_HOME/client/log4j.jar SimplePublisher
```

Note that we have added the log4j.jar to the classpath because this is used by JBossMQ clients for logging.

The `default_properties` hashtable is probably something you've seen before as a mechanism for passing in various properties that are used to establish context. We provide the settings for JNDI that are used by default in JBoss. We've done this here for simplicity's sake. A more flexible method is to pass in these settings through the command line rather than keeping them in the code. For example:

```
java -classpath .;%JBOSS_HOME%\client\jbossall-
client.jar;%JBOSS_HOME%\client\log4j.jar -
Djava.naming.factory.initial=org.jnp.interfaces.NamingContextFactory
-Djava.naming.provider.url=localhost:1099 SimplePublisher.
```

For the settings to be used, keep in mind that you have to remove the code that passes in the default_properties to the InitialContext constructor.

We also have JNDI lookups for the TopicConnectionFactory and the Topic. The JNDI names that these are bound under vary with different application servers, and even settings.

CROSS-REFERENCE **The SnoopJNDI servlet from Chapter 8 is a great way to browse the JNDI space of an application server.**

By now, the program should execute without any errors but how can we tell if the message is really being sent? In order to do that, we need to complete the other side of the messaging chain. Namely, we need to write a receiver counterpart to our sender program. Here's the code for `SimpleSubscriber.java`:

```
import java.util.*;
import javax.jms.*;
import javax.naming.*;

/**
 *  Simple JMS Subscriber.
 *
 *@author   stng
 *@created    January 19, 2003
 */
public class SimpleSubscriber
{

  /**
   *  The main program for the SimpleSubscriber class
   *
   *@param  args The command-line arguments
   *@since
   */
  public static void main( String[] args )
  {
    TopicConnection connection = null;
    TopicSession session = null;
    try
    {
      // --- Create default properties to find JBoss's JNDI. ---
      Hashtable default_properties = new Hashtable();
      default_properties.put(
              Context.INITIAL_CONTEXT_FACTORY,
              "org.jnp.interfaces.NamingContextFactory" );
```

```
default_properties.put( Context.PROVIDER_URL, "localhost:1099" );

// --- Create and cache various JMS resources. ---
// -- Note that we are using the transaction aware versions of
// -- everything.
Context context = new InitialContext( default_properties );
TopicConnectionFactory factory = (TopicConnectionFactory)
    context.lookup( "java:/XAConnectionFactory" );
connection = factory.createTopicConnection();
session = connection.createTopicSession(
        true, Session.AUTO_ACKNOWLEDGE );
Topic topic = (Topic) context.lookup( "topic/testTopic" );

// -- We use topic/testTopic as the topic to publish to because it
// -- is defined by default by JBossMQ. You can find the queues
// -- and topics available in the jbossmq-destinations-service.xml
// -- file within the %JBOSS_HOME%\server\default directory.
TopicSubscriber subscriber = session.createSubscriber( topic );
subscriber.setMessageListener(
  new MessageListener()
  {
    public void onMessage( Message message )
    {
      System.out.println( "Got " + message );
      try
      {
        if( message instanceof TextMessage )
        {
          String message_body =
            ( (TextMessage) message ).getText();

          // -- Do something useful with the message body.
          // -- We'll use the time value that is the body
          // -- of the message sent by SimplePublisher
          // -- and calculate the elapsed time in secs.
          double elapsed_time = ( ( new Date() ).getTime() -
            Long.parseLong( message_body ) ) / 1000.0;
          System.out.println(
            "Message has spent " +
            elapsed_time + " in transit." );
        }
      }
      catch( Exception e )
      {
        e.printStackTrace();
      }
    }
  }
```

```
      );

      connection.start();


      // --- Keep running until enter is pressed. ---

      System.out.println( "Press enter to quit." );
      System.out.println( "Awaiting messages..." );
      System.in.read();
      session.commit();
    }
    catch( Exception e )
    {
      e.printStackTrace();
    }
    finally
    {
      try
      {
        if( session != null )
        {
          session.close();
        }
      }
      catch( JMSException e2 )
      {
        e2.printStackTrace();
      }
      try
      {
        if( connection != null )
        {
          connection.close();
        }
      }
      catch( JMSException e2 )
      {
        e2.printStackTrace();
      }
    }
  }
}
```

You can compile the program with the following command:

```
javac -classpath .;%JBOSS_HOME%\client\jbossall-client.jar SimpleSubscriber.java
```

For Linux clients, replace the command with:

```
javac -classpath .:$JBOSS_HOME/client/jbossall-client.jar SimpleSubscriber.java
```

After it is compiled, try running SimpleSubscriber. As before, you'll need JBoss to be running.

In Windows, SimpleSubscriber can be run with following command:

```
java -classpath .;%JBOSS_HOME%\client\jbossall-
client.jar;%JBOSS_HOME%\client\log4j.jar SimpleSubscriber
```

In Linux, the command is:

```
java -classpath .:$JBOSS_HOME/client/jbossall-
client.jar:$JBOSS_HOME/client/log4j.jar SimpleSubscriber
```

At this point, the SimpleSubscriber should be patiently awaiting messages. In a new command shell, run the SimplePublisher program. You should get some output showing the details of the JMS message, as well as a short line on the time elapsed. At this stage, we know the basic JMS pub/sub messaging is working, so everything is configured right.

NOTE If you're having problems with the messaging, check that JBoss is running. You can check by surfing to the JMX console at `http://localhost:8080/jmx-console`**. If you see a HTML page for JBoss, then you're good to go. Please note that the JMX module is not available if you are using the standalone JBossMQ configuration.**

The code for SimpleSubscriber is very similar to that of SimplePublisher. The main addition is the anonymous inner class that serves as the incoming message handler. This is the section of code that looks like:

```
subscriber.setMessageListener(
    new MessageListener()
    {
        public void onMessage( Message message )
        {
            ....
        }
    }
);
```

Also, it uses the JMS subscriber counterparts. This is an exercise of pub/sub messaging, but PTP can be easily swapped in by substituting the appropriate PTP classes, which is an example of how the domain unification in JMS 1.1 pays off. Prior to 1.1, the interfaces for pub/sub were different from those for PTP. The older interface is still there, so if you want to trade off flexibility for backward compatibility, you can do so.

With the programs, our text message body is a string representation of the time. We can visually verify that the JMS message header contains an attribute called `jmsTimeStamp` that matches up with our calculations.

Now, let's take a look at the JMX console and see how it fits into the JMS picture. JMX is a Java management specification that exposes MBeans, which are management components. In the JMX console, these MBeans correspond to subsystems within JBoss. Run JBoss and open a browser to show the JMX console (shown in Figure 9.1), which can be found at `http://localhost:8080/jmx-console`.

As you can see in Figures 9.1 and 9.2, the JMX console has a vast array of MBeans displayed. This top-level view of the JBoss server is called the JMX Agent view. We're interested in looking at the JBossMQ queues and topics, so let's skip on down to the section titled `jboss.mq.destination`. This is where all the queues and topics are listed. Let's take a more in-depth look at testTopic. Click on the `service=Topic,name=testTopic` link. We are now presented with a view of the MBean for testTopic. Here, we can see what's going on inside the JBoss server. For example, there's an attribute called `JNDI Name` with the value `topic/testTopic`. This is the JNDI name to which the testTopic is bound. Let's try changing that to `topic/testTopic2`. Click Apply Changes, and try running the SimplePublisher program again. As you can see from the stack trace, the JNDI name has been changed, and testTopic is no longer available under `topic/testTopic`. Now, let's go back and change the `JNDIName` back to `topic/testTopic`. If you run SimplePublisher again, you'll see that everything is back to the way it was.

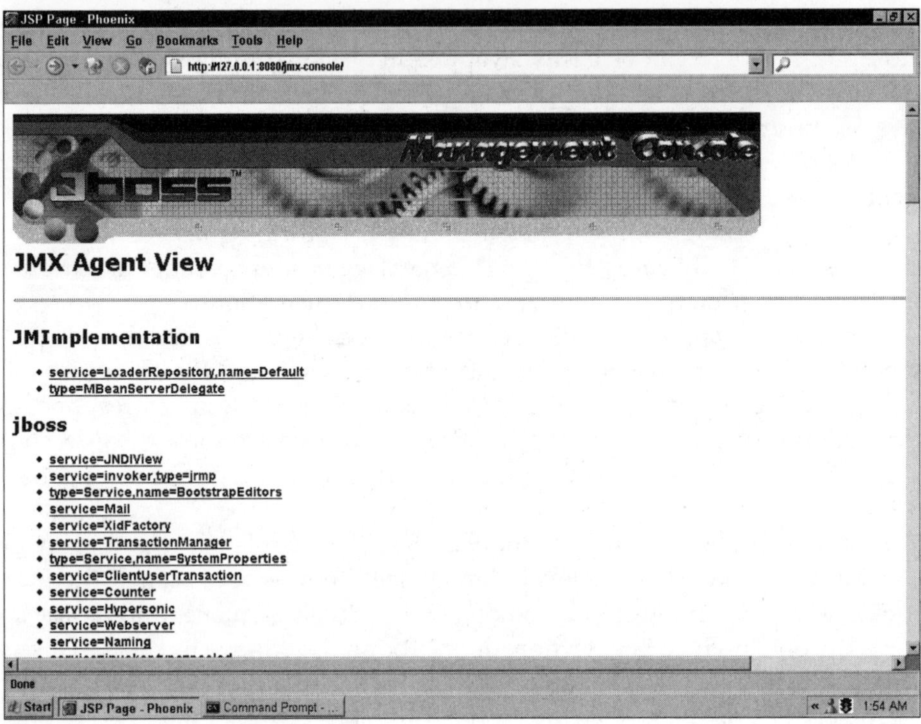

Figure 9.1 JBoss's JMX console.

Let's take a look at how we can add and remove queues and topics via the JMX console. Go back up to the top-level JMX Agent view. Now, look for the `jboss.mq` section. There will be a link called `service=Destination Manager`. This is the MBean that controls the creation and destruction of JMS destinations. Click on the link. We changed MBean attributes before, but we also have the ability to execute MBean operations. Go to the `void create Topic()` operation and type in **testTopic2** for `arg0`, which is the name of the topic we want to create. Click Invoke, and you should see a message like `Operation completed successfully without a return value.` So far so good! Now, go back to the JMX Agent view and check out the `jboss.mq.destination` section. You should find your newly created JMS topic there. If you drill down into the MBean view for `testTopic2`, you'll see that it is bound to the JNDI name `topic/testTopic2` by default. The JNDI names that things are bound under can vary between J2EE application servers. In this case, JBoss uses the `topic/` for JMS topics.

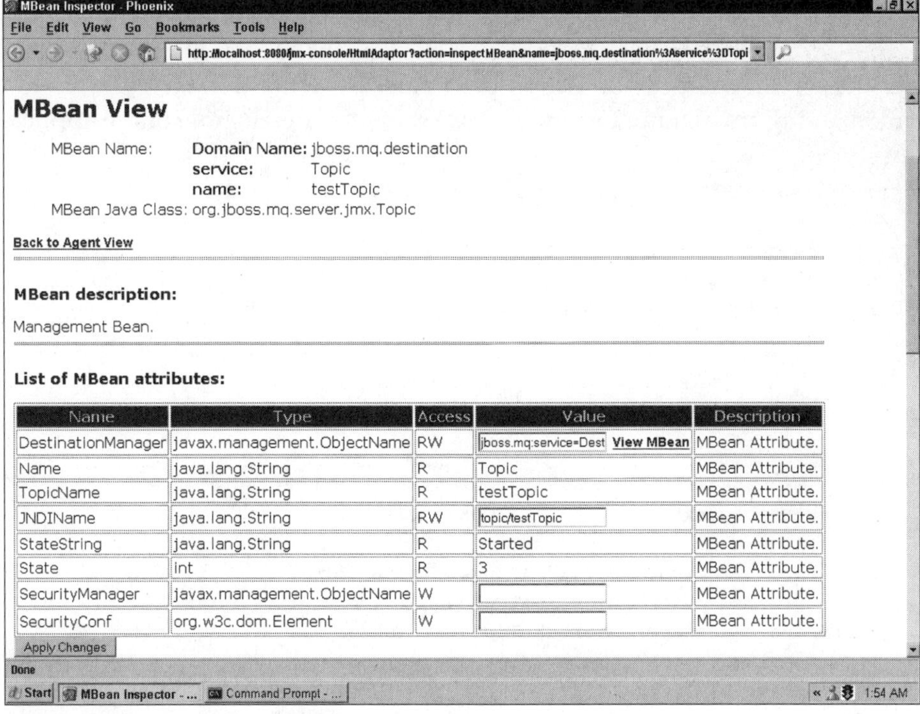

Figure 9.2 JBossMQ Topic Mbean.

CAUTION From our experience, developer assumptions about the JNDI naming can be the source of much wasted time and frustration, so tread carefully. The JMX console is a powerful tool, but you can also potentially make changes that disrupt the system. Use it carefully for changes. Even if you're not making changes, the JMX console is excellent for getting information on the state of a running system.

Okay, we've got JBossMQ's basic JMS functionality running. Now, let's try using it from within the J2EE framework, namely from a servlet and then a MDB.

Servlet JMS Clients

Servlets can use JMS messaging with pretty much the same syntax as the standalone JMS clients do. Unlike standalone clients, servlets cannot consume messages asynchronously. For this reason, servlet clients should only be used as producers.

The most noteworthy change is that the construction InitialContext doesn't require additional parameters. This is so because the J2EE container that manages the servlet will provide the proper values by default. In fact, you should avoid passing any parameters in, because this subverts the role of the application server.

Here's a sample from servlet code that uses JMS:

```
public void doGet( HttpServletRequest request,
HttpServletResponse response )
throws IOException, ServletException {
  String s = "";

  TopicConnection connection = null;
  TopicSession session = null;
  try {
    // --- Create various JMS resources to use testTopic. ---
    Context context = new InitialContext();
    TopicConnectionFactory factory = (TopicConnectionFactory)
      context.lookup( "java:/XAConnectionFactory" );
    connection = factory.createTopicConnection();
    session = connection.createTopicSession(
      true, Session.AUTO_ACKNOWLEDGE );
    Topic topic = (Topic)
      context.lookup( "java:comp/env/jms/testTopic" );
    TopicPublisher publisher = session.createPublisher( topic );

    // --- Publish a trivial text message. ---
    TextMessage message = session.createTextMessage();
    message.setText( "" + new Date().getTime() );
    publisher.publish( message );
    session.commit();
    s = "Published " + message;
  }
  catch( Exception e ) {
    s = s + e;
    e.printStackTrace();
  }
  response.getWriter().println( s );
  System.out.println( s );
}
```

You should add references in the `web.xml` descriptor for any external resources that are used so that your servlet code won't be dependent on the JNDI naming. By isolating those mappings into descriptor files, we can move beyond different J2EE application servers or make changes in the JNDI naming scheme without breaking things. Here's an excerpt from the `web.xml` file that declares the local reference, `jms/testTopic`, which we used from the `java:comp/env/` JDNI space:

```
<resource-ref >
   <description><![CDATA[TestTopic resource reference]]></description>
   <res-ref-name>jms/testTopic</res-ref-name>
   <res-type>javax.jms.Topic</res-type>
   <res-auth>Container</res-auth>
</resource-ref>
```

NOTE Don't forget that order matters within the XML descriptor files. Be sure to add these entries at the right location.

Now, we need to define the actual mapping for our application server. In the case of JBoss, that would be in the `jboss-web.xml` file that resides at the same directory level as the `web.xml` file. This is the application-server-specific counterpart to `web.xml`. You'll see this pattern quite often in J2EE descriptors.

Here's our complete `jboss-web.xml` file:

```
<?xml version="1.0" encoding="UTF-8"?>
<!DOCTYPE jboss-web PUBLIC
    "-//JBoss//DTD Web Application 2.3//EN"
    "http://www.jboss.org/j2ee/dtd/jboss-web_3_0.dtd">

<jboss-web>

   <context-root>/myweb</context-root>

   <!— Resource references —>
   <resource-ref>
      <res-ref-name>jms/testTopic</res-ref-name>
      <jndi-name>topic/testTopic</jndi-name>
   </resource-ref>

   <!— EJB References —>

</jboss-web>
```

TIP For quick-and-dirty development in JBoss, you can skip all the descriptor hoops and just refer to the JNDI name you know that the queue or topic will be bound under (for example, "`topic/testTopic`"). Not a great idea from a software engineering perspective, but great for quick prototyping.

Stateless Session Beans

We won't actually show an entire code example involving a stateless session bean using messaging. A lot of that is similar to the standalone client. Instead we'll cover the important differences involved in using JMS from the context of a stateless session bean.

As with any component managed by a J2EE application server, stateless session beans will get the proper InitialContext without having to provide any additional parameters.

The other thing to note is that if you are using container-managed transaction, then you should not call `commit()` or `rollback()` explicitly. Normally, the bean will automatically commit if it returns without exception and rollback if an exception occurs. Note that this also implies that the parameters passed into the JMS session creation methods are ignored in favor of the J2EE container's settings. Using container-managed transactions is recommended for most cases.

NOTE There's an exception to every rule: In the current implementation of JBossMQ an explicit commit is required before the message is sent in a transacted environment.

Normally, you keep a reference to the topic and the topic connection for efficiency. These references are created in `ejbCreate()` and released in `ejbRemove()`.

Here's a small snippet from a typical stateless session bean messaging façade:

```
public void ejbCreate() throws CreateException
{
  try
  {
    // -- Allocate JMS resources --
    InitialContext context = new InitialContext();
    TopicConnectionFactory factory = (TopicConnectionFactory)
        context.lookup( "ConnectionFactory" );
      m_topic = (Topic) context.lookup( "topic/testTopic" );
      m_connection = factory.createTopicConnection();
  }
  catch( Exception e )
  {
    throw new CreateException( e.getMessage() );
  }
}
```

That's about it! There aren't even any changes to the descriptors.

Message-Driven Beans

Message-driven beans are the recommended choice for implementing server-side messaging in J2EE. Because they are EJBs, message-driven beans gain all the same benefits from the container management. They are very simple to write compared to other types of EJBs, and we'll cover them in detail in Chapter 10, "Implementing an EJB Container."

Message-Design Considerations

We've seen how JMS fits into the enterprise picture and have written some JMS clients. In fact, we've covered many areas of messaging and JMS, but until now we've neglected the actual message itself. What kinds of considerations are involved in designing messages?

A message consists of the following parts:

The header. The header contains useful information about the message delivery. The JMSPriority in the header is of greatest interest to us here. By tweaking this, you can vary the quality of service. Bump up the priority of administration messages and drop down less critical messages. Good prioritization is critical for maintaining responsiveness under load.

The message properties section. Message selectors use message properties to select messages to consume. By carefully using the properties, we can avoid wasting resources on processing a message we're not interested in. Be sure to use message selectors to filter your messages, because using your own code to filter within message consumers is inefficient. In the same vein, avoid creating multiple queues or topics when it makes more sense to use message selectors. A good rule of thumb is that the more consumption overlap, either physically or logically, the more likely you should be using selectors.

The message body. The message body is pretty much dependent on the message type. In our examples, we've encountered the TextMessage type. The other types are: BytesMessage, MapMessage, ObjectMessage, and StreamMessage, which is one of the neatest types. StreamMessage is very useful for encoding a playback sequence into a single message. It does use Java serialization, so be aware that it is more resource-intensive than the other message types.

Designing a good message is not too complicated. Try to stay as lightweight as possible. Usually a minimal message is all that's needed. You can always create a second message with more detail for those cases that do require additional information.

NOTE Keep in mind that a message could potentially be published to many subscribers, so an increase in overhead multiplied many times over is a very real possibility.

Summary

JMS is a very unique piece of the J2EE toolset that is often overlooked in the mainstream. Nevertheless, messaging and JMS have many roles to play within the enterprise architecture.

In this chapter, we showed you how to set up JBossMQ, which lets you explore ways to improve your applications by adding JMS. Sometimes it takes a little time to get your head wrapped around asynchronous communications. However, when used properly, JMS will reduce complexity and increase architectural flexibility, while improving scalability, responsiveness, and performance.

CHAPTER

10

Implementing an EJB Container

We've seen the presentation layers, such as servlets and JSPs, that provide the outward facing interfaces to enterprise applications, and have examined some of the lower-level infrastructure such as messaging. Now, we will tackle the meat and potatoes of the enterprise application: Enterprise Java Beans (EJB). EJBs are managed software components within the J2EE architecture.

This chapter surveys the available open source options to develop and deploy EJBs. We will provide an overview of general EJB usage and issues, especially as concerns application architecture, and evaluate the EJB containers JBoss and JOnAS, the two current open source leaders.

Architectural Considerations

EJBs form the basis for distributed components in an enterprise application and are the worker bees of the J2EE world. Most of the heavy lifting in terms of business logic is done here. By design, they allow the developers to focus on coding the business logic, while being able to declaratively manage the aspects to be delegated to the container. Most important among these container-managed aspects are transactions, security, and distributed deployment. The life cycle of an EJB is also left in the hands of the EJB container and is rigidly set within the EJB specification.

There are different types of EJBs defined by the specification. Each type was created to address a preexisting domain of problems and through real-world use; general consensus has emerged regarding where each is most applicable. Among the types of EJBs to choose from are:

- Stateless session beans
- Stateful session beans
- Container-managed persistence beans
- Bean-managed persistence beans
- Message-driven beans

In this chapter, we cover each of these types of EJBs as well as where they fit into the enterprise architecture. First, though, we will focus on the entire EJB layer as a whole.

Java is built upon the object-oriented programming model, and this is evident in the way problems are solved in Java. EJBs try to extend this object model to distributed, enterprise-level applications, but the design of EJBs is component based. This means that certain object-oriented programming paradigms we take for granted are not available. For example, the notion of inheritance is not supported on the EJB level, although this can often be worked around by deferring the EJB classes and interfaces to the last child or by using aggregation.

EJBs are also limited in the things they are allowed to do. These restrictions are chiefly designed to allow the EJB container to retain management over the EJBs. For this reason, EJBs are not allowed to use any threading or synchronization. In fact, they aren't even technically allowed to access the file system! In reality, these rules are not enforced, but it is dangerous to work outside the specification. Breaking the EJB contract can and will lead to errors because the EJB container will assume certain operating parameters. Luckily, though, there is often a better solution that fits more within the spirit of enterprise applications.

A large body of literature exists on the topic of EJBs. It is a large and complicated topic that has already been covered in great detail in many other places. Yet, as an evolving technology the EJB specification continues to grow and will surely be the subject of much future discussion. For these reasons, we do not cover EJBs in an exhaustive manner. We do, however, provide some overview of interesting subsets within the EJB domain. Our primary goal is to get you familiar with the open source EJB containers. Any EJB examples and related topics exist to aid in achieving that goal.

Beans

Beans are the standard component architecture in Java. Originally introduced with the Java Bean specification to simplify the creation of reusable software components, EJBs (Enterprise Java Beans) are the natural extension of that philosophy on the server side. Unlike JavaBeans, EJBs are managed by a EJB container that handles tasks such as transaction management and security. EJBs are a combination of naming conventions, interfaces, and descriptors. They also come in a variety of flavors, each suitable for a certain subset of common server-side tasks. In the following sections, we'll break down how they work, examine the relationship between EJBs and their container, and dig into the various types of EJBs.

How an EJB Works

Container management is what drives the power and flexibility of EJBs. The EJB specification's genius lies not in what is included in the spec, but what is excluded. Contracts provide the interfaces that decouple the EJB from the client and also the container. The remote and local interfaces specify how a client should work with an EJB, but leave room for the EJB container to provide added value atop the interaction. On the server side, the home interface enables the EJB container to figure out how to manage the management of an EJB. Through these interfaces, the EJB container is free to manage EJBs based on a holistic view and provide life-cycle management for them. In addition, the container manages resources for the EJBs through the Context object, which is a conduit for communication between the EJB and its container. As we will show, this combination is very effective in achieving the goal of simplifying the construction of server-side software components.

Home, Remote, and Local Interfaces

There are number of interfaces linked with EJBs, each of which tells the EJB container how the EJB expects to interact with a client:

Home interface. The home interface tells a client how to work with the EJB container. The home interface is used by a client to ask the EJB container to perform certain actions. These are usually acts such as creating an EJB, locating EJBs by some criteria, or removing an EJB. The home interface's operations are largely management related.

Remote interface. The remote interface spells out what things a remote client can do with an EJB. When the client wants to work with a specific EJB, it uses the remote interface (or its local counterpart as we will see). The remote interface exposes a business-oriented component view into the EJB. This means that the operations in the remote interface are generally business methods.

Local interface. In version 2.0 of the EJB specification, local interfaces were added to parallel the remote versions. The local interface offers optimized access for clients co-located within the same JVM as the EJB. Local interfaces give developers the option to gain performance when working with EJBs that are co-located within the same JVM. One caveat is that this means that you can only take advantage of local interfaces from within server-side clients and that care must be taken to ensure that this locality is guaranteed. It is easy for local interfaces to break during a refactoring of the deployment architecture. By and large, these performance gains are the result of switching from a pass-by-value model to a pass-by-reference model. Both client and EJB developers need to be aware of this, because objects passed as a parameter can be inadvertently modified. This can work out to your advantage, as nonserializable parameters can be used in local interface methods.

One of the original goals of the J2EE EJB specifications has been to shield the developer from the distinctions between a local and a remote object, but this has proven to be unworkable due in part to the fundamental differences between a remote and a local component. Local interfaces are a recapitulation to this unavoidable fact. There is a positive side to this separation—it is utilized in J2EE applications to resurrect scoping. Co-located EJBs can be more tightly coupled and expose methods for local consumption without having to make them publicly accessible. The result is a pseudo-package/public component interface on the EJB level. Please note that this is a way to manage method visibility, not to restrict of method access, which should remain in the hands of declarative container-managed authentication and access control.

An EJB container combines information provided in the deployment descriptor to generate a managed implementation of the EJB. Usually, there is a platform-independent descriptor file that conveys standard information such as what the Java classname is for a particular interface, what type of EJB it is, or what transactional support is required for so-and-so method. In addition, there is platform-specific descriptor file that provides important cues about the EJB for the EJB container. Here, we'll find such information as what JNDI names to bind an EJB under, how to persist an EJB, and so on.

Generating Interface Files with X-Doclet

When creating an EJB you will create the EJB class, a home interface, at least one remote or local interfaces and an XML deployment descriptor. Furthermore specific containers may require additional files beyond the basic deployment descriptor to support the EJB deployment in that container. If you think that the specification of an EJB seems to be spread throughout far too many files, you're right. Making a single change to an EJB can often require modification to three or four files. It is a tedious, and therefore error-prone, process to write an EJB by hand. Rest assured that there have historically been good reasons for this modularity.

When the EJB drafts were first written, Java reflection and dynamic proxies were not in standard use. As a result, the J2EE container had to insert management code into the EJB classes. At that time, this was done through an additional compilation step where the container deduced what code to generate by examining interfaces and deployment descriptors. Because each container had to generate its own management code that sat between the client and the code written by the developer, this was a necessary evil.

The spec writers expected much of this housekeeping to be done through tools, such as might be found in an IDE. Luckily, managing the myriad of files is easier today because these types of tools do exist. One of our favorites is XDoclet, which can be integrated into the build process to automatically generate the various interface files as well as the descriptors from metadata encoded throughout Javadoc comments in a single class file. This makes the management and development of EJBs much less painstaking. The following table gives a summary of XDoclet.

Product	XDoclet
Category	Code generation
URL	http://xdoclet.sourceforge.net
Supported Platforms	Java 1.4 and above
License	XDoclet Open Source License
Features	Automated generation of EJB interfaces and descriptor files

Most EJB containers have also adopted dynamic proxy generation to skip the extra compilation step. This is a welcome change and simplifies the development process. (As a historical note, this approach was first utilized by JBoss.)

Containers and EJB Life Cycle

Now that you have a good grasp on the various interfaces that an EJB can be composed of, let's take a look at the life cycle of an EJB and how the container management fits into that picture.

The EJB container provides services for the EJBs housed within it. This is done by wrapping the EJBs and managing access to them. The focus is usually on the benefits added by the EJB container, but to provide them, the EJB container must manage the life cycle of EJBs. As developers, it is important to understand this life cycle model and what effect it has on the way EJBs are coded.

EJBs share many aspects of the life cycle. The EJB life cycle consists of just a handful of possible states. All EJBs start and end in the Does Not Exist state. At the prime of their life cycle, they are in the Ready state and can service requests.

In the following sections, we'll briefly go over the general life cycle of each type of EJB. Life cycle state and sequence diagrams are available in the official EJB specifications, which are available for downloading from Sun's Web site at `http://java.sun.com/j2ee/`.

Life Cycle of a Stateless Session Bean

A stateless session bean does not maintain state between method calls. This makes any instance of a stateless session bean interchangeable with any other instance. The stateless session bean has a simple life cycle as follows:

1. `setSessionContext()` is called to establish the EJB's context.
2. `ejbCreate()` is called to initialize the EJB.
3. The EJB enters the ready state and can accept business method calls.
4. `ejbRemove()` is called to let the EJB wrap up before the end of its life cycle.

Life Cycle of a Stateful Session Bean

The life cycle of a stateful session bean is pretty much the same as that of the stateless session bean. A stateful session bean manages state between method calls. This makes the stateful session bean non-interchangeable with other instances of the same bean. As a result of this, the EJB container creates separate instances of the stateful session bean for each client. In addition, a stateful session bean must be able to handle *passivation* and *activation*. Passivation occurs when the container needs to put the EJB aside to save resources. Activation occurs when the container returns the bean to the Ready state so that it can handle business method calls again.

1. Creation is requested by the client via a `create()` method in the home or local home interface.
2. `setSessionContext()` is called to establish the EJB's context.
3. `ejbCreate()` is called to initialize the EJB.
4. The EJB is in the ready stage and can take business method calls. The container can optionally passivate and activate the EJB, usually for resource-allocation purposes.
5. Removal is requested by the client via a `remove()` method in the home or local home interface.
6. `ejbRemove()` is called to let the EJB wrap up before the end of its life cycle.

Life Cycle of an Entity Bean

Entity beans continue to build on the stateful session bean life cycle by adding the Pooled state. Many containers may pool instances of session beans, but the specification doesn't require it of the container. However, the specification does require support for pooling Entity beans. In addition, because entity beans have unique object IDs, they cannot be interchangeably pooled. This makes pooling something that must be addressed explicitly. The Pooled state sits between the Does Not Exist state and the Ready state of the entity bean. In order for this to work, the entity bean must be able to faithfully set and unset the requisite state. An Entity bean when in the pool effectively has no state. When the Entity bean is taken from the pool its state is established by assigning values from the underlying persistent store. In other words, there are no differences between pooled instances of the same entity bean. But each Entity bean in Ready state is unique. This is the contract that lets the EJB container optimize resources with entity beans.

With that in mind, the entity bean life cycle looks something like this:

1. `setEntityContext()` is called to establish the EJB's context. The EJB now goes into the Pooled state.
2. Creation is requested by the client via a `create()` method in the home or local home interface.
3. `ejbCreate()` is called to initialize the EJB.
4. `ejbPostCreate()` is called after the entity bean's key is available. This means that code in this method can now use the context object's `getEntityObject()` as well as its own `getPrimaryKey()`.

5. The EJB is in the Ready state and can take business method calls. The container can optionally passivate and activate the EJB, which moves the entity bean back and forth from the Pooled state to the Ready state. This is usually done for resource-allocation purposes.
6. Removal is requested by the client via a `remove()` method in the home or local home.
7. `ejbRemove()` is called to let the EJB wrap up before the end of its life cycle. The entity bean is returned to the pool and enters the Pooled state.

Life Cycle of a Message-Driven Bean

Message beans serve as end points for JMS (Java Messaging Service) messages. The message-driven bean's life cycle is a clean and simple one, as follows:

1. `setMessageDrivenContext()` is called to establish the EJB's context.
2. `ejbCreate()` is called to initialize the EJB.
3. The EJB enters the Ready state and is ready to accept asynchronous messages, which are handled by callbacks to the `onMessage()` method.
4. `ejbRemove()` is called to let the EJB wrap up before the end of its life cycle.

Transaction Management

Transaction management is one of the primary tasks under the control of EJB containers. In a transactional operation, your EJB can abort by either throwing a RemoteException or using the EJB context to call `setRollbackOnly()`. All this is transparent to the EJB developer and works in calls that span many EJBs. Container-managed transactions are really convenient compared to having to code your own transactions. There are many choices for declarative transactional behavior ranging from `NotSupported` to `Mandatory`. If you are interested in knowing about all the sordid details, please consult the EJB specification. A good guideline to follow is that when in doubt, leave it on `Required`. When many EJBs interact with each other; it is all too easy to get edge cases where the transactional behavior is not consistent with what you have in mind. It's a good idea to clearly plan out the tree of possible interactions before making a decision.

Resource Management

EJB containers also serve a critical role as the manager of resources. These resources are made available to the EJB through the context object, which is passed into the EJB during its construction.

There are three different types of context objects: `EntityContext`, `SessionContext`, and `MessageDrivenContext`. These differ slightly, depending on the limitations placed upon the EJB type, but are very similar for the most part. All allow lookups for container-managed resources. These resources are often mapped by the J2EE container to a local JNDI namespace, usually bound under `java:comp/env`. This has the advantage of decoupling the physical resource mapping from the EJB.

The context object also provides the means for the EJB to communicate with its container. It can be used to signal a transaction rollback, for example. Another valuable service is that the context object can be used to determine access privileges and call context, which is useful for specialized access control checks.

Sharing the JVM with the Servlet Container

EJB containers are just one layer in the J2EE application server stack. Quite often EJB containers will also include a servlet container. The reasons for this marriage are better performance and increased convenience. Examples of EJB containers bundled with a servlet container include commercial products such as the WebLogic application server as well as open source products such as JBoss.

JBoss is actually offered in two different bundles:

- The default bundle with the Jetty servlet container integrated with it
- A bundle featuring JBoss integrated with Apache Tomcat

The choice of bundles preserves the developer's freedom to choose a servlet container, while maintaining the benefits of a shared JVM. It also highlights an important point: You can integrate different servlet containers for use with an EJB container in the same JVM. Although the J2EE specification does not mandate this, some EJB containers and servlet containers have worked out the necessary API hooks to allow for this customization.

Sharing a JVM improves performance by reducing the cost of communication. These are significant improvements, too, on the scale of an order of magnitude. For example, an EJB invocation by a servlet across separate physical machines will require network resources such as a socket, incur marshalling and demarshalling costs, and cross through many more abstraction layers. By comparison, some EJB containers can optimize a shared JVM EJB invocation to a level of performance roughly equivalent to that of a method call.

Having a shared JVM also makes development tasks more convenient. For example:

- There's no need to start up separate processes for the EJB container and the servlet container.
- There are fewer configuration files to adjust in order to get the two to talk to one another.
- Tracing a servlet to EJB call is easy with a shared JVM, whereas trying to debug a call that crosses JVMs is nigh impossible.

Of course, sharing is not without its problems:

- The fate of the EJB container becomes tied with that of the servlet container. Should one cause an instability or crash the JVM, the other will suffer as well.
- Sharing a JVM limits the horizontal and vertical scalability of the EJB and servlet container to exactly one machine. This limit is acceptable as long as a single machine can handle the peak load, but with larger applications, it's just not possible.
- Operating system limits now apply to the combined requirements of the two. For example, if process has a limit of 16 semaphores, that must now be split between the EJB container and the servlet container. Many systems will manage multiple servlet and EJB processes better than a single gargantuan process. Of course, through proper tuning of the operating system and JVM parameters, this drawback can be mitigated.

In general, the drawbacks are not too worrisome. However, when the application needs to scale out to multiple machines, sharing the JVM becomes impossible to do. Sharing a JVM on a single machine is often ideal for development and prototyping purposes; however, this decision needs to be made separately for deployment systems. This topic is covered in more detail in Chapter 15.

Session Beans

Session beans are short-lived and well suited for scalable server-side components. They come in two flavors: stateless and stateful. Stateless session beans are the Swiss army knives of EJBs; they serve a multitude of roles largely due to their lean approach to server-side components. By contrast, stateful session beans fall into an uninteresting niche because they are seldom the optimal choice. The following sections give you a look at both of these types of session beans in more detail.

Stateless Beans

Stateless session beans are EJBs that have neither state nor persistence characteristics. By foregoing those characteristics, stateless session beans gain increased scalability. These are great for handling requests that can be completed within a single request.

Because they are stateless, an EJB container can create or destroy stateless session beans as necessary, to match the processing load. They are interchangeable and can be easily distributed to many nodes within a clustered application server.

Stateless session beans can perform most tasks. They often act as facades that coordinate the activity of many other components, such as other EJBs, for a client. Another great use pattern is to have them front a distributed persistence mechanism such as JDO or Hibernate, thus gaining the benefits of container management without having to deal with heavy component-oriented persistence schemes such as container-managed beans.

Stateful Session Beans

Stateful session beans are like their stateless counterparts, except that their state is maintained over a client session. This makes stateful session beans a logical way to hold client information on the server side. In this regard, a stateful session bean can be thought of as an extension of the client's session storage. Items in a shopping cart, for example, can be stored within a stateful session bean that maps to a single client. This is the theory behind stateful session beans.

Note that a client session has a relatively short lifespan, as opposed to persistent EJBs that keep their state indefinitely. Nevertheless, the addition of state makes stateful session beans much more expensive for an EJB container to maintain. This becomes more of an issue in the case of clustered deployments. Although this is technically transparent to the developer, in real-world usage you have to pay careful attention to the use of stateful session beans and their impact on the scalability of your application. Note also that, unlike stateless session beans, stateful session beans do not support concurrent calls, which further erodes their performance.

Developers often opt for lighter-weight mechanisms that store the state closer to the client. For a Web-based interface, one might choose to store the session state in an HttpSession instead. The advantage with this approach is that you can save the extra expense of EJB hoop jumping, such as having to perform an EJB lookup to find the stateful session bean. However, the solution then becomes tied to that type of client. For each additional client type, say a WAP (Wireless Application Protocol) client or a thick Java GUI client, new state-handling mechanisms must be added.

Entity Beans

Entity beans are EJBs that serve conceptually as a component view into persistent storage. This means that they have state and keep that state for their entire life cycle. There are two types of entity beans: *container-managed* and *bean-managed* beans. Container-managed beans have traditionally been scorned (you'll see why in the next section), but the latest release, CMP 2.1, has a lot to offer enterprise developers. As container-managed persistence (or CMP) becomes more suitable for real-world applications, the need for bean-managed persistence (or BMP) beans is declining. We'll take a more detailed look into both types of entity beans in the following sections.

Container-Managed Persistence 1.0

CMP beans are meant to present a shared, object-oriented view into persistent data, notably relational databases. In many ways, CMP 1.0 is a naive approach that merely maps the object interface to the data source. By attempting to be minimalist, key features were omitted from the specification. Among the list of problems are:

- No ability to define relationships between CMP beans
- Limited query options
- No ability to order results
- No way to model fine-grained objects
- Huge disconnect from proven RDBMS (relational database management system) concepts

The list goes on and on. For applications that have the luxury of creating brand-new database schemas and need an EJB-centric view of the data, CMP 1.0 can be made to work. There are also a number of design patterns to work around some of its shortcomings. These days, CMP 1.0 is an outdated, very simplistic, lowest-common-denominator data mapping. In the grand scheme of things, CMP 1.0 never really took off, and because it shouldn't be used in newer projects, will likely fade away quite soon.

Container-Managed Persistence 2.1

CMP 2.1 addresses many of the issues that limited earlier releases of CMP (namely CMP 1.0) from being accepted by developers. The end result is that CMP 2.1 can be used for complex data mappings to the EJB model in an efficient manner. CMP 2.1 tries very hard to bring back into the fold concepts that have worked well in databases and integrate them into the component model. There is still an impedance mismatch between the two worlds, but it's nice to see the signs of reconciliation.

Specifically, the 2.1 specification added support for the following features:

Relationships. Now, in addition to managing beans that map to records within individual tables, the container has the ability to manage relationships between beans representing data from multiple tables. This relationship management was left to the programmer prior to the EJB 2.0 specification.

Abstract interfaces. Abstract interfaces are a great boon for the EJB container. By having abstract getters/setters, the EJB Container can intercept method calls. This is beneficial for both passively gathering access pattern statistics and for actively manipulating the call. In the older 1.0 specification, access to raw fields was allowed, making it much more difficult for the EJB container to get involved.

The EJB Query Language (or EJB QL). The EJB Query Language is an improvement over the limited and tedious finders in the 1.0 specification. EJB QL draws heavily from SQL, which makes it easy to pick up and ready to apply to solve real-world problems. On some level, it feels wrong to have parallel technologies that are so similar, but the bottom line is that EJB QL is vital to making CMPs independent of the underlying database.

Dependent classes. Dependent classes are important for aggregation. Often it is nice to model contained items without the costs of a heavyweight EJB. For example, an Order EJB might consist of one or more line items. Prior to the dependent classes, each of those would have had to be modeled as its own EJB. This modeling was inefficient, difficult to manage, and made CMP more difficult to use in earlier version of the specification.

Cascading deletes. Cascading deletes are important for maintaining relationships between objects. When a parent object is deleted, the deletion is cascaded to the child objects.

Automatic primary key generation. Automatic primary key generation removes the burden of generating unique primary keys from the application. This task can often be delegated to the native database for greater performance, while maintaining key integrity.

Cascading deletes and automatic primary key generation are also concepts borrowed from the relational database world.

CMP beans still have extra, but normally negligible, overhead. There are many declarative deployment options that can drastically change the performance profile of your enterprise application, depending on how the CMP is used within the J2EE application. For example, if updates are minimal, then the CMP can be more aggressively cached.

CAUTION **These declarative options can also be dangerous. For example, specifying the wrong type of caching has far-reaching consequences beyond just reducing performance—it is actually possible to undermine transactional correctness! This type of issue is not limited to CMP beans, but is mentioned here to remind us that declarative options can add complexity outside the scope of the code.**

A counterintuitive result of all this is that CMP EJBs can actually be faster than handcrafted persistence code in the grand scheme of things because the container is able to use the deployment hints along with runtime behavior to optimize data access. Because the EJB container knows the relationships between data and the access patterns, it can act as a smart cache. To analogize, the effect is that the EJB container can do for data what the HotSpot JVM does for code. As always, though, your mileage may vary.

Bean-Managed Persistence

Bean-managed persistence is the catchall fallback EJB to data sources. By leaving the code to work with the data in the hands of the developer, BMP is both extremely powerful and limited at the same time. The premise behind the EJB container is to simplify the development of enterprise components; the result, though, is that by dropping back into hand-coded persistence, many of the benefits of container management are lost. The analogy we like to use is that

BMP is to persistent components as Java Native Interface (JNI) is to Java. Sure, there are times when we need to access things at a lower level but it is contrary to the spirit of the architecture. Our advice to you is to take some concrete benchmarks and verify that there isn't a more elegant way to do things before diving into Bean-managed persistence.

One huge drawback to BMP is the way the interface is specified. Namely, BMP manages on a per key basis. This means that retrieving each BMP bean will have to incur the overhead of an entire roundtrip. This translates to a $1+n$ database query overhead. For example, let's say we have a BMP bean that models a customer object and uses JDBC to persist itself. If the client uses the finder and locates 100 customers, then 101 database queries must be used. To give a sense of the inefficiency of this, the same thing can be accomplished in a single database query.

The consensus view in the industry is that BMP is a legacy technology now. It still has a place within the J2EE framework, but it is getting squeezed out by more appropriate solutions such as CMP and Java Data Objects (JDO). Often a stateless session bean facade to JDO or JDBC can be substituted for a BMP and get you more bang for the buck. Also, keep in mind that with CMP, the EJB container can make these optimizations and you have the added benefit of not needing to hand-code the solution. Be sure to check out the changes in CMP 2.1 before dismissing CMP, because it is much improved over the justifiably maligned CMP 1.0.

Message-Driven Beans

Message-driven beans (MDBs) are the asynchronous EJBs. They work hand-in-hand with JMS to handle messaging and are highly scalable because they're short-lived and stateless. The MDB specification is wonderfully elegant, providing a great cornerstone for messaging, albeit one that is not necessarily very object-oriented. MDBs tend to look like event handlers, because that is the core activity they are tasked with. Message-driven beans are the only way to develop message consumers within the EJB layer of J2EE. Quite often, the MDB will be just the first in a chain of EJBs that must work together to fulfill a request.

CROSS-REFERENCE **We cover the benefits of asynchronous messaging in Chapter 9.**

Tool Selection

Once again, we must select a single project from the multitude of free, open source projects. There used to be lots of interest in constructing EJB containers, but that time has passed. Nowadays, three survivors remain from the days of EJB container proliferation: JBoss, JOnAS, and OpenEJB.

Survey and Analysis

A survey of the scene shows that JBoss and JOnAS are the two major open source EJB containers available today. Both are excellent products with a solid history of development and deployment. We'll try to illustrate that by giving some background into these two projects.

JBoss

Marc Fleury, a former Sun employee, started JBoss in March 1999. JBoss is currently at version 3.0 and is a full-featured J2EE application server that contains everything from the HTTP server to the EJB container. JBoss is open source and freely available. Over the years, important contributions have come from great developers all over the world. The current core team has many members who are involved in setting the future direction of the J2EE specification standards, so JBoss tends to be a leading-edge J2EE application server.

JBoss takes a very unique approach to implementing the EJB container. Marc Fleury likes to refer to JBoss as the "webOS." At the heart of this notion is the microkernel-based structure. The microkernel allows JBoss to offer services and modules on granular level. For example, the EJB container is implemented through the combination of services and modules. Everything is tied together and managed through JMX, which makes it easy to see what's going on and manipulate the container. Overall, it's a very advanced infrastructure.

Other noteworthy capabilities include the easy clustering through net boot and the farm deployment feature. In addition, the hot redeployment is a great timesaver that allows you to drop new .ear and .war files into the deployment directory, where JBoss will automatically pick them up, cycle the existing application, and deploy the updated version.

NOTE **JBoss is the most downloaded J2EE application server ever, and its reputation and popularity continue to climb. There are no hard numbers yet, but from our experience, the vast majority of JBoss deployments are for development or internal consumption rather than production. This is not to say that JBoss isn't ready for production; quite the contrary. There are some highly visible rollouts with JBoss from such clients as the Dow Jones Indexes and BASF.**

The JBoss team embraces leading-edge techniques, and the new 4.0 version promises to go above and beyond the J2EE paradigm. Aspect-oriented programming is the driving force behind this latest version. Through aspects, much of the declarative power of the EJB specification can be generalized and applied to plain old Java objects (POJOs). This is a good thing because EJBs have gained the not-altogether-undeserved reputation for being overly complex and unnecessary. Time will tell whether JBoss will succeed in this respect. Nevertheless, you can rest assured that they will always be pushing the frontiers of J2EE. The following table provides a summary of JBoss.

Product	JBoss
Category	J2EE application server/EJB container
URL	http://www.jboss.org
Supported Platforms	Java 1.3 and above
License	LGPL Open Source License
Features	Leading-edge specification compliance, very popular, easy-to-use

JOnAS

JOnAS is another leading open source, freely available J2EE application server. It has roots in a J2EE implementation built by Bull, a leading French IT and consulting firm. The implementation was open sourced and its development is now under the umbrella of the ObjectWeb consortium, the same folks who are involved with the JORAM project. The ObjectWeb consortium is a collaboration between Bull, the Research & Development Division of France Telecom and INRIA, and The French National Institute for Research in Computer Science and Control.

Some superb research went into creating JOnAS, including advanced transaction handling and a nice persistence engine. The persistence engine is based on JORM/MEDOR, ObjectWeb's persistence framework, and provides a fairly good, but not complete, subset of the CMP 2.1 specification. JORM/MEDOR has implicit database mapping as well as the ability to use other backing stores such as a file system. ObjectWeb has several advanced prototypes available that have research technology in them. These aren't ready for production use yet, but some of the stuff looks very interesting from a theoretical standpoint.

JOnAS also offers many of the same optimizations as JBoss. Their Jeremie protocol, for example, optimizes local RMI calls similarly to the way JBoss does. Performance tests show the two running very close together. The big plus with JOnAS is that the container has proven vertical scalability and a very nice degradation of performance after it hits the peak of its scalability.

The documentation available on the Web site is quite extensive and of very good quality; kudos to the ObjectWeb guys for tackling the one area that tends to receive the least attention in open source projects.

When downloading JOnAS, you have to go through the drill of filling out a form with some contact information and a license agreement. It's not a big deal, but it's one more hoop to jump through. JOnAS is definitely worth checking out. Its characteristics are described in the following table.

Product	JOnAS
Category	J2EE application server/EJB container
URL	http://www.objectweb.org/jonas/
Supported Platforms	Java 1.3 and above
License	LGPL Open Source License
Features	Good documentation, great vertical scalability

OpenEJB

OpenEJB is an EJB container that is designed for ease of use. OpenEJB ships with Apple's WebObjects and was designed for speed and low resource consumption. OpenEJB implements the EJB 1.1 specification with support for CMP 2.0 beans. The following table provides a summary for OpenEJB.

Product	OpenEJB
Category	EJB container
URL	http://openejb.sourceforge.net
Supported Platforms	Java 1.3 and above
License	BSD-like open source license
Features	Easy to integrate and use EJB 1.1 container with CMP 2.0 support

OpenEJB may be a good container for those who want an easy-to-install and-configure container for learning EJB basics. However, because OpenEJB currently only implements the 1.1 EJB specification, we will not consider it further in this chapter.

Needs and Features Analysis

Now, we must consider the needs and requirements of a layer in the J2EE stack. In this case, we are dealing with the EJB container, but as you may notice, what we need here is very similar to the list we assembled for servlet containers. These needs are:

Conformance to J2EE standards. Conformance to J2EE standards is a must. The picture becomes less clear, however, because there are incrementally more complicated versions of the EJB specifications. The original 1.0 specification spanned 181 pages, while the current 2.1 specification draft has grown to around 640 pages. Clearly, the EJB specification is getting ever more complicated, and there will be important distinctions among EJB containers, which are struggling to keep up with the latest specification.

Support for integration within the J2EE stack. As with any element of the J2EE stack, support for integrating it with other components, such as Web servers, servlet containers, and relational database management systems, is vital. Most EJB containers, especially the open source ones, are designed to play well with other J2EE components.

Project stability and continuing support. Stability and continuing support are important in any piece of software, but more so in the EJB container. Recent times have seen a huge reduction in the number of free, open source EJB container projects that are being actively developed. We also need stability so that as the EJB container evolves and new versions are released, the product continues to work correctly and efficiently. The notion of support is related to this definition of stability. There will be subtle differences that will require technical support. When choosing an EJB container, we need to ensure that this level of support exists and can be reasonably expected to exist for the lifetime of the deployment.

Scalability. Scalability, both vertical and horizontal, is perhaps the most important feature in production deployment. Good vertical scalability is crucial for reducing the number of machines you'll need to handle. Once the application's footprint exceeds a single machine, then having an EJB container that scales well horizontally is crucial. Advanced clustering techniques can be a great boon in terms of horizontal scalability.

Ease of use. EJBs have a reputation for being excessively complicated. By trimming down the number of steps and automating tasks, an EJB container with good ease of use can reduce the overhead borne by the developer.

Documentation. Documentation is good to have available in any situation and is critical for EJB containers because much of the power of having container-managed behavior lies within the configuration. Without proper and sufficient documentation, it would be difficult to understand the expected behavior of the EJB applications we are building.

Evaluation of EJB Containers

We have our list of free, open source EJB containers, and the list of features that we will use to judge the EJB containers. Let's go down the list of features and see how JBoss compares with JOnAS in each area.

We'll start with conformance with J2EE standards. JOnAS is a bit behind the J2EE 1.3 specification as of the time of writing. There are some features specified in CMP 2.1 that are missing: cascading deletes, auto-primary-key-generation, ejbSelect, and some EJB QL operators. Based on past performance, these issues will probably be addressed by the time you read this. So why bring it up? Well, the odds are that the new J2EE 1.4 specification will be out by now, too. The point is that JOnAS tends to be 6 to 12 months behind JBoss. This is a double-edged sword in that JBoss may outrun the standards. Code written to specifications that are still in flux may need to be rewritten once a standard is established.

In the area of J2EE integration, both JBoss and JOnAS deliver standout performances. They are both available integrated with Tomcat, the servlet container we selected for use in Chapter 5. They are easily integrated with other key pieces of the J2EE architecture. This is a draw simply because both EJB containers get full marks in this category.

JBoss stands out in the category for project stability and continued support. As the most downloaded J2EE application server, the prospects of continued project stability and support are extremely bright. The recent formation of the JBoss Group for professional paid support shows that there is a thriving market for commercial deployments of JBoss. Both containers have commercial deployments to show as references, but the JBoss deployments have been the more visible and impressive of the two. In general, JBoss seems to have more mindshare and developer support than JOnAS, so this round goes to JBoss.

It's a split decision in terms of scalability. JOnAS offers better vertical scalability than JBoss. Studies indicate that JOnAS can not only handle greater load, but offers a much nicer degradation curve once the peak load is exceeded. The peak load handled by JBoss is quite good, but performance drops considerably after the load surpasses the peak. On the other hand, JBoss offers a very nice clustering solution. JBoss allows an application to be automatically deployed on the master server and then automatically pushed out as an updated application to a cluster of servers. Scaling up is as simple as adding machines to the cluster. This is a great feature for deployments that require more than one machine or that might need additional machines in the future.

JBoss provides a wonderful experience out of the box. Things are integrated in an intelligent manner, and the entire J2EE application server stack is right there should you need it. In particular, the Hypersonic database that is included coupled with the JBoss create table descriptor allows quick testing of CMP EJBs. (Keep in mind that this is not so much a real database per se as it is a development tool substitute for an RDBMS; more information on Hypersonic is available at `http://hsqldb.sourceforge.net/`.) JOnAS is also available integrated with either Tomcat or Jetty, which makes it easy to get started right away.

Documentation is an area where the two have significant differences. JOnAS has all of its documentation available online, and access to it is free and unrestricted. JBoss has taken a two-pronged approach to documentation. There is a freely available version of the documentation written by community volunteers. The quality of this documentation is good, but the version of JBoss covered can lag behind the latest one available for downloading. This type of document lag can be frustrating for users. JBoss also offers a professional set of documentation available for purchase at a reasonable price. This documentation is always up to date and is written by the core developers, so it is of high quality. Nevertheless, JOnAS wins out in this department for making good-quality documentation freely available to the public.

Product Selection

In the feature comparison between JBoss and JOnAS, both had great showings. The two projects have somewhat differing philosophies behind them. JBoss wants to push the envelope and is spending a lot of effort in getting more deployments. In the case of JOnAS, the emphasis seems to be on creating a more refined product that is rooted in a more orthodox approach to the J2EE specifications. No doubt due in part to its origins as an in-house product developed by Bull, JOnAS has more of the fit and finish of a commercial product. Ultimately, though, what won us over was JBoss's ease of use.

For research-and-development purposes, JBoss is the better product. The hot redeployment feature is an absolute timesaver in development. More importantly, JBoss allows you to have a running implementation of tomorrow's J2EE. Projects can be developed against the latest technology and then deployed to commercial J2EE containers as vendors release versions that comply with those specifications. The clustering support is a nice bonus feature to have available, even though most deployments will not need this.

On the other hand, JOnAS seems to offer a more conservative approach to the J2EE specifications that mirrors commercial J2EE containers. It has greater vertical scalability, or better scaling on a single machine, but more limited horizontal scalability, which is applicable in scenarios with clustered deployments. The emphasis seems to be on incremental improvement rather than revolutionary changes.

JBoss held the edge in the feature comparison. In addition, our target deployment is development first and production second. Because JBoss tends to be more on the cutting edge, it makes it possible to get hands-on experience with the latest standards. For these reasons, we will be using JBoss in the remainder of this chapter to explore EJBs in more depth.

Installation and Configuration

We showed you how to install JBoss in Chapter 9. The same setup will work just fine for testing the examples in this chapter. So, instead of recapping the same setup process, what we'll touch upon here are some of the advanced installation options for JBoss.

Installing JBoss in Windows

Perhaps the most common Windows question in using Java on the server side is, "How can I get my Java application to run as a service?" A *service* in Windows (similar to a daemon in Linux) executes a program independently of the user login and allows it to automatically start when the computer starts. The service will constantly be running in the background, allowing JBoss to be available at all times. In addition, a service can be configured by a system administrator to give it specific access privileges, permissions, and resources. This is crucial for a production deployment of JBoss and something that must be addressed for any server-type application, such as the servlet containers and databases.

In the early days, there were some products that wrapped themselves inside of a Java application to allow themselves to run as a service. They worked for the most part but had some minor annoyances. Happily, the situation is much improved. The best product to date is Java Service by Alexandria Software Consulting, which is a free open source program that installs any Java program as an NT Service. The process is simple, and there is ample documentation available on their site to help you customize your configuration. The following table gives a summary of Java Service.

Product	Java Service
Category	Windows service wrapper for Java applications
URL	http://wrapper.tanukisoftware.org/doc/english/index.html
Supported Platforms	Java 1.3 and above
License	MIT License
Features	Allows Java applications to execute as a Windows services

The exact script will depend a lot on your settings, but on our machine the script looks like this:

```
JavaService.exe -install JBoss %JAVA_HOME%\jre\bin\server\jvm.dll -
Djava.class.path=%JAVA_HOME%\lib\tools.jar;%JBOSS_HOME%\bin\run.jar -
start org.jboss.Main -stop org.jboss.Main -method systemExit -current
%JBOSS_HOME%\bin
```

NOTE **Be sure that your** `JAVA_HOME` **and** `JBOSS_HOME` **environment variables are properly set.**

This script installs JBoss as a service under the name JBoss. If you open up the Services administration panel, located under Control Panel ➪ Administrative Tools, you'll see your newly installed service as shown in Figure 10.1

NOTE **To uninstall this program, just run** `JavaService.exe -uninstall JBoss.`

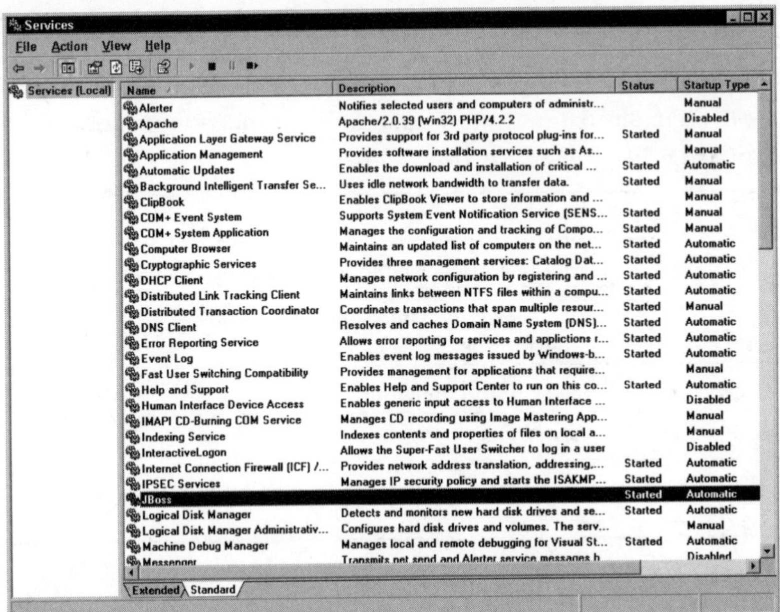

Figure 10.1 The Windows Services administration panel.

The Services administration panel makes it easy for you to start and stop services. Other management tasks can be performed here as well. The two most important tasks are setting the startup type and setting the account associated with the service. In most cases, you will want to change the startup type from its default setting to Automatic. To change the account associated with the JBoss service, check under the "Log On As" column: this shows the account associated with the JBoss service. Depending on your security configuration, you may want to change the account to a user account specifically created for JBoss. This way, you can manage permissions in a more fine-grained manner. By default, JBoss is associated with the Local System account. We will leave it alone because this account is normally used by Windows for server services such as IIS. The following table gives a summary of the JBoss service.

Product	JBoss Service
Category	Service wrapper
URL	http://www.alexandriasc.com/software/JavaService/index.html
Supported Platforms	Java 1.2 and above
License	BSD-style open source license
Features	Wraps any Java program as an NT service; scripts are available for JBoss and Tomcat

Installing JBoss in Linux

In Chapter 9, we showed you how to install JBoss for personal use on Linux. This time, we will tackle setting up JBoss as a shared server running as a daemon. To facilitate sharing, we also need to tweak ownership and file permissions. In order to perform these tasks, you will need to have root permissions.

Ownership and File Permissions

The question of ownership and file permissions is a sticky one. Typically, programs are either owned by the user or, in the case of shared programs, owned by a user ID that is created just for that purpose. We'll be going that route in this case. First, create a new user ID and user group for JBoss:

```
useradd -c "Special JBoss user" -r jboss
```

Next, you need to move your JBoss directory to the location where shared programs are commonly installed. This varies among different Linux distributions. A good place to put the JBoss directory is under `/usr/local/jboss`.

NOTE Be sure to update the `JBOSS_HOME` environment variable to point to the shared directory.

Now, let's move the ownership over to the new `jboss` user ID.

```
chown -R jboss:jboss /usr/local/jboss
```

That's it! Next, we'll look at how to start our new shared JBoss program as a daemon within Linux.

Running JBoss as a Daemon

This is similar to setting up the servlet container as a service. Once again, we add the `jbossd` script to the `/etc/init.d` director, then run the `chkconfig` command to install the script.

Here's the source for `jbossd`:

```
#!/bin/sh
#
# Startup script for JBoss.
#
# chkconfig: 2345 95 15
# description: JBoss is a J2EE EJB container.
# processname: jboss
# pidfile: /var/run/jboss.pid
```

```
# config: /usr/local/jboss/conf/default/jboss.conf
# logfile: /usr/local/jboss/log/server.log

#==========================================================================
#=== IMPORTANT NOTE:
#=== The comments above are required for the chkconfig script to work
#=== correctly. Please do not remove them. Read the man pages for
#=== chkconfig if you need to know more.
#==========================================================================

# Source function library.
# Set environment variables needed by JVM and JBoss
JAVA_HOME=/usr/java/j2sdk1.4.1_01
JBOSS_HOME=/usr/local/jboss
# Update the path with JRE and JBoss references.
PATH=$PATH:$JAVA_HOME/jre/bin:$JAVA_HOME/bin:$JBOSS_HOME/bin

#==========================================================================
# This function will be executed when the system is starting up.
#==========================================================================
start() {
  # Start daemon
  echo "Starting JBoss: "
  su -l jboss -s /bin/bash -c "/usr/local/jboss/bin/run.sh"
  RETVAL=$?
  if [ $RETVAL -eq 0 ]; then
    echo "JBoss started!"
  else
    echo "JBoss failed to start!"
  fi
  echo
  touch /var/lock/subsys/jboss
}

#==========================================================================
# This function will be executed when the system is stopping.
#==========================================================================
stop() {
# Stop daemon.
  echo "Stopping JBoss: "
  su -l jboss -s /bin/bash -c "/usr/local/jboss/bin/shutdown.sh"
  RETVAL=$?
  if [ $RETVAL -eq 0 ]; then
    echo "JBoss stopped!"
  else
    echo "Problem stopping JBoss!"
  fi
  echo
  rm -f /var/lock/subsys/jboss
```

```
}

restart() {
  echo "Stopping JBoss for restart..."
  stop
  sleep 15
  echo "Restarting JBoss:"
  start
}

# See how we were called.
case "$1" in
  start)
  start
  ;;
  stop)
  stop
  ;;
  restart)
    restart
  ;;
  *)
  echo "Usage:" "$0" "{start|stop|restart}\n"
  exit 1
esac

exit 0
```

To install the script, run the following command:

```
chkconfig -add jbossd
```

JBoss should now be installed as a daemon (the "d" in `jbossd` stands for daemon) and will start up and shut down with the machine it is installed on.

Binding JBoss to Port 80

The last thing we need to do is bind JBoss to the default HTTP port. This step is only important if you want to use the servlet container that is integrated with JBoss. If you'll recall, this is the exact same issue we faced when we were installing the servlet container on its own. Any port below 1024 is a privileged port and requires root-level access to bind to it. The recommended solution in most deployments is to use `mod_jk` in conjunction with Apache.

CROSS-REFERENCE **Chapter 5 gives you details on binding Tomcat to port 80 by using the Apache Web server.**

Testing JBoss

By now, JBoss should be happily installed and ready to go. In the following sections, we'll show you how to test it by developing some code to exercise JBoss as an EJB container. You will also get the opportunity to examine the code and deployment descriptors of the various types of EJBs. We'll start out with a simple project that consists of a single stateless session bean and continue to add EJBs into it.

In these examples, we'll be deploying the EJBs separately from any other code. Often, an enterprise application is packaged all together into a single .ear file. In Part IV, we'll show the development of an entire enterprise application. For now, let's focus on the EJB side of things.

Session Bean Tests and Sample Code

Stateless session beans are the best starting point for developing scalable components containing business logic. They are extremely useful and relatively easy to code. In this section, we show you how to develop a trivial "Hello World" type of stateless session bean EJB and use a JSP page to interact with it. There will be quite a few classes, so it is probably easiest to organize everything in a new directory.

First, let's create our core EJB class. This actually implements the business methods (just a simple "Hello" in this case).

Here's the code for `GreeterBean.java`:

```
package test.ejb;

import javax.ejb.*;
import java.util.*;
import java.rmi.*;

public class GreeterBean implements SessionBean
{
    private String msLastGreeted = null;
    private SessionContext moContext;

    // --- Standard EJB life cycle stuff ---

    public void ejbActivate() {}
    public void ejbCreate() {}
    public void ejbRemove() {}
    public void ejbPassivate() {}
```

```
    public void setSessionContext( SessionContext oContext )
    {
        moContext = oContext;
    }


    // --- Our "business" methods ---

    public String sayHello( String sName )
    {
        String s = "Hello " + sName + "! ";
        if( msLastGreeted != null )
        {
            s = s + "I just saw " + msLastGreeted + ".";
        }
        msLastGreeted = sName;
        return s;
    }


    // -- This method is only exposed via the local interface, so this
    // -- is effectively hidden from the scope of remote clients.
    public String getLastGreeted()
    {
        return msLastGreeted;
    }
}
```

Now, let's save that file under `test\ejb\GreeterBean.java` and take a look at the various EJB interface classes.

The home interface is used to create our bean. We've kept it very minimal. Here's the code for `GreeterHome.java`:

```
package test.interfaces;

public interface GreeterHome
   extends javax.ejb.EJBHome
{
    public test.interfaces.Greeter create()
        throws javax.ejb.CreateException, java.rmi.RemoteException;
}
```

The local home interface looks quite similar. It's basically the same as the home interface minus the remote exception and extending a different base interface.

Here's the code for GreeterHomeLocal.java:

```
package test.interfaces;

public interface GreeterLocalHome
   extends javax.ejb.EJBLocalHome
{
    public test.interfaces.GreeterLocal create()
        throws javax.ejb.CreateException;
}
```

Now, let's look at the interface classes that tell an EJB client what methods are available. We'll look at Greeter.java, the remote interface, first:

```
package test.interfaces;

public interface Greeter
   extends javax.ejb.EJBObject
{
    public String sayHello( String name ) throws
java.rmi.RemoteException;
}
```

In the local interface version, we're going to expose an additional method that we didn't want remote clients to access. Remote and local interfaces are used as tools to manage scope and method visibility. In a real-world application, this can be used to hide tightly coupled code behind the local interface.

Compared with the remote interface version, the general form for the local interface is the same, except that it extends EJBLocalObject rather than EJBObject and the methods don't throw remote exceptions.

Here's the code for GreeterLocal.java:

```
package test.interfaces;

public interface GreeterLocal
   extends javax.ejb.EJBLocalObject
{
    public String sayHello( String name );
    public String getLastGreeted();
}
```

The differences are very minimal as far as the interfaces go. There are five different files, yet they don't really hold a lot of different information. This is part of the grunt work that can and should be automated by tools such as XDoclet, which can generate these interface files from a single source file. To see XDoclet in action, skip ahead to the section on CMP beans.

Let's try compiling the files. Be sure that the files are saved under the correct directory, as indicated by their package.

We're going to separate the commands for compiling the interfaces and the EJB because the client often needs the interface files. Unless the interface changes, we should use the same compiled class files for compatibility reasons. If the interface files are recompiled, they will need to be updated in the client as well.

The command for compiling the interfaces on Windows is as follows:

```
javac -classpath .;%JBOSS_HOME%\client\jboss-j2ee.jar
test\interfaces\Greeter.java test\interfaces\GreeterLocal.java
test\interfaces\GreeterHome.java test\interfaces\GreeterLocalHome.java
```

And for the EJB:

```
javac -classpath .;%JBOSS_HOME%\client\jboss-j2ee.jar test\ejb\GreeterBean.java
```

On Linux, the command for compiling the interfaces as follows:

```
javac -classpath .:$JBOSS_HOME/client/jboss-j2ee.jar
test/interfaces/Greeter.java test/interfaces/GreeterLocal.java
test/interfaces/GreeterHome.java test/interfaces/GreeterLocalHome.java
```

And the Linux command for compiling the EJB is:

```
javac -classpath .:$JBOSS_HOME/client/jboss-j2ee.jar test/ejb/GreeterBean.java
```

The files should be all compiled and ready to be packaged into a .jar file for the EJB, along with the descriptor files that we are about to write. If the compilation failed, be sure to check that the JDK is in your path and that the environment variable for `JBOSS_HOME` is set properly.

The last step before we package up our stateless session bean EJB is to write some descriptor files. These tell the EJB container about the EJB we've created. You need to place these files under the `META-INF` subdirectory.

First, we need to write a J2EE standard descriptor file for the EJB. This is the `ejb-jar.xml` file and it should look like this:

```
<?xml version="1.0" encoding="UTF-8"?>
<!DOCTYPE ejb-jar PUBLIC "-//Sun Microsystems, Inc.//DTD Enterprise
JavaBeans 2.0//EN" "http://java.sun.com/dtd/ejb-jar_2_0.dtd">
<ejb-jar >
   <enterprise-beans>
      <session >
         <ejb-name>Greeter</ejb-name>
         <home>test.interfaces.GreeterHome</home>
```

```
            <remote>test.interfaces.Greeter</remote>
            <local-home>test.interfaces.GreeterLocalHome</local-home>
            <local>test.interfaces.GreeterLocal</local>
            <ejb-class>test.ejb.GreeterBean</ejb-class>
            <session-type>Stateful</session-type>
            <transaction-type>Container</transaction-type>
         </session>
      </enterprise-beans>
   </ejb-jar>
```

Notice how we specified the files that compose our EJB and declared what type of EJB our Greeter EJB is. We also have declarative information about how the EJB should function—namely that transactions should be managed by the container. There are many options available, and you should consult an EJB reference for all the details.

Next, we need to write the EJB container-specific descriptor file. This declares things that are specific to JBoss such as where to bind our little EJB. This file is named `jboss.xml`. We've kept it as minimal as possible, but there are also many options available here. Please consult the JBoss documentation for more details.

Here are the contents of `jboss.xml`:

```
<?xml version="1.0" encoding="UTF-8"?>
<!DOCTYPE jboss PUBLIC "-//JBoss//DTD JBOSS 3.0//EN"
"http://www.jboss.org/j2ee/dtd/jboss_3_0.dtd">

<jboss>
   <enterprise-beans>
      <session>
         <ejb-name>Greeter</ejb-name>
         <jndi-name>ejb/Greeter</jndi-name>
         <local-jndi-name>ejb/GreeterLocal</local-jndi-name>
      </session>
   </enterprise-beans>
</jboss>
```

Okay, so now we have our class files and the descriptors. It's now time to package them together into an EJB .jar file that we can deploy to the EJB container! We'll be using the command line `jar` command, but this task is often handled by your IDE or Ant build script.

On Windows the command is:

```
jar cvf greeter-ejb.jar test\ejb\GreeterBean.class test\interfaces\Greeter.class
test\interfaces\GreeterLocal.class test\interfaces\GreeterHome.class
test\interfaces\GreeterLocalHome.class META-INF\ejb-jar.xml META-INF\jboss.xml
```

And on Linux the command is:

```
jar cvf greeter-ejb.jar test/ejb/GreeterBean.class test/interfaces/Greeter.class
test/interfaces/GreeterLocal.class test/interfaces/GreeterHome.class
test/interfaces/GreeterLocalHome.class META-INF/ejb-jar.xml META-INF/jboss.xml
```

Now, we have our EJB Jar file! Check to make sure that JBoss is up and running. Once that's done we can deploy the EJB by simply copying the EJB .jar file into JBoss's deploy directory, usually the following:

```
%JBOSS_HOME%%\server\default\deploy
```

JBoss should pick up the addition within a couple seconds and begin deploying it. Once the deployment is complete, check the JMX console to make sure it's really deployed. There should now be an entry under the `jboss.management.single` section that looks something like:

```
J2EEApplication= ,J2EEServer=Single,j2eeType=EJBModule,name=greeter-ejb.jar
```

If that's the case, your EJB is properly deployed and running! Now, we need to test it from the client's perspective. For that purpose, we'll be whipping up a simple JSP page that calls on the Greeter EJB. Actually, it won't be too simple, because we'll need to create a .war file and include the proper Web application descriptor files to let the EJB container know what we plan on doing.

The JSP page uses the session to hold a reference to the Greeter EJB. This saves us the expense of performing the JNDI lookup each time. In real-world applications, the presentation layer wouldn't be concerned with these issues and this kind of stuff would be pushed back into the servlet or a stateless session bean facade that coordinates things. We're just using JSP as a quick-and-dirty way to exercise the EJBs.

Here's the code for `index.jsp`:

```
<%@ page
   session="true"
   isThreadSafe="true"
   isErrorPage="false"
   import="javax.naming.*, javax.rmi.*, test.interfaces.*"
%>
<html>
<head>
  <title>jsp ejb client</title>
</head>
<body>
<h4>Ejb web-client test</h4>
```

```
<p>
  It is now <%= new java.util.Date() %>.
</p>
<p>
  Exercising the right to vote!
</p>
<p>
<%
  try
  {
    // -- Generate a list of names to choose from. --
    String names[] = { "judy", "alex", "eric", "alice" };

    // - Retrieve the reference to our Greeter EJB from the JSP
    // - session if possible.

    Greeter greeter = (Greeter) session.getAttribute( "greeter" );
    if( greeter == null )
    {
      out.println( "<br> Creating new EJB reference to greeter." );
      Context context = new InitialContext();
      GreeterHome home = (GreeterHome)
        PortableRemoteObject.narrow( context.lookup( "ejb/Greeter" ),
        GreeterHome.class );
      greeter = (Greeter)
        PortableRemoteObject.narrow( home.create(), Greeter.class );
      session.setAttribute( "greeter", greeter );
    }


    // -- Exercise the EJB by getting a couple greetings. --

    for( int i=0; i<10; ++i )
    {
      out.println( "<br>"
        + greeter.sayHello(
          names[ (int)( Math.random() * names.length ) ] ) );
    }
  }
  catch( Exception e )
  {
    out.println( "Caught exception: "
      + e.getMessage() + " Details: "
      + e );
    e.printStackTrace();
  }
%>
</p>
</body>
</html>
```

Almost there! We just have to add a couple of Web-application descriptors. The standard J2EE Web-application descriptor is `web.xml`. In addition, JBoss-specific descriptors are housed in the `jboss-web.xml` file. Both of these files reside within the `WEB-INF` subdirectory.

Here's the code for `web.xml`:

```
<?xml version="1.0" encoding="UTF-8"?>
<!DOCTYPE web-app PUBLIC
"-//Sun Microsystems, Inc.//DTD Web Application 2.3//EN"
"http://java.sun.com/dtd/web-app_2_3.dtd">

<web-app >
    <welcome-file-list>
        <welcome-file>index.jsp</welcome-file>
    </welcome-file-list>
    <ejb-ref>
        <description>Greeter</description>
        <ejb-ref-name>Greeter</ejb-ref-name>
        <ejb-ref-type>Session</ejb-ref-type>
        <home>test.interfaces.GreeterHome</home>
        <remote>test.interfaces.Greeter</remote>
        <ejb-link>Greeter</ejb-link>
    </ejb-ref>
</web-app>
```

And here's the code for `jboss-web.xml`:

```
<?xml version="1.0" encoding="UTF-8"?>
<!DOCTYPE jboss-web PUBLIC
"-//JBoss//DTD Web Application 2.3//EN"
"http://www.jboss.org/j2ee/dtd/jboss-web_3_0.dtd">

<jboss-web>
    <context-root>/ejb_tests</context-root>

    <!-- EJB References -->
    <ejb-ref>
        <ejb-ref-name>Greeter</ejb-ref-name>
        <jndi-name>ejb/Greeter</jndi-name>
    </ejb-ref>
</jboss-web>
```

To create the .war file, we just need to `jar` up `index.jsp`, the descriptor files, and the interface class files. Create the `WEB-INF\classes` directory, and copy all the interface files into it. Then `jar` everything up and copy the .war file into the JBoss deploy directory.

For example, on Windows the commands are:

```
mkdir WEB-INF\classes
copy test\interfaces\Greeter.class WEB-INF\classes
copy test\interfaces\GreeterLocal.class WEB-INF\classes
copy test\interfaces\GreeterHome.class WEB-INF\classes
copy test\interfaces\GreeterLocalHome.class WEB-INF\classes
jar cvf greeter.war WEB-INF index.jsp
copy greeter.war %JBOSS_HOME%\server\default\deploy
```

On Linux the commands are:

```
mkdir WEB-INF/classes
cp test/interfaces/Greeter.class WEB-INF/classes
cp test/interfaces/GreeterLocal.class WEB-INF/classes
cp test/interfaces/GreeterHome.class WEB-INF/classes
cp test/interfaces/GreeterLocalHome.class WEB-INF/classes
jar cvf greeter.war WEB-INF index.jsp
cp greeter.war $JBOSS_HOME/server/default/deploy
```

Now that we've got it running, let's step back and take a look at what the application does.

In the JSP page, we draw a random name and ask the Greeter EJB to greet us. The greeting will also include the name of the last person it greeted. Go ahead and visit the page a couple times. The URL for it is `http://localhost:8080/ejb_tests/`.

NOTE **If you get an error message stating that the** `Tools.jar` **file is not found, the most likely culprit is a missing or incorrect** `JAVA_HOME` **setting. Be sure to set the** `JAVA_HOME` **environment variable to point to the directory where the JDK is installed.**

The Greeter EJB basically greets the user based on the name passed in and mentions the last person it has greeted. In a stateless session bean, we are not guaranteed anything regarding the state of our EJB between method calls. You should avoid keeping stateful information for that reason, even though this restriction is not strictly enforced by the EJB container. Besides, the very notion runs contrary to the spirit of the stateless session bean.

One way to see how this state is unreliable is to see what happens when you use two different client sessions. This can be done by using two different computers or by having two browsers (not browser windows). Open up the page and refresh it. Just based on the information displayed by the last browser greeted, it may seem as if state is maintained. However, this is a dangerous assumption because the EJB container is free to create a pool of stateless session beans and dole them out as it deems fit. If we want the state to be consistent to a client, we need to use a stateful session bean.

It is just a simple matter of modifying a descriptor file to switch the Greeter from a stateless session bean to a stateful session bean. Just edit `ejb-jar.xml` and replace Stateless with Stateful. Make an updated EJB .jar file and redeploy. That's all there is to it! Now, if you access the Greeter with multiple clients, you'll find that it is consistent within the client session—which is how stateful session beans are designed to be! The typical example of the shopping cart or user preferences makes it easy to see the usefulness of this construct.

NOTE The stateful session bean is a server-side component. It is only reachable as long as the client retains a reference to it, which is why our JSP page holds the reference within the session. There are many methods and locations where an enterprise application can choose to hold and retain state for a client. Knowing how the stateful session bean works will, hopefully, make it easier to tackle the problem.

CMP 2.*x* Entity Bean Tests and Sample Code

Rather than go through the tedium of creating all the files in the last section by hand again, we'll show you how XDoclet can simplify your life. The idea behind XDoclet is the automatic generation of support files, such as deployment descriptors, based on Javadoc comments within the source code. As we shall see, this is an eminently practical concept.

Also, we will start using Ant build scripts to simplify the build process, because this is fast becoming the standard for building Java projects in any capacity, and it works like a charm.

The following examples will assume that you have already installed Ant. Please refer to Chapter 4 for more information on installing these tools. There is a multitude of really good Ant build scripts, projects layouts, and other configuration-related material available. This project layout, and the Ant build script associated with it, is a stripped down version of one Stan normally uses for new projects. It has roots in the original XDoclet samples, but has evolved over the course of usage in real-world projects. As always, it is only a starting point, and each project tends to have unique requirements that warrant new tweaks and changes.

The Ant build script we'll be using will only generate the EJB .jar file. Often, the build will generate .war and .ear files. Automatic deployment, JUnit tests, and source control management round out the other favorites. You'll find an extensive list of extra capabilities in Ant. For more details, check out their Web site at `http://ant.apache.org/`.

Okay, let's get started with the basic directory structure for this simple project. The layout is as follows, where the `$PROJECT_ROOT` is the base directory for this application:

```
$PROJECT_ROOT\
    |-src
    |----java
    |--------test
    |------------ejb
    |-gen-src
    |-gen-meta
    |-build
    |-dist
    |-lib
```

Our source files will go into the `src` directory. The `gen-src` and `gen-meta` directories are where the Xdoclet-generated code and descriptors go, respectively. The build directory just holds temporary build classes and other miscellaneous files. The `dist` directory is where the final EJB .jar file is placed when the build script completes its work. Finally, the `lib` directory houses the .jar files that are referenced in building the code. For this project, the only file needed is `jboss-j2ee.jar`, which can be copied from `%JBOSS_HOME%\client\`.

In the project's root directory, we have two files: `build.xml` and `build.properties`. The `build.xml` file is a standard Ant build script. If you run Ant from the project root directory, this file will be detected and used to build the project.

TIP **You can use the** `build.properties` **file to hold properties that can change from machine to machine. This way configuration changes are limited to the** `build.properties` **file, and the** `build.xml` **file can be used by all.**

Here are the contents of the `build.xml` file:

```
<?xml version="1.0"?>
<project name="j2ee-app" default="clean-build" basedir=".">

    <!-- Grab overrides for any properties. -->
    <property file="build.properties" />
    <property file="${user.home}/build.properties" />
```

```
<!-- Default property values. -->
<property name="project.ejb.file" value="${project.name}-ejb.jar" />

<property name="project.dir" value="." />
<property name="project.dist.dir" value="${project.dir}/dist" />
<property name="project.lib.dir" value="${project.dir}/lib" />

<property name="project.src.dir" value="${project.dir}/src" />
<property name="project.src.java.dir"
          value="${project.src.dir}/java" />

<property name="project.gen-src.dir"
          value="${project.dir}/gen-src" />
<property name="project.gen-meta.dir"
          value="${project.dir}/gen-meta" />

<property name="project.build.dir" value="${project.dir}/build" />
<property name="project.build.classes.dir"
          value="${project.build.dir}/classes" />

<property name="xdoclet.lib.dir"
          value="${project.lib.dir}" />
<property name="project.xdoclet.force" value="false" />

<!-- These are here to test the use of properties in @tags. -->
<!-- WARNING: Allowing jBOSS to create or destroy
             tables may lead to a loss of data. -->
<property name="jboss.create_table" value="true" />
<property name="jboss.remove_table" value="false" />

<!-- Set up the classpath to all jars, including those in
     the project and affliated tools like xdoclet, etc. -->
<path id="project.class.path">

    <!-- Add all jars in the lib directory. -->
    <fileset dir="${project.lib.dir}">
        <include name="**/*.jar" />
    </fileset>

    <!-- Add all jars in the xdoclet lib directory. -->
    <fileset dir="${xdoclet.lib.dir}">
        <include name="**/*.jar" />
    </fileset>

    <!-- Append the external classpath last. -->
    <pathelement path="${java.class.path}" />

</path>
```

```
    <!-- Init -->
    <target name="init">
        <tstamp>
            <format property="TODAY" pattern="yyyy-MM-dd"/>
        </tstamp>
        <taskdef
            name="xdoclet"
            classname="xdoclet.DocletTask"
            classpathref="project.class.path"
            />
        <taskdef
            name="ejbdoclet"
            classname="xdoclet.modules.ejb.EjbDocletTask"
            classpathref="project.class.path"
            />
        <taskdef
            name="webdoclet"
            classname="xdoclet.modules.web.WebDocletTask"
            classpathref="project.class.path"
            />
        <taskdef
            name="replacecopy"
            classname="xdoclet.ant.ReplaceCopy"
            classpathref="project.class.path"
            />
    </target>

    <target name="ejbdoclet" depends="init">
        <ejbdoclet
            destdir="${project.gen-src.dir}"
            mergedir=""
            excludedtags="@version,@author,@todo"
            addedtags="@xdoclet-generated at ${TODAY},@copyright
holder,@author author"
            ejbspec="2.0"
            force="${project.xdoclet.force}"
            verbose="false"
            >
            <!-- Includes EJBs in test.ejb package only -->
            <fileset dir="${project.src.java.dir}">
                <include name="test/ejb/*Bean.java" />
                <exclude name="test/ejb/Base*.java" />
            </fileset>

            <packageSubstitution
               packages="ejb" substituteWith="interfaces"/>
```

```
        <remoteinterface/>
        <localinterface/>
        <homeinterface/>
        <localhomeinterface/>

        <dataobject/>
        <valueobject/>
        <entitypk/>
        <entitycmp/>
        <entitybmp/>
        <session/>

        <utilobject cacheHomes="true" includeGUID="true"/>

        <deploymentdescriptor
            destdir="${project.gen-meta.dir}"
            validatexml="true"
            mergedir="fake-to-debug"
            >
            <configParam name="clientjar" value="blah.jar"/>
        </deploymentdescriptor>

        <jboss
            version="3.0"
            unauthenticatedPrincipal="nobody"
            xmlencoding="UTF-8"
            destdir="${project.gen-meta.dir}"
            validatexml="true"
            preferredrelationmapping="relation-table"
            createTable="${jboss.create_table}"
            removetable="${jboss.remove_table}"
            />
    </ejbdoclet>
</target>


<!-- Compile -->
<target name="compile" depends="init">
    <javac srcdir="${project.src.java.dir};${project.gen-src.dir}"
        destdir="${project.build.classes.dir}"
        includes="**/*.java"
        debug="on">
        <classpath refid="project.class.path" />
    </javac>
</target>
```

```
    <!-- Create EJB .jar file. -->
    <target name="ejb-jar" depends="init">
        <jar jarfile="${project.dist.dir}/${project.ejb.file}" >
            <!-- Includes EJBs in test.ejb package only -->
            <fileset
                dir="${project.build.classes.dir}"
                includes="test/ejb/**,test/interfaces/**"
            />
            <metainf
                dir="${project.gen-meta.dir}"
                includes="**.*"
            />
            <fileset
                dir="${project.dist.dir}"
                includes="${project.war.file}"
            />
        </jar>
    </target>


    <!-- Clean everything. -->
    <target name="clean" depends="init">
        <delete dir="${project.build.dir}" quiet="true" />
        <delete dir="${project.dist.dir}" quiet="true" />
        <delete dir="${project.gen-src.dir}" quiet="true" />
        <delete dir="${project.gen-meta.dir}" quiet="true" />

        <mkdir dir="${project.build.dir}" />
        <mkdir dir="${project.build.classes.dir}" />
        <mkdir dir="${project.dist.dir}" />
        <mkdir dir="${project.gen-src.dir}" />
        <mkdir dir="${project.gen-meta.dir}" />
    </target>

    <!--Clean build -->
    <target name="clean-build" depends="clean, main" />

    <!-- Main -->
    <target name="main" depends="ejbdoclet, compile, ejb-jar" />

</project>
```

You should be able to read through the build.xml file and get a good understanding of what it does. Some points that bear mentioning are the autogeneration of database tables, which is a JBoss-specific feature, and the ejbdoclet stuff.

CAUTION **In the two lines following the WARNING comment, you'll see that a property telling JBoss to create new database tables for CMP persistence is set. This information is used by XDoclet to generate the deployment descriptors in** `jboss-ejb.xml` **that in turn instruct JBoss. Because we're just testing out CMP on JBoss with the Hypersonic database, this is not an issue. As a general rule, though, setting** `jboss createTable` **to true can be a dangerous because it will overwrite or erase data in your database. Use this with caution!**

The other thing is that we are instructing XDoclet to only work on certain files. The lines to note are bolded and appear immediately below comments that read:

```
<!— Includes EJBs in test.ejb package only —>
```

These lines work off of an implicit knowledge of the project's organization and naming scheme.

The `build.properties` file is very straightforward. You'll need to modify this file to fit your configuration. The only real property to specify is the home directory where XDoclet is installed.

Here are the contents of `build.properties`:

```
# --- Project properties ---
project.name = simple_entity
xdoclet.dir=c:/java/xdoclet
xdoclet.lib.dir = ${xdoclet.dir}/lib
```

And that's it for the infrastructure! Now, let's check out the source code. The first thing to note is that it is all contained within a single source file. We no longer have to write each interface file by hand thanks to XDoclet. However, we could start refactoring our design into more classes that would promote the sharing of common code. Through such architecture, we can gain some object-oriented reuse, while staying within the bounds of the EJB specification.

Here is the source for `SimpleEntity.java`:

```
package test.ejb;

import javax.ejb.*;
import java.rmi.RemoteException;


/**
 * Just a simple CMP entity bean with a name and a number
 *
```

```
 * @ejb.bean           name="SimpleEntity"
 *                     type="CMP"
 *                     jndi-name="ejb/SimpleEntity"
 *                     view-type="both"
 *                     primkey-field="name"
 *
 * @ejb.persistence
 *   table-name="simple_entity"
 *
 * @ejb.pk
 *   class="java.lang.String"
 *   generate="false"
 *   unchecked="true"
 */
public abstract class SimpleEntityBean
    implements EntityBean
{
    private EntityContext moContext = null;


    /** @ejb.create-method */
    public java.lang.String ejbCreate( String name, int number )
        throws CreateException
    {
        setName( name );
        setNumber( number );
        return null;
    }

    public void ejbPostCreate( String name, int number )
        throws CreateException
    {}

    public void ejbActivate() throws EJBException
    {}

    public void ejbPassivate() throws EJBException
    {}

    public void ejbLoad() throws EJBException
    {}

    public void ejbStore() throws EJBException
    {}

    public void ejbRemove() throws RemoveException, EJBException
    {}
```

```
    public void setEntityContext( EntityContext oContext )
        throws EJBException
    {
        moContext = oContext;
    }

    public void unsetEntityContext()
        throws EJBException
    {
        moContext = null;
    }

    /**
     * @ejb.pk-field
     * @ejb.interface-method
     * @ejb.persistent-field
     * @ejb.persistence column-name="name"
     */
    public abstract String getName();

    /**
     * @ejb.interface-method
     */
    public abstract void setName( String name );

    /**
     * @ejb.interface-method
     * @ejb.persistent-field
     * @ejb.persistence column-name="number"
     */
    public abstract int getNumber();

    /**
     * @ejb.interface-method
     */
    public abstract void setNumber( int number );

}
```

Looking through the source code, you'll find Javadoc lines that contain `@ejb.*`. These are used to cue XDoclet on how to generate files. For example, the `@ejb.interface-method` comment tags the method as one that should be exposed via the remote interface. Other tags such as `@ejb.persistence column-name="number"` are used to pass on information on the data schema that the CMP works with. There are many more tags, including ones to generate distribution-specific information for such diverse offerings as JBoss, WebLogic, Orion, Resin, Oracle, WebSphere, and many others.

Building the project is as simple as running Ant from the project's root directory, then copying the newly minted .jar file from the `dist` directory to the JBoss `deploy` directory.

Here are the Windows instructions:

```
cd \%PROJECT_ROOT%
ant
copy dist\simple-entity-ejb.jar %JBOSS_HOME%\server\default\deploy
```

And here are the Linux instructions:

```
cd /$PROJECT_ROOT
ant
cp dist/simple-entity-ejb.jar $JBOSS_HOME/server/default/deploy
```

The SimpleEntity CMP bean should now be deployed automatically. Because we have specified the appropriate JBoss-specific tags within the source code, JBoss will also create the appropriate table structure in the Hypersonic database. This means our CMP bean is ready to go.

Here's the code for a quick-and-dirty Swing client program to test out the CMP bean. It will let you add, load, and remove SimpleEntity CMP beans.

Here's the source for `SimpleEntityClient.java`:

```
import java.awt.*;
import java.awt.event.*;
import java.util.*;
import javax.naming.*;
import javax.rmi.*;
import javax.swing.*;

import test.interfaces.*;


public class SimpleEntityClient
  extends JFrame
  implements ActionListener
{
  private Context moContext = null;
  private JButton moAddButton = null;
  private JButton moRemoveButton = null;
  private JButton moLoadButton = null;
  private JTextField moNameField = null;
  private JTextField moNumberField = null;
  private JTextArea moMessageArea = null;

  public SimpleEntityClient() {
    super( "Simple Entity Client" );
    setupContext();
```

```
    createGui();
  }

  protected void setupContext() {
    // --- Create default properties to find JBoss's JNDI. ---

    Hashtable default_properties = new Hashtable();
    default_properties.put(
    Context.INITIAL_CONTEXT_FACTORY,
    "org.jnp.interfaces.NamingContextFactory" );
    default_properties.put(
    Context.PROVIDER_URL, "localhost:1099" );


    // --- Create various JMS resources. ---
    // -- Note that we are using the transaction aware versions of
    // -- everything.

    try {
      moContext = new InitialContext( default_properties );
    }
    catch( NamingException e ) {
      e.printStackTrace();
      System.exit( 1 );
    }
  }

  protected void createGui() {
    setBounds( 50, 50, 500, 500 );

    moAddButton = new JButton( "add" );
    moAddButton.addActionListener( this );
    moRemoveButton = new JButton( "remove by name" );
    moRemoveButton.addActionListener( this );
    moLoadButton = new JButton( "load by name" );
    moLoadButton.addActionListener( this );

    moMessageArea = new JTextArea();

    moNameField = new JTextField();
    moNumberField =  new JTextField();

    JPanel oLabelPanel = new JPanel( new GridLayout( 2, 1 ) );
    oLabelPanel.add( new JLabel( "Name:" ) );
    oLabelPanel.add( new JLabel( "Number:" ) );

    JPanel oFieldPanel = new JPanel( new GridLayout( 2, 1 ) );
    oFieldPanel.add( moNameField );
    oFieldPanel.add( moNumberField );
```

```
    JPanel oButtonPanel = new JPanel();
    oButtonPanel.add( moAddButton, BorderLayout.SOUTH );
    oButtonPanel.add( moRemoveButton, BorderLayout.SOUTH );
    oButtonPanel.add( moLoadButton, BorderLayout.SOUTH );

    JPanel oTopPanel = new JPanel( new BorderLayout() );
    oTopPanel.add( oLabelPanel, BorderLayout.WEST );
    oTopPanel.add( oFieldPanel );
    oTopPanel.add( oButtonPanel, BorderLayout.SOUTH );

    JPanel oPanel = new JPanel( new BorderLayout() );
    oPanel.add( oTopPanel, BorderLayout.NORTH );
    oPanel.add( new JScrollPane( moMessageArea ) );

    getContentPane().add( oPanel );
    setDefaultCloseOperation( JFrame.EXIT_ON_CLOSE );
  }

  public void actionPerformed( ActionEvent oActionEvent ) {
    if( oActionEvent.getSource() == moAddButton ) {
      addSimpleEntity();
    }

    if( oActionEvent.getSource() == moRemoveButton ) {
      removeSimpleEntity();
    }

    if( oActionEvent.getSource() == moLoadButton ) {
      loadSimpleEntity();
    }
  }

  protected void addSimpleEntity() {
    try {
      SimpleEntityHome oHome = (SimpleEntityHome)
      PortableRemoteObject.narrow(
        moContext.lookup( "ejb/SimpleEntity" ),
        SimpleEntityHome.class );
      SimpleEntity oSimpleEntity = (SimpleEntity)
        PortableRemoteObject.narrow(
        oHome.create( moNameField.getText(),
        Integer.parseInt( moNumberField.getText() ) ),
        SimpleEntity.class );
      moMessageArea.setText( "Added " + oSimpleEntity );
    }
    catch( Exception e ) {
      JOptionPane.showMessageDialog(
        null,
        e.toString(),
        "Whoops!",
```

```
        JOptionPane.ERROR_MESSAGE );
    }
  }

  protected void removeSimpleEntity() {
    try {
      SimpleEntityHome oHome = (SimpleEntityHome)
        PortableRemoteObject.narrow(
        moContext.lookup( "ejb/SimpleEntity" ),
        SimpleEntityHome.class );
      String sPK = moNameField.getText();
      SimpleEntity oSimpleEntity = (SimpleEntity)
        PortableRemoteObject.narrow(
        oHome.findByPrimaryKey( sPK ),
        SimpleEntity.class );
      oSimpleEntity.remove();
      moMessageArea.setText( "Removed " + oSimpleEntity );
    }
    catch( Exception e ) {
      JOptionPane.showMessageDialog( null,
      e.toString(),
      "Whoops!",
      JOptionPane.ERROR_MESSAGE );
    }
  }

  protected void loadSimpleEntity() {
    try {
      SimpleEntityHome oHome = (SimpleEntityHome)
        PortableRemoteObject.narrow(
        moContext.lookup( "ejb/SimpleEntity" ),
        SimpleEntityHome.class );
      String sPK = moNameField.getText();
      SimpleEntity oSimpleEntity = (SimpleEntity)
        PortableRemoteObject.narrow(
        oHome.findByPrimaryKey( sPK ),
        SimpleEntity.class );
      moNumberField.setText( "" + oSimpleEntity.getNumber() );
      moMessageArea.setText( "Loaded " + oSimpleEntity );
    }
    catch( Exception e ) {
      JOptionPane.showMessageDialog(
        null,
        e.toString(),
        "Whoops!",
        JOptionPane.ERROR_MESSAGE );
    }
  }

  public static void main( String args[] ) {
```

```
        SimpleEntityClient client = new SimpleEntityClient();
        client.show();
    }
}
```

To compile and run the client, the `jbossall-client.jar`, `log4j.jar`, and `simple-entity-ejb.jar` files will be required. These .jar files contain classes that are referenced within the client.

Here's the command for compiling the client in Windows:

```
javac -classpath .;%JBOSS_HOME%\client\jbossall-client.jar;simple-entity-ejb.jar
SimpleEntityClient.java
```

And here's the command for compiling the client in Linux:

```
javac -classpath .:$JBOSS_HOME/client/jbossall-client.jar:simple-entity-ejb.jar
SimpleEntityClient.java
```

Now, to run the client we also need to have those .jar files available. Here's the command to run the client in Windows:

```
java -classpath .;%JBOSS_HOME%\client\jbossall-
client.jar;%JBOSS_HOME%\client\log4j.jar;simple-entity-ejb.jar
SimpleEntityClient
```

And here's the command to run the client in Linux:

```
java -classpath .:$JBOSS_HOME/client/jbossall-
client.jar:$JBOSS_HOME/client/log4j.jar:simple-entity-ejb.jar SimpleEntityClient
```

The interface is fairly self-explanatory. Text fields are available to set values. The Add button adds the CMP based on those values. The Remove button removes a CMP with the name specified in the field. The load button loads a CMP based on the name field. Because the client will print out exceptions, you can try out combinations such as removing nonexistent CMPs and creating duplicates to see what the exception will look like in those instances. Finally, the List button just dumps a list of all SimpleEntity CMP beans into the message area. With the client, you can now see that the CMP bean is deployed and works as expected.

So there you have it! We're able to get a simple CMP EJB deployed on JBoss. This is just the tip of the iceberg as far as CMP is concerned. There are more CMP features and deployment optimizations to explore, as well as a plethora of design patterns that can make your CMP beans better. All this is beyond the scope of this chapter, but you'll see some of these techniques put to use as we build the sample application in the later part of this book.

Message-Driven Beans

We will now cover the steps to create an MDB for use with JBossMQ. Believe it or not, MDBs are one of the simplest J2EE components to write and deploy. The example does assume some knowledge of JMS, which is covered in Chapter 9.

This is an MDB we like that works with queues. We'll be creating what we call an interceptor component. Let's say you have an existing component that communicates with a queue Q1. Essentially, we will create an MDB that is registered to listen on Q2, and change the mapping for the client to have its messages routed to Q2 instead. Then, with the MDB, we can inspect the messages and pass them on to Q1. This is useful for debugging JMS environments without disrupting existing components.

Here's the code for `InterceptorMessageBean.java`:

```
import javax.ejb.*;
import javax.jms.*;
import javax.naming.*;


public class InterceptorMessageBean
  implements MessageDrivenBean, MessageListener
{
  protected MessageDrivenContext m_context = null;
  protected Queue m_queue = null;
  protected QueueConnection m_connection = null;
  protected QueueSession m_session = null;


  public void setMessageDrivenContext( MessageDrivenContext context )
  throws EJBException {
    m_context = context;
  }


  /**
   * Create the message-driven bean.
   **/
  public void ejbCreate() throws CreateException {
    try {
      // --- Allocate JMS resources. ---

      InitialContext context = new InitialContext();
      QueueConnectionFactory factory = (QueueConnectionFactory)
        context.lookup( "XAConnectionFactory" );
      m_queue = (Queue)
        context.lookup( "java:comp/env/jms/destinationQueue" );
      m_connection = factory.createQueueConnection();
```

```
    }
    catch( Exception e ) {
      throw new CreateException( e.getMessage() );
    }
  }


  public void ejbRemove() {
    // --- Release cached JMS resources. ---

    if( m_queue != null ) {
      m_queue = null;
    }

    if( m_connection != null ) {
      try {
        m_connection.close();
      }
      catch( JMSException e ) {
        e.printStackTrace();
      }
      m_connection = null;
    }
  }


  public void onMessage( Message message ) {
    QueueSession session = null;

    System.out.println( "Interceptor got message " + message );
    try {
      // --- Forward the message. ---

      session = m_connection.createQueueSession( false, 0 );
      QueueSender sender = session.createSender( m_queue );
      sender.send( message );

      System.out.println( "Message forwarded." );
    }
    catch( Exception e ) {
      e.printStackTrace();
    }
    finally {
      try {
        session.close();
      }
      catch( JMSException e ) {
        e.printStackTrace();
      }
    }
```

```
    }
}
```

We can compile this with the following command in Windows:

```
javac -classpath .;%JBOSS_HOME%\client\jboss-
j2ee.jar;%JBOSS_HOME%\client\log4j.jar InterceptorMessageBean.java
```

And in Linux:

```
javac -classpath .:$JBOSS_HOME/client/jboss-
j2ee.jar:$JBOSS_HOME/client/log4j.jar InterceptorMessageBean.java
```

Now, we'll have to create the deployment descriptors for this MDB. There are two deployment descriptor files required for the EJB .jar file that we will be using for the InterceptorMessageBean: `ejb-jar.xml` and `jboss.xml`. The `ejb-jar.xml` file is a standard J2EE deployment descriptor file, and the `jboss.xml` deployment descriptor file holds the JBoss-specific settings. These should reside in a directory called `META-INF` under the base directory where the `InterceptorMessageBean.class` file resides.

Here's the listing for `ejb-jar.xml`:

```
<?xml version="1.0" encoding="UTF-8"?>
<!DOCTYPE ejb-jar PUBLIC
"-//Sun Microsystems, Inc.//DTD Enterprise JavaBeans 2.0//EN"
"http://java.sun.com/dtd/ejb-jar_2_0.dtd">

<ejb-jar >

   <description><![CDATA[No Description.]]></description>
   <display-name>Interceptor MDB</display-name>
   <enterprise-beans>
      <message-driven >
         <description>
           <![CDATA[Message Driven Bean Template]]>
         </description>
         <display-name>Interceptor MDB</display-name>
         <ejb-name>InterceptorMessageBean</ejb-name>
         <ejb-class>InterceptorMessageBean</ejb-class>
         <transaction-type>Container</transaction-type>
         <acknowledge-mode>Auto-acknowledge</acknowledge-mode>
         <message-driven-destination>
           <destination-type>javax.jms.Queue</destination-type>
           <subscription-durability>NonDurable</subscription-durability>
         </message-driven-destination>
         <resource-ref >
            <res-ref-name>jms/destinationQueue</res-ref-name>
            <res-type>javax.jms.Queue</res-type>
```

```
            <res-auth>Container</res-auth>
         </resource-ref>
         <resource-ref >
            <res-ref-name>jms/testQueue2</res-ref-name>
            <res-type>javax.jms.Queue</res-type>
            <res-auth>Container</res-auth>
         </resource-ref>
      </message-driven>
   </enterprise-beans>
</ejb-jar>
```

And the listing for `jboss.xml` is:

```
<?xml version="1.0" encoding="UTF-8"?>
<!DOCTYPE jboss PUBLIC
"-//JBoss//DTD JBOSS 3.0//EN"
"http://www.jboss.org/j2ee/dtd/jboss_3_0.dtd">

<jboss>
   <unauthenticated-principal>nobody</unauthenticated-principal>
   <enterprise-beans>
      <message-driven>
         <ejb-name>InterceptorMessageBean</ejb-name>
         <destination-jndi-name>jms/testQueue2</destination-jndi-name>
         <resource-ref>
            <res-ref-name>jms/destinationQueue</res-ref-name>
            <jndi-name>queue/testQueue</jndi-name>
         </resource-ref>
         <resource-ref>
            <res-ref-name>jms/testQueue2</res-ref-name>
            <jndi-name>queue/testQueue2</jndi-name>
         </resource-ref>
      </message-driven>
   </enterprise-beans>
</jboss>
```

Now, let's create our EJB jar file for deployment. We will use the `jar` command to do so:

```
jar cvf InterceptorMDB.jar InterceptorMessageBean.class META-INF\ejb-
jar.xml META-INF\jboss.xml
```

In Linux, use:

```
jar cvf InterceptorMDB.jar InterceptorMessageBean.class META-INF/ejb-
jar.xml META-INF/jboss.xml
```

To deploy the EJB jar file, just copy it into JBoss's deploy directory, usually `%JBOSS_HOME%\server\default\deploy`. If JBoss is running, you should see a message along the lines of:

```
"Deployed package: file:C:/jboss-
3.0.4/server/default/deploy/InterceptorMDB.jar"
```

That's all there is to it!

As you can see, message-driven beans are just a single class. The descriptors are minimal, and they are very powerful part of the enterprise architecture. Clean and simple! Just the way things should be!

Summary

In this chapter, we covered EJB containers, which provides the middle-tier enterprise architecture connecting the top presentation-oriented tiers with the bottom tier of enterprise systems. There's a lot of power in the EJB component architecture, not the least of which is the flexibility of descriptors and container-managed aspects. We saw a close race between JBoss and JOnAS. Each is a superb implementation of perhaps the most complex J2EE layer. In the end, we selected JBoss for ease of use and cutting-edge EJB specification compliance.

CHAPTER

11

Providing Web Services

Web services provide a powerful, platform-independent way to support distributed computing by leveraging the ubiquitous infrastructure used for the World Wide Web. With Web services, Java functions can be made easily accessible to other languages. Java can also access Web services written in other languages and hosted on other platforms.

In this chapter, we discuss the use of open source tools for implementing Web services. The primary tool we're going to use is Apache Axis, which is the leading open source implementation of Sun's JAX/RPC standard. JAX/RPC is a Java-centric Web services API that builds upon other Web services standards such as SOAP and WSDL. We'll look at all these standards and examine their role within the J2EE enterprise architecture.

Architectural Considerations

The primary function of Web services is to facilitate interaction with external systems and clients. For this reason, Java Web services are at the edges of the J2EE architecture. Web services need to be accessible and understandable by those external systems and clients at the very least. These issues are addressed by SOAP and WSDL, respectively. These two World Wide Web Consortium (W3C) standards are the basic building blocks of platform-independent Web services today. The JAX/RPC API and the Apache Axis implementation of that API are used to expose those Web services according to standards.

Existing components, such as EJBs, can be wrapped and made accessible as Java Web services. The procedure for doing so is exactly the same as writing any other EJB client. On the other side of the fence, almost any Java component, from servlets to EJBs, can consume Web services. This process is made much easier by Apache Axis's Java stub generator. We will examine this in more detail in the examples in this chapter.

Java Web services are typically deployed in the servlet engine. In fact, Axis itself is commonly deployed as a Web application, with Web services processed via JSP. Architecturally, the comparison is very valid and a useful analogy for thinking about how the pieces fit together.

A Brief Introduction to Web Services and SOAP

When people think of Web services, SOAP is usually the standard that comes to mind. SOAP (Simple Object Access Protocol) is an XML-based invocation protocol whose success is due in large part to its simplicity. Essentially, SOAP offers the same functionality of remote procedure calls (RPCs).

Platform and language independence are two of the key SOAP design goals. This approach is validated by the widespread support from major companies for SOAP. A Java Web services client can interact with a Web service hosted on a Microsoft .NET server just as easily as one on Apache Axis. Tangible benefits are realized by the standardization of open protocols such as SOAP.

Again, harking to the goal of simplicity, SOAP is much more loosely coupled than previous RPC standards. As with the case of scripting, loose coupling makes SOAP easy to use at the expense of strict checking and language integration. Apache Axis, with its stub-generation capability, brings back those benefits by building stubs on top of the SOAP layer.

Another important point is that SOAP is not actually tied to any single transport protocol, although most deployments use HTTP. In theory, this flexibility is a good separation of design. Unfortunately, this leaves key issues like session management and transaction support up in the air. Many vendors have forged on ahead with proprietary implementations for the time being.

Figure 11.1 shows the basic structure of a SOAP message:

For the most part, we can focus our attention on the SOAP body. The SOAP headers are usually generated for us by the APIs we'll be using. Also, note that the AttachmentPart sections are an extension to the basic SOAP message that is covered by the SAAJ API (see the definition of SAAJ in the upcoming list).

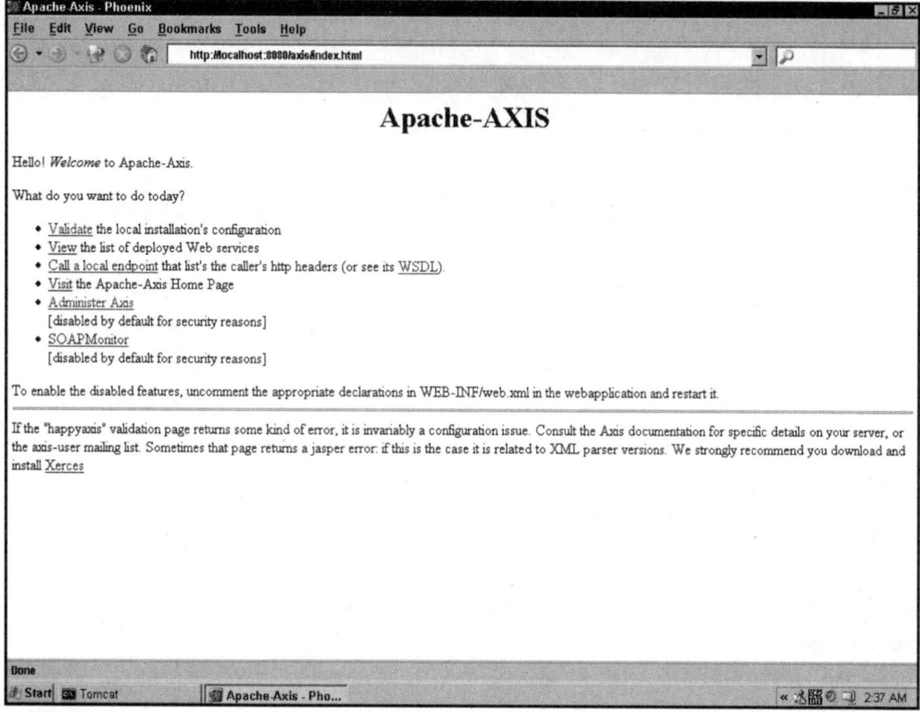

Figure 11.1 Structure of a SOAP message.

Despite all its fame, SOAP alone is not enough to create a useful Web services ecosystem. It is mostly just an invocation protocol, and there is a need for many other standards for things such as discovery, description, and standardized schemas. In addition to SOAP, a number of standards are either in use or being pushed as solutions to the higher-level problems faced by Web services. These include the following standards:

BPELWS. Business Process Execution Language for Web Services enables complex business conversations and workflows, a critical next step for Web services.

ebXML. Electronic Business Extensible Markup Language is a set of specifications covering electronic business. The Java APIs that implement approved standards include JAX-RPC, JAXM, and JAXR.

JAX/RPC. This is the most important Java API, because it handles the binding between the underlying language-independent protocols, such as SOAP and WSDL, to Java objects and interfaces.

JAXM. Java API for XML Messaging implements the SAAJ API and extends SOAP with additional functionality.

JAXR. Java API for XML Registries is used to access various Web service registries, those specified under the umbrella of UDDI (Universal Description, Discovery and Integration) and ebXML.

SOAP. This is the invocation protocol for using Web services.

SAAJ. SOAP with Attachments API for Java is the Java API for working with SOAP messages that have additional MIME (Multipurpose Internet Mail Extensions) data attached.

UDDI. Universal Description, Discovery and Integration of Web services is a discovery mechanism that lets clients find Web services in a public directory.

WSDL. Web Services Description Language governs the description of a Web service and how to use it.

XML Schema. This is the schema description of cross-platform data types used in SOAP messages.

NOTE **The Java Web Services Developer Pack (JWSDP), available at the following URL:**

```
http://java.sun.com/webservices/webservicespack.html
```

contains the reference implementations of the Java standards mentioned here. These APIs will be required of future J2EE 1.4–compliant application servers. Until then, it may be necessary to download the JWSDP for some of the examples.

Most industry heavyweights already support SOAP, and it will very likely be a linchpin of the new Web landscape. Web services will continue developing upon and around SOAP.

Where Web Services Fit into an Enterprise Architecture

New enterprise applications will likely be both providers and consumers of Web services. The network effects, in which the degree of interconnectedness increases the value to all parties involved, are just beginning to be realized. Web services give flexibility to the enterprise architecture to meet changing collaborative needs. Because many of these systems are outside of your control, Web services must not only be simple and easy to access, but must conform to shared standards.

The basic standard for Web services is SOAP, which is used by JAX-RPC as well as other platforms, such as Microsoft's .Net architecture. SOAP provides the basic protocol for the Web services conversation, and it can be used with a number of underlying transport protocols such as HTTP, SMTP, or HTTPS. Nevertheless, SOAP/HTTP is used in the majority of cases.

The SOAP/HTTP connection leads us to another problem: firewalls. Traditionally, RPC solutions, such as DCOM and IIOP, communicated over special ports. By using HTTP, SOAP is able to cross most firewalls, which allow port 80 traffic. This is a double-edged sword. Gone are the issues of configuring firewalls to open up special ports or adding tunneling to support RPC traffic. On the other hand, now it becomes much more complicated to lock down and manage services. Firewalls are beginning to analyze HTTP traffic to allow filtering of SOAP and other tunneled traffic. The whole endeavor bogs down into one of those messy, real-world situations of point and counterpoint. The best solution is to have good network administrators on staff to keep on top of things.

With Apache Axis, Web services are hosted in the servlet container. This is a quite sensible, given that we are talking about *Web* services. It is reasonably accurate to treat the Web-services layer the same as Web-application layer. Developing a Web service can be done with no more effort than developing a JSP. In a real application, however, Web services would likely follow more of the servlet pattern. That is to say, the Web service would call upon other elements of the J2EE architecture, such as EJBs, to achieve its function.

On the client side of the Web services architecture, things are a bit less standardized. As testament to the open and interoperable nature of Web services, the variety of different clients range from standalone programs written in other languages to Java servlets.

NOTE **Web services are often long, synchronous calls. Some clients can benefit by placing a JMS layer between the client application and the Web services stubs. This way, the client can benefit from JMS queuing without any changes on the server side.**

Recently, Amazon and Google introduced Web services interfaces to their businesses. Being able to integrate with their services brings value to both parties involved, even when they cannot foresee how and by whom those services are used. Those services that should be openly accessible are prime candidates for Web services. In other cases, the benefits of a building on the Web services standard must be weighed against such services inefficiency and immaturity. Often RMI or IIOP are better choices within your own tightly coupled systems.

As usual, the architecture for securing systems is lagging behind our ability to open up systems. There are existing security standards that cover various pieces of the security picture, but there's no standard for putting everything together to secure Web services. Web services need to be able to guarantee the following:

Authentication. The identity of the provider and client must be verified.

Authorization. There must be permissions for controlling access and Web service usage.

Confidentiality. The contents of the conversation must be protected.

Integrity. It must ensure that a conversation isn't changed or altered.

Broad outlines and prototypes for a standard security layer are underway. The WS-Security standard is one to keep an eye on. WS-Security supercedes the SOAP-Security proposal and specifies a set of standard SOAP extensions to use. XML Encryption and XML Digital Signatures are both a part of the WS-Security standard. The encryption of message contents is covered by XML Encryption, while XML Digital Signatures are used to sign the contents and guarantee their integrity. SSL is often used to secure the Web service call on the wire. For now, WS-Security looks to be the front-runner for a Java standard. Nevertheless, it remains an early adopter technology because a Sun standard does not exist for it yet.

NOTE **Be aware that many existing Web services are not conformant with WS-Security. In fact, most Web services are either unsecured or secured in an ad hoc manner.**

Enterprise applications should definitely be designed with an eye on Web services. The Web services security question is being addressed, and a standard should emerge shortly. This is simply too critical a piece of the enterprise architecture for that not to happen. Within a J2EE enterprise application, JAX-RPC represents the best path to Web services and receives our recommendation.

Java and Web Services

Web services are implemented through the platform-independent and language-independent standards. Indeed, the existence of Web services standards is already giving rise to more interoperable systems. Established Internet leaders, such as Google and Amazon.com, are opening up access to their systems through SOAP and WSDL. As J2EE developers, it would benefit us to be able to use and write Web services in a Java-centric manner. Luckily for us, there is support for working with Web services at all those levels.

Most Java Web services will be developed using the JAX-RPC API. JAX-RPC is a Java API designed for working with XML-based Web services. In particular, it handles the forward and reverse mapping from Java objects to their platform-independent counterparts. The forward mapping maps an existing Web service into the equivalent Java interface. The reverse mapping takes a Java object and generates the necessary framework to expose it as a platform-independent Web service.

Using JAX-RPC will improve productivity and drop the entry barrier to working with Java Web services. JAX-RPC is the best choice for most scenarios. Best of all, we can reasonably expect that JAX-RPC will be available because it will be required as a part of the upcoming J2EE 1.4 specification.

Axis

Apache Axis provides a great implementation of Java Web services. It is an open source implementation of JAX-RPC that is available right now. Axis actually sports an amazing lineage, enjoying its start as SOAP4J from IBM and later as the Apache SOAP project. The most current incarnation, renamed Axis, is the result of a complete rewrite of Apache SOAP. The new code is built around SAX for higher performance. As far as open source Java Web services projects go, Apache Axis is the best around, and we'll be using it for all of the Java Web services examples in this chapter.

Installation and Configuration

Apache Axis is actually implemented as a J2EE Web application. This means that we can use Axis to provide Web services on any J2EE-compliant servlet engine. In the following sections, we'll show you how to install and configure Apache Axis.

NOTE **The instructions for this chapter assume that you're using Tomcat.**

Basic Install

To start off, we need to download a copy of the Apache Axis project. The latest release is available at `http://ws.apache.org/axis/releases.html`. At the time of writing, this is version 1.1rc2. Download the `axis-1_1rc2.zip` file (for Windows) or the `axis-1_1rc2.tar.gz file` file (for Linux).

After downloading the file, extract the files from the archive. Unlike many of the other installations, we don't need to extract them to a common directory. The Axis files will be packaged and deployed as part of a J2EE Web application. Normally, J2EE Web applications are packaged as .war files. However, to make it easier to access Java Web services, we're going to deploy Apache Axis in Tomcat as an unpackaged Web application. This is basically a directory with the same structure and files as the .war archive.

To deploy the unpackaged Axis Web application, copy the `webapps/axis` folder into the Tomcat `webapps` folder.

On Windows, the command is:

```
copy webapps\axis %TOMCAT_HOME%\webapps
```

On Linux, the command is:

```
cp -r webapps/axis $TOMCAT_HOME/webapps
```

If you look inside the `WEB-INF/libs` directory within the Axis Web application, you'll find library .jar files for JAX/RPC, SAAJ, and WSDL among others. These are some of the standard APIs we covered earlier in our discussions about Java Web services and XML. Apache Axis depends on these Web services standards to provide the foundation. Often the Axis interfaces will give us streamlined access to the APIs.

NOTE **Due to some changes in the way Java 1.4 handles package naming, the `jaxrpc.jar` and `saaj.jar` files may cause problems when packaged within the `WEB-INF/lib` directory. If you encounter such an error, the solution is to move the .jar files into the `%TOMCAT_HOME%\common\lib` directory and then restart Tomcat for the .jar files to be loaded.**

Go ahead and start Tomcat if it isn't already running. Tomcat will pick up the new Web application automatically and deploy the Axis servlet. By default, the Web application is deployed under the Web application's directory name, `axis`. This is fine for now. In the *Binding Axis under a Different Name* section later in the chapter, we'll demonstrate how to deploy it under a different name and as a .war file.

Axis Admin Page

Let's verify that Axis is working. Using your Web browser, open up the Axis index page (`http://localhost:8080/axis/index.html`), which should look like Figure 11.2.

The first thing to do is verify that Axis is running okay. To do so, click on the Validate link to open the `happyaxis.jsp` page. You should see a page similar to Figure 11.3.

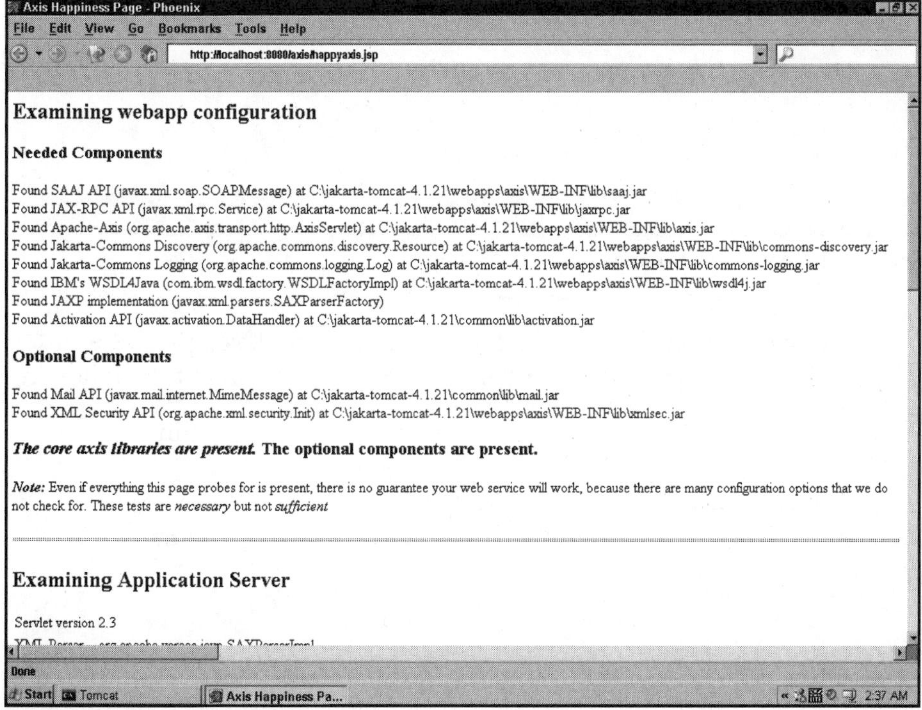

Figure 11.2 Axis index page.

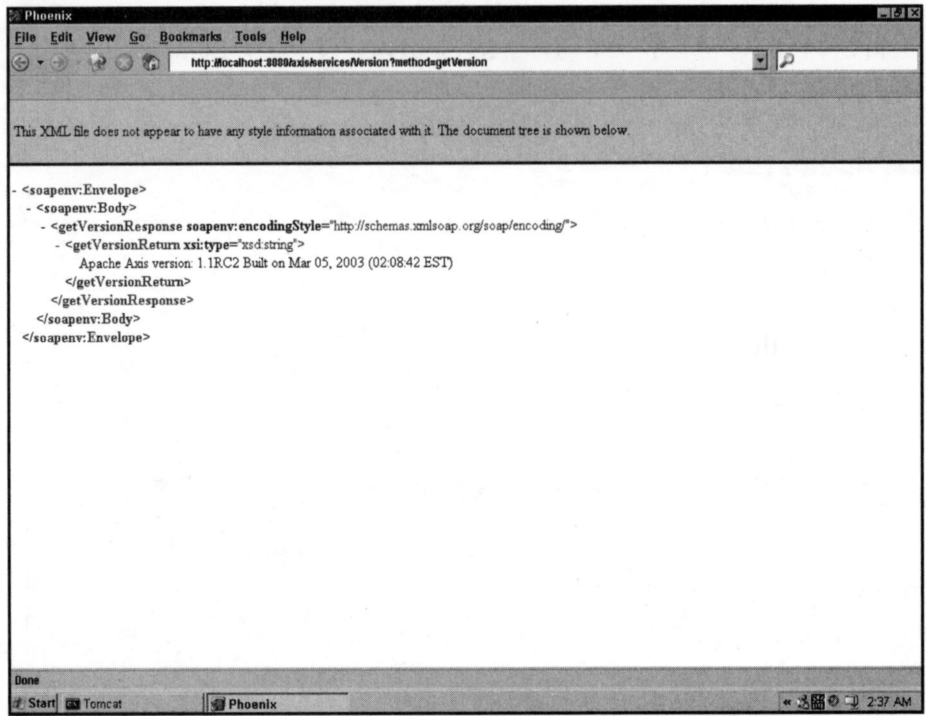

Figure 11.3 happyaxis.jsp page.

The admin page will probably be disabled by default. If so, go to `WEB-INF/web.xml` file within the Axis Web application and uncomment the following segment:

```
<!--
  <servlet-mapping>
    <servlet-name>AdminServlet</servlet-name>
    <url-pattern>/servlet/AdminServlet</url-pattern>
  </servlet-mapping>
 -->
```

This will reenable the admin link on the Axis index page. Currently, the admin page seems rather sparse and provides little in the way of useful information. This may change in the future, but until then we recommend that you leave the admin page disabled.

Adding XML Security

You'll notice that the XML Security module is not installed. The XML Security module adds support for the XML Signatures and XML Encryption standards.

Let's go ahead and install that because we'll be covering it later in this chapter. To do so, go to the XML Security page (http://xml.apache.org/security) and follow the instructions to download the current distribution. At the time of writing, this is xml-security-bin-1_0_4.zip. After it is downloaded, extract the distribution. Then, simply copy the build/xmlsec.jar into the WEB-INF/libs file with the other library .jar files.

On Windows, the command is:

```
copy build\xmlsec.jar %TOMCAT_HOME%\webapps\axis\WEB-INF\libs
```

On Linux, the command is:

```
cp build/xmlsec.jar $TOMCAT_HOME/webapps/axis/WEB-INF/libs
```

Restart Tomcat, and check happyaxis.jsp again. XML Security should be available now.

Binding Axis under a Different Name

Axis is just a regular J2EE Web application. By default, it is deployed in an extracted .war directory. You can change the name by which Axis is bound under Tomcat.

To expose the Axis Web services under a different binding, simply rename the Web application folder and restart Tomcat. Now, try changing the bound name from axis to mywebservices.

NOTE You may not be able to change the Web application's name while Tomcat is running. If that's the case, you'll have to shut down Tomcat before renaming.

On Windows, use:

```
ren %TOMCAT_HOME%\webapps\axis %TOMCAT_HOME%\webapps\mywebservices
```

On Linux, use:

```
mv $TOMCAT_HOME/webapps/axis $TOMCAT_HOME/webapps/mywebservices
```

Restart Tomcat, and now you'll see that Axis is available at http://localhost:8080/mywebservices/.

See, nothing magical about it at all! As you can see, using Java Web services via Apache Axis is a piece of cake.

Integration and Testing

Now that Axis is up and running, let's test Web services. Axis comes with several sample services that are available by default. To reach a Web service, you need to know the SOAP endpoint at which that the service is available; this SOAP endpoint is in the form of a standard URL. In the official specifications, SOAP calls should be sent via HTTP POST. To make things easier to debug, Axis also allows HTTP `GET` requests. With a HTTP `GET` request, we can encode some SOAP parameters in the query string of the URL, which is everything from the question mark on.

Let's try calling one of the default Axis Web services. We'll retrieve the Axis version information by calling the `getVersion` method in the Version Web service. The URL to access that is:

```
http://localhost:8080/axis/services/Version?method=getVersion
```

NOTE **Don't worry if you encounter a message stating, "`Problem with servlet engine config file: /WEB-INF/server-config.wsdd.`" This configuration file is automatically created as soon as a Web service is deployed.**

You should see something similar to Figure 11.4.

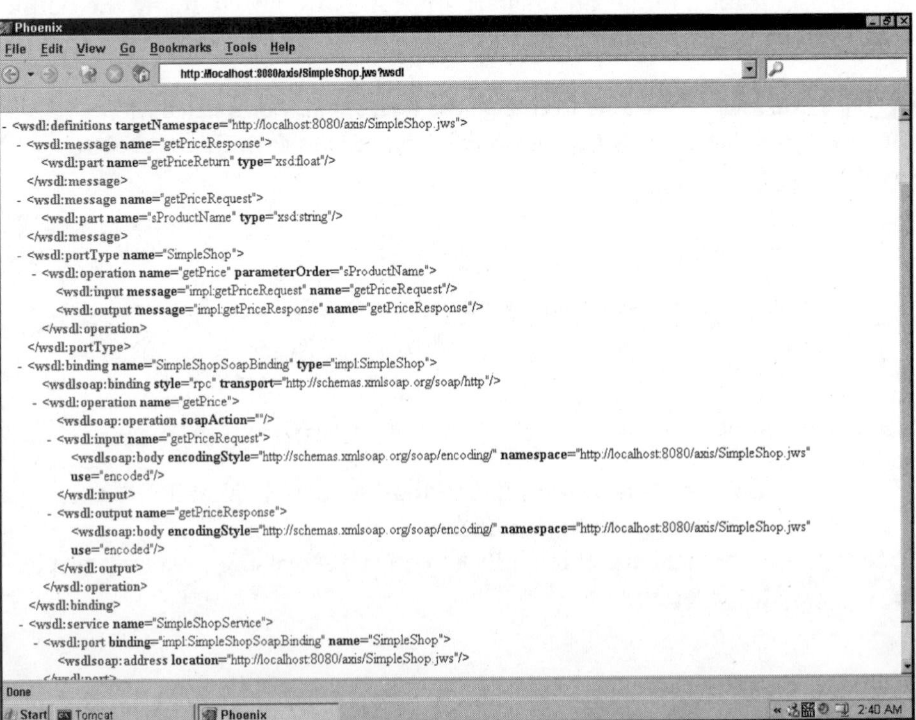

Figure 11.4 Results from calling getVersion.

Now that we know Web services are working, let's move on to the interesting stuff: writing and deploying our own Web services.

Constructing Web Services

Apache Axis comes with many excellent examples. We would recommend studying those to learn more about Java Web services. To get you started, we'll show you how to construct Java Web services and clients, with an emphasis on the Java-centric technologies.

Building a Basic Web Service

In this section, we'll show you how to build a simple price-quoting Web service called SimpleShop. There are several ways to construct a Java Web service with Apache Axis. SimpleShop will use the simplest method: writing the service in the form of a Java source file. This basic Web service has a single exposed method, `getPrice`. To begin, we'll just write the Web service as if it were a normal Java class.

Here's the source code for `SimpleShop.java`:

```
import java.util.*;


public class SimpleShop
{
    protected Map moPrices = null;

    public SimpleShop()
    {
        setupMockPrices();
    }


    protected void setupMockPrices()
    {
        moPrices = new HashMap();
        moPrices.put( "t-shirt", new Float( 19.99 ) );
        moPrices.put( "coffee cup", new Float( 10.00 ) );
        moPrices.put( "poster", new Float( 14.95 ) );
    }


    public float getPrice( String sProductName ) throws Exception
    {
        // --- Check that the product exists, otherwise throw an
exception. ---
```

```
        if( !moPrices.containsKey( sProductName ) )
        {
            throw new Exception( "ProductNotFound" );
        }


        // --- Return the float price of the product. ---

        Float f = (Float) moPrices.get( sProductName );
        return f.floatValue();
    }

}
```

Deployment is as simple as renaming the source file with the .jws extension and making available in the Axis Web application's main directory. Note that we don't even need to compile it—that's handled automatically by Apache Axis.

NOTE If you renamed the Axis directory, be sure to either change the name back or adjust the destination directory to the new name. The instructions are going to assume that it's still bound under `axis`.

On Windows, the command is:

```
copy SimpleShop.java %TOMCAT_HOME%\webapps\axis\SimpleShop.jws
```

On Linux, it is:

```
cp SimpleShop.java $TOMCAT_HOME/webapps/axis/SimpleShop.jws
```

The .jws method of creating a Web service is very similar to JSP in terms of ease and operation. When the Web service is accessed, Axis will generate the appropriate WSDL description and SOAP endpoint from the .jws file.

The URL for retrieving the WSDL description of a Web service can be retrieved from Axis by calling the Web service with wsdl as a query parameter. For example, to see the WSDL for the SimpleShop Web service, the URL is:

```
http://localhost:8080/axis/SimpleShop.jws?wsdl
```

Here's what the WSDL generated for the SimpleShop should look like:

```
<wsdl:definitions targetNamespace="http://localhost:8080/axis/SimpleShop.jws">

  <wsdl:message name="getPriceResponse">
    <wsdl:part name="getPriceReturn" type="xsd:float"/>
  </wsdl:message>
```

```
<wsdl:message name="getPriceRequest">
  <wsdl:part name="sProductName" type="xsd:string"/>
</wsdl:message>

<wsdl:portType name="SimpleShop">
  <wsdl:operation name="getPrice" parameterOrder="sProductName">
    <wsdl:input message="impl:getPriceRequest" name="getPriceRequest"/>
    <wsdl:output message="impl:getPriceResponse" name="getPriceResponse"/>
  </wsdl:operation>
</wsdl:portType>

<wsdl:binding name="SimpleShopSoapBinding" type="impl:SimpleShop">
  <wsdlsoap:binding style="rpc"
              transport="http://schemas.xmlsoap.org/soap/http"/>
  <wsdl:operation name="getPrice">
    <wsdlsoap:operation soapAction=""/>
    <wsdl:input name="getPriceRequest">
      <wsdlsoap:body encodingStyle="http://schemas.xmlsoap.org/soap/encoding/"
         namespace="http://localhost:8080/axis/SimpleShop.jws" use="encoded"/>
    </wsdl:input>
    <wsdl:output name="getPriceResponse">
      <wsdlsoap:body encodingStyle="http://schemas.xmlsoap.org/soap/encoding/"
         namespace="http://localhost:8080/axis/SimpleShop.jws" use="encoded"/>
    </wsdl:output>
  </wsdl:operation>
</wsdl:binding>

<wsdl:service name="SimpleShopService">
  <wsdl:port binding="impl:SimpleShopSoapBinding" name="SimpleShop">
    <wsdlsoap:address location="http://localhost:8080/axis/SimpleShop.jws"/>
  </wsdl:port>
</wsdl:service>

</wsdl:definitions>
```

Note that we only had to write one Java source file. The WSDL describing our service is generated from that, as are the SOAP and Java Web service endpoints. See? Writing Java Web services with Apache Axis is a snap!

Next, we'll write a simple client application to access the SimpleShop Web service. There are two ways of writing the client, and we will cover both. The first client, SimpleShopClient, is written using the Axis interface to SOAP. It is a simple Swing application that lets you enter the URL of the Web service and the item whose price should be retrieved. By default, it gets the price of a T-shirt from the SimpleShop Web service we wrote earlier. Tinkering with SimpleShop and the SimpleShopClient is an easy way to get a good picture of the entire process behind a SOAP-based Web service.

Setting up the Web service call and parameters is handled within our code. While not raw XML/SOAP processing, the abstraction level we're dealing with in this client code is pretty close to that. We will show you a better method using generated Java stubs in SimpleShopClient2 in the next section. For now, let's take a look at the hand-coded method of processing a Web services call.

Here's the source code for `SimpleShopClient.java`:

```
import java.awt.*;
import java.awt.event.*;
import java.net.*;
import java.util.*;
import javax.naming.*;
import javax.rmi.*;
import javax.swing.*;
import javax.xml.namespace.*;
import javax.xml.rpc.*;
import org.apache.axis.*;
import org.apache.axis.client.Call;
import org.apache.axis.client.Service;
import org.apache.axis.encoding.*;


public class SimpleShopClient extends JFrame implements ActionListener
{
    private Context moContext = null;
    private JButton moGetPriceButton = null;
    private JTextField moServiceUrlField = null;
    private JTextField moItemNameField = null;
    private JTextArea moMessageArea = null;


    public SimpleShopClient()
    {
        super( "Simple Shop Client" );
        createGui();
    }


    protected void createGui()
    {
        setBounds( 50, 50, 500, 500 );

        moGetPriceButton = new JButton( "Get Price!" );
        moGetPriceButton.addActionListener( this );

        moServiceUrlField = new JTextField();
        moServiceUrlField.setText(
          "http://localhost:8080/axis/SimpleShop.jws" );

    moItemNameField = new JTextField();
        moItemNameField.setText( "t-shirt" );
```

```
        moMessageArea = new JTextArea();

        JPanel oLabelPanel = new JPanel( new GridLayout( 2, 1 ) );
        oLabelPanel.add( new JLabel( "Service URL:" ) );
        oLabelPanel.add( new JLabel( "Item:" ) );

        JPanel oFieldPanel = new JPanel( new GridLayout( 2, 1 ) );
        oFieldPanel.add( moServiceUrlField );
        oFieldPanel.add( moItemNameField );

        JPanel oTopPanel = new JPanel( new BorderLayout() );
        oTopPanel.add( oLabelPanel, BorderLayout.WEST );
        oTopPanel.add( oFieldPanel );
        oTopPanel.add( moGetPriceButton, BorderLayout.SOUTH );

        JPanel oPanel = new JPanel( new BorderLayout() );
        oPanel.add( oTopPanel, BorderLayout.NORTH );
        oPanel.add( new JScrollPane( moMessageArea ) );

        getContentPane().add( oPanel );
        setDefaultCloseOperation( JFrame.EXIT_ON_CLOSE );
    }


    public void actionPerformed( ActionEvent oActionEvent )
    {
        if( oActionEvent.getSource() == moGetPriceButton )
        {
            getPrice();
        }

    }


    protected void getPrice()
    {
        try
        {
            Service oService = new Service();
            Call oCall = (Call) oService.createCall();
            oCall.setTargetEndpointAddress( new URL(
              moServiceUrlField.getText() ) );
            oCall.setOperationName( "getPrice" );
            oCall.addParameter( "product_name",
              XMLType.XSD_STRING,
              ParameterMode.IN );
            oCall.setReturnType( XMLType.XSD_FLOAT );

            Object[] oInputParams = new Object[]
                   { moItemNameField.getText()  };
```

```
                Object oReturn = oCall.invoke( oInputParams );
                oReturn = (Float) oReturn;

                moMessageArea.append( "The price for a "
                  + moItemNameField.getText()
                  + " is " + oReturn + ".\n" );
            }
            catch( Exception e )
            {
                JOptionPane.showMessageDialog( null,
                  e.toString(), "Whoops!",
                  JOptionPane.ERROR_MESSAGE );
            }
        }


        public static void main( String args[] )
        {
            SimpleShopClient oClient = new SimpleShopClient();
            oClient.show();
        }
    }
```

Notice that in the example we coded the data type specifications for marshaling. Because the Web service's WSDL description contains the necessary information, we can actually automate the process. Apache Axis provides just the tool for the task, WSDL2Java. In the next section, we'll show you how to build SimpleShopClient2 using this tool.

A Web Service Client Using Generated Stubs

In the first example in the previous section, we had to write a client using a generic interface. Luckily for us Java developers, Apache Axis comes with a Java client stub generator that completes the usability loop on the client side. Given the WSDL for a Web service, the appropriate Java client stubs are generated. In this example, we'll use the generator to simplify the code of the SimpleShopClient.

The generator program, WSDL2Java, is contained within the `wsdl4j.jar` file. The only parameter required is the URL pointing to the WSDL description. We'll be using it on the SimpleShop Web service we deployed earlier on Tomcat. Make sure that Tomcat is running before generating the stubs because we'll be relying on the WSDL that Apache Axis automatically created from `SimpleShop.jws`.

NOTE **You can also use a WSDL file within the local file system. Just use the appropriate URL(that is,** `file:///temp/SimpleShop.wsdl`**).**

To run WSDL2Java on Windows, use the following (extremely long) command:

```
java -classpath .;%TOMCAT_HOME%\webapps\axis\WEB-
INF\lib\axis.jar;%TOMCAT_HOME%\webapps\axis\WEB-
INF\lib\jaxrpc.jar;%TOMCAT_HOME%\webapps\axis\WEB-INF\lib\wsdl4j.jar;%TO
MCAT_HOME%\webapps\axis\WEB-INF\lib\commons-
logging.jar;%TOMCAT_HOME%\webapps\axis\WEB-INF\lib\commons-
discovery.jar;%TOMCAT_HOME%\common\lib\servlets.jar;%TOMCAT_HOME%\webapp
s\axis\WEB-INF\lib\saaj.jar org.apache.axis.wsdl.WSDL2Java
http://localhost:8080/axis/SimpleShop.jws?wsdl
```

On Linux, use the following command instead:

```
java -classpath .;%TOMCAT_HOME%\webapps\axis\WEB-
INF\lib\axis.jar;%TOMCAT_HOME%\webapps\axis\WEB-
INF\lib\jaxrpc.jar;%TOMCAT_HOME%\webapps\axis\WEB-INF\lib\wsdl4j.jar;%TO
MCAT_HOME%\webapps\axis\WEB-INF\lib\commons-
logging.jar;%TOMCAT_HOME%\webapps\axis\WEB-INF\lib\commons-
discovery.jar;%TOMCAT_HOME%\common\lib\servlets.jar;%TOMCAT_HOME%\webapp
s\axis\WEB-INF\lib\saaj.jar org.apache.axis.wsdl.WSDL2Java
http://localhost:8080/axis/SimpleShop.jws?wsdl
```

After the generator is completed, there should be a new folder named `localhost` in the directory. The generator uses the namespace of the Web service in generating the stubs. In our case, the service is located under the `localhost\axis` directory. The package name for the new stubs will match that same hierarchy.

Here's an example of one of the generated stubs, SimpleShopService:

```
/**
 * SimpleShop.java
 *
 * This file was auto-generated from WSDL
 * by the Apache Axis WSDL2Java emitter.
 */

package localhost.axis.SimpleShop_jws;

public interface SimpleShop extends java.rmi.Remote
{
    public float getPrice(java.lang.String sProductName)
      throws java.rmi.RemoteException;
}
```

The resemblance to our source file for `SimpleShop.jws` is no coincidence. The client stub and the Web service are synchronized through the WSDL description. Using the stubs, we no longer have to set the endpoints, data types, and operation names. An important side effect is that we no longer need to enter the Web service's URL, which also means that the generated stub only works with one particular endpoint. However, now we can focus on using the Web service as just another Java object. To illustrate the difference, we'll create SimpleShopClient2, using the stubs to communicate with our Web service.

Here's the source code for SimpleShopClient2:

```
import localhost.axis.SimpleShop_jws.SimpleShop;
import localhost.axis.SimpleShop_jws.SimpleShopService;
import localhost.axis.SimpleShop_jws.SimpleShopServiceLocator;

public class SimpleShopClient2
{
    public static void main( String args[] )
    {
        try
        {
            SimpleShopService oServiceLocator =
              new SimpleShopServiceLocator();
            SimpleShop oService = oServiceLocator.getSimpleShop();
            float fPrice = oService.getPrice( "coffee cup" );
            System.out.println( "The price is " + fPrice );
        }
        catch( Exception e )
        {
            e.printStackTrace();
        }
    }
}
```

As you can see, it is much easier to write a Web services client using the generated stub classes. Stubs can be generated for existing public Web services, such as Google's Web Services API and Amazon.com's Amazon Web Services 2.0. Integrating these external Web services into your applications is easy and opens up new avenues for collaboration. Following are the URLs to access these services:

- Google Web Services API:

  `http://www.google.com/apis/`

- Amazon Web Services 2.0:

  `http://associates.amazon.com/exec/panama/associates/join/developer/kit.html`

Apache Axis is able to generate stubs that work with the ASP.NET Web services without any problems. The Microsoft SOAP Interoperability server (`http://mssoapinterop.org/`) lets you test cross-platform Web services integration with a .NET server. This is a good place to get more information on interoperability.

Generating client stubs from the WSDL description is just one side of the story. It is also possible to generate the server-side skeleton at the same time as the client stubs. So instead of starting from the .jws file, you would begin by authoring a description of your Web service. Then, the WSDL file would be used to generate the client stubs and the server-side skeleton for your Web service. This approach is rarely used, so we won't be covering it in this book. This feature is similar to what we have already seen and more detail is beyond the scope of this book; however, if you are interested, the details are available on the Apache Axis Web site.

Using Web Service Deployment Descriptors as Web Services

Deploying Java Web services through .jws files is quick and easy, but oftentimes we'll need something more powerful. For example, perhaps we would like to expose an existing EJB as a Web service or exercise more control over the service handlers. Apache Axis provides advanced custom deployment of Java Web services through the Web Service Deployment Descriptor (WSDD) method.

The WSDD deployment method requires you to write an XML deployment descriptor file and an undeployment descriptor file. These files tell Axis how to process a particular call to a Java Web service. Following we have a minimal WSDD deployment file for the SimpleShop service we used as an example earlier in this chapter: `SimpleShop.wsdd`:

```
<?xml version="1.0" encoding="UTF-8"?>
<deployment xmlns="http://xml.apache.org/axis/wsdd/"
    xmlns:java="http://xml.apache.org/axis/wsdd/providers/java">
 <service name="SimpleShopWsdd" provider="java:RPC">
  <parameter name="className" value="SimpleShop"/>
  <parameter name="allowedMethods" value="*"/>
 </service>
</deployment>
```

As you can see, this is a very basic file that maps a request to a Java class for handling. We'll be using the `SimpleShop.class` file from earlier. Be sure to copy the `SimpleShop.class` into `WEB-INF/classes` so that Tomcat can find the file. Next, check that Axis and Tomcat are running.

Okay, we're ready to deploy the WSDD for SimpleShop now. Apache Axis has an AdminClient tool that we'll be using.

On Windows, you use the following command:

```
java -classpath .;%TOMCAT_HOME%\webapps\axis\WEB-
INF\lib\axis.jar;%TOMCAT_HOME%\webapps\axis\WEB-
INF\lib\jaxrpc.jar;%TOMCAT_HOME%\webapps\axis\WEB-INF\lib\commons-logging.jar;%T
OMCAT_HOME%\webapps\axis\WEB-INF\lib\commons-
discovery.jar;%TOMCAT_HOME%\webapps\axis\WEB-INF\lib\saaj.jar
org.apache.axis.client.AdminClient SimpleShop.wsdd
```

On Linux, you use this command instead:

```
java -classpath .:$TOMCAT_HOME/webapps/axis/WEB-
INF/lib/axis.jar:$TOMCAT_HOME/webapps/axis/WEB-
INF/lib/jaxrpc.jar:$TOMCAT_HOME/webapps/axis/WEB-INF/lib/commons-logging.jar:$TO
MCAT_HOME/webapps/axis/WEB-INF/lib/commons-
discovery.jar:$TOMCAT_HOME/webapps/axis/WEB-INF/lib/saaj.jar
org.apache.axis.client.AdminClient SimpleShop.wsdd
```

Now, let's check to see if deploying the SimpleShop service through WSDD worked. Open up the following URL:

```
http://localhost:8080/axis/services/SimpleShopWsdd?method=getPrice&item=t-shirt
```

Now, let's try undeploying the service. Create the `SimpleShopUndeploy.wsdd` file.

```
<?xml version="1.0" encoding="UTF-8"?>
<undeployment xmlns="http://xml.apache.org/axis/wsdd/"
    xmlns:java="http://xml.apache.org/axis/wsdd/providers/java">
 <service name="SimpleShopWsdd" provider="java:RPC" />
</undeployment>
```

Run the Axis AdminClient program again, this time with the undeployment WSDD file to remove the SimpleShop service.

On Windows, use this command:

```
java -classpath .;%TOMCAT_HOME%\webapps\axis\WEB-
INF\lib\axis.jar;%TOMCAT_HOME%\webapps\axis\WEB-
INF\lib\jaxrpc.jar;%TOMCAT_HOME%\webapps\axis\WEB-INF\lib\commons-logging.jar;%T
OMCAT_HOME%\webapps\axis\WEB-INF\lib\commons-
discovery.jar;%TOMCAT_HOME%\webapps\axis\WEB-INF\lib\saaj.jar
org.apache.axis.client.AdminClient SimpleShopUndeploy.wsdd
```

On Linux, use this command:

```
java -classpath .:$TOMCAT_HOME/webapps/axis/WEB-
INF/lib/axis.jar:$TOMCAT_HOME/webapps/axis/WEB-
INF/lib/jaxrpc.jar:$TOMCAT_HOME/webapps/axis/WEB-INF/lib/commons-logging.jar:$TO
MCAT_HOME/webapps/axis/WEB-INF/lib/commons-
```

```
discovery.jar:$TOMCAT_HOME/webapps/axis/WEB-INF/lib/saaj.jar
org.apache.axis.client.AdminClient SimpleShopUndeploy.wsdd
```

Although it is a tad bit more complicated than deploying a Web service as a .jws file, the WSDD deployment method can do things that cannot be done with the simpler deployment method. For example, if you don't have the source file, you can still deploy using just the class file with the WSDD deployment method. The most useful WSDD deployment feature is the ability to specify alternate providers. For example, Axis has a java:EJB provider that hooks into EJBs.

Deploying EJBs as Web Services

An example WSDD for an EJB might look like this:

```
<?xml version="1.0" encoding="UTF-8"?>
<deployment xmlns="http://xml.apache.org/axis/wsdd/"
    xmlns:java="http://xml.apache.org/axis/wsdd/providers/java">
 <service name="Greeter" provider="java:EJB" >
    <parameter name="className" value="test.ejb.GreeterBean" />
    <parameter name="beanJndiName" value="ejb/Greeter" />
    <parameter name="homeInterfaceName"
value="test.interfaces.GreeterHome" />
    <parameter name="remoteInterfaceName"
value="test.interfaces.Greeter" />
    <parameter name="jndiContextClass"
      value="com.sun.jndi.rmi.registry.RegistryContextFactory"/>
    <parameter name="jndiURL" value="rmi://localhost:1099"/>
    <parameter name="allowedMethods" value="*"/>
  </service>
</deployment>
```

Be sure that the Axis Web application is deployed in JBoss. You can do so by copying the axis folder into JBoss's deployment directory. You'll also need to make sure that Axis can load the class files for the Greeter EJB. The easiest way to do that is to add a copy of the `greeter-ejb.jar` to the `axis\lib` directory. Thus, there will be two copies of `greeter-ejb.jar`, one in the `deploy` directory for JBoss and one in the `lib` directory for Axis.

In Windows, use the following command:

```
xcopy %AXIS_HOME%\webapps\axis %JBOSS_HOME%\server\default\deploy\axis.war\ /s
```

In Linux, use this command instead:

```
cp -r $AXIS_HOME/webapps/axis $JBOSS_HOME/server/default/deploy/axis.war
```

NOTE You must change the folder name to `axis.war` **in order for JBoss to recognize it as a Web application.**

We need to use the Axis AdminClient once again to deploy our Web service. On Windows, the command is as follows:

```
java -classpath .;%TOMCAT_HOME%\webapps\axis\WEB-
INF\lib\axis.jar;%TOMCAT_HOME%\webapps\axis\WEB-
INF\lib\jaxrpc.jar;%TOMCAT_HOME%\webapps\axis\WEB-INF\lib\commons-logging.jar;%T
OMCAT_HOME%\webapps\axis\WEB-INF\lib\commons-
discovery.jar;%TOMCAT_HOME%\webapps\axis\WEB-INF\lib\saaj.jar
org.apache.axis.client.AdminClient Greeter.wsdd
```

On Linux, the command is as follows:

```
java -classpath .:$TOMCAT_HOME/webapps/axis/WEB-
INF/lib/axis.jar:$TOMCAT_HOME/webapps/axis/WEB-
INF/lib/jaxrpc.jar:$TOMCAT_HOME/webapps/axis/WEB-INF/lib/commons-logging.jar:$TO
MCAT_HOME/webapps/axis/WEB-INF/lib/commons-
discovery.jar:$TOMCAT_HOME/webapps/axis/WEB-INF/lib/saaj.jar
org.apache.axis.client.AdminClient Greeter.wsdd
```

You can test to see if it works by calling the Web service via HTTP GET:

```
http://localhost:8080/axis/services/Greeter?method=sayHello&name=World
```

You should get an XML response with a sayHelloResponse. This is a useful approach to deploying EJBs as Web services, but with JBoss things are even more interesting. JBoss has a module called JBoss.NET, which is an integrated Axis implementation with some value-added features such as additional handlers for authentication, transaction management, and much more. What we're going to do is deploy the Greeter stateless session bean from Chapter 10 as a JBoss.NET Web service.

First, we need to add the JBoss.NET module into the default server configuration. Copy the `server\all\deploy\jboss-net.sar` directory to `server\default\deploy`.

Let's check to see if JBoss.NET is working. The following URL should list the services:

```
http://localhost:8080/jboss-net/servlet/AxisServlet
```

Okay, that's done. Now, JBoss.NET is basically Axis repackaged and integrated with JBoss. Deployment relies on a .wsr file, which is basically a packaged up version of the Axis's WSDD. The .wsr file is a standard .jar file with a single XML Web services descriptor under `META-INF\web-service.xml`.

Following is the `web-service.xml` file for creating a JBoss.NET Web service using the Greeter EJB.

Here are the contents of `web-service.xml`:

```
<?xml version="1.0" encoding="UTF-8"?>
<deployment
    name="Greeter"
    xmlns="http://xml.apache.org/axis/wsdd/"
    xmlns:java="http://xml.apache.org/axis/wsdd/providers/java"
>

  <service name="Greeter" provider="Handler">
    <parameter name="handlerClass"
        value="org.jboss.net.axis.server.EJBProvider" />
    <parameter name="beanJndiName" value="ejb/Greeter" />
    <parameter name="homeInterfaceName" value="test.interfaces.GreeterHome" />
    <parameter name="allowedMethods" value="*" />
     <requestFlow name="GreeterRequest">
      <handler type="java:org.jboss.net.axis.server.TransactionRequestHandler"/>
    </requestFlow>

     <responseFlow name="GreeterResponse">
      <handler
          type="java:org.jboss.net.axis.server.SerialisationResponseHandler"/>
      <handler
          type="java:org.jboss.net.axis.server.TransactionResponseHandler"/>
    </responseFlow>
  </service>
</deployment>
```

NOTE **You can also use XDoclet to generate the JBoss.NET Web services deployment descriptor. The XDoclet module for that can be retrieved from JBoss's CVS repository. There's an excellent summary online at** `http://www.nsdev.org/jboss/stories/jboss-net.html`**, with information about using XDoclet with JBoss.NET.**

Although it is very similar to the WSDD file, you'll note that JBoss uses different classes to handle the calls. Let's package up the `greeter.wsr` file and use JBoss's hot deploy to try out the service.

On Windows, the commands are:

```
jar cvf greeter.wsr META-INF\web-service.xml
copy greeter.wsr %JBOSS_HOME%\server\default\deploy
```

On Linux, the commands are:

```
jar cvf greeter.wsr META-INF/web-service.xml
copy greeter.wsr $JBOSS_HOME/server/default/deploy
```

JBoss will detect this file and deploy it. When used this way, the .wsr file is loosely deployed. We will find it deployed under the following URL:

```
http://localhost:8080/jboss-net/services/Greeter?wsdl
```

TIP A handy option for debugging is to use `-Daxis.enableListQuery=true` **when starting JBoss. This exposes the JBoss.NET configuration at** `http://localhost:8080/jboss-net/services/Administration?list.` **It's very useful for development, but a potential security issue when running in a production environment.**

A better-organized method, recommended for production, is to have the .wsr file residing inside your application's .ear file. The .wsr file should be at the same level as an EJB .jar file within the .ear file. You'll also need to add a reference to the .wsr in the <module> tag within the .ear's `META-INF\application.xml file.` Following are the additions you'll need to make to the .ear's `META-INF\application.xml` file:

```
<module>
     <java>greeter.wsr</java>
</module>
```

As you can see, JBoss.NET is a powerful mechanism for deploying Java Web services. The toolset is a bit rough, and there are still some issues with reloading a Web service at times, necessitating a restart of the server to detect new changes. The option to use a vanilla installation of Apache's Axis is still available, so you can choose the method that works best for your application. It has some quirks, but JBoss.NET is shaping up to be a great distinguishing feature in favor of JBoss.

Testing and Troubleshooting Web Services

Web services are fairly easy to develop, but there are still gray areas that aren't spelled out by the standard specifications yet. In the following sections, we'll share some tips for testing and troubleshooting key areas of Web services that can be problematic.

Data-Type Marshaling

Data-type marshaling is still tricky with SOAP. Serializers handle common data types such as strings, floats, integers, and so on. However, there are still potential compatibility problems when serializing and deserializing complex types across different platforms. To be safe, try to compose complex types from the common data types. Otherwise, you may end up with having to troubleshoot cross-platform issues! Table 11.1 lists the XML Schema and Java data types.

NOTE Nillable values, the WSDL version of a Java variable that can be null, are always represented by the Java object equivalent (that is, a nillable xsd:int maps to an Integer object).

Care must be taken as far as what objects can be serialized in a SOAP message. Naturally, objects that refer to local resources should never be passed. These include GUI objects, I/O handles, and database objects. It's important to note that just because an object is Java serializable doesn't imply that it can be used in a cross-platform, interoperable manner.

Table 11.1 XML Schema and Java Data Types

XML SCHEMA DATA TYPE (USED BY SOAP)	JAVA DATA TYPE
xsd:base64Binary	byte []
xsd:boolean	Boolean
xsd:byte	byte
xsd:dateTime	java.util.Calendar
xsd:decimal	java.math.BigDecimal
xsd:double	double
xsd:float	float
xsd:hexBinary	byte[]
xsd:int	int
xsd:integer	java.math.BigInteger
xsd:long	long
xsd:QName	javax.xml.namespace.QName
xsd:short	short
xsd:string	java.lang.String

Exceptions

Exceptions seem to be handled inconsistently. Indeed, the semantics are not very well defined in the SOAP standard. In the structure of a SOAP message, there is a SOAPFault section. This seems to be reserved for exceptions. In Axis, RemoteExceptions are indeed marshaled through the SOAPFault section. However, application-level exceptions—pretty much anything that's not a RemoteException—are marshaled as <wsdl:exception> elements within the response. Unfortunately, the semantics of an exception still vary from one SOAP implementation to another. In an interoperability scenario, this can cause problems in detailed exception management. On the plus side, the notification of an exception can still be relied on.

Monitoring TCP/SOAP Messages

Apache Axis comes with a nice tool called the Axis TCP Monitor. Using the Axis TCP Monitor, it is possible to trace TCP communication during a Java Web service call. Because SOAP runs on HTTP over TCP/IP, the SOAP messages can be seen as well.

The TCP Monitor is included in `axis.jar`. We'll use port 9080 as the debugging port. So to trace a message, have the client use port 9080. The server will still be listening on port 8080. Because TCP Monitor acts as a proxy, it will send traffic that it sees on 9080 through to 8080.

Normally, TCP Monitor is a passive listener that just displays the traffic. However, with the `resend` command, you can actually modify a request. Just edit the text of the request on the left or top window, depending on your layout, and then hit the Resend button to resend it to the server and see how it behaves.

The command for running TCP Monitor is:

```
java -classpath axis.jar org.apache.axis.utils.tcpmon 9080 localhost 8080
```

In the previous example, we specified three parameters: the port to listen on, the host to forward to, and the port to forward to. If you launch the application without any command-line parameters, TCP Monitor will present a GUI interface for specifying the settings.

To see it in action, launch the TCP Monitor with port 9080 as the source and localhost, port 8080 as the destination. Then, try calling the SimpleShop Web service by opening the following URL:

```
http://localhost:9080/axis/SimpleShop.jws?method=getPrice&item=t-shirt
```

You should see TCP Monitor capture the traffic and display it in the application (see Figure 11.5).

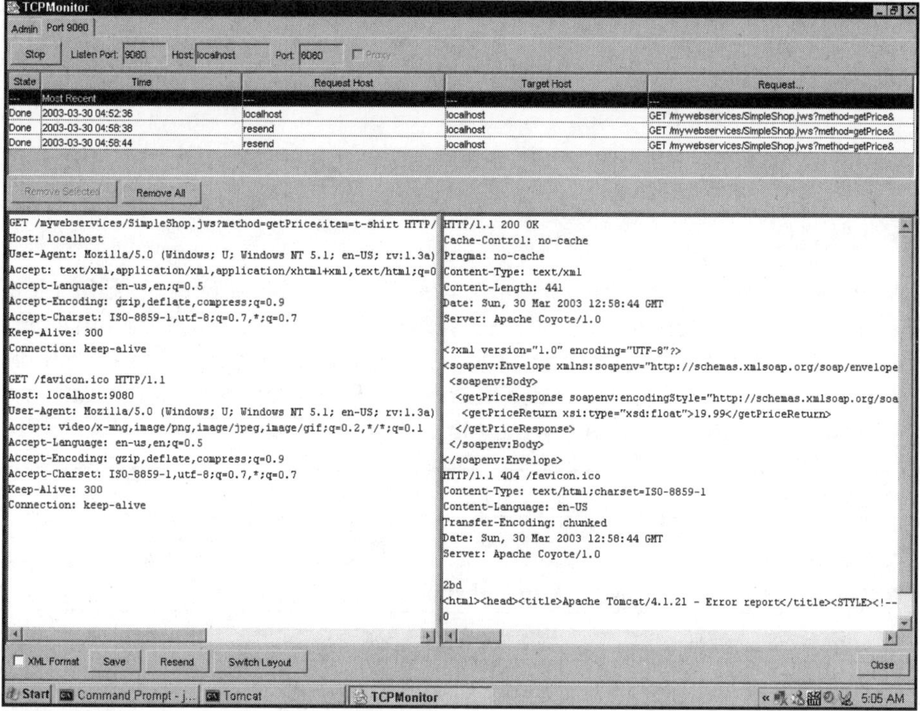

Figure 11.5 A captured SOAP conversation.

This is great for gaining insight into the SOAP conversation. It is also a fantastic tool in its own right for debugging any type of TCP communication, such as servlets or JSPs.

Web Service Registries

SOAP standardizes the invocation of Web services. WSDL standardizes the description, explaining how a Web service can be accessed. That still leaves the question of where, which is the problem that Web service registries are meant to solve.

Registry services are necessary for the discovery of Web services. They serve as a directory through which appropriate Web services can be placed and found. Without registries, a lot of effort would be spent on the discovery of Web services. A registry standard is important for Web services to scale up to a large audience.

JAXR is an API that abstracts access to a registry. The two registry standards of note are the UDDI Registry and ebXML Registry. The UDDI Registry and ebXML Registry standards differ in the scope of features that are mandated. JAXR uses the concept of level conformance to support the two registry standards. Level 1 is required by all JAXR implementations and corresponds to the feature set in a UDDI Registry. Meanwhile, Level 2 is optional and defines the interfaces to more advanced features, as in the ebXML standard.

Because Apache Axis does not implement a Web service registry, we won't cover it in detail. There are some open source projects out there that are working on building registry implementations, including ebXMLRR and jUDDI.

ebXMLRR

ebXMLRR is implements the version 2.1 of the ebXML Registry specification. The project is fairly active and tracking right along with the specifications. One caveat is that ebXMLRR relies on a SQL-92-compliant JDBC database. Postgres is the recommended choice because the ebXMLRR developers do the majority of their testing with it. The following table provides a summary of ebXMLRR.

Product	ebXMLRR
Category	Web services registry
URL	http://ebxmlrr.sourceforge.net/
Supported Platforms	Java 1.4 and above
License	Apache Open Source License
Features	An open implementation of the ebXML Registry v. 2.0 specification

jUDDI

Meanwhile, jUDDI provides an implementation of the UDDI Registry specification. The project developers are still working towards version 1.0, so as of yet there isn't a packaged release. You have to get jUDDI from CVS and build it yourself for the time being. Also, jUDDI only supports UDDI Registry version 2.0 and not the latest version, 3.0.

The following table gives you more information if you're interested in researching jUDDI.

Product	jUDDI
Category	Web services registry
URL	http://www.juddi.org
Supported Platforms	Java 1.3 and above
License	BSD Open Source License
Features	An open implementation of the UDDI Registry specification

Summary

In this chapter, we've shown how Apache Axis can be used to implement Java Web services within the J2EE architecture. From a technical standpoint, most of the Web services pieces, other than security, are in place. The promise of Web services is an unheralded period of interoperable systems, an ecosystem of interdependent services from myriad companies. Whether this promise is realized or not, Web services are going to be an important part of every company's business strategy.

CHAPTER

12

Adding XML Power Tools

XML is sprouting up all over the place. From Web services to configuration files, XML has indeed proven itself to be an extensible markup language. In this chapter, we'll examine XML and what it is, cover all the new Java specifications based on XML, and show how you can use XML in your open source J2EE applications.

Architectural Considerations

Like the explosion of interconnectivity after the adoption of HTTP, XML is a glue technology that serves as a common data interchange format and facilitates interoperability. With XML, the semantics and metadata are not lost in the encoding of data. XML can be manipulated, transformed, and validated. We continually encounter it with new interoperability technology, such as Web services and document interchange. There's no doubt that XML has its place in any software architecture and definitely within the J2EE architecture.

Overview

XML stands for the Extensible Markup Language and is a descriptive markup language that lets you organize information into a structured format. Primarily conceived to address issues with existing markup languages in handling structured documents on the Web, XML has filled that role grandly.

The recent focus on XML to achieve interoperability is evident from the new projects being worked by public companies. Business integration, an area traditionally served by EDI (electronic data interchange), is gradually making the transition to new XML-based standards. Why? Because EDI relies on a fixed format that is neither extensible nor standardized, both of which are attributes that XML documents possess. Practically every interoperability technology we've seen since XML's introduction has relied on XML. Following are a few examples of how XML is changing industry standards even as you read this:

- RDF (Resource Description Framework) is a ubiquitous system for lightweight knowledge description and interchange that is based on XML.
- RSS (Rich Site Summary) as a site syndication format is a concrete use of RDF that has taken off. News syndication, blogging (Web logs), software version updates, and other forms of content syndication all depend on RSS.
- SOAP and XML over HTTP are widely used for remote procedure calls.
- Even HTML itself is being updated to be XML based with the new XHTML standard.

XML has proven to be useful in other contexts beyond just the Internet. A few examples follow:

- The most popular Java build system, Ant, has build files that are based on XML.
- Jelly is an amazing XML-based scripting system.
- J2EE deployment descriptors are XML documents.
- Configuration files in general are shifting towards XML.
- Even traditionally binary formats, such as graphic file formats, can benefit from the XML, as can be seen by the W3C's SVG (Scalable Vector Graphics) standard.

As you can see, people continue to innovate with XML and use it to solve new problems; this provides compelling evidence that XML is wildly successful in meeting its original design goals. Having all this interoperability is a great boon to everyone's productivity.

XML and Other Markup Languages

In this section, we'll examine the roots of the XML standard and the way it has grown to fit within today's software architectures.

SGML

XML is in many ways a simplified descendant of SGML (Standard Generalized Markup Language), a powerful markup language used by large corporations for organizing large document repositories. SGML was created prior to the proliferation of the Internet and so suffers from not taking into account issues that arise in that context. For example, SGML does not support Unicode in names. In addition, SGML is often too complex and generalized to be used over the limited bandwidth of an Internet connection. These issues were taken into account when creating XML.

XML draws upon greatly on its SGML heritage. Their documents share a similar tree structure. SGML and XML are consistent in enforcing elements to be well formed. Both are composed of documents having nodes, elements, and attributes. Perhaps the only part of XML that doesn't derive from SGML is the notion of namespaces, which has proven to be a useful addition. Using namespaces allows hybrid documents to combine elements drawn from different documents without any ambiguity. The fully qualified name will always be unique and allows snippets to be validated against the proper schema.

HTML

Another markup language similar to XML is the well-known HTML (Hypertext Markup Language). HTML is used to write the majority of Web pages today and also has roots that draw from the ideas in SGML. However, unlike XML and SGML, HTML is neither extensible nor consistent. Some of the problems with HTML include the following:

- Only a fixed set of tags is defined for use in the document.
- Case sensitivity in tag names is not enforced.
- Tags are not required to be properly closed and nested. For example, the <li> tag does not require a matching </li> tag.
- Attributes within tags are not required to be quoted, which results in greater ambiguity and makes HTML harder to parse.

All in all, this lack of consistency poses problems for the use of HTML as the primary markup language of documents on the Web. HTML tags are generally focused on presentation rather than structure, undermining its usefulness as a data interchange format. Today the push is on to replace HTML with its XML equivalent, XHTML.

Where Do XML Tools Fit?

XML is already integrated into the standard edition of Java. The new APIs are geared toward basic XML parsing and transformations. The next release of Sun's J2EE specification, version 1.4, will include many new XML specifications targeted at enterprise XML tasks. The list of specifications is rapidly growing, and it is a lot of work just keeping up with the flood. Slated for official arrival in J2EE 1.4 are the following APIs:

- JAX-RPC (Java API for XML-based Remote Procedure Calls) facilitates the use of Java Web services based on WSDL and SOAP.
- JAXB (Java Architecture for XML Binding) provides automated binding between Java objects and XML.
- JAXM (Java API for XML Messaging) builds upon the SAAJ to provide higher-level XML messaging.
- JAXR (Java API for XML Registries) is used for accessing XML registries, such as UDDI and ebXML registries.
- SAAJ (SOAP with Attachments API for Java) implements the SOAP 1.1 messaging standard for Java.

The default implementation of these APIs is currently available in the Java Web Services Developer Pack, which can be downloaded from Sun's Web site (`http://java.sun.com`). The pack is licensed under the usual Sun Binary Code License Agreement and covers many of the emerging Web services technologies, including ebXML (Electronic Business Using XML), SOAP (Simple Object Access Protocol), UDDI (Universal Description, Discovery, and Integration of Web Services), and WSDL. These all build upon XML, but we'll defer elaboration about Java Web services until Chapter 13.

XML fits into the J2EE model in many areas, as the wide array of future J2EE standard APIs shows. There are perhaps too many APIs, spurred on by excessive optimism about the applicability of XML. Many of these standards will be simplified or merged, as we've already seen happen in the case of Web services.

Before applying XML as a universal hammer to every problem, keep in mind that XML is primarily a data interchange and interoperability technology. The edges of a J2EE application are where XML will be the most useful. As yet, there is no compelling reason to use XML throughout an application. As an anti-pattern, take the notion of using XML to internally represent business or data objects. This seems appealing because the process of binding is skipped, but the impedance mismatch is just too high to make it worthwhile. Java object representations are more compact, don't require a conceptual shift to program, and benefit from the wealth of existing code. There are other areas where XML is marginally taking hold, such as in the case of XML databases. Time will tell whether this is a viable niche, but historically the relational model is very good at handling data storage and querying, and XML databases are tragically similar to the hierarchical model that preceded the relational age.

There are many new XML specifications and tools. We will survey some of the more interesting open source XML tools in this chapter. With the breadth of products around, our focal point will remain on the tools that have already proven useful in J2EE environments.

XML Parsers

There are a variety of XML tools available for use with Java. As of version 1.4, the Java JDK comes with built-in XML libraries. These libraries are low-level compared to the others available and will serve as a starting point for us to explore XML.

The bundled libraries provide Java interfaces to the standard W3C standards:

- DOM Level 1 and Level 2 (Document Object Model)
- SAX Level 2 (Simple API for XML)
- XSL 1.0 (Extensible Stylesheet Language), which includes XSLT (Extensible Stylesheet Transformations) and XPath (XML Path Language)

The Apache's Crimson and Xalan projects provide the basic implementation for JDK 1.4. Java's XML interfaces are standardized and pluggable, so the implementation can be changed without affecting any code written against the standard. Many of the XML tools we review here provide implementations that implement the standard interfaces, while providing better performance and more features.

SAX Parsing

SAX (Simple API for XML) is lightweight interface for working with XML. SAX uses an event-driven method of parsing that minimizes resource usage because it's not working with the entire document at once. The input source is read, and events are generated as tags are encountered, making SAX ideal for straight-though read-only usage and some transformation tasks.

SAX is a key part of the larger Java XML framework. Of all the standard Java APIs dealing with XML, SAX is perhaps the lowest level. As such, it serves an important role as the foundation for the other XML tools. Many implementations of DOM, for example, use SAX to read in XML data.

DOM Parsing

DOM is the W3C standard for language-neutral object model for representing and working with XML. DOM represents XML as a treelike structure of objects. Working with DOM is more in line with the object-oriented programming design of Java, although it is still not as natural as some of the higher-level XML tools because DOM objects represent documents rather than business objects.

Because DOM keeps the entire XML document in memory, it requires more resources than SAX. The benefit is that operations require less processing after the initial memory is allocated. Certain implementations use tricks such as compact representations and deferred the parsing of subtrees to minimize the initial resource hit.

For situations that require heavy manipulation of the XML document, extensive querying, or XML schemas, DOM is better than SAX. Despite this, DOM is best viewed as a common denominator technology that is best used as the basis for higher-level tools.

XML Parser Selection

There's no doubt that Sun has caught on to the XML trend early. By bundling the JAXP (Java API for XML Processing) APIs, which include DOM, SAX, and XSLT, JDK 1.4 has made it easy for Java programmers to work with XML. JAXP keeps with Java's tradition of specifying APIs, not implementations.

The bundled implementation is decent but for best performance, features, and ease –of use you'll want to build your applications using some of the open source XML tools available. For what it's worth, these tools generally build upon the standard JAXP interfaces. Many of these implementations offer improved performance and resource usage, which is nice in and of itself. The real benefits, though, come from the higher-level interfaces. More can be accomplished in far fewer lines with JDOM or dom4j, and it makes sense to use them instead of the default APIs. Other projects offer even more elaborate features, such as automated binding of Java objects to XML, which makes data objects directly from an XML document. In the next section, we'll cover many of the open source Java XML tools available.

Other XML Tools

There are many open source Java XML tools available. Almost all build upon or implement the W3C standards of SAX, DOM, and XSL. Some are focused on parsing XML, while others provide higher-level services built upon XML, such as transformation services. Perhaps the only exceptions are the XmlPull parsers, which must operate in leaner environments.

This section will concentrate on giving an overview of the most notable projects, with an emphasis on what value they add in comparison to the default implementations and also spelling the differences in philosophy behind the XML projects. Each project takes a different tack on exposing the functionality to parsing and working with XML. Depending on the type of project and the developers, a particular tool may prove to be the best fit. No one design approach is inherently better or worse than any other.

Apache XML Projects

Quite a few good open source XML projects are hosted under the Apache banner. They target different problem domains, ranging from basic parsing to XML databases. The most famous of these is Xerces, which implements the basic DOM/SAX interfaces. In fact, the default implementation of Java's XML interfaces is based on an older version of Xerces and is now hosted under the Crimson name.

Some of the projects will be covered in the sections ahead. There isn't enough room to discuss each of these projects in detail but we will list a brief description of the most useful projects:

Xerces. A SAX/DOM parser

Xalan. An XSL processor, also bundled with JDK 1.4

Cocoon. An XML Web-publishing framework

FOP. An XSL formatting object processor for transforming XML documents into other formats, such as HTML, PDF, or MS Word

Apache SOAP. An implementation of the W3C SOAP protocol standard that grew out of IBM's SOAP4J project

Crimson. A SAX/DOM parser that was the basis for the XML implementation bundled with JDK 1.4

Xindice. An XML database

The Apache Web site is fast becoming the hub for many of the best open source Java projects. Some of the XML projects we cover here are in their infancy, like XIndice, while others, such as Crimson, are clearly in their decline. This turmoil is a positive sign of the developmental energy here.

TIP **Before undergoing any Java development, we recommend that you visit the Apache site and check to see if there are any new tools that your application can take advantage of.**

Xalan

Xalan is the Apache project that implements the XSL technologies. Two major specifications that fall under that heading are XSLT and XPath. XSLT is used to specify transformations on an XML document, while XPath is used to query and access information from an XML document. The following table provides a summary of Xalan.

Product	Xalan
Category	XSL
URL	http://xml.apache.org/xalan-j
Supported Platforms	Java 1.2 and above, bundled with Java 1.4 and above
License	Apache Open Source License
Features	Standard implementation of XSL technologies such as XSLT and Xpath

XSLT is the language for specifying transformations. Like the documents it transforms, XSLT itself is based on XML. It uses a stylesheet to specify the transformation rules, which are basically XML elements within the XSLT namespace that contain a prerequisite pattern and a template. If an element in the source XML document matches that pattern, then the template is applied to generate the transformed document. We'll see examples of XSLT in the *Integration and Testing* section later in this chapter.

XPath is one of the more promising XML technologies. It's somewhat akin to a query language for XML, although there are competing standards coming down the pipeline. Writing queries in XPath is more natural and compact than using the programmatic interface. For example, the XPath query to find all nodes named line_item looks like this:

```
//line_item
```

XPath also supports conditionals and attributes. For example, to find all nodes named line_item with a count greater than 5, the XPath expression is as follows:

```
//line_item[ @count > 5 ]
```

Here's the rough equivalent in JDOM without using XPath:

```
Collection oMatchingElements = new ArrayList();
Iterator itr = oElement.getChildren();
while( itr.hasNext() )
{
    Element oChild = (Element) itr.next();
    String sCount = oChild.getAttributeValue( "count" );
    if( Integer.parseInt( sCount ) > 5 )
    {
        oMatchingElements.add( oChild );
    }
}
```

As you can see, XPath syntax is much more compact than the comparable Java code using a programmatic model. In fact, the JDOM code only iterates through the first level of children—additional code would be needed to recurse through all children at any depth in order to match the functionality in the XPath expression. XPath has expressiveness of SQL and can be applied to similar types of situations.

Overall, Xalan provides high-quality implementations of XSLT and XPath. Because it is included with Java as of version 1.4, you can rely on Xalan being available for use in most environments. However, in most cases a higher-level XML tool, such as dom4j or JDOM, is a better choice for harnessing the power of XSLT and XPath. The drawback is that the application will then be relying on proprietary APIs and libraries, which may not be possible in some cases.

Apache FOP

The Apache FOP (formatting object processor) project consists of specialized XSL transformation objects. These stylesheets help realize much of the theoretical benefits of keeping data in an independent, structured format such as XML. Through the use of FOP, a source document can be transformed to target the needs of the clients. The following table gives a summary of FOP.

Product	Apache FOP
Category	Formatting object processing
URL	http://xml.apache.org/xalan-j
Supported Platforms	Java 1.2 and above, bundled with Java 1.4 and above
License	Apache Open Source License
Features	Generates PDF, PS, SVG, and other presentational formats from the XML-based FO document

FOP supports transformation to the following target formats, with more being added continually:

- Adobe PDF (Portable Document Format)
- Hewlett-Packard PCL (Page Control Language)
- PostScript
- SVG (Scalable Vector Graphics)
- Print (direct to print spool)
- AWT (Abstract Window Toolkit)
- Framemaker MIF (Maker Interchange Format)
- Text

The original source file is marked up in a manner that isn't concerned about the final presentational elements. Typically, there are two transformation steps:

1. XSLT is used to transform the source file into an XML document that is properly marked up for presentation. This intermediate XML document is referred to as the FO (formatting object) document.
2. The FO document is transformed into the final representation via FOP.

Zeus

Zeus is part of the Enhydra project and is a tool for binding Java objects to their XML equivalents. This makes working with XML documents as simple as working with a Java object. So, instead of calling `oDocument.getElement ( "line_item" )`, now you can write the code as `orderObject.getLineItem()`. This is more natural Java code. See the following table for a summary of Zeus.

Product	Zeus
Category	Java to XML binding
URL	http://zeus.enhydra.org
Supported Platforms	Java 1.2 and above preferred
License	Enhydra Public License
Features	Allows you to work with XML as a first-class object

Through the use of binding constraints and rules, the underlying XML can change without breaking the Java code. Only the binding constraints and rules need to be updated to accommodate the new format of the bound XML document.

Zeus generates the source code from a description of constraints upon the XML document. Normally, this constraints file will be in the form of a DTD (document type description) or an XML schema that describes the form of an XML document. Each element in the constraints file is mapped to an object by the source generator. The object will be represented by two files, a Java file that holds the object's interface and another containing implementation for that class. You can then use the generated Java source files within your own code.

Zeus is a nice tool, but Castor is a better choice for Java to XML binding. Requiring the preprocessing step complicates the build process and makes it more difficult to maintain the source in the long run if the mapping changes. Overall, Zeus builds on a good idea but its implementation lacks the elegance and flexibility of Castor's.

Castor

Castor is a data-binding tool that's similar to Zeus. It performs a role similar to JAXB's within JAX suite of APIs. In addition to the Java to XML binding, Castor offers Java to JDO binding and Java to LDAP binding. The following table provides a summary of Castor.

Product	Castor
Category	Java data binding
URL	http://castor.exolab.org
Supported Platforms	Java 1.2 and above preferred
License	BSD-like Open Source License
Features	The most comprehensive and flexible Java data-binding tool

The framework is constructed to allow new bindings to be added in the future. Castor's feature set is very complete and includes:

- Automatic Java binding to XML
- Automatic OQL (Object Query Language) mapping to SQL
- Transaction support
- Caching

Castor is by far the most comprehensive and flexible Java object-binding tool available. These bindings can be automated, generated from an existing schema, or defined within a configuration file.

Like Zeus, Castor builds upon the work of other projects. The dependencies include Xerces, Jakarta ORO, and Jakarta Regexp.

JDOM

JDOM is an unabashedly Java-centric interface to XML. JDOM builds upon a JAXP-compliant parser, and its goal is to let programs work with XML within the style and syntax of Java. As a result, JDOM is very easy for Java programmers to learn. See the following table for a summary of JDOM.

Product	JDOM
Category	XML parser
URL	http://www.jdom.org
Supported Platforms	Java 1.2 and above preferred
License	JDOM Open Source License (BSD-like)
Features	Java-centric interface to XML

One key architectural decision of JDOM is the focus away from object factories. This makes it possible to construct a new Element object without needing a reference to the parent document or calling a static method in a factory. Overall, the code is cleaner and there's less overhead involved.

The biggest criticism against JDOM is that it is not as object oriented as it should be, and objects don't make use of shared base classes. Inheritance used properly makes for a more cogent object model that is both easier to understand and fits the Java model better. dom4j is a good example of a proper object-oriented design.

JDOM is an excellent tool for parsing and manipulating XML documents. The simple object model is refreshingly easy-to-use. Performance is decent, but not a major selling point. To quote one of the project goals, JDOM aims to solve 80 percent of your XML needs with 20 percent of the work.

dom4j

dom4J is very similar in scope to JDOM, but has a different take on its design approach. Whereas JDOM works hard to avoid factory design patterns and having deep object hierarchies, dom4J embraces them. Although initially cumbersome, the design patterns make dom4J more extensible in the long run. The following table provides a summary of dom4j.

Product	dom4j
Category	XML Parser
URL	http://www.dom4j.org
Supported Platforms	Java 1.2 and above preferred
License	BSD-like Open Source License
Features	Very comprehensive and high-level Java API for XML. Includes XPath support, XSLT, and XML Data Schema Data Type

Other than the design-pattern overhead, the interface is well thought out and powerful. The way the object hierarchy is built is very clean and nice. For example, the Element interface extends the Node interface, with the appropriate functionality in each.

dom4J is very feature-complete and includes a very good XPath implementation and XSLT support. It is also one of the best-performing XML solutions. There isn't much that dom4J can't do, and it is definitely worth checking out for any of your XML needs.

kXML

kXML is an excellent XML parser for limited Java environments, such as a Java applet or a J2ME client. Most of the other XML tools are meant to be used either on the server side or within the desktop environment. It would be nice to have the same XML data formats even when communicating with smaller clients. These clients typically have access to fewer resources and may not even have the full Java API available. kXML is designed to meet these requirements. While not as full-featured as the other tools, just having the ability to work with XML is a great boon. The following table gives a summary of kXML.

Product	kXML
Category	XML parser
URL	http://kxml.enhydra.org
Supported Platforms	Java 1.1 and above, J2ME
License	Enhydra Public License
Features	XML pull parser for use in limited Java environments

The kXML parser uses the pull model of XML parsing. The pull model of parsing defers retrieval of XML elements until they are referenced. The model has proven to be very easy to use and ideal for limited environments. While not as widely known as SAX or DOM, the XML pull model is standardized via the Common API for XML Pull Parsing (XmlPull). More information on the standard is available at `http://www.xmlpull.org`. Naturally, kXML complies with the XmlPull standard.

XPP3

From the folks at Indiana University comes XPP3 (XML Pull Parser), another XML pull parser that conforms to the XmlPull standard. Because of its small size and limited feature set, XPP3 is targeted towards the same environments as kXML. XPP3's performance is even better than that of kXML. What it lacks is the visibility and support behind the kXML project. XPP3 is an excellent product that benefits from the freedom to innovate that comes from being an academic research project. See the following table for a summary of XPP3.

Product	XPP3
Category	XML pull parser
URL	http://www.extreme.indiana.edu/xgws/xsoap/xpp/
Supported Platforms	Java 1.1 and above, J2ME
License	Indiana University Extreme! Lab Software License
Features	XML pull parser for use in limited Java environments

Integration and Testing

We've covered the many XML tools available, now we're going to write some examples using those tools. The parser tests are mostly to demonstrate the different styles and design philosophies behind the various parsers. The Castor example shows how to use a more advanced Java-object-to-XML binding model. The JDBC example covers the common task of making legacy data available for interchange as XML. Finally, we will explore a pair of J2EE examples that cover using XML within the servlet layer and the EJB layer.

Testing Code

We start off with a demonstration parsing the same XML document with a variety of tools. Seeing the code makes it easier to determine which style you're most comfortable with. These parsing examples are necessarily academic to facilitate comparison.

The examples often reference `order.xml`, an XML document we made up for the purpose of testing the parsers. This document needs to be available in the same directory as the sample code. In some examples, `order.xml` will be automatically generated by the code. Nevertheless, the contents of the `order.xml` should remain consistent.

The contents of `order.xml` are:

```
<?xml version="1.0" encoding="UTF-8"?>
<order>
  <line_item name="T-shirt"
             count="1"
             color="red"
             size="XL">
    <notes>Please ship before next week.</notes>
  </line_item>
</order>
```

The ability to validate XML is one of this document's great strengths. The DTD standard was popular in the past, but DTDs are being phased out because they can only enforce structural validity. If you've worked with HTML, you may recall seeing DTDs before. The following is an example of a DTD reference in an HTML document:

```
<!DOCTYPE HTML PUBLIC "-//W3C//DTD HTML 4.01 Transitional//EN">
```

The most likely new standard for validating XML documents is XML Schema. This is a W3C recommendation for defining the schema and rules governing a valid XML document. With XML Schema, we can define what is and is not permissible data, what format data should be in, and how it should be structured. As an added bonus, XML schemas are themselves written in XML.

The XML schema for our simple `order.xml` is contained in the `order.xsd` file.

Following are the contents of `order.xsd`:

```
<schema
    xmlns="http://www.w3.org/2001/XMLSchema"
    xmlns:soml="http://www.theculprit.com/test/simple_order_ml" >
    <element name="order">
        <complexType>
            <element name="line_item">
            type="decimal"/>
                <attribute name="name" type="string"/>
                <attribute name="count" type="integer">
                    <minInclusive value="0" />
                </attribute>
                <attribute name="color" type="string" >
                    <maxLength value="14" />
                </attribute>
                <attribute name="size" type="soml:ItemSize" />
                <element name="notes" type="string" />
            </element>
        </complexType>
    </element>
    <simpleType name="ItemSize" base="string">
        <enumeration value="XS" />
        <enumeration value="S" />
        <enumeration value="M" />
        <enumeration value="L" />
        <enumeration value="XL" />
        <enumeration value="XXL" />
    </simpleType>
</schema>
```

The schema is pretty self-explanatory. The structure of the schema document looks similar to the document it is describing. There are rules and restrictions, known as *data facets*, sprinkled throughout it. For example, the maxLength element is a data facet. We can also create new types, as in the case of the itemSize element. The XML Schema specification provides a number of standard types we can use to enforce type on our XML data. There are also some alternate methods of validating XML available. These include Regular Language Description for XML (RELAX), RELAX Next Generation (RELAX NG), and Tree Regular Expression for XML (TREX). RELAX NG is basically the combination of RELAX and TREX, so moving forward, it is the most likely to achieve to achieve popularity. More information can be found on RELAX NG at `http://www.relaxng.org`.

XML Schema represents a great way to perform validation and is a huge improvement over the DTD standard.

NOTE Validation is a relatively expensive operation, so use it accordingly. Because there is still not a definitive standard for validation, we're going to avoid getting into the topic in great depth. What we can tell you is that XML validation plays a vital role in enterprise systems.

SAX Parser Test

This is a minimal example demonstrating the use of the standard SAX interfaces. The example relies on the default implementation that is shipped as part of JDK 1.4. SAX operates at a fairly low level and is generally used for parsing input from an input source. We'll use it in a similar manner in this example to print out the names and attributes of elements as they are pushed to the program by SAX.

A survey of SAX usage shows that it is rarely output oriented. Higher-level XML tools, such as dom4j and JDOM, provide "pretty printers" for formatting XML output in a way that makes it easier to read by human beings. This example program provides the beginnings of what could be a primitive output program based on SAX.

NOTE Because XML is human-readable text, it is trivial to output a valid XML document through the traditional output methods such as `println()`.

Note that we create a subclass of the DefaultHandler class to hook in the logic we want performed when a SAX event is encountered. MyDocHandler only handles two events: `startElement` and `endElement`. There's not much processing involved. The most complicated code loops through the element's attributes and prints them out.

Here's the source for `jdk14_sax_test.java`:

```
import java.io.*;
import org.xml.sax.*;
import org.xml.sax.helpers.DefaultHandler;
import javax.xml.parsers.*;

class MyDocHandler extends DefaultHandler {
  public void startElement(
    String sNamespace,
    String sLocalName,
    String sQualifiedName,
    Attributes oAttributes )
  throws SAXException
  {
    // --- Print out what the element we are passed in is. ---
```

```
    System.out.println( sQualifiedName + " started." );
    for( int idxAttribute = 0;
             idxAttribute < oAttributes.getLength();
             ++idxAttribute )
    {
      System.out.println( "   (" + oAttributes.getQName( idxAttribute ) +
                          " = " + oAttributes.getValue( idxAttribute ) +
                          ")" );
    }
  }


  public void endElement(
    String sNamespace,
    String sLocalName,
    String sQualifiedName )
  {
    System.out.println( sQualifiedName + " ended." );
  }
}


public class jdk14_sax_test {
  public static void main( String args[] )
  {
    // --- Parse order.xml. ---
    DefaultHandler oHandler = new MyDocHandler();
    SAXParserFactory oFactory = SAXParserFactory.newInstance();
    try {
      SAXParser oParser = oFactory.newSAXParser();
      oParser.parse( "order.xml", oHandler );
    }
    catch( Exception e ) {
      e.printStackTrace();
    }
  }
}
```

To compile `jdk14_sax_test.java`, run the following command:

```
javac jdk14_sax_test.java
```

Running the example program is equally simple. Use:

```
java jdk14_sax_test
```

DOM Parser Test

The DOM parser example is the template for the other parser tests. First, a new XML document is created and written to the file system. Then, the sample code will parse back in the `order.xml` file.

In the code, you'll notice a hack using the XSL interfaces to dump a copy of the XML document to `System.out`. Other high-level XML tools provide output classes and pretty printers for writing out XML, so that we don't need to use this trick.

Here's the source code for `jdk14_dom_test.java`:

```
import java.io.*;
import javax.xml.parsers.*;
import javax.xml.transform.*;
import javax.xml.transform.dom.DOMSource;
import javax.xml.transform.stream.*;
import org.w3c.dom.*;


public class jdk14_dom_test {
  public static void main( String args[] ) {
    try {
      //--- Create a new DOM document. ---

      DocumentBuilder oBuilder =
          DocumentBuilderFactory.newInstance().newDocumentBuilder();
      Document oDocument =
          oBuilder.getDOMImplementation().createDocument(
              null, "order", null);
      Element oOrderElement = oDocument.getDocumentElement();
      Element oLineItem = oDocument.createElement( "line_item" );
      oLineItem.setAttribute( "name", "T-shirt" );
      oLineItem.setAttribute( "count",  "1" );
      oLineItem.setAttribute( "color", "red" );
      oLineItem.setAttribute( "size", "XL" );
      Element oNoteElement = oDocument.createElement( "notes" );
      Text oNoteText =
        oDocument.createTextNode( "Please ship before next week." );
      oNoteElement.appendChild( oNoteText );
      oLineItem.appendChild( oNoteElement );
      oOrderElement.appendChild( oLineItem );

      //--- Print out the document using a null XSL transformation.
      Transformer oTransformer =
        TransformerFactory.newInstance().newTransformer();
      oTransformer.transform(
          new DOMSource( oDocument ),
          new StreamResult( System.out ) );
```

```
// --- Parse the order.xml document. ---
oDocument = oBuilder.parse( new File( "order.xml" ) );


      // --- Document is parsed now. ---
      System.out.println( "document is now: " + oDocument );


    }
    catch( Exception e ) {
      e.printStackTrace();
    }
  }
}
```

To compile the example, run the following command:

```
javac jdk14_dom_test.java
```

To run the program, use the following command:

```
java jdk14_dom_test
```

The example will output the state of the XML document as the program executes. First, the XML document is created. Then, the program writes the XML to disk. Finally, it parses the newly written file to reconstruct the XML document.

The DOM interface gives us fairly complete control over parsing and manipulating XML in Java. For a standard interface, it's quite good, but it forces us to do a lot of same tasks over and over. This is where JDOM and dom4j shine in simplifying the model.

dom4j Parser Test

This code example for dom4j is functionally equivalent to the DOM parser test. The difference is that the dom4j shields the developer from a lot of the overhead and grunt work. The ability to specify details remains, but the default interface hides that complexity from us.

Installation

Unlike the previous examples, which rely on the bundled JAXP implementation, dom4j requires installation. This is a straightforward affair that follows the usual download and unzip model.

First, go to the dom4j Web site (`http://www.dom4j.org`) and download the latest version. Then, extract the files into a directory for dom4j. The exact directory will depend on your personal preferences. On a Windows system, you can extract to something like `\java\dom4j`. On Linux, you could try `/usr/local/dom4j`. After the files are extracted, set the `DOM4J_HOME` environment variable to point to the directory where the files are located.

CAUTION **It is not recommended that you put XML library .jars into the JRE's** `lib\ext` **directory. This is because the new .jar files can cause conflicts with .jar files that are packaged with some J2EE application containers.**

Code Examples

This code example shows the design patterns that are consciously avoided by JDOM due to the syntactic overhead. In my opinion, its biggest quirk is the need to have a reference to the parent document in order to create new elements. Although there are valid architectural reasons for this requirement, it forces us to keep references to the parent document in a lot of our code. This makes it difficult to create elements and attach them later to a document.

Here's the source code for `Dom4jTest.java`:

```
import java.io.*;
import org.dom4j.*;
import org.dom4j.io.*;

public class Dom4jTest {

  public static void main( String args[] ) {
    // --- Creating an XML document ---
    Document oDocument = DocumentHelper.createDocument();
    Element oOrder = oDocument.addElement( "order" );
    Element oLineItem = oOrder.addElement( "line_item" );
    oLineItem.addAttribute( "name", "T-shirt" );
    oLineItem.addAttribute( "count",  "1" );
    oLineItem.addAttribute( "color", "red" );
    oLineItem.addAttribute( "size", "XL" );
    oLineItem.addElement( "notes" ).addText(
        "Please ship before next week." );
    System.out.println( "Document after creation: " +
      oDocument + oDocument.asXML() );

    // --- Save the XML to a file. ---
    try {
      XMLWriter oWriter = new XMLWriter(
         new FileWriter( "order.xml" ) );
      oWriter.write( oDocument );
      oWriter.close();
    }
```

```
        catch( Exception e ) {
          e.printStackTrace();
        }

        // --- Load the XML document back from the file. ---
        oDocument = null;
        System.out.println( "Document after nulling: " + oDocument );
        SAXReader oReader = new SAXReader();
        try {
          oDocument = oReader.read( "order.xml" );
        }
        catch( Exception e ) {
          e.printStackTrace();
        }
        System.out.println( "Document after loading: " +
          oDocument + oDocument.asXML() );
      }
    }
```

Make sure that the environment variable for DOM4J_HOME is set to point to the directory where dom4j is installed.

To compile the example on Windows, run the following command:

```
javac -classpath .;%DOM4J_HOME%\dom4j-full.jar Dom4jTest.java
```

On Linux, the compile command is:

```
javac -classpath .:$DOM4J_HOME/dom4j-full.jar Dom4jTest.java
```

After compiling the example, you can run it with the following command on Windows:

```
java -classpath .;%DOM4J_HOME\dom4j-full.jar Dom4jTest
```

On Linux, the command is:

```
java -classpath .:$DOM4J_HOME/dom4j-full.jar Dom4jTest
```

Like the DOM example program, the dom4j example outputs the XML document after it is first constructed. Then, it parses the newly generated `order.xml` and shows the results of the parsing. Fairly run-of-the-mill activity, but it gives a good sense for how the dom4j interface is designed.

JDOM Parser Test

JDOM is one of the two best high-level tools for working with XML documents, along with dom4j. The two have different design philosophies. JDOM focuses on providing Java-centric interfaces, while dom4J is more inclined to forgo syntactic niceness in favor of strong design patterns. Keep an eye on the effortless manner with which JDOM handles creation of XML documents and elements.

Installation

The latest JDOM release can be downloaded from the Web site (`http://www.jdom.org`). Installation is very straightforward. After downloading the file, extract the files into your JDOM directory. On Windows, that could be something like `c:\java\jdom`. On Linux, something like `/usr/local/jdom` would be appropriate. Be sure to set the `JDOM_HOME` environment variable to point to the directory where the JDOM files are located.

Code Examples

JDOM goes out of its way to make things work the way you would expect from a Java object viewpoint. The code example shows how easy it is to create new XML documents and elements, as well as performing I/O.

Here's the source for `jdom_test.java`

```
import java.io.*;
import org.jdom.*;
import org.jdom.input.*;
import org.jdom.output.*;

public class jdom_test {

  public static void main( String args[] ) {

    // --- Creating an XML document ---
    Document oDocument = new Document( new Element( "order" ) );
    Element oLineItem = new Element( "line_item" );
    oLineItem.setAttribute( "name", "T-shirt" );
    oLineItem.setAttribute( "count",  "1" );
    oLineItem.setAttribute( "color", "red" );
    oLineItem.setAttribute( "size", "XL" );
    oLineItem.addContent(
    new Element( "notes" ).setText(
    "Please ship before next week." ) );
    oDocument.getRootElement().addContent( oLineItem );
    System.out.println( "Document after creation: " + oDocument );

    // --- Saving the XML to a file ---
    XMLOutputter oOutputter = new XMLOutputter();
    try {
      oOutputter.output( oDocument,
      new FileWriter( "order.xml" ) );
    }
```

```
        catch( Exception e ) {
          e.printStackTrace();
        }

        // --- Loading the XML document back from the file ---
        oDocument = null;
        System.out.println( "Document after nulling: " + oDocument );

        SAXBuilder oBuilder = new SAXBuilder();
        try {
          oDocument = oBuilder.build( new FileReader( "order.xml" ) );
        }
        catch( Exception e ) {
          e.printStackTrace();
        }
        System.out.println( "Document after loading: " + oDocument );
      }
    }
```

To compile the example on Windows, use the following command:

```
javac -classpath .;%JDOM_HOME%\build\jdom.jar jdom_test.java
```

On Linux, it is:

```
javac -classpath .:$JDOM_HOME/build/jdom.jar jdom_test.java
```

To run the example after you've compiled it, run the following command on Windows:

```
java -classpath .;%JDOM_HOME%\build\jdom.jar jdom_test
```

On Linux, the command is:

```
java -classpath .:$JDOM_HOME/build/jdom.jar jdom_test
```

The program should generate output very similar to the dom4j example. In fact, the JDOM and dom4j examples do exactly the same thing, using a different tool. The important thing is to compare and contrast the code for the two. In my opinion, the code using JDOM is cleaner and easier to follow.

Castor Test

We'll be working with `order.xml` again, but this time we're going to put a different spin on things. Castor allows us to create Java object bindings to the XML document, in this case `order.xml`. Now instead of dealing with objects that model XML documents, we can work directly with the Order object. Likewise, changing attributes is now done via mutator methods on the `LineItem` object. Basically, with Castor, first class objects can be generated to and from data in the XML documents. The easiest way to see how this works is to check out the code example.

Installation

Before installing Castor, please download and install Xerces Java 2 from the Apache XML site (`http://xml.apache.org/xerces2-j/index.html`). You'll need to download version 2.3 or above. The binaries are all that we need for the example. Once the archive is downloaded, extract the files into the directory where you want to house Xerces. Then, set the `XERCES_HOME` environment variable to point to this directory. On a Windows system, you can install it into a directory such as `c:\java\xerces2`. On Linux, you could use `/usr/local/xerces2`.

The latest Castor release can be downloaded from the project's Web site (`http://castor.exolab.org`). You can download either the .jar file or a full distribution. For this example, we'll only need the Castor XML .jar file, which is `castor-0.9.42-xml.jar` as of the time of writing. Be sure to copy this .jar file to the directory where you're going to put the Castor example.

Code Examples

The first feature we'll want to check out in Castor is the automated mapping. In the code example, we're going to use that with the order object. Then, we'll show how to use a custom-mapping file to create a binding with the `order.xml` file we've been using in the other examples.

Here's the `order.java` source code:

```
import java.io.*;
import java.util.*;

public class Order implements Serializable
{
    private ArrayList moLineItems = new ArrayList();
    private String msNotes;

    public void setNotes( String sNotes )
    {
        msNotes = sNotes;
    }


    public String getNotes()
    {
```

```
        return msNotes;
    }


    public ArrayList getLineItems()
    {
        return moLineItems;
    }


    public void setLineItems( ArrayList oLineItems )
    {
        moLineItems = oLineItems;
    }

    public void addLineItem( LineItem oLineItem )
    {
        getLineItems().add( oLineItem );
    }


    public String toString()
    {
        StringBuffer sb = new StringBuffer();
        sb.append( "Order Notes: " )
          .append( getNotes() )
          .append( "\nLine Items: " );
        Iterator itr = getLineItems().iterator();
        while( itr.hasNext() )
        {
            sb.append( itr.next().toString() );
        }
        return sb.toString();
    }
}
```

Each order can have one or more line items. The source code to implement the `LineItem` class is:

```
import java.io.*;

public class LineItem implements Serializable
{
    private String msName;
    private String msColor;
    private String msSize;
    private int miCount;
```

```
public LineItem()
{}


public LineItem(
   String sName,
   int    iCount,
   String sColor,
   String sSize )
{
    setName( sName );
    setCount( iCount );
    setColor( sColor );
    setSize( sSize );
}


public void setName( String sName )
{
    msName = sName;
}


public void setCount( int iCount )
{
    miCount = iCount;
}


public void setColor( String sColor )
{
    msColor = sColor;
}


public void setSize( String sSize )
{
    msSize = sSize;
}


public String getName()
{
    return msName;
}


public int getCount()
{
```

```
            return miCount;
        }


        public String getColor()
        {
            return msColor;
        }


        public String getSize()
        {
            return msSize;
        }


        public String toString()
        {
            return "\nLine Item " + getName() +
                   " " + getCount() +
                   " " + getColor() +
                   " " + getSize();
        }
    }
```

Now, we'll look at the test program that will generate a simple order and use the XML binding to persist it to and from disk. This example relies on the automated binding. Castor will inspect the Java object and generate a binding based on the accessor methods (those starting with `get*`). Note that in order for the automated binding to work, Castor must have access to concrete classes with an empty public constructor. These restrictions are quite reasonable and are the same as required by Java Beans.

Here's the source for `test_castor.java`:

```
import java.io.*;
import org.exolab.castor.mapping.*;
import org.exolab.castor.xml.*;

public class castor_test
{

    public static void main( String args[] )
    {
        // --- Creating the order object ---

        Order oOrder = new Order();
        oOrder.setNotes( "This is just a test order." );
        oOrder.addLineItem( new LineItem( "T-shirt", 2, "red", "M" ) );
```

```
        oOrder.addLineItem( new LineItem( "T-shirt", 1, "blue", "S" ) );
        System.out.println( "After construction: " + oOrder );


        // --- Write out to disk. ---

        Mapping oMapping = new Mapping();
        // The above will be used for explicit mapping.

        try
        {
//NOTE: Uncomment the next line to use a custom mapping file.
            //oMapping.loadMapping( "mapping.xml" );
            Marshaller oMarshaller = new Marshaller(
               new FileWriter( "order.xml" ) );
//NOTE: Uncomment the next line to use a custom mapping file.
            //oMarshaller.setMapping( oMapping );
            oMarshaller.marshal( oOrder );
        }
        catch( Exception e )
        {
            e.printStackTrace();
        }


        // --- Read back the object. ---

        oOrder = null;
        Unmarshaller oUnmarshaller = new Unmarshaller( Order.class );
        try
        {
//NOTE: Uncomment the next line to use a custom mapping file.
            //oUnmarshaller.setMapping( oMapping );
            oOrder = (Order) oUnmarshaller.unmarshal(
               new FileReader( "order.xml" ) );
        }
        catch( Exception e )
        {
            e.printStackTrace();
        }
        System.out.println( "After unmarshalling: " + oOrder );
    }
}
```

To compile the program in Windows, use the following command:

```
javac -classpath .;castor-0.9.4.3-xml.jar castor_test.java Order.java
LineItem.java
```

On Linux, the compile command is:

```
javac -classpath .:castor-0.9.4.3-xml.jar castor_test.java Order.java
LineItem.java
```

NOTE **This may be different depending on the version of the Castor jar you downloaded.**

To run the example on Windows, use:

```
java -classpath .;castor-0.9.4.3-xml.jar;%XERCES_HOME%\xercesImpl.jar
castor_test
```

On Linux, the command is:

```
java -classpath .:castor-0.9.4.3-xml.jar:$XERCES_HOME/xercesImpl.jar
castor_test
```

NOTE **Make sure you have installed Xerces because Castor depends on it to run.**

Running the example will show that the automated binding does work, but an examination of the `order.xml` file that is generated shows that the format is not the same as that we've seen in previous examples. By using a custom mapping file, we can fix that.

Here's the `order.xml` that is autogenerated, reformatted for readability:

```
<?xml version="1.0" encoding="UTF-8"?>
<order>
  <notes>This is just a test order.</notes>
  <line-items count="2"
    xsi:type="java:LineItem"
    xmlns:xsi="http://www.w3.org/2001/XMLSchema-instance">
    <color>red</color>
    <name>T-shirt</name>
    <size>M</size>
  </line-items>
  <line-items count="1"
      xsi:type="java:LineItem"
      xmlns:xsi="http://www.w3.org/2001/XMLSchema-instance">
    <color>blue</color>
    <name>T-shirt</name>
    <size>S</size>
  </line-items>
</order>
```

To specify a mapping file, uncomment the lines that specify the mapping. These are the three lines preceded by a note comment in `test_castor.java`.

Now, we need to write the `mapping.xml` file and save that in the same directory.

Here's the source for `mapping.xml`:

```
<?xml version="1.0"?>
<!DOCTYPE mapping PUBLIC
  "-//EXOLAB/Castor Object Mapping DTD Version 1.0//EN"
  "http://castor.exolab.org/mapping.dtd">

<mapping>
    <class name="Order">
        <map-to xml="order" />

        <field name="Notes"
               type="java.lang.String">
            <bind-xml name="notes"
                      node="attribute" />
        </field>

        <field name="LineItems"
               type="LineItem"
               collection="arraylist">
            <bind-xml name="line-item" node="element" />
        </field>
    </class>

    <class name="LineItem">
        <field name="Name" type="java.lang.String">
            <bind-xml name="name"
                      node="attribute" />
        </field>
        <field name="Count" type="integer">
            <bind-xml name="count"
                      node="attribute" />
        </field>
        <field name="Color" type="java.lang.String">
            <bind-xml name="color"
                      node="attribute" />
        </field>
        <field name="Size" type="java.lang.String">
            <bind-xml name="size"
                      node="attribute" />
        </field>
    </class>
</mapping>
```

Run the Castor example again to try out the manual mapping. Not much is different judging from the output. However, if you look at the `order.xml` file in a text viewer, you'll see that it is now clean of the metadata that Castor generates for the automated mappings. That same metadata is now explicitly coded within binding rules in the `mapping.xml` file.

As you can see, Castor introduces a totally different way to work with XML documents. Bound Java objects are a far more natural way to work with XML. Castor is very handy for generating Java objects from existing XML data. Actually, Castor is primarily a binding tool, and it can be used to bind Java objects with other sources, most notably relational databases. The ability to map to existing XML documents is especially handy!

Stylesheet Formatting Test

XSLT is one of the reasons why XML documents are such a great intermediary format. Because XML documents are structured and carry the metadata to describe themselves, we can easily transform a proper XML document into any number of intermediate or final formats. In this example, we'll tackle the common task of transforming a custom XML document into HTML for presentation to a Web client.

Our source XML document will be the `order.xml` file once again. We'll need to create a stylesheet to detail the transformations we want. This is a simple stylesheet that generates an HTML view of the order.

Source for the `order_to_html.xsl` stylesheet:

```
<?xml version="1.0"?>
<xsl:stylesheet
    xmlns:xsl="http://www.w3.org/1999/XSL/Transform" version="1.0">
    <xsl:output method="html" indent="yes"/>

    <xsl:template match="/" >
        <xsl:apply-templates />
    </xsl:template>

    <xsl:template match="order">
        <html>
            <head><title>Order</title></head>
            <body>
                <h3>My Order</h3>
                <table border="1">
                    <tr>
                        <th>Name</th>
                        <th>Count</th>
                        <th>Color</th>
                        <th>Size</th>
                    </tr>
```

```
                <xsl:apply-templates select="line_item" />
            </table>
        </body>
    </html>
</xsl:template>

<xsl:template match="line_item">
    <tr>
        <td><xsl:value-of select="@name" /></td>
        <td><xsl:value-of select="@count" /></td>
        <td><xsl:value-of select="@color" /></td>
        <td><xsl:value-of select="@size" /></td>
    </tr>
    <tr>
        <td colspan="4" >
          <emphasis>
            <xsl:apply-templates select="notes" />
          </emphasis>
        </td>
    </tr>
</xsl:template>
</xsl:stylesheet>
```

Note that it makes use of XML namespaces. Line 2 specifies that the full XML namespace for elements starting with the xsl: namespace prefix. We've defined patterns to match against our order XML document elements. These elements are then used in the template delimited by the contents of each <xsl:template> element.

The sample program will depend on dom4j, so be sure to have that installed. It will load the `order.xml` document, transform it with the `order_to_html.xsl` stylesheet, and then write the output back to `order.html`.

Here's the source for `xslt_test.java`:

```
import java.io.*;
import javax.xml.transform.*;
import javax.xml.transform.stream.*;
import org.dom4j.*;
import org.dom4j.io.*;


public class xslt_test {
  public static void main( String args[] ) {
    try {
      // --- Read in order.xml. ---
      SAXReader oReader = new SAXReader();
      Document oDocument = oReader.read( "order.xml" );
```

```
      // --- Create the stylesheet and transformer. ---
      StreamSource oStylesheetSource =
          new StreamSource( new File( "order_to_html.xsl" ) );
      Transformer oTransformer = TransformerFactory
        .newInstance()
        .newTransformer( oStylesheetSource );

      // --- Transform the order XML document and
      // --- output it as order.html. ---
      DocumentSource oDocumentSource = new DocumentSource( oDocument );
      StreamResult oResult = new StreamResult( "order.html" );
      oTransformer.transform( oDocumentSource, oResult );
    }
    catch( Exception e ) {
      e.printStackTrace();
    }
  }
}
```

To compile this on Windows, run the following:

```
javac -classpath .;%DOM4J_HOME%\dom4j-full.jar xslt_test.java
```

On Linux, run:

```
javac -classpath .:$DOM4J_HOME/dom4j-full.jar xslt_test
```

To run the example on Windows, use the following:

```
java -classpath .;%DOM4J_HOME%\dom4j-full.jar xslt_test
```

To run the example on Linux, use:

```
java -classpath .:$DOM4J_HOME/dom4j-full.jar xslt_test
```

After executing the sample program, the `order.html` file will be created. Open that file and compare it with the `order.xml` file. With a bit of examination, the transformations should be evident. We've only scratched the surface of XSLT's transformation rules. The language is considerably more powerful than simple matching and templating, but more in-depth coverage is beyond the scope of this book.

There's been a push to offload the XSLT processing to the client side. The latest browsers, such as Mozilla 1.*x*, support XSLT transformations. This not only saves processing time on the server, but also gives the user more control over the presentation. A user could choose to apply different stylesheets or use a client program that can operate on the source XML before applying the stylesheet for presentation. Currently, this is still not a feasible solution for most applications because the percentage of clients conforming to the full W3C XSLT standard is quite low. In more controlled environments, this can be a good architecture.

We've witnessed the use of XSLT to create presentational HTML from an XML source. The XSLT language is quite flexible and powerful enough to be used in other, more creative ways. This example has only shown a small glimpse of XSLT's true power. Hopefully, you'll be compelled to learn more about this fascinating technology.

Integration

As earlier sections of this chapter attest, there are literally hundreds of places to use XML within the J2EE environment. Now, we'll take a look at three examples of common integration points of XML within the J2EE: JDBC, EJBs, and servlets.

JDBC Example

JDBC and XML are natural partners in providing open access to an enterprise's data. JDBC offers standardized Java access to many data stores, and XML is ideal for interchanging data. In our example, we'll be extracting from legacy JDBC and making it available as XML.

This is written as a standalone Java program, but it could easily be an EJB or a Java Web service. The JDBC portion connects with the example database we used in Chapter 9. Our program will connect to the JDBC source, run a user-specified SQL query against it, and present the result set as XML.

Here's the source code for `xml_jdbc_test.java`:

```
import java.awt.*;
import java.awt.event.*;
import java.io.*;
import java.net.*;
import java.sql.*;
import java.util.*;
import javax.swing.*;
import org.jdom.*;
import org.jdom.output.*;

public class xml_jdbc_test extends JFrame {
  private String msDriver;
  private String msUrl;
  private String msUser;
  private String msPassword;
```

```
private JButton moQueryButton;
private JTextArea moQueryArea;
private JTextArea moResultsArea;
private Connection moConnection;


public xml_jdbc_test(
  String sDriver,
  String sUrl,
  String sUser,
  String sPassword )
{
  super( "XML-JDBC test" );
  msDriver = sDriver;
  msUrl = sUrl;
  msUser = sUser;
  msPassword = sPassword;

  try {
    setupConnection();
  }
  catch( Exception e ) {
    e.printStackTrace();
    System.exit( 1 );
  }


  createGui();
}


protected void setupConnection()
throws Exception
{
  Class.forName( msDriver );
  moConnection = DriverManager.getConnection( msUrl, msUser, msUrl );
}

protected void createGui()
{
  setBounds( 50, 50, 500, 500 );
  moQueryArea = new JTextArea();
  moResultsArea = new JTextArea();
  moQueryButton = new JButton( "Query" );
  moQueryButton.addActionListener(
    new ActionListener()
    {
      public void actionPerformed( ActionEvent oActionEvent )
      {
        doQuery();
```

```
            }
          }
        );

        // --- Build the query panel. ---
        JPanel oQueryPanel = new JPanel( new BorderLayout() );
        oQueryPanel.add( new JScrollPane( moQueryArea ) );
        oQueryPanel.add(
          new JLabel( "Enter the SQL Query here: " ),
          BorderLayout.NORTH );

        // --- Build the results panel. ---
        JPanel oResultsPanel = new JPanel( new BorderLayout() );
        oResultsPanel.add( new JScrollPane( moResultsArea ) );
        oResultsPanel.add(
          new JLabel( "XML representation of the query results: " ),
          BorderLayout.NORTH );

        // --- Aggregate the text area panels. ---
        JPanel oTextAreasPanel = new JPanel( new GridLayout( 2, 1 ) );
        oTextAreasPanel.add( oQueryPanel );
        oTextAreasPanel.add( oResultsPanel );

        // --- Construct the main panel. ---
        JPanel oPanel = new JPanel( new BorderLayout() );
        oPanel.add( oTextAreasPanel );
        oPanel.add( moQueryButton, BorderLayout.SOUTH );

        getContentPane().add( oPanel );
        setDefaultCloseOperation( JFrame.EXIT_ON_CLOSE );
      }


      public void doQuery() {
        // --- Clear the textareas. ---
        String sQuery = moQueryArea.getText();
        moResultsArea.setText( "Query: " + sQuery + "\n\n" );

        try {
          Statement oStatement = moConnection.createStatement();
          ResultSet oResultSet = oStatement.executeQuery( sQuery );
          ResultSetMetaData oMetaData = oResultSet.getMetaData();

          Document oDocument = new Document(
            new Element( "query-results" ) );
          Element oQueryElement = new Element( "sql-query" );
          oQueryElement.setText( sQuery );
          oDocument.getRootElement().addContent( oQueryElement );
```

```
      Element oResultSetElement = new Element( "result-set" );
      oDocument.getRootElement().addContent( oResultSetElement );

      int iRowCount = 0;
      while( oResultSet.next() ) {
        ++iRowCount;

        // --- Export each row to XML as it is retrieved.---
        // Note: uses base 1 indexing.
        Element oRowElement = new Element( "row" );
        oResultSetElement.addContent( oRowElement );
        oRowElement.setAttribute( "index", "" + iRowCount );
        for( int idxColumn = 1;
             idxColumn <= oMetaData.getColumnCount(); ++idxColumn ) {
          Element oColumnElement = new Element( "column" );
          oColumnElement.setAttribute(
            "name",
            oMetaData.getColumnName( idxColumn ) );
          oColumnElement.setAttribute(
            "type",
            oMetaData.getColumnTypeName( idxColumn ) );
          oColumnElement.setAttribute(
            "value",
            oResultSet.getString( idxColumn ) );
          oRowElement.addContent( oColumnElement );
        }
      }
      oResultSet.close();
      oResultSetElement.setAttribute( "count", "" + iRowCount );


      // --- Append the document to the text area. ---
      XMLOutputter oOutputter = new XMLOutputter( "  ", true );
      moResultsArea.setText(
        moResultsArea.getText() +
        oOutputter.outputString( oDocument ) );
    }
    catch( Exception e ) {
      moResultsArea.setText(
        "Exception encountered. " +
        e.getMessage() );
      if( !( e instanceof SQLException ) ) {
        e.printStackTrace();
      }
    }
  }


  public static void main( String args[] ) {
    String sDriver = "org.hsqldb.jdbcDriver";
```

```
    String sUrl = "jdbc:hsqldb:d:/openjava/hsqldb/data/hsqltest";
    String sUser = "sa";
    String sPassword = "";

    if( args.length > 0 && args[0] != "" )
      sDriver = args[0];
    if( args.length > 1 && args[1] != "" )
      sUrl = args[1];
    if( args.length > 2 && args[2] != "" )
      sUser = args[2];
    if( args.length > 3 && args[3] != "" )
      sPassword = args[3];

    System.out.println( "Driver: " + sDriver );
    System.out.println( "URL    : " + sUrl );
    System.out.println( "User   : " + sUser );
    System.out.println( "Passwd: " + sPassword );

    xml_jdbc_test oTest =
      new xml_jdbc_test( sDriver, sUrl, sUser, sPassword );
    oTest.show();
  }
}
```

To compile in Windows, use the following command:

```
javac -classpath .;%JDOM_HOME%\build\jdom.jar xml_jdbc_test.java
```

In Linux, the command is:

```
javac -classpath .:$JDOM_HOME/build/jdom.jar xml_jdbc_test.java
```

NOTE You'll need to have a reference to the JDBC driver .jar file in your classpath to run the example.

To run the example on Windows, use the following command:

```
java -classpath .;mysql-connector-java-3.0.6-stable.jar;%JDOM-
HOME%\build\jdom.jar xml_jdbc_test
```

In Linux, the command is:

```
java -classpath .: mysql-connector-java-3.0.6-
stable.jar:$JDOM_HOME/build/jdom.jar xml_jdbc_test
```

The `xml_jdbc_test` is a Swing program. There are two text areas at the top and a query button at the bottom. SQL queries can be entered into the top text area. The bottom text area shows the result of the SQL query as XML. To run the query, press the "Query" button.

The `xml_jdbc_test` example is a rather academic program. However, it can be used as a basis for more useful programs. It's possible to extract existing relational database schemas and expose those as XML documents. The XML can be persisted or made available via a servlet. You can also use the mapping the other way, importing data from an XML document and storing it in a JDBC database.

The goal of this example is give you an idea of how the two technologies can work together. [NR1]

EJB Example

XML is just as easy to use within an EJB. We'll modify the XSLT example to work as a message-driven bean. This is a useful model because you can queue up XSLT transformations that often take up a lot of processing time.

In this example, our sample XSLT MDB will transform documents received in JMS messages. Our source document will once again be the `order.xml`, sent as a string within JMS text messages. Once transformed, the resultant HTML is saved to a directory for future access.

There are several files we need to package in the EJB .jar file. In addition to the usual descriptors in `META-INF`, we also store resources used by the message-driven bean under the `WEB-INF` directory. The library .jar for dom4j, which we'll be using for our XML work, is stored here. The other resource file is our XSLT stylesheet, `order_to_html.xsl`, which is used by the EJB to transform incoming messages. The contents of the `order_to_html.xsl` file are the same as in our XSLT example earlier in this chapter.

The layout for the directory is as follows:

```
\META-INF\ejb-jar.xml
\META-INF\jboss.xml
\WEB-INF\order_to_html.xsl
\WEB-INF\lib\dom4j-full.jar
```

Be sure that the directory and file layout match the above example. When we create the EJB .jar, that directory layout is expected. Any missing files will cause problems upon deployment in the EJB container.

Here's the source for `SampleXsltMessageBean.java`:

```
import java.io.*;
import javax.ejb.*;
import javax.jms.*;
import javax.naming.*;
import javax.xml.transform.*;
```

```
import javax.xml.transform.stream.*;
import org.dom4j.*;
import org.dom4j.io.*;


public class SampleXsltMessageBean
implements MessageDrivenBean, MessageListener {
  public static final String OUTPUT_DIRECTORY = "/temp/";
  protected MessageDrivenContext m_context = null;
  protected Topic m_topic = null;
  protected TopicConnection m_connection = null;
  protected TopicSession m_session = null;


  public void setMessageDrivenContext( MessageDrivenContext context )
  throws EJBException {
    m_context = context;
  }


  /**
   * Create the message-driven bean.
   **/
  public void ejbCreate() throws CreateException {
    try {
      // --- Allocate JMS resources ---

      InitialContext context = new InitialContext();
      TopicConnectionFactory factory = (TopicConnectionFactory)
        context.lookup( "XAConnectionFactory" );
      m_topic = (Topic)
        context.lookup( "java:comp/env/jms/destinationTopic" );
      m_connection = factory.createTopicConnection();
    }
    catch( Exception e ) {
      throw new CreateException( e.getMessage() );
    }
  }


  public void ejbRemove() {
    // --- Release cached JMS resources. ---

    if( m_topic != null ) {
      m_topic = null;
    }

    if( m_connection != null ) {
      try {
        m_connection.close();
```

```
      }
      catch( JMSException e ) {
        e.printStackTrace();
      }
      m_connection = null;
    }
  }


  public void onMessage( Message oMessage ) {

//= Retrieve from message ---
    if( oMessage instanceof TextMessage ) {
      TextMessage oTextMessage = (TextMessage) oMessage;
      try {

//===   Read in the document from the JMS message. ---
        SAXReader oReader = new SAXReader();
        Document oDocument = oReader.read(
          new StringReader( oTextMessage.getText() ) );


//===   Create the stylesheet and transformer. ---
        InputStream oStylesheetInputStream =
          getClass().getResourceAsStream( "WEB-INF/order_to_html.xsl" );
        StreamSource oStylesheetSource =
          new StreamSource( oStylesheetInputStream );
        Transformer oTransformer =
          TransformerFactory
            .newInstance().newTransformer( oStylesheetSource );

//===   Transform the order XML document and output it as order.html.
        DocumentSource oDocumentSource =
          new DocumentSource( oDocument );
        File oOutputFile = new File( OUTPUT_DIRECTORY + "order.html" );
        StreamResult oResult = new StreamResult( oOutputFile );
        System.out.println( "transformed and save to: " + oOutputFile );
        oTransformer.transform( oDocumentSource, oResult );
      }
      catch( Exception e ) {
        e.printStackTrace();
      }
    }
  }
}
```

To compile `SampleXsltMessageBean.java` on Windows, the command is:

```
javac -classpath .;%JBOSS_HOME%\client\jbossall-client.jar;WEB-
INF\lib\dom4j-full.jar SampleXsltMessageBean.java
```

On Linux, it is:

```
javac -classpath .:$JBOSS_HOME/client/jbossall-client.jar:WEB-
INF/lib/dom4j-full.jar SampleXsltMessageBean.java
```

After the `SampleXsltMessageBean` is compiled, we need to jar up the directory for deployment as an EJB .jar file.

The command to create package `SampleXsltMDB.jar` is:

```
jar cvf SampleXsltMDB.jar SampleXsltMessageBean.class META-INF WEB-INF
```

The next step is to deploy the MDB. On JBoss, merely copy the `SampleXsltMDB.jar` to the deployment folder.

On Windows, this is:

```
copy SampleXsltMDB.jar %JBOSS_HOME%\server\default\deploy
```

On Linux, it is:

```
cp SampleXsltMDB.jar $JBOSS_HOME/server/default/deploy
```

If the EJB container is running, the .jar file should be automatically deployed. Now in order to test it, we still need a client to send JMS messages to the MDB.

The client to our message-driven bean is a simple Java application that publishes a text message to the topic that the MDB is hooked into. The program is based on the `SimplePublisher.java` from Chapter 9, except that we replace the contents of the message with the text of `order.xml`. The code is repeated here for your convenience.

Here's the source for the modified `SimplePublisher.java`:

```
import java.io.*;
import java.util.*;
import javax.jms.*;
import javax.naming.*;

/**
 *  Simple JMS Publisher
 */
public class SimplePublisher {
  public static void main( String[] args ) {
    TopicConnection connection = null;
    TopicSession session = null;
    try {
      // --- Create default properties to find JBoss's JNDI. ---

      Hashtable default_properties = new Hashtable();
```

```
    default_properties.put(
      Context.INITIAL_CONTEXT_FACTORY,
      "org.jnp.interfaces.NamingContextFactory" );
    default_properties.put( Context.PROVIDER_URL, "localhost:1099" );


    // --- Create various JMS resources. ---
    // -- Note that we are using the transaction aware versions of
    // -- everything.

    Context context = new InitialContext( default_properties );
    TopicConnectionFactory factory = (TopicConnectionFactory)
      context.lookup( "java:/XAConnectionFactory" );
    connection = factory.createTopicConnection();
    session = connection
      .createTopicSession( true, Session.AUTO_ACKNOWLEDGE );
    Topic topic = (Topic) context.lookup( "topic/testTopic" );

    // -- We use topic/testTopic as the topic to publish to because it
    // -- is defined by default by JBossMQ. You can find the queues
    // -- and topics available at JBoss startup time within the
    // -- jbossmq-destinations-service.xml file inside the
    // -- %JBOSS_HOME%\server\default directory.
    TopicPublisher publisher = session.createPublisher( topic );

    // --- Publish an order.xml text message. ---
    StringBuffer sb = new StringBuffer();
    BufferedReader oReader =
      new BufferedReader( new FileReader( "order.xml" ) );
    while( oReader.ready() ) {
      sb.append( oReader.readLine() );
    }

    TextMessage message = session.createTextMessage();
    message.setText( sb.toString() );

    publisher.publish( message );
    session.commit();
    System.out.println( "Published " + message );
  }
  catch( Exception e ) {
    e.printStackTrace();
  }
  finally {
    try {
      if( session != null ) {
        session.close();
      }
    }
```

```
        catch( JMSException e2 ) {
          e2.printStackTrace();
        }
        try {
          if( connection != null ) {
            connection.close();
          }
        }
        catch( JMSException e2 ) {
          e2.printStackTrace();
        }
      }
    }
  }
```

Compilation is the same as before. On Windows, the command is:

```
javac -classpath .;%JBOSS_HOME%\client\jbossall-client.jar
SimplePublisher.java
```

On Linux, it is:

```
javac -classpath .:$JBOSS_HOME/client/jbossall-client.jar
SimplePublisher.java
```

To run the client on Windows, use the following command:

```
java -classpath .;%JBOSS_HOME%\client\jbossall-
client.jar;%JBOSS_HOME%\client\log4j.jar SimplePublisher
```

On Linux, use:

```
java -classpath .:$JBOSS_HOME/client/jbossall-
client.jar:$JBOSS_HOME/client/log4j.jar SimplePublisher
```

Assuming that the MDB is deployed, you can run the client program to trigger the transformation. With the default settings, the `order.html` file will be created under `c:\temp\order.html`.

To recap, we constructed a MDB that uses dom4j to transform documents received via JMS messages. Queued transformations are quite useful in many scenarios. Our example does a trivial transformation, but the documents, stylesheets, and output can all be easily changed to fit your own needs. Best of all, you can see that these pieces can work together in various combinations to get the behavior and meet the constraints that are required to solve the problems you face.

Servlet Example

This time we're going to integrate the XML toolset into the Web layer. The Apache FOP tool is commonly used in J2EE applications to present data in .pdf format, so that's the example we'll tackle. We'll build a servlet that takes in the FO document as a parameter and transforms that XML document into a .pdf file.

Our servlet code is actually quite simple. All the heavy lifting is done for us by the Apache FOP library. In order to test this, you'll need to have Tomcat running. If you haven't set this up already, please refer to Chapter 5.

Here's the source code for `SimpleFopServlet.java`:

```
import java.util.*;
import java.io.*;
import javax.servlet.*;
import javax.servlet.http.*;
import org.xml.sax.*;
import org.apache.fop.apps.*;


public class SimpleFopServlet extends HttpServlet
{
  public void doGet(
    HttpServletRequest oRequest,
    HttpServletResponse oResponse )
  throws IOException, ServletException
  {
    try {
      String sSource = oRequest.getParameter( "src" );
      oResponse.setContentType( "application/pdf" );
      Driver oDriver = new Driver(
        new InputSource( sSource ),
        oResponse.getOutputStream() );
      oDriver.setRenderer( Driver.RENDER_PDF );
      oDriver.run();
    }
    catch( Exception e ) {
      e.printStackTrace();
      throw new ServletException( e.getMessage() );
    }
  }
}
```

We need to make the FOP libraries available for use by the servlet. The best way to package a library .jar for use with a servlet is within the `WEB-INF/lib` directory of the .war file. These .jar files will typically be loaded by the Web application server in such a manner as to make them accessible only to the files packaged in that .war.

Apache FOP is broken out into several different .jar files. The primary .jar file is `fop.jar`, but it has several dependencies on other projects. These .jar files are included in the distribution, and we need to provide these .jar files even though we won't be directly calling upon them in the SimpleFopServlet. The .jar files needed to use FOP are:

- `avalon-framework-???.jar` FOP relies on the Avalon common framework.

NOTE **The name of the avalon framework jar file will vary depending on the version of FOP you're using. The name that is current with the writing of this book is `avalon-framework-cvs-20020806.jar`.**

- `batik.jar`. Provides the SVG capabilities for the FOP project.
- `fop.jar`. The actual jar containing the Apache FOP classes.

Be sure to copy these jar files into `WEB-INF\lib`. The directory structure for the .war file will resemble the following:

```
/WEB-INF/web.xml
/WEB-INF/classes/SimpleFopServlet.class
/WEB-INF/lib/avalon-framework-???.jar
/WEB-INF/lib/batik.jar
/WEB-INF/lib/fop.jar
```

Here's the source for `web.xml`:

```
<?xml version="1.0" encoding="ISO-8859-1"?>
<!DOCTYPE web-app PUBLIC
  "-//Sun Microsystems, Inc.//DTD Web Application 2.2//EN"
  "http://java.sun.com/j2ee/dtds/web-app_2_2.dtd">
<web-app>
  <servlet>
    <servlet-name>SimpleFop</servlet-name>
    <servlet-class>SimpleFopServlet</servlet-class>
  </servlet>
  <servlet-mapping>
    <servlet-name>SimpleFop</servlet-name>
    <url-pattern>/simpleFop</url-pattern>
  </servlet-mapping>
</web-app>
```

We'll need to compile our servlet and package the compiled classes, the Web application deployment descriptor file, and library .jar files all into one .war file for deployment. Copy the Apache FOP jar and its dependencies into the `WEB-INF\lib` directory. The .jar files we'll need are:

- The Apache FOP .jar (`fop.jar`)
- The Java Servlet .jar (`servlet.jar`)

On Windows, the process is:

```
javac -classpath .;.\WEB-
INF\lib\fop.jar;%TOMCAT_HOME%\common\lib\servlet.jar
SimpleFopServlet.java
copy SimpleFopServlet.class WEB-INF\classes
jar cvf fop-servlet.war WEB-INF
```

On Linux, the process is as follows:

```
javac -classpath .:./WEB-
INF/lib/fop.jar:$TOMCAT_HOME/common/lib/servlet.jar
SimpleFopServlet.java
cp SimpleFopServlet.class WEB-INF/classes
jar cvf fop-servlet.war WEB-INF
```

The compiled class files are placed under the `WEB-INF/classes` directory. In this case, we only have one servlet class file for `SimpleFopServlet`. This servlet is mapped to the URL pattern `/simpleFop`. The only parameter recognized by the servlet is `src`, which should contain the URL to the source FO document.

Here's a sample FO document (`simple.fo`) for testing:

```
<?xml version="1.0" encoding="utf-8"?>

<fo:root xmlns:fo="http://www.w3.org/1999/XSL/Format">

    <!-- Defines a template for content layouts called simple -->
    <fo:layout-master-set>
        <fo:simple-page-master master-name="simple"
                               page-height="8.5in"
                               page-width="11.0in"
                               margin-top="1.0in"
                               margin-bottom="1.0in"
                               margin-left="1.0in"
```

```
                                        margin-right="1.0in">
            <fo:region-body margin-top="0.75in"
                            margin-bottom="0.5in" />
        </fo:simple-page-master>
    </fo:layout-master-set>

    <!-- Actual content page. -->
    <fo:page-sequence master-reference="simple" >
        <fo:flow flow-name="xsl-region-body">
            <fo:block text-align="center" language="en">
Hello world!
            </fo:block>
        </fo:flow>
    </fo:page-sequence>
    <fo:page-sequence master-reference="simple" >
        <fo:flow flow-name="xsl-region-body">
            <fo:block text-align="justify" language="en">
Page 2. More content here.
            </fo:block>
        </fo:flow>
    </fo:page-sequence>
</fo:root>
```

To try out the servlet, deploy the .war file to your Web application server. Once you have deployed the code on Tomcat, the URL used to invoke the FOP processing via a servlet is:

```
http://localhost:8080/fop-servlet/simpleFop?src=file:///C:/temp/simple.fo
```

Naturally, this depends on how Tomcat is set up on your system. The first part of the URL, `http:// localhost:8080`, specifies the server and port for our Tomcat installation. `/fop-servlet` is the subtree where the .war file is bound by default. This is followed by the URL mapping we specified in the `web.xml` file, `simpleFop`. Finally we have the portion of the URL containing the `src` parameter. The result can be seen in Figure 12.1.

As a reporting tool, the servlet/FOP combination is great. Not only can you generate .pdf and other printable formats, but it is also possible to create output SVG images. With an additional transformation step, SVG can be rendered into PNG, GIF, or JPEG. The packaging is similar to the EJB integration example, but servlets are nice because they can be directly accessed by HTTP. You'll find that servlets are one of the best and most common places to integrate XML.

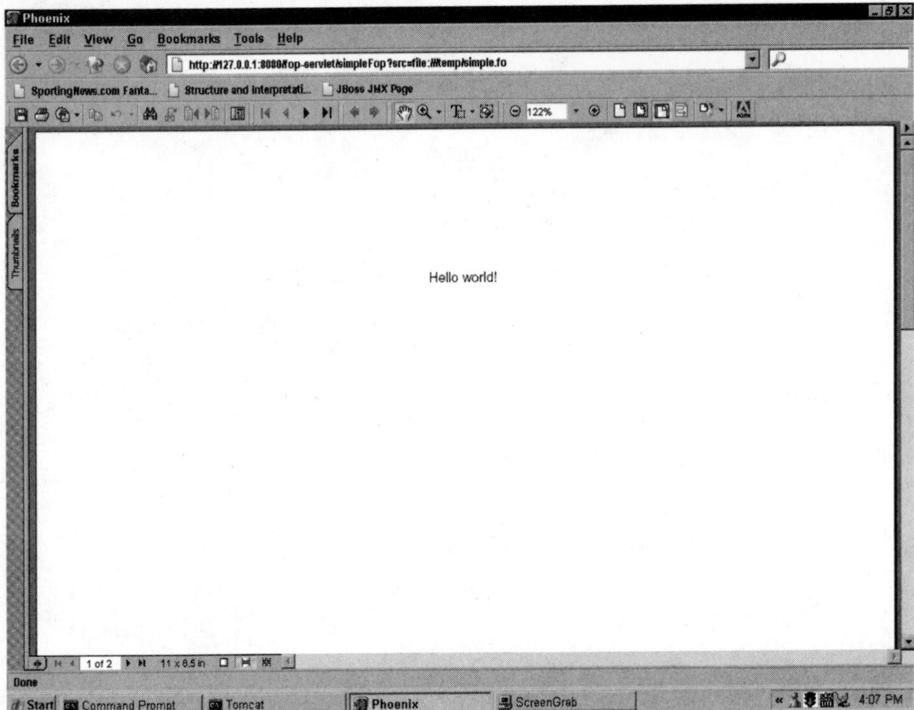

Figure 12.1 Screenshot of the rendered PDF of simple.Fop.

Summary

The standard JAXP APIs provide a solid foundation for using XML with Java. With the next release of the J2EE specification, version 1.4, we can expect even more standard XML interfaces to be provided. Even now, there is a rich set of open source XML tools we can use. These tools can be used in many different combinations within the context of the J2EE architecture. In this chapter, we've tried to lay out the possibilities and familiarize you with some of the most useful projects.

PART

Four

Test Driving the Platform

Up to this point, our focus has been selecting and integrating the components of our platform. In some ways, this has been like building a car from a kit. For the kit-car, a chassis, body, and drive train are selected and combined to build the car. Once the car has been assembled, you take it for a test drive. In our case, we have selected a number of components from open source tools to assemble our enterprise platform. Now, it is time to take the platform out for a test drive, so to speak. This part of the book provides that test-drive. It does this by implementing some of the key aspects of the sample application that was introduced in Chapter 3. The final chapter deals with issues related to deploying applications on the platform for real-world production scenarios.

CHAPTER

13

Building an Application: Assembling the Back End

Up to this point, our focus has been selecting and integrating the components of our platform. Now that we've finished building the platform, it's time to demonstrate building and deploying an application on it. The application we'll create is based on the Old Friends Incorporated application introduced in Chapter 3. This chapter builds the back end, or enterprise layers, of the application using the components introduced to the platform in the previous section. The next chapter shows you how to build the presentation layer.

CROSS-REFERENCE Although this chapter and Chapter 14 give you a good overview of how to build an application with open source tools, *Java Open Source Programming* by Joe Walnes et al. (Wiley Publishing, Inc. 2003), a companion book to this one that's also part of the Java Open Source Library, discusses the topic in far more detail.

Setup for a Test Drive

Figure 13.1 shows an overview of the platform components that we will exercise in this example. We will start building our example from the bottom tier or "back end" and work our way up to the middle and, in Chapter 14, the front end. This is a common approach in enterprise system development because often a number of back-end components already exist. This approach allows us to start with the domain model that may already exist in our enterprise environment and move forward.

In this chapter, we are developing the component, connection, and enterprise tiers that make up the middle and back end, as shown in the figure. The steps we will take to create this example are:

1. Create the database and tables.
2. Connect the EJB container to the database.
3. Create the EJBs.
4. Install and test the EJBs.

In the next chapter, we will show you how to:

- Create the Struts Action Classes.
- Create the Struts Java Server Pages.
- Test the application.

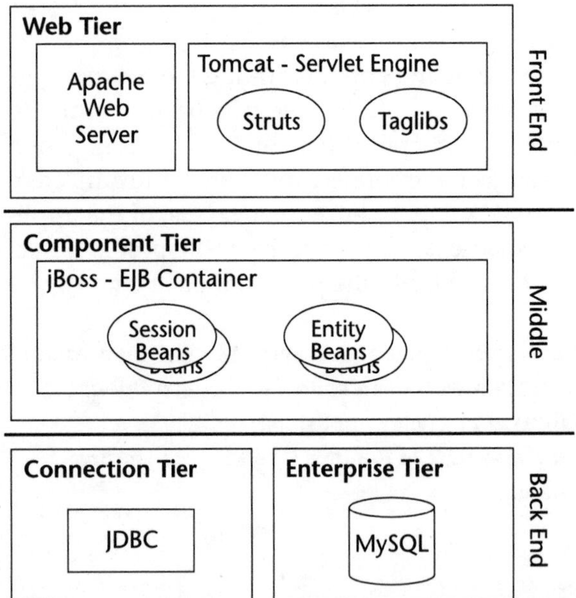

Figure 13.1 Platform components used for the user profile example.

The sample application covered in this chapter assumes that the following platform components have been downloaded and installed:

- **Ant.** See Chapter 4.
- **JDBC Driver for MySql.** See Chapter 9.
- **MySql database.** See Chapter 8.
- **JBoss EJB container.** See Chapter 10.

Understanding the Scenario

Our goal in this chapter and in Chapter 14 is to provide a demonstration of the platform that is complete enough to exercise the platform's features, while at the same time being simple enough to be clear and instructive. To do this, we will focus on a particular aspect of the Old Friends Incorporated example introduced in Chapter 3. As a reminder, Old Friends Incorporated is creating software to aid in planning class or group reunions.

For our scenario, we note that all reunions involve people getting together. This implies a requirement to track those people who are interested in participating in the reunion or at least in keeping in touch with their classmates. This application will allow class members to register and provide contact information to share with other class members.

Understanding the Use Cases

Figure 13.2 shows a UML (Unified Modeling Language) use case diagram, illustrating the use cases developed for this scenario. A *use case diagram* shows users in roles and illustrates how those users interact with the system. The users within a role are portrayed as stick figures. The ovals represent actions that a user in a role can perform on the system.

Two roles are shown in the diagram.

VerifiedUser. A verified user is a user who has been logged into the system. A verified user can modify his or her own user profile information and can log out.

NewUser. A new user is one who is not logged in. A new user can log in, becoming a verified user or can create a new user record.

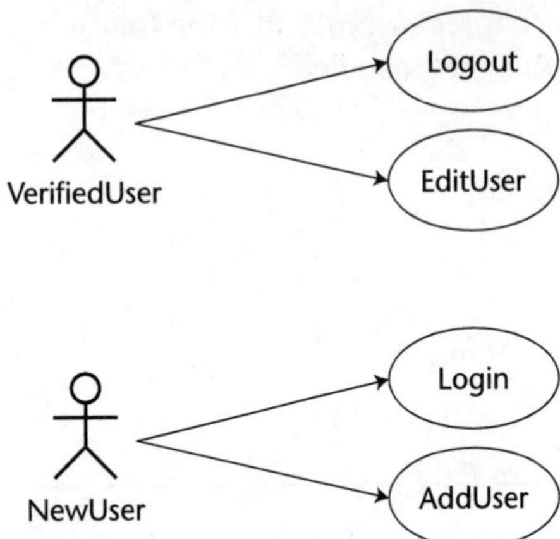

Figure 13.2 UML use case diagram.

Creating a Domain Model

From the previous section, it should be clear that we will need a class to represent the information we know about a user. This user class is an example of a domain class. Domain classes describe the people, places, and things, or nouns that are a part of the business problem. A domain class is often implemented as the base layer for an application. In our case, the domain classes represent potential Enterprise Java Beans. The UML class diagram shown in Figure 13.3 shows two classes and the relationship between them.

The model shows that each user has exactly one graduating class (the number one next to the GradClass box) and that each graduating class has a one-to-many relationship (the 1..* next to the User box) with the users. In reality, some users are faculty members and are associated with many graduating classes. We will handle this case by adding faculty as a separate instance of GradClass.

We will use these models as the basis for understanding the application as we develop it.

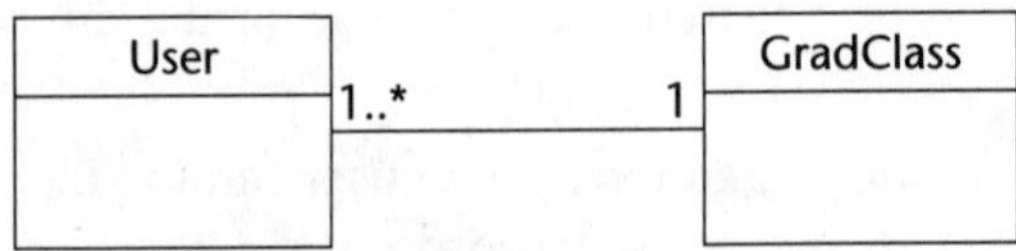

Figure 13.3 Domain classes.

Normally, we would create a separate class to store information common to a specific Graduation class, however for simplicity we will only provide the User class and associate a user with a Graduating class by collecting the year the user graduated.

Directory Structure

It is helpful to have a predefined directory structure when starting on any project involving EJB development. The directory structure we used when developing this software is provided here as a reference.

DIRECTORY	WHAT IT CONTAINS
/chapter13/.	Serves as the base directory for all files and subdirectories. The ant `build.xml`, the test client, and the final deployment .jar file are all in this directory. All other subdirectories are below this one.
./com/oldfriends.	The base for all packages in the project.
./com/oldfriends/entity.	All entity beans and their interfaces.
./com/oldfriends/session.	All session beans and their interfaces.
./com/oldfriends/dto.	Data transfer objects or value beans.
./com/oldfriends/utils.	Utility classes.
./etc.	Deployment descriptors.
./sql.	SQL scripts.

Supporting User Profiles

The first part of the example that we will explore is adding information about the users to the system. A *user profile* is an object that provides information about the user of the system. Most systems have some sort of user profile object, but that object is normally customized either for the system or for the needs of the enterprise. The primary functions that our user profile system needs to support are:

- Adding a new user
- Finding an existing user
- Editing an existing user

We also want to maintain the following information about each user:

- First name
- Last name
- Middle initial
- Maiden name
- Graduating class
- Login ID
- Password
- Email address

If we were creating more than just a sample application, we might also want to collect address, phone number, and other information about the user, but in this case, we want to make the examples simple enough for easy understanding. Because adding these attributes do not significantly change what we are trying to illustrate, we will ignore them here.

Creating the Database

For this example, we will use the MySQL database. Make sure that MySQL has been installed according to the instructions in Chapter 8. The following script can be executed to create the database.

```
use oldfriends;
drop table users;
create table users (
  userid varchar(36) NOT NULL PRIMARY KEY,
  first_name varchar(20),
  last_name varchar(20),
  mi varchar(2),
  maiden_name varchar(20),
  grad_class int,
  login_id varchar(20) NOT NULL UNIQUE,
  password varchar(20) NOT NULL,
  email varchar(128) NOT NULL
);
```

The scripts can be executed either from the MySQL command-line interface or from the MySQL Control Center application. We can add some records into this database for test data as shown here:

```
Insert into users
(userid, first_name, last_name, mi, maiden_name,
grad_class, login_id, password, email)
```

```
values ("0000000-000000-00000000-0-00000000-1", "John", "Doe", "X.",
"", 76, "jdoe","password","jdoe@someaddr.org");

Insert into users
(userid, first_name, last_name, mi, maiden_name,
grad_class, login_id, password, email)
values ("0000000-000000-00000000-0-00000000-2", "Jane", "Doe", "Y.",
"Smith", 76, "janedoe","password","janedoe@someaddr.org");

Insert into users
(userid, first_name, last_name, mi, maiden_name,
grad_class, login_id, password, email)
values ("0000000-000000-00000000-0-00000000-3", "Jack", "Smith", "Z.",
"", 77, "jsmith","password","smitty@someaddr.org");
```

The table uses a 36-character field as the primary key. This allows us to use Globally Unique Identifiers (GUIDs) for our primary key. While GUIDs are not as simple to use in some cases as integer-based keys, GUIDs work very well in clustered environments where simpler key systems are often challenged. A GUID is guaranteed to be unique no matter which machine it was generated on. In our case, these scripts only need a special value to distinguish our test data from real data inserted into the system. The values entered here are not legitimate GUIDs but they will also never clash with a real GUID. We will discuss GUIDs further later in the chapter.

For security reasons, we will also want to create a special user to access the database. We will call the user `dbuser`, and at this time we will grant all privileges to this user. The following commands create the user and grant the privileges:

```
GRANT ALL PRIVILEGES ON oldfriends TO dbuser@'192.168.%'
  INDENTIFIED BY 'passwd';
```

This new user is restricted in that it cannot grant privileges to others and it is only valid for connections coming from the same network. You will want to replace `'passwd'` with an appropriate password for your system.

Squirrel or the `JdbcTest` program from Chapter 8 can be used as a quick test of the JDBC connection to the database. The following command should be entered as one line to run `JdbcTest`:

```
java -cp mysql-connector-java-2.0.14-bin.jar JdbcTest \
  com.mysql.jdbc.Driver jdbc:mysql://localhost:3306/oldfriends \
  dbuser passwd
```

Now, we need to configure the EJB container to provide us with a DataSource for our database.

Configuring the DataSource in the EJB Container

We will be using the JBoss EJB container for this application. The EJB container needs to be configured with a DataSource for our database. JBoss 3.0 supports databases using the Java Connector Architecture (JCA). However, most databases do not come with JCA support at this time. JBoss addresses this concern by creating a JCA wrapper around an existing JDBC driver. An XML file describing the information needed to deploy the database configures the JCA wrapper. Samples of these XML files can be found in the `docs/examples/jca` directory below the directory where JBoss has been installed. The following XML file is based on the `mysql-service.xml` sample, but has been edited to make it easier to understand:

```
<?xml version="1.0" encoding="UTF-8"?>
<server>
  <mbean
    code="org.jboss.resource.connectionmanager.LocalTxConnectionManager"
    name="jboss.jca:service=LocalTxCM,name=MySqlDS">
    <depends optional-attribute-name="ManagedConnectionFactoryName">
      <!--embedded mbean-->
      <mbean
        code="org.jboss.resource.connectionmanager.RARDeployment"
        name="jboss.jca:service=LocalTxDS,name=MySqlDS">

        <attribute name="JndiName">MySqlDS</attribute>
        <attribute name="ManagedConnectionFactoryProperties">
          <properties>
            <config-property
              name="ConnectionURL"
              type="java.lang.String">\
jdbc:mysql://localhost:3306/oldfriends</config-property>
            <config-property
              name="DriverClass"
              type="java.lang.String">\
com.mysql.jdbc.Driver</config-property>
           <config-property
              name="UserName"
              type="java.lang.String">dbuser</config-property>
            <config-property
              name="Password"
              type="java.lang.String">passwd</config-property>
          </properties>
        </attribute>
        <depends
          optional-attribute-name="OldRarDeployment">\
jboss.jca:service=\
RARDeployment,name=JBoss LocalTransaction JDBC Wrapper</depends>
      </mbean>
```

```
    </depends>
<depends optional-attribute-name="ManagedConnectionPool">
      <!--embedded mbean-->
      <mbean
code="org.jboss.resource.connectionmanager.JBossManagedConnectionPool"
        name="jboss.jca:service=LocalTxPool,name=MySqlDS">

        <attribute name="MinSize">0</attribute>
        <attribute name="MaxSize">50</attribute>
        <attribute name="BlockingTimeoutMillis">5000</attribute>
        <attribute name="IdleTimeoutMinutes">15</attribute>
        <attribute name="Criteria">ByContainer</attribute>
      </mbean>

    </depends>
    <depends
      optional-attribute-name="CachedConnectionManager">
jboss.jca:service=CachedConnectionManager</depends>

    <depends
      optional-attribute-name="JaasSecurityManagerService">
jboss.security:service=JaasSecurityManager</depends>

    <attribute
      name="TransactionManager">\
java:/TransactionManager</attribute>
    <!--make the rar deploy! hack till better deployment-->
    <depends>jboss.jca:service=RARDeployer</depends>
  </mbean>
</server>
```

There are five elements in this file that we are primarily interested in and are used to configure the database. All of these have a name attribute that is used to identify the element. All but one of these is a <config-property> element. The elements we are interested in, by name, are:

- JndiName
- ConnectionURL
- DriverClass
- UserName
- Password

The JndiName specifies that name that will be used to look up the connection in the future. The other names correspond to the arguments that are needed to establish a JDBC connection. These values should be edited within the file to reflect the values in your system. In our case, the values are set as follows:

- JndiName is "MySqlDS"
- ConnectionURL is "jdbc:mysql://localhost:3306/oldfriends"
- DriverClass is "com.mysql.jdbc.Driver"
- UserName is "dbuser"
- Password is "passwd"

After the XML file has been edited, there are two steps to deploying it. First, copy the .jar file for the JDBC driver into the lib directory below your JBoss server configuration. This will most likely be jbossversion/server/default/lib. Next, copy the edited XML file into the deploy directory. After this is done, JBoss should be restarted.

We can easily check to see if the resource was installed by using the JBoss jmx-console application. Using a browser from the same machine as JBoss, enter in the following URL:

```
http://localhost:8080/jmx-console
```

Scroll down to the section titled jboss.jca and look for lines that begin with name=MySqlDS, as shown in Figure 13.4.

Once this is successful, we are ready to start writing some Java code.

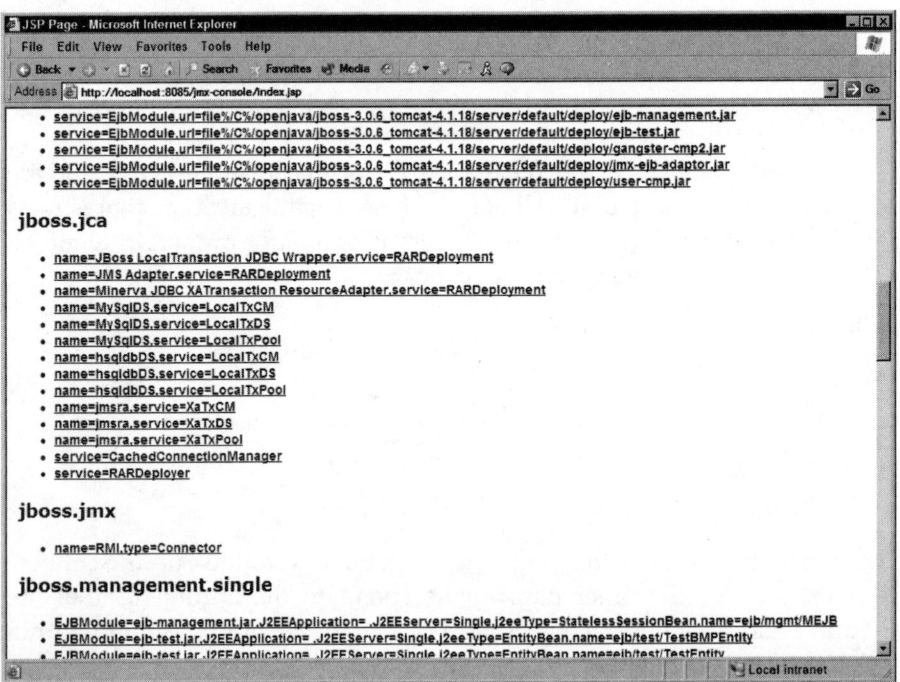

Figure 13.4 JBoss jmx-console screen.

Creating the Data Transfer Object

We will need to be able to pass user objects around between the different layers of our application. Java Beans provide a convenient means to do this. A simple Java Bean that just has `get` and `set` methods for its attributes is called a *value bean* and can be used as a data transfer object (or DTO). The DTO is a standard J2EE design pattern. We will use the DTO to store the state or value of a specific row in the database and pass that state between layers of the application. Although an EJB entity bean also provides access to the state, the entity bean is not convenient to pass around within the application. Also, changes to the entity beans immediately modify the database. We may want to change the value bean and confirm that those changes are valid before we update the database. The following code represents the value bean for our user table:

```
package com.oldfriends.dto;

public class UserDTO extends Object implements java.io.Serializable
{
  private String userid = null;
  private String firstName = null;
  private String lastName = null;
  private String mi = null;
  private String maidenName= null;
  private int gradYear = 0;
  private String email = null;
  private String loginId = null;
  private String password = null;

  /** Creates new BasicUserBean */
  public UserDTO()
  {
  }

  public String getFirstName()
  {
    return( firstName );
  }
  public void setFirstName( String s )
  {
    firstName = s;
  }

  public String getLastName()
  {
    return( lastName);
  }
  public void setLastName( String s )
  {
```

```
    lastName = s;
  }

  public String getMi()
  {
    return( mi );
  }
  public void setMi( String s )
  {
    mi = s;
  }

  public String getMaidenName()
  {
    return( maidenName );
  }
  public void setMaidenName( String s )
  {
    maidenName = s;
  }

  public int getGradYear()
  {
    return( gradYear );
  }
  public void setGradYear( int grad_year )
  {
    gradYear = grad_year;
  }

  public String getLoginId()
  {
    return( loginId );
  }
  public void setLoginId( String s )
  {
    loginId = s;
  }

  public String getPassword()
  {
    return( password );
  }
  public void setPassword( String s )
  {
    password = s;
  }

  public String getEmail()
  {
    return( email );
  }
```

```
    public void setEmail( String s )
    {
      email = s;
    }
    public String getUserid()
    {
        return userid;
    }
    public void setUserid( String uid)
    {
        userid = uid;
    }
  }
```

Once again, we have kept this simple. Normally, you might have added several constructors and functions to test for equality, generate hash values, and clone instances of the class. The userDTO class implements the serializable interface. Serializable is a *marker interface* that has no methods. Marker interfaces allow others classes to easily test if a class supports a particular feature. This one is provided to inform other classes that instances of this class can be written and read from streams.

Creating the User Entity Bean

Entity beans are persistent Enterprise Java Beans. It is easiest to think of an entity bean as corresponding to a specific row in a database table or result set. Entity bean persistence can be managed either by the EJB container (CMP) or by the programmer (BMP). We will implement a CMP bean for the User domain object. The CMP Bean class must be an abstract class that implements the `javax.ejb.EntityBean` interface. The EJB container generates a concrete class that extends this class when the bean is deployed. The following code shows this class:

```
package com.oldfriends.ejb;

import com.oldfriends.dto.UserDTO;
import com.oldfriends.utils.KeyMaker;
import java.lang.*;

/** Entity bean representing an application user
 * @author John T. Bell
 */
public abstract class UserEjb implements javax.ejb.EntityBean
{
  public UserEjb(){}
  public String ejbCreate(
    String firstName,
    String lastName,
```

```
  String mi,
  String maidenName,
  int gradYear,
  String loginId,
  String email,
  String password
  )
  throws javax.ejb.CreateException
{
  setUserid();//Dynamically generates a new key value
  setFirstName( firstName );
  setLastName( lastName );
  setMi(mi);
  setMaidenName( maidenName);
  setGradYear( gradYear );
  setLoginId( loginId );
  setPassword( password );
  setEmail( email);
  return null;
}

public String ejbCreate( UserDTO userBean )
  throws javax.ejb.CreateException
{
  setUserid();//Dynamically generates a new key value
  setFirstName( userBean.getFirstName());
  setLastName( userBean.getLastName() );
  setMi(userBean.getMi());
  setMaidenName( userBean.getMaidenName());
  setGradYear( userBean.getGradYear());
  setLoginId( userBean.getLoginId() );
  setPassword( userBean.getPassword() );
  setEmail( userBean.getEmail() );
  return null;
}

public void ejbPostCreate(
  String firstName,
  String lastName,
  String mi,
  String maidenName,
  int gradYear,
  String loginId,
  String email,
  String password
)
{}

private void setUserid()
{
    this.setUserid(KeyMaker.getNewKey());
```

```
    }

    public void ejbPostCreate( UserDTO userBean ){}

    public abstract String getUserid();
    public abstract void setUserid( String uid );

    public abstract String getFirstName() ;
    public abstract void setFirstName( String firstName ) ;
    public abstract String getLastName() ;
    public abstract void setLastName( String lastName ) ;
    public abstract String getMi() ;
    public abstract void setMi( String mi ) ;
    public abstract String getMaidenName() ;
    public abstract void setMaidenName( String maidenName ) ;
    public abstract int getGradYear() ;
    public abstract void setGradYear( int gradYear ) ;
    public abstract String getLoginId() ;
    public abstract void setLoginId( String loginId ) ;
    public abstract String getPassword() ;
    public abstract void setPassword( String password ) ;
    public abstract String getEmail() ;
    public abstract void setEmail( String email ) ;

    public void ejbLoad(){}
    public void ejbStore(){}
    public void ejbActivate(){}
    public void ejbPassivate(){}
    public void setEntityContext(javax.ejb.EntityContext ctx){}
    public void unsetEntityContext(){}
    public void ejbRemove() throws javax.ejb.RemoveException{}

}
```

Notice that the only code is in the `ejbCreate` methods and the private `setUserid()` method. The `setUserid()` method is called by the `ejbCreate` methods to generate a new GUID when adding a record to the database. Neither `ejbCreate` method accepts a value for the userid column of the database. Instead, it calls the `setUserid()` method, which in turn calls a utility class that generates a new value for the primary key. The following code shows this utility class:

```
package com.oldfriends.utils;
import org.jboss.util.id.GUID;

public class KeyMaker
{
    void KeyMaker(){}
    public static String getNewKey()
    {
```

```
        GUID guid = new GUID();
        return guid.toString();
    }
}
```

We want this in a separate class because we have used a function that is specific to JBoss to create the key.

NOTE **When you want to move this code to another container besides JBoss, you will want to replace this class with one that is not tied to this JBoss function. We are using the JBoss function just because it is convenient to do so when running in this JBoss environment.**

Creating the Home and LocalHome Interfaces

Normally, an entity bean should never be referenced from outside of the EJB container. Instead, session beans residing in the same container should use the entity bean and provide a facade layer for the outside world. So for entity beans, we want to create a LocalHome interface that session beans can use to create and retrieve instances of the entity bean. If we were going to expose this bean outside of the container, we would also create a home interface. In our case, we will create a home interface just so that we have a convenient means of testing the bean.

GUIDS AND JBOSS

The JBoss GUID() function does not create a standard GUID. A standard GUID is a hex representation of a 128-bit unsigned integer. This 128-bit number can be represented as 16 bytes. Normally, each byte is translated into two hexadecimal digits and represented as a string with dashes inserted to aid in the reading. By convention, the 128 bits are constructed from a combination of the network card Media Access Control (MAC) address, the system clock down to the current tenth of a millisecond, and a random number. This combination is supposed to guarantee uniqueness for the next 100 years or so.

Although there are a number of Java-based GUID generators, most true GUID generators are unsuitable for use in an EJB environment because a native library is needed to read the MAC address from the network card. Some GUID generators get around this by having the MAC address optionally provided as a configuration parameter. Other programs use different values to replace the MAC address. Floyd Marinescu provides a good example of an alternative GUID generator in the book *EJB Design Patterns* (Wiley Publishing, Inc. 2002). The JBoss GUID generator, although not standard, does generate keys that are the correct length and are unique. But notice that the strings are not hexadecimal digits. Still, this is good enough for our current needs.

The following code shows the LocalHome interface:

```
package com.oldfriends.ejb;

import javax.ejb.FinderException;

public interface UserLocalHome extends javax.ejb.EJBLocalHome
{
  public LocalUser create(
    String firstName,
    String lastName,
    String mi,
    String maidenName,
    String loginId,
    String email,
    String password
  );
  public LocalUser create( com.oldfriends.user.UserDTO userBean  );
  public LocalUser findByPrimaryKey(int id) throws FinderException;
  public LocalUser findByLoginId(String id) throws FinderException;
  public LocalUser findByEmail(String email) throws FinderException;
}
```

The LocalHome interface provides two create methods matching the `ejbCreate` methods on our bean. We also expose three finder methods:

findByPrimaryKey. This retrieves an instance based on the userid or primary key of the record.

findByLoginId. This retrieves an instance based on the login_id column.

findByEmail. This retrieves an instance based on the email address.

The container will implement these methods based on values in our deployment descriptor when we deploy the EJB.

The following code shows the `Home` interface:

```
package com.oldfriends.entity;

import com.oldfriends.user.*;
import java.rmi.RemoteException;
import javax.ejb.*;

public interface UserRemoteHome extends javax.ejb.EJBHome
{
  public UserRemote create(
    String firstName,
    String lastName,
    String mi,
    String maidenName,
```

```
      int gradYear,
      String loginId,
      String email,
      String password
    ) throws CreateException, RemoteException;

    public com.oldfriends.entity.UserRemote create( UserDTO userBean  )
      throws CreateException, RemoteException;
    public com.oldfriends.entity.UserRemote findByPrimaryKey(String id)
      throws FinderException, RemoteException;
    public com.oldfriends.entity.UserRemote findByLoginId(String id)
      throws FinderException, RemoteException;
    public com.oldfriends.entity.UserRemote findByEmail(String email)
      throws FinderException, RemoteException;
  }
```

The primary difference here is that the methods on the RemoteHome interface must also throw RemoteException. It is possible to expose different functions in the home and local home interfaces. But remember that in this case we would ordinarily only provide the LocalHome interface; we are providing a home interface just to facilitate testing.

Creating the LocalUser Interface

The local and remote interfaces expose the methods that can be used by the clients of the entity bean. The remote interface is only created for external clients. Because this is an entity bean, we normally only create a local interface but here we will also create a remote interface for testing purposes. Session beans within the same container as the entity bean will use the local interface. When the bean is deployed, the container will create an object that implements this interface. This object is returned when the `create()` and `findByXxx()` methods are executed on the home interface. The following code shows the local interface:

```
package com.oldfriends.entity;

import java.lang.*;
import java.rmi.RemoteException;

public interface UserLocal extends javax.ejb.EJBLocalObject
{

  public String getUserid();
//  public void setUserid(Integer i);
```

```
    public String getFirstName();
    public void setFirstName( String firstName );
    public String getLastName();
    public void setLastName( String lastName );
    public String getMi();
    public void setMi( String mi );
    public String getMaidenName();
    public void setMaidenName( String maidenName );
    public int getGradYear();
    public void setGradYear( int year );
    public String getLoginId();
    public void setLoginId( String loginId );
    public String getPassword();
    public void setPassword( String password );
    public String getEmail();
    public void setEmail( String email );
}
```

The local interface for this bean simply exposes the `getXxx()` and `setXxx()` methods created in the abstract EJB class.

Creating an EJB Deployment Descriptor

Every EJB needs to have an entry in a deployment descriptor. This is the first EJB in our package, so we will create a complete deployment descriptor here and then edit it as we move forward. We will build this file up from fragments so we can explain things as we go along. The deployment descriptor for an EJB is named `ejb-jar.xml` and must appear in the `META-INF` directory of the .jar file that contains the EJB. We will create and edit the file in the `/etc` directory and put it into the `META-INF` directory when we build the .jar file. The opening lines of the file are shown in the following code:

```
<?xml version="1.0" encoding="UTF-8"?>
<!DOCTYPE ejb-jar PUBLIC
  '-//Sun Microsystems, Inc.//DTD Enterprise JavaBeans 2.0//EN'
  'http://java.sun.com/dtd/ejb-jar_2_0.dtd'>
```

The first line is standard for most XML documents and provides the XML version and the document encoding information. The second line provides the reference for the DTD or data type definition for the document. The first quoted string after `PUBLIC` is the public ID. This is specific to the version of the DTD. The next quoted string is a URL that describes where a copy of the DTD can be found. Often, it is handy to replace the DTD URL with a URL for local copy of the DTD. If you are using an XML editor, it is useful to have the DTDs because the editor can assist with identifying errors as you create the document.

All EJB deployment descriptors start with the <ejb-jar> element, as shown in the following fragment:

```
<ejb-jar>
    <display-name>chapter13</display-name>
    <enterprise-beans>
<!-- Define the Entity Beans here -->
```

The display name is optional but is recommended for those environments that provide a management interface for the container. The <enterprise-beans> tag starts the section for describing the beans that will be deployed with this file.

The <entity> tag (shown in the following fragment below) starts the definition of our entity bean. There is one entity tag for each entity bean being deployed:

```
<entity>
    <display-name>UserEJB</display-name>
    <ejb-name>UserEJB</ejb-name>
    <home>com.oldfriends.entity.UserRemoteHome</home>
    <remote>com.oldfriends.entity.UserRemote</remote>
    <local-home>com.oldfriends.entity.UserLocalHome</local-home>
    <local>com.oldfriends.entity.UserLocal</local>
    <ejb-class>com.oldfriends.entity.UserEjb</ejb-class>
```

The display name is again optional but useful to have. The <home>, <remote>, <local-home>, and <local> tags provide the fully qualified class names for the matching interfaces. The <ejb-class> tag provides the fully qualified class name for the class that implements the entity bean. The next piece of our deployment descriptor follows:

```
    <persistence-type>Container</persistence-type>
    <prim-key-class>java.lang.String</prim-key-class>
    <reentrant>False</reentrant>
```

The <persistence-type> describes who has the responsibility for storing the bean and must be either Container or Bean. The <prim-key-class> provides the fully qualified class name of the class that represents the primary key in the database. Note that if the key column in the database were an integer, you would want to use java.lang.Integer because the Java int type is not a class and cannot be used. reentrant describes whether the bean code is suitable for reentrant calls; a reentrant is a call on a method before a previous call to the same method has completed. This is normally set to False.

NOTE The values for all elements are case sensitive. For example the values True and False must be represented with the uppercase first letter, and the Container value in the <persistence-type> element must start with an uppercase C.

The next fragment of the deployment descriptor (shown below) provides information required for container-managed persistence:

```
<cmp-version>2.x</cmp-version>
<abstract-schema-name>User</abstract-schema-name>
<cmp-field>
    <field-name>userid</field-name>
</cmp-field>
<cmp-field>
    <field-name>email</field-name>
</cmp-field>
<cmp-field>
    <field-name>firstName</field-name>
</cmp-field>
<cmp-field>
    <field-name>gradYear</field-name>
</cmp-field>
<cmp-field>
    <field-name>lastName</field-name>
</cmp-field>
<cmp-field>
    <field-name>loginId</field-name>
</cmp-field>
<cmp-field>
    <field-name>maidenName</field-name>
</cmp-field>
<cmp-field>
    <field-name>mi</field-name>
</cmp-field>
<cmp-field>
    <field-name>password</field-name>
</cmp-field>
```

The <cmp-version> tag describes the version of container-managed persistence we will be supporting. Our bean is written for the CMP 2.0 version of the specification, as should be the case for all new entity beans. <abstract-schema-name> is required and provides a reference to the schema that will be used in EJB QL statements. For a CMP bean, every attribute that needs to be managed by the container must be listed within <cmp-field> tags, as shown.

Next, we have to identify which of the fields defined above represents the primary key. This is done with the <primkey-field> as follows:

```
<primkey-field>userid</primkey-field>
```

Our entity bean supports two custom queries beyond the standard `findByPrimaryKey` method. In CMP 2.0, the container implements these methods, but we have to provide it with the queries. The queries provided to the container are not standard SQL as you might expect but are instead a specialized variant called EJB QL. The first query shown below implements the `findByLoginId` method exposed in the home and LocalHome interfaces.

```
<query>
    <query-method>
      <method-name>findByLoginId</method-name>
      <method-params>
        <method-param>java.lang.String</method-param>
      </method-params>
    </query-method>
    <ejb-ql>
    <![CDATA[SELECT OBJECT(u) FROM User u WHERE u.loginId=?1]]>
    </ejb-ql>
</query>
```

The value of the <method-name> tag must correspond to the method in the home interfaces. Each <method-param> tag provides the fully qualified class name for the arguments for the query. Our query accepts a single `java.lang.String` argument. The query itself appears in the <ejb-ql> element.

NOTE The query must appear within a CDATA element so that the query does confuse the XML parser and get mistaken for XML markup.

The query in this case is:

```
SELECT OBJECT(u) FROM User u WHERE u.loginId=?1
```

The `?1` will be replaced with the string described in the <method-param> tag when the query is executed. The word `User` after `FROM` in `FROM User` is the <abstract-schema-name> described previously. The following code shows the second query for `findByEmail`:

```
<query>
    <query-method>
      <method-name>findByEmail</method-name>
      <method-params>
```

```
            <method-param>java.lang.String</method-param>
          </method-params>
        </query-method>
        <ejb-ql>
        <![CDATA[SELECT OBJECT(u) FROM User u WHERE u.email=?1]]>
        </ejb-ql>
    </query>
```

The final fragment, which closes the open tags, completes the `ejb-jar` file for now:

```
        </entity>
    </enterprise-beans>
</ejb-jar>
```

But wait, there's more. JBoss has some JBoss-specific deployment information that it needs. The next section gives you a look at these files.

Object Relational Mapping and the jbosscmp-jdbc.xml File

As we have discussed previously, the container generates most of the code for a CMP entity bean. The process of mapping columns in a relational database to object attributes is called object relational mapping or O/R Mapping. The container needs to have some means to know how the columns in the database correspond to `get` and `set` methods in the entity bean. Unfortunately, the EJB standard does not prescribe a uniform way to do this. Each EJB container normally has its own container-specific way to map database columns to class attributes. For CMP 2.0, JBoss uses an XML file named `jbosscmp-jdbc.xml` to describe this mapping. This file must appear in the `META-INF` directory of the EJB .jar file along with the `ejb-jar.xml` file described in the previous section.

The following code shows the first fragment containing the document description and the root element:

```
<?xml version="1.0" encoding="UTF-8"?>
<!DOCTYPE jbosscmp-jdbc PUBLIC
  '-//JBoss//DTD JBOSSCMP-JDBC 3.0//EN'
  'file://C:\jboss-3.0.6_tomcat-4.1.18\docs\dtd\jbosscmp-jdbc_3_0.dtd'>
<jbosscmp-jdbc>
    <enterprise-beans>
```

Instead of using the remote URL for the DTD, we have elected to use the local copy installed by JBoss. The <jbosscmp-jdbc> element is the root element, and the <enterprise-beans> element provides a container for the entity elements to follow.

```
<entity>
    <ejb-name>UserEJB</ejb-name>
    <datasource>java:/jdbc/MySqlDS</datasource>
    <datasource-mapping>mySQL</datasource-mapping>
    <create-table>false</create-table>
    <remove-table>false</remove-table>
    <table-name>users</table-name>
```

The value of the <ejb-name> element must match the corresponding name in the `ejb-jar.xml` file. The <datasource> element contains the JNDI (Java Naming and Directory Interface) name for the DataSource that will be used to retrieve and store the data. This is the same DataSource that we set up earlier in the chapter. The <datasource-mapping> element is used by JBoss to perform database-specific conversions.

JBoss provides the ability to automatically create and destroy the appropriate tables in the database as the bean is deployed or undeployed. In general, we find that this is a bad idea. The database will be dropped and lose all of its data whenever the bean is undeployed from the container if <remove-table> is set to true. We find that we are too likely to undeploy my beans without consideration for the database so this is too dangerous for our tastes. Finally, the <table-name> tag must be an exact match of the table name in the database.

The following code shows the mapping between the columns of the table and the attributes of the EJB:

```
<cmp-field>
    <field-name>userid</field-name>
    <column-name>userid</column-name>
</cmp-field>
<cmp-field>
    <field-name>email</field-name>
    <column-name>email</column-name>
</cmp-field>
<cmp-field>
    <field-name>firstName</field-name>
    <column-name>first_name</column-name>
</cmp-field>
<cmp-field>
    <field-name>gradYear</field-name>
    <column-name>grad_class</column-name>
</cmp-field>
<cmp-field>
    <field-name>lastName</field-name>
    <column-name>last_name</column-name>
</cmp-field>
<cmp-field>
    <field-name>loginId</field-name>
    <column-name>login_id</column-name>
```

```
</cmp-field>
<cmp-field>
    <field-name>maidenName</field-name>
    <column-name>maiden_name</column-name>
</cmp-field>
<cmp-field>
    <field-name>mi</field-name>
    <column-name>mi</column-name>
</cmp-field>
<cmp-field>
    <field-name>password</field-name>
    <column-name>password</column-name>
</cmp-field>
```

Each attribute with a `get` or `set` method in the local (or remote) interface must be covered here. The <field-name> element corresponds to the `get` and `set` method names exposed in the interface. For example, `password` corresponds to the `getPassword` and `setPassword` methods in the UserLocal and UserRemote interfaces. The value of the <column-name> attribute must be an exact match with the column name in the database.

The three tags shown below close the open tags in the file and complete the `jbosscmp-jdbc.xml` file.

```
        </entity>
    </enterprise-beans>
</jbosscmp-jdbc>
```

NOTE JBoss also supports the older CMP 1.0 persistence mechanism. For CMP 1.0, JBoss requires a different file, named `jaws.xml`,to handle the O/R mapping for CMP 1.0 beans. Because CMP 1.0 is being depricated, we do not cover it here.

NOTE The file `jbosscmp-jdbc.xml` is not required for bean-managed persistence (BMP) beans.

There is still one more JBoss-specific file that is needed for our bean, as discussed in the next section.

The JBoss.xml File

JNDI is used to retrieve home and LocalHome interfaces from the EJB container. The `jboss.xml` file tells the JBoss container how to assign JNDI names to the interfaces. The following code shows the entire jboss.xml file for our current example:

```
<?xml version="1.0" encoding="UTF-8"?>
<!DOCTYPE jboss PUBLIC
  "-//JBoss//DTD JBOSS//EN"
  'file://C:\openjava\jboss-3.0.6_tomcat-4.1.18\docs\dtd\jboss_3_0.dtd'>
<jboss>
    <enterprise-beans>
        <entity>
            <ejb-name>UserEJB</ejb-name>
            <jndi-name>ejb/UserEJB</jndi-name>
            <local-jndi-name>ejb/LocalUserEJB</local-jndi-name>
        </entity>
    </enterprise-beans>
</jboss>
```

An entry should exist in this file for each bean to be deployed. The <ejb-name> corresponds to the <ejb-name> that appears in the ejb-jar.xml file. The <jndi-name> provides the JNDI name that will be used to retrieve the home interface. The <local-jndi-name> provides the JNDI name that will be used to retrieve the LocalHome interface.

Compiling the Bean

We will use Ant to compile the bean. Ant uses a file named build.xml to describe how to build a project. In this section, we will cover the build.xml file needed to compile our code, construct the .jar file, and deploy the .jar file to JBoss. This build file is based on Ant version 1.5. Following are the first two lines of this file:

```
<?xml version="1.0" encoding="UTF-8"?>
<project basedir="." default="compile" name="oldfriends">
```

Each Ant build file must start with a project. The project attributes define the base directory for the project, the default target for the project, and the project name. The base directory is used as the relative directory for all directory accesses. The default target will be executed if no other target is requested on the command line. The name serves as the project name and is available as a reference through the build file.

Ant provides the ability to set properties that can used throughout the file. These can also be stored in a properties file, as is shown in Chapter 10.

```
<property name="app.name" value="oldfriends"/>
<property name="jar.name" value="user-cmp"/>
```

```
<property name="jboss.home" value="C:/jboss-3.0.6_tomcat-4.1.18"/>
<property name="jboss.deploy"
    value="${jboss.home}/server/default/deploy"/>
<property name="lib.dir" value="${jboss.home}/client"/>
```

These lines should be edited to reflect the values needed for your system. You can replace these parameters with their values by using the `${parameter_name}` notation within the attributes of any tag.

Ant provides a very useful capability to build classpaths. The next lines build a classpath that includes every .jar file in the client subdirectory of the JBoss distribution.

```
<path id="oldfriends.classpath">
    <fileset dir="${lib.dir}">
        <include name="*.jar"/>
    </fileset>
</path>
```

The next line is the first target in the build file. A target is something that Ant will try to build. This target is the "`init`" target and is designed to handle any initialization that might be needed. It doesn't do anything yet, but is provided as a placeholder to meet future needs.

```
<target name="init"/>
```

The next target, shown here, has the responsibility for compiling our code:

```
<target depends="init" name="compile">
    <javac classpathref="oldfriends.classpath"
           debug="true"
           deprecation="true"
           destdir="."
           srcdir=".">
    </javac>
</target>
```

The target invokes the Java compiler by using the `javac` task. A task is something that Ant knows how to do. Ant has a number of predefined tasks, and new tasks can be added by writing Java code for Ant. The `javac` task uses the previously defined `classpath` by including a `classpathref` attribute. The `destdir` and `srcdir` attributes provide the option to compile the code in one directory and send the class files to a different directory. The other attributes correspond to compiler command-line arguments. This target depends on the `init` target. This means that Ant will not execute this target until after the `init` target is up to date.

The next target, shown in the following code, builds the .jar file:

```
<target depends="compile" name="jar">
    <jar jarfile="${jar.name}.jar" update="no">
        <fileset dir=".">
            <include name="**/*.class"/>
        </fileset>
        <metainf dir="etc"/>
    </jar>
</target>
```

The .jar task will run the .jar utility and copy all of the files described in the fileset to the .jar file. The `metainf` element within the .jar task copies the files in the `/etc` directory into the `META-INF` directory of the .jar file.

NOTE If we try to name the source directory for the `meta-inf` **file** `meta-inf`**, the task copies the files into the .jar directory** `meta-inf/meta-inf`**. This is incorrect. and the best workaround is not to name the directory** `meta-inf`**. Therefore, we call our directory** `/etc`**.**

This is how our `ejb-jar.xml`, `jboss.xml`, and `jbosscmp-jdbc.xml` files are moved to the correct directory within the .jar file.

The next two targets, shown here, provide a convenient means to deploy the .jar file to JBoss or to undeploy it.

```
<target depends="jar" name="deploy">
    <copy file="${jar.name}.jar" todir="${jboss.deploy}"/>
</target>
<target depends="" name="undeploy">
    <delete file="${jboss.deploy}/${jar.name}.jar"/>
</target>
```

The `deploy` target depends on the `jar` target, which in turn depends on the `compile` target. In this way, Ant automatically rebuilds anything that is needed before deploying the .jar file.

One very nice feature of JBoss is that you can start the deployment process simply by copying the .jar file into the proper deployment directory. Likewise, you can simply delete the file to undeploy it. We defined the deployment directory as the default directory earlier in the parameter section of the `build.xml` file.

The next target is a useful utility for removing all of the compiled files.

```
<target depends="init"
    description="Clean all build products." name="clean">
```

```
    <delete>
        <fileset dir=".">
            <include name="**/*.class"/>
        </fileset>
    </delete>
    <delete file="${jar.name}.jar"/>
    <delete dir="apidoc"/>
</target>
</project >
```

We close the XML file by providing the project end tag.
You can run the file using the command:

```
ant deploy
```

If you are successful, the output should look something like the following:

```
Buildfile: build.xml

init:

compile:
    [javac] Compiling 16 source files to C:\mysrc\chapter13

jar:
      [jar] Building jar: C:\mysrc\chapter13\user-cmp.jar

deploy:
     [copy] Copying 1 file to C:\jboss-3.0.6_tomcat-4.1.18\server\
default\deploy

BUILD SUCCESSFUL
Total time: 5 seconds
```

If JBoss is running, the output in the JBoss console when you deploy the bean should be something similar to the following:

```
00:38:29,403 INFO  [EjbModule] Creating
00:38:29,433 INFO  [EjbModule] Deploying UserEJB
00:38:29,503 INFO  [EjbModule] Created
00:38:29,503 INFO  [EjbModule] Starting
00:38:29,753 INFO  [EjbModule] Started
00:38:29,753 INFO  [MainDeployer] Deployed package:
file:/C:/openjava/jboss-3.0.6_tomcat-4.1.18/server/default/deploy/user-
cmp.jar
```

Testing the Bean

Now that we have built and deployed our bean, we want to test it. This was the reason for providing home and remote interfaces for the entity bean. To test the bean, we will create a very small command line-based client. An EJB client in general needs to:

1. Get an InitialContext
2. Use the context to lookup the home interface
3. Get a remote interface from the home interface
4. Execute the methods on the remote interface

The code for the test client follows:

```
import javax.naming.*;
import javax.rmi.PortableRemoteObject;
import javax.ejb.DuplicateKeyException;

import com.oldfriends.entity.UserRemoteHome;
import com.oldfriends.entity.UserRemote;
import com.oldfriends.user.UserDTO;
import java.lang.ClassCastException;
import javax.ejb.EJBHome;
import javax.naming.NamingException;

public class TestUserEJB
{
  private EJBHome getHomeInterface(
    String jndiName, Class theHomeClass )
    throws NamingException, ClassCastException
  {
    Context myctx = null;
    EJBHome home = null;
    try{
      myctx = new InitialContext();
      Object obj = myctx.lookup(jndiName);
      home = (EJBHome)PortableRemoteObject.narrow( obj, theHomeClass );
    }
    catch( Exception e )
    {
      e.printStackTrace();
    }
    return home;
  }

  public void userEntityTest()
  {
    try
```

```
  {
    System.out.println( "Getting Home Interface");
    UserRemoteHome home = (UserRemoteHome)
      getHomeInterface( "ejb/UserEJB",
      com.oldfriends.entity.UserRemoteHome.class);

    System.out.println( "\nRetrieving Records");
    System.out.println( "\nFindByPrimaryKey");
    UserRemote ur =
    home.findByPrimaryKey("0000000-000000-00000000-0-00000000-1");
    System.out.println( "Name:"+
    ur.getFirstName() + " " +
    ur.getLastName()+" "+ur.getUserid());

    System.out.println( "\nFindByEmail");
    ur = home.findByEmail("janedoe@someaddr.org");
    System.out.println( "Name:"+
    ur.getFirstName() + " " +
    ur.getLastName()+" "+ur.getUserid());

    System.out.println("\nFindByLoginId");
    ur = home.findByLoginId("jsmith");
    System.out.println( "Name:"+
    ur.getFirstName() + " " +
    ur.getLastName()+" "+ur.getUserid());

    System.out.println( "\nCreating Record");
    ur = home.create(
    "first",
    "last",
    "x",
    "",
    2003,
    "login",
    "email",
    "password");
    System.out.println( "\nNew user="+ur.getUserid());
    System.out.print( "\nDone ");
  }
  catch (Exception ex)
  {
    System.err.println("Caught an unexpected exception!");
    ex.printStackTrace();
  }
  finally
  {
    System.out.println( "Finally");
  }
}
```

```
    public static void main(String[] args)
    {
      UserClient uc = new UserClient();
      uc.userEntityTest();
    }
  }
```

The private `getHomeInterface` method is used to get the InitialContext and perform the lookup and type conversion for retrieving the home interface from JNDI. The rest of the program performs various lookups on the test data we inserted when we created the database and then adds a new record to the table.

You can use Ant to run the program. The following Ant task configures the classpath and runs the program:

```
<target depends="compile" name="run-test">
  <java classname="TestUserEJB" dir="." fork="true">
    <classpath>
       <pathelement location="."/>
       <path refid="oldfriends.classpath"/>
    </classpath>
  </java>
</target>
```

To execute the program using Ant, enter the following command on the command line:

```
ant run-test
```

The output should look something like the text shown below:

```
Buildfile: build.xml

init:

compile:

run-test:
     [java] Getting Home Interface

     [java] Retrieving Records

     [java] FindByPrimaryKey
     [java] Name:John Doe 0000000-000000-00000000-0-00000000-1

     [java] FindByEmail
     [java] Name:Jane Doe 0000000-000000-00000000-0-00000000-2
```

```
     [java] FindByLoginId
     [java] Name:Jack Smith 0000000-000000-00000000-0-00000000-3

     [java] Creating Record

     [java] New user=5c4o042-zbp0i6-ddzhbn2w-1-ddzip0ay-6

     [java] Done Finally

BUILD SUCCESSFUL
Total time: 3 seconds
```

Notice that the new user has a GUID automatically generated for the primary key.

Now that we know we have a working entity bean, we are ready to wrap it with a session bean. The session bean is what servlets and other clients will access to retrieve data from the database.

Creating a Session Facade

The *session facade* is a primary design pattern for enterprise Java development. In general, the facade pattern presents a simpler interface to a complex set of underlying interfaces. The session facade can improve performance in distributed systems. Facades are normally course grained; for example, instead of making many small network round trips to read each field of an entity bean a session facade bundles the fields up into a value bean or DTO for single network transfer. The facade can also represent a single entry point for accessing all of the data related to a particular domain object. In our case, all of the information that can be tied to a user record can be made accessible via the facade. As the underlying application becomes more complex, the facade can remain fairly simple from the client's perspective. The facade also acts as an adapter layer between the client programs and the underlying business components. As the underlying infrastructure changes the clients are only dependent on the facade remaining the same.

Our facade is a stateless session bean that accesses and uses the entity bean we have just created to provide clients with access to the information about users. This information is not necessarily limited to data in the user table. As the system is expanded, we should be able to use this session bean to retrieve information that is stored throughout the database.

Following is the source code for our session bean:

```
package com.oldfriends.session;

import com.oldfriends.entity.UserLocal;
```

```
import com.oldfriends.entity.UserLocalHome;
import com.oldfriends.user.UserDTO;
import com.oldfriends.utils.*;
import java.lang.ClassCastException;
import javax.ejb.*;
import javax.naming.Context;
import javax.naming.NamingException;
import javax.rmi.PortableRemoteObject;

public class UserSessionEJB implements javax.ejb.SessionBean
{
  protected UserLocalHome userHome = null;
  protected SessionContext sessionCtx = null;

  public UserSessionEJB() throws EJBException
  {
  }

  public String getHello() throws EJBException
  {
    return "Hello from UserSessionEJB";
  }

  public UserDTO getUserByUserid(String uid)
  throws EJBException
  {
    UserLocal lu;
    UserDTO user;
    try
    {
      UserLocalHome lh = lookupUserLocalHome();
      lu = lh.findByPrimaryKey(uid);
      return buildUserBean( lu );
    }
    catch(FinderException fe )
    {
      throw new EJBException( "getUser: Could not findkey("+uid+")",fe);
    }
    catch(Exception e)
    {
      throw new EJBException( "getUserByUserid: UID="+uid ,e);
    }
    //      return buildUserBean( lu );
  }

  public UserDTO getUserByLogin( String login )
  throws EJBException
  {
    UserLocal lu;
    try
```

```
    {
      UserLocalHome lh = lookupUserLocalHome();
      lu = lh.findByLoginId(login);
    }
    catch(FinderException fe )
    {
      throw new EJBException( "getUser: Could not findkey("
        + login
        + ")",fe);
    }
    return buildUserBean( lu );
  }

  public UserDTO getUserByEmail( String email )
  throws EJBException
  {
    UserLocal lu;
    try
    {
      UserLocalHome lh = lookupUserLocalHome();
      lu = lh.findByEmail(email);
    }
    catch(FinderException fe )
    {
      throw new EJBException( "getUser: Could not findkey("
        + email
        + ")",fe);
    }
    return buildUserBean( lu );
  }

  private UserDTO buildUserBean( UserLocal lu )
  {
    UserDTO u = new UserDTO();
    u.setFirstName(lu.getFirstName());
    u.setLastName(lu.getLastName());
    u.setMi(lu.getMi());
    u.setMaidenName(lu.getMaidenName());
    u.setGradYear(lu.getGradYear());
    u.setLoginId(lu.getLoginId());
    u.setPassword(lu.getPassword());
    u.setEmail(lu.getEmail());
    u.setUserid(lu.getUserid());
    return u;
  }


  public void updateUser( UserDTO user )
  {
    UserLocal lu;
```

```
    try
    {
      UserLocalHome lh = lookupUserLocalHome();
      lu = lh.findByPrimaryKey(user.getUserid());
      setUser( user, lu );
    }
    catch(FinderException fe )
    {
      throw new EJBException(
      "setUser: Could not findkey("+user.getUserid()+")",fe);
    }
    catch( Exception ex )
    {
      throw new EJBException(
      "updateUser: Unexpected Exception ",ex);
    }
  }

  public UserDTO addUser( UserDTO user )
  {
    UserLocal lu;
    try
    {
      UserLocalHome lh = lookupUserLocalHome();
      lu = lh.create(user);
    }
    catch(CreateException cx )
    {
      throw new EJBException(
      "addUser: could not create user", cx);
    }
    return buildUserBean( lu );
  }

  private void setUser( UserDTO u, UserLocal lu)
  throws EJBException
  {
    lu.setFirstName(u.getFirstName());
    lu.setLastName(u.getLastName());
    lu.setMi(lu.getMi());
    lu.setMaidenName(u.getMaidenName());
    lu.setGradYear(u.getGradYear());
    lu.setLoginId(u.getLoginId());
    lu.setPassword(u.getPassword());
    lu.setEmail(u.getEmail());
  }

  private UserLocalHome lookupUserLocalHome()
  throws EJBException
  {
```

```
    UserLocalHome home;
    if( userHome != null)
      return userHome;
    try
    {
      Context ctx = ResourceLocator.getInitialContext();
      home = (UserLocalHome)ctx.lookup("ejb/LocalUserEJB");
      userHome = home;
    }
    catch( NamingException ne )
    {
      throw(
      new EJBException("UserSessionBean: Problem finding User EJB", ne)
      );
    }
    catch( ClassCastException cce )
    {
      throw(new EJBException("UserSessionBean: Class Cast Fail", cce));
    }
    catch( Exception cce )
    {
      throw new EJBException(
        "lookupUserLocalHome: unexpected exception:", cce);
    }
    return home;
  }

  public UserDTO[] getUsersByYear( int year )
  throws EJBException
  {
    return null;
  }

  public UserDTO[] getAllUsers()
  throws EJBException
  {
    return null;
  }

  public void ejbCreate()
  {
  }

  public void ejbActivate()
  throws javax.ejb.EJBException, java.rmi.RemoteException
  {
  }

  public void ejbPassivate()
  throws javax.ejb.EJBException, java.rmi.RemoteException
```

```
    {
    }

    public void ejbRemove()
    throws javax.ejb.EJBException, java.rmi.RemoteException
    {
    }

    public void setSessionContext(SessionContext sc)
    throws javax.ejb.EJBException, java.rmi.RemoteException
    {
      sessionCtx = sc;
    }
}
```

This should be placed in the `com.oldfriends.session` directory of our project.

The first interesting method here is `getHello()`. `getHello()` is used here as an aid to troubleshooting. This method should always work unless there is something wrong with your deployment.

There are several private methods here that perform useful work for the bean. The private `setUser()` method sets the fields of a UserEJB entity bean from a User DTO object. The `buildUserBean` method does the opposite: it builds the UserDTO based on the contents of a UserEJB instance. The `lookup UserLocalHome()` method does a context lookup once and then stores the home interface for subsequent use. It uses a utility class to provide it with the InitialContext. We will look at this class after the current discussion.

The three methods are

- getUserByUserid
- getUserByLogin
- getUserByEmail

These methods are all used to retrieve individual records from the user table. The record is copied into a UserDTO instance and returned to the client. The attributes of this UserDTO object can be modified, and then the object can be sent to the update user method, which retrieves the matching user record and updates it in the database. The `addUser` method accepts a UserDTO object and creates a new record in the database. The method returns the new record, which makes the primary key available to the client.

Two methods are provided to return arrays of UserDTO objects. The first, `getUsersByYear()` returns an array of all of the users that share the same graduating class as passed as an argument. This method does not use the user entity bean. Instead, it performs a query directly against the MySql DataSource and converts the records in the resulting recordset to an array of UserDTO objects. This array of object is returned. `getAllUsers` is similar, except that it returns the entire user table as an array of UserDTO objects. The reason for doing direct queries is that for this type of data the direct query is normally more efficient than a set of individual queries on the entity beans. The rest of the methods are standard EJB life-cycle methods.

Locating Resources

The ResourceLocator class provides a place to put the code that is used to look up resources in the system. Often resources only need to be looked up once and can be cached for subsequent uses. The ResourceLocator is designed so it can be used by many classes, and it caches the things that it can cache. The source code for the ResourceLocator is provided below:

```
package com.oldfriends.utils;

import java.sql.*;
import javax.ejb.*;
import javax.naming.*;
import javax.rmi.PortableRemoteObject;
import javax.sql.DataSource;

public class ResourceLocator
{
  private static Context ctx;
  private static DataSource datasource;
  private static final String DSNAME = "MySqlDS";

  public static Context getInitialContext()
  throws NamingException, ClassCastException
  {
    Context myctx;
    if( ResourceLocator.ctx == null )
    {
      myctx = new InitialContext();
      ResourceLocator.ctx = myctx;
    }
    else
      myctx = ResourceLocator.ctx;
    return myctx;
  }

  public static EJBHome getLocalHomeInterface(String jndiName)
  throws NamingException, ClassCastException
  {
    Context myctx = ResourceLocator.getInitialContext();
    EJBHome home = (EJBHome)myctx.lookup(jndiName);
    return home;
```

```
    }

    public static EJBHome getHomeInterface(
    String jndiName, Class theHomeClass )
    throws NamingException, ClassCastException
    {
      EJBHome home;
      Context myctx = ResourceLocator.getInitialContext();
      Object obj = myctx.lookup(jndiName);
      home = (EJBHome)PortableRemoteObject.narrow( obj, theHomeClass );
      return home;
    }

    public static DataSource getDataSource( String jndiName )
    throws NamingException
    {
      DataSource ds = null;
      if( ResourceLocator.ctx == null )
      {
        ResourceLocator.ctx = new InitialContext();
      }
      ds = (DataSource)ResourceLocator.ctx.lookup(jndiName);
      return ds;
    }

    public static Connection getConnection()
    throws NamingException, SQLException
    {
      Connection conn;
      if(datasource==null)
      {
        datasource = ResourceLocator
                     .getDataSource(ResourceLocator.DSNAME);
      }
      conn = datasource.getConnection();
      return conn;
    }
  }
```

The ResourceLocator shown here is a very simple, almost minimalist, one. It provides methods to:

- Retrieve and cache the initial context
- Look up and convert LocalHome interfaces
- Look up and convert home interfaces
- Look up and cache DataSources
- Get DataBase connections

Using a ResourceLocator often provides for more efficient access to resources and minimizes the knowledge needed to access the resources in various classes. Use of a ResourceLocator is considered to be a J2EE best practice.

The Home Interface

The following code is the home interface for our session bean. This will be used to create and return an instance of the remote interface to the client:

```
package com.oldfriends.session;

import com.oldfriends.session.UserSessionRemote;
import java.rmi.RemoteException;
import javax.ejb.*;

public interface UserSessionHome extends EJBHome
{
     UserSessionRemote create() throws RemoteException, CreateException;
}
```

The only method we add here is the create method.

The Remote Interface

The code remote interface is shown below. It exposes the methods of the EJB for access by the client:

```
package com.oldfriends.session;

import com.oldfriends.user.UserDTO;
import java.rmi.RemoteException;
import javax.ejb.*;

public interface UserSessionRemote extends javax.ejb.EJBObject
{
  public String getHello()
    throws RemoteException, EJBException;
  public UserDTO getUserByUserid( String userid )
    throws RemoteException, EJBException;
  public UserDTO getUserByLogin( String login)
    throws RemoteException, EJBException;
  public UserDTO getUserByEmail( String login)
    throws RemoteException, EJBException;
  public UserDTO addUser( UserDTO user )
    throws RemoteException, EJBException;
  public void updateUser( UserDTO user )
    throws RemoteException, EJBException;
  public UserDTO[] getUsersByYear( int year )
```

```
    throws RemoteException, EJBException;
  public UserDTO[] getAllUsers()
    throws RemoteException, EJBException;
}
```

Creating a Deployment Descriptor

Now, we need to modify the EJB deployment descriptor `ejb-jar.xml` to add our new session bean. We will start with the file we created earlier, and this time just focus on the additions needed to add our session bean. The first part of this addition is shown below. It should be added immediately after the closing </entity> tag:

```
<session>
  <display-name>UserSession</display-name>
  <ejb-name>UserSession</ejb-name>
  <home>com.oldfriends.session.UserSessionHome</home>
  <remote>com.oldfriends.session.UserSessionRemote</remote>
  <ejb-class>com.oldfriends.session.UserSessionEJB</ejb-class>
  <session-type>Stateless</session-type>
  <transaction-type>Container</transaction-type>
```

The values here are almost identical to those we have already discussed for the entity bean. There are a couple of differences here. The <session-type> can be either `Stateless` or `Stateful`. Ours is a stateless bean. The transaction type is set for the container to manage transactions.

The next section, which follows, is the <ejb-local-ref> element, which is needed so that we can find the entity bean:

```
<ejb-local-ref>
  <ejb-ref-name>ejb/LocalUserEJB</ejb-ref-name>
  <ejb-ref-type>Entity</ejb-ref-type>
  <local-home>com.oldfriends.entity.UserLocalHome</local-home>
  <local>com.oldfriends.entity.UserLocal</local>
  <ejb-link>UserEJB</ejb-link>
</ejb-local-ref>
```

The <ejb- ref-name> value should be set to the JNDI name that is used in our code to retrieve the LocalHome interface of the entity bean. The `<ejb-link>` provides the connection between this JNDI name and the entry for the bean. This will be used in the `jboss.xml` file to complete the JNDI mapping. The <ejb-ref-type> tells the container whether we are referencing an entity bean or a session bean. The <local-home> and <local> elements provide the fully qualified class names for the LocalHome and local interfaces for the bean we are referencing.

The next section is also a reference, but it is a resource reference that will be used to get the DataSource from the container, as you can see in the following code:

```
  <resource-ref>
    <description>DataSource for oldfriends database</description>
    <res-ref-name>java:/jdbc/MySqlDS</res-ref-name>
    <res-type>javax.sql.DataSource</res-type>
    <res-auth>Container</res-auth>
    <res-sharing-scope>Sharable</res-sharing-scope>
  </resource-ref>
</session>
```

The <res-ref-name> is the JNDI name that we use in our code to get the DataSource. The <res-type> element provides the fully qualified class name of the class that is returned by the lookup. The <res-auth> element says that the container has the responsibility for providing username and password needed to generate connections from the DataSource. Finally, <res-sharing-scope> says that this resource is sharable with other beans. The </session> tag ends the changes to the `ejb-jar.xml` file.

Changing the jboss.xml File

Because this is not an entity bean, we do not need to modify the `jbosscmp-jdbc.xml` file. The final changes we need to make for deploying our session bean are made to the `jboss.xml` file. The change is the four following lines:

```
<session>
  <ejb-name>UserSession</ejb-name>
  <jndi-name>ejb/UserSession</jndi-name>
</session>
```

These lines should be added immediately after the </entity> tag that we put into the file earlier.

Rebuilding the .jar File

We do not need to make any changes to the existing Ant script to rebuild the .jar file. It will happily build the new EJB and install the new .jar file by executing the following command:

```
ant deploy
```

If nothing goes wrong, the output will be similar to what we saw earlier when we compiled and deployed the bean under the *Compiling the Bean* section.

Building the Test Client

We will add a new method to our test client to test the new session bean, as shown in the following code:

```
public void userSessionTest()
  {
    UserSessionRemote remote;
    UserSessionHome home;
    System.out.println("userSessionTest:");
    try
    {
      System.out.println( "Getting Home Interface");
      home = (UserSessionHome)getHomeInterface(
      "ejb/UserSession",
      com.oldfriends.session.UserSessionHome.class);

      System.out.println( "Getting Remote Interface");
      remote = home.create();

      System.out.println(remote.toString());

      System.out.println( "Calling getHello");
      System.out.println("Hello:"+remote.getHello());

      System.out.println( "Retrieving Records");
      System.out.println( "getUserByUserid");
      UserDTO udata =
        remote.getUserByUserid("0000000-000000-00000000-0-00000000-1");
      System.out.println( "Name:"+
      udata.getFirstName() + " " +
      udata.getLastName()+" "+udata.getUserid());

      System.out.println( "getUserByLogin");
      udata = remote.getUserByLogin("jsmith");
      System.out.println( "Name:"+
      udata.getFirstName() + " " +
      udata.getLastName()+" "+udata.getUserid());

      System.out.println( "Update User");
      udata.setFirstName("NotJack");
      remote.updateUser(udata);
```

```
        udata = remote.getUserByLogin("jsmith");
        System.out.println( "Name:"+
        udata.getFirstName() + " " +
        udata.getLastName()+" "+udata.getUserid());

        System.out.println( "Add User");
        udata.setFirstName("One");
        udata.setLastName("LastName");
        udata.setMi("Z");
        udata.setMaidenName("");
        udata.setLoginId("lgid");
        udata.setPassword("somepwd");
        udata.setEmail("email@foo.bar");

        udata = remote.addUser(udata);
        System.out.println( "Name:"+
        udata.getFirstName() + " " +
        udata.getLastName()+" "+udata.getUserid());

        remote.remove();
      }
      catch( Exception ex )
      {
        System.err.println(
          "userSessionTest: Caught an unexpected exception!");
        ex.printStackTrace();
      }
      finally
      {
        remote = null;
        home = null;
        System.out.println( "userSessionTest: Finally");
      }
    }
```

The new `userSessionTest` method is similar to the `userEntityTest` method covered earlier, except that it uses the UserDTO object to move user data between the client the EJB container. We demonstrate the session bean methods for retrieving users, updating users, and adding a user to the system. We also need to make a change to the main method so that our new method is executed. The new main method follows:

```
public static void main(String[] args)
{
  UserClient uc = new UserClient();
  uc.userEntityTest();
  uc.userSessionTest();
}
```

We can execute this from Ant without any further changes. Use the following command to run this by using Ant:

```
ant run-test
```

The output will be similar to the output previously observed for the entity bean under the *Testing the Bean* section.

Summary

In this chapter, we presented some of the back-end components for an application that demonstrates some of the capabilities of the J2EE platform that we have created. We introduced some of the relevant use cases and the domain objects, created a database for storing our data, and then created a DataSource within our EJB container to access the database. Then, we went through the entire process for developing, deploying, and testing a container-managed persistence (CMP) entity bean.

After testing the entity bean, we created a session bean that accesses the entity bean and that will serve as a facade for accessing user data on the system. We went through the process of creating the session bean and modifying the deployment files to deploy the session bean with the entity bean previously deployed. Finally, we tested session bean.

The database created in this chapter sits in the enterprise tier of our J2EE platform and represents the data layer of our application. The EJB container is used to access the database and isolate us from database changes. It provides the repository in the business tier of the J2EE platform for our application's business logic. The session facade will be the only interface that is exposed between these layers and the layers to come in the next chapter.

The next chapter builds upon the code created in this chapter. It covers the creation of the presentation layers of the application using a Model-View-Controller design pattern. The presentation layer provides a Web-based user interface for accessing these back-end components.

Throughout the chapter, we have tried to demonstrate best practices for creating J2EE applications, while remaining within the constraints of creating examples that are both complete and easy to understand. The ResourceLocator class is one example of this effort. The code for this chapter and all of the chapters in the book is available as a download from the publisher's Web site supporting this book. We encourage all readers to download the source code and experiment with it themselves.

CHAPTER

14

Building an Application: Assembling the Front End

In this chapter, we continue to build upon the Old Friends Incorporated example that we have used in previous chapters of the book. In Chapter 13, we showed you how to build the back end and middle tiers of an application. In this chapter, we will look at the front-end components that are used to create the presentation layers of the application.

Just to recap, in the previous chapter, we

- Created a database to store our application data
- Created supporting Enterprise Java Beans
- Tested the Enterprise Java Beans

In this chapter, we will

- Create a Servlet that uses the EJBs from the Chapter 13
- Create a Struts application that uses Enterprise Java Beans

The sample applications covered in this chapter assume that the following applications have been downloaded and installed:

- **Tomcat (standalone).** See Chapter 5.
- **Struts.** See Chapter 7.
- **MySql database.** See Chapter 8.

- **JDBC Driver for MySql.** See Chapter 8.
- **JBoss EJB container.** See Chapter 10.
- **The code from Chapter 13.** See Chapter 13.
- **Ant.** See Chapter 4.

NOTE You may also find that the source code from Chapter 7 is useful as a starting point for this chapter.

NOTE As with all chapters, the source code files for this application are all available from the books companion Web site at `http://www.wiley.com/compbooks/bell`.

Building a Test Servlet

We start out by creating a test servlet for the UserSessionEJB that we created in Chapter 13. The test servlet will serve several purposes:

- It demonstrates that the communications between the servlet container and the EJB container are working.
- It provides us with a simple example of how to create and deploy a servlet that accesses an EJB.
- It provides us with an opportunity to create and test an implementation of the BusinessDelegate design pattern. We will reuse this Business Delegate object when we create a Struts-based application later in the chapter.

The Business Delegate Pattern

The Business Delegate pattern is a design pattern that is an example of a reusable design, in same vein as the Model-View-Controller pattern that has been discussed in previous chapters. The purpose of the Business Delegate pattern is to hide the implementation details of the business logic exposed by the business delegate. In this case, we want to hide the fact that the business logic is implemented as an EJB from the servlet or control layer. This layer of abstraction allows us to replace the EJB implementation with another technology if needed at some point in the future. The delegate exposes the methods of the EJB's remote interface as its own methods, but hides the fact that the implementation is implemented through an EJB by performing the operations to get the EJB home and remote interfaces. The source code for our sample UserDelegate class is:

```
package com.oldfriends.user;

import com.oldfriends.session.UserSessionHome;
import com.oldfriends.session.UserSessionRemote;
import com.oldfriends.utils.ResourceLocator;
import java.rmi.RemoteException;
import javax.ejb.EJBException;

public class UserDelegate
{
  UserSessionHome home;
  UserSessionRemote remote;

  /** Creates a new instance of UserDelegate */
  public UserDelegate()
  {
    this.init();
  }
  protected void init()
  {
    try
    {
      home = (UserSessionHome)ResourceLocator.getHomeInterface(
      "ejb/UserSession",
      com.oldfriends.session.UserSessionHome.class);
      remote = home.create();
    }
    catch(Exception e )
    {
    }
  }

  public String getHello()
  throws RemoteException, EJBException
  {
    return remote.getHello();
  }

  public UserDTO getUserByUserid( String userid )
  throws RemoteException, EJBException
  {
    return remote.getUserByUserid(userid);
  }
```

```
    public UserDTO getUserByLogin( String login)
    throws RemoteException, EJBException
    {
      return remote.getUserByLogin(login);
    }

    public UserDTO getUserByEmail( String email )
    throws RemoteException, EJBException
    {
      return remote.getUserByEmail(email);
    }

    public UserDTO addUser( UserDTO user )
    throws RemoteException, EJBException
    {
      return remote.addUser( user );
    }

    public void updateUser( UserDTO user )
    throws RemoteException, EJBException
    {
      remote.updateUser( user );
    }

    public UserDTO[] getUsersByYear( int year )
    throws RemoteException, EJBException
    {
      return remote.getUsersByYear( year );
    }

    public UserDTO[] getAllUsers()
    throws RemoteException, EJBException
    {
      return remote.getAllUsers();
    }

    public void refresh()
    {
      this.init();
    }
  }
```

The `init()` method handles the task of looking up both the home and remote interfaces of our session facade that is implemented as the User SessionEJB. It uses the Resource Locator pattern discussed in the Chapter 13 to get the home interface. The other methods expose the methods of the User SessionRemote interface. This UserDelegate can now be used by any class that needs to access the User information within the system without requiring the class to have any knowledge of how that information is stored or accessed.

The TestUserEJB Servlet

The next step is to create a servlet that uses the UserDelegate class. The source code for the servlet follows:

```
import java.io.*;
import java.net.*;

import javax.servlet.*;
import javax.servlet.http.*;

import com.oldfriends.user.*;
import javax.ejb.*;

public class TestUserEJB extends HttpServlet
{
protected void doGet(
  HttpServletRequest request,
  HttpServletResponse response)
  throws ServletException, IOException
  {
    PrintWriter out = response.getWriter();
    UserDelegate ud;
    try
    {
      ud = new UserDelegate();
      UserDTO udata =
         ud.getUserByUserid("0000000-000000-00000000-0-00000000-1");
      out.println("Hello:"+ud.getHello());
      out.println( "Name:"+
      udata.getFirstName() + " " +
      udata.getLastName()+" "+udata.getUserid());
    }
    catch( Exception e )
    {
      e.printStackTrace(out);
    }

  }
}
```

Note that the servlet has no knowledge that the actual implementation of UserDelegate occurs via an EJB.

Deploying the TestUserEJB Servlet

Web applications are deployed as .war files. .war files require a specific directory structure and a deployment descriptor file called `web.xml`. The directory structure and the required files for this application should appear as follows:

```
TestUserEJB
./WEB-INF/jboss-web.xml
./WEB-INF/web.xml
./WEB-INF/classes/TestUserDelegate.java
./WEB-INF/classes/com/oldfriends/session/UserSessionRemote.java
./WEB-INF/classes/com/oldfriends/session/UserSessionHome.java
./WEB-INF/classes/com/oldfriends/user/UserDelegate.java
./WEB-INF/classes/com/oldfriends/user/UserDTO.java
./WEB-INF/classes/com/oldfriends/utils/ResourceLocator.java
```

The files in bold are new. The other files are reused from the EJB project in the previous chapter. We need to create a deployment descriptor (`web.xml` file) for the application. The `web.xml` file is:

```
<?xml version="1.0" encoding="UTF-8"?>

<!DOCTYPE web-app
    PUBLIC "-//Sun Microsystems, Inc.//DTD Web Application 2.3//EN"
    "http://java.sun.com/dtd/web-app_2_3.dtd">

<web-app>
  <servlet>
    <servlet-name>TestUserEJB</servlet-name>
    <servlet-class>TestUserEJB</servlet-class>
  </servlet>
  <servlet-mapping>
    <servlet-name>TestUserEJB</servlet-name>
    <url-pattern>/servlet/TestUserEJB</url-pattern>
  </servlet-mapping>

  <ejb-ref>
       <ejb-ref-name>ejb/UserSession</ejb-ref-name>
       <ejb-ref-type>Session</ejb-ref-type>
       <home>com.oldfriends.session.UserSessionHome</home>
       <remote>com.oldfriends.session.UserSessionRemote</remote>
       <ejb-link>UserSession</ejb-link>
  </ejb-ref>
</web-app>
```

Note the <ejb-ref> element. It tells the container that an Enterprise Java Bean will be used by the Web application and provides the class and reference information needed to use the bean. This is very similar to the <ejb-ref> tag discussed in the previous chapter for the EJB deployment descriptor.

If we will be deploying this in a servlet container that is configured within JBoss, then we also need a file to provide JBoss-specific deployment information. This file is called `jboss-web.xml` and is included as follows:

```
<?xml version="1.0" encoding="UTF-8"?>
<!DOCTYPE jboss-web PUBLIC
  "-//JBoss//DTD Web Application 2.3//EN"
  'file://C:\openjava\jboss-3.0.6_tomcat-4.1.18\docs\dtd\jboss-
web_3_0.dtd'>

<jboss-web>
  <ejb-ref>
    <ejb-ref-name>ejb/UserSession</ejb-ref-name>
    <jndi-name>UserSession</jndi-name>
  </ejb-ref>
</jboss-web>
```

This simply provides the mapping between the jndi-name used to locate the home interface of the EJB and the reference used on the servlet code. This file is not needed if the servlet container is external to JBoss.

Compiling the TestUserEJB Application

The following `build.xml` file can be used with Ant to compile the application and create a .war file for deployment into JBoss.

```
<?xml version="1.0" encoding="UTF-8"?>
<project basedir="." default="compile" name="ch14">
  <property name="app.name" value="ch14"/>
  <property name="jboss.home"
            value="C:/openjava/jboss-3.0.6_tomcat-4.1.18"/>
  <property name="jboss.deploy"
            value="${jboss.home}/server/default/deploy"/>
  <property name="lib.dir" value="${jboss.home}/client"/>

  <path id="build.classpath">
    <fileset dir="${lib.dir}">
      <include name="*.jar"/>
    </fileset>
  </path>

  <target name="init">
  </target>

  <target depends="init" name="compile">
    <javac
      classpathref="build.classpath"
      debug="true"
```

```
        deprecation="true"
        destdir="./WEB-INF/classes"
        srcdir="./WEB-INF/classes">
      </javac>
    </target>

    <target depends="compile" name="war">
      <war destfile="${app.name}.war"
         update="no"
         excludes="build.xml"
         webxml="./WEB-INF/web.xml">
        <fileset dir=".">
          <include name="**/*.jar"/>
          <include name="**/*.class"/>
          <include name="**/*.java"/>
          <include name="**/*.xml"/>
          <exclude name="**/web.xml"/>
        </fileset>
      </war>
    </target>

    <target depends="war" name="all"/>
    <target depends="war" name="deploy">
      <copy file="${app.name}.war" todir="${jboss.deploy}"/>
    </target>
    <target depends="war" name="undeploy">
      <delete file="${jboss.deploy}/${app.name}.war"/>
    </target>
  </project>
```

The .war target compiles any code that still needs to be compiled and builds the .war file. Make certain you edit the `jboss.home` and `app.name` properties near the top of the file to reflect the values for your system. You can include the Java source code in your .war files so that they can be edited in place. If you do not want to include the source code, then remove the line in the .war task that reads:

```
<include name="**/*.java"/>
```

Running the TestUserEJB Application

The application can be deployed into JBoss using the deploy task in the `build.xml` file. The application can then be executed with the following URL:

```
http://localhost:8080/ch14/servlet/TestUserEJB
```

The response should consist of the following lines:

```
Hello:Hello World!
Name:John Doe 0000000-000000-00000000-0-00000000-1
```

Using a Remote EJB Container

The application can be executed on an instance of Tomcat that is separate from the JBoss instance by providing it with the JBoss client files and changing the way the ResourceLocator class finds the InitialContext. To do this, copy the files from the client folder below the `JBOSS_HOME` directory into the `WEB-INF/lib` directory for the application.

Next, add the following method to the ResourceLocator class. This method allows us to provide initialization parameters to specify a particular `InitContext()` instance:

```
public static Context getInitialContext(Properties props)
    throws NamingException, ClassCastException
{
    Context myctx;
    if( ResourceLocator.ctx == null )
    {
        myctx = new InitialContext( props );
        ResourceLocator.ctx = myctx;
    }
    else{
        myctx = ResourceLocator.ctx;
    }
    return myctx;
}
```

The simplest thing to do here is to change the call to `getInitialContext()` so that it passes in an initialized Properties instance as follows:

```
Properties props = new Properties();
props.setProperty(
  "java.naming.factory.initial",
  "org.jnp.interfaces.NamingContextFactory");
props.setProperty(
  "java.naming.factory.url.pkgs",
  "org.jboss.naming:org.jnp.interfaces");
props.setProperty(
  "java.naming.provider.url",
  "localhost:1099");
ResourceLocator.getInitialContext( props );
```

The line that reads "`localhost:1099`" should be set to the machine name for the JBoss server and the port that the JNDI service is configured on. After this is completed, the code can be recompiled and deployed on a separate Tomcat server by dropping the .war file into Tomcat's `webapps` directory.

NOTE On a production system, you would want to read the properties from the `web.xml` file or a `jndi.properties` file and not use String constants. This allows the parameters to be changed at deployment time without editing and recompiling the program.

A better method to perform this initialization is shown in the following servlet code. This servlet can be deployed with the application to preconfigure the ResourceLocator with information passed from the `web.xml` file.

```
import com.oldfriends.utils.ResourceLocator;
import java.io.*;
import java.net.*;
import java.util.Properties;
import javax.naming.NamingException;

import javax.servlet.*;
import javax.servlet.http.*;

public class AppInit extends HttpServlet
{
  public void init()
  throws ServletException
  {
    super.init();
    Properties props = new Properties();
    props.setProperty("java.naming.factory.initial",
      getInitParameter("java.naming.factory.initial"));
    props.setProperty("java.naming.factory.url.pkgs",
      getInitParameter("java.naming.factory.url.pkgs"));
    props.setProperty("java.naming.provider.url",
      getInitParameter("java.naming.provider.url"));
    try
    {
      ResourceLocator.getInitialContext(props);
    }
    catch( NamingException ne )
    {
      throw new ServletException("Could not get InitialContext", ne );
    }
  }
}
```

The following entries should be made to the `web.xml` file to support this servlet:

```
<servlet>
    <servlet-name>AppInit</servlet-name>
    <servlet-class>AppInit</servlet-class>
    <init-param>
      <param-name>java.naming.factory.initial</param-name>
      <param-value>org.jnp.interfaces.NamingContextFactory</param-value>
    </init-param>
    <init-param>
      <param-name>java.naming.factory.url.pkgs</param-name>
      <param-value>org.jboss.naming:org.jnp.interfaces</param-value>
    </init-param>
    <init-param>
      <param-name>java.naming.provider.url</param-name>
      <param-value>localhost:1099</param-value>
    </init-param>
    <load-on-startup>1</load-on-startup>
  </servlet>
```

The parameter value for the `java.naming.provider.url` parameter should be set to the machine name or IP address and port of the machine running the JBoss server. The <load-on-startup> element ensures that the `init` function of this servlet will be executed before any other servlets within the application. Now, we can change the JBoss container being used simply by editing the `web.xml` file and restarting the application.

Build an Application Using Struts

Now, we are ready to build our application using the Struts framework. Struts provides an implementation of the Model-View-Controller (MVC) design pattern for implementing the presentation layers of our application. Struts is built on servlet and JSP technology.

CROSS-REFERENCE Chapter 7 provides an overview of Struts and the example in Chapter 7 provides the starting point for our code in this chapter.

The Scenario

We will provide a very brief version of the scenario here. (If you would like more information please see the discussion in the Chapter 13.) Old Friends Incorporated is creating a software package for high-school reunions. In this sample program, we are supporting two primary functions against the user database: self-registration, where a new user record is created and added to the database, and profile editing, which allows the editing of the user record. In addition, we will support listing the names and email addresses of other members in the same class. The supporting database and Enterprise Java Beans were developed in Chapter 13. This chapter develops the presentation layer, or user interface, to those functions. We will use the code presented as an example in Chapter 7 as a starting point.

Setting Up the Directory Structure for Development

There are several things we need to do to prepare for developing our application. We will start by creating the directory structure we need to support the software development and then copying the files we need into the appropriate directories. This project will build on source code introduced in previous chapters, so we need to copy those classes so that they are available to our new classes.

It is helpful to have a predefined directory structure when starting on any project involving EJB development. A sample directory structure is provided here. You should create a similar directory structure and copy the needed files into the proper directories

DIRECTORY	WHAT IT CONTAINS
/chapter14/.	Serves as the base directory for all files and subdirectories. The ant `build.xml` and the final deployment .war file are all located in this directory. All other subdirectories are below this one.
./oldfriends/.	The base directory for the .war file. Our HTML and JSP files will reside here.
./oldfriends/WEB-INF.	This is the servlet WEB-INF directory. The `web.xml` file is found here.
./WEB-INF/classes/com/oldfriends/utils.	Copy the classes from the EJB `utils` directory here.
./WEB-INF/classes/com/oldfriends/user.	Copy the classes from the EJB `user` directory here.
./WEB-INF/classes/com/oldfriends/session.	The home and remote interfaces for the session bean are needed here.
./WEB-INF/lib.	`struts.jar` goes here. If you will be using a remote instance of JBoss, you will also need to have the JBoss client files here.

The UserDTO class is a data transfer object (DTO), sometimes called a *value bean*. It stores a representation of the user record that is convenient to pass between the various layers of the application. The UserDTO class was developed in the Chapter 13 and should be located in the following directory:

```
chapter14/oldfriends/WEB-INF/classes/com/oldfriends/user
```

We will also use the resource locator class to help us look up and find the home interface for the UserSession bean. This class should be located in the following directory:

```
chapter14/oldfriends/WEB-INF/classes/com/oldfriends/utils
```

The `struts.jar` file must go in the `lib` directory. Depending on how we deploy the application, we may add additional .jar files to this directory later. For now, we will just place `struts.jar` here.

We will reuse the UserDelegate class that we created as a part of the Test UserEJB example presented earlier in this chapter.

Application Flow

The diagram in Figure 14.1 represents the page-navigation structure of our application. In the diagram, each JSP is shown as being connected to one or more actions. Each action supports either a simple success or a failure of the action that determines the next JSP page to present.

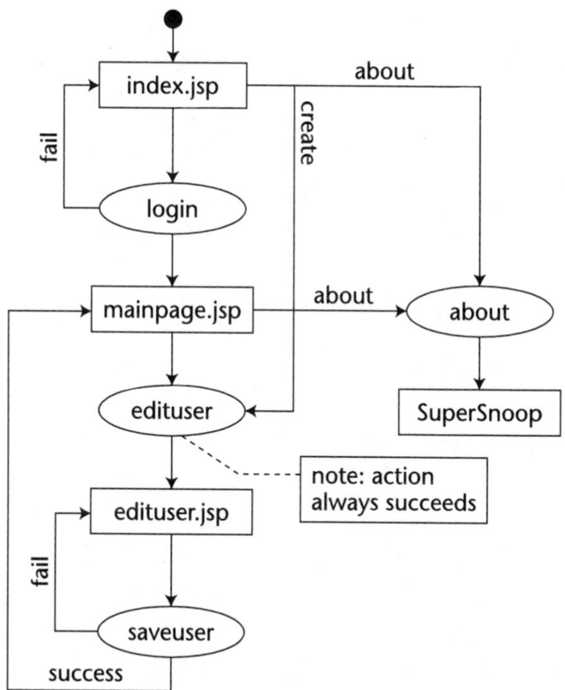

Figure 14.1 Our application's page-navigation structure.

The initial page is `index.jsp`, which presents three choices of "actions" to the user. The actions are accessed by the user via buttons that will be presented in the Web pages generated by the JSP. Figure 14.2 shows the initial application screen.

The user is presented with three choices: log in by completing the form with a login ID and password, register a new account, or click the About button. The connection to the `about` action is shown on the side to help make the illustration of the primary paths through the application clearer. Once logged in, the user is presented with the main page where the user may update his or her profile or click the About button. Later, additional choices will be added here to allow the user to list classmates and sign up for events.

Login

We start by creating the code needed to log into the site. In this case, we will start by creating an ActionForm class LoginForm.java. The source code for the class follows:

```
import javax.servlet.http.*;
import org.apache.struts.action.*;

public class LoginForm extends ActionForm
{
  private String loginId = null;
  private String password = null;
  private int noValidate = 0;

  public String getLoginId()
  {
    return loginId;
  }
  public void setLoginId( String login )
  {
    loginId=login;
  }

  public String getPassword()
  {
    return password;
  }
  public void setPassword( String pass )
  {
    password=pass;
  }

  public ActionErrors validate(
  ActionMapping aMapping,
```

```
    HttpServletRequest aR)
    {
      ActionErrors err = new ActionErrors();
      if( noValidate==0)
      {
        if ((loginId == null) || (loginId.length() < 1))
          err.add("loginId", new ActionError("error.loginid"));
        if ((password == null) || (password.length() < 1))
          err.add("password", new ActionError("error.password"));
      }
      return err;
    }

    public void noValidate(int in)
    {
      noValidate=in;
    }

    public void reset(ActionMapping aMapping, HttpServletRequest aR)
    {
      loginId = null;
      password = null;
    }
}
```

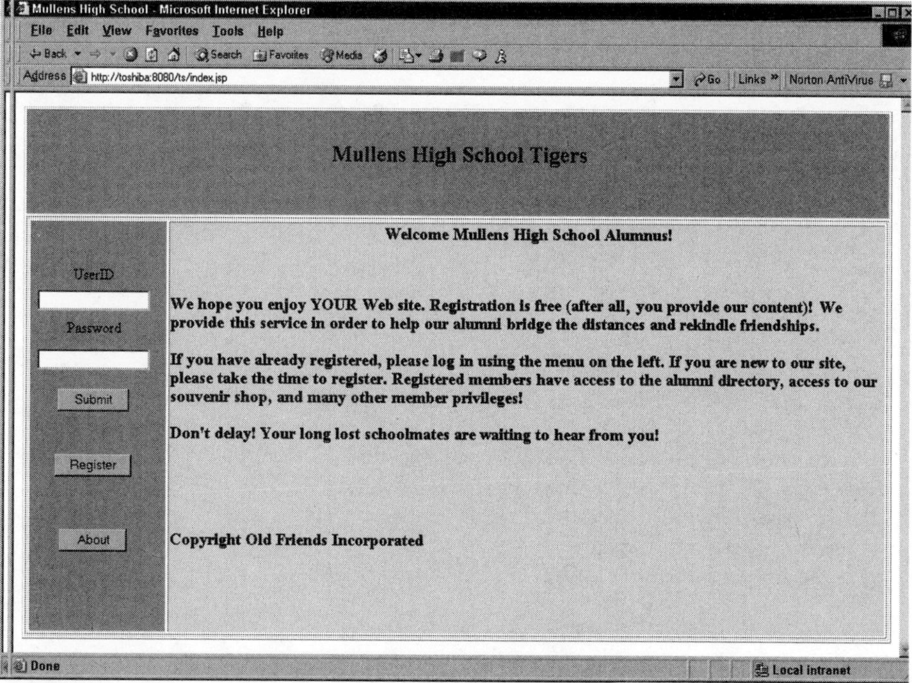

Figure 14.2 Initial screen for Old Friends Incorporated application.

This class collects the login ID and password information from the login form represented in the file `index.jsp` (the listing for `index.jsp` can be found in Chapter 7). We will use this ActionForm in the Action class to validate our user against the database.

The following line should be inserted into the <form-beans> element `struts-config.xml`:

```
<form-bean name="loginForm" type="LoginForm" />
```

where `name` is the name that we will use to reference this bean in our code and JSP files, and `type` is the name of the class that implements the bean.

Creating the LoginAction Class

The action class represents the controller logic for the application. For the Login Action, we need to accept the credentials offered and try to find a matching record in the database. If a match is found, then we will go to the main page. Otherwise, we need to print an error message and return to the login page. The code for the LoginAction class is:

```
import javax.servlet.http.*;
import org.apache.struts.action.*;
import com.oldfriends.user.*;

public class LoginAction extends Action
{

  /** Creates a new instance of LoginAction */
  public LoginAction()
  {
  }

  public ActionForward execute(
  ActionMapping actionMapping,
  ActionForm actionForm,
  HttpServletRequest request,
  HttpServletResponse response)
  throws java.io.IOException, javax.servlet.ServletException
  {
    ActionErrors errors = new ActionErrors();
    HttpSession session = request.getSession();
    LoginForm form = (LoginForm)actionForm;
    UserDelegate ud = null;
    UserDTO user = null;

    session.removeAttribute("user");
    //== see if we can find the user
```

```
      try
      {
        ud = new UserDelegate();
        user = ud.getUserByLogin(form.getLoginId());
      }
      catch(UserNotFoundException e )
      {
        user = null;
        errors.add(
        ActionErrors.GLOBAL_ERROR,
        new ActionError("error.wrong.loginid", form.getLoginId()));
      }

      //== Check that the password matches.
      if( user != null )
      {
        if(!user.getPassword().equals(form.getPassword()))
        {
          errors.add( "password",
          new ActionError("error.wrong.password"));
        }
      }

      //== Something went wrong.
      if (!errors.isEmpty())
      {
        saveErrors(request, errors);
        return (new ActionForward(actionMapping.getInput()));
      }

      //== Everything is A-OK, so put the user into the session.
      session.setAttribute("user", user );

      //== We don't want the form bean anymore.
      if(actionMapping.getAttribute() != null)
      {
        if ("request".equals(actionMapping.getScope()))
          request.removeAttribute(actionMapping.getAttribute());
        else
          session.removeAttribute(actionMapping.getAttribute());
      }
      return actionMapping.findForward("success");
    }
  }
```

We start by looking for a user in the session. If there is one, we want to remove it because we have a new login in progress. Next, we create an instance of the UserDelegate class. UserDelegate is the class that we use to access the underlying EJB implementation, as was shown earlier in this chapter. If this fails, or if we cannot find the user, we generate an error; otherwise, we compare the password entered with the password stored in the database to see if we have a match.

If we do not have a match, we add another error to our errors collection. If the passwords do match, then we need to store the user record in the session so that we can use it again later, and delete the LoginForm from the session or request because we no longer need it. LoginAction will return the action mapping for success, which will be used by the Struts ActionServlet to determine which JSP page will be rendered next. In the case of a successful login, that will be `mainpage.jsp`.

Adding and Editing Users

On the opening page (`index.jsp`), the user has the option to click the Register button to register a new account. This action essentially inserts a new user profile into the database. Once logged in, the user has an option to edit his or her profile. This feature allows the updating of existing user records in the database. Both of these actions are very similar, so we want to use the same code for them both. The source code for the UserForm class follows:

```
import javax.servlet.http.*;
import org.apache.struts.action.*;

public class UserForm extends ActionForm {

  private String action = null;
  private String firstName = null;
  private String mi = null;
  private String lastName = null;
  private String maidenName = null;
  private String gradYear = null;
  private String email = null;
  private String loginId = null;
  private String password1 = null;
  private String password2 = null;

  public UserForm() {
  }

  public String getAction() {
    return action;
  }
  public void setAction(String _action) {
    action = _action;
  }

  public String getFirstName() {
```

```
    return firstName;
  }
  public void setFirstName(String aFName) {
    firstName = aFName;
  }

  public String getMi() {
    return mi;
  }
  public void setMi(String aMName) {
    mi = aMName;
  }

  public String getLastName() {
    return lastName;
  }
  public void setLastName(String aLName) {
    lastName = aLName;
  }

  public String getMaidenName() {
    return maidenName;
  }
  public void setMaidenName(String aMDName) {
    maidenName = aMDName;
  }

  public String getGradYear() {
    return gradYear;
  }
  public void setGradYear(String aGradYR) {
    gradYear = aGradYR;
  }


  public String getEmail() {
    return email;
  }
  public void setEmail(String aEmail) {
    email = aEmail;
  }

  public String getLoginId() {
    return loginId;
  }
  public void setLoginId(String aLoginId) {
    loginId = aLoginId;
  }

  public String getPwd1() {
```

```
    return password1;
  }
  public void setPwd1(String aPasswd) {
    password1 = aPasswd;
  }

  public String getPwd2(){
    return password2;
  }

  public void setPwd2(String aPasswd2){
    password2 = aPasswd2;
  }

  public ActionErrors validate(
  ActionMapping aMapping,
  HttpServletRequest aR) {
    ActionErrors err = new ActionErrors();
    if ((loginId == null) || (loginId.length() < 1))
      err.add("loginId", new ActionError("error.loginid"));
    if ((password1 == null) || (password1.length() < 1))
      err.add("password1", new ActionError("error.password"));
    if ((password2 == null) || (!password1.equals(password2)))
      err.add("password1", new ActionError("error.password.match"));
    if ((firstName == null) || (firstName.length() < 1))
      err.add("firstName", new ActionError("error.first.name"));
    if ((lastName == null) || (lastName.length() < 1))
      err.add("lastName", new ActionError("error.last.name"));
    return err;
  }

  public void reset(ActionMapping aMapping, HttpServletRequest aR)
  {
    reset();
  }
  public void reset()
  {
    action = null;
    firstName = null;
    mi = null;
    lastName = null;
    maidenName = null;
    gradYear = null;
    email = null;
    loginId = null;
    password1 = null;
    password2 = null;
  }
}
```

This code is similar to the RegistrationForm class presented in Chapter 7. We do want to make sure that the following line will be inserted into the <form-beans> element `struts-config.xml`:

```
<form-bean name="userForm" type="UserForm" />
```

where `name` is the name that we will use to reference this bean in our code and JSP files, and `type` is the name of the class that implements the bean. The `complete struts-config.xml` file is discussed more completely in the *Configuring Struts* section later in this chapter.

We also need to create an EditUserAction class to handle the `create` and `edit` functions that need to be supported.

EditUserAction Class

For Struts 1.1, we want to overload the `execute()` method of the Action class to implement our action code. If we were writing for Struts 1.0, we would overload the `perform()` method instead. The open lines of the class are shown in the following code:

```
import com.oldfriends.user.*;
import javax.servlet.http.*;
import org.apache.struts.action.*;

public class EditUserAction extends Action
{
  public EditUserAction()
  {
  }

  public ActionForward execute(
  ActionMapping actionMapping,
  ActionForm actionForm,
  HttpServletRequest request,
  HttpServletResponse response)
  throws java.io.IOException, javax.servlet.ServletException
  {
    HttpSession session = request.getSession();
    UserForm form = (UserForm)actionForm;
    UserDTO user = null;
    ActionErrors errors = new ActionErrors();
```

We need to determine if we are going to be editing an existing instance of a user or creating a new one. If the user is logged in, then there should be an existing user instance stored in the session scope. If there is no user in the session, then we will need to create a new user. However, the user may have returned to the login screen and may want to create a new user even if he or she is already logged in. If that is the case, we need to delete the existing user in the session and start fresh. If we are not creating a new user, then we will be editing the user stored in the current session:

```
// See if we are editing or adding a user.
String action = request.getParameter("action");
user = (UserDTO)session.getAttribute("user");
if((user == null)||("Create".equals(action)))
{
  action="Create";
  session.removeAttribute( "user" );
  user = new UserDTO();
}
else
{
  action="Edit";
}
```

Normally, the ActionServlet will have already created an empty instance of the UserForm for us, but in case this has not been done, we create one and store it into the proper context, based on the scope attribute for current action in the `struts-config.xml` file:

```
    // If there is no form instance, create one and store it.
if (form == null)
{
  form = new UserForm();
  if ("request".equals(actionMapping.getScope()))
    request.setAttribute(actionMapping.getAttribute(), form);
  else
    session.setAttribute(actionMapping.getAttribute(), form);
}
```

If we are not creating a new form, then we want to copy the information from the instance of the UserDTO class that we stored in the session to the UserForm class. This will prepopulate the fields on the form rendered by the JSP to show the current state of the data. We also save the value of the `action` parameter in the form for convenience:

```
if( !"Create".equals(action))
{
  userToForm(user, form);
  action = "Edit";
}
form.setAction(action);
```

If there are errors, we want to make sure they are available for us to list them. However, in this case we should not expect to ever encounter any errors. The section of code that follows serves as a placeholder in case we want to treat parameters other than `Edit` or `Create` as errors or if other error conditions are recognized at a later time. Finally, we return our action mapping and end our method. For this class, the action mapping will always return the `success` mapping:

```
    if( !errors.isEmpty() )
    {
      saveErrors(request, errors);
      return new ActionForward(actionMapping.getInput());
    }
    return actionMapping.findForward("success");
  }
```

We complete the class by providing two utility methods for copying an instance of UserForm to an instance of UserDTO, and vice versa. This can be automated by using classes from the Jakarta commons beanUtils project, but here we choose to do it ourselves for clarity. These methods are protected so that we can use them when we extend the class:

```
  protected void formToUser(UserForm form, UserDTO user )
  {
    user.setFirstName(form.getFirstName());
    user.setLastName(form.getLastName());
    user.setMi(form.getMi());
    user.setMaidenName(form.getMaidenName());
    user.setEmail(form.getEmail());
    user.setGradYear(Integer.parseInt(form.getGradYear()));
    user.setLoginId(form.getLoginId());
    user.setPassword(form.getPwd1());
  }

  protected void userToForm(UserDTO user, UserForm form  )
  {
    form.setFirstName(user.getFirstName());
    form.setLastName(user.getLastName());
    form.setMi(user.getMi());
    form.setMaidenName(user.getMaidenName());
    form.setEmail(user.getEmail());
    form.setGradYear(Integer.toString(user.getGradYear()));
    form.setLoginId(user.getLoginId());
    form.setPwd1(user.getPassword());
    form.setPwd2(user.getPassword());
  }
}
```

The SaveUserAction Class

We require two separate actions when editing or adding user records. The first action we have just seen serves to initialize the data that will be presented in the form that will be displayed to the user. The JSP file `edituser.jsp` will be used both for editing existing and adding new users. After the information provided by the EditUserAction has been modified, we need an action to save it to the database. That is the purpose of the SaveUserAction class. This action has the responsibility for calling the UserDelegate to persist the data by adding a new record or updating an existing one. We begin by extending the EditUserAction class that we created previously. This gives us access to the protected `userToForm()` and `formToUser()` methods of the parent class:

```
import com.oldfriends.user.UserDTO;
import com.oldfriends.user.UserDelegate;
import javax.servlet.http.*;
import org.apache.struts.action.*;

public class SaveUserAction extends EditUserAction
{

  /** Creates a new instance of SaveUserAction */
  public SaveUserAction()
  {
  }
```

Next, we extend the `execute` method of the Struts Action class. This overloads the extension of the method in the parent EditUserAction class. In this next section of code, we also initialize our variables:

```
  public ActionForward execute(
  ActionMapping actionMapping,
  ActionForm actionForm,
  HttpServletRequest request,
  HttpServletResponse response)
  throws java.io.IOException, javax.servlet.ServletException
  {
    HttpSession session = request.getSession();
    UserForm form = (UserForm)actionForm;
    String action = null;
    ActionErrors errors = null;
    UserDTO user = (UserDTO)session.getAttribute("user");
    UserDelegate ud = null;
```

Note that we look for a user instance in the session and attempt to get it. If we have an existing user record, we need it for updating because it also stores the primary key for the record we want to update. In the following section, we create an instance of the UserDelegate. The UserDelegate serves as our interface to the underlying session bean that we use to access the user data:

```
try
{
  ud = new UserDelegate();
  if( user == null )
  {
    user = new UserDTO();
    formToUser( form, user );
    UserDTO newuser = ud.addUser(user);
    user = newuser;
    session.setAttribute("user", user);
  }
  else
  {
    formToUser( form, user );
    ud.updateUser(user);
  }
}
```

In the preceding code, if the user was found earlier in the session then the data from the form is copied to the user instance of the UserDTO class and then the user object is passed to the `updateUser()` method of the User Delegate. This will, in turn, call the session bean to update the user information stored in the database.

If no user was found in the session, then we create a blank user. This user does not have a userid or primary key field at this point. We copy the User Form instance into the new UserDTO instance and then call `addUser()` on the UserDelgate. If `addUser` fails and throws an exception, we do not want to lose the data we have already entered, so we store it temporarily into a `newuser` instance of UserDTO. If it does not throw an exception then we assign `newuser` to `user` and then store it into the session.

If an exception occurs, we add an error to the errors collection as follows:

```
catch(Exception e)
{
  errors = new ActionErrors();
  errors.add(ActionErrors.GLOBAL_ERROR,
  new ActionError("error.userupdate", action, e.getMessage()));
}
```

The `error.userupdate` message accepts two parameters. In this case, we want to report what went wrong and so we pass the message from the exception that was caught as a parameter. Although this is not user-friendly, it is very helpful for debugging purposes.

The following code completes our implementation of the class:

```
        if(( errors == null) || (errors.isEmpty()) )
        {
          if(actionMapping.getAttribute() != null)
          {
            if ("request".equals(actionMapping.getScope()))
              request.removeAttribute(actionMapping.getAttribute());
            else
              session.removeAttribute(actionMapping.getAttribute());
          }
          return actionMapping.findForward("success");
        }
        else
        {
          saveErrors(request, errors);
          return new ActionForward(actionMapping.getInput());
        }
      }
    }
```

If there are no errors, then we remove the form from the request or session scope as determined by the `struts-config.xml` for the current action. Then, we return the action mapping for the success target of the current action (as defined in `struts-config.xml`). Otherwise, we store the errors and return to the form used to provide the input.

Configuring Struts

Struts uses a file called, by default, `struts-config.xml` to describe how the various components of a Struts application interact with each other. Here we will examine the configuration file for our application. We start with the introductory header information and the `struts-config` root element as follows:

```
<?xml version="1.0" encoding="ISO-8859-1" ?>

<!DOCTYPE struts-config PUBLIC
      "-//Apache Software Foundation//DTD Struts Configuration 1.1//EN"
     "http://jakarta.apache.org/struts/dtds/struts-config_1_1.dtd">
<struts-config>
```

The next section provides a mapping for the form beans that will be used. The name of the bean is the name that will be used to reference that bean in the session or request scope. The type of the bean is the fully qualified class name of the class that implements the bean. Because we have elected not to place our beans in a package, the type is simply the class name:

```
<form-beans>
  <form-bean name="emptyForm" type="EmptyForm" />
  <form-bean name="loginForm" type="LoginForm" />
  <form-bean name="userForm" type="UserForm" />
</form-beans>
```

We will not use any global forwards for this application. A global forward can be used anytime there is a common target page that many actions will want to forward the request to:

```
<global-forwards>
</global-forwards>
```

Action Mappings

The next section of the XML file covers the action mappings. The action mappings provide the information that is used by the Struts ActionServlet to determine which forms to load and which action classes to invoke for a specific request. The action mapping for the login action is as follows:

```
<action-mappings>
  <!-- Handles the opening page -->
  <action path="/login"
    type="LoginAction"
    name="loginForm"
    input="/index.jsp"
    >
    <forward name="success" path="/mainpage.jsp"/>
    <forward name="fail" path="/index.jsp"/>
  </action>
```

In the file `index.jsp` is a line that reads:

```
<html:form action="login">
```

When the Submit button is clicked, this form sends a `POST` request to the Struts ActionServlet with `/login.do` appended to the end of the URL. The ActionServlet looks at the request and then finds the matching action, in this case `login`, in the `struts-config.xml` file. The servlet then uses the value of the name attribute in the action element to determine which form class it should load. It loads the form class if needed and copies the information from the form into the class by matching the names of the input fields on the form with the names of the `set` methods on the class. Once the fields have been set, the servlet calls the `validation` method on the form bean. If the validation fails, the servlet forwards the request to the page identified in the `input` attribute. If it succeeds, then it calls the `Action` class. The name of the action class is provided through the `type` attribute of the action element. In our case it is `type="LoginAction"`.

The action class returns an ActionMapping that is used to forward the request. These are listed as forward elements contained within the action element. Each forward is named, and the names are used in the code to select the forward element that will be used. The `path` attribute of the forward element determines the URL that the request will be forwarded to. If a matching name for a forward is not found in the local forward element, the global forward elements will be searched for a match as well.

There are several additional action mappings that we want to configure for our application, as described in the following sections.

The about Action

We use the about action mapping to select an about page. The action tag is:

```
<!-- Handles the about page -->
<action path="/about"
  type="EmptyAction"
  name="emptyForm">
  <forward name="success" path="/servlet/SuperSnoop"/>
</action>
```

During development, we like to have the about function mapped to the SuperSnoop servlet that we showed in Chapter 5. This illustrates one of the strengths of the Struts architecture: Once we have completed development, we can have the About button forward to an information page simply by changing the path attribute in the forward element.

About, uses the EmptyAction and EmptyForm classes that were developed in Chapter 7. These classes are useful when you want to leverage the Struts infrastructure but you do not have a traditional form that needs to be processed.

The Mainpage Action

Once we have successfully logged into the system, either by entering our login ID and password and clicking Login or by registering as a new user, we want to go to the main page. The following action does this.

```
<!-- Handles the mainmenu page -->
  <action path="/mainpage"
    type="EmptyAction"
    name="emptyForm">
    <forward name="success" path="/mainpage.jsp"/>
  </action>
```

It also uses the EmptyAction and EmptyForm classes from Chapter 7.

NOTE **Just a reminder, when we are at the main page, we should always be logged in. The current software does not enforce this. It is possible for a user to directly enter the URL for** `mainpage.jsp` **and arrive at mainpage without authentication. There are numerous ways of preventing this, but they are beyond the scope of this book.**

EditUser Action

The following `EditUser` action is used when we want to invoke the `edituser.jsp`, which is the page we use if we want to add a new user or edit an existing user's information:

```
<action path="/edituser"
    type="EditUserAction"
    name="userForm"
    input="/edituser.jsp"
    validate="false">
    <forward name="success" path="/edituser.jsp"/>
  </action>
```

The action can be invoked with an argument passed as a parameter on the URL to determine if a new user should be created or if an existing user will be edited.

We set `validate="false"` here so that the servlet does not call the validate method of the form class. The `validate` method will be called when the form is submitted to be saved, but here we are just populating the form with existing data.

The action method `EditUserAction` should always map to success. The JSP file `edituser.jsp` will never invoke this method. Instead it invokes the `SaveUser` action.

SaveUser Action

The `edituser.jsp` file uses the `SaveUser` action to update the database with the user's new or modified information. The action tag for this follows:

```
<action path="/saveuser"
    type="SaveUserAction"
    name="userForm"
    input="/edituser.jsp">
    <forward name="success" path="/mainpage.jsp"/>
  </action>
</action-mappings>
</struts-config>
```

When this task succeeds, the user is returned to the main page of the application. Here, we also close the <action-mapping> element and the root element of the document. This completes our `struts-config.xml` file.

Configuring the Servlet Container

The `web.xml` file is used to provide configuration information for the Web application and the servlet container. In this section, we look at the `web.xml` file needed for this application. The first part of the file, which follows, provides the document information and the root <web-app> element:

```
<?xml version="1.0" encoding="ISO-8859-1"?>
<!DOCTYPE web-app
  PUBLIC "-//Sun Microsystems, Inc.//DTD Web Application 2.3//EN"
  "http://java.sun.com/dtd/web-app_2_3.dtd">
<web-app>
```

Next, we configure the Struts ActionServlet:

```
<servlet>
<servlet-name>action</servlet-name>
<servlet-class>org.apache.struts.action.ActionServlet</servlet-class>
  <init-param>
    <param-name>application</param-name>
    <param-value>ApplicationResources</param-value>
  </init-param>
  <init-param>
    <param-name>config</param-name>
    <param-value>/WEB-INF/struts-config.xml</param-value>
  </init-param>
  <init-param>
    <param-name>debug</param-name>
    <param-value>2</param-value>
  </init-param>
  <init-param>
    <param-name>detail</param-name>
    <param-value>2</param-value>
  </init-param>
  <init-param>
    <param-name>validate</param-name>
    <param-value>true</param-value>
  </init-param>
  <load-on-startup>2</load-on-startup>
  </servlet>
```

We use the <init-param> elements to provide Struts with the information it needs to find resources. The application parameter provides the name of the properties file that is used to look up messages. The `config` parameter provides the name of file used for Struts configuration. This is normally set to `struts-config.xml`.

Struts uses the <load-on-startup> element to request that the container load the Struts servlet when the container is started. The number 2 informs the container to load the Struts servlet after any application with a number lower than 2.

The next servlet definition is used for the SuperSnoop servlet. This is handy to install when developing code, and for this example, we have configured it to be invoked by the application when the About button is clicked within the application:

```
<servlet>
  <servlet-name>Servlet_SuperSnoop</servlet-name>
  <display-name>Servlet SuperSnoop</display-name>
  <servlet-class>SuperSnoop</servlet-class>
</servlet>
```

Next, we cover the servlet mappings:

```
<servlet-mapping>
    <servlet-name>action</servlet-name>
    <url-pattern>*.do</url-pattern>
</servlet-mapping>
<servlet-mapping>
    <servlet-name>Servlet_SuperSnoop</servlet-name>
    <url-pattern>/servlet/SuperSnoop</url-pattern>
</servlet-mapping>
```

Note that the Struts ActionServlet will be invoked for any URL pattern ending with a .do.

In the next fragment, we tell the container to use `index.jsp` as the `welcome` file. The container returns this file when only the application name is provided in the URL:

```
<welcome-file-list>
  <welcome-file>index.jsp</welcome-file>
</welcome-file-list>
```

The next fragment identifies the JSP tag libraries that will be supported in the application:

```
<taglib>
  <taglib-uri>/WEB-INF/struts-bean.tld</taglib-uri>
  <taglib-location>/WEB-INF/struts-bean.tld</taglib-location>
</taglib>
<taglib>
```

```
    <taglib-uri>/WEB-INF/struts-html.tld</taglib-uri>
    <taglib-location>/WEB-INF/struts-html.tld</taglib-location>
  </taglib>
  <taglib>
    <taglib-uri>/WEB-INF/struts-logic.tld</taglib-uri>
    <taglib-location>/WEB-INF/struts-logic.tld</taglib-location>
  </taglib>
  <taglib>
    <taglib-uri>/struts</taglib-uri>
    <taglib-location>/WEB-INF/lib/struts.jar</taglib-location>
  </taglib>
```

Now, we need to add the necessary reference information that's required to access the EJB that we created to access the information from the database. This is done using the <ejb-ref> element, as shown in the following code. This section is identical to the reference information shown and discussed in the first example in this chapter:

```
  <ejb-ref>
    <ejb-ref-name>ejb/UserSession</ejb-ref-name>
    <ejb-ref-type>Session</ejb-ref-type>
    <home>com.oldfriends.session.UserSessionHome</home>
    <remote>com.oldfriends.session.UserSessionRemote</remote>
    <ejb-link>UserSession</ejb-link>
  </ejb-ref>
```

A final note on the `web.xml` file: If you are planning to run the application on an instance of Tomcat that is not embedded inside of JBoss, then you should add the AppInit servlet and the appropriate elements to the `web.xml` file, as shown in the TestUserEJB example covered earlier in this chapter. Doing this allows you to debug the application using the embedded version of Tomcat found in the Netbeans IDE. We will discuss another technique that is useful for development and debugging shortly, in the *A Final Development Aid* section. But first we need to look at the `jboss-web.xml` file.

Configuring JBoss

If we will be deploying this application under JBoss we need to add the JBoss-specific file `jboss-web.xml`. In this case, the `jboss-web.xml` file is identical to the version shown in the TestUserEJB example covered in the beginning of the chapter.

Setting Properties

Struts uses a properties file for accessing messages. The properties file we use for this example follows:

```
error.loginid=<li>LoginId is required</li>
error.password=<li>Password is required</li>
error.wrong.password=Wrong Password
error.wrong.loginid=Could not find userid {0}
error.password.match=Passwords must both be the same
error.first.name=First name is required
error.last.name=Last name is required
error.system.baduser=User record could not be retrieved - system error
error.userupdate=User Update failed-:{0}:- {1}
oldfriends.highschool=Mullens High School
```

Numbers inside of curly braces correspond to parameters that are passed into calls to the `errors.add()` method in the code examples.

Building the Application

We are ready now to start building the application. As before, we will use Ant. A basic Ant `build.xml` file that can be used to build this application follows:

```
<?xml version="1.0" encoding="UTF-8"?>
<project basedir="." default="compile" name="ch14">
  <property name="app.name" value="ch14ex2"/>
  <property name="jboss.home"
     value="C:/openjava/jboss-3.0.6_tomcat-4.1.18"/>
  <property name="jboss.deploy"
     value="${jboss.home}/server/default/deploy"/>
  <property name="lib.dir" value="${jboss.home}/client"/>

  <path id="build.classpath">
    <fileset dir="${lib.dir}">
      <include name="*.jar"/>
    </fileset>
  </path>

  <target name="init">
  </target>

  <target depends="init" name="compile">
    <javac
      classpathref="build.classpath"
```

```
        debug="true"
        deprecation="true"
        destdir="./WEB-INF/classes"
        srcdir="./WEB-INF/classes">
      </javac>
    </target>

    <target depends="compile" name="war">
      <war destfile="${app.name}.war"
         update="no"
         excludes="build.xml"
         webxml="./WEB-INF/web.xml">
        <fileset dir=".">
          <exclude name="**/web.xml"/>
          <include name="**/*.class"/>
          <include name="**/*.gif"/>
          <include name="**/*.html"/>
          <include name="**/*.jar"/>
          <include name="**/*.java"/>
          <include name="**/*.jpg"/>
          <include name="**/*.jsp"/>
          <include name="**/*.properties"/>
          <include name="**/*.tld"/>
          <include name="**/*.xml"/>
        </fileset>
      </war>
    </target>

    <target depends="war" name="all"/>
    <target depends="war" name="deploy">
      <copy file="${app.name}.war" todir="${jboss.deploy}"/>
    </target>
    <target depends="war" name="undeploy">
      <delete file="${jboss.deploy}/${app.name}.war"/>
    </target>
  </project>
```

NOTE **You will need to change the values of the properties at the top of the file to reflect your system's configuration.**

This build file does not assume that your source code files and your class files are stored in different directories. Instead, it builds the application in place. The source code files will also be stored in the .war file.

If you are deploying the application on a standalone instance of Tomcat, then you will want to modify the deployment task. Tomcat will not automatically redeploy a .war file if it is updated. Instead, you will need to delete the previous installation and replace the .war file with the new one for Tomcat to deploy. As an alternative, you can extract the .war file into the Tomcat `webapps` directory yourself.

Running the Application

Remember that this application has dependencies on the EJBs developed and deployed in Chapter 13. After the different components have been built and deployed, the application can be accessed through the browser. The following URL should bring up the login screen:

```
http://localhost:8080/ch14ex2
```

where `localhost:8080` should be replaced by the machine name and port where the application is running and `ch14ex2` is the name of the .war file that was deployed.

This should bring up the screen shown earlier in Figure 14.2. We should have at least three entries in the database from Chapter 13. We can use the login ID of `jdoe` and the password `password` to log into the system. This brings us to the `mainpage.jsp` screen, as shown in Figure 14.3.

Clicking the Edit button allows us to edit the profile of the currently logged in user. This is almost the same as the registration screen, except that the fields are prepopulated. The screen is shown in Figure 14.4.

Successfully editing the screen or canceling out of it brings us back to the main page. Finally, clicking the About button on the open page or the main page runs the `SuperSnoop` servlet, as shown in Figure 14.5.

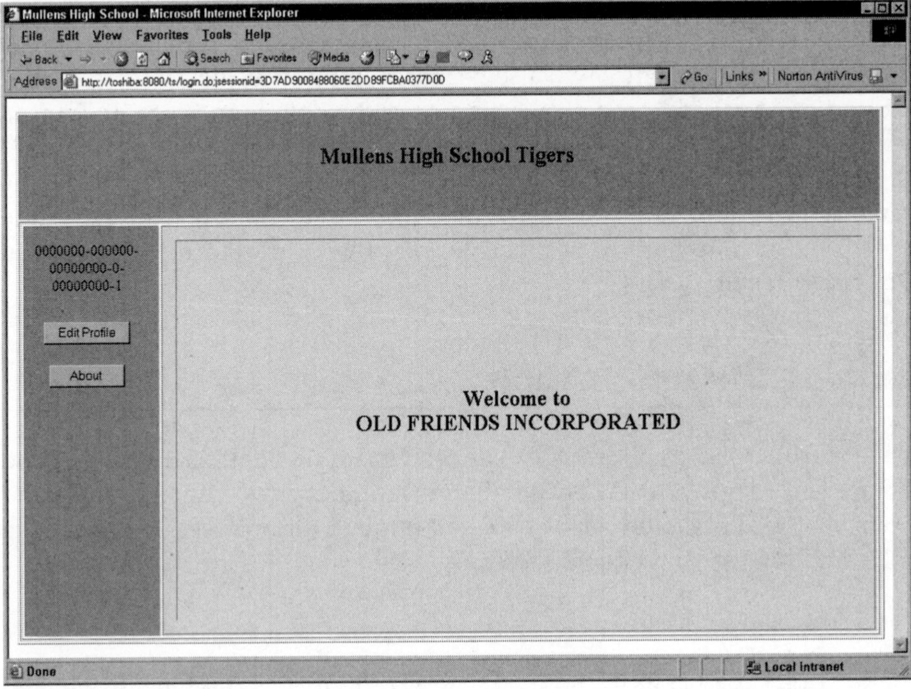

Figure 14.3 The Old Friends Incorporated main page.

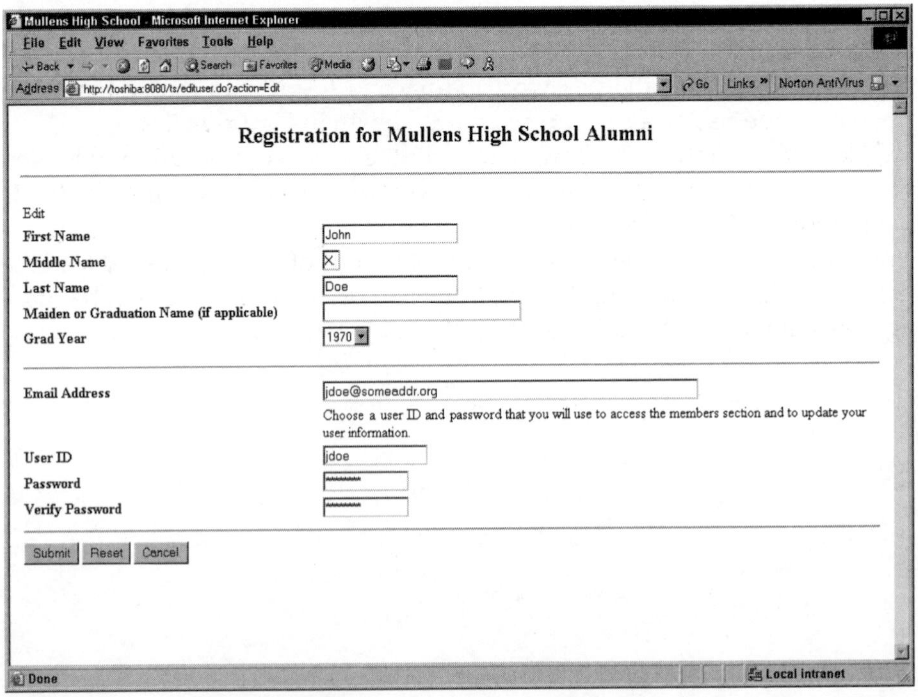

Mullens High School - Microsoft Internet Explorer
File Edit View Favorites Tools Help
Back Search Favorites Media
Address http://toshiba:8080/ts/edituser.do?action=Edit
Go Links Norton AntiVirus

Registration for Mullens High School Alumni

Edit
First Name John
Middle Name X
Last Name Doe
Maiden or Graduation Name (if applicable)
Grad Year 1970

Email Address jdoe@someaddr.org
Choose a user ID and password that you will use to access the members section and to update your user information.
User ID jdoe
Password
Verify Password

Submit Reset Cancel

Done
Local intranet

Figure 14.4 Editing a user profile.

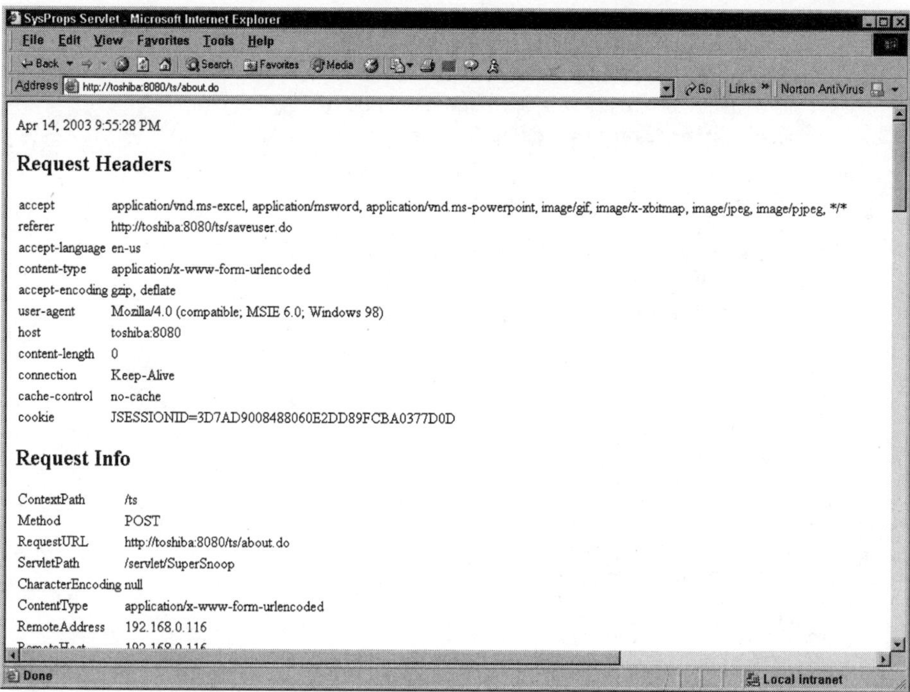

Figure 14.5 Results of clicking the About button.

A Final Development Aid

Before we end this chapter, let's look at one thing we can do to really ease the testing and development of the user interface side of the application. The problem we are faced with is that distributed development is, by its very nature, a complex process. It is often difficult to find errors and fix code when multiple elements of an application are all changing at the same time. Also, it can be difficult testing and debugging whenever multiple platforms are involved. In many environments, the EJB server will be on one machine, the database on another, and the servlet container on a third (this is discussed in more detail in the next chapter). This section offers a single simple idea that can often be used to address most of the user-interface development issues without you having to be concerned about the other components. The idea is this: Replace the BusinessDelegate instance with a stub implementation that has the same behavior but does not actually use the underlying infrastructure. A sample replacement for the UserDelegate is shown in the following code:

```
package com.oldfriends.user;

import com.oldfriends.session.UserSessionHome;
import com.oldfriends.session.UserSessionRemote;
import com.oldfriends.utils.ResourceLocator;

public class UserDelegate
{
  UserDTO user = null;
  /** Creates a new instance of UserDelegate */
  public UserDelegate()
  {
    this.init();
  }

  protected void init()
  {
    user = new UserDTO();
    user.setFirstName("John");
    user.setLastName("Doe");
    user.setMi("X");
    user.setLoginId("jdoe");
    user.setPassword("xxxx");
    user.setGradYear(1991);
    user.setMaidenName("");
    user.setUserid("STUB-00-000000-00000000-0-00000000-1");
    user.setEmail("jdoe@email.com");
  }

  public String getHello()
  {
    return "Hello";
  }

  public UserDTO getUserByUserid( String userid )
  throws UserNotFoundException
  {
    if(userid.equals(user.getUserid()))
      return user;
    else
      throw new UserNotFoundException("Couldn't find userId:"+userid);
  }

  public UserDTO getUserByLogin( String login)
  throws UserNotFoundException
  {
    if(login.equals(user.getLoginId()))
      return user;
    else
      throw new UserNotFoundException("Couldn't find loginId"+login);
  }
```

```
    public UserDTO getUserByEmail( String email )
    {
      return user;
    }

    public UserDTO addUser( UserDTO newuser )
    {
      user.setFirstName(newuser.getFirstName());
      user.setLastName(newuser.getLastName());
      user.setMi(newuser.getMi());
      user.setLoginId(newuser.getLoginId());
      user.setPassword(newuser.getPassword());
      user.setGradYear(newuser.getGradYear());
      user.setMaidenName(newuser.getMaidenName());
      user.setUserid("STUB-00-000000-00000000-0-00000000-1");
      user.setEmail(newuser.getEmail());
      return user;
    }

    public void updateUser( UserDTO newuser )
    {
      addUser( newuser );
    }

    public UserDTO[] getUsersByYear( int year )
    {
      return null;
    }

    public UserDTO[] getAllUsers()
    {
      return null;
    }

    public void refresh()
    {
      this.init();
    }
  }
```

Instead of using an EJB, this simple class just keeps a single hard-coded instance of a UserDTO as a member variable. If we needed something a little more complex, we could use a small array of instances. Because the client code uses the UserDelegate to access the underlying infrastructure, the client does not even know that the underlying infrastructure is not there. This version of the UserDelegate provides the same client interface as the real one that we use to access the session bean. However, this UserDelegate can be used to test the client application before the session bean exists, or while you are still trying to work through server issues.

What we have demonstrated here is a very simple example. A more sophisticated approach would support the accessing of delegates through interfaces and the dynamic loading of delegate classes based on configuration parameters in `web.xml` or stored in properties files. This allows the Delegates to be swapped in and out as needed just by changing configuration values. Finally, the delegate can be used to change how you access the underlying systems. You can start with a delegate to use EJB as the underlying technology, but if you later need to support the application in an environment without EJB support you can implement an alternate set of delegates, using JDO or some other technology.

Summary

In this chapter, we created the user-interface components, or presentation layers, of an application designed to test-drive the J2EE platform that we have assembled from open source components.

The chapter demonstrates some of the effective techniques for using Struts as a controller in a MVC application architecture. Struts provides the tools required to separate business components from presentation components. Yet, Struts allows us to work with the familiar JSP model for developing Web pages. While implementing these examples, we explored some of the design patterns that have emerged from J2EE development. These include the Resource Locator design pattern, the Business Delegate design pattern, and through Struts, the Model-View-Controller design pattern.

We have also demonstrated that we can support the building of the many layers of a modern Java-based enterprise application on a platform that has been assembled entirely from open source components. Although this is important from a developer's viewpoint, it is not enough. We also must have the ability to deploy the application in a way that supports the expected user base.

In the next chapter, we discuss how to deploy this open source J2EE platform for production environments. In other words, now that we have built an application, we will look at what it takes to deploy the application in a scalable environment that can grow to accommodate any size of user base.

CHAPTER

15

Deploying and Running Your Application

In previous chapters of this book, we have selected and assembled components to create a platform that we can use to build and deploy J2EE-based applications using only open source components. In Chapters 13 and 14, we demonstrated building an application using these platform components. This chapter examines application deployment, or moving an application from the development cycle into an operational cycle.

NOTE **As we mentioned in other chapters, the focus of this book is on creating the platform rather than on creating applications. *Java Open Source Programming* by Joe Walnes et al (Wiley Publishing, Inc., 2003), a companion book to this one in the Java Open Source Library, discusses actually creating applications using open source tools in far more detail.**

After the Development Cycle

Once your enterprise platform has been developed, it will need to be deployed and run on its intended target system. In some cases, you may be deploying it on a system that is similar to the development system. In others, you may be deploying it on a different system entirely. After the software is deployed, it is said to be operational. We will look at several considerations that need to be taken into account for the deployment and operations of enterprise software developed and running on our open source J2EE platform, including:

- Application portability
- Physical architecture of the system
- Performance testing and tuning
- Deployment processes
- Operations and maintenance

Portability

Often when it comes time to deploy your enterprise application, you will not be deploying it on the same system that it was developed on. There are a number of reasons for this, including:

- Normally the development system does not have to be as large or have the capacity to handle as much load as a production system.
- Development systems have different visibility to the outside world and thus have different security requirements.
- Development systems normally do not have to be operated in continuous 24/7 mode.
- Your development system may have different connections to the underlying enterprise systems.
- It is common to have training and test versions of enterprise systems to support development, testing, and training needs without interrupting the normal information-management needs of the business.

The fact that deployment environments may be different from the development environment needs to be considered as you develop and test the software. Yes, Java is the "write once, run anywhere" language, and this eases the task considerably; this is the reason that we are able to develop an application on one system and deploy it on another. Every so often, though, you will find that enterprise software written on one platform may be difficult to get working on another J2EE platform.

There are, however, some basic rules that can be followed to ensure that your software moves easily to a new platform:

Program to the standard not to the platform. You should always write your applications to conform to the version of the standard that you will support in your project, eschewing platform-specific code like the plague. If the supported standard is servlet specification 2.3 and EJB 2.0, then write to those standards. Don't be tempted by the enhanced features or extensions of the platform you are using.

When you can't avoid environmental- or platform-specific code, isolate it. The environment is the set of external things your code needs to function. This includes database connections, configuration parameters, JNDI names, directory names, and classes or services that need to be available to your application. Another way to describe this is that your system should be loosely coupled with its environment. Here are three easy steps that you should use to isolate system dependencies:

1. Create interfaces that reflect how a specific type of resource needs to be accessed.
2. Create classes that implement the interfaces for the various environments that will be supported.
3. Create factories to create instances of the classes for your programs.

Use an interface to define a uniform standardized way that your program will access the resource or service. Any class can implement the interface, thus giving you the flexibility to have multiple implementations that may work differently but all behave the same way. The servlet interface is a classic example. The servlet container does not have any specific knowledge of a servlet other than that the servlet implements the servlet interface. The factory classes need to support loading and constructing the correct class instances based on the configuration parameters for the application. The application itself should not have to be aware of how these class instances were created. This allows the application to be reconfigured to support a new deployment without modifying source code.

Avoid using hard-coded values in your system. Put another way, don't put hard-coded strings into your code. There are several reasons for this. First if you place the strings in your code, you must change the code to change the strings. This is obvious in applications that need to support multilanguage use. They need to have the strings stored externally so that the language-specific string can be presented. What is less obvious is the need to do this to give you the ability to support multiple databases. In spite of the standardized SQL that is supposed to be supported, the reality is that SQL statements to perform specific tasks vary from database to database. If you may have to support more than one database, it is lot easier to change the strings in a file of parameterized SQL statements than it is to have to go through and reedit all of the code that uses each SQL statement.

Choosing a System for Deployment

There are generally three different scenarios for deployment systems:

- You are writing an application to be deployed on an existing in-place system. In this scenario, you have little or no choice about the deployment environment, but you do know what the environment will be and can plan accordingly. This is often the case for internal company development projects.
- You are writing an application to support multiple deployments on various systems. This is a common case if you are creating software for resale. The customer selects the system, typically from a set of options that you support. In some cases, the customer is willing to pay more for support on the platform of their choice.
- You are writing the software and also specifying the deployment system. In this case, you have complete control (within whatever project guidelines or constraints have been established) over the selection of hardware and software. This is a common case for new projects or customers that do not already have an infrastructure to support the application.

If you do have the freedom to choose the deployment system, then you will be faced with a number of decisions. We will look at some of those decision points in this section. You will, of course, have to decide on the hardware and operating system. It is recommended that, if possible, you develop the application on a system that is similar to the system you will deploy the application on. This and following the portability suggestions given previously should help to minimize surprises at deployment time.

NOTE This discussion is designed to help create an order of magnitude estimate for designing and creating a system to use for deployment purposes. Each application has its own particular quirks and needs that may affect its performance and the validity of this estimate. There is no good substitute for the load testing and performance modeling of an application to validate system choices.

There are several factors that need to be taken into account when determining the hardware and operating system for the deployment system:

- Performance is often the factor that first comes to mind. However, in today's environment of commodity hardware, we feel that your choice of hardware and operating system should have more to do with your organization's ability to support the system than its performance characteristics.
- The acquisition cost of the system is always a factor, but once again it is normally not as important as the ability to support the system.
- Another primary consideration is the availability of a current JVM. Unfortunately, some systems tend to lag behind others in JVM support. Before a final decision is made, this should be investigated. As a general rule, you can count on current JVM support for Windows, Linux for Intel's 80*x*86 processors (including the Pentium family), and Sun-based systems.

Performance and Platform Sizing

Determining the characteristics of the deployment system goes beyond deciding which hardware to purchase. You also need to decide *how much* hardware should be purchased. This process is called *sizing* the system. Your performance requirements should help to establish the size of the system that you need. One of the advantages of modern distributed computing systems is the ability to grow a system by adding more machines, rather than replacing existing machines with new, larger, faster machines. When you make your hardware and operating system choice, one of the cost considerations you should take into account is the incremental cost of expanding, or growing, the system. Normally, when a system is expanded, you want to be able to use the same hardware and software as the other existing components. When you run out of capacity in the current system, you can then incrementally add capacity and grow the system simply by adding more machines.

There are several things to remember when determining the size of the system. First is that sizing a system is an order of magnitude exercise and does not have to be too precise. If you size a system to be too large, you may be wasting money, but you can always use the system to host additional applications. If you size a system to be too small, you can always grow the system but there may be a delay while the additional hardware comes online.

There are a number of questions that can be answered to aid in resolving the sizing issue. These include:

How many total users are there for the system? This may not be easy to answer for open Web applications but if you are creating an application for use by an organization, determine the total number of the users within the organization that will use the application. For example, if a company has 4,000 employees and you are creating a timecard application, then you can expect a total of 4,000 users. This will help you answer the next question.

How many users will be accessing the system at the same time? Or put another way, how many active sessions will there be at any time? Even if you have 4,000 users, it is not likely that they will all be using the system at the same time. For many applications, you can use a rule of thumb that no more than 2 percent of the total user base will be actively using the system at any point in time. This means that for our hypothetical case of 4,000 users, we can typically expect 80 users at once. Remember that just because a user has the browser open to the application, doesn't mean that he or she is actively using it. For many applications, the 2 percent figure may be high; for others, it may be low. You need to get an understanding for how your application will be used and adjust this number accordingly.

Are there certain times when the system will be hit more heavily than others? This is a very important consideration that many developers forget about. For example, if timecards are due in at a certain time, you may find that there is a peak load during a period just before the time when the timecard information is due, when everyone is trying to access the system. This becomes a peak load or usage time. These peaks are regular and normally fairly easy to anticipate and account for. On a public Web site, there may be events such as sales promotions that drive traffic to the application, causing peaks that harder to plan for unless you have some history of previous performance.

An example of this was observed as John supported a dealer application for a major manufacturing company. The company had dealers distributed across the United States, and the application represented the primary means of information exchange between the company and it's dealers. Each morning at 8:00, 9:00, 10:00, and 11:00 A.M., we observed a series of peaks in usage. After 11:00 A.M., system usage would stabilize for the rest of the day. In this situation, each dealer tended to open at 8:00 A.M., and the first thing the dealer would do is hit the system to check that day's information. At 8:00 A.M., the east coast dealers came online, then at 9:00 A.M. and 10:00 A.M., the dealers in the Central and Mountain time zones connected in, respectively. By 11:00 A.M. Eastern Standard Time, the west coast was online and the system usage settled down. Understanding these types of usage patterns can be critical in right-sizing your system.

What are the response time goals? Response time measures the time it takes for the system to generate a response to a specific request. This is easy to measure and is captured in the log files of the various Web components. Although response time is easy to measure, it is highly dependent on a number of things, including system load, the mix of static and dynamic content, and the performance characteristics of the application. To provide a uniform measurement that can be used in sizing, we need to compare the performance of the system with no load to the system loaded at some level above the maximum expected load. Application response time requirements should always be expressed for an unloaded system. Then, the requirements for a loaded system can be expressed as a degradation of performance from the unloaded state. These numbers can normally be determined by load testing on a similar platform. An example might help to make this clearer. Let's say that a certain sequence of operations takes 10 seconds on an unloaded system and that we expect a peak user load of 120 concurrent active users. We can now state that the system should not experience any degradation of performance supporting a peak load of 120 users, and we have a solid measurable requirement. We could alternately state that the system will experience less than a 50 percent increase in response time due to a load of 120 users. This means that with 120 users we would expect the same sequence of requests and responses to be completed in 15 seconds or less instead of the 10 seconds of the unloaded system.

Determining the Number of CPUs

The questions we have asked till now have focused on issues that will help us to determine how many CPUs we will need and how fast they need to be. To generate our estimate, we will use the rule of thumb that each concurrent user requires 10 MHz of CPU speed. Applying this rule means that our 4,000-user timecard application that supports 80 concurrent users can run on a modest single 800-MHz CPU. This assumes that the Web application server and EJB container and databases are each on their own independent servers. In this case of 80 concurrent users, it is very likely that we will deploy the application on the same type of system that we developed it on. On the other hand, if we had 40,000 users, 800 of them concurrent at peak times, we might select a system with 4 CPUs, each running at 2 GHz. How this processing power is distributed through the layers of the architecture will be discussed in the *Hardware Scaling* section later in this chapter.

Determining Memory Requirements

For our purposes, memory falls into two general categories: short-term memory (RAM) and long-term memory (hard drive storage). If we do not have enough short-term memory, then the system will slow down as it swaps memory with slower long-term storage. Long-term memory is primarily a database- and content-sizing effort.

Short-Term Storage

To determine short-term memory-sizing requirements, in addition to the information we have already collected, we also need to know the estimated amount of data that will be stored per active user. Essentially, this is equivalent to the amount of data that will be available in the servlet session, session beans, and active entity beans for a user as he or she uses the application. Once we have this number, we double it so that we can handle inactive sessions, and then add a fixed amount for operating system and application overhead. For our payroll application, let's assume that we will have about 8 KB of short-term data on average per user. Multiply this by 80 users and double it, and we need only about 1.2 MB of additional memory beyond our baseline. That's not very much when you consider that the baseline for many systems today is about 256 MB. If we use 1 MB of memory per user, then we still only need 160 MB beyond the 256-MB baseline. This is less the 512-MB total.

We do run into some issues if we have a much larger user base or per user memory requirement. Many low-cost systems have limitations on the amount of RAM they support. Operating systems too may have limitations on the amount of RAM they can address. Typically on today's Intel *x*86-based hardware, it is difficult to add more than 2 GB of RAM per CPU. On many systems, the limit is half of that. If you are planning to use low-cost hardware and your memory requirements are greater than those supported by the hardware, then you will need to use multiple servers.

Long-Term Storage

The next consideration is long-term, or hard disk, storage, which isn't quite as simple to pin down as short-term storage. The calculation is similar to the previous discussion of short-term storage in that we start with a baseline and add a number for each user. This time, though, we need to consider all users of the system over time and not just concurrent users or total users. We also need to consider static data or content and data that is not user related. This ends up breaking down into a number of exercises, which are discussed in the following sections:

- *Estimating Database Requirements*
- *Estimating System Requirements*
- *Estimating Content Requirements*

After each of these estimates has been determined, the long-term storage requirements can be calculated by summing the estimates. Normally, a fixed percentage (25 to 50 percent) of additional storage is then added in because most operating systems work more efficiently with larger areas of free space available on the disk subsystem.

Estimating Database Requirements

Entire books have been written on database sizing. The simple method that we describe in this section should be good enough for the purposes of this book. It is based on four pieces of information for each table in each database:

rec_size. An estimate of the average record size.

num_recs. An estimate the number of records that will be initially stored in each table (always at least 1).

growth_rate. An estimate of the pace that the table will grow over a period of time.

periods. The number of time periods the data must be maintained. For example, will the data be maintained for 6 months, a year, or 5 years before it can be purged?

The amount of data per table in megabytes can then by calculated using the following formula:

```
table_size = rec_size * ( 1+num_recs * growth_rate * periods)
```

This amount is then summed for all tables. We also add a multiplier to account for the cost of indices and other database overhead. Table 15.1 shows an example of the calculation for three tables of a hypothetical payroll application.

Table 15.1 Estimate of Database Size

TABLE NAME	RECORD SIZE (IN BYTES)	INITIAL RECORD COUNT	ANNUAL GROWTH RATE	FINAL RECORD RETENTION	COUNT	TABLE SIZE (IN MEGABYTES)
Employee	200	4,000	50 percent	5 years	14,000	2.7
Pay Record	80	4,000	1200 percent	5 years	244,000	18.6
TaxLookup	10,000	1	100 percent	5 years	6	0.1
					Total:	21.3
					Overhead:	50 percent
					Size:	32.0

The table assumes an initial population of 4,000 employee records. We expect to add 2,000 employee records per year to the user table in the database. We have to keep each employee record whether or not the employee is still employed, so even though we expect the work force to remain at 4,000 employees, the database will grow to 14,000 records over a period of 5 years. Each employee can be paid 12 times per year, so the pay record table in the database grows at a rate of 1,200 percent per year. Tax information must also be retained but it only changes once a year.

Estimating System Requirements

The system requirements are the amounts of storage needed for the operating system in addition to system software required to run the application. This estimate includes the Web server, application server, database software, and any other software that is required to operate the system. This can be determined by examining the amount of storage consumed on a freshly installed system prior to the installation of specific databases or the code and content for the application being deployed.

When estimating the system requirements, do not forget to consider the amount of space that will be required for system logging. Most operating systems have an automated logging facility. You need to determine how the system logs will be managed and ensure that you have enough space to accommodate your needs.

Estimating Content Requirements

The content requirement is the space required for the enterprise-application code that you have developed along with any static content that is needed to support the application. Static content includes HTML and image files. If you need this estimate before the application has been created, make an estimate of the number of pages in the application, and then estimate the size of each page based on a percentage of text and graphics content for the average page. If you have trouble coming up with a number, capture several complete pages from similar applications and use the sizes of the captured pages as a basis for your estimate.

Determining Bandwidth Requirements

Bandwidth represents the amount of data that can flow over a period of time. For computer applications, bandwidth is normally measured in bps (bits per second). Bandwidth also represents a limiting factor in the performance of your application. For example, suppose that you are deploying your application over the Internet, using a fractional T1 line supporting 256 Kbps, and the average response to each request is a modest 1,024 bytes, or 8,192 bits. This means that you will be limited to 256K divided by 8K, which equals 32 responses per second.

If your content is a little more graphics intensive and your average response is 4,096 bytes, the number of requests that can be handled drops to eight. If this is the case, it does not matter how fast the rest of your hardware is, you will be limited by the bandwidth of your Internet connection.

Going back to the first example, 32 responses per second does not necessarily correspond to 32 users. If your application is one that requires a lot of user interactivity as users move from page to page, it is likely that you can support considerably more then 32 users. What you are interested in when modeling how your application uses bandwidth is the time per page view. If a user takes, on average, 20 seconds to view a page in your application, there will be an average of 20 seconds between requests, and the same 256 Kbps pipe can support 640 users with an average page size of 1,024 bytes.

Performance Testing

Performance testing is used to help tune system performance and determine if the system and the software meet the performance requirements that will be placed upon the system. Although performance testing may identify problems in the software, its primary purpose is to aid in the architecture and tuning of the system. Performance testing is normally accomplished by placing increasingly greater amounts of load onto the system until performance targets are met or performance degradation occurs.

Performance testing may occur from the perspective of a user of the application. In this case, the test generates user requests and collects the responses generated by the system. The test generator can simulate many users accessing the system at the same time. Several differing scenarios can be provided to simulate typical usage patterns if they are known. This is how Apache jMeter (discussed in Chapter 4) works. The tests are not built with knowledge of the underlying structure of the application. Instead, the tests are designed based on knowledge of how the users will use the system. In general, this is known as *black box testing*.

Unlike black box testing, where no knowledge of the structure of the underlying system is applied, *white box testing* leverages a user's knowledge of the underlying system to test specific points of interest within the system. White box tests may focus on specific user transactions that we know exercise certain elements within the system. White box testing may also be performed at layers or tiers other than the front-end, or presentation, layer. For example, we may want to exercise Enterprise Java Beans and measure the performance that we can expect from the EJB container. This would be useful to tell us if we had enough processing power supporting that tier of the platform.

System Configurations

Now that we have discussed sizing and performance testing, it is time for us to look at how we can put a system together. One of the real strengths in J2EE and distributed computing is that it provides a great deal of flexibility when it comes to configuring a system to meet application needs. If your application is a small one, it is possible to host the entire application on a single machine. On the other hand, if the user base grows, the system used to serve the application can be grown incrementally along with the user base. This feature is called scalability, and it is one of the real strengths of J2EE. The system can be scaled to meet the demands of the users by adding hardware without making changes to the software. The hardware is added incrementally, leaving the existing hardware in place and growing the system to meet increasing user demand.

Hardware Scaling

Let's assume for sake of this discussion that we are starting out with a single machine hosting all of the primary components of our platform, as depicted in Figure 15.1.

The first thing we can do to grow the system is to replace the system with a single system that is more capable. For example, if we started out with a single CPU system operating at 1.0 GHz, we could upgrade the system to a Quad CPU system with each CPU running at 2.0 GHz. This gives us almost a fourfold increase in performance and ability to support users (the real number will be closer to 3.7). Although this approach may work for a while, this technique of growth has limitations in that eventually you may not be able to buy a big enough single box.

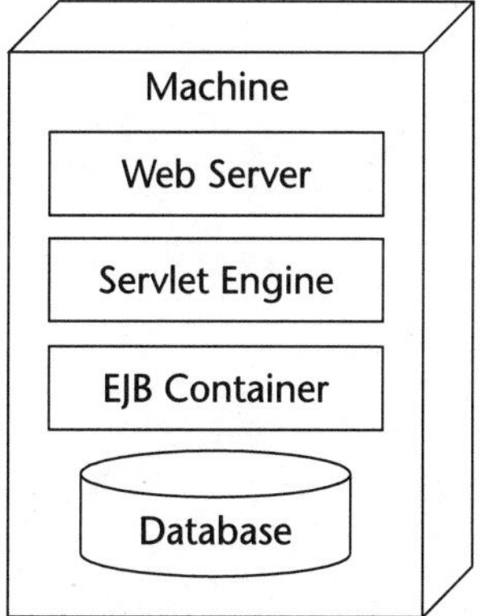

Figure 15.1 Single computer hosting entire platform.

The solution to this problem is to use more than one machine. Now, the question becomes, "How do I split my application between machines?" The first approach that we will look at we call *scaling*. The following sections discuss the two types of scaling: vertical scaling and horizontal scaling.

Vertical Scaling

In vertical scaling, we divide an application according to the tiers of the application. These tiers correspond to the different platform components, as shown earlier in Figure 15.1. In many cases, the database is already being hosted on a separate machine anyway, so this is often a first step in vertical scaling. Figure 15.2 shows this and a second step with the EJB container separated.

This process can continue to its logical conclusion of a separate machine for each tier.

Horizontal Scaling

While vertical scaling separates tiers into different machines, horizontal scaling replicates machines across tiers. The difference is illustrated in Figure 15.3.

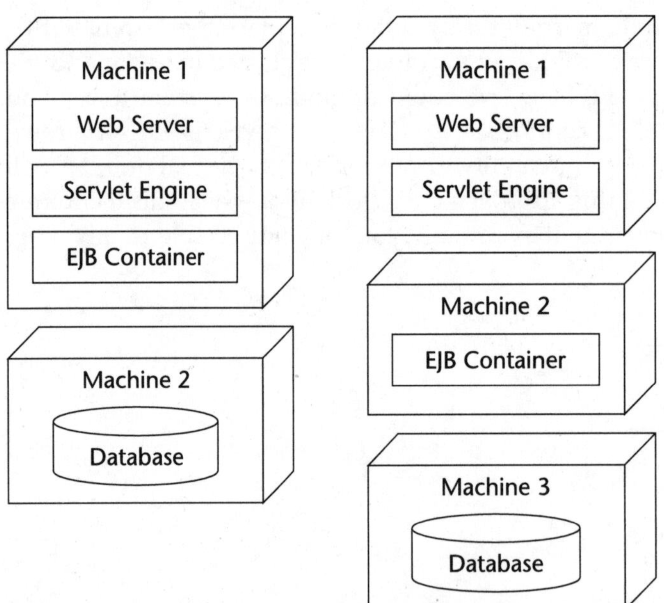

Figure 15.2 Vertical scaling by separating tiers.

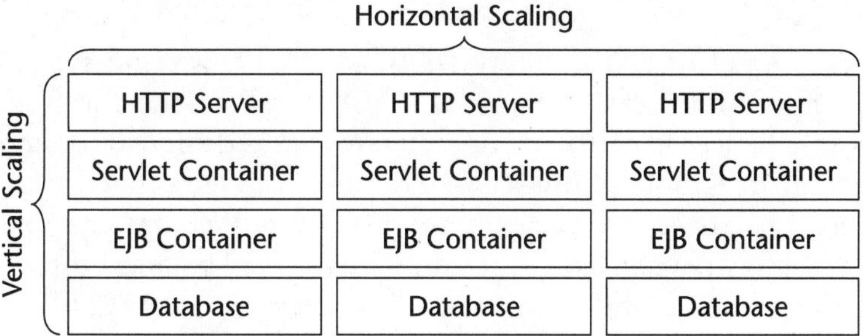

Figure 15.3 Horizontal versus vertical scaling.

When scaling horizontally, it is not necessary to scale each tier by the same amount. Different tiers may have different scaling needs, and it is possible to scale only those tiers that need to see an improvement in performance-handling characteristics. This may lead to configurations such as those shown in Figure 15.4.

At this point, it is not apparent how horizontal scaling works. Horizontal scaling does not provide a clear separation of duties, as in vertical scaling where the functional components each have clearly defined separate responsibilities. Although it is often possible to break an application up horizontally, this can create difficulty in the management and deployment of the software. One way of doing this can be implemented with Apache as a front end for Tomcat. In this case, Apache is configured to direct certain URLs to a particular instance of Tomcat running on one machine. Requests for other URLs can be routed to different instances of Tomcat running on other machines. Unfortunately, you will lose some of the management features that Tomcat provides if you do this. This represents a simple form of load balancing. More sophisticated load-balancing techniques can be used to distribute requests across multiple servers.

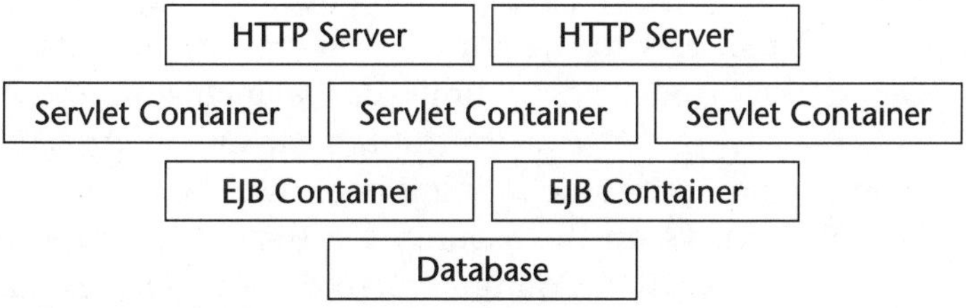

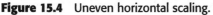

Figure 15.4 Uneven horizontal scaling.

Load Balancing

Load balancing can be performed in many ways, each with varying system implications. One of the simplest techniques is to use a load balancer in front of the tier. This load balancer is hardware or software that is designed to send requests for services to different machines based on some predetermined set of rules. Hardware load balancers are very common for large Web-based applications. In its simplest form, when a request comes in, the load balancer directs that request to one of several identical servers, as shown in Figure 15.5:

A problem arises if the server needs to maintain state. If the load balancer sends the first request to one server and the next request from the same session to a different server, the second server does not have the previous state information needed to maintain the state of the session. One way of addressing this concern is to use "sticky" addresses. In this approach, once a request is routed to a particular server, all future requests for some predetermined period of time will continue to be routed that same server. This allows the server to maintain state information. Often, this is done using the IP address of the incoming packet. This technique of load balancing does have some peril associated with it in that many users access Web applications through proxy servers or network address translation firewalls. These techniques mean that many requests will appear to originate from the same IP address effectively negating the value of the load balancer for those users.

One way of addressing this limitation in a Web environment is for the load balancer to recognize session cookies set by a particular server. The load balancer can then route the request to the server that created the session cookie.

Again, Apache can be configured to serve as a load balancer supporting multiple Tomcat servers. In this case, however, each instance of Tomcat is identical to the other instances. Apache is configured to have all requests for servlets or JSP sent to one of several instances of Tomcat. Each instance can be weighted to receive more or less load. This allows multiple Tomcat instances to be running on different hardware and requests to be sent according to the relative weights of the hardware. Apache will automatically track session cookies and send subsequent requests to the correct Tomcat instance. If an instance of Tomcat goes down, Apache will limit its balancing to those instances that remain. When a new instance of Tomcat returns online, Apache will recognize it and automatically restart including it back into the rotation.

This form of load balancing works on the assumption that each machine handles the same load (or a proportional amount if weighted) if it receives the same number of requests as the other machines. It is also possible for the load balancer to monitor the systems that it is distributing tasks to and adjust how it distributes the load so that machines that are less busy get requests preferentially over those machines that are busier. This normally requires more intimate knowledge of the product being managed than is normally used by simple load balancers. Clustering is another technique based on the idea that the product knows itself.

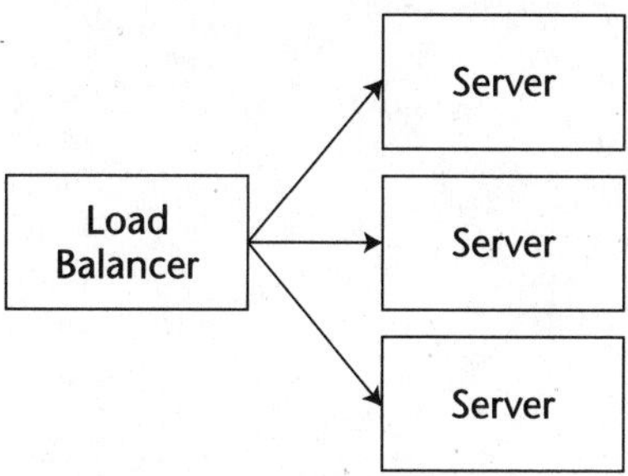

Figure 15.5 Load balancing.

Clustering

Clustering is an alternate technique for distributing load across multiple systems. Clustering is a feature that can be built into individual platform components. The feature allows an instance of one server to find and share tasks with other instances of the server, working cooperatively with the other servers of the same type in a system. Support for clustering is built into both JBoss and Apache.

Clustering may provide a number of advantages over the simple load-balancing schemes discussed in previous sections. Each instance of the software usually knows how to determine the amount of load it is currently handling in relation to its siblings in the cluster, which allows new tasks or requests to be routed to the machine that is most available rather than just a blind random distribution of tasks, as in the previous example.

Normally, it is possible to remove a machine from a cluster, leaving the rest of the cluster intact and operating. This provides a failover mechanism and can help to ensure reliable operation of your application.

Firewalls and Security

One final point before we conclude this section on system configurations. As we are dividing our physical architecture, we need to account for other elements of the environment we will be working within. Where this is most critical is in the area of security. A Web-based application should never be deployed unless it is behind some sort of firewall. A *firewall* restricts access to network paths that outside systems can use to access the system behind the firewall. Firewalls can be implemented either in hardware or software. Linux systems often come with a firewall preconfigured for the system. A firewall will only allow messages sent to specific IP addresses and ports to pass. Figure 15.6 shows a typical system deployment in relation to firewalls.

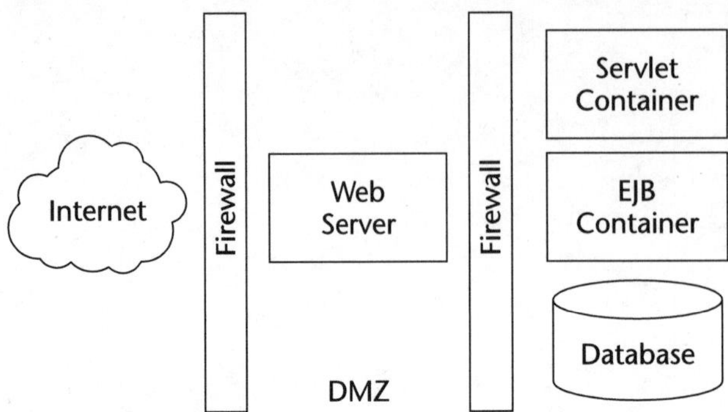

Figure 15.6 Firewalls.

The first firewall on the left of the figure provides access from the Internet only to ports 80 and 443 in support of the HHTP and HTTPS protocols. The second firewall protects the rest of the systems of the enterprise in case the first firewall is breached. This second firewall may, for example, only open port 8009 to support communications to the Tomcat servlet container. The area between the two firewalls is called the *demilitarized zone* (DMZ). Machines located in this area should not be considered trusted by other machines in the corporate network. In the scenario just described, database access and access to other enterprise systems is limited to those systems that are behind the second firewall.

Operations and Maintenance

Once the application has been written and the hardware is in place, we deploy the software and let the users come and enjoy it. We move from the development phase into the operations-and-maintenance portion of the software's life cycle. You may think that the hard part is over. The reality, from a software-engineering perspective, is that operation and maintenance represents 70 percent of the software life-cycle cost. This is more than twice the amount spent to write and deploy the software.

There is another consideration here as well: Now that we have people actually using the software, what is the impact on those users and on the business if the software is unavailable? There is one major chain of hotels that claims it loses 3 million dollars each day that its Web-based reservation system is down. This is 125,000 dollars per hour. Your application may or may not have that kind of impact but it is important to access what the impact of system downtime is.

Processes

In our experience, the establishment of processes for managing a system is the most critical factor overall in system reliability. It is process failures more than any other that seem to cause system failures. Process failures then compound the problem, making troubleshooting and recovery more difficult. We recommend that processes be established and, when possible, automated for all system operations tasks. Examples of some of the processes that need to be established are:

- Software and content deployment
- Error reporting and tracking
- System monitoring and alerting
- System backups
- Security auditing

The following sections discuss each of these processes in more detail.

Content and Software Deployment

We can't count how many times we've seen folks deploy a new piece of software just to find out it broke the system, and then had to scramble to restore the system to its previous state before it was required to be available again. It helps if adequate testing occurs before deployment, but even so sometimes problems slip into the system. In an ideal situation, both deployment and rollback should be automated. This is easy to do with many of the open source tools that we have already seen. Chapters 13 and 14 both showed examples of using Ant to deploy application software. Ant can be also used to check the software out from a repository such as CVS (covered in Chapter 4). An Ant script can be created that checks out the new version of software to be deployed from the CVS repository and automatically deploys it to the servers. If the deployment fails, then the Ant script should be able to repeat the deployment of the previous version to restore the system to its previous state. If deployment processes are scripted, then it is less likely that new deployment errors will be introduced into the process.

Error Reporting and Tracking

Once something does go wrong on a system, it is important to have a means of assigning the correct resources to handle the problem and monitor and track the progress of the fix. It is important to understand what actions were taken to fix the problem so that if the issue ever arises again the history of the problem can be found and examined. There are a number of open source bug-tracking packages that can be used for this. Scarab is an open source bug-tracking project available from `http://www.tigris.org` that is designed to work in a Java servlet environment.

System Monitoring and Alerting

Apache, Tomcat, Jboss, and most of the other tools we have examined have the ability to support generation of log files. The current Java and J2EE standards provide support for application logging. Log4J and commons-logging are complementary logging frameworks available from `http://jakarta.apache.org` that can be used within applications to generate log messages at various levels of detail, depending on runtime configuration of the package. Your application software should make generous use of these packages and generate meaningful log messages when things don't work or if you need to track significant events. Programs can then be executed on the log files to generate reports and messages that can be used both for auditing the system and identifying problems.

Unfortunately, automated system monitoring seems to be one of the weaker areas in open source software. There do not seem to be a large number of tools for monitoring log files and automatically sending notifications of critical events. However, it is not difficult to write software for these tasks, and it can be created to support the specific features of your environment.

System Backups

System backups need to be a basic feature for any computer operation. The backup requirements for each site will vary but in most cases a regular automated backup should be scheduled. Backups should be grandfathered so that a minimum of two previous versions of the system exists at any time. At least one copy should always be kept offsite or in a different facility.

John once had a client who regularly backed his system up and rotated his tapes so that he always had three recent versions of a complete backup. But the client never took any of the tapes home with him at night or stored them in a different facility. One weekend, the office above his had a water leak. His office was flooded and all of his computers were under water. The backup tapes, which were stored next to the computers, were also underwater and ruined. Fortunately, John was able to recover the system's hard drive, but this could have been a real disaster for his client's company.

Security Auditing

Security auditing is another of those tasks that people shouldn't have to be reminded about, but they still neglect. Both Linux and Windows provide numerous tools to assist in managing the security of computers running their respective operating systems. These tools should be used on a regularly scheduled basis, and the reports should be examined for discrepancies.

Operational Requirements

When you are determining the processes that make sense for your organization, it helps to understand the operational requirements for the system. Your operational requirements can be determined through the answers to questions such as:

- What are the primary hours of operation for the software?
- What is the maximum allowable time for the system to be down for a planned outage?
- What is the maximum allowable time for the system to be down for an unplanned outage?
- How often will content be changed on the system?
- How often will software be updated on the system?

As for primary hours of operation, does your application need to be available 24 hours 7 days a week or is 9 to 5 support enough? These are two extremes but both are reasonably common. Let's take a look at some of the things a 24/7 operational cycle implies:

- 24-hour support staff
- No downtime for system maintenance
- Redundant fault-tolerant systems with failover capability
- Graceful degradation of system performance as failure occurs

It can be very expensive to implement the features needed for 24/7 support. You should be certain that the cost of having the system down justifies the expense of operations.

Summary

In this chapter, we have examined a number of issues related to the deployment and operations of software created for our platform. We have looked at various mechanisms for scaling the systems environment to support large numbers of users. We have discussed performance testing and finally system operations.

Throughout this book, we have examined open source components that can be leveraged to create a complete Java enterprise development platform. In earlier chapters we have tried to show how to

- Select open source J2EE components
- Install the components
- Integrate each component with the others and
- Test the components to make certain they are working

In this chapter, we have tried to show you how these components can be deployed in a fashion that meets the operational needs of any size of application.

We have tried to demonstrate that Open Source Java tools offer many of the same features as their commercial counterparts, and often these tools provide features that go beyond commercial offerings. Our goal has not been to say that open source is the only way to go. Rather, it has been to provide you with the knowledge to help you to use open source tools effectively and help you to select the tools that are right for the job, whether they are commercial or open source. Hopefully, when you make your tool selections in the future, you will now be prepared consider the value that open source tools have to offer.

Index

SYMBOLS

A

B

C

U

X

Z